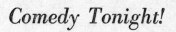

Comedy Tonight!

Comedy Tonight!

Broadway Picks
Its Favorite Plays

EDITED BY
MARY SHERWIN

With an Introduction by
Nancy Stark
Editor
Fireside Theatre

DOUBLEDAY & COMPANY, INC.
Garden City, New York

Printed in the United States of America

We wish to express our appreciation to the following people for their assistance on this anthology:

Woody Allen, Heywood Hale Broun,
Abe Burrows, Jules Feiffer,
Bob Fosse, William Goldman,
Helen Hayes, Garson Kanin,
Walter Kerr, Joshua Logan,
Edwin Newman, George Oppenheimer,
Hal Prince, Richard Rodgers,
Dore Schary, Roger Stevens,
Howard Teichmann, Earl Wilson,
and others.

Contents

Introduction

THE IDEA of eliciting the suggestions of some of Broadway's most distinguished writers, producers, directors, actors, and critics in putting together an anthology of ten comedies was a compromise. And, as it turned out, an inspired compromise. Although the thought of a questionnaire had been mentioned early on, those of us involved with the project—Jim Charlton, Managing Editor of the Publishing Group; Mary Sherwin, the editor who put the book together; and I—were confident that the task of agreeing on ten outstanding plays could easily be done without resorting to higher authorities.

Each of us drew up a preliminary list of ten to fifteen choices. When we sat down to compare them we discovered we had a number of overlaps as well as disagreements—and a bulky list of over thirty plays. Then the discussions started: Should the anthology be post-War? What about the classics, Wilde and Shaw? Might not the list be top-heavy with Neil Simon hits? And if we wanted to avoid that problem, then which Simon should we choose? There was some concern that our list would lean too heavily on English playwrights, that it wasn't "American" enough, and wouldn't properly represent Broadway's contribution to the comic tradition. A question cropped up about musical comedies like *Guys and Dolls,* and about tragicomedies. We agonized over *Mister Roberts* and *Harvey* (our agony later vindicated by their being included here)—two plays that, because they left us misty-eyed rather than in stitches, we feared might not be true comedies after all.

Then we came to Neil Simon.

I assumed that Jim and Mary had of course picked *Barefoot in the Park* as Neil Simon's greatest play. Certainly *I* had. Despite their insistence that *The Odd Couple* is Simon's best comedy, I was not convinced. *Barefoot in the Park* is just about the funniest play I have ever seen. I was reminded of those wonderful lines from *The Prime of Miss Jean Brodie* in which Miss Brodie asks her class: "Can anyone tell me who is the greatest Italian painter?" A pupil answers: "Leonardo da

Vinci, Miss Brodie." And Miss Brodie responds: "That is incorrect. The answer is Giotto; he is my favorite." So *Barefoot in the Park* is *my* favorite Simon play and I wasn't about to give it up without a fight. And I wasn't at all willing to concede that "everyone" would feel that *The Odd Couple* is Simon's best work.

That's when we went back to our original idea of asking theatre luminaries to name their favorite comedies.

The questionnaire we sent out was prepared in the following way: More than thirty-five plays were listed with ample room for comments. Extra sheets of paper were provided so that the respondents could suggest additional favorites that we hadn't included. This was mailed along with a letter from me describing what we were doing and asking for their assistance.

Three weeks later we had received exactly one response—Edwin Newman's. It seemed we were destined to experience a real-life version of that old joke: "The letter poured in." And then the answers suddenly began to arrive—two and three a day. We were gratified by the intense interest and personal warmth of these busy people in the comments they took the trouble to provide, and we think you, also, will be interested in what they had to say about the comedies in this collection. We have reproduced their comments for you as an introduction to each play. There were also many other distinguished figures in the American Theatre who contributed their choices to our list of comedies, but they either chose to remain anonymous or noted their favorites without comment.

The style in which each respondent replied was often quite revealing. Woody Allen awarded checkmarks the way Wanda Hale awards stars. Joshua Logan gave forth with a virtual crescendo of "yeses" for his pet choices, and an intimidating crescendo of "noes" when he thought a suggestion of ours was completely off-base.

Helen Hayes lost our questionnaire but fortunately retained the envelope in which it was sent, and wrote us back a charming, if puzzled, letter explaining her dilemma and asking what she could do for us. When we mailed her a new form, she was kind enough to respond to it in a matter of days.

It was a good thing that we allowed a great deal of space for comments and additions, for additions there were! We had relegated *Guys and Dolls* to the musical comedy slot and several respondents lifted it from there and put it down as one of their favorite comedies. Another play, *Three Men on a Horse,* the 1935 comedy by George Abbott, was not included on our list but showed up on a number of others as a write-in.

When we started consolidating the responses we began to notice—miracle of all miracles—a consensus emerging. And a truly representative consensus at that—including classics as well as modern comedies, and featuring not more than one play by any playwright. *Harvey* and *Mister Roberts,* the plays that might have been considered too poignant to be thought of as comedies, appeared on a majority of lists. Noël Coward and Oscar Wilde both garnered a majority of votes even though they were neither American nor modern. (One person, though, did acknowledge our original dilemma. Jules Feiffer asked rhetorically: "How do you add quality to present-day Broadway? Of course, you import it.") And more people chose *The Odd Couple* than picked *Barefoot in the Park*. Both vintage Simon, I'd say magnanimously.

Nancy Stark
Editor
Fireside Theatre

The Importance of Being Earnest

OSCAR WILDE

Why our respondents liked

 THE IMPORTANCE OF
BEING EARNEST

"Always a favorite—anywhere."
HELEN HAYES

"The wittiest ever? For me, yes."
WILLIAM GOLDMAN

"As perfect as a Swiss clock, its appeal is in the very smoothness of its working, a working which the author is happy to have us observe."
HEYWOOD HALE BROUN

The Importance of Being Earnest, noted for its witticisms and ingenious situations, is a satire on the English nobility and clergy. This comedy farce was written by the Irish-born dramatist and poet Oscar Wilde, who also authored critical essays, poems, works of fiction, including *The Picture of Dorian Gray,* in addition to his popular light comedies. *The Importance of Being Earnest* was first produced in London in February 1895. The day before it was to open, a friend of Oscar Wilde asked him if he thought his play would succeed. Wilde's answer was: "My dear fellow, the play is a success." The only question is whether the audience will be a success." Within several months the play appeared on the New York stage at the Empire Theatre. This was the first of many subsequent Broadway runs—1902, 1921, and 1926, when its cast members included Vernon Steele, Reginald Owen, and Lucile Watson. In 1927 the play was transformed into a musical comedy entitled *Oh, Ernest.* After its 1939 revival starring Clifton Webb and Estelle Winwood, a London company production directed by and featuring John Gielgud appeared in 1947 at New York's Royale Theatre and was much praised for its delightful, high-styled production. Many subsequent revivals over the years attest to *The Importance of Being Earnest* being one of the classics of the theatre.

The Importance of Being Earnest was first performed in the United States on April 22, 1895, at the Empire Theatre in New York. It was revived by The Theatre Guild and John C. Wilson in association with H. M. Tennent, Ltd., of London, on March 3, 1947, at the Royale Theatre, New York City. The cast was as follows:

Lane	Richard Wordsworth
Algernon Moncrieff	Robert Flemyng
John Worthing, J.P.	John Gielgud
Lady Bracknell	Margaret Rutherford
Hon. Gwendolen Fairfax	Pamela Brown
Cecily Cardew	Jane Baxter
Miss Prism	Jean Cadell
Rev. Canon Chasuble, D.D.	John Kidd
Merriman	Stringer Davis
Footman	Donald Bain

Staged by John Gielgud
Settings by Motley
Lighting by William Conway

ACT ONE

Algernon Moncrieff's flat in Half-Moon Street, London, W.

ACT TWO

The garden at the Manor House, Woolton.

ACT THREE

Drawing-room of the Manor House, Woolton.

ACT ONE

Scene. Morning-room in ALGERNON'S *flat in Half-Moon Street. The room is luxuriously and artistically furnished. The sound of a piano is heard in the adjoining room.*

(LANE *is arranging afternoon tea on the table, and after the music has ceased, Algernon enters.*)

ALGERNON: Did you hear what I was playing, Lane?

LANE: I didn't think it polite to listen, sir.

ALGERNON: I'm sorry for that, for your sake. I don't play accurately—anyone can play accurately—but I play with wonderful expression. As far as the piano is concerned, sentiment is my forte. I keep science for life.

LANE: Yes, sir.

ALGERNON: And, speaking of the science of life, have you got the cucumber sandwiches cut for Lady Bracknell?

LANE: Yes, sir. (*Hands them on a salver.*)

ALGERNON (*inspects them, takes two, and sits down on the sofa*): Oh! . . . by the way, Lane, I see from your book that on Thursday night, when Lord Shoreman and Mr. Worthing were dining with me, eight bottles of champagne are entered as having been consumed.

LANE: Yes, sir; eight bottles and a pint.

ALGERNON: Why is it that at a bachelor's establishment the servants invariably drink the champagne? I ask merely for information.

LANE: I attribute it to the superior quality of the wine, sir. I have often observed that in married households the champagne is rarely of a first-rate brand.

ALGERNON: Good Heavens! Is marriage so demoralizing as that?

LANE: I believe it *is* a very pleasant state, sir. I have had very little experience of it myself up to the present. I have only been married once. That was in consequence of a misunderstanding between myself and a young person.

ALGERNON (*languidly*): I don't know that I am much interested in your family life, Lane.

LANE: No, sir; it is not a very interesting subject. I never think of it myself.

ALGERNON: Very natural, I am sure. That will do, Lane, thank you.

LANE: Thank you, sir. (LANE *goes out*.)

ALGERNON: Lane's views on marriage seem somewhat lax. Really, if the lower orders don't set us a good example, what on earth is the use of them? They seem, as a class, to have absolutely no sense of moral responsibility.

(*Enter* LANE.)

LANE: Mr. Ernest Worthing.

(*Enter* JACK.) (LANE *goes out*.)

ALGERNON: How are you, my dear Ernest? What brings you up to town?

JACK: Oh, pleasure, pleasure! What else should bring one anywhere? Eating as usual, I see, Algy!

ALGERNON (*stiffly*): I believe it is customary in good society to take some slight refreshment at five o'clock. Where have you been since last Thursday?

JACK (*sitting down on the sofa*): In the country.

ALGERNON: What on earth do you do there?

JACK (*pulling off his gloves*): When one is in town one amuses oneself. When one is in the country one amuses other people. It is excessively boring.

ALGERNON: And who are the people you amuse?

JACK (*airily*): Oh, neighbours, neighbours.

ALGERNON: Got nice neighbours in your part of Shropshire?

JACK: Perfectly horrid! Never speak to one of them.

ALGERNON: How immensely you must amuse them! (*Goes over and takes sandwich.*) By the way, Shropshire is your county, is it not?

JACK: Eh? Shropshire? Yes, of course. Hallo! Why all these cups? Why cucumber sandwiches? Why such reckless extravagance in one so young? Who is coming to tea?

ALGERNON: Oh! merely Aunt Augusta and Gwendolen.

JACK: How perfectly delightful!

ALGERNON: Yes, that is all very well; but I am afraid Aunt Augusta won't quite approve of your being here.

JACK: May I ask why?

ALGERNON: My dear fellow, the way you flirt with Gwendolen is perfectly disgraceful. It is almost as bad as the way Gwendolen flirts with you.

JACK: I am in love with Gwendolen. I have come up to town expressly to propose to her.

ALGERNON: I thought you had come up for pleasure? . . . I call that business.

JACK: How utterly unromantic you are!

ALGERNON: I really don't see anything romantic in proposing. It is very romantic to be in love. But there is nothing romantic about a definite proposal. Why, one may be accepted. One usually is, I believe. Then the excitement is all over. The very essence of romance is uncertainty. If ever I get married, I'll certainly try to forget the fact.

JACK: I have no doubt about that, dear Algy. The Divorce Court was specially invented for people whose memories are so curiously constituted.

ALGERNON: Oh! there is no use speculating on that subject. Divorces are made in Heaven—(JACK *puts out his hand to take a sandwich.* ALGERNON *at once interferes.*) Please don't touch the cucumber sandwiches. They are ordered specially for Aunt Augusta. (*Takes one and eats it.*)

JACK: Well, you have been eating them all the time.

ALGERNON: That is quite a different matter. She is my aunt. (*Takes plate from below.*) Have some bread and butter. The bread and butter is for Gwendolen. Gwendolen is devoted to bread and butter.

JACK (*advancing to table and helping himself*): And very good bread and butter it is too.

ALGERNON: Well, my dear fellow, you need not eat as if you were going to eat it all. You behave as if you were married to her already. You are not married to her already, and I don't think you ever will be.

JACK: Why on earth do you say that?

ALGERNON: Well, in the first place girls never marry the men they flirt with. Girls don't think it right.

JACK: Oh, that is nonsense!

ALGERNON: It isn't. It is a great truth. It accounts for the extraordinary numbers of bachelors that one sees all over the place. In the second place, I don't give my consent.

JACK: Your consent!

ALGERNON: My dear fellow, Gwendolen is my first cousin. And before I allow you to marry her, you will have to clear up the whole question of Cecily. (*Rings bell.*)

JACK: Cecily! What on earth do you mean? What do you mean, Algy, by Cecily? I don't know anyone of the name of Cecily.

(*Enter* LANE.)

ALGERNON: Bring me that cigarette case Mr. Worthing left in the smoking-room the last time he dined here.

LANE: Yes, sir. (LANE *goes out.*)

JACK: Do you mean to say you have had my cigarette case all this time? I wish to goodness you had let me know. I have been writing frantic letters to Scotland Yard about it. I was very nearly offering a large reward.

ALGERNON: Well, I wish you would offer one. I happen to be more than usually hard up.

JACK: There is no good offering a large reward now that the thing is found.

(*Enter* LANE *with the cigarette case on a salver.* ALGERNON *takes it at once.* LANE *goes out.*)

ALGERNON: I think that is rather mean of you, Ernest, I must say. (*Opens case and examines it.*) However, it makes no matter, for, now that I look at the inscription inside, I find that the thing isn't yours after all.

JACK: Of course it's mine. (*Moving to him.*) You have seen me with it a hundred times, and you have no right whatsoever to read what is written inside. It is a very ungentlemanly thing to read a private cigarette case.

ALGERNON: Oh! it is absurd to have a hard-and-fast rule about what one should read and what one shouldn't. More than half of modern culture depends on what one shouldn't read.

JACK: I am quite aware of the fact, and I don't propose to discuss modern culture. It isn't the sort of thing one should talk of in private. I simply want my cigarette case back.

ALGERNON: Yes; but this isn't your cigarette case. This cigarette case is a present from someone of the name of Cecily, and you said you didn't know anyone of that name.

JACK: Well, if you want to know, Cecily happens to be my aunt.

ALGERNON: Your aunt!

JACK: Yes. Charming old lady she is, too. Lives at Tunbridge Wells. Just give it back to me, Algy.

ALGERNON (*retreating to back of sofa*): But why does she call herself Cecily if she is your aunt and lives at Tunbridge Wells? (*Reading.*) "From little Cecily with her fondest love."

JACK (*moving to sofa and kneeling upon it*): My dear fellow, what on earth is there in that? Some aunts are tall, some aunts are not tall. That is a matter that surely an aunt may be allowed to decide for herself. You seem to think that every aunt should be exactly like your aunt! That is absurd! For Heaven's sake give me back my cigarette case. (*Follows* ALGERNON *round the room.*)

ALGERNON: Yes. But why does your aunt call you her uncle? "From little Cecily, with her fondest love to her dear Uncle Jack." There is no objection, I admit, to an aunt being a small aunt, but why an aunt, no matter what her size may be, should call her own nephew her uncle, I can't quite make out. Besides, your name isn't Jack at all; it is Ernest.

JACK: It isn't Ernest; it's Jack.

ALGERNON: You have always told me it was Ernest. I have introduced you to everyone as Ernest. You answer to the name of Ernest. You look as if your name was Ernest. You are the most earnest looking person I ever saw in my life. It is perfectly absurd your saying that your name isn't Ernest. It's on your cards. Here is one of them. (*Taking it from case.*) "Mr. Ernest Worthing, B. 4, The Albany." I'll keep this as a proof that your name is Ernest if ever you attempt to deny it to me, or to Gwendolen, or to anyone else. (*Puts the card in his pocket.*)

JACK: Well, my name is Ernest in town and Jack in the country, and the cigarette case was given to me in the country.

ALGERNON: Yes, but that does not account for the fact that your small Aunt Cecily, who lives at Tunbridge Wells, calls you her dear uncle. Come, old boy, you had much better have the thing out at once.

JACK: My dear Algy, you talk exactly as if you were a dentist. It is very vulgar to talk like a dentist when one isn't a dentist. It produces a false impression.

ALGERNON: Well, that is exactly what dentists always do. Now, go on! Tell me the whole thing. I may mention that I have always suspected you of being a confirmed and secret Bunburyist; and I am quite sure of it now.

JACK: Bunburyist? What on earth do you mean by a Bunburyist?

ALGERNON: I'll reveal to you the meaning of that incomparable expression as soon as you are kind enough to inform me why you are Ernest in town and Jack in the country.

JACK: Well, produce my cigarette case first.

ALGERNON: Here it is. (*Hands cigarette case.*) Now produce your explanation, and pray make it improbable. (*Sits on sofa.*)

JACK: My dear fellow, there is nothing improbable about my explanation at all. In fact it's perfectly ordinary. Old Mr. Thomas Cardew, who adopted me when I was a little boy, made me in his will guardian to his granddaughter, Miss Cecily Cardew. Cecily, who addresses me as her uncle from motives of respect that you could not possibly appreciate, lives at my place in the country under the charge of her admirable governess, Miss Prism.

ALGERNON: Where is that place in the country, by the way?

JACK: That is nothing to you, dear boy. You are not going to be invited. . . . I may tell you candidly that the place is not in Shropshire.

ALGERNON: I suspected that, my dear fellow! I have Bunburyed all over Shropshire on two separate occasions. Now, go on. Why are you Ernest in town and Jack in the country?

JACK: My dear Algy, I don't know whether you will be able to understand my real motives. You are hardly serious enough. When one is placed in the position of guardian, one has to adopt a very high moral tone on all subjects. It's one's duty to do so. And as a high moral tone can hardly be said to conduce very much to either one's health or one's happiness, in order to get up to town I have always pretended to have a younger brother of the name of Ernest, who lives in the Albany, and gets into the most dreadful scrapes. That, my dear Algy, is the whole truth pure and simple.

ALGERNON: The truth is rarely pure and never simple. Modern life would be very tedious if it were either, and modern literature a complete impossibility!

JACK: That wouldn't be at all a bad thing.

ALGERNON: Literary criticism is not your forte, my dear fellow. Don't try it. You should leave that to people who haven't been at a University. They do it so well in the daily papers. What you really are is a Bunburyist. I was quite right in saying you were a Bunburyist. You are one of the most advanced Bunburyists I know.

JACK: What on earth do you mean?

ALGERNON: You have invented a very useful young brother called Ernest, in order that you may be able to come up to town as often as you like. I have invented an invaluable permanent invalid called Bunbury, in order that I may be able to go down into the country whenever I choose. Bunbury is perfectly invaluable. If it wasn't for Bunbury's extraordinary bad health, for instance, I wouldn't be able to dine with you at Willis's tonight, for I have been really engaged to Aunt Augusta for more than a week.

JACK: I haven't asked you to dine with me anywhere tonight.

ALGERNON: I know. You are absurdly careless about sending out invitations. It is very foolish of you. Nothing annoys people so much as not receiving invitations.

JACK: You had much better dine with your Aunt Augusta.

ALGERNON: I haven't the smallest intention of doing anything of the kind. To begin with, I dined there on Monday, and once a week is quite enough to dine with one's own relations. In the second place, whenever I do dine there I am always treated as a member of the family, and sent down with either no woman at all, or two. In the third place, I know perfectly well whom she will place me next to, tonight. She will place me next Mary Farquhar, who always flirts with her own husband across the dinner-table. That is not very pleasant. Indeed, it is not even decent . . . and that sort of thing is enormously on the increase. The amount of women in London who flirt with their own husbands is perfectly scandalous. It looks so bad. It is simply washing one's clean linen in public. Besides, now that I know you to be a confirmed Bunburyist, I naturally want to talk to you about Bunburying. I want to tell you the rules.

JACK: I'm not a Bunburyist at all. If Gwendolen accepts me, I am going to kill my brother, indeed I think I'll kill him in any case. Cecily is a little too much interested in him. It is rather a bore. So I am going to get rid of Ernest. And I strongly advise you to do the same with Mr. . . . with your invalid friend who has the absurd name.

ALGERNON: Nothing will induce me to part with Bunbury, and if you ever get married, which seems to me extremely problematic, you will be very glad to know Bunbury. A man who marries without knowing Bunbury has a very tedious time of it.

JACK: That is nonsense. If I marry a charming girl like Gwendolen, and she is the only girl I ever saw in my life that I would marry, I certainly won't want to know Bunbury.

ALGERNON: Then your wife will. You don't seem to realize, that in married life three is company and two is none.

JACK (*sententiously*): That, my dear young friend, is the theory that the corrupt French Drama has been propounding for the last fifty years.

ALGERNON: Yes; and that the happy English home has proved in half the time.

JACK: For heaven's sake, don't try to be cynical. It's perfectly easy to be cynical.

ALGERNON: My dear fellow, it isn't easy to be anything nowadays. There's such a lot of beastly competition about. (*The sound of an electric bell is heard.*) Ah! that must be Aunt Augusta. Only relatives, or creditors, ever ring in that Wagnerian manner. Now, if I get her out of the way for ten minutes, so that you can have an opportunity for proposing to Gwendolen, may I dine with you tonight at Willis's?

JACK: I suppose so, if you want to.

ALGERNON: Yes, but you must be serious about it. I hate people who are not serious about meals. It is so shallow of them.

(*Enter* LANE.)

LANE: Lady Bracknell and Miss Fairfax.

(ALGERNON *goes forward to meet them. Enter* LADY BRACKNELL *and* GWENDOLEN.)

LADY BRACKNELL: Good afternoon, dear Algernon, I hope you are behaving very well.

ALGERNON: I'm feeling very well, Aunt Augusta.

LADY BRACKNELL: That's not quite the same thing. In fact the two things rarely go together. (*Sees* JACK *and bows to him with icy coldness.*)

ALGERNON (*to* GWENDOLEN): Dear me, you are smart!

GWENDOLEN: I am always smart! Aren't I, Mr. Worthing?

JACK: You're quite perfect, Miss Fairfax.

GWENDOLEN: Oh! I hope I am not that. It would leave no room for developments, and I intend to develop in many directions. (GWENDOLEN *and* JACK *sit down together in the corner.*)

LADY BRACKNELL: I'm sorry if we are a little late, Algernon, but I was obliged to call on dear Lady Harbury. I hadn't been there since her poor husband's death. I never saw a woman so altered; she looks quite twenty years younger. And now I'll have a cup of tea, and one of those nice cucumber sandwiches you promised me.

ALGERNON: Certainly, Aunt Augusta. (*Goes over to tea-table.*)

LADY BRACKNELL: Won't you come and sit here, Gwendolen?

GWENDOLEN: Thanks, Mamma, I'm quite comfortable where I am.

ALGERNON (*picking up empty plate in horror*): Good heavens! Lane! Why are there no cucumber sandwiches? I ordered them specially.

LANE (*gravely*): There were no cucumbers in the market this morning, sir. I went down twice.

ALGERNON: No cucumbers!

LANE: No, sir. Not even for ready money.

ALGERNON: That will do, Lane, thank you.

LANE: Thank you, sir.

ALGERNON: I am greatly distressed, Aunt Augusta, about there being no cucumbers, not even for ready money.

LADY BRACKNELL: It really makes no matter, Algernon. I had some crumpets with Lady Harbury, who seems to me to be living entirely for pleasure now.

ALGERNON: I hear her hair has turned quite gold from grief.

LADY BRACKNELL: It certainly has changed its colour. From what cause I, of course, cannot say. (ALGERNON *crosses and hands tea.*) Thank you. I've quite a treat for you tonight, Algernon. I am going to send you down with Mary Farquhar. She is such a nice woman, and so attentive to her husband. It's delightful to watch them.

ALGERNON: I am afraid, Aunt Augusta, I shall have to give up the pleasure of dining with you tonight after all.

LADY BRACKNELL (*frowning*): I hope not, Algernon. It would put my table completely out. Your uncle would have to dine upstairs. Fortunately he is accustomed to that.

ALGERNON: It is a great bore, and, I need hardly say, a terrible disappointment to me, but the fact is I have just had a telegram to say that my poor friend Bunbury is very ill again. (*Exchanges glances with* JACK.) They seem to think I should be with him.

LADY BRACKNELL: It is very strange. This Mr. Bunbury seems to suffer from curiously bad health.

ALGERNON: Yes, poor Bunbury is a dreadful invalid.

LADY BRACKNELL: Well, I must say, Algernon, that I think it is high time that Mr. Bunbury made up his mind whether he was going to live or to die. This shilly-shallying with the question is absurd. Nor do I in any way approve of the modern sympathy with invalids. I consider it morbid. Illness of any kind is hardly a thing to be encouraged in others. Health is the primary duty of life. I am always telling that to your poor uncle, but he never seems to take much notice . . . as far as any improvement in his ailments goes. I should be obliged if you would ask Mr. Bunbury, from me, to be kind enough not to have a relapse on Saturday, for I rely on you to arrange my music for me. It is my last reception, and one wants something that will encourage conversation, particularly at the end of the season when everyone has practically said whatever they had to say, which, in most cases, was probably not much.

ALGERNON: I'll speak to Bunbury, Aunt Augusta, if he is still conscious, and I think I can promise you he'll be all right by Saturday. Of course the music is a great difficulty. You see, if one plays good music, people don't listen, and if one plays bad music, people don't talk. But I'll run over the programme I've drawn out, if you will kindly come into the next room for a moment.

LADY BRACKNELL: Thank you, Algernon. It is very thoughtful of you. (*Rising, and following* ALGERNON.) I'm sure the programme will be delightful, after a few expurgations. French songs I cannot possibly allow. People always seem to think that they are improper, and either look shocked, which is vulgar, or laugh, which is worse. But German sounds a thoroughly respectable language, and indeed, I believe is so. Gwendolen, you will accompany me.

GWENDOLEN: Certainly, Mamma.

(LADY BRACKNELL *and* ALGERNON *go into the music-room,* GWENDOLEN *remains behind.*)

JACK: Charming day it has been, Miss Fairfax.

GWENDOLEN: Pray don't talk to me about the weather, Mr. Worthing. Whenever people talk to me about the weather, I always feel quite certain that they mean something else. And that makes me so nervous.

JACK: I do mean something else.

GWENDOLEN: I thought so. In fact, I am never wrong.

JACK: And I would like to be allowed to take advantage of Lady Bracknell's temporary absence. . . .

GWENDOLEN: I would certainly advise you to do so. Mamma has a way of coming back suddenly into a room that I have often had to speak to her about.

JACK (*nervously*): Miss Fairfax, ever since I met you I have admired you more than any girl . . . I have ever met since . . . I met you.

GWENDOLEN: Yes, I am quite aware of the fact. And I often wish that in public, at any rate, you had been more demonstrative. For me you have always had an irresistible fascination. Even before I met you I was far from indifferent to you. (JACK *looks at her in amazement.*) We live, as I hope you know, Mr. Worthing, in an age of ideals. The fact is constantly mentioned in the more expensive monthly magazines, and has reached the provincial pulpits I am told: and my ideal has always been to love someone of the name of Ernest. There is something in that name that inspires absolute confidence. The moment Algernon first mentioned to me that he had a friend called Ernest, I knew I was destined to love you.

JACK: You really love me, Gwendolen?

GWENDOLEN: Passionately!

JACK: Darling! You don't know how happy you've made me.

GWENDOLEN: My own Ernest!

JACK: But you don't really mean to say that you couldn't love me if my name wasn't Ernest?

GWENDOLEN: But your name is Ernest.

JACK: Yes, I know it is. But supposing it was something else? Do you mean to say you couldn't love me then?

GWENDOLEN (*glibly*): Ah! that is clearly a metaphysical speculation, and like most metaphysical speculations has very little reference at all to the actual facts of real life, as we know them.

JACK: Personally, darling, to speak quite candidly, I don't much care about the name of Ernest . . . I don't think the name suits me at all.

GWENDOLEN: It suits you perfectly. It is a divine name. It has a music of its own. It produces vibrations.

JACK: Well, really, Gwendolen, I must say that I think there are lots of other much nicer names. I think Jack, for instance, a charming name.

GWENDOLEN: Jack? . . . No, there is very little music in the name Jack, if any at all, indeed. It does not thrill. It produces absolutely no vibrations. . . . I have known several Jacks, and they all, without exception, were more than usually plain. Besides, Jack is a notorious domesticity for John! And I pity any woman who is married to a man called John. She would probably never be allowed to know the entrancing pleasure of a single moment's solitude. The only really safe name is Ernest.

JACK: Gwendolen, I must get christened at once—I mean we must get married at once. There is no time to be lost.

GWENDOLEN: Married, Mr. Worthing?

JACK (astounded): Well . . . surely. You know that I love you, and you led me to believe, Miss Fairfax, that you were not absolutely indifferent to me.

GWENDOLEN: I adore you. But you haven't proposed to me yet. Nothing has been said at all about marriage. The subject has not even been touched on.

JACK: Well . . . may I propose to you now?

GWENDOLEN: I think it would be an admirable opportunity. And to spare you any possible disappointment, Mr. Worthing, I think it only fair to tell you quite frankly beforehand that I am fully determined to accept you.

JACK: Gwendolen!

GWENDOLEN: Yes, Mr. Worthing, what have you got to say to me?

JACK: You know what I have got to say to you.

GWENDOLEN: Yes, but you don't say it.

JACK: Gwendolen, will you marry me? (Goes on his knees.)

GWENDOLEN: Of course I will, darling. How long you have been about it! I am afraid you have had very little experience in how to propose.

JACK: My own one, I have never loved anyone in the world but you.

GWENDOLEN: Yes, but men often propose for practice. I know my brother Gerald does. All my girl-friends tell me so. What wonderfully blue eyes you have, Ernest! They are quite, quite blue. I hope you will always look at me just like that, especially when there are other people present.

(Enter LADY BRACKNELL.)

LADY BRACKNELL: Mr. Worthing! Rise, sir, from this semi-recumbent posture. It is most indecorous.

GWENDOLEN: Mamma! (*He tries to rise; she restrains him.*) I must beg you to retire. This is no place for you. Besides, Mr. Worthing has not quite finished yet.

LADY BRACKNELL: Finished what, may I ask?

GWENDOLEN: I am engaged to Mr. Worthing, Mamma. (*They rise together.*)

LADY BRACKNELL: Pardon me, you are not engaged to anyone. When you do become engaged to someone, I, or your father, should his health permit him, will inform you of the fact. An engagement should come on a young girl as a surprise, pleasant or unpleasant, as the case may be. It is hardly a matter that she could be allowed to arrange for herself. . . . And now I have a few questions to put to you, Mr. Worthing. While I am making these inquiries, you, Gwendolen, will wait for me below in the carriage.

GWENDOLEN (*reproachfully*): Mamma!

LADY BRACKNELL: In the carriage, Gwendolen! (GWENDOLEN *goes to the door. She and* JACK *blow kisses to each other behind* LADY BRACKNELL'S *back.* LADY BRACKNELL *looks vaguely about as if she could not understand what the noise was. Finally turns round.*) Gwendolen, the carriage!

GWENDOLEN: Yes, Mamma. (*Goes out, looking back at* JACK.)

LADY BRACKNELL (*sitting down*): You can take a seat, Mr. Worthing.

(*Looks in her pocket for note-book and pencil.*)

JACK: Thank you, Lady Bracknell, I prefer standing.

LADY BRACKNELL (*pencil and note-book in hand*): I feel bound to tell you that you are not down on my list of eligible young men, although I have the same list as the dear Duchess of Bolton has. We work together, in fact. However, I am quite ready to enter your name, should your answers be what a really affectionate mother requires. Do you smoke?

JACK: Well, yes, I must admit I smoke.

LADY BRACKNELL: I am glad to hear it. A man should always have an occupation of some kind. There are far too many idle men in London as it is. How old are you?

JACK: Twenty-nine.

LADY BRACKNELL: A very good age to be married at. I have always been of opinion that a man who desires to get married should know either everything or nothing. Which do you know?

JACK (*after some hesitation*): I know nothing, Lady Bracknell.

LADY BRACKNELL: I am pleased to hear it. I do not approve of anything that tampers with natural ignorance. Ignorance is like a delicate exotic fruit; touch it and the bloom is gone. The whole theory of modern education is radically unsound. Fortunately in England, at any rate, education produces no effect whatsoever. If it did, it would prove a serious danger to the upper classes, and probably lead to acts of violence in Grosvenor Square. What is your income?

JACK: Between seven and eight thousand a year:

LADY BRACKNELL (*makes a note in her book*): In land, or in *investments?*

JACK: In investments, chiefly.

LADY BRACKNELL: That is satisfactory. What between the duties expected of one during one's lifetime, and the duties exacted from one after one's death, land has ceased to be either a profit or a pleasure. It gives one position, and prevents one from keeping it up. That's all that can be said about land.

JACK: I have a country house with some land, of course, attached to it, about fifteen hundred acres, I believe; but I don't depend on that for my real income. In fact, as far as I can make out, the poachers are the only people who make anything out of it.

LADY BRACKNELL: A country house! How many bedrooms? Well, that point can be cleared up afterwards. You have a town house, I hope? A girl with a simple, unspoiled nature, like Gwendolen, could hardly be expected to reside in the country.

JACK: Well, I own a house in Belgrave Square, but it is let by the year to Lady Bloxham. Of course, I can get it back whenever I like, at six months' notice.

LADY BRACKNELL: Lady Bloxham? I don't know her.

JACK: Oh, she goes about very little. She is a lady considerably advanced in years.

LADY BRACKNELL: Ah, nowadays that is no guarantee of respectability of character. What number in Belgrave Square?

JACK: 149.

LADY BRACKNELL (*shaking her head*): The unfashionable side. I thought there was something. However, that could easily be altered.

JACK: Do you mean the fashion, or the side?

LADY BRACKNELL (*sternly*): Both, if necessary, I presume. What are your politics?

JACK: Well, I am afraid I really have none. I am a Liberal Unionist.

LADY BRACKNELL: Oh, they count as Tories. They dine with us. Or come in the evening, at any rate. Now to minor matters. Are your parents living?

JACK: I have lost both my parents.

LADY BRACKNELL: Both? . . . That seems like carelessness. Who was your father? He was evidently a man of some wealth. Was he born in what the Radical papers call the purple of commerce, or did he rise from the ranks of aristocracy?

JACK: I am afraid I really don't know. The fact is, Lady Bracknell, I said I had lost my parents. It would be nearer the truth to say that my parents seem to have lost me. . . . I don't actually know who I am by birth. I was . . . well, I was found.

LADY BRACKNELL: Found!

JACK: The late Mr. Thomas Cardew, an old gentleman of a very charitable and kindly disposition, found me, and gave me the name of Worthing, because he happened to have a first-class ticket for Worthing in his pocket at the time. Worthing is a place in Sussex. It is a seaside resort.

LADY BRACKNELL: Where did the charitable gentleman who had a first-class ticket for this seaside resort find you?

JACK (*gravely*): In a handbag.

LADY BRACKNELL: A handbag?

JACK (*very seriously*): Yes, Lady Bracknell. I was in a handbag—a somewhat large, black leather handbag, with handles to it—an ordinary handbag, in fact.

LADY BRACKNELL: In what locality did this Mr. James, or Thomas, Cardew come across this ordinary handbag?

JACK: In the cloakroom at Victoria Station. It was given to him in mistake for his own.

LADY BRACKNELL: The cloakroom at Victoria Station?

JACK: Yes. The Brighton line.

LADY BRACKNELL: The line is immaterial. Mr. Worthing, I confess I feel somewhat bewildered by what you have just told me. To be born, or at any rate, bred in a handbag, whether it had handles or not, seems to me to display a contempt for the ordinary decencies of family life that remind one of the worst excesses of the French Revolution. And I presume you know what that unfortunate movement led to? As for the particular locality in which the handbag was found, a cloakroom at a railway station might serve to conceal a social indiscretion—has probably, indeed, been used for that purpose before now—but it could hardly be regarded as an assured basis for a recognized position in good society.

JACK: May I ask you then what you would advise me to do? I need hardly say I would do anything in the world to ensure Gwendolen's happiness.

LADY BRACKNELL: I would strongly advise you, Mr. Worthing, to try and acquire some relations as soon as possible, and to make a definite effort to produce at any rate one parent, of either sex, before the season is quite over.

JACK: Well, I don't see how I could possibly manage to do that. I can produce the handbag at any moment. It is in my dressing-room at home. I really think that should satisfy you, Lady Bracknell.

LADY BRACKNELL: Me, sir! What has it to do with me? You can hardly imagine that I and Lord Bracknell would dream of allowing our only daughter—a girl brought up with the utmost care—to marry into a cloakroom, and form an alliance with a parcel? Good morning, Mr. Worthing!

(LADY BRACKNELL *sweeps out in majestic indignation.*)

JACK: Good morning! (ALGERNON, *from the other room, strikes up the* Wedding March. JACK *looks perfectly furious, and goes to the door.*) For goodness' sake don't play that ghastly tune, Algy! How idiotic you are!

(*The music stops, and* ALGERNON *enters cheerily.*)

ALGERNON: Didn't it go off all right, old boy? You don't mean to say Gwendolen refused you? I know it is a way she has. She is always refusing people. I think it is most ill-natured of her.

JACK: Oh, Gwendolen is as right as a trivet. As far as she is concerned, we are engaged. Her mother is perfectly unbearable. Never met such a gorgon . . . I don't really know what a gorgon is like, but I am quite sure that Lady Bracknell is one. In any case, she is a monster, without being a myth, which is rather unfair . . . I beg your pardon, Algy, I suppose I shouldn't talk about your own aunt in that way before you.

ALGERNON: My dear boy, I love hearing my relations abused. It is the only thing that makes me put up with them at all. Relations are simply a tedious pack of people who haven't got the remotest knowledge of how to live, nor the smallest instinct about when to die.

JACK: Oh, that is nonsense!

ALGERNON: It isn't!

JACK: Well, I won't argue about the matter. You always want to argue about things.

ALGERNON: That is exactly what things were originally made for.

JACK: Upon my word, if I thought that, I'd shoot myself. . . . (*A pause.*) You don't think there is any chance of Gwendolen becoming like her mother in about a hundred and fifty years, do you, Algy?

ALGERNON: All women become like their mothers. That is their tragedy. No man does. That's his.

JACK: Is that clever?

ALGERNON: It is perfectly phrased! and quite as true as any observation in civilized life should be.

JACK: I am sick to death of cleverness. Everybody is clever nowadays. You can't go anywhere without meeting clever people. The thing has become an absolute public nuisance. I wish to goodness we had a few fools left.

ALGERNON: We have.

JACK: I should extremely like to meet them. What do they talk about?

ALGERNON: The fools! Oh! about the clever people, of course.

JACK: What fools!

ALGERNON: By the way, did you tell Gwendolen the truth about your being Ernest in town, and Jack in the country?

JACK (*in a very patronizing manner*): My dear fellow, the truth isn't quite the sort of thing one tells to a nice sweet refined girl. What extraordinary ideas you have about the way to behave to a woman!

ALGERNON: The only way to behave to a woman is to make love to her, if she is pretty, and to someone else if she is plain.

JACK: Oh, that is nonsense.

ALGERNON: What about your brother? What about that profligate Ernest?

JACK: Oh, before the end of the week I shall have got rid of him. I'll say he died in Paris of apoplexy. Lots of people die of apoplexy, quite suddenly, don't they?

ALGERNON: Yes, but it's hereditary, my dear fellow. It's a sort of thing that runs in families. You had much better say a severe chill.

JACK: You are sure a severe chill isn't hereditary, or anything of that kind?

ALGERNON: Of course it isn't!

JACK: Very well, then. My poor brother Ernest is carried off suddenly in Paris, by a severe chill. That gets rid of him.

ALGERNON: But I thought you said that . . . Miss Cardew was a little too much interested in your poor brother Ernest? Won't she feel his loss a good deal?

JACK: Oh, that is all right. Cecily is not a silly romantic girl, I am glad to say. She has got a capital appetite, goes long walks, and pays no attention at all to her lessons.

ALGERNON: I would rather like to see Cecily.

JACK: I will take very good care you never do. She is excessively pretty, and she is only just eighteen.

ALGERNON: Have you told Gwendolen yet that you have an excessively pretty ward who is only just eighteen?

JACK: Oh! one doesn't blurt these things out to people. Cecily and Gwendolen are perfectly certain to be extremely great friends. I'll bet you anything you like that half an hour after they have met, they will be calling each other sister.

ALGERNON: Women only do that when they have called each other a lot of other things first. Now, my dear boy, if we want to get a good table at Willis's, we really must go and dress. Do you know it is nearly seven?

JACK (*irritably*): Oh! it always is nearly seven.

ALGERNON: Well, I'm hungry.

JACK: I never knew you when you weren't. . . .

ALGERNON: What shall we do after dinner? Go to the theatre?

JACK: Oh no! I loathe listening.

ALGERNON: Well, let us go to the club?

JACK: Oh, no! I hate talking.

ALGERNON: Well, we might trot round to the Empire at ten?

JACK: Oh no! I can't bear looking at things. It is so silly.

ALGERNON: Well, what shall we do?

JACK: Nothing!

ALGERNON: It is awfully hard work doing nothing. However, I don't mind hard work where there is no definite object of any kind.

(*Enter* LANE.)

LANE: Miss Fairfax.

(*Enter* GWENDOLEN. LANE *goes out.*)

ALGERNON: Gwendolen, upon my word!

GWENDOLEN: Algy, kindly turn your back. I have something very particular to say to Mr. Worthing.

ALGERNON: Really, Gwendolen, I don't think I can allow this at all.

GWENDOLEN: Algy, you always adopt a strictly immoral attitude towards life. You are not quite old enough to do that. (ALGERNON *retires to the fireplace.*)

JACK: My own darling!

GWENDOLEN: Ernest, we may never be married. From the expression on Mamma's face I fear we never shall. Few parents nowadays pay any regard to what their children say to them. The old-fashioned respect for the young is fast dying out. Whatever influence I ever had over Mamma, I lost at the age of three. But although she may prevent us from becoming man and wife, and I may marry someone else, and marry often, nothing that she can possibly do can alter my eternal devotion to you.

JACK: Dear Gwendolen!

GWENDOLEN: The story of your romantic origin, as related to me by Mamma, with unpleasing comments, has naturally stirred the deeper fibres of my nature. Your Christian name has an irresistible fascination. The simplicity of your character makes you exquisitely incomprehensible to me. Your town address at the Albany I have. What is your address in the country?

JACK: The Manor House, Woolton, Hertfordshire.

(ALGERNON, *who has been carefully listening, smiles to himself, and writes the address on his shirt-cuff. Then picks up the Railway Guide.*)

GWENDOLEN: There is a good postal service, I suppose? It may be necessary to do something desperate. That of course will require serious consideration. I will communicate with you daily.

JACK: My own one!

GWENDOLEN: How long do you remain in town?

JACK: Till Monday.

GWENDOLEN: Good! Algy, you may turn round now.

ALGERNON: Thanks, I've turned round already.

GWENDOLEN: You may also ring the bell.

JACK: You will let me see you to your carriage, my own darling?

GWENDOLEN: Certainly.

JACK (*to* LANE, *who now enters*): I will see Miss Fairfax out.

LANE: Yes, sir. (JACK *and* GWENDOLEN *go off.*)

(LANE *presents several letters on a salver to* ALGERNON. *It is to be surmised that they are bills, as* ALGERNON *after looking at the envelopes, tears them up.*)

ALGERNON: A glass of sherry, Lane.

LANE: Yes, sir.

ALGERNON: Tomorrow, Lane, I'm going Bunburying.

LANE: Yes, sir.

ALGERNON: I shall probably not be back till Monday. You can put up my dress clothes, my smoking jacket, and all the Bunbury suits. . . .

LANE: Yes, sir. (*Handing sherry.*)

ALGERNON: I hope tomorrow will be a fine day, Lane.

LANE: It never is, sir.

ALGERNON: Lane, you're a perfect pessimist.

LANE: I do my best to give satisfaction, sir.

(*Enter* JACK. LANE *goes off.*)

JACK: There's a sensible, intellectual girl! The only girl I ever cared for in my life. (ALGERNON *is laughing immoderately.*) What on earth are you so amused at?

ALGERNON: Oh, I'm a little anxious about poor Bunbury, that is all.

JACK: If you don't take care, your friend Bunbury will get you into a serious scrape some day.

ALGERNON: I love scrapes. They are the only things that are never serious.

JACK: Oh, that's nonsense, Algy. You never talk anything but nonsense.

ALGERNON: Nobody ever does.

(JACK *looks indignantly at him, and leaves the room.* ALGERNON *lights a cigarette, reads his shirt-cuff, and smiles.*)

ACT-DROP.

ACT TWO

Scene. Garden at the Manor House. A flight of grey stone steps leads up to the house. The garden, an old-fashioned one, full of roses. Time of year, July. Basket chairs, and a table covered with books, are set under a large yew tree.

(MISS PRISM *discovered seated at the table.* CECILY *is at the back watering flowers.*)

MISS PRISM (*calling*): Cecily, Cecily! Surely such a utilitarian occupation as the watering of flowers is rather Moulton's duty than yours? Especially at a moment when intellectual pleasures await you. Your German grammar is on the table. Pray open it at page fifteen. We will repeat yesterday's lesson.

CECILY (*coming over very slowly*): But I don't like German. It isn't at all a becoming language. I know perfectly well that I look quite plain after my German lesson.

MISS PRISM: Child, you know how anxious your guardian is that you should improve yourself in every way. He laid particular stress on your German, as he was leaving for town yesterday. Indeed, he always lays stress on your German when he is leaving for town.

CECILY: Dear Uncle Jack is so very serious! Sometimes he is so serious that I think he cannot be quite well.

MISS PRISM (*drawing herself up*): Your guardian enjoys the best of health, and his gravity of demeanour is especially to be commended in one so comparatively young as he is. I know no one who has a higher sense of duty and responsibility.

CECILY: I suppose that is why he often looks a little bored when we three are together.

MISS PRISM: Cecily! I am surprised at you. Mr. Worthing has many troubles in his life. Idle merriment and triviality would be out of place in his conversation. You must remember his constant anxiety about that unfortunate young man his brother.

CECILY: I wish Uncle Jack would allow that unfortunate young man, his brother, to come down here sometimes. We might have a good influence over him, Miss Prism. I am sure you certainly would. You know German, and Geology, and things of that kind influence a man very much. (CECILY *begins to write in her diary.*)

MISS PRISM (*shaking her head*): I do not think that even I could produce any effect on a character that according to his own brother's admission is irretrievably weak and vacillating. Indeed I am not sure that I would desire to reclaim him. I am not in favour of this modern mania for turning bad people into good people at a moment's notice. As a man sows so let him reap. You must put away your diary, Cecily. I really don't see why you should keep a diary at all.

CECILY: I keep a diary in order to enter the wonderful secrets of my life. If I didn't write them down I should probably forget all about them.

MISS PRISM: Memory, my dear Cecily, is the diary that we all carry about with us.

CECILY: Yes, but it usually chronicles the things that have never happened, and couldn't possibly have happened. I believe that memory is responsible for nearly all the three-volume novels that Mudie sends us.

MISS PRISM: Do not speak slightingly of the three-volume novel, Cecily. I wrote one myself in earlier days.

CECILY: Did you really, Miss Prism? How wonderfully clever you are! I hope it did not end happily? I don't like novels that end happily. They depress me so much.

MISS PRISM: The good ended happily, and the bad unhappily. That is what fiction means.

CECILY: I suppose so. But it seems very unfair. And was your novel ever published?

MISS PRISM: Alas! no. The manuscript unfortunately was abandoned. I use the word in the sense of lost or mislaid. To your work, child, these speculations are profitless.

CECILY (*smiling*): But I see dear Dr. Chasuble coming up through the garden.

MISS PRISM (*rising and advancing*): Dr. Chasuble! This is indeed a pleasure.

(*Enter* CANON CHASUBLE.)

CHASUBLE: And how are we this morning? Miss Prism, you are, I trust, well?

CECILY: Miss Prism has just been complaining of a slight headache. I think it would do her so much good to have a short stroll with you in the Park, Dr. Chasuble.

MISS PRISM: Cecily, I have not mentioned anything about a headache.

CECILY: No, dear Miss Prism, I know that, but I felt instinctively that you had a headache. Indeed I was thinking about that, and not about my German lesson, when the Rector came in.

CHASUBLE: I hope, Cecily, you are not inattentive.

CECILY: Oh, I am afraid I am.

CHASUBLE: That is strange. Were I fortunate enough to be Miss Prism's pupil, I would hang upon her lips. (MISS PRISM *glares*.) I spoke metaphorically.—My metaphor was drawn from bees. Ahem! Mr. Worthing, I suppose, has not returned from town yet?

MISS PRISM: We do not expect him till Monday afternoon.

CHASUBLE: Ah yes, he usually likes to spend his Sunday in London. He is not one of those whose sole aim is enjoyment, as, by all accounts, that unfortunate young man his brother seems to be. But I must not disturb Egeria and her pupil any longer.

MISS PRISM: Egeria? My name is Lætitia, Doctor.

CHASUBLE (*bowing*): A classical allusion merely, drawn from the pagan authors. I shall see you both no doubt at Evensong?

MISS PRISM: I think, dear Doctor, I will have a stroll with you. I find I have a headache after all, and a walk might do it good.

CHASUBLE: With pleasure, Miss Prism, with pleasure. We might go as far as the schools and back.

MISS PRISM: That would be delightful. Cecily, you will read your Political Economy in my absence. The chapter on the Fall of the Rupee you may omit. It is somewhat too sensational. Even these metallic problems have their melodramatic side.

(*Goes down the garden with* DR. CHASUBLE.)

CECILY (*picks up books and throws them back on table*): Horrid Political Economy! Horrid Geography! Horrid, horrid German!

(*Enter* MERRIMAN *with a card on a salver.*)

MERRIMAN: Mr. Ernest Worthing has just driven over from the station. He has brought his luggage with him.

CECILY (*takes the card and reads it*): "Mr. Ernest Worthing, B. 4, The Albany, W." Uncle Jack's brother! Did you tell him Mr. Worthing was in town?

MERRIMAN: Yes, Miss. He seemed very much disappointed. I mentioned that you and Miss Prism were in the garden. He said he was anxious to speak to you privately for a moment.

CECILY: Ask Mr. Ernest Worthing to come here. I suppose you had better talk to the housekeeper about a room for him.

MERRIMAN: Yes, Miss. (MERRIMAN *goes off.*)

CECILY: I have never met any really wicked person before. I feel rather frightened. I am so afraid he will look just like everyone else.

(*Enter* ALGERNON, *very gay and debonair.*)

He does!

ALGERNON (*raising his hat*): You are my little cousin Cecily, I'm sure.

CECILY: You are under some strange mistake. I am not little. In fact, I believe I am more than usually tall for my age. (ALGERNON *is rather taken aback.*) But I am your cousin Cecily. You, I see from your card, are Uncle Jack's brother, my cousin Ernest, my wicked cousin Ernest.

ALGERNON: Oh! I am not really wicked at all, cousin Cecily. You mustn't think that I am wicked.

CECILY: If you are not, then you have certainly been deceiving us all in a very inexcusable manner. I hope you have not been leading a double life, pretending to be wicked and being really good all the time. That would be hypocrisy.

ALGERNON (*looks at her in amazement*): Oh! Of course I have been rather reckless.

CECILY: I am glad to hear it.

ALGERNON: In fact, now you mention the subject, I have been very bad in my own small way.

CECILY: I don't think you should be so proud of that, though I am sure it must have been very pleasant.

ALGERNON: It is much pleasanter being here with you.

CECILY: I can't understand how you are here at all. Uncle Jack won't be back till Monday afternoon.

ALGERNON: That is a great disappointment. I am obliged to go up by the first train on Monday morning. I have a business appointment that I am anxious . . . to miss.

CECILY: Couldn't you miss it anywhere but in London?

ALGERNON: No; the appointment is in London.

CECILY: Well, I know, of course, how important it is not to keep a business engagement, if one wants to retain any sense of the beauty of life, but still I think you had better wait till Uncle Jack arrives. I know he wants to speak to you about your emigrating.

ALGERNON: About my what?

CECILY: Your emigrating. He has gone up to buy your outfit.

ALGERNON: I certainly wouldn't let Jack buy my outfit. He has no taste in neckties at all.

CECILY: I don't think you will require neckties. Uncle Jack is sending you to Australia.

ALGERNON: Australia? I'd sooner die.

CECILY: Well, he said at dinner on Wednesday night, that you would have to choose between this world, the next world, and Australia.

ALGERNON: Oh, well! The accounts I have received of Australia and the next world are not particularly encouraging. This world is good enough for me, cousin Cecily.

CECILY: Yes, but are you good enough for it?

ALGERNON: I'm afraid I'm not that. That is why I want you to reform me. You might make that your mission, if you don't mind, cousin Cecily.

CECILY: I'm afraid I've no time, this afternoon.

ALGERNON: Well, would you mind my reforming myself this afternoon?

CECILY: It is rather quixotic of you. But I think you should try.

ALGERNON: I will. I feel better already.

CECILY: You are looking a little worse.

ALGERNON: That is because I am hungry.

CECILY: How thoughtless of me. I should have remembered that when one is going to lead an entirely new life, one requires regular and wholesome meals. Won't you come in?

ALGERNON: Thank you. Might I have a button-hole first? I never have any appetite unless I have a button-hole first.

CECILY: A Maréchal Niel? (*Picks up scissors.*)

ALGERNON: No, I'd sooner have a pink rose.

CECILY: Why? (*Cuts a flower.*)

ALGERNON: Because you are like a pink rose, cousin Cecily.

CECILY: I don't think it can be right for you to talk to me like that. Miss Prism never says such things to me.

ALGERNON: Then Miss Prism is a short-sighted old lady. (CECILY *puts the rose in his button-hole.*) You are the prettiest girl I ever saw.

CECILY: Miss Prism says that all good looks are a snare.

ALGERNON: They are a snare that every sensible man would like to be caught in.

CECILY: Oh! I don't think I would care to catch a sensible man. I shouldn't know what to talk to him about.

(*They pass into the house.* MISS PRISM *and* DR. CHASUBLE *return.*)

MISS PRISM: You are too much alone, dear Dr. Chasuble. You should get married. A misanthrope I can understand—a womanthrope, never!

CHASUBLE (*with a scholar's shudder*): Believe me, I do not deserve so neologistic a phrase. The precept as well as the practice of the Primitive Church was distinctly against matrimony.

MISS PRISM (*sententiously*): That is obviously the reason why the Primitive Church has not lasted up to the present day. And you do not seem to realize, dear Doctor, that by persistently remaining single, a man converts himself into a permanent public temptation. Men should be more careful; this very celibacy leads weaker vessels astray.

CHASUBLE: But is a man not equally attractive when married?

MISS PRISM: No married man is ever attractive except to his wife.

CHASUBLE: And often, I've been told, not even to her.

MISS PRISM: That depends on the intellectual sympathies of the woman. Maturity can always be depended on. Ripeness can be trusted. Young women are green. (DR. CHASUBLE *starts.*) I spoke horticulturally. My metaphor was drawn from fruits. But where is Cecily?

CHASUBLE: Perhaps she followed us to the schools.

(*Enter* JACK *slowly from the back of the garden. He is dressed in the deepest mourning, with crepe hatband and black gloves.*)

MISS PRISM: Mr. Worthing!

CHASUBLE: Mr. Worthing?

MISS PRISM: This is indeed a surprise. We did not look for you till Monday afternoon.

JACK (*shakes* MISS PRISM'S *hand in a tragic manner*): I have returned sooner than I expected. Dr. Chasuble, I hope you are well?

CHASUBLE: Dear Mr. Worthing, I trust this garb of woe does not betoken some terrible calamity?

JACK: My brother.

MISS PRISM: More shameful debts and extravagance?

CHASUBLE: Still leading his life of pleasure?

JACK (*shaking his head*): Dead!

CHASUBLE: Your brother Ernest dead?

JACK: Quite dead.

MISS PRISM: What a lesson for him! I trust he will profit by it.

CHASUBLE: Mr. Worthing, I offer you my sincere condolence. You have at least the consolation of knowing that you were always the most generous and forgiving of brothers.

JACK: Poor Ernest! He had many faults, but it is a sad, sad blow.

CHASUBLE: Very sad indeed. Were you with him at the end?

JACK: No. He died abroad; in Paris, in fact. I had a telegram last night from the manager of the Grand Hotel.

CHASUBLE: Was the cause of death mentioned?

JACK: A severe chill, it seems.

MISS PRISM: As a man sows, so shall he reap.

CHASUBLE (*raising his hand*): Charity, dear Miss Prism, charity! None of us are perfect. I myself am peculiarly susceptible to draughts. Will the interment take place here?

JACK: No. He seemed to have expressed a desire to be buried in Paris.

CHASUBLE: In Paris! (*Shakes his head.*) I fear that hardly points to any very serious state of mind at the last. You would no doubt wish me to make some slight allusion to this tragic domestic affliction next Sunday. (JACK *presses his hand convulsively.*) My sermon on the meaning of the manna in the wilderness can be adapted to almost any occasion, joyful, or, as in the present case, distressing. (*All sigh.*) I have preached it at harvest celebrations, christenings, confirmations, on days of humiliation and festal days. The last time I delivered it was in the Cathedral, as a charity sermon on behalf of the Society for the Prevention of Discontent among the Upper Orders. The Bishop, who was present, was much struck by some of the analogies I drew.

JACK: Ah! that reminds me, you mentioned christenings, I think, Dr. Chasuble? I suppose you know how to christen all right? (DR. CHASUBLE *looks astounded.*) I mean, of course, you are continually christening, aren't you?

MISS PRISM: It is, I regret to say, one of the Rector's most constant duties in this parish. I have often spoken to the poorer classes on the subject. But they don't seem to know what thrift is.

CHASUBLE: But is there any particular infant in whom you are interested, Mr. Worthing? Your brother was, I believe, unmarried, was he not?

JACK: Oh, yes.

MISS PRISM (*bitterly*): People who live entirely for pleasure usually are.

JACK: But it is not for any child, dear Doctor. I am very fond of children. No! the fact is, I would like to be christened myself, this afternoon, if you have nothing better to do.

CHASUBLE: But surely, Mr. Worthing, you have been christened already?

JACK: I don't remember anything about it.

CHASUBLE: But have you any grave doubts on the subject?

JACK: I certainly intend to have. Of course I don't know if the thing would bother you in any way, or if you think I am a little too old now.

CHASUBLE: Not at all. The sprinkling, and, indeed, the immersion of adults is a perfectly canonical practice.

JACK: Immersion!

CHASUBLE: You need have no apprehensions. Sprinkling is all that is necessary, or indeed I think advisable. Our weather is so changeable. At what hour would you wish the ceremony performed?

JACK: Oh, I might trot round about five if that would suit you.

CHASUBLE: Perfectly, perfectly! In fact I have two similar ceremonies to perform at that time. A case of twins that occurred recently in one of the outlying cottages on your own estate. Poor Jenkins the carter, a most hard-working man.

JACK: Oh! I don't see much fun in being christened along with other babies. It would be childish. Would half-past five do?

CHASUBLE: Admirably! Admirably! (*Takes out watch.*) And now, dear Mr. Worthing, I will not intrude any longer into a house of sorrow. I would merely beg you not to be too much bowed down by grief. What seems to us bitter trials are often blessings in disguise.

MISS PRISM: This seems to me a blessing of an extremely obvious kind.

(*Enter* CECILY *from the house.*)

CECILY: Uncle Jack! Oh, I am pleased to see you back. But what horrid clothes you have got on! Do go and change them.

MISS PRISM: Cecily!

CHASUBLE: My child! my child! (CECILY *goes towards* JACK; *he kisses her brow in a melancholy manner.*)

CECILY: What is the matter, Uncle Jack? Do look happy! You look as if you had toothache, and I have got such a surprise for you. Who do you think is in the dining-room? Your brother!

JACK: Who?

CECILY: Your brother Ernest. He arrived about half an hour ago.

JACK: What nonsense! I haven't got a brother!

CECILY: Oh, don't say that. However badly he may have behaved to you in the past he is still your brother. You couldn't be so heartless as to disown him. I'll tell him to come out. And you will shake hands with him, won't you, Uncle Jack? (*Runs back into the house.*)

CHASUBLE: These are very joyful tidings.

MISS PRISM: After we had all been resigned to his loss, his sudden return seems to me peculiarly distressing.

JACK: My brother is in the dining-room? I don't know what it all means. I think it is perfectly absurd.

(*Enter* ALGERNON *and* CECILY *hand in hand. They come slowly up to* JACK.)

JACK: Good heavens! (*Motions* ALGERNON *away.*)

ALGERNON: Brother John, I have come down from town to tell you that I am very sorry for all the trouble I have given you, and that I intend to lead a better life in the future. (JACK *glares at him and does not take his hand.*)

CECILY: Uncle Jack, you are not going to refuse your own brother's hand?

JACK: Nothing will induce me to take his hand. I think his coming down here disgraceful. He knows perfectly well why.

CECILY: Uncle Jack, do be nice. There is some good in everyone. Ernest has just been telling me about his poor invalid friend Mr. Bunbury whom he goes to visit so often. And surely there must be much good in one who is kind to an invalid, and leaves the pleasures of London to sit by a bed of pain.

JACK: Oh! he has been talking about Bunbury, has he?

CECILY: Yes, he has told me all about poor Mr. Bunbury, and his terrible state of health.

JACK: Bunbury! Well, I won't have him talk to you about Bunbury or about anything else. It is enough to drive one perfectly frantic.

ALGERNON: Of course I admit that the faults were all on my side. But I must say that I think that Brother John's coldness to me is peculiarly painful. I expected a more enthusiastic welcome, especially considering it is the first time I have come here.

CECILY: Uncle Jack, if you don't shake hands with Ernest, I will never forgive you.

JACK: Never forgive me?

CECILY: Never, never, never!

JACK: Well, this is the last time I shall ever do it. (*Shakes hands with* ALGERNON *and glares.*)

CHASUBLE: It's pleasant, is it not, to see so perfect a reconciliation? I think we might leave the two brothers together.

MISS PRISM: Cecily, you will come with us.

CECILY: Certainly, Miss Prism. My little task of reconciliation is over.

CHASUBLE: You have done a beautiful action today, dear child.

MISS PRISM: We must not be premature in our judgments.

CECILY: I feel very happy. (*They all go off.*)

JACK: You young scoundrel, Algy, you must get out of this place as soon as possible. I don't allow any Bunburying here.

(*Enter* MERRIMAN.)

MERRIMAN: I have put Mr. Ernest's things in the room next to yours, sir. I suppose that is all right?

JACK: What?

MERRIMAN: Mr. Ernest's luggage, sir. I have unpacked it and put it in the room next to your own.

JACK: His luggage?

MERRIMAN: Yes, sir. Three portmanteaus, a dressing-case, two hat boxes, and a large luncheon-basket.

ALGERNON: I am afraid I can't stay more than a week this time.

JACK: Merriman, order the dog-cart at once. Mr. Ernest has been suddenly called back to town.

MERRIMAN: Yes, sir. (*Goes back into the house.*)

ALGERNON: What a fearful liar you are, Jack. I have not been called back to town at all.

JACK: Yes, you have.

ALGERNON: I haven't heard anyone call me.

JACK: Your duty as a gentleman calls you back.

ALGERNON: My duty as a gentleman has never interfered with my pleasures in the smallest degree.

JACK: I can quite understand that.

ALGERNON: Well, Cecily is a darling.

JACK: You are not to talk of Miss Cardew like that. I don't like it.

ALGERNON: Well, I don't like your clothes. You look perfectly ridiculous in them. Why on earth don't you go up and change? It is perfectly childish to be in deep mourning for a man who is actually staying for a whole week with you in your house as a guest. I call it grotesque.

JACK: You are certainly not staying with me for a whole week as a guest or anything else. You have got to leave . . . by the four-five train.

ALGERNON: I certainly won't leave you so long as you are in mourning. It would be most unfriendly. If I were in mourning you would stay with me, I suppose. I should think it very unkind if you didn't.

JACK: Well, will you go if I change my clothes?

ALGERNON: Yes, if you are not too long. I never saw anybody take so long to dress, and with such little result.

JACK: Well, at any rate, that is better than being always overdressed as you are.

ALGERNON: If I am occasionally a little overdressed, I make up for it by being always immensely overeducated.

JACK: Your vanity is ridiculous, your conduct an outrage, and your presence in my garden utterly absurd. However, you have got to catch the four-five, and I hope you will have a pleasant journey back to town. This Bunburying, as you call it, has not been a great success for you. (*Goes into the house.*)

ALGERNON: I think it has been a great success. I'm in love with Cecily, and that is everything.

(*Enter* CECILY *at the back of the garden. She picks up the can and begins to water the flowers.*)

But I must see her before I go, and make arrangements for another Bunbury. Ah, there she is.

CECILY: Oh, I merely came back to water the roses. I thought you were with Uncle Jack.

ALGERNON: He's gone to order the dog-cart for me.

CECILY: Oh, is he going to take you for a nice drive?

ALGERNON: He's going to send me away.

CECILY: Then have we got to part?

ALGERNON: I am afraid so. It's very painful parting.

CECILY: It is always painful to part from people whom one has known for a very brief space of time. The absence of old friends one can endure with equanimity. But even a momentary separation from anyone to whom one has just been introduced is almost unbearable.

ALGERNON: Thank you.

(*Enter* MERRIMAN.)

MERRIMAN: The dog-cart is at the door, sir. (ALGERNON *looks appealingly at* CECILY.)

CECILY: It can wait, Merriman . . . for . . . five minutes.

MERRIMAN: Yes, Miss. (*Exit* MERRIMAN.)

ALGERNON: I hope, Cecily, I shall not offend you if I state quite frankly and openly that you seem to me to be in every way the visible personification of absolute perfection.

CECILY: I think your frankness does you great credit, Ernest. If you will allow me I will copy your remarks into my diary. (*Goes over to table and begins writing in diary.*)

ALGERNON: Do you really keep a diary? I'd give anything to look at it. May I?

CECILY: Oh no. (*Puts her hand over it.*) You see, it is simply a very young girl's record of her own thoughts and impressions, and consequently meant for publication. When it appears in volume form I hope you will order a copy. But pray, Ernest, don't stop. I delight in taking down from dictation. I have reached "absolute perfection." You can go on. I am quite ready for more.

ALGERNON (*somewhat taken aback*): Ahem! Ahem!

CECILY: Oh, don't cough, Ernest. When one is dictating one should speak fluently and not cough. Besides, I don't know how to spell a cough.

(*Writes as* ALGERNON *speaks.*)

ALGERNON (*speaking very rapidly*): Cecily, ever since I first looked upon your wonderful and incomparable beauty, I have dared to love you wildly, passionately, devotedly, hopelessly.

CECILY: I don't think that you should tell me that you love me wildly, passionately, devotedly, hopelessly. Hopelessly doesn't seem to make much sense, does it?

ALGERNON: Cecily!

(*Enter* MERRIMAN.)

MERRIMAN: The dog-cart is waiting, sir.

ALGERNON: Tell it to come round next week, at the same hour.

MERRIMAN (*looks at* CECILY, *who makes no sign*): Yes, sir. (MERRIMAN *retires.*)

CECILY: Uncle Jack would be very much annoyed if he knew you were staying on till next week, at the same hour.

ALGERNON: Oh, I don't care about Jack. I don't care for anybody in the whole world but you. I love you, Cecily. You will marry me, won't you?

CECILY: You silly boy! Of course. Why, we have been engaged for the last three months.

ALGERNON: For the last three months?

CECILY: Yes, it will be exactly three months on Thursday.

ALGERNON: But how did we become engaged?

CECILY: Well, ever since dear Uncle Jack first confessed to us that he had a younger brother who was very wicked and bad, you of course have formed the chief topic of conversation between myself and Miss

Prism. And of course a man who is much talked about is always very attractive. One feels there must be something in him after all. I daresay it was foolish of me, but I fell in love with you, Ernest.

ALGERNON: Darling! And when was the engagement actually settled?

CECILY: On the 14th of February last. Worn out by your entire ignorance of my existence, I determined to end the matter one way or the other, and after a long struggle with myself I accepted you under this dear old tree here. The next day I bought this little ring in your name, and this is the little bangle with the true lovers' knot I promised you always to wear.

ALGERNON: Did I give you this? It's very pretty, isn't it?

CECILY: Yes, you've wonderfully good taste, Ernest. It's the excuse I've always given for your leading such a bad life. And this is the box in which I keep all your dear letters. (*Kneels at table, opens box, and produces letters tied up with blue ribbon.*)

ALGERNON: My letters! But my own sweet Cecily, I have never written you any letters.

CECILY: You need hardly remind me of that, Ernest. I remember only too well that I was forced to write your letters for you. I always wrote three times a week, and sometimes oftener.

ALGERNON: Oh, do let me read them, Cecily?

CECILY: Oh, I couldn't possibly. They would make you far too conceited. (*Replaces box.*) The three you wrote me after I had broken off the engagement are so beautiful, and so badly spelled, that even now I can hardly read them without crying a little.

ALGERNON: But was our engagement ever broken off?

CECILY: Of course it was. On the 22nd of last March. You can see the entry if you like. (*Shows diary.*) "Today I broke off my engagement with Ernest. I feel it is better to do so. The weather still continues charming."

ALGERNON: But why on earth did you break it off? What had I done? I had done nothing at all. Cecily, I am very much hurt indeed to hear you broke it off. Particularly when the weather was so charming.

CECILY: It would hardly have been a really serious engagement if it hadn't been broken off at least once. But I forgave you before the week was out.

ALGERNON (*crossing to her, and kneeling*): What a perfect angel you are, Cecily.

CECILY: You dear romantic boy. (*He kisses her, she puts her fingers through his hair.*) I hope your hair curls naturally, does it?

ALGERNON: Yes, darling, with a little help from others.

CECILY: I am so glad.

ALGERNON: You'll never break off our engagement again, Cecily?

CECILY: I don't think I could break it off now that I have actually met you. Besides, of course, there is the question of your name.

ALGERNON: Yes, of course. (*Nervously.*)

CECILY: You must not laugh at me, darling, but it had always been a girlish dream of mine to love someone whose name was Ernest. (ALGERNON *rises,* CECILY *also.*) There is something in that name that seems to inspire absolute confidence. I pity any poor married woman whose husband is not called Ernest.

ALGERNON: But, my dear child, do you mean to say you could not love me if I had some other name?

CECILY: But what name?

ALGERNON: Oh, any name you like—Algernon—for instance. . . .

CECILY: But I don't like the name of Algernon.

ALGERNON: Well, my own dear, sweet, loving little darling, I really can't see why you should object to the name of Algernon. It is not at all a bad name. In fact, it is rather an aristocratic name. Half of the chaps who get into the Bankruptcy Court are called Algernon. But seriously, Cecily . . . (*Moving to her.*) . . . if my name was Algy, couldn't you love me?

CECILY (*rising*): I might respect you, Ernest, I might admire your character, but I fear that I should not be able to give you my undivided attention.

ALGERNON: Ahem! Cecily! (*Picking up hat.*) Your Rector here is, I suppose, thoroughly experienced in the practice of all the rites and ceremonials of the Church?

CECILY: Oh, yes. Dr. Chasuble is a most learned man. He has never written a single book, so you can imagine how much he knows.

ALGERNON: I must see him at once on a most important christening—I mean on most important business.

CECILY: Oh!

ALGERNON: I shan't be away more than half an hour.

CECILY: Considering that we have been engaged since February the 14th, and that I only met you today for the first time, I think it is rather hard that you should leave me for so long a period as half an hour. Couldn't you make it twenty minutes?

ALGERNON: I'll be back in no time.

(*Kisses her and rushes down the garden.*)

CECILY: What an impetuous boy he is! I like his hair so much. I must enter his proposal in my diary.

(*Enter* MERRIMAN.)

MERRIMAN: A Miss Fairfax has just called to see Mr. Worthing. On very important business Miss Fairfax states.

CECILY: Isn't Mr. Worthing in his library?

MERRIMAN: Mr. Worthing went over in the direction of the Rectory some time ago.

CECILY: Pray ask the lady to come out here; Mr. Worthing is sure to be back soon. And you can bring tea.

MERRIMAN: Yes, Miss. (*Goes out.*)

CECILY: Miss Fairfax! I suppose one of the many good elderly women who are associated with Uncle Jack in some of his philanthropic work in London. I don't quite like women who are interested in philanthropic work. I think it is so forward of them.

(*Enter* MERRIMAN.)

MERRIMAN: Miss Fairfax.

(*Enter* GWENDOLEN.) (*Exit* MERRIMAN.)

CECILY (*advancing to meet her*): Pray let me introduce myself to you. My name is Cecily Cardew.

GWENDOLEN: Cecily Cardew? (*Moving to her and shaking hands.*) What a very sweet name! Something tells me that we are going to be great friends. I like you already more than I can say. My first impressions of people are never wrong.

CECILY: How nice of you to like me so much after we have known each other such a comparatively short time. Pray sit down.

GWENDOLEN (*still standing up*): I may call you Cecily, may I not?

CECILY: With pleasure!

GWENDOLEN: And you will always call me Gwendolen, won't you?

CECILY: If you wish.

GWENDOLEN: Then that is all quite settled, is it not?

CECILY: I hope so. (*A pause. They both sit down together.*)

GWENDOLEN: Perhaps this might be a favourable opportunity for my mentioning who I am. My father is Lord Bracknell. You have never heard of Papa, I suppose?

CECILY: I don't think so.

GWENDOLEN: Outside the family circle, Papa, I am glad to say, is entirely unknown. I think that is quite as it should be. The home seems to me to be the proper sphere for the man. And certainly once a man begins to neglect his domestic duties he becomes painfully effeminate, does he not? And I don't like that. It makes men so very attractive. Cecily, Mamma, whose views on education are remarkably strict, has brought me up to be extremely short-sighted; it is part of her system; so do you mind my looking at you through my glasses?

CECILY: Oh! not at all, Gwendolen. I am very fond of being looked at.

GWENDOLEN (*after examining* CECILY *carefully through a lorgnette*): You are here on a short visit I suppose.

CECILY: Oh no! I live here.

GWENDOLEN (*severely*): Really? Your mother, no doubt, or some female relative of advanced years, resides here also?

CECILY: Oh no! I have no mother, nor, in fact, any relations.

GWENDOLEN: Indeed?

CECILY: My dear guardian, with the assistance of Miss Prism, has the arduous task of looking after me.

GWENDOLEN: Your guardian?

CECILY: Yes, I am Mr. Worthing's ward.

GWENDOLEN: Oh! It is strange he never mentioned to me that he had a ward. How secretive of him! He grows more interesting hourly. I am not sure, however, that the news inspires me with feelings of unmixed delight. (*Rising and going to her.*) I am very fond of you, Cecily; I have liked you ever since I met you! But I am bound to state that now that I know that you are Mr. Worthing's ward, I cannot help expressing a wish you were—well just a little older than you seem to be—and not quite so very alluring in appearance. In fact, if I may speak candidly—

CECILY: Pray do! I think that whenever one has anything unpleasant to say, one should always be quite candid.

GWENDOLEN: Well, to speak with perfect candour, Cecily, I wish that you were fully forty-two, and more than usually plain for your age. Ernest has a strong upright nature. He is the very soul of truth and honour. Disloyalty would be as impossible to him as deception. But even men of the noblest possible moral character are extremely susceptible to the influence of the physical charms of others. Modern, no less than ancient history, supplies us with many most painful examples of what I refer to. If it were not so, indeed, history would be quite unreadable.

CECILY: I beg your pardon, Gwendolen, did you say Ernest?

GWENDOLEN: Yes.

CECILY: Oh, but it is not Mr. Ernest Worthing who is my guardian. It is his brother—his elder brother.

GWENDOLEN (*sitting down again*): Ernest never mentioned to me that he had a brother.

CECILY: I am sorry to say they have not been on good terms for a long time.

GWENDOLEN: Ah! that accounts for it. And now that I think of it I have never heard any man mention his brother. The subject seems distasteful to most men. Cecily, you have lifted a load from my mind. I was growing almost anxious. It would have been terrible if any cloud had come across a friendship like ours, would it not? Of course you are quite, quite sure that it is not Mr. Ernest Worthing who is your guardian?

CECILY: Quite sure. (*A pause.*) In fact, I am going to be his.

GWENDOLEN (*enquiringly*): I beg your pardon?

CECILY (*rather shy and confidingly*): Dearest Gwendolen, there is no reason why I should make a secret of it to you. Our little county newspaper is sure to chronicle the fact next week. Mr. Ernest Worthing and I are engaged to be married.

GWENDOLEN (*quite politely, rising*): My darling Cecily, I think there must be some slight error. Mr. Ernest Worthing is engaged to me. The announcement will appear in the *Morning Post* on Saturday at the latest.

CECILY (*very politely, rising*): I am afraid you must be under some misconception. Ernest proposed to me exactly ten minutes ago. (*Shows diary.*)

GWENDOLEN (*examines diary through her lorgnette carefully*): It is certainly very curious, for he asked me to be his wife yesterday afternoon at 5:30. If you would care to verify the incident, pray do so.

(*Produces diary of her own.*) I never travel without my diary. One should always have something sensational to read in the train. I am so sorry, dear Cecily, if it is any disappointment to you, but I am afraid *I* have the prior claim.

CECILY: It would distress me more than I can tell you, dear Gwendolen, if it caused you any mental or physical anguish, but I feel bound to point out that since Ernest proposed to you he clearly has changed his mind.

GWENDOLEN (*meditatively*): If the poor fellow has been entrapped into any foolish promise I shall consider it my duty to rescue him at once, and with a firm hand.

CECILY (*thoughtfully and sadly*): Whatever unfortunate entanglement my dear boy may have got into, I will never reproach him with it after we are married.

GWENDOLEN: Do you allude to me, Miss Cardew, as an entanglement? You are presumptuous. On an occasion of this kind it becomes more than a moral duty to speak one's mind. It becomes a pleasure.

CECILY: Do you suggest, Miss Fairfax, that I entrapped Ernest into an engagement? How dare you? This is no time for wearing the shallow mask of manners. When I see a spade I call it a spade.

GWENDOLEN (*satirically*): I am glad to say that I have never seen a spade. It is obvious that our social spheres have been widely different.

(*Enter* MERRIMAN, *followed by the footman. He carries a salver, table cloth, and plate stand.* CECILY *is about to retort. The presence of the servants exercises a restraining influence, under which both girls chafe.*)

MERRIMAN: Shall I lay tea here as usual, Miss?

CECILY (*sternly, in a calm voice*): Yes, as usual. (MERRIMAN *begins to clear table and lay cloth. A long pause.* CECILY *and* GWENDOLEN *glare at each other.*)

GWENDOLEN: Are there many interesting walks in the vicinity, Miss Cardew?

CECILY: Oh! yes! a great many. From the top of one of the hills quite close one can see five counties.

GWENDOLEN: Five counties! I don't think I should like that. I hate crowds.

CECILY (*sweetly*): I suppose that is why you live in town? (GWENDOLEN *bites her lip, and beats her foot nervously with her parasol.*)

GWENDOLEN (*looking round*): Quite a well-kept garden this is, Miss Cardew.

CECILY: So glad you like it, Miss Fairfax.

GWENDOLEN: I had no idea there were any flowers in the country.

CECILY: Oh, flowers are as common here, Miss Fairfax, as people are in London.

GWENDOLEN: Personally I cannot understand how anybody manages to exist in the country, if anybody who is anybody does. The country always bores me to death.

CECILY: Ah! This is what the newspapers call agricultural depression, is it not? I believe the aristocracy are suffering very much from it just at present. It is almost an epidemic amongst them, I have been told. May I offer you some tea, Miss Fairfax?

GWENDOLEN (*with elaborate politeness*): Thank you. (*Aside.*) Detestable girl! But I require tea!

CECILY (*sweetly*): Sugar?

GWENDOLEN (*superciliously*): No, thank you. Sugar is not fashionable any more. (CECILY *looks angrily at her, takes up the tongs and puts four lumps of sugar into the cup.*)

CECILY (*severely*): Cake or bread and butter?

GWENDOLEN (*in a bored manner*): Bread and butter, please. Cake is rarely seen at the best houses nowadays.

CECILY (*cuts a very large slice of cake, and puts it on the tray*): Hand that to Miss Fairfax.

(MERRIMAN *does so, and goes out with footman.* GWENDOLEN *drinks the tea and makes a grimace. Puts down cup at once, reaches out her hand to the bread and butter, looks at it, and finds it is cake. Rises in indignation.*)

GWENDOLEN: You have filled my tea with lumps of sugar, and though I asked most distinctly for bread and butter, you have given me cake. I am known for the gentleness of my disposition, and the extraordinary sweetness of my nature, but I warn you, Miss Cardew, you may go too far.

CECILY (*rising*): To save my poor, innocent, trusting boy from the machinations of any other girl there are no lengths to which I would not go.

GWENDOLEN: From the moment I saw you I distrusted you. I felt that you were false and deceitful. I am never deceived in such matters. My first impressions of people are invariably right.

CECILY: It seems to me, Miss Fairfax, that I am trespassing on your valuable time. No doubt you have many other calls of a similar character to make in the neighbourhood.

(*Enter* JACK.)

GWENDOLEN (*catching sight of him*): Ernest! My own Ernest!

JACK: Gwendolen! Darling! (*Offers to kiss her.*)

GWENDOLEN (*drawing back*): A moment! May I ask if you are engaged to be married to this young lady? (*Points to* CECILY.)

JACK (*laughing*): To dear little Cecily! Of course not! What could have put such an idea into your pretty little head?

GWENDOLEN: Thank you. You may! (*Offers her cheek.*)

CECILY (*very sweetly*): I knew there must be some misunderstanding, Miss Fairfax. The gentleman whose arm is at present round your waist is my dear guardian, Mr. John Worthing.

GWENDOLEN: I beg your pardon?

CECILY: This is Uncle Jack.

GWENDOLEN (*receding*): Jack! Oh!

(*Enter* ALGERNON.)

CECILY: Here is Ernest.

ALGERNON (*goes straight over to* CECILY *without noticing anyone else*): My own love! (*Offers to kiss her.*)

CECILY (*drawing back*): A moment, Ernest! May I ask you—are you engaged to be married to this young lady?

ALGERNON (*looking round*): To what young lady? Good heavens! Gwendolen!

CECILY: Yes! to good heavens, Gwendolen, I mean to Gwendolen.

ALGERNON (*laughing*): Of course not! What could have put such an idea into your pretty little head?

CECILY: Thank you. (*Presenting her cheek to be kissed.*) You may. (ALGERNON *kisses her.*)

GWENDOLEN: I felt there was some slight error, Miss Cardew. The gentleman who is now embracing you is my cousin, Mr. Algernon Moncrieff.

CECILY (*breaking away from* ALGERNON): Algernon Moncrieff! Oh! (*The two girls move towards each other and put their arms round each other's waists as if for protection.*)

CECILY: Are you called Algernon?

ALGERNON: I cannot deny it.

CECILY: Oh!

GWENDOLEN: Is your name really John?

JACK (*standing rather proudly*): I could deny it if I liked. I could deny anything if I liked. But my name certainly is John. It has been John for years.

CECILY (*to* GWENDOLEN): A gross deception has been practised on both of us.

GWENDOLEN: My poor wounded Cecily!

CECILY: My sweet wronged Gwendolen!

GWENDOLEN (*slowly and seriously*): You will call me sister, will you not? (*They embrace.* JACK *and* ALGERNON *groan and walk up and down.*)

CECILY (*rather brightly*): There is just one question I would like to be allowed to ask my guardian.

GWENDOLEN: An admirable idea! Mr. Worthing, there is just one question I would like to be permitted to put to you. Where is your brother Ernest? We are both engaged to be married to your brother Ernest, so it is a matter of some importance to us to know where your brother Ernest is at present.

JACK (*slowly and hesitatingly*): Gwendolen—Cecily—it is very painful for me to be forced to speak the truth. It is the first time in my life that I have ever been reduced to such a painful position, and I am really quite inexperienced in doing anything of the kind. However I will tell you quite frankly that I have no brother Ernest. I have no brother at all. I never had a brother in my life, and I certainly have not the smallest intention of ever having one in the future.

CECILY (*surprised*): No brother at all?

JACK (*cheerily*): None!

GWENDOLEN (*severely*): Had you never a brother of any kind?

JACK (*pleasantly*): Never. Not even of any kind.

GWENDOLEN: I am afraid it is quite clear, Cecily, that neither of us is engaged to be married to anyone.

CECILY: It is not a very pleasant position for a young girl suddenly to find herself in. Is it?

GWENDOLEN: Let us go into the house. They will hardly venture to come after us there.

CECILY: No, men are so cowardly, aren't they?

(*They retire into the house with scornful looks.*)

JACK: This ghastly state of things is what you call Bunburying, I suppose?

ALGERNON: Yes, and a perfectly wonderful Bunbury it is. The most wonderful Bunbury I have ever had in my life.

JACK: Well, you've no right whatsoever to Bunbury here.

ALGERNON: That is absurd. One has a right to Bunbury anywhere one chooses. Every serious Bunburyist knows that.

JACK: Serious Bunburyist! Good heavens!

ALGERNON: Well, one must be serious about something, if one wants to have any amusement in life. I happen to be serious about Bunburying. What on earth you are serious about I haven't got the remotest idea. About everything, I should fancy. You have such an absolutely trivial nature.

JACK: Well, the only small satisfaction I have in the whole of this wretched business is that your friend Bunbury is quite exploded. You won't be able to run down to the country quite so often as you used to do, dear Algy. And a very good thing too.

ALGERNON: Your brother is a little off colour, isn't he, dear Jack? You won't be able to disappear to London quite so frequently as your wicked custom was. And not a bad thing either.

JACK: As for your conduct towards Miss Cardew, I must say that your taking in a sweet, simple, innocent girl like that is quite inexcusable. To say nothing of the fact that she is my ward.

ALGERNON: I can see no possible defence at all for your deceiving a brilliant, clever, thoroughly experienced young lady like Miss Fairfax. To say nothing of the fact that she is my cousin.

JACK: I wanted to be engaged to Gwendolen, that is all. I love her.

ALGERNON: Well, I simply wanted to be engaged to Cecily. I adore her.

JACK: There is certainly no chance of your marrying Miss Cardew.

ALGERNON: I don't think there is much likelihood, Jack, of you and Miss Fairfax being united.

JACK: Well, that is no business of yours.

ALGERNON: If it was my business, I wouldn't talk about it. (*Begins to eat muffins.*) It is very vulgar to talk about one's business. Only people like stockbrokers do that, and then merely at dinner parties.

JACK: How you can sit there, calmly eating muffins when we are in this horrible trouble, I can't make out. You seem to me to be perfectly heartless.

ALGERNON: Well, I can't eat muffins in an agitated manner. The butter would probably get on my cuffs. One should always eat muffins quite calmly. It is the only way to eat them.

JACK: I say it's perfectly heartless your eating muffins at all, under the circumstances.

ALGERNON: When I am in trouble, eating is the only thing that consoles me. Indeed, when I am in really great trouble, as anyone who knows me intimately will tell you, I refuse everything except food and drink. At the present moment I am eating muffins because I am unhappy. Besides, I am particularly fond of muffins. (*Rising.*)

JACK (*rising*): Well, that is no reason why you should eat them all in that greedy way. (*Takes muffins from* ALGERNON.)

ALGERNON (*offering tea-cake*): I wish you would have tea-cake instead. I don't like tea-cake.

JACK: Good heavens! I suppose a man may eat his own muffins in his own garden.

ALGERNON: But you have just said it was perfectly heartless to eat muffins.

JACK: I said it was perfectly heartless of you, under the circumstances. That is a very different thing.

ALGERNON: That may be. But the muffins are the same. (*He seizes the muffin-dish from* JACK.)

JACK: Algy, I wish to goodness you would go.

ALGERNON: You can't possibly ask me to go without having some dinner. It's absurd. I never go without my dinner. No one ever does, except vegetarians and people like that. Besides I have just made arrangements with Dr. Chasuble to be christened at a quarter to six under the name of Ernest.

JACK: My dear fellow, the sooner you give up that nonsense the better. I made arrangements this morning with Dr. Chasuble to be christened myself at 5:30, and I naturally will take the name of Ernest. Gwendolen would wish it. We can't both be christened Ernest. It's absurd. Besides, I have a perfect right to be christened if I like. There is no evidence at all that I ever have been christened by anybody. I should think it extremely probable I never was, and so does Dr. Chasuble. It is entirely different in your case. You have been christened already.

ALGERNON: Yes, but I have not been christened for years.

JACK: Yes, but you have been christened. That is the important thing.

ALGERNON: Quite so. So I know my constitution can stand it. If you are not quite sure about your ever having been christened, I must say I think it rather dangerous your venturing on it now. It might make you very unwell. You can hardly have forgotten that someone very closely connected with you was very nearly carried off this week in Paris by a severe chill.

JACK: Yes, but you said yourself that a severe chill was not hereditary.

ALGERNON: It usen't to be, I know—but I daresay it is now. Science is always making wonderful improvements in things.

JACK (*picking up the muffin-dish*): Oh, that is nonsense; you are always talking nonsense.

ALGERNON: Jack, you are at the muffins again! I wish you wouldn't. There are only two left. (*Takes them.*) I told you I was particularly fond of muffins.

JACK: But I hate tea-cake.

ALGERNON: Why on earth then do you allow tea-cake to be served up for your guests? What ideas you have of hospitality!

JACK: Algernon! I have already told you to go. I don't want you here. Why don't you go!

ALGERNON: I haven't quite finished my tea yet! and there is still one muffin left. (JACK *groans, and sinks into a chair,* ALGERNON *still continues eating.*)

ACT-DROP.

ACT THREE

Scene. Morning-room at the Manor House.
    (GWENDOLEN *and* CECILY *are at the window, looking out into the garden.*)

GWENDOLEN: The fact that they did not follow us at once into the house, as anyone else would have done, seems to me to show that they have some sense of shame left.

CECILY: They have been eating muffins. That looks like repentance.

GWENDOLEN (*after a pause*): They don't seem to notice us at all. Couldn't you cough?

CECILY: But I haven't got a cough.

GWENDOLEN: They're looking at us. What effrontery!

CECILY: They're approaching. That's very forward of them.

GWENDOLEN: Let us preserve a dignified silence.

CECILY: Certainly. It's the only thing to do now.

    (*Enter* JACK *followed by* ALGERNON. *They whistle some dreadful popular air from a British opera.*)

GWENDOLEN: This dignified silence seems to produce an unpleasant effect.

CECILY: A most distasteful one.

GWENDOLEN: But we will not be the first to speak.

CECILY: Certainly not.

GWENDOLEN: Mr. Worthing, I have something very particular to ask you. Much depends on your reply.

CECILY: Gwendolen, your common sense is invaluable. Mr. Moncrieff, kindly answer me the following question. Why did you pretend to be my guardian's brother?

ALGERNON: In order that I might have an opportunity of meeting you.

CECILY (*to* GWENDOLYN): That certainly seems a satisfactory explanation, does it not?

GWENDOLEN: Yes, dear, if you can believe him.

CECILY: I don't. But that does not affect the wonderful beauty of his answer.

GWENDOLEN: True. In matters of grave importance, style, not sincerity, is the vital thing. Mr. Worthing, what explanation can you offer to me for pretending to have a brother? Was it in order that you might have an opportunity of coming up to town to see me as often as possible?

JACK: Can you doubt it, Miss Fairfax?

GWENDOLEN: I have the gravest doubts upon the subject. But I intend to crush them. This is not the moment for German scepticism. (*Moving to* CECILY.) Their explanations appear to be quite satisfactory, especially Mr. Worthing's. That seems to me to have the stamp of truth upon it.

CECILY: I am more than content with what Mr. Moncrieff said. His voice alone inspires one with absolute credulity.

GWENDOLEN: Then you think we should forgive them?

CECILY: Yes. I mean no.

GWENDOLEN: True! I had forgotten. There are principles at stake that one cannot surrender. Which of us should tell them? The task is not a pleasant one.

CECILY: Could we not both speak at the same time?

GWENDOLEN: An excellent idea! I nearly always speak at the same time as other people. Will you take the time from me?

CECILY: Certainly. (GWENDOLEN *beats time with uplifted finger.*)

GWENDOLEN AND CECILY (*speaking together*): Your Christian names are still an insuperable barrier. That is all!

JACK AND ALGERNON (*speaking together*): Our Christian names! Is that all? But we are going to be christened this afternoon.

GWENDOLEN (*to* JACK): For my sake you are prepared to do this terrible thing?

JACK: I am.

CECILY (*to* ALGERNON): To please me you are ready to face this fearful ordeal?

ALGERNON: I am!

GWENDOLEN: How absurd to talk of the equality of the sexes! Where questions of self-sacrifice are concerned, men are infinitely beyond us.

JACK: We are. (*Clasps hands with* ALGERNON.)

CECILY: They have moments of physical courage of which we women know absolutely nothing.

GWENDOLEN (*to* JACK): Darling!

ALGERNON (*to* CECILY): Darling. (*They fall into each other's arms.*)

(*Enter* MERRIMAN. *When he enters he coughs loudly, seeing the situation.*)

MERRIMAN: Ahem! Ahem! Lady Bracknell!

JACK: Good heavens!

(*Enter* Lady Bracknell. *The couples separate in alarm. Exit* MERRIMAN.)

LADY BRACKNELL: Gwendolen! What does this mean?

GWENDOLEN: Merely that I am engaged to be married to Mr. Worthing Mamma.

LADY BRACKNELL: Come here. Sit down. Sit down immediately. Hesitation of any kind is a sign of mental decay in the young, of physical weakness in the old. (*Turns to* JACK.) Apprised, sir, of my daughter's sudden flight by her trusty maid, whose confidence I purchased by means of a small coin, I followed her at once by a luggage train. Her unhappy father is, I am glad to say, under the impression that she is attending a more than usually lengthy lecture by the University Extension Scheme on the influence of a permanent income on thought. I do not propose to undeceive him. Indeed I have never undeceived him on any question. I would consider it wrong. But of course, you will clearly understand that all communication between yourself and my daughter must cease immediately from this moment. On this point, as indeed on all points, I am firm.

JACK: I am engaged to be married to Gwendolen, Lady Bracknell!

LADY BRACKNELL: You are nothing of the kind, sir. And now, as regards Algernon! . . . Algernon!

ALGERNON: Yes, Aunt Augusta.

LADY BRACKNELL: May I ask if it is in this house that your invalid friend Mr. Bunbury resides?

ALGERNON (*stammering*): Oh! No! Bunbury doesn't live here. Bunbury is somewhere else at present. In fact, Bunbury is dead.

LADY BRACKNELL: Dead! When did Mr. Bunbury die? His death must have been extremely sudden.

ALGERNON (*airily*): Oh! I killed Bunbury this afternoon. I mean poor Bunbury died this afternoon.

LADY BRACKNELL: What did he die of?

ALGERNON: Bunbury? Oh, he was quite exploded.

LADY BRACKNELL: Exploded! Was he the victim of a revolutionary outrage? I was not aware that Mr. Bunbury was interested in social legislation. If so, he is well punished for his morbidity.

ALGERNON: My dear Aunt Augusta, I mean he was found out! The doctors found out that Bunbury could not live, that is what I mean—so Bunbury died.

LADY BRACKNELL: He seems to have had great confidence in the opinion of his physicians. I am glad, however, that he made up his mind at the last to some definite course of action, and acted under proper medical advice. And now that we have finally got rid of this Mr. Bunbury, may I ask, Mr. Worthing, who is that young person whose hand my nephew Algernon is now holding in what seems to me a peculiarly unnecessary manner?

JACK: That lady is Miss Cecily Cardew, my ward. (LADY BRACKNELL *bows coldly to* CECILY.)

ALGERNON: I am engaged to be married to Cecily, Aunt Augusta.

LADY BRACKNELL: I beg your pardon?

CECILY: Mr. Moncrieff and I are engaged to be married, Lady Bracknell.

LADY BRACKNELL (*with a shiver, crossing to the sofa and sitting down*): I do not know whether there is anything peculiarly exciting in the air of this particular part of Hertfordshire, but the number of engagements that go on seems to me considerably above the proper average that statistics have laid down for our guidance. I think some preliminary enquiry on my part would not be out of place. Mr. Worthing, is Miss Cardew at all connected with any of the larger railway stations in London? I merely desire information. Until yesterday I had no idea that there were any families or persons whose origin was a Terminus. (JACK *looks perfectly furious, but restrains himself.*)

JACK (*in a clear, cold voice*): Miss Cardew is the granddaughter of the late Mr. Thomas Cardew of 149, Belgrave Square, S.W.; Gervase Park, Dorking, Surrey; and the Sporran, Fifeshire, N.B.

LADY BRACKNELL: That sounds not unsatisfactory. Three addresses always inspire confidence, even in tradesmen. But what proof have I of their authenticity?

JACK: I have carefully preserved the Court Guides of the period. They are open to your inspection, Lady Bracknell.

LADY BRACKNELL (*grimly*): I have known strange errors in that publication.

JACK: Miss Cardew's family solicitors are Messrs. Markby, Markby, and Markby.

LADY BRACKNELL: Markby, Markby, and Markby? A firm of the very highest position in their profession. Indeed I am told that one of the Mr. Markbys is occasionally to be seen at dinner parties. So far I am satisfied.

JACK (*very irritably*): How extremely kind of you, Lady Bracknell! I have also in my possession, you will be pleased to hear, certificates of Miss Cardew's birth, baptism, whooping cough, registration, vaccination, confirmation, and the measles; both the German and the English variety.

LADY BRACKNELL: Ah! A life crowded with incident, I see; though perhaps somewhat too exciting for a young girl. I am not myself in favour of premature experiences. (*Rises, looks at her watch.*) Gwendolen! the time approaches for our departure. We have not a moment to lose. As a matter of form, Mr. Worthing, I had better ask you if Miss Cardew has any little fortune?

JACK: Oh! about a hundred and thirty thousand pounds in the Funds. That is all. Good-bye, Lady Bracknell. So pleased to have seen you.

LADY BRACKNELL (*sitting down again*): A moment, Mr. Worthing. A hundred and thirty thousand pounds! And in the Funds! Miss Cardew seems to me a most attractive young lady, now that I look at her. Few girls of the present day have any really solid qualities, any of the qualities that last, and improve with time. We live, I regret to say, in an age of surfaces. (*To* CECILY.) Come over here, dear. (CECILY *goes across.*) Pretty child! your dress is sadly simple, and your hair seems almost as nature might have left it. But we can soon alter all that. A thoroughly experienced French maid produces a really marvellous result in a very brief space of time. I remember recommending one to young Lady Lancing, and after three months her own husband did not know her.

JACK (*aside*): And after six months nobody knew her.

LADY BRACKNELL (*glares at* JACK *for a few moments. Then bends, with a practised smile, to* CECILY): Kindly turn round, sweet child. (CECILY *turns completely round.*) No, the side view is what I want. (CECILY *presents her profile.*) Yes, quite as I expected. There are distinct social possibilities in your profile. The two weak points in our age are its want of principle and its want of profile. The chin a little higher, dear. Style largely depends on the way the chin is worn. They are worn very high, just at present. Algernon!

ALGERNON: Yes, Aunt Augusta!

LADY BRACKNELL: There are distinct social possibilities in Miss Cardew's profile.

ALGERNON: Cecily is the sweetest, dearest, prettiest girl in the whole world. And I don't care twopence about social possibilities.

LADY BRACKNELL: Never speak disrespectfully of Society, Algernon. Only people who can't get into it do that. (*To* CECILY.) Dear child, of course you know that Algernon has nothing but his debts to depend upon. But I do not approve of mercenary marriages. When I married Lord Bracknell I had no fortune of any kind. But I never dreamed for a moment of allowing that to stand in my way. Well, I suppose I must give my consent.

ALGERNON: Thank you, Aunt Augusta.

LADY BRACKNELL: Cecily, you may kiss me!

CECILY (*kisses her*): Thank you, Lady Bracknell.

LADY BRACKNELL: You may also address me as Aunt Augusta for the future.

CECILY: Thank you, Aunt Augusta.

LADY BRACKNELL: The marriage, I think, had better take place quite soon.

ALGERNON: Thank you, Aunt Augusta.

CECILY: Thank you, Aunt Augusta.

LADY BRACKNELL: To speak frankly, I am not in favour of long engagements. They give people the opportunity of finding out each other's character before marriage, which I think is never advisable.

JACK: I beg your pardon for interrupting you, Lady Bracknell, but this engagement is quite out of the question. I am Miss Cardew's guardian, and she cannot marry without my consent until she comes of age. That consent I absolutely decline to give.

LADY BRACKNELL: Upon what grounds may I ask? Algernon is an extremely, I may almost say an ostentatiously, eligible young man. He has nothing, but he looks everything. What more can one desire?

JACK: It pains me very much to have to speak frankly to you, Lady Bracknell, about your nephew, but the fact is that I do not approve at all of his moral character. I suspect him of being untruthful. (ALGERNON *and* CECILY *look at him in indignant amazement.*)

LADY BRACKNELL: Untruthful! My nephew Algernon? Impossible! He is an Oxonian.

JACK: I fear there can be no possible doubt about the matter. This afternoon, during my temporary absence in London on an important question of romance, he obtained admission to my house by means of the false pretence of being my brother. Under an assumed name he drank, I've just been informed by my butler, an entire pint bottle of my Perrier-Jouet, Brut, '89; a wine I was specially reserving for myself. Continuing his disgraceful deception, he succeeded in the course of the afternoon in alienating the affections of my only ward. He subsequently stayed to tea, and devoured every single muffin. And what makes his conduct all the more heartless is, that he was perfectly well aware from the first that I have no brother, that I never had a brother, and that I don't intend to have a brother, not even of any kind. I distinctly told him so myself yesterday afternoon.

LADY BRACKNELL: Ahem! Mr. Worthing, after careful consideration I have decided entirely to overlook my nephew's conduct to you.

JACK: That is very generous of you, Lady Bracknell. My own decision, however, is unalterable. I decline to give my consent.

LADY BRACKNELL (to CECILY): Come here, sweet child. (CECILY goes over.) How old are you, dear?

CECILY: Well, I am really only eighteen, but I always admit to twenty when I go to evening parties.

LADY BRACKNELL: You are perfectly right in making some slight alteration. Indeed, no woman should ever be quite accurate about her age. It looks so calculating. . . . (In a meditative manner.) Eighteen, but admitting to twenty at evening parties. Well, it will not be very long before you are of age and free from the restraints of tutelage. So I don't think your guardian's consent is, after all, a matter of any importance.

JACK: Pray excuse me, Lady Bracknell, for interrupting you again, but it is only fair to tell you that according to the terms of her grandfather's will Miss Cardew does not come legally of age till she is thirty-five.

LADY BRACKNELL: That does not seem to me to be a grave objection. Thirty-five is a very attractive age. London society is full of women of the very highest birth who have, of their own free choice, remained thirty-five for years. Lady Dumbleton is an instance in point. To my own knowledge she has been thirty-five ever since she arrived at the age of forty, which was many years ago now. I see no reason why our dear Cecily should not be even still more attractive at the age you mention than she is at present. There will be a large accumulation of property.

CECILY: Algy, could you wait for me till I was thirty-five?

ALGERNON: Of course I could, Cecily. You know I could.

CECILY: Yes, I felt it instinctively, but I couldn't wait all that time. I hate waiting even five minutes for anybody. It always makes me rather cross. I am not punctual myself, I know, but I do like punctuality in others, and waiting, even to be married, is quite out of the question.

ALGERNON: Then what is to be done, Cecily?

CECILY: I don't know, Mr. Moncrieff.

LADY BRACKNELL: My dear Mr. Worthing, as Miss Cardew states positively that she cannot wait till she is thirty-five—a remark which I am bound to say seems to me to show a somewhat impatient nature—I would beg of you to reconsider your decision.

JACK: But my dear Lady Bracknell, the matter is entirely in your own hands. The moment you consent to my marriage with Gwendolen, I will most gladly allow your nephew to form an alliance with my ward.

LADY BRACKNELL (*rising and drawing herself up*): You must be quite aware that what you propose is out of the question.

JACK: Then a passionate celibacy is all that any of us can look forward to.

LADY BRACKNELL: That is not the destiny I propose for Gwendolen. Algernon, of course, can choose for himself. (*Pulls out her watch.*) Come, dear (GWENDOLEN *rises*), we have already missed five, if not six, trains. To miss any more might expose us to comment on the platform.

(*Enter* DR. CHASUBLE.)

CHASUBLE: Everything is quite ready for the christenings.

LADY BRACKNELL: The christenings, sir! Is not that somewhat premature?

CHASUBLE (*looking rather puzzled, and pointing to* JACK *and* ALGERNON): Both these gentlemen have expressed a desire for immediate baptism.

LADY BRACKNELL: At their age? The idea is grotesque and irreligious! Algernon, I forbid you to be baptized. I will not hear of such excesses. Lord Bracknell would be highly displeased if he learned that that was the way in which you wasted your time and money.

CHASUBLE: Am I to understand then that there are to be no christenings at all this afternoon?

JACK: I don't think that, as things are now, it would be of much practical value to either of us, Dr. Chasuble.

CHASUBLE: I am grieved to hear such sentiments from you, Mr. Worthing. They savour of the heretical views of the Anabaptists, views that I have completely refuted in four of my unpublished sermons. However, as your present mood seems to be one peculiarly secular, I will return to the church at once. Indeed, I have just been informed by the pew-opener that for the last hour and a half Miss Prism has been waiting for me in the vestry.

LADY BRACKNELL (*starting*): Miss Prism! Did I hear you mention a Miss Prism?

CHASUBLE: Yes, Lady Bracknell. I am on my way to join her.

LADY BRACKNELL: Pray allow me to detain you for a moment. This matter may prove to be one of vital importance to Lord Bracknell and myself. Is this Miss Prism a female of repellent aspect, remotely connected with education?

CHASUBLE (*somewhat indignantly*): She is the most cultivated of ladies, and the very picture of respectability.

LADY BRACKNELL: It is obviously the same person. May I ask what position she holds in your household?

CHASUBLE (*severely*): I am a celibate, madam.

JACK (*interposing*): Miss Prism, Lady Bracknell, has been for the last three years Miss Cardew's esteemed governess and valued companion.

LADY BRACKNELL: In spite of what I hear of her, I must see her at once. Let her be sent for.

CHASUBLE (*looking off*): She approaches; she is nigh.

(*Enter* MISS PRISM *hurriedly.*)

MISS PRISM: I was told you expected me in the vestry, dear Canon. I have been waiting for you there for an hour and three quarters. (*Catches sight of* LADY BRACKNELL *who has fixed her with a stony glare.* MISS PRISM *grows pale and quails. She looks anxiously round as if desirous to escape.*)

LADY BRACKNELL (*in a severe, judicial voice*): Prism! (MISS PRISM *bows her head in shame.*) Come here, Prism! (MISS PRISM *ap-*

proaches in a humble manner.) Prism! Where is that baby? (*General consternation. The* CANON *starts back in horror.* ALGERNON *and* JACK *pretend to be anxious to shield* CECILY *and* GWENDOLEN *from hearing the details of a terrible public scandal.*) Twenty-eight years ago, Prism, you left Lord Bracknell's house, Number 104, Upper Grosvenor Street, in charge of a perambulator that contained a baby, of the male sex. You never returned. A few weeks later, through the elaborate investigations of the Metropolitan police, the perambulator was discovered at midnight, standing by itself in a remote corner of Bayswater. It contained the manuscript of a three-volume novel of more than usually revolting sentimentality. (MISS PRISM *starts in involuntary indignation.*) But the baby was not there! (*Everyone looks at* MISS PRISM.) Prism! Where is that baby? (*A pause.*)

MISS PRISM: Lady Bracknell, I admit with shame that I do not know. I only wish I did. The plain facts of the case are these. On the morning of the day you mention, a day that is for ever branded on my memory, I prepared as usual to take the baby out in its perambulator. I had also with me a somewhat old, but capacious handbag, in which I had intended to place the manuscript of a work of fiction that I had written during my few unoccupied hours. In a moment of mental abstraction, for which I never can forgive myself, I deposited the manuscript in the bassinette, and placed the baby in the handbag.

JACK (*who has been listening attentively*): But where did you deposit the handbag?

MISS PRISM: Do not ask me, Mr. Worthing.

JACK: Miss Prism, this is a matter of no small importance to me. I insist on knowing where you deposited the handbag that contained the infant.

MISS PRISM: I left it in the cloakroom of one of the larger railway stations in London.

JACK: What railway station?

MISS PRISM (*quite crushed*): Victoria. The Brighton line. (*Sinks into a chair.*)

JACK: I must retire to my room for a moment. Gwendolen, wait here for me.

GWENDOLEN: If you are not too long, I will wait here for you all my life. (*Exit* JACK *in great excitement.*)

CHASUBLE: What do you think this means, Lady Bracknell?

LADY BRACKNELL: I dare not even suspect, Dr. Chasuble. I need hardly tell you that in families of high position strange coincidences are not supposed to occur. They are hardly considered the thing.

(*Noises heard overhead as if someone was throwing trunks about. Everyone looks up.*)

CECILY: Uncle Jack seems strangely agitated.

CHASUBLE: Your guardian has a very emotional nature.

LADY BRACKNELL: This noise is extremely unpleasant. It sounds as if he was having an argument. I dislike arguments of any kind. They are always vulgar, and often convincing.

CHASUBLE (*looking up*): It has stopped now. (*The noise is redoubled.*)

LADY BRACKNELL: I wish he would arrive at some conclusion.

GWENDOLEN: This suspense is terrible. I hope it will last.

(*Enter* JACK *with a handbag of black leather in his hand.*)

JACK (*rushing over to* MISS PRISM): Is this the handbag, Miss Prism? Examine it carefully before you speak. The happiness of more than one life depends on your answer.

MISS PRISM (*calmly*): It seems to be mine. Yes, here is the injury it received through the upsetting of a Gower Street omnibus in younger and happier days. Here is the stain on the lining caused by the explosion of a temperance beverage, an incident that occurred at Leamington. And here, on the lock, are my initials. I had forgotten that in an extravagant mood I had had them placed there. The bag is undoubtedly mine. I am delighted to have it so unexpectedly restored to me. It has been a great inconvenience being without it all these years.

JACK (*in a pathetic voice*): Miss Prism, more is restored to you than this handbag. I was the baby you placed in it.

MISS PRISM (*amazed*): You?

JACK (*embracing her*): Yes . . . mother!

MISS PRISM (*recoiling in indignant astonishment*): Mr. Worthing! I am unmarried!

JACK: Unmarried! I do not deny that is a serious blow. But after all, who has the right to cast a stone against one who has suffered? Cannot repentance wipe out an act of folly? Why should there be one law for men, and another for women? Mother, I forgive you. (*Tries to embrace her again.*)

MISS PRISM (*still more indignant*): Mr. Worthing, there is some error. (*Pointing to* LADY BRACKNELL.) There is the lady who can tell you who you really are.

JACK (*after a pause*): Lady Bracknell, I hate to seem inquisitive, but would you kindly inform me who I am?

LADY BRACKNELL: I am afraid that the news I have to give you will not altogether please you. You are the son of my poor sister, Mrs. Moncrieff, and consequently Algernon's elder brother.

JACK: Algy's elder brother! Then I have a brother after all. I knew I had a brother! I always said I had a brother! Cecily,—how could you have ever doubted that I had a brother? (*Seizes hold of* ALGERNON.) Dr. Chasuble, my unfortunate brother. Miss Prism, my unfortunate brother. Gwendolen, my unfortunate brother. Algy, you young scoundrel, you will have to treat me with more respect in the future. You have never behaved to me like a brother in all your life.

ALGERNON: Well, not till today, old boy, I admit. I did my best, however, though I was out of practice. (*Shakes hands.*)

GWENDOLEN (*to* JACK): My own! But what own are you? What is your Christian name, now that you have become someone else?

JACK: Good heavens! . . . I had quite forgotten that point. Your decision on the subject of my name is irrevocable, I suppose?

GWENDOLEN: I never change, except in my affections.

CECILY: What a noble nature you have, Gwendolen!

JACK: Then the question had better be cleared up at once. Aunt Augusta, a moment. At the time when Miss Prism left me in the handbag, had I been christened already?

LADY BRACKNELL: Every luxury that money could buy, including christening, had been lavished on you by your fond and doting parents.

JACK: Then I was christened! That is settled. Now, what name was I given? Let me know the worst.

LADY BRACKNELL: Being the eldest son you were naturally christened after your father.

JACK (*irritably*): Yes, but what was my father's Christian name?

LADY BRACKNELL (*meditatively*): I cannot at the present moment recall what the General's Christian name was. But I have no doubt he had one. He was eccentric, I admit. But only in later years. And that was the result of the Indian climate, and marriage, and indigestion, and other things of that kind.

JACK: Algy! Can't you recollect what our father's Christian name was?

ALGERNON: My dear boy, we were never even on speaking terms. He died before I was a year old.

JACK: His name would appear in the Army Lists of the period, I suppose, Aunt Augusta?

LADY BRACKNELL: The General was essentially a man of peace, except in his domestic life. But I have no doubt his name would appear in any military directory.

JACK: The Army Lists of the last forty years are here. These delightful records should have been my constant study. (*Rushes to bookcase and tears the books out.*) M. Generals . . . Mallam, Maxbohm, Magley, what ghastly names they have—Markby, Migsby, Mobbs, Moncrieff! Lieutenant 1840, Captain, Lieutenant-Colonel, Colonel, General 1869, Christian names, Ernest John. (*Puts book very quietly down and speaks quite calmly.*) I always told you, Gwendolen, my name was Ernest, didn't I? Well, it is Ernest after all. I mean it naturally is Ernest.

LADY BRACKNELL: Yes, I remember now that the General was called Ernest. I knew I had some particular reason for disliking the name.

GWENDOLEN: Ernest! My own Ernest! I felt from the first that you could have no other name!

JACK: Gwendolen, it is a terrible thing for a man to find out suddenly that all his life he has been speaking nothing but the truth. Can you forgive me?

GWENDOLEN: I can. For I feel that you are sure to change.

JACK: My own one!

CHASUBLE (*to* MISS PRISM): Lætitia! (*Embraces her.*)

MISS PRISM (*enthusiastically*): Frederick! At last!

ALGERNON: Cecily! (*Embraces her.*) At last!

JACK: Gwendolen! (*Embraces her.*) At last!

LADY BRACKNELL: My nephew, you seem to be displaying signs of triviality.

JACK: On the contrary, Aunt Augusta, I've now realized for the first time in my life the vital Importance of Being Earnest.

CURTAIN.

58593

Private Lives

NOËL COWARD

Why our respondents liked

 PRIVATE LIVES

"Best pure Coward. Still a great great work."
JOSHUA LOGAN

*"Coward at his best BUT it has to be done with
just the right style and elegance."*
GEORGE OPPENHEIMER

"An apotheosis of style."
HEYWOOD HALE BROUN

Private Lives, a witty, sophisticated comedy about the English "leisure class," was authored by Noël Coward, prolific English playwright, actor, and composer. Coward's writings encompass comedies (e.g., *Blithe Spirit,* 1941), musical plays (e.g., *Bitter Sweet,* 1929), songs and sketches, autobiography (*Present Indicative,* 1937; *Future Indefinite,* 1954); he also produced several films based on his own scripts, including *In Which We Serve* and *Brief Encounter. Private Lives,* after its original production in London, came to Broadway in January 1931. It was scheduled for only a three-month run, and Noël Coward, who cast himself in one of the principal roles, refused to continue in the part after the three months was over. On May 11, 1931, Madge Kennedy and Otto Kruger were brought in for the starring roles. A 1947 revival on Broadway, which starred Tallulah Bankhead, also had a very successful run. More recently, in 1969, this play, which has been so popular in repertory over the years, returned to Broadway with Tammy Grimes and Brian Bedford in the roles of Amanda and Elyot.

Private Lives was presented by Charles B. Cochran on January 27, 1931, at the Times Square Theatre, New York City. The cast was as follows:

Sibyl Chase	Jill Esmond
Elyot Chase	Noël Coward
Victor Prynne	Laurence Olivier
Amanda Prynne	Gertrude Lawrence
Louise	Therese Quadri

Staged by Noël Coward

ACT ONE

Terrace of a hotel in France. Summer evening.

ACT TWO

Amanda's flat in Paris. A few days later. Evening.

ACT THREE

Amanda's flat in Paris. The next morning.

ACT ONE

The Scene is the terrace of a hotel in France. There are two French windows at the back opening on to two separate suites. The terrace space is divided by a line of small trees in tubs, and, down-stage, running parallel with the footlights, there is a low stone balustrade. Upon each side of the line of tree tubs is a set of suitable terrace furniture, a swinging seat, two or three chairs, and a table. There are orange and white awnings shading the windows, as it is summer.

When the curtain rises it is about eight o'clock in the evening. There is an orchestra playing not very far off. Sibyl Chase opens the windows on the Right, and steps out on to the terrace. She is very pretty and blonde, and smartly dressed in travelling clothes. She comes down stage, stretches her arms wide with a little sigh of satisfaction, and regards the view with an ecstatic expression.

SIBYL (*calling*): Elli, Elli dear, do come out. It's so lovely.

ELYOT (*inside*): Just a minute.

(After a pause ELYOT *comes out. He is about thirty, quite slim and pleasant looking, and also in travelling clothes. He walks right down to the balustrade and looks thoughtfully at the view.* SIBYL *stands beside him, and slips her arm through his.)*

ELYOT: Not so bad.

SIBYL: It's heavenly. Look at the lights of that yacht reflected in the water. Oh dear, I'm so happy.

ELYOT (*smiling*): Are you?

SIBYL: Aren't you?

ELYOT: Of course I am. Tremendously happy.

SIBYL: Just to think, here we are, you and I, married!

ELYOT: Yes, things have come to a pretty pass.

SIBYL: Don't laugh at me, you mustn't be *blasé* about honeymoons just because this is your second.

ELYOT (*frowning*): That's silly.

SIBYL: Have I annoyed you by saying that?

ELYOT: Just a little.

SIBYL: Oh, darling, I'm so sorry. (*She holds her face up to his.*) Kiss me.

ELYOT (*doing so*): There.

SIBYL: Ummm, not so very enthusiastic.

ELYOT (*kissing her again*): That better?

SIBYL: Three times, please, I'm superstitious.

ELYOT: (*kissing her*): You really are very sweet.

SIBYL: Are you glad you married me?

ELYOT: Of course I am.

SIBYL: How glad?

ELYOT: Incredibly, magnificently glad.

SIBYL: How lovely.

ELYOT: We ought to go in and dress.

SIBYL: Gladder than before?

ELYOT: Why do you keep harping on that?

SIBYL: It's in my mind, and yours too, I expect.

ELYOT: It isn't anything of the sort.

SIBYL: She was pretty, wasn't she? Amanda?

ELYOT: Very pretty.

SIBYL: Prettier than I am?

ELYOT: Much.

SIBYL: Elyot!

ELYOT: She was pretty and sleek, and her hands were long and slim, and her legs were long and slim, and she danced like an angel. You dance very poorly, by the way.

SIBYL: Could she play the piano as well as I can?

ELYOT: She couldn't play the piano at all.

SIBYL (*triumphantly*): Aha! Had she my talent for organisation?

ELYOT: No, but she hadn't your mother either.

SIBYL: I don't believe you like mother.

ELYOT: Like her! I can't bear her.

SIBYL: Elyot! She's a darling, underneath.

ELYOT: I never got underneath.

SIBYL: It makes me unhappy to think you don't like mother.

ELYOT: Nonsense. I believe the only reason you married me was to get away from her.

SIBYL: I married you because I loved you.

ELYOT: Oh dear, oh dear, oh dear, oh dear!

SIBYL: I love you far more than Amanda loved you. I'd never make you miserable like she did.

ELYOT: We made each other miserable.

SIBYL: It was all her fault, you know it was.

ELYOT (*with vehemence*): Yes, it was. Entirely her fault.

SIBYL: She was a fool to lose you.

ELYOT: We lost each other.

SIBYL: She lost you, with her violent tempers and carryings on.

ELYOT: Will you stop talking about Amanda?

SIBYL: But I'm very glad, because if she hadn't been uncontrolled, and wicked, and unfaithful, we shouldn't be here now.

ELYOT: She wasn't unfaithful.

SIBYL: How do you know? I bet she was. I bet she was unfaithful every five minutes.

ELYOT: It would take a far more concentrated woman than Amanda to be unfaithful every five minutes.

SIBYL (*anxiously*): You do hate her, don't you?

ELYOT: No, I don't hate her. I think I despise her.

SIBYL (*with satisfaction*): That's much worse.

ELYOT: And yet I'm sorry for her.

SIBYL: Why?

ELYOT: Because she's marked for tragedy; she's bound to make a mess of everything.

SIBYL: If it's all her fault, I don't see that it matters much.

ELYOT: She has some very good qualities.

SIBYL: Considering what a hell she made of your life, I think you are very nice about her. Most men would be vindictive.

ELYOT: What's the use of that? It's all over now, such a long time ago.

SIBYL: Five years isn't very long.

ELYOT (*seriously*): Yes it is.

SIBYL: Do you think you could ever love her again?

ELYOT: Now then, Sibyl.

SIBYL: But could you?

ELYOT: Of course not, I love you.

SIBYL: Yes, but you love me differently; I know that.

ELYOT: More wisely perhaps.

SIBYL: I'm glad. I'd rather have that sort of love.

ELYOT: You're right. Love is no use unless it's wise, and kind, and undramatic. Something steady and sweet, to smooth out your nerves when you're tired. Something tremendously cosy; and unflurried by scenes and jealousies. That's what I want, what I've always wanted really. Oh my dear, I do hope it's not going to be dull for you.

SIBYL: Sweetheart, as tho' you could ever be dull.

ELYOT: I'm much older than you.

SIBYL: Not so very much.

ELYOT: Seven years.

SIBYL (*snuggling up to him*): The music has stopped now and you can hear the sea.

ELYOT: We'll bathe tomorrow morning.

SIBYL: I mustn't get sunburnt.

ELYOT: Why not?

SIBYL: I hate it on women.

ELYOT: Very well, you shan't then. I hope you don't hate it on men.

SIBYL: Of course I don't. It's suitable to men.

ELYOT: You're a completely feminine little creature, aren't you?

SIBYL: Why do you say that?

ELYOT: Everything in its place.

SIBYL: What do you mean?

ELYOT: If you feel you'd like me to smoke a pipe, I'll try and master it.

SIBYL: I like a man to be a man, if that's what you mean.

ELYOT: Are you going to understand me, and manage me?

SIBYL: I'm going to try to understand you.

ELYOT: Run me without my knowing it?

SIBYL (*withdrawing slightly*): I think you're being a little unkind.

ELYOT: No, I don't mean to be. I was only wondering.

SIBYL: Well?

ELYOT: I was wondering what was going on inside your mind, what your plans are really?

SIBYL: Plans; oh, Elli!

ELYOT: Apart from loving me and all that, you must have plans.

SIBYL: I haven't the faintest idea what you're talking about.

ELYOT: Perhaps it's subconscious then, age-old instincts working away deep down, mincing up little bits of experience for future use, watching me carefully like a little sharp-eyed, blonde kitten.

SIBYL: How can you be so horrid.

ELYOT: I said Kitten, not Cat.

SIBYL: Kittens grow into cats.

ELYOT: Let that be a warning to you.

SIBYL (*slipping her arm through his again*): What's the matter, darling; are you hungry?

ELYOT: Not a bit.

SIBYL: You're very strange all of a sudden, and rather cruel. Just because I'm feminine. It doesn't mean that I'm crafty and calculating.

ELYOT: I didn't say you were either of those things.

SIBYL: I hate these half masculine women who go banging about.

ELYOT: I hate anybody who goes banging about.

SIBYL: I should think you needed a little quiet womanliness after Amanda.

ELYOT: Why will you keep on talking about her?

SIBYL: It's natural enough, isn't it?

ELYOT: What do you want to find out?

SIBYL: Why did you really let her divorce you?

ELYOT: She divorced me for cruelty, and flagrant infidelity. I spent a whole week-end at Brighton with a lady called Vera Williams. She had the nastiest looking hair brush I have ever seen.

SIBYL: Misplaced chivalry, I call it. Why didn't you divorce her?

ELYOT: It would not have been the action of a gentleman, whatever that may mean.

SIBYL: I think she got off very lightly.

ELYOT: Once and for all will you stop talking about her.

SIBYL: Yes, Elli dear.

ELYOT: I don't wish to see her again or hear her name mentioned.

SIBYL: Very well, darling.

ELYOT: Is that understood?

SIBYL: Yes, darling. Where did you spend your honeymoon?

ELYOT: St. Moritz. Be quiet.

SIBYL: I hate St. Moritz.

ELYOT: So do I, bitterly.

SIBYL: Was she good on skis?

ELYOT: Do you want to dine downstairs here, or at the Casino?

SIBYL: I love you, I love you, I love you.

ELYOT: Good, let's go in and dress.

SIBYL: Kiss me first.

ELYOT (*kissing her*): Casino?

SIBYL: Yes. Are you a gambler? You never told me.

ELYOT: Every now and then.

SIBYL: I shall come and sit just behind your chair and bring you luck.

ELYOT: That will be fatal.

(*They go off into their suite. There is a slight pause and the*
VICTOR PRYNNE *enters from the Left suite. He is quite nice looking*
about thirty or thirty-five. He is dressed in a light travelling suit. H
sniffs the air, looks at the view, and then turns back to the window.)

VICTOR (*calling*): Mandy.

AMANDA (*inside*): What?

VICTOR: Come outside, the view is wonderful.

AMANDA: I'm still damp from the bath. Wait a minute—(VICTOR *light*
a cigarette. Presently AMANDA *comes out on to the terrace. She i*
quite exquisite with a gay face and a perfect figure. At the momer
she is wearing a negligee.) I shall catch pneumonia, that's what
shall catch.

VICTOR (*looking at her*): God!

AMANDA: I beg your pardon?

VICTOR: You look wonderful.

AMANDA: Thank you, darling.

VICTOR: Like a beautiful advertisement for something.

AMANDA: Nothing peculiar, I hope.

VICTOR: I can hardly believe it's true. You and I, here alone together, married!

AMANDA (*rubbing her face on his shoulder*): That stuff's very rough.

VICTOR: Don't you like it?

AMANDA: A bit hearty, isn't it?

VICTOR: Do you love me?

AMANDA: Of course, that's why I'm here.

VICTOR: More than—

AMANDA: Now then, none of that.

VICTOR: No, but do you love me more than you loved Elyot?

AMANDA: I don't remember, it's such a long time ago.

VICTOR: Not so very long.

AMANDA (*flinging out her arms*): All my life ago.

VICTOR: I'd like to break his damned neck.

AMANDA (*laughing*): Why?

VICTOR: For making you unhappy.

AMANDA: It was mutual.

VICTOR: Rubbish! It was all his fault, you know it was.

AMANDA: Yes, it was, now I come to think about it.

VICTOR: Swine!

AMANDA: Don't be so vehement, darling.

VICTOR: I'll never treat you like that.

AMANDA: That's right.

VICTOR: I love you too much.

AMANDA: So did he.

VICTOR: Fine sort of love that is. He struck you once, didn't he?

AMANDA: More than once.

VICTOR: Where?

AMANDA: Several places.

VICTOR: What a cad.

AMANDA: I struck him too. Once I broke four gramophone records over his head. It was very satisfying.

VICTOR: You must have been driven to distraction.

AMANDA: Yes, I was, but don't let's talk about it, please. After all, it's a dreary subject for our honeymoon night.

VICTOR: He didn't know when he was well off.

AMANDA: Look at the lights of that yacht reflected in the water. I wonder whose it is.

VICTOR: We must bathe tomorrow.

AMANDA: Yes. I want to get a nice sunburn.

VICTOR (*reproachfully*): Mandy!

AMANDA: Why, what's the matter?

VICTOR: I hate sunburnt women.

AMANDA: Why?

VICTOR: It's somehow, well, unsuitable.

AMANDA: It's awfully suitable to me, darling.

VICTOR: Of course if you really want to.

AMANDA: I'm absolutely determined. I've got masses of lovely oil to rub all over myself.

VICTOR: Your skin is so beautiful as it is.

AMANDA: Wait and see. When I'm done a nice crisp brown, you'll fall in love with me all over again.

VICTOR: I couldn't love you more than I do now.

AMANDA: Oh, dear. I did so hope our honeymoon was going to be progressive.

VICTOR: Where did you spend the last one?

AMANDA (*warningly*): Victor.

VICTOR: I want to know.

AMANDA: St. Moritz. It was very attractive.

VICTOR: I hate St. Moritz.

AMANDA: So do I.

VICTOR: Did he start quarreling with you right away?

AMANDA: Within the first few days. I put it down to the high altitudes.

VICTOR: And you loved him?

AMANDA: Yes, Victor.

VICTOR: You poor child.

AMANDA: You must try not to be pompous, dear. (*She turns away.*)

VICTOR (*hurt*): Mandy!

AMANDA: I don't believe I'm a bit like what you think I am.

VICTOR: How do you mean?

AMANDA: I was never a poor child.

VICTOR: Figure of speech, dear, that's all.

AMANDA: I suffered a good deal, and had my heart broken. But it wasn't an innocent girlish heart. It was jagged with sophistication. I've always been sophisticated, far too knowing. That caused many of my rows with Elyot, I irritated him because he knew I could see through him.

VICTOR: I don't mind how much you see through me.

AMANDA: Sweet. (*She kisses him.*)

VICTOR: I'm going to make you happy.

AMANDA: Are you?

VICTOR: Just by looking after you, and seeing that you're all right, you know.

AMANDA (*a trifle wistfully*): No, I don't know.

VICTOR: I think you love me quite differently from the way you loved Elyot.

AMANDA: Do stop harping on Elyot.

VICTOR: It's true, though, isn't it?

AMANDA: I love you much more calmly, if that's what you mean.

VICTOR: More lastingly?

AMANDA: I expect so.

VICTOR: Do you remember when I first met you?

AMANDA: Yes. Distinctly.

VICTOR: At Marion Vale's party.

AMANDA: Yes.

VICTOR: Wasn't it wonderful?

AMANDA: Not really, dear. It was only redeemed from the completely commonplace by the fact of my having hiccoughs.

VICTOR: I never noticed them.

AMANDA: Love at first sight.

VICTOR: Where did you first meet Elyot?

AMANDA: To hell with Elyot.

VICTOR: Mandy!

AMANDA: I forbid you to mention his name again. I'm sick of the sound of it. You must be raving mad. Here we are on the first night of our honeymoon, with the moon coming up, and the music playing, and all you can do is to talk about my first husband. It's downright sacrilegious.

VICTOR: Don't be angry.

AMANDA: Well, it's very annoying.

VICTOR: Will you forgive me?

AMANDA: Yes; only don't do it again.

VICTOR: I promise.

AMANDA: You'd better go and dress now, you haven't bathed yet.

VICTOR: Where shall we dine, downstairs here, or at the Casino?

AMANDA: The Casino is more fun, I think.

VICTOR: We can play Boule afterwards.

AMANDA: No, we can't, dear.

VICTOR: Don't you like dear old Boule?

AMANDA: No, I hate dear old Boule. We'll play a nice game of Chemin de fer.

VICTOR (*apprehensively*): Not at the big table?

AMANDA: Maybe at the biggest table.

VICTOR: You're not a terrible gambler, are you?

AMANDA: Inveterate. Chance rules my life.

VICTOR: What nonsense.

AMANDA: How can you say it's nonsense? It was chance meeting you. It was chancing falling in love; it's chance that we're here, particularly after your driving. Everything that happens is chance.

VICTOR: You know I feel rather scared of you at close quarters.

AMANDA: That promises to be very embarrassing.

VICTOR: You're somehow different now, wilder than I thought you were, more strained.

AMANDA: Wilder! Oh Victor, I've never felt less wild in my life. A little strained, I grant you, but that's the newly married atmosphere; you can't expect anything else. Honeymooning is a very overrated amusement.

VICTOR: You say that because you had a ghastly experience before.

AMANDA: There you go again.

VICTOR: It couldn't fail to embitter you a little.

AMANDA: The honeymoon wasn't such a ghastly experience really; it was afterwards that was so awful.

VICTOR: I intend to make you forget it all entirely.

AMANDA: You won't succeed by making constant references to it.

VICTOR: I wish I knew you better.

AMANDA: It's just as well you don't. The "woman"—in italics—should always retain a certain amount of alluring feminine mystery for the "man"—also in italics.

VICTOR: What about the man? Isn't he allowed to have any mystery?

AMANDA: Absolutely none. Transparent as glass.

VICTOR: Oh, I see.

AMANDA: Never mind, darling; it doesn't necessarily work out like that; it's only supposed to.

VICTOR: I'm glad I'm normal.

AMANDA: What an odd thing to be glad about. Why?

VICTOR: Well, aren't you?

AMANDA: I'm not so sure I'm normal.

VICTOR: Oh, Mandy, of course you are, sweetly, divinely normal.

AMANDA: I haven't any peculiar cravings for Chinamen or old boots, if that's what you mean.

VICTOR (*scandalised*): Mandy!

AMANDA: I think very few people are completely normal really, deep down in their private lives. It all depends on a combination of circumstances. If all the various cosmic thingummys fuse at the same moment, and the right spark is struck, there's no knowing what one mightn't do. That was the trouble with Elyot and me, we were like two violent acids bubbling about in a nasty little matrimonial bottle.

VICTOR: I don't believe you're nearly as complex as you think you are.

AMANDA: I don't think I'm particularly complex, but I know I'm unreliable.

VICTOR: You're frightening me horribly. In what way unreliable?

AMANDA: I'm so apt to see things the wrong way round.

VICTOR: What sort of things?

AMANDA: Morals. What one should do and what one shouldn't.

VICTOR (*fondly*): Darling, you're so sweet.

AMANDA: Thank you, Victor, that's most encouraging. You really must have your bath now. Come along.

VICTOR: Kiss me.

AMANDA (*doing so*): There, dear, hurry now; I've only got to slip my dress on and then I shall be ready.

VICTOR: Give me ten minutes.

AMANDA: I'll bring the cocktails out here when they come.

VICTOR: All right.

AMANDA: Go along now, hurry.

(*They both disappear into their suite. After a moment's pause* ELYOT *steps carefully on to the terrace carrying a tray upon which are two champagne cocktails. He puts the tray down on the table.*)

ELYOT (*calling*): Sibyl.

SIBYL (*inside*): Yes.

ELYOT: I've brought the cocktails out here, hurry up.

SIBYL: I can't find my lipstick.

ELYOT: Never mind, send down to the kitchen for some cochineal.

SIBYL: Don't be so silly.

ELYOT: Hurry.

(ELYOT *saunters down to the balustrade. He looks casually over on to the next terrace, and then out at the view. He looks up at the moon and sighs, then he sits down in a chair with his back towards the line of tubs, and lights a cigarette.* AMANDA *steps gingerly on to her terrace carrying a tray with two champagne cocktails on it. She is wearing a charmingly simple evening gown, her cloak is flung over her right shoulder. She places the tray carefully on the table, puts her cloak over the back of a chair, and sits down with her back towards* ELYOT. *She takes a small mirror from her handbag, and scrutinises her face in it. The orchestra downstairs strikes up a new melody. Both* ELYOT *and* AMANDA *give a little start. After a moment,* ELYOT *pensively begins to hum the tune the band is playing. It is a sentimental, romantic little tune.* AMANDA *hears him, and clutches at her throat suddenly as though she were suffocating. Then she jumps up noiselessly, and peers over the line of tubs.* ELYOT, *with his back to her, continues to sing obliviously. She sits down again, relaxing with a gesture almost of despair. Then she looks anxiously over her shoulder at the window in case Victor should be listening, and then, with a little smile, she takes up the melody herself, clearly.* ELYOT *stops dead and gives a gasp, then he jumps up, and stands looking at her. She continues to sing, pretending not to know that he is there. At the end of the song, she turns slowly, and faces him.*)

AMANDA: Thoughtful of them to play that, wasn't it?

ELYOT (*in a stifled voice*): What are you doing here?

AMANDA: I'm on honeymoon.

ELYOT: How interesting, so am I.

AMANDA: I hope you're enjoying it.

ELYOT: It hasn't started yet.

AMANDA: Neither has mine.

ELYOT: Oh, my God!

AMANDA: I can't help feeling that this is a little unfortunate.

ELYOT: Are you happy?

AMANDA: Perfectly.

ELYOT: Good. That's all right, then, isn't it?

AMANDA: Are you?

ELYOT: Ecstatically.

AMANDA: I'm delighted to hear it. We shall probably meet again some-time. Au revoir! (*She turns.*)

ELYOT (*firmly*): Good-bye.

(*She goes indoors without looking back. He stands gazing after her with an expression of horror on his face.* SIBYL *comes brightly on to the terrace in a very pretty evening frock.*)

SIBYL: Cocktail, please. (ELYOT *doesn't answer.*) Elli, what's the matter?

ELYOT: I feel very odd.

SIBYL: Odd, what do you mean, ill?

ELYOT: Yes, ill.

SIBYL (*alarmed*): What sort of ill?

ELYOT: We must leave at once.

SIBYL: Leave!

ELYOT: Yes, dear. Leave immediately.

SIBYL: Elli!

ELYOT: I have a strange foreboding.

SIBYL: You must be mad.

ELYOT: Listen, darling. I want you to be very sweet, and patient, and understanding, and not be upset, or ask any questions, or anything. I have an absolute conviction that our whole future happiness depends upon our leaving here instantly.

SIBYL: Why?

ELYOT: I can't tell you why.

SIBYL: But we've only just come.

ELYOT: I know that, but it can't be helped.

SIBYL: What's happened, what has happened?

ELYOT: Nothing has happened.

SIBYL: You've gone out of your mind.

ELYOT: I haven't gone out of my mind, but I shall if we stay here another hour.

SIBYL: You're not drunk, are you?

ELYOT: Of course I'm not drunk. What time have I had to get drunk?

SIBYL: Come down and have some dinner, darling, and then you'll feel ever so much better.

ELYOT: It's no use trying to humour me. I'm serious.

SIBYL: But darling, please be reasonable. We've only just arrived; everything's unpacked. It's our first night together. We can't go away now.

ELYOT: We can have our first night together in Paris.

SIBYL: We shouldn't get there until the small hours.

ELYOT (*with a great effort at calmness*): Now please, Sibyl, I know it sounds crazy to you, and utterly lacking in reason and sense, but I've got second sight over certain things. I'm almost psychic. I've got the most extraordinary sensation of impending disaster. If we stay here something appalling will happen. I know it.

SIBYL (*firmly*): Hysterical nonsense.

ELYOT: It isn't hysterical nonsense. Presentiments are far from being nonsense. Look at the woman who cancelled her passage on the *Titanic*. All because of a presentiment.

SIBYL: I don't see what that has to do with it.

ELYOT: It has everything to do with it. She obeyed her instincts, that's what she did, and saved her life. All I ask is to be allowed to obey my instincts.

SIBYL: Do you mean that there's going to be an earthquake or something?

ELYOT: Very possibly, very possibly indeed, or perhaps a violent explosion.

SIBYL: They don't have earthquakes in France.

ELYOT: On the contrary, only the other day they felt a distinct shock at Toulon.

SIBYL: Yes, but that's in the South where it's hot.

ELYOT: Don't quibble, Sibyl.

SIBYL: And as for explosions, there's nothing here that can explode.

ELYOT: Oho, isn't there.

SIBYL: Yes, but Elli—

ELYOT: Darling, be sweet. Bear with me. I beseech you to bear with me.

SIBYL: I don't understand. It's horrid of you to do this.

ELYOT: I'm not doing anything. I'm only asking you, imploring you to come away from this place.

SIBYL: But I love it here.

ELYOT: There are thousands of other places far nicer.

SIBYL: It's a pity we didn't go to one of them.

ELYOT: Now, listen, Sibyl—

SIBYL: Yes, but why are you behaving like this, why, why, why?

ELYOT: Don't ask why. Just give in to me. I swear I'll never ask you to give in to me over anything again.

SIBYL (*with complete decision*): I won't think of going tonight. It's utterly ridiculous. I've done quite enough travelling for one day, and I'm tired.

ELYOT: You're as obstinate as a mule.

SIBYL: I like that, I must say.

ELYOT (*hotly*): You've got your nasty little feet dug into the ground, and you don't intend to budge an inch, do you?

SIBYL (*with spirit*): No, I do not.

ELYOT: If there's one thing in the world that infuriates me, it's sheer wanton stubbornness. I should like to cut off your head with a meat axe.

SIBYL: How dare you talk to me like that, on our honeymoon night.

ELYOT: Damn our honeymoon night. Damn it, damn it, damn it!

SIBYL (*bursting into tears*): Oh, Elli, Elli—

ELYOT: Stop crying. Will you or will you not come away with me to Paris?

SIBYL: I've never been so miserable in my life. You're hateful and beastly. Mother was perfectly right. She said you had shifty eyes.

ELYOT: Well, she can't talk. Hers are so close together, you couldn't put a needle between them.

SIBYL: You don't love me a little bit. I wish I were dead.

ELYOT: Will you or will you not come to Paris?

SIBYL: No, no I won't.

ELYOT: Oh, my God! (*He stamps indoors.*)

SIBYL (*following him, wailing*): Oh, Elli, Elli, Elli—

(VICTOR *comes stamping out of the French windows on the left,* *followed by* AMANDA.)

VICTOR: You were certainly right when you said you weren't normal. You're behaving like a lunatic.

AMANDA: Not at all. All I have done is to ask you a little favour.

VICTOR: Little favour indeed.

AMANDA: If we left now we could be in Paris in a few hours.

VICTOR: If we crossed Siberia by train we could be in China in a fortnight, but I don't see any reason to do it.

AMANDA: Oh, Victor darling—please, please—be sensible, just for my sake.

VICTOR: Sensible!

AMANDA: Yes, sensible. I shall be absolutely miserable if we stay here. You don't want me to be absolutely miserable all through my honeymoon, do you?

VICTOR: But why on earth didn't you think of your sister's tragedy before?

AMANDA: I forgot.

VICTOR: You couldn't forget a thing like that.

AMANDA: I got the places muddled. Then when I saw the Casino there in the moonlight, it all came back to me.

VICTOR: When did all this happen?

AMANDA: Years ago, but it might just as well have been yesterday. I can see her now lying dead, with that dreadful expression on her face. Then all that awful business of taking the body home to England. It was perfectly horrible.

VICTOR: I never knew you had a sister.

AMANDA: I haven't any more.

VICTOR: There's something behind all this.

AMANDA: Don't be silly. What could there be behind it?

VICTOR: Well, for one thing, I know you're lying.

AMANDA: Victor!

VICTOR: Be honest. Aren't you?

AMANDA: I can't think how you can be so mean and suspicious.

VICTOR (*patiently*): You're lying, Amanda. Aren't you?

AMANDA: Yes, Victor.

VICTOR: You never had a sister, dead or alive?

AMANDA: I believe there was a stillborn one in 1902.

VICTOR: What is your reason for all this?

AMANDA: I told you I was unreliable.

VICTOR: Why do you want to leave so badly?

AMANDA: You'll be angry if I tell you the truth.

VICTOR: What is it?

AMANDA: I warn you.

VICTOR: Tell me. Please tell me.

AMANDA: Elyot's here.

VICTOR: What!

AMANDA: I saw him.

VICTOR: When?

AMANDA: Just now, when you were in the bath.

VICTOR: Where was he?

AMANDA (*hesitatingly*): Down there, in a white suit. (*She points over the balustrade.*)

VICTOR (*sceptically*): White suit?

AMANDA: Why not? It's summer, isn't it?

VICTOR: You're lying again.

AMANDA: I'm not. He's here. I swear he is.

VICTOR: Well, what of it?

AMANDA: I can't enjoy a honeymoon with you, with Elyot liable to bounce in at any moment.

VICTOR: Really, Mandy.

AMANDA: Can't you see how awful it is? It's the most embarrassing thing that ever happened to me in my whole life.

VICTOR: Did he see you?

AMANDA: No, he was running.

VICTOR: What was he running for?

AMANDA: How on earth do I know? Don't be so annoying.

VICTOR: Well, as long as he didn't see you it's all right, isn't it?

AMANDA: It isn't all right at all. We must leave immediately.

VICTOR: But why?

AMANDA: How can you be so appallingly obstinate?

VICTOR: I'm not afraid of him.

AMANDA: Neither am I. It isn't a question of being afraid. It's just a horrible awkward situation.

VICTOR: I'm damned if I can see why our whole honeymoon should be upset by Elyot.

AMANDA: My last one was.

VICTOR: I don't believe he's here at all.

AMANDA: He is I tell you. I saw him.

VICTOR: It was probably an optical illusion. This half light is very deceptive.

AMANDA: It was no such thing.

VICTOR: I absolutely refuse to change all our plans at the last moment, just because you think you've seen Elyot. It's unreasonable and ridiculous of you to demand it. Even if he is here I can't see that it matters. He'll probably feel much more embarrassed than you, and a damned good job too; and if he annoys you in any way I'll knock him down.

AMANDA: That would be charming.

VICTOR: Now don't let's talk about it any more.

AMANDA: Do you mean to stand there seriously and imagine that the whole thing can be glossed over as easily as that?

VICTOR: I'm not going to leave, Mandy. If I start giving in to you as early as this, our lives will be unbearable.

AMANDA (*outraged*): Victor!

VICTOR (*calmly*): You've worked yourself up into a state over a situation which really only exists in your mind.

AMANDA (*controlling herself with an effort*): Please, Victor, please for this last time I implore you. Let's go to Paris now, tonight. I mean it with all my heart—please—

VICTOR (*with gentle firmness*): No, Mandy!

AMANDA: I see quite clearly that I have been foolish enough to marry a fat old gentleman in a club armchair.

VICTOR: It's no use being cross.

AMANDA: You're a pompous ass.

VICTOR (*horrified*): Mandy!

AMANDA (*enraged*): Pompous ass, that's what I said, and that's what I meant. Blown out with your own importance.

VICTOR: Mandy, control yourself.

AMANDA: Get away from me. I can't bear to think I'm married to such rugged grandeur.

VICTOR (*with great dignity*): I shall be in the bar. When you are ready to come down and dine, let me know.

AMANDA (*flinging herself into a chair*): Go away, go away.

(VICTOR *stalks off, at the same moment that* ELYOT *stamps on, on the other side, followed by* SIBYL *in tears.*)

ELYOT: If you don't stop screaming, I'll murder you.

SIBYL: I wish to heaven I'd never seen you in my life, let alone married you. I don't wonder Amanda left you, if you behaved to her as you've behaved to me. I'm going down to have dinner by myself and you can just do what you like about it.

ELYOT: Do, and I hope it chokes you.

SIBYL: Oh Elli, Elli—

(*She goes wailing indoors.* ELYOT *stamps down to the balustrade and lights a cigarette, obviously trying to control his nerves.* AMANDA *sees him, and comes down too.*)

AMANDA: Give me one for God's sake.

ELYOT (*hands her his case laconically*): Here.

AMANDA (*taking a cigarette*): I'm in such a rage.

ELYOT (*lighting up*): So am I.

AMANDA: What are we to do?

ELYOT: I don't know.

AMANDA: Whose yacht is that?

ELYOT: The Duke of Westminster's I expect. It always is.

AMANDA: I wish I were on it.

ELYOT: I wish you were too.

AMANDA: There's no need to be nasty.

ELYOT: Yes there is, every need. I've never in my life felt a greater urge to be nasty.

AMANDA: And you've had some urges in your time, haven't you?

ELYOT: If you start bickering with me, Amanda, I swear I'll throw you over the edge.

AMANDA: Try it, that's all, just try it.

ELYOT: You've upset everything, as usual.

AMANDA: I've upset everything! What about you?

ELYOT: Ever since the first moment I was unlucky enough to set eyes on you, my life has been insupportable.

AMANDA: Oh do shut up, there's no sense in going on like that.

ELYOT: Nothing's any use. There's no escape, ever.

AMANDA: Don't be melodramatic.

ELYOT: Do you want a cocktail? There are two here.

AMANDA: There are two over here as well.

ELYOT: We'll have my two first. (*Amanda crosses over into* ELYOT's *part of the terrace. He gives her one, and keeps one himself.*)

AMANDA: Shall we get roaring screaming drunk?

ELYOT: I don't think that would help. We did it once before and it was a dismal failure.

AMANDA: It was lovely at the beginning.

ELYOT: You have an immoral memory Amanda. Here's to you. (*They raise their glasses solemnly and drink.*)

AMANDA: I tried to get away the moment after I'd seen you, but he wouldn't budge.

ELYOT: What's his name.

AMANDA: Victor, Victor Prynne.

ELYOT (*toasting*): Mr. and Mrs. Victor Prynne. (*He drinks.*) Mine wouldn't budge either.

AMANDA: What's her name?

ELYOT: Sibyl.

AMANDA (*toasting*): Mr. and Mrs. Elyot Chase. (*She drinks.*) God pity the poor girl.

ELYOT: Are you in love with him?

AMANDA: Of course.

ELYOT: How funny.

AMANDA: I don't see anything particularly funny about it; you're in love with yours aren't you?

ELYOT: Certainly.

AMANDA: There you are then.

ELYOT: There we both are then.

AMANDA: What's she like?

ELYOT: Fair, very pretty, plays the piano beautifully.

AMANDA: Very comforting.

ELYOT: How's yours?

AMANDA: I don't want to discuss him.

ELYOT: Well, it doesn't matter, he'll probably come popping out in a minute and I shall see for myself. Does he know I'm here?

AMANDA: Yes, I told him.

ELYOT (*with sarcasm*): That's going to make things a whole lot easier.

AMANDA: You needn't be frightened, he won't hurt you.

ELYOT: If he comes near me I'll scream the place down.

AMANDA: Does Sibyl know I'm here?

ELYOT: No, I pretended I'd had a presentiment. I tried terribly hard to persuade her to leave for Paris.

AMANDA: I tried too, it's lucky we didn't both succeed, isn't it? Otherwise we should probably all have joined up in Rouen or somewhere.

ELYOT (*laughing*): In some frowsy little hotel.

AMANDA (*laughing too*): Oh dear, it would have been much, much worse.

ELYOT: I can see us all sailing down in the morning for an early start.

AMANDA (*weakly*): Lovely, oh lovely.

ELYOT: Glorious! (*They both laugh helplessly.*)

AMANDA: What's happened to yours?

ELYOT: Didn't you hear her screaming? She's downstairs in the dining-room I think.

AMANDA: Mine is being grand, in the bar.

ELYOT: It really is awfully difficult.

AMANDA: Have you known her long?

ELYOT: About four months. We met in a house party in Norfolk.

AMANDA: Very flat, Norfolk.

ELYOT: How old is dear Victor?

AMANDA: Thirty-four, or five; and Sibyl?

ELYOT: I blush to tell you, only twenty-three.

AMANDA: You've gone a mucker alright.

ELYOT: I shall reserve my opinion of your choice until I've met dear Victor.

AMANDA: I wish you wouldn't go on calling him "Dear Victor." It's extremely irritating.

ELYOT: That's how I see him. Dumpy, and fair, and very considerate, with glasses. Dear Victor.

AMANDA: As I said before I would rather not discuss him. At least I have good taste enough to refrain from making cheap gibes at Sibyl.

ELYOT: You said Norfolk was flat.

AMANDA: That was no reflection on her, unless she made it flatter.

ELYOT: Your voice takes on an acid quality whenever you mention her name.

AMANDA: I'll never mention it again.

ELYOT: Good, and I'll keep off Victor.

AMANDA (*with dignity*): Thank you.

(*There is silence for a moment. The orchestra starts playing the same tune that they were singing previously.*)

ELYOT: That orchestra has a remarkable small repertoire.

AMANDA: They don't seem to know anything but this, do they? (*She sits down on the balustrade, and sings it, softly. Her eyes are looking out to sea, and her mind is far away.* ELYOT *watches her while she sings. When she turns to him at the end, there are tears in her eyes. He looks away awkwardly and lights another cigarette.*)

ELYOT: You always had a sweet voice, Amanda.

AMANDA (*a little huskily*): Thank you.

ELYOT: I'm awfully sorry about all this, really I am. I wouldn't have had it happen for the world.

AMANDA: I know. I'm sorry too. It's just rotten luck.

ELYOT: I'll go away tomorrow whatever happens, so don't you worry.

AMANDA: That's nice of you.

ELYOT: I hope everything turns out splendidly for you, and that you'll be very happy.

AMANDA: I hope the same for you, too.

(*The music, which has been playing continually through this little scene, returns persistently to the refrain. They both look at one another and laugh.*)

ELYOT: Nasty insistent little tune.

AMANDA: Extraordinary how potent cheap music is.

ELYOT: What exactly were you remembering at that moment?

AMANDA: The Palace Hotel Skating Rink in the morning, bright strong sunlight, and everybody whirling round in vivid colours, and you kneeling down to put on my skates for me.

ELYOT: You'd fallen on your fanny a few moments before.

AMANDA: It was beastly of you to laugh like that, I felt so humiliated.

ELYOT: Poor darling.

AMANDA: Do you remember waking up in the morning, and standing on the balcony, looking out across the valley?

ELYOT: Blue shadows on white snow, cleanness beyond belief, high above everything in the world. How beautiful it was.

AMANDA: It's nice to think we had a few marvellous moments.

ELYOT: A few. We had heaps really, only they slip away into the background, and one only remembers the bad ones.

AMANDA: Yes. What fools we were to ruin it all. What utter, utter fools.

ELYOT: You feel like that too, do you?

AMANDA (*wearily*): Of course.

ELYOT: Why did we?

AMANDA: The whole business was too much for us.

ELYOT: We were so ridiculously over in love.

AMANDA: Funny wasn't it?

ELYOT (*sadly*): Horribly funny.

AMANDA: Selfishness, cruelty, hatred, possessiveness, petty jealousy. All those qualities came out in us just because we loved each other.

ELYOT: Perhaps they were there anyhow.

AMANDA: No, it's love that does it. To hell with love.

ELYOT: To hell with love.

AMANDA: And yet here we are starting afresh with two quite different people. In love all over again, aren't we? (ELYOT *doesn't answer*.) Aren't we?

ELYOT: No.

AMANDA: Elyot.

ELYOT: We're not in love all over again, and you know it. Good night, Amanda. (*He turns abruptly, and goes towards the French windows.*)

AMANDA: Elyot—don't be silly—come back.

ELYOT: I must go and find Sibyl.

AMANDA: I must go and find Victor.

ELYOT (*savagely*): Well, why don't you?

AMANDA: I don't want to.

ELYOT: It's shameful, shameful of us.

AMANDA: Don't: I feel terrible. Don't leave me for a minute, I shall go mad if you do. We won't talk about ourselves any more, we'll talk about outside things, anything you like, only just don't leave me until I've pulled myself together.

ELYOT: Very well. (*There is a dead silence.*)

AMANDA: What have you been doing lately? During these last years?

ELYOT: Travelling about. I went round the world you know after—

AMANDA (*hurriedly*): Yes, yes, I know. How was it?

ELYOT: The world?

AMANDA: Yes.

ELYOT: Oh, highly enjoyable.

AMANDA: China must be very interesting.

ELYOT: Very big, China.

AMANDA: And Japan—

ELYOT: Very small.

AMANDA: Did you eat sharks' fins, and take your shoes off, and use chopsticks and everything?

ELYOT: Practically everything.

AMANDA: And India, the burning Ghars, or Ghats, or whatever they are, and the Taj Mahal. How was the Taj Mahal?

ELYOT (*looking at her*): Unbelievable, a sort of dream.

AMANDA: That was the moonlight I expect, you must have seen it in the moonlight.

ELYOT (*never taking his eyes off her face*): Yes, moonlight is cruelly deceptive.

AMANDA: And it didn't look like a biscuit box did it? I've always felt that it might.

ELYOT (*quietly*): Darling, darling, I love you so.

AMANDA: And I do hope you met a sacred Elephant. They're lint white I believe, and very, very sweet.

ELYOT: I've never loved anyone else for an instant.

AMANDA (*raising her hand feebly in protest*): No, no, you mustn't— Elyot—stop.

ELYOT: You love me, too, don't you? There's no doubt about it anywhere, is there?

AMANDA: No, no doubt anywhere.

ELYOT: You're looking very lovely you know, in this damned moonlight. Your skin is clear and cool, and your eyes are shining, and
you're growing lovelier and lovelier every second as I look at you.
You don't hold any mystery for me, darling, do you mind? There
isn't a particle of you that I don't know, remember, and want.

AMANDA (*softly*): I'm glad, my sweet.

ELYOT: More than any desire anywhere, deep down in my deepest heart
I want you back again—please—

AMANDA (*putting her hand over his mouth*): Don't say any more,
you're making me cry so dreadfully.

(*He pulls her gently into his arms and they stand silently, completely oblivious to everything but the moment, and each other.
When finally, they separate, they sit down, rather breathlessly, on the
balustrade.*)

AMANDA: What now? Oh darling, what now?

ELYOT: I don't know, I'm lost, utterly.

AMANDA: We must think quickly, oh quickly—

ELYOT: Escape?

AMANDA: Together?

ELYOT: Yes, of course, now, now.

AMANDA: We can't, we can't, you know we can't.

ELYOT: We must.

AMANDA: It would break Victor's heart.

ELYOT: And Sibyl's too probably, but they're bound to suffer anyhow.
Think of the hell we'd lead them into if we stayed. Infinitely worse
than any cruelty in the world, pretending to love them, and loving
each other, so desperately.

AMANDA: We must tell them.

ELYOT: What?

AMANDA: Call them, and tell them.

ELYOT: Oh no, no, that's impossible.

AMANDA: It's honest.

ELYOT: I can't help how honest it is, it's too horrible to think of. How
should we start? What should we say?

AMANDA: We should have to trust to the inspiration of the moment.

ELYOT: It would be a moment completely devoid of inspiration. The most appalling moment imaginable. No, no, we can't, you must see that, we simply can't.

AMANDA: What do you propose to do then? As it is they might appear at any moment.

ELYOT: We've got to decide instantly one way or another. Go away together now, or stay with them, and never see one another again, ever.

AMANDA: Don't be silly, what choice is there?

ELYOT: No choice at all, come—(*He takes her hand.*)

AMANDA: No, wait. This is sheer raving madness, something's happened to us, we're not sane.

ELYOT: We never were.

AMANDA: Where can we go?

ELYOT: Paris first, my car's in the garage, all ready.

AMANDA: They'll follow us.

ELYOT: That doesn't matter, once the thing's done.

AMANDA: I've got a flat in Paris.

ELYOT: Good.

AMANDA: It's in the Avenue Montaigne. I let it to Freda Lawson, but she's in Biarritz, so it's empty.

ELYOT: Does Victor know?

AMANDA: No, he knows I have one but he hasn't the faintest idea where.

ELYOT: Better and better.

AMANDA: We're being so bad, so terribly bad, we'll suffer for this, I know we shall.

ELYOT: Can't be helped.

AMANDA: Starting all those awful rows all over again.

ELYOT: No, no, we're older and wiser now.

AMANDA: What difference does that make? The first moment either of us gets a bit nervy, off we'll go again.

ELYOT: Stop shilly-shallying, Amanda.

AMANDA: I'm trying to be sensible.

ELYOT: You're only succeeding in being completely idiotic.

AMANDA: Idiotic indeed! What about you?

ELYOT: Now look here Amanda—

AMANDA (*stricken*): Oh my God!

ELYOT (*rushing to her and kissing her*): Darling, darling, I didn't mean it—

AMANDA: I won't move from here unless we have a compact, a sacred, sacred compact never to quarrel again.

ELYOT: Easy to make but difficult to keep.

AMANDA: No, no, it's the bickering that always starts it. The moment we notice we're bickering, either of us, we must promise on our honour to stop dead. We'll invent some phrase or catchword, which when either of us says it, automatically cuts off all conversation for at least five minutes.

ELYOT: Two minutes dear, with an option of renewal.

AMANDA: Very well, what shall it be?

ELYOT (*hurriedly*): Solomon Isaacs.

AMANDA: All right, that'll do.

ELYOT: Come on, come on.

AMANDA: What shall we do if we meet either of them on the way downstairs?

ELYOT: Run like stags.

AMANDA: What about clothes?

ELYOT: I've got a couple of bags I haven't unpacked yet.

AMANDA: I've got a small trunk.

ELYOT: Send the porter up for it.

AMANDA: Oh this is terrible—terrible—

ELYOT: Come on, come on, don't waste time.

AMANDA: Oughtn't we to leave notes or something?

ELYOT: No, no, no, we'll telegraph from somewhere on the road.

AMANDA: Darling, I daren't, it's too wicked of us, I simply daren't.

ELYOT (*seizing her in his arms and kissing her violently*): Now will you behave?

AMANDA: Yes, but Elyot darling—

ELYOT: Solomon Isaacs!

(*They rush off together through* ELYOT'*s suite. After a moment or so,* VICTOR *steps out on to the terrace and looks round anxiously. Then he goes back indoors again, and can be heard calling "Mandy." Finally he again comes out on to the terrace and comes despondently down to the balustrade. He hears* SIBYL'*s voice calling "Elli" and looks round as she comes out of the French windows. She jumps slightly upon seeing him.*)

VICTOR: Good evening.

SIBYL (*rather flustered*): Good-evening—I was—er—looking for my husband.

VICTOR: Really, that's funny. I was looking for my wife.

SIBYL: Quite a coincidence. (*She laughs nervously.*)

VICTOR (*after a pause*): It's very nice here isn't it?

SIBYL: Lovely.

VICTOR: Have you been here long?

SIBYL: No, we only arrived today.

VICTOR: Another coincidence. So did we.

SIBYL: How awfully funny.

VICTOR: Would you care for a cocktail?

SIBYL: Oh no thank you—really—

VICTOR: There are two here on the table.

(SIBYL *glances at the two empty glasses on the balustrade, and tosses her head defiantly.*)

SIBYL: Thanks very much, I'd love one.

VICTOR: Good, here you are. (SIBYL *comes over to* VICTOR's *side of the terrace. He hands her one and takes one himself.*)

SIBYL: Thank you.

VICTOR (*with rather forced gaiety*): To absent friends. (*He raises his glass.*)

SIBYL (*raising hers*): To absent friends. (*They both laugh rather mirthlessly and then sit down on the balustrade, pensively sipping their cocktails and looking at the view.*) It's awfully pretty isn't it? The moonlight, and the lights of that yacht reflected in the water—

VICTOR: I wonder who it belongs to.

THE CURTAIN SLOWLY FALLS

ACT TWO

The Scene is AMANDA's *flat in Paris. A few days have elapsed since Act 1. The flat is charmingly furnished, its principal fea-*

tures being a Steinway Grand on the Left, facing slightly up stage. Down stage centre, a very large comfortable sofa, behind which is a small table. There is also another sofa somewhere about, and one or two small tables, and a gramophone. The rest can be left to the discretion and taste of the decorator.

When the Curtain Rises it is about ten o'clock in the evening. The windows are wide open, and the various street sounds of Paris can be heard but not very loudly as the apartment is high up.

AMANDA and ELYOT are seated opposite one another at the table. They have finished dinner and are dallying over coffee and liqueurs. AMANDA is wearing pajamas, and ELYOT a comfortable dressing-gown.

AMANDA: I'm glad we let Louise go. I am afraid she is going to have a cold.

ELYOT: Going to have a cold; she's been grunting and snorting all the evening like a whole herd of bison.

AMANDA (*thoughtfully*): Bison never sounds right to me somehow. I have a feeling it ought to be bisons, a flock of bisons.

ELYOT: You might say a covey of bisons, or even a school of bisons.

AMANDA: Yes, lovely. The Royal London School of Bisons. Do you think Louise is happy at home?

ELYOT: No, profoundly miserable.

AMANDA: Family beastly to her?

ELYOT (*with conviction*): Absolutely vile. Knock her about dreadfully I expect, make her eat the most disgusting food, and pull her fringe.

AMANDA (*laughing*): Oh, poor Louise.

ELYOT: Well, you know what the French are.

AMANDA: Oh yes, indeed. I know what the Hungarians are too.

ELYOT: What are they?

AMANDA: Very wistful. It's all those Pretzles I shouldn't wonder.

ELYOT: And the Poostza; I always felt the Poostza was far too big, Danube or no Danube.

AMANDA: Have you ever crossed the Sahara on a camel?

ELYOT: Frequently. When I was a boy we used to do it all the time. My grandmother had a lovely seat on a camel.

AMANDA: There's no doubt about it, foreign travel's the thing.

ELYOT: Would you like some brandy?

AMANDA: Just a little. (*He pours some into her glass and some into his own.*)

ELYOT: I'm glad we didn't go out tonight.

AMANDA: Or last night.

ELYOT: Or the night before.

AMANDA: There's no reason to, really, when we're cosy here.

ELYOT: Exactly.

AMANDA: It's nice, isn't it?

ELYOT: Strangely peaceful. It's an awfully bad reflection on our characters. We ought to be absolutely tortured with conscience.

AMANDA: We are, every now and then.

ELYOT: Not nearly enough.

AMANDA: We sent Victor and Sibyl a nice note from wherever it was; what more can they want?

ELYOT: You're even more ruthless than I am.

AMANDA: I don't believe in crying over my bridge before I've eaten it.

ELYOT: Very sensible.

AMANDA: Personally I feel grateful for a miraculous escape. I know now that I should never have been happy with Victor. I was a fool ever to consider it.

ELYOT: You did a little more than consider it.

AMANDA: Well, you can't talk.

ELYOT: I wonder whether they met each other, or whether they've been suffering alone.

AMANDA: Oh dear, don't let's go on about it, it really does make one feel rather awful.

ELYOT: I suppose one or other or both of them will turn up here eventually.

AMANDA: Bound to; it won't be very nice, will it?

ELYOT (*cheerfully*): Perfectly horrible.

AMANDA: Do you realise that we're living in sin?

ELYOT: Not according to the Catholics, Catholics don't recognise divorce. We're married as much as ever we were.

AMANDA: Yes, dear, but we're not Catholics.

ELYOT: Never mind, it's nice to think they'd sort of back us up. We were married in the eyes of heaven, and we still are.

AMANDA: We may be alright in the eyes of Heaven, but we look like being in the hell of a mess socially.

ELYOT: Who cares?

AMANDA: Are we going to marry again, after Victor and Sibyl divorce us?

ELYOT: I suppose so. What do you think?

AMANDA: I feel rather scared of marriage really.

ELYOT: It is a frowsy business.

AMANDA: I believe it was just the fact of our being married, and clamped together publicly, that wrecked us before.

ELYOT: That, and not knowing how to manage each other.

AMANDA: Do you think we know how to manage each other now?

ELYOT: This week's been very successful. We've hardly used Solomon Isaacs at all.

AMANDA: Solomon Isaacs is so long, let's shorten it to Sollocks.

ELYOT: All right.

AMANDA: Darling, you do look awfully sweet in your little dressing-gown.

ELYOT: Yes, it's pretty ravishing, isn't it?

AMANDA: Do you mind if I come round and kiss you?

ELYOT: A pleasure, Lady Agatha.

(AMANDA *comes round the table, kisses him, picks up the coffee pot, and returns to her chair.*)

AMANDA: What fools we were to subject ourselves to five years' unnecessary suffering.

ELYOT: Perhaps it wasn't unnecessary, perhaps it mellowed and perfected us like beautiful ripe fruit.

AMANDA: When we were together, did you really think I was unfaithful to you?

ELYOT: Yes, practically every day.

AMANDA: I thought you were too; often I used to torture myself with visions of your bouncing about on divans with awful widows.

ELYOT: Why widows?

AMANDA: I was thinking of Claire Lavenham really.

ELYOT: Oh Claire.

AMANDA (*sharply*): What did you say "Oh Claire" like that for? It sounded far too careless to me.

ELYOT (*wistfully*): What a lovely creature she was.

AMANDA: Lovely, lovely, lovely!

ELYOT (*blowing her a kiss*): Darling!

AMANDA: Did you ever have an affair with her? Afterwards I mean?

ELYOT: Why do you want to know?

AMANDA: Curiosity, I suppose.

ELYOT: Dangerous.

AMANDA: Oh not now, not dangerous now. I wouldn't expect you to have been celibate during those five years, any more than I was.

ELYOT (*jumping*): What?

AMANDA: After all, Claire was undeniably attractive. A trifle over vivacious I always thought, but that was probably because she was fundamentally stupid.

ELYOT: What do you mean about not being celibate during those five years?

AMANDA: What do you think I mean?

ELYOT: Oh God. (*He looks down miserably.*)

AMANDA: What's the matter?

ELYOT: You know perfectly well what's the matter.

AMANDA (*gently*): You mustn't be unreasonable, I was only trying to stamp out the memory of you. I expect your affairs well outnumbered mine anyhow.

ELYOT: That is a little different. I'm a man.

AMANDA: Excuse me a moment while I get a caraway biscuit and change my crinoline.

ELYOT: It doesn't suit women to be promiscuous.

AMANDA: It doesn't suit men for women to be promiscuous.

ELYOT (*with sarcasm*): Very modern dear; really your advanced views quite startle me.

AMANDA: Don't be cross, Elyot, I haven't been so dreadfully loose actually. Five years is a long time, and even if I did nip off with someone every now and again, they were none of them very serious.

ELYOT: (*rising from the table and walking away*): Oh, do stop it please—

AMANDA: Well, what about you?

ELYOT: Do you want me to tell you?

AMANDA: No, no, I don't—I take everything back—I don't.

ELYOT (*viciously*): I was madly in love with a woman in South Africa.

AMANDA: Did she have a ring through her nose?

ELYOT: Don't be revolting.

AMANDA: We're tormenting one another. Sit down, sweet, I'm scared.

ELYOT (*slowly*): Very well. (*He sits down thoughtfully.*)

AMANDA: We should have said Sollocks ages ago.

ELYOT: We're in love alright.

AMANDA: Don't say it so bitterly. Let's try to get the best out of it this time, instead of the worst.

ELYOT (*stretching his hand across the table*): Hand please.

AMANDA (*clasping it*): Here.

ELYOT: More comfortable?

AMANDA: Much more.

ELYOT (*after a slight pause*): Are you engaged for this dance?

AMANDA: Funnily enough I was, but my partner was suddenly taken ill.

ELYOT (*rising and going to the gramophone*): It's this damned small-pox epidemic.

AMANDA: No, as a matter of fact it was kidney trouble.

ELYOT: You'll dance it with me I hope?

AMANDA (*rising*): I shall be charmed.

ELYOT (*as they dance*): Quite a good floor, isn't it?

AMANDA: Yes, I think it needs a little Borax.

ELYOT: I love Borax.

AMANDA: Is that the Grand Duchess Olga lying under the piano?

ELYOT: Yes, her husband died a few weeks ago, you know, on his way back from Pulborough. So sad.

AMANDA: What on earth was he doing in Pulborough?

ELYOT: Nobody knows exactly, but there have been the usual stories.

AMANDA: I see.

ELYOT: Delightful parties Lady Bundle always gives, doesn't she?

AMANDA: Entrancing. Such a dear old lady.

ELYOT: And so gay. Did you notice her at supper blowing all those shrimps through her ear trumpet?

(*The tune comes to an end.* AMANDA *sits on the edge of the sofa, pensively.*)

ELYOT: What are you thinking about?

AMANDA: Nothing in particular.

ELYOT: Come on, I know that face.

AMANDA: Poor Sibyl.

ELYOT: Sibyl?

AMANDA: Yes, I suppose she loves you terribly.

ELYOT: Not as much as all that, she didn't have a chance to get really under way.

AMANDA: I expect she's dreadfully unhappy.

ELYOT: Oh, do shut up, Amanda, we've had all that out before.

AMANDA: We've certainly been pretty busy trying to justify ourselves.

ELYOT: It isn't a question of justifying ourselves; it's the true values of the situation that are really important. The moment we saw one another again we knew it was no use going on. We knew it instantly really, although we tried to pretend to ourselves that we didn't. What we've got to be thankful for is that we made the break straight away, and not later.

AMANDA: You think we should have done it anyhow?

ELYOT: Of course, and things would have been in a worse mess than they are now.

AMANDA: And what if we'd never happened to meet again. Would you have been quite happy with Sibyl?

ELYOT: I expect so.

AMANDA: Oh, Elyot!

ELYOT: You needn't look so stricken. It would have been the same with you and Victor. Life would have been smooth, and amicable, and quite charming, wouldn't it?

AMANDA: Poor dear Victor. He certainly did love me.

ELYOT: Splendid.

AMANDA: When I met him I was so lonely and depressed, I felt that I was getting old, and crumbling away unwanted.

ELYOT: It certainly is horrid when one begins to crumble.

AMANDA (*wistfully*): He used to look at me hopelessly like a lovely spaniel, and I sort of melted like snow in the sunlight.

ELYOT: That must have been an edifying spectacle.

AMANDA: Victor really had a great charm.

ELYOT: You must tell me all about it.

AMANDA: He had a positive mania for looking after me, and protecting me.

ELYOT: That would have died down in time, dear.

AMANDA: You mustn't be rude, there's no necessity to be rude.

ELYOT: I wasn't in the least rude; I merely made a perfectly rational statement.

AMANDA: Your voice was decidedly bitter.

ELYOT: Victor had glorious legs, hadn't he? And fascinating ears.

AMANDA: Don't be silly.

ELYOT: He probably looked radiant in the morning, all flushed and tumbled on the pillow.

AMANDA: I never saw him on the pillow.

ELYOT: I'm surprised to hear it.

AMANDA (*angrily*): Elyot!

ELYOT: There's no need to be cross.

AMANDA: What did you mean by that?

ELYOT: I'm sick of listening to you yap, yap, yap, yap, yap, yapping about Victor.

AMANDA: Now listen Elyot, once and for all—

ELYOT: Oh my dear, Sollocks! Sollocks!—two minutes—Sollocks.

AMANDA: But—

ELYOT (*firmly*): Sollocks! (*They sit in dead silence, looking at each other.* AMANDA *makes a sign that she wants a cigarette.* ELYOT *gets up, hands her the box, and lights one for her and himself.* AMANDA *rises and walks over to the window, and stands there, looking out for a moment. Presently* ELYOT *joins her. She slips her arm through his, and they kiss lightly. They draw the curtains and then come down and sit side by side on the sofa.* ELYOT *looks at his watch.* AMANDA *raises her eyebrows at him and he nods, then they both sigh, audibly.*) That was a near thing.

AMANDA: It was my fault. I'm terribly sorry, darling.

ELYOT: I was very irritating, I know I was. I'm sure Victor was awfully nice, and you're perfectly right to be sweet about him.

AMANDA: That's downright handsome of you. Sweetheart! (*She kisses him.*)

ELYOT (*leaning back with her on the sofa*): I think I love you more than ever before. Isn't it ridiculous? Put your feet up.

(*She puts her legs across his, and they snuggle back together in the corner of the sofa, his head resting on her shoulder.*)

AMANDA: Comfortable?

ELYOT: Almost, wait a minute. (*He struggles a bit and then settles down with a sigh.*)

AMANDA: How long, Oh Lord, how long?

ELYOT (*drowsily*): What do you mean, "How long, Oh Lord, how long?"

AMANDA: This is far too perfect to last.

ELYOT: You have no faith, that's what's wrong with you.

AMANDA: Absolutely none.

ELYOT: Don't you believe in—? (*He nods upwards.*)

AMANDA: No, do you?

ELYOT (*shaking his head*): No. What about—? (*He points downwards.*)

AMANDA: Oh dear no.

ELYOT: Don't you believe in anything?

AMANDA: Oh yes, I believe in being kind to everyone, and giving money to old beggar women, and being as gay as possible.

ELYOT: What about after we're dead?

AMANDA: I think a rather gloomy merging into everything, don't you?

ELYOT: I hope not, I'm a bad merger.

AMANDA: You won't know a thing about it.

ELYOT: I hope for a glorious oblivion, like being under gas.

AMANDA: I always dream the most peculiar things under gas.

ELYOT: Would you be young always? If you could choose?

AMANDA: No, I don't think so, not if it meant having awful bull's glands popped into me.

ELYOT: Cows for you dear. Bulls for me.

AMANDA: We certainly live in a marvellous age.

ELYOT: Too marvellous. It's alright if you happen to be a specialist at something, then you're too concentrated to pay attention to all the other things going on. But, for the ordinary observer, it's too much.

AMANDA (*snuggling closer*): Far, far too much.

ELYOT: Take the radio for instance.

AMANDA: Oh darling, don't let's take the radio.

ELYOT: Well, aeroplanes then, and Cosmic Atoms, and Television, and those gland injections we were talking about just now.

AMANDA: It must be so nasty for the poor animals, being experimented on.

ELYOT: Not when the experiments are successful. Why in Vienna I believe you can see whole lines of decrepit old rats carrying on like Tiller Girls.

AMANDA (*laughing*): Oh, how very, very sweet.

ELYOT (*burying his face in her shoulder*): I do love you so.

AMANDA: Don't blow, dear heart, it gives me the shivers.

ELYOT (*trying to kiss her*): Swivel your face round a bit more.

AMANDA (*obliging*): That better?

ELYOT (*kissing her lingeringly*): Very nice, thank you kindly.

AMANDA (*twining her arms around his neck*): Darling, you're so terribly, terribly dear, and sweet, and attractive. (*She pulls his head down to her again and they kiss lovingly.*)

ELYOT (*softly*): We were raving mad, ever to part, even for an instant.

AMANDA: Utter imbeciles.

ELYOT: I realised it almost immediately, didn't you?

AMANDA: Long before we got our decree.

ELYOT: My heart broke on that damned trip round the world. I saw such beautiful things, darling. Moonlight shining on old temples, strange barbaric dances in jungle villages, scarlet flamingoes flying over deep, deep blue water. Breathlessly lovely, and completely unexciting because you weren't there to see them with me.

AMANDA (*kissing him again*): Take me please, take me at once, let's make up for lost time.

ELYOT: Next week?

AMANDA: Tomorrow.

ELYOT: Done.

AMANDA: I must see those dear flamingoes. (*There is a pause.*) Eight years all told, we've loved each other. Three married and five divorced.

ELYOT: Angel. Angel. Angel. (*He kisses her passionately.*)

AMANDA (*struggling slightly*): No, Elyot, stop now, stop—

ELYOT: Why should I stop? You know you adore being made love to.

AMANDA (*through his kisses*): It's so soon after dinner.

ELYOT (*jumping up rather angrily*): You really do say most awful things.

AMANDA (*tidying her hair*): I don't see anything particularly awful about that.

ELYOT: No sense of glamour, no sense of glamour at all.

AMANDA: It's difficult to feel really glamorous with a crick in the neck.

ELYOT: Why didn't you say you had a crick in your neck?

AMANDA (*sweetly*): It's gone now.

ELYOT: How convenient. (*He lights a cigarette.*)

AMANDA (*holding out her hand*): I want one please.

ELYOT (*throwing her one*): Here.

AMANDA: Match?

ELYOT (*impatiently*): Wait a minute, can't you?

AMANDA: Chivalrous little love.

ELYOT (*throwing the matches at her*): Here.

AMANDA (*coldly*): Thank you very much indeed. (*There is a silence for a moment.*)

ELYOT: You really can be more irritating than anyone in the world.

AMANDA: I fail to see what I've done that's so terribly irritating.

ELYOT: You have no tact.

AMANDA: Tact. You have no consideration.

ELYOT (*walking up and down*): Too soon after dinner indeed.

AMANDA: Yes, much too soon.

ELYOT: That sort of remark shows rather a common sort of mind I'm afraid.

AMANDA: Oh it does, does it?

ELYOT: Very unpleasant, makes me shudder.

AMANDA: Making all this fuss just because your silly vanity is a little upset.

ELYOT: Vanity. What do you mean, vanity?

AMANDA: You can't bear the thought that there are certain moments when our chemical, what d'you call 'ems, don't fuse properly.

ELYOT (*derisively*): Chemical what d'you call 'ems. Please try to be more explicit.

AMANDA: You know perfectly well what I mean, and don't you try to patronise me.

ELYOT (*loudly*): Now look here, Amanda——

AMANDA (*sudenly*) : Darling, Sollocks! Oh, for God's sake, Sollocks!

ELYOT: But listen—

AMANDA: Sollocks, Sollocks, Oh dear—triple Sollocks!

(*They stand looking at one another in silence for a moment, then* AMANDA *flings herself down on the sofa and buries her face in the cushions.* ELYOT *looks at her, then goes over to the piano. He sits down and begins to play idly.* AMANDA *raises her head, screws herself round on the sofa, and lies there listening.* ELYOT *blows a kiss to her and goes on playing. He starts to sing softly to her, never taking his eyes off her. When he has finished the little refrain, whatever it was, he still continues to play it looking at her.*)

AMANDA: Big romantic stuff, darling.

ELYOT (*smiling*) : Yes, big romantic stuff.

(*He wanders off into another tune.* AMANDA *sits up crossed legged on the sofa, and begins to sing it, then, still singing, she comes over and perches on the piano. They sing several old refrains from dead and gone musical comedies finishing with the song that brought them together again in the first Act. Finally* AMANDA *comes down and sits next to him on the piano stool, they both therefore have their backs half turned to the audience. She rests her head on his shoulder, until finally his fingers drop off the keys, and they melt into one another's arms.*)

ELYOT (*after a moment*): You're the most thrilling, exciting woman that was ever born.

AMANDA (*standing up, and brushing her hand lightly over his mouth*): Dearest, dearest heart—

(*He catches at her hand and kisses it, and then her arm, until he is standing up, embracing her ardently. She struggles a little, half laughing, and breaks away, but he catches her, and they finish up on the sofa again, clasped in each other's arms, both completely given up to the passion of the moment, until the telephone bell rings violently, and they both spring apart.*)

ELYOT: Good God!

AMANDA: Do you think it's them?

ELYOT: I wonder.

AMANDA: Nobody knows we're here except Freda, and she wouldn't ring up.

ELYOT: It must be them then.

AMANDA: What are we to do?

ELYOT (*suddenly*): We're alright darling, aren't we—whatever happens?

AMANDA: Now and always, Sweet.

ELYOT: I don't care then. (*He gets up and goes defiantly over to the telephone, which has been ringing incessantly during the little preceding scene.*)

AMANDA: It was bound to come sooner or later.

ELYOT (*at telephone*): Hallo—hallo—what—comment? Madame, qui? 'allo—'allo—oui c'est ça. Oh, Madame Duvallon—Oui, oui, oui. (*He puts his hand over the mouthpiece.*) It's only somebody wanting to talk to the dear Madame Duvallon.

AMANDA: Who's she?

ELYOT: I haven't the faintest idea. (*At telephone.*) Je regrette beaucoup Monsieur, mais Madam Duvallon viens de partir—cette après midi, pour Madagascar. (*He hangs up the telephone.*) Whew; that gave me a fright.

AMANDA: It sent shivers up my spine.

ELYOT: What shall we do if they suddenly walk in on us?

AMANDA: Behave exquisitely.

ELYOT: With the most perfect poise?

AMANDA: Certainly, I shall probably do a Court Curtsey.

ELYOT (*sitting on the edge of the sofa*): Things that ought to matter dreadfully, don't matter at all when one's happy, do they?

AMANDA: What is so horrible is that one can't stay happy.

ELYOT: Darling, don't say that.

AMANDA: It's true. The whole business is a very poor joke.

ELYOT: Meaning that sacred and beautiful thing, Love?

AMANDA: Yes, meaning just that.

ELYOT (*striding up and down the room dramatically*): What does it all mean, that's what I ask myself in my ceaseless quest for ultimate truth. Dear God, what does it all mean?

AMANDA: Don't laugh at me, I'm serious.

ELYOT (*seriously*): You mustn't be serious, my dear one, it's just what they want.

MANDA: Who's they?

LYOT: All the futile moralists who try to make life unbearable. Laugh at them. Be flippant. Laugh at everything, all their sacred shibboleths. Flippancy brings out the acid in their damned sweetness and light.

MANDA: If I laugh at everything, I must laugh at us too.

LYOT: Certainly you must. We're figures of fun alright.

MANDA: How long will it last, this ludicrous, overbearing love of ours?

LYOT: Who knows?

MANDA: Shall we always want to bicker and fight?

LYOT: No, that desire will fade, along with our passion.

MANDA: Oh dear, shall we like that?

LYOT: It all depends on how well we've played.

MANDA: What happens if one of us dies? Does the one that's left still laugh?

LYOT: Yes, yes, with all his might.

MANDA (*wistfully clutching his hand*): That's serious enough, isn't it?

LYOT: No, no, it isn't. Death's very laughable, such a cunning little mystery. All done with mirrors.

MANDA: Darling, I believe you're talking nonsense.

LYOT: So is everyone else in the long run. Let's be superficial and pity the poor Philosophers. Let's blow trumpets and squeakers, and enjoy the party as much as we can, like very small, quite idiotic school-children. Let's savour the delight of the moment. Come and kiss me darling, before your body rots, and worms pop in and out of your eye sockets.

MANDA: Elyot, worms don't pop.

LYOT (*kissing her*): I don't mind what you do see? You can paint yourself bright green all over, and dance naked in the Place Vendome, and rush off madly with all the men in the world, and I shan't say a word, as long as you love me best.

MANDA: Thank you, dear. The same applies to you, except that if I catch you so much as looking at another woman, I'll kill you.

LYOT: Do you remember that awful scene we had in Venice?

MANDA: Which particular one?

LYOT: The one when you bought that little painted wooden snake on the Piazza, and put it on my bed.

MANDA: Oh Charles. That was his name, Charles. He did wriggle so beautifully.

ELYOT: Horrible thing, I hated it.

AMANDA: Yes, I know you did. You threw it out of the window into the Grand Canal. I don't think I'll ever forgive you for that.

ELYOT: How long did the row last?

AMANDA: It went on intermittently for days.

ELYOT: The worst one was in Cannes when your curling irons burnt a hole in my new dressing-gown. (*He laughs.*)

AMANDA: It burnt my comb too, and all the towels in the bathroom.

ELYOT: That was a rouser, wasn't it?

AMANDA: That was the first time you ever hit me.

ELYOT: I didn't hit you very hard.

AMANDA: The manager came in and found us rolling on the floor, biting and scratching like panthers. Oh dear, oh dear—(*She laughs helplessly.*)

ELYOT: I shall never forget his face. (*They both collapse with laughter.*)

AMANDA: How ridiculous, how utterly, utterly ridiculous.

ELYOT: We were very much younger then.

AMANDA: And very much sillier.

ELYOT: As a matter of fact the real cause of that row was Peter Burden.

AMANDA: You knew there was nothing in that.

ELYOT: I didn't know anything of the sort, you took presents from him.

AMANDA: Presents: only a trivial little brooch.

ELYOT: I remember it well, bristling with diamonds. In the worst possible taste.

AMANDA: Not at all, it was very pretty. I still have it, and I wear it often.

ELYOT: You went out of your way to torture me over Peter Burden.

AMANDA: No, I didn't, you worked the whole thing up in your jealous imagination.

ELYOT: You must admit that he was in love with you, wasn't he?

AMANDA: Just a little perhaps. Nothing serious.

ELYOT: You let him kiss you. You said you did.

AMANDA: Well, what of it?

ELYOT: What of it!

AMANDA: It gave him a lot of pleasure, and it didn't hurt me.

ELYOT: What about me?

AMANDA: If you hadn't been so suspicious and nosey you'd never have known a thing about it.

ELYOT: That's a nice point of view I must say.

AMANDA: Oh dear, I'm bored with this conversation.

ELYOT: So am I, bored stiff. (*He goes over to the table.*) Want some brandy?

AMANDA: No thanks.

ELYOT: I'll have a little, I think.

AMANDA: I don't see why you want it, you've already had two glasses.

ELYOT: No particular reason, anyhow they were very small ones.

AMANDA: It seems so silly to go on, and on, and on with a thing.

ELYOT (*pouring himself out a glassful*): You can hardly call three liqueur glasses in a whole evening going on, and on, and on.

AMANDA: It's become a habit with you.

ELYOT: You needn't be so grand, just because you don't happen to want any yourself at the moment.

AMANDA: Don't be so stupid.

ELYOT (*irritably*): Really Amanda—

AMANDA: What?

ELYOT: Nothing. (AMANDA *sits down on the sofa, and, taking a small mirror from her bag, gazes at her face critically, and then uses some lipstick and powder. A trifle nastily.*) Going out somewhere dear?

AMANDA: No, just making myself fascinating for you.

ELYOT: That reply has broken my heart.

AMANDA: The woman's job is to allure the man. Watch me a minute will you?

ELYOT: As a matter of fact that's perfectly true.

AMANDA: Oh, no, it isn't.

ELYOT: Yes it is.

AMANDA (*snappily*): Oh be quiet.

ELYOT: It's a pity you didn't have any more brandy; it might have made you a little less disagreeable.

AMANDA: It doesn't seem to have worked such wonders with you.

ELYOT: Snap, snap, snap; like a little adder.

AMANDA: Adders don't snap, they sting.

ELYOT: Nonsense, they have a little bag of venom behind their fangs and they snap.

AMANDA: They sting.

ELYOT: They snap.

AMANDA (*with exasperation*): I don't care, do you understand? I don't care. I don't mind if they bark, and roll about like hoops.

ELYOT: (*after a slight pause*): Did you see much of Peter Burden after our divorce?

AMANDA: Yes, I did, quite a lot.

ELYOT: I suppose you let him kiss you a good deal more then.

AMANDA: Mind your own business.

ELYOT: You must have had a riotous time. (AMANDA *doesn't answer, so he stalks about the room.*) No restraint at all—very enjoyable—you never had much anyhow.

AMANDA: You're quite insufferable; I expect it's because you're drunk.

ELYOT: I'm not in the least drunk.

AMANDA: You always had a weak head.

ELYOT: I think I mentioned once before that I only had three minute liqueur glasses of brandy the whole evening long. A child of two couldn't get drunk on that.

AMANDA: On the contrary, a child of two could get violently drunk on only one glass of brandy.

ELYOT: Very interesting. How about a child of four, and a child of six, and a child of nine?

AMANDA (*turning her head away*): Oh do shut up.

ELYOT (*witheringly*): We might get up a splendid little debate about that, you know, Intemperate Tots.

AMANDA: Not very funny, dear; you'd better have some more brandy.

ELYOT: Very good idea, I will. (*He pours out another glass and gulps it down defiantly.*)

AMANDA: Ridiculous ass.

ELYOT: I beg your pardon?

AMANDA: I said ridiculous ass!

ELYOT (*with great dignity*): Thank you. (*There is a silence.* AMANDA *gets up, and turns the gramophone on.*) You'd better turn that off, I think.

AMANDA (*coldly*): Why?

ELYOT: It's very late and it will annoy the people upstairs.

AMANDA: There aren't any people upstairs. It's a photographer's studio.

ELYOT: There are people downstairs, I suppose?

AMANDA: They're away in Tunis.

ELYOT: This is no time of the year for Tunis. (*He turns the gramophone off.*)

AMANDA (*icily*): Turn it on again, please.

ELYOT: I'll do no such thing.

AMANDA: Very well, if you insist on being boorish and idiotic. (*She gets up and turns it on again.*)

ELYOT: Turn it off. It's driving me mad.

AMANDA: You're far too temperamental. Try to control yourself.

ELYOT: Turn it off.

AMANDA: I won't. (ELYOT *rushes at the gramophone.* AMANDA *tries to ward him off. They struggle silently for a moment, then the needle screeches across the record.*) There now, you've ruined the record. *She takes it off and scrutinises it.*)

ELYOT: Good job, too.

AMANDA: Disagreeable pig.

ELYOT (*suddenly stricken with remorse*): Amanda darling—Sollocks.

AMANDA (*furiously*): Sollocks yourself. (*She breaks the record over his head.*)

ELYOT (*staggering*): You spiteful little beast. (*He slaps her face. She screams loudly and hurls herself sobbing with rage on to the sofa, with her face buried in the cushions.*)

AMANDA (*wailing*): Oh, oh, oh—

ELYOT: I'm sorry, I didn't mean it—I'm sorry, darling, I swear I didn't mean it.

AMANDA: Go away, go away, I hate you. (ELYOT *kneels on the sofa and tries to pull her round to look at him.*)

ELYOT: Amanda—listen—listen—

AMANDA (*turning suddenly, and fetching him a welt across the face*): Listen indeed; I'm sick and tired of listening to you, you damned sadistic bully.

ELYOT (*with great grandeur*): Thank you. (*He stalks towards the door, in stately silence. Amanda throws a cushion at him, which misses him and knocks down a lamp and a vase on the side table.* ELYOT *laughs falsely.*) A pretty display I must say.

AMANDA (*wildly*): Stop laughing like that.

ELYOT (*continuing*): Very amusing indeed.

AMANDA (*losing control*): Stop—stop—stop—(*She rushes at him, he grabs her hands and they sway about the room, until he manages to twist her round by the arms so that she faces him, closely, quivering with fury*)—I hate you—do you hear? You're conceited, and over-bearing, and utterly impossible!

ELYOT (*shouting her down*): You're a vile tempered loose-living wicked little beast, and I never want to see you again so long as I live. (*He flings her away from him, she staggers, and falls against a chair. They stand gasping at one another in silence for a moment.*)

AMANDA (*very quietly*): This is the end, do you understand? The end, finally and forever. (*She goes to the door, which opens on to the landing, and wrenches it open. He rushes after her and clutches her wrist.*)

ELYOT: You're not going like this.

AMANDA: Oh yes I am.

ELYOT: You're not.

AMANDA: I am; let go of me— (*He pulls her away from the door, and once more they struggle. This time a standard lamp crashes to the ground.* AMANDA, *breathlessly, as they fight.*) You're a cruel fiend, and I hate and loathe you; thank God I've realised in time what you're really like; marry you again, never, never, never. . . . I'd rather die in torment—

ELYOT (*at the same time*): Shut up; shut up. I wouldn't marry you again if you came crawling to me on your bended knees, you're a mean, evil minded, little vampire—I hope to God I never set eyes on you again as long as I live—

(*At this point in the proceedings they trip over a piece of carpet, and fall on to the floor, rolling over and over in paroxysms of rage.* VICTOR *and* SIBYL *enter quietly, through the open door, and stand staring at them in horror. Finally* AMANDA *breaks free and half gets up,* ELYOT *grabs her leg, and she falls against a table, knocking it completely over.*)

AMANDA (*screaming*): Beast; brute; swine; cad; beast; beast; brute; devil— (*She rushes back at* ELYOT *who is just rising to his feet, and gives him a stinging blow, which knocks him over again. She rushes blindly off Left, and slams the door, at the same moment that he jumps up and rushes off Right, also slamming the door.* VICTOR *and* SIBYL *advance apprehensively into the room, and sink on to the sofa—*

THE CURTAIN FALLS

ACT THREE

*The Scene is the same as Act 2. It is the next morning. The
time is about eight-thirty.* VICTOR *and* SIBYL *have drawn the
two sofas across the doors Right, and Left, and are stretched
on them, asleep.* VICTOR *is in front of* AMANDA'S *door, and*
SIBYL *in front of* ELYOT'S.

The room is in chaos, as it was left the night before.

*As the curtain rises, there is the rattling of a key in the lock
of the front door, and* LOUISE *enters. She is rather a frowsy
looking girl, and carries a string bag with various bundles of
eatables crammed into it, notably a long roll of bread, and a
lettuce. She closes the door after her, and in the half light trips
over the standard lamp lying on the floor. She puts her string
bag down, and gropes her way over to the window. She draws
the curtains, letting sunlight stream into the room. When she
looks round, she gives a little cry of horror. Then she sees*
VICTOR *and* SIBYL *sleeping peacefully, and comes over and
scrutinises each of them with care, then she shakes* SIBYL *by the
shoulder.*

SIBYL (*waking*): Oh dear.

LOUISE: Bon jour, Madame.

SIBYL (*bewildered*): What?—Oh—bon jour.

LOUISE: Qu'est-ce que vous faites ici, madame?

SIBYL: What—what?—Wait a moment, attendez un instant—oh dear—

VICTOR (*sleepily*): What's happening? (*Jumping up.*) Of course, I
remember now. (*He sees* LOUISE.) Oh!

LOUISE (*firmly*): Bon jour, Monsieur.

VICTOR: Er—bon jour—What time is it?

LOUISE (*rather dully*): Eh, Monsieur?

SIBYL (*sitting up on the sofa*): Quelle heure est-il s'il vous plaît?

LOUISE: C'est neuf heures moins dix, madame.

VICTOR: What did she say?

SIBYL: I think she said nearly ten o'clock.

VICTOR (*taking situation in hand*): Er—voulez—er—wake—reveillez Monsieur et Madame—er—toute suite?

LOUISE (*shaking her head*): Non, Monsieur. Il m'est absolument defendu de les appeler jusqu'à ce qu'ils sonnent. (*She takes her bag and goes off into the kitchen.* VICTOR *and* SIBYL *look at each other helplessly.*)

SIBYL: What are we to do?

VICTOR (*with determination*): Wake them ourselves. (*He goes towards* AMANDA's *door.*)

SIBYL: No, no, wait a minute.

VICTOR: What's the matter?

SIBYL (*plaintively*): I couldn't face them yet, really, I couldn't; I feel dreadful.

VICTOR: So do I. (*He wanders gloomily over to the window.*) It's a lovely morning.

SIBYL: Lovely. (*She bursts into tears.*)

VICTOR (*coming to her*): I say, don't cry.

SIBYL: I can't help it.

VICTOR: Please don't, please—

SIBYL: It's all so squalid, I wish we hadn't stayed; what's the use?

VICTOR: We've got to see them before we go back to England, we must get things straightened out.

SIBYL (*sinking down on to the sofa*): Oh dear, oh dear, oh dear, I wish I were dead.

VICTOR: Hush, now, hush. Remember your promise. We've got to see this through together and get it settled one way or another.

SIBYL (*sniffling*): I'll try to control myself, only I'm so . . . so tired, I haven't slept properly for ages.

VICTOR: Neither have I.

SIBYL: If we hadn't arrived when we did, they'd have killed one another.

VICTOR: They must have been drunk.

SIBYL: She hit him.

VICTOR: He'd probably hit her, too, earlier on.

SIBYL: I'd no idea anyone ever behaved like that; it's so disgusting, so degrading, Elli of all people—oh dear— (*She almost breaks down again, but controls herself.*)

VICTOR: What an escape you've had.

SIBYL: What an escape we've both had.

(AMANDA *opens her door and looks out. She is wearing travelling clothes, and is carrying a small suit-case. She jumps, upon seeing* SIBYL *and* VICTOR.)

AMANDA: Oh!—good morning.

VICTOR (*with infinite reproach in his voice*): Oh, Amanda.

AMANDA: Will you please move this sofa, I can't get out.

(VICTOR *moves the sofa, and she advances into the room and goes towards the door.*)

VICTOR: Where are you going?

AMANDA: Away.

VICTOR: You can't.

AMANDA: Why not?

VICTOR: I want to talk to you.

AMANDA (*wearily*): What on earth is the use of that?

VICTOR: I must talk to you.

AMANDA: Well, all I can say is, it's very inconsiderate. (*She plumps the bag down by the door and comes down to* VICTOR.)

VICTOR: Mandy, I—

AMANDA (*gracefully determined to rise above the situation*): I suppose you're Sibyl; how do you do? (SIBYL *turns her back on her.*) Well, if you're going to take up that attitude, I fail to see the point of your coming here at all.

SIBYL: I came to see Elyot.

AMANDA: I've no wish to prevent you, he's in there, probably wallowing in an alcoholic stupor.

VICTOR: This is all very unpleasant, Amanda.

AMANDA: I quite agree, that's why I want to go away.

VICTOR: That would be shirking; this must be discussed at length.

AMANDA: Very well, if you insist, but not just now, I don't feel up to it. Has Louise come yet?

VICTOR: If Louise is the maid, she's in the kitchen.

AMANDA: Thank you. You'd probably like some coffee, excuse me a moment. (*She goes off into the kitchen.*)

SIBYL: Well! How dare she?

VICTOR (*irritably*): How dare she what?

SIBYL: Behave so calmly, as though nothing had happened.

VICTOR: I don't see what else she could have done.

SIBYL: Insufferable I call it.

(ELYOT *opens his door and looks out.*)

ELYOT (*seeing them*): Oh God. (*He shuts the door again quickly.*)

SIBYL: Elyot—Elyot— (*She rushes over to the door and bangs on it.*)
Elyot—Elyot—Elyot—

ELYOT (*inside*): Go away.

SIBYL (*falling on to the sofa*): Oh, oh, oh. (*She bursts into tears
again.*)

VICTOR: Do pull yourself together for heaven's sake.

SIBYL: I can't, I can't—oh, oh, oh—

(AMANDA *reenters.*)

AMANDA: I've ordered some coffee and rolls, they'll be here soon. I
must apologise for the room being so untidy. (*She picks up a cushion, and pats it into place on the sofa. There is silence except for
SIBYL's sobs. AMANDA looks at her, then at VICTOR; then she goes
off into her room again, and shuts the door.*)

VICTOR: It's no use crying like that, it doesn't do any good.

(*After a moment, during which SIBYL makes renewed efforts to
control her tears, ELYOT opens the door immediately behind her,
pushes the sofa, with her on it, out of the way, and walks towards the
front door. He is in travelling clothes, and carrying a small suitcase.*)

SIBYL (*rushing after him*): Elyot, where are you going?

ELYOT: Canada.

SIBYL: You can't go like this, you can't.

ELYOT: I see no point in staying.

VICTOR: You owe it to Sibyl to stay.

ELYOT: How do you do, I don't think we've met before.

SIBYL: You must stay, you've got to stay.

ELYOT: Very well, if you insist. (*He plumps his bag down.*) I'm afraid the room is in rather a mess. Have you seen the maid Louise?

VICTOR: She's in the kitchen.

ELYOT: Good. I'll order some coffee. (*He makes a movement towards the kitchen.*)

VICTOR (*stopping him*): No, your—er—my—er—Amanda has already ordered it.

ELYOT: Oh, I'm glad the old girl's up and about.

VICTOR: We've got to get things straightened out, you know.

ELYOT (*looking around the room*): Yes, it's pretty awful. We'll get the concierge up from downstairs.

VICTOR: You're being purposely flippant, but it's no good.

ELYOT: Sorry. (*He lapses into silence.*)

VICTOR (*after a pause*): What's to be done?

ELYOT: I don't know.

SIBYL (*with spirit*): It's all perfectly horrible. I feel smirched and unclean as though slimy things had been crawling all over me.

ELYOT: Maybe they have, that's a very old sofa.

VICTOR: If you don't stop your damned flippancy, I'll knock your head off.

ELYOT (*raising his eyebrows*): Has it ever struck you that flippancy might cover a very real embarrassment?

VICTOR: In a situation such as this, it's in extremely bad taste.

ELYOT: No worse than bluster, and invective. As a matter of fact, as far as I know, this situation is entirely without precedent. We have no prescribed etiquette to fall back upon. I shall continue to be flippant.

SIBYL: Oh Elyot, how can you—how can you.

ELYOT: I'm awfully sorry, Sibyl.

VICTOR: It's easy enough to be sorry.

ELYOT: On the contrary. I find it exceedingly difficult. I seldom regret anything. This is a very rare and notable exception, a sort of red-letter day. We must all make the most of it.

SIBYL: I'll never forgive you, never. I wouldn't have believed anyone could be so callous and cruel.

ELYOT: I absolutely see your point, and as I said before, I'm sorry.

(*There is silence for a moment. Then* AMANDA *comes in again. She has obviously decided to carry everything off in a high-handed manner.*)

AMANDA (*in social tones*): What! Breakfast not ready yet? Really, these French servants are too slow for words. (*She smiles gaily.*) What a glorious morning. (*She goes to the window.*) I do love Paris, it's so genuinely gay. Those lovely trees in the Champs Elysées, and the little roundabouts for the children to play on, and those shiny red taxis. You can see Sacre Coeur quite clearly today, sometimes it's a bit misty, particularly in August, all the heat rising up from the pavements you know.

ELYOT (*drily*): Yes, dear, we know.

AMANDA (*ignoring him*): And it's heavenly being so high up. I found this flat three years ago, quite by merest chance. I happened to be staying at the Plaza Athenée, just down the road—

ELYOT (*enthusiastically*): Such a nice hotel, with the most enchanting courtyard with a fountain that goes plopplopplopplopplopplopplop-plopplop—

VICTOR: This is ridiculous, Amanda.

ELYOT: (*continuing*): Plop plop plop plop plop plop plop plop plop plop—

AMANDA: (*overriding him*): Now, Victor, I refuse to discuss anything in the least important until after breakfast. I couldn't concentrate now, I know I couldn't.

ELYOT (*sarcastically*): What manner. What poise. How I envy it. To be able to carry off the most embarrassing situation with such tact, and delicacy, and above all—such subtlety. Go on Amanda, you're making everything so much easier. We shall all be playing Hunt the Slipper in a minute.

AMANDA: Please don't address me, I don't wish to speak to you.

ELYOT: Splendid.

AMANDA: And what's more, I never shall again as long as I live.

ELYOT: I shall endeavour to rise above it.

AMANDA: I've been brought up to believe that it's beyond the pale, for a man to strike a woman.

ELYOT: A very poor tradition. Certain women should be struck regularly, like gongs.

AMANDA: You're an unmitigated cad, and a bully.

ELYOT: And you're an ill mannered, bad tempered slattern.

AMANDA (*loudly*): Slattern indeed.

ELYOT: Yes, slattern, slattern, slattern, and fishwife.

VICTOR: Keep your mouth shut, you swine.

ELYOT: Mind your damned business.

(*They are about to fight, when* SIBYL *rushes between them.*)

SIBYL: Stop, stop, it's no use going on like this. Stop, please. (*To* AMANDA.) Help me, do, do, do, help me—

AMANDA: I'm not going to interfere. Let them fight if they want to, it will probably clear the air anyhow.

SIBYL: Yes but—

AMANDA: Come into my room, perhaps you'd like to wash or something.

SIBYL: No, but—

AMANDA (*firmly*): Come along.

SIBYL: Very well. (*She tosses her head at* ELYOT, *and* AMANDA *drags her off.*)

VICTOR (*belligerently*): Now then!

ELYOT: Now then what?

VICTOR: Are you going to take back those things you said to Amanda?

ELYOT: Certainly, I'll take back anything, if only you'll stop bellowing at me.

VICTOR (*contemptuously*): You're a coward too.

ELYOT: They want us to fight, don't you see?

VICTOR: No, I don't, why should they?

ELYOT: Primitive feminine instincts—warring males—very enjoyable.

VICTOR: You think you're very clever, don't you?

ELYOT: I think I'm a bit cleverer than you, but apparently that's not saying much.

VICTOR (*violently*): What?

ELYOT: Oh, do sit down.

VICTOR: I will not.

ELYOT: Well, if you'll excuse me, I will, I'm extremely tired. (*He sits down.*)

VICTOR: Oh, for God's sake, behave like a man.

ELYOT (*patiently*): Listen a minute, all this belligerency is very right and proper and highly traditional, but if only you'll think for a moment, you'll see that it won't get us very far.

VICTOR: To hell with all that.

ELYOT: I should like to explain that if you hit me, I shall certainly hit you, probably equally hard, if not harder. I'm just as strong as you should imagine. Then you'd hit me again, and I'd hit you again, and we'd go on until one or the other was knocked out. Now if you'll explain to me satisfactorily how all that can possibly improve the situation, I'll tear off my coat, and we'll go at one another hammer and tongs, immediately.

VICTOR: It would ease my mind.

ELYOT: Only if you won.

VICTOR: I should win alright.

ELYOT: Want to try?

VICTOR: Yes.

ELYOT (*jumping up*): Here goes then—(*He tears off his coat.*)

VICTOR: Just a moment.

ELYOT: Well?

VICTOR: What did you mean about them wanting us to fight?

ELYOT: It would be balm to their vanity.

VICTOR: Do you love Amanda?

ELYOT: Is this a battle or a discussion? If it's the latter I shall put on my coat again, I don't want to catch a chill.

VICTOR: Answer my question, please.

ELYOT: Have a cigarette?

VICTOR (*stormily*): Answer my question.

ELYOT: If you analyse it, it's rather a silly question.

VICTOR: Do you love Amanda?

ELYOT (*confidentially*): Not very much this morning, to be perfectly frank, I'd like to wring her neck. Do you love her?

VICTOR: That's beside the point.

ELYOT: On the contrary, it's the crux of the whole affair. If you do love her still, you can forgive her, and live with her in peace and harmony until you're ninety-eight.

VICTOR: You're apparently even more of a cad than I thought you were.

ELYOT: You are completely in the right over the whole business, don't imagine I'm not perfectly conscious of that.

VICTOR: I'm glad.

ELYOT: It's all very unfortunate.

VICTOR: Unfortunate. My God!

ELYOT: It might have been worse.

VICTOR: I'm glad you think so.

ELYOT: I do wish you'd stop about being so glad about everything.

VICTOR: What do you intend to do? That's what I want to know. What do you intend to do?

ELYOT (*suddenly serious*): I don't know, I don't care.

VICTOR: I suppose you realise that you've broken that poor little woman's heart?

ELYOT: Which poor little woman?

VICTOR: Sibyl, of course.

ELYOT: Oh, come now, not as bad as that. She'll get over it, and forget all about me.

VICTOR: I sincerely hope so . . . for her sake.

ELYOT: Amanda will forget all about me too. Everybody will forget all about me. I might just as well lie down and die in fearful pain and suffering, nobody would care.

VICTOR: Don't talk such rot.

ELYOT: You must forgive me for taking rather a gloomy view of everything but the fact is, I suddenly feel slightly depressed.

VICTOR: I intend to divorce Amanda, naming you as corespondent.

ELYOT: Very well.

VICTOR: And Sibyl will divorce you for Amanda. It would be foolish of either of you to attempt any defence.

ELYOT: Quite.

VICTOR: And the sooner you marry Amanda again, the better.

ELYOT: I'm not going to marry Amanda.

VICTOR: What?

ELYOT: She's a vile tempered wicked woman.

VICTOR: You should have thought of that before.

ELYOT: I did think of it before.

VICTOR (*firmly*): You've got to marry her.

ELYOT: I'd rather marry a ravening Leopard.

VICTOR (*angrily*): Now look here. I'm sick of all this shilly-shallying. You're getting off a good deal more lightly than you deserve; you can consider yourself damned lucky I didn't shoot you.

ELYOT (*with sudden vehemence*): Well, if you'd had a spark of manliness in you, you would have shot me. You're all fuss and fume, one of these cotton-wool Englishmen. I despise you.

VICTOR (*through clenched teeth*): You despise me?

ELYOT: Yes, utterly. You're nothing but a rampaging gas bag! (*He goes off into his room and slams the door, leaving* VICTOR *speechless with fury*, AMANDA *and* SIBYL *reenter.*)

AMANDA (*brightly*): Well, what's happened?

VICTOR (*sullenly*): Nothing's happened.

AMANDA: You ought to be ashamed to admit it.

SIBYL: Where's Elyot?

VICTOR: In there.

AMANDA: What's he doing?

VICTOR (*turning angrily away*): How do I know what he's doing?

AMANDA: If you were half the man I thought you were, he'd be bandaging himself.

SIBYL (*with defiance*): Elyot's just as strong as Victor.

AMANDA (*savagely*): I should like it proved.

SIBYL: There's no need to be so vindictive.

AMANDA: You were abusing Elyot like a pickpocket to me a little while ago, now you are standing up for him.

SIBYL: I'm beginning to suspect that he wasn't quite so much to blame as I thought.

AMANDA: Oh really?

SIBYL: You certainly have a very unpleasant temper.

AMANDA: It's a little difficult to keep up with your rapid changes of front, but you're young and inexperienced, so I forgive you freely.

SIBYL (*heatedly*): Seeing the depths of degradation to which age and experience have brought you, I'm glad I'm as I am!

AMANDA (*with great grandeur*): That was exceedingly rude. I think you'd better go away somewhere. (*She waves her hand vaguely.*)

SIBYL: After all, Elyot is my husband.

AMANDA: Take him with you, by all means.

SIBYL: If you're not very careful, I will! (*She goes over to* ELYOT's *door and bangs on it.*) Elyot—Elyot—

ELYOT (*inside*): What is it?

SIBYL: Let me in. Please, please let me in; I want to speak to you!

AMANDA: Heaven preserve me from nice women!

SIBYL: Your own reputation ought to do that.

AMANDA (*irritably*): Oh, go to hell!

(ELYOT *opens the door, and* SIBYL *disappears inside,* AMANDA *looks at* VICTOR, *who is standing with his back turned, staring out of the window, then she wanders about the room, making rather inadequate little attempts to tidy up. She glances at* VICTOR *again.*)

AMANDA: Victor.

VICTOR (*without turning*): What?

AMANDA (*sadly*): Nothing. (*She begins to wrestle with one of the sofas in an effort to get it in place.* VICTOR *turns, sees her, and comes down and helps her, in silence.*)

VICTOR: Where does it go?

AMANDA: Over there. (*After they have placed it,* AMANDA *sits on the edge of it and gasps a little.*) Thank you, Victor.

VICTOR: Don't mention it.

AMANDA (*after a pause*): What did you say to Elyot?

VICTOR: I told him he was beneath contempt.

AMANDA: Good.

VICTOR: I think you must be mad, Amanda.

AMANDA: I've often thought that myself.

VICTOR: I feel completely lost, completely bewildered.

AMANDA: I don't blame you. I don't feel any too cosy.

VICTOR: Had you been drinking last night?

AMANDA: Certainly not!

VICTOR: Had Elyot been drinking?

AMANDA: Yes—gallons.

VICTOR: Used he to drink before? When you were married to him?

AMANDA: Yes, terribly. Night after night he'd come home roaring and hiccoughing.

VICTOR: Disgusting!

AMANDA: Yes, wasn't it?

VICTOR: Did he really strike you last night?

AMANDA: Repeatedly. I'm bruised beyond recognition.

VICTOR (*suspecting slight exaggeration*): Amanda!

AMANDA (*putting her hand on his arm*): Oh, Victor, I'm most awfully sorry to have given you so much trouble, really I am! I've behaved badly, I know, but something strange happened to me. I can't explain it, there's no excuse, but I am ashamed of having made you unhappy.

VICTOR: I can't understand it at all. I've tried to, but I can't. It all seems so unlike you.

AMANDA: It isn't really unlike me, that's the trouble. I ought never to have married you; I'm a bad lot.

VICTOR: Amanda!

AMANDA: Don't contradict me. I know I'm a bad lot.

VICTOR: I wasn't going to contradict you.

AMANDA: Victor!

VICTOR: You appal me—absolutely!

AMANDA: Go on, go on, I deserve it.

VICTOR: I didn't come here to accuse you; there's no sense in that!

AMANDA: Why did you come?

VICTOR: To find out what you want me to do.

AMANDA: Divorce me, I suppose, as soon as possible. I won't make any difficulties. I'll go away, far away, Morocco, or Tunis, or somewhere. I shall probably catch some dreadful disease, and die out there, all alone—oh dear!

VICTOR: It's no use pitying yourself.

AMANDA: I seem to be the only one who does. I might just as well enjoy it. (*She sniffs.*) I'm thoroughly unprincipled; Sibyl was right!

VICTOR (*irritably*): Sibyl's an ass.

AMANDA (*brightening slightly*): Yes, she is rather, isn't she? I can't think why Elyot ever married her.

VICTOR: Do you love him?

AMANDA: She seems so insipid, somehow—

VICTOR: Do you love him?

AMANDA: Of course she's very pretty, I suppose, in rather a shallow way, but still—

VICTOR: Amanda!

AMANDA: Yes, Victor?

VICTOR: You haven't answered my question.

AMANDA: I've forgotten what it was.

VICTOR (*turning away*): You're hopeless—hopeless.

AMANDA: Don't be angry, it's all much too serious to be angry about.

VICTOR: You're talking utter nonsense!

AMANDA: No, I'm not, I mean it. It's ridiculous for us all to stand round arguing with one another. You'd much better go back to England and let your lawyers deal with the whole thing.

VICTOR: But what about you?

AMANDA: I'll be all right.

VICTOR: I only want to know one thing, and you won't tell me.

AMANDA: What is it?

VICTOR: Do you love Elyot?

AMANDA: No, I hate him. When I saw him again suddenly at Deauville, it was an odd sort of shock. It swept me away completely. He attracted me; he always has attracted me, but only the worst part of me. I see that now.

VICTOR: I can't understand why? He's so terribly trivial and superficial.

AMANDA: That sort of attraction can't be explained, it's a sort of a chemical what d'you call 'em.

VICTOR: Yes; it must be!

AMANDA: I don't expect you to understand, and I'm not going to try to excuse myself in any way. Elyot was the first love affair of my life, and in spite of all the suffering he caused me before, there must have been a little spark left smouldering, which burst into flame when I came face to face with him again. I completely lost grip of myself and behaved like a fool, for which I shall pay all right, you needn't worry about that. But perhaps one day, when all this is dead and done with, you and I might meet and be friends. That's something to hope for, anyhow. Good-bye, Victor dear. (*She holds out her hand.*)

VICTOR (*shaking her hand mechanically*): Do you want to marry him?

AMANDA: I'd rather marry a boa constrictor.

VICTOR: I can't go away and leave you with a man who drinks, and knocks you about.

AMANDA: You needn't worry about leaving me, as though I were a sort of parcel. I can look after myself.

VICTOR: You said just now you were going away to Tunis, to die.

AMANDA: I've changed my mind, it's the wrong time of the year for Tunis. I shall go somewhere quite different. I believe Brioni is very nice in the summer.

VICTOR: Why won't you be serious for just one moment?

AMANDA: I've told you, it's no use.

VICTOR: If it will make things any easier for you, I won't divorce you.

AMANDA: Victor!

VICTOR: We can live apart until Sibyl has got her decree against Elyot, then, some time after that, I'll let you divorce me.

AMANDA (*turning away*): I see you're determined to make me serious, whether I like it or not.

VICTOR: I married you because I loved you.

AMANDA: Stop it, Victor! Stop it! I won't listen!

VICTOR: I expect I love you still; one doesn't change all in a minute. You never loved me. I see that now, of course, so perhaps everything has turned out for the best really.

AMANDA: I thought I loved you, honestly I did.

VICTOR: Yes, I know, that's all right.

AMANDA: What an escape you've had.

VICTOR: I've said that to myself often during the last few days.

AMANDA: There's no need to rub it in.

VICTOR: Do you agree about the divorce business?

AMANDA: Yes. It's very, very generous of you.

VICTOR: It will save you some of the mud-slinging. We might persuade Sibyl not to name you.

AMANDA (*ruefully*): Yes, we might.

VICTOR: Perhaps she'll change her mind about divorcing him.

AMANDA: Perhaps. She certainly went into the bedroom with a predatory look in her eye.

VICTOR: Would you be pleased if that happened?

AMANDA: Delighted. (*She laughs suddenly. Victor looks at her, curiously.* SIBYL *and* ELYOT *come out of the bedroom. There is an awkward silence for a moment.*)

SIBYL (*looking at* AMANDA *triumphantly*): Elyot and I have come to a decision.

AMANDA: How very nice!

VICTOR: What is it?

AMANDA: Don't be silly, Victor. Look at their faces.

ELYOT: Feminine intuition, very difficult.

AMANDA (*looking at* SIBYL): Feminine determination, very praiseworthy.

SIBYL: I am not going to divorce Elyot for a year.

AMANDA: I congratulate you.

ELYOT (*defiantly*): Sibyl has behaved like an angel.

AMANDA: Well, it was certainly her big moment.

(LOUISE *comes staggering in with a large tray of coffee and rolls, etc. She stands peering over the edge of it, not knowing where to put it.*)

ELYOT: Il faut le mettre sur la petite table là-bas.

LOUISE: Oui, monsieur.

(ELYOT *and* VICTOR *hurriedly clear the things off the side table, and* LOUISE *puts the tray down, and goes back into the kitchen.* AMANDA *and* SIBYL *eye one another.*)

AMANDA: It all seems very amicable.

SIBYL: It is, thank you.

AMANDA: I don't wish to depress you, but Victor isn't going to divorce me either.

ELYOT (*looking up sharply*): What!

AMANDA: I believe I asked you once before this morning, never to speak to me again.

ELYOT: I only said "What." It was a general exclamation denoting extreme satisfaction.

AMANDA (*politely to* SIBYL): Do sit down, won't you?

SIBYL: I'm afraid I must be going now. I'm catching the Golden Arrow; it leaves at twelve.

ELYOT (*coaxingly*): You have time for a little coffee surely?

SIBYL: No, I really must go!

ELYOT: I shan't be seeing you again for such a long time.

AMANDA (*brightly*): Living apart? How wise!

ELYOT (*ignoring her*): Please, Sibyl, do stay!

SIBYL (*looking at* AMANDA *with a glint in her eye*): Very well, just for a little.

AMANDA: Sit down, Victor, darling.

(*They all sit down in silence.* AMANDA *smiles sweetly at* SIBYL *and holds up the coffee pot and milk jug.*) Half and half?

SIBYL: Yes, please.

AMANDA (*sociably*): What would one do without one's morning coffee? That's what I often ask myself.

ELYOT: Is it?

AMANDA (*withering him with a look*): Victor, sugar for Sibyl. (*To* SIBYL.) It would be absurd for me to call you anything but Sibyl, wouldn't it?

SIBYL (*not to be outdone*): Of course, I shall call you Mandy.

(AMANDA *represses a shudder*.)

ELYOT: Oh God! We're off again. What weather! (AMANDA *hands* SIBYL *her coffee*.)

SIBYL: Thank you.

VICTOR: What's the time?

ELYOT: If the clock's still going after last night, it's ten-fifteen.

AMANDA (*handing* VICTOR *cup of coffee*): Here, Victor dear.

VICTOR: Thanks.

AMANDA: Sibyl, sugar for Victor.

ELYOT: I should like some coffee, please.

(AMANDA *pours some out for him, and hands it to him in silence*.)

AMANDA (*to* VICTOR): Brioche?

VICTOR (*jumping*): What?

AMANDA: Would you like a brioche?

VICTOR: No, thank you.

ELYOT: I would. And some butter, and some jam. (*He helps himself*.)

AMANDA (*to* SIBYL): Have you ever been to Brioni?

SIBYL: No. It's in the Adriatic, isn't it?

VICTOR: The Baltic, I think.

SIBYL: I made sure it was the Adriatic.

AMANDA: I had an aunt who went there once.

ELYOT (*with his mouth full*): I once had an aunt who went to Tasmania.

(AMANDA *looks at him stonily. He winks at her, and she looks away hurriedly*.)

VICTOR: Funny how the South of France has become so fashionable in the summer, isn't it?

SIBYL: Yes, awfully funny.

ELYOT: I've been laughing about it for months.

AMANDA: Personally, I think it's a bit too hot, although of course one can lie in the water all day.

SIBYL: Yes, the bathing is really divine!

VICTOR: A friend of mine has a house right on the edge of Cape Ferrat.

SIBYL: Really?

VICTOR: Yes, right on the edge.

AMANDA: That must be marvellous!

VICTOR: Yes, he seems to like it very much.

(*The conversation languishes slightly.*)

AMANDA (*with great vivacity*): Do you know, I really think I love travelling more than anything else in the world! It always gives me such a tremendous feeling of adventure. First of all, the excitement of packing, and getting your passport visa'd and everything, then the thrill of actually starting, and trundling along on trains and ships, and then the most thrilling thing of all, arriving at strange places, and seeing strange people, and eating strange foods—

ELYOT: And making strange noises afterwards.

(AMANDA *chokes violently.* VICTOR *jumps up and tries to offer assistance, but she waves him away, and continues to choke.*)

VICTOR (*to* ELYOT): That was a damned fool thing to do.

ELYOT: How did I know she was going to choke?

VICTOR (*to* AMANDA): Here, drink some coffee.

AMANDA (*breathlessly gasping*): Leave me alone. I'll be all right in a minute.

VICTOR (*to* ELYOT): You waste too much time trying to be funny.

SIBYL (*up in arms*): It's no use talking to Elyot like that; it wasn't his fault.

VICTOR: Of course it was his fault entirely, making rotten stupid jokes—

SIBYL: I thought what Elyot said was funny.

VICTOR: Well, all I can say is, you must have a very warped sense of humour.

SIBYL: That's better than having none at all.

VICTOR: I fail to see what humour there is in incessant trivial flippancy.

SIBYL: You couldn't be flippant if you tried until you were blue in the face.

VICTOR: I shouldn't dream of trying.

SIBYL: It must be very sad not to be able to see any fun in anything.

(AMANDA *stops choking, and looks at* ELYOT. *He winks at her again, and she smiles.*)

VICTOR: Fun! I should like you to tell me what fun there is in—

SIBYL: I pity you, I really do. I've been pitying you ever since we left Deauville.

VICTOR: I'm sure it's very nice of you, but quite unnecessary.

SIBYL: And I pity you more than ever now.

VICTOR: *Why* now particularly?

SIBYL: If you don't see why, I'm certainly not going to tell you.

VICTOR: I see no reason for you to try to pick a quarrel with me. I've tried my best to be pleasant to you, and comfort you.

SIBYL: You weren't very comforting when I lost my trunk.

VICTOR: I have little patience with people who go about losing luggage.

SIBYL: I don't go about losing luggage. It's the first time I've lost anything in my life.

VICTOR: I find that hard to believe.

SIBYL: Anyhow, if you'd tipped the porter enough, everything would have been all right. Small economies never pay; it's absolutely no use—

VICTOR: Oh, for God's sake be quiet!

(AMANDA *lifts her hand as though she were going to interfere, but* ELYOT *grabs her wrist. They look at each other for a moment, she lets her hand rest in his.*)

SIBYL (*rising from the table*): How dare you speak to me like that!

VICTOR (*also rising*): Because you've been irritating me for days.

SIBYL (*outraged*): Oh!

VICTOR (*coming down to her*): You're one of the most completely idiotic women I've ever met.

SIBYL: And you're certainly the rudest man I've ever met!

VICTOR: Well then, we're quits, aren't we?

SIBYL (*shrilly*): One thing, you'll get your deserts all right.

VICTOR: What do you mean by that?

SIBYL: You know perfectly well what I mean. And it'll serve you right for being weak-minded enough to allow that woman to get round you so easily.

VICTOR: What about you? Letting that unprincipled roué persuade you to take him back again!

(AMANDA *and* ELYOT *are laughing silently.* ELYOT *blows her a lingering kiss across the table.*)

SIBYL: He's nothing of the sort, he's just been victimized, as you were victimized.

VICTOR: Victimized! What damned nonsense!

SIBYL (*furiously*): It isn't damned nonsense! You're very fond of swearing and blustering and threatening, but when it comes to the point you're as weak as water. Why, a blind cat could see what you've let yourself in for.

VICTOR (*equally furious*): Stop making those insinuations.

SIBYL: I'm not insinuating anything. When I think of all the things you said about her, it makes me laugh, it does really; to see how completely she's got you again.

VICTOR: You can obviously speak with great authority; having had the intelligence to marry a drunkard.

SIBYL: So that's what she's been telling you. I might have known it! I suppose she said he struck her too!

VICTOR: Yes, she did, and I'm quite sure it's perfectly true.

SIBYL: I expect she omitted to tell you that she drank fourteen glasses of brandy last night straight off; and that the reason their first marriage was broken up was that she used to come home at all hours of the night, screaming and hiccoughing.

VICTOR: If he told you that, he's a filthy liar.

SIBYL: He isn't—he isn't!

VICTOR: And if you believe it, you're a silly scatter-brained little fool.

SIBYL (*screaming*): How dare you speak to me like that! How dare you! I've never been so insulted in my life! How dare you!

(AMANDA *and* ELYOT *rise quietly, and go, hand in hand, towards the front door.*)

VICTOR (*completely giving way*): It's a tremendous relief to me to have an excuse to insult you. I've had to listen to your weeping and wailings for days. You've clacked at me, and snivelled at me until you've nearly driven me insane, and I controlled my nerves and continued to try to help you and look after you, because I was sorry for you. I always thought you were stupid from the first, but I must say I never realised that you were a malicious little vixen as well!

SIBYL (*shrieking*): Stop it! Stop it! You insufferable great brute. (*She slaps his face hard, and he takes her by the shoulders and shakes her like a rat, as* AMANDA *and* ELYOT *go smilingly out of the door, with their suitcases, and—*

THE CURTAIN FALLS.

The Man Who Came to Dinner

MOSS HART

and

GEORGE S. KAUFMAN

To
Alexander Woollcott
for reasons
that are nobody's business
The Authors

Why our respondents liked

 THE MAN WHO CAME
TO DINNER

"To me this is the funniest comedy I have seen—a perfect portrait of Woollcott and a brilliantly constructed play with twists and turns in typical Kaufman-Hart manner. I have seen, acted in it, read it and consider it unique."

GEORGE OPPENHEIMER

"One of the best Kaufman & Hart."

JOSHUA LOGAN

"A miracle which burns venom into champagne."

HEYWOOD HALE BROUN

"Obvious. It made fun of a nightmare each of us had about being stuck with an unwanted guest."

DORE SCHARY

The Man Who Came to Dinner is one of the many critical successes that playwrights George S. Kaufman and Moss Hart collaborated on, and it proved to be one of the main highlights of the 1939–40 Broadway theatre season. The play was modeled on the character of Kaufman and Hart's friend, raconteur and writer Alexander Woollcott, and took six months to write. Woollcott was delighted with the script from the start. However, he turned down the opportunity to play the lead character, Sheridan Whiteside, because he was identified with the part and didn't want to be embarrassed if the show was unsuccessful. Moreover, he felt that even if *The Man Who Came to Dinner* became a hit he didn't want to spend the next two years in New York. The search for another actor led to Monty Woolley, a former drama teacher at Yale with a few minor Broadway roles to his credit. Word of mouth of the play's tryouts in Boston was so enthusiastic that there was a large advance ticket sale at Broadway's Music Box Theatre— $3.30 for an orchestra seat. A Chicago company was soon organized with former dancer Clifton Webb cast as Sheridan Whiteside. Alexander Woollcott, having changed his mind, played the lead role in the West Coast Company and later in performances on the East Coast. Confirming the acclaim that the play was receiving across the nation, the entire company was invited to a White House reception by the Roosevelts. The many performances of *The Man Who Came to Dinner* staged around the world annually attest to the play's continuing popularity.

The Man Who Came to Dinner was presented by Sam H. Harris on October 16, 1939, at the Music Box Theatre, New York City. The cast was as follows:

Mrs. Ernest W. Stanley	Virginia Hammond
Miss Preen	Mary Wickes
Richard Stanley	Gordon Merrick
June Stanley	Barbara Wooddell
John	George Probert
Sarah	Mrs. Priestley Morrison
Mrs. Dexter	Barbara Adams
Mrs. McCutcheon	Edmonia Nolley
Mr. Stanley	George Lessey
Maggie Cutler	Edith Atwater
Dr. Bradley	Dudley Clements
Sheridan Whiteside	Monty Woolley
Harriet Stanley	Ruth Vivian
Bert Jefferson	Theodore Newton
Professor Metz	LeRoi Operti
The Luncheon Guests	Phil Sheridan
	Charles Washington
	William Postance
Mr. Baker	Carl Johnson
Expressman	Harold Woolf
Lorraine Sheldon	Carol Goodner
Sandy	Michael Harvey
Beverly Carlton	John Hoysradt
Westcott	Edward Fisher
Radio Technicians	Rodney Stewart
	Carl Johnson
Six Young Boys	Daniel Leone
	Jack Whitman
	Daniel Landon

	Donald Landon
	DeWitt Purdue
	Robert Rea
Banjo	David Burns
Two Deputies	Curtis Karpe
	Phil Sheridan
A Plainclothes Man	William Postance

Staged by Bernard Hart
Setting by Donald Oenslager

With thanks to Cole Porter for the music and lyrics

The scene is the home of Mr. and Mrs. Stanley,
in a small town in Ohio.

ACT ONE

ACT TWO

*Another week has passed
Christmas Eve*

ACT THREE

Christmas Morning

ACT ONE

SCENE I

SCENE—*The curtain rises on the attractive living room in the home of* MR. *and* MRS. ERNEST W. STANLEY, *in a small town in Ohio. The* STANLEYS *are obviously people of means. The room is large, comfortable, tastefully furnished. Double doors lead into a library; there is a glimpse of a dining room at the rear, and we see the first half dozen steps of a handsome curved staircase. At the other side, bay windows, the entrance hall, the outer door.*

MRS. STANLEY *is hovering nervously near the library doors, which are tightly closed. She advances a step or two, retreats, advances again and this time musters up enough courage to listen at the door. Suddenly the doors are opened and she has to leap back.*

A NURSE *in full uniform emerges—scurries, rather, out of the room.*

An angry voice from within speeds her on her way: "Great dribbling cow!"

MRS. STANLEY (*eagerly*): How is he? Is he coming out?

(*But the* NURSE *has already disappeared into the dining room.*)
(*Simultaneously the doorbell rings—at the same time a young lad of twenty-one,* RICHARD STANLEY, *is descending the stairs.*)

RICHARD: I'll go, Mother.

(JOHN, *a white-coated servant, comes hurrying in from the dining room and starts up the stairs, two at a time.*)

MRS. STANLEY: What's the matter? What is it?

JOHN: They want pillows. (*And he is out of sight.*)

(*Meanwhile the* NURSE *is returning to the sick room. The voice is heard again as she opens the doors. "Don't call yourself a doctor in my presence! You're a quack if I ever saw one!"*)

(RICHARD *returns from the hall, carrying two huge packages and a sheaf of cablegrams.*)

RICHARD: Four more cablegrams and more packages. . . . Dad is going crazy upstairs, with that bell ringing all the time.

(*Meanwhile* JUNE, *the daughter of the house, has come down the stairs. An attractive girl of twenty. At the same time the telephone is ringing.*)

MRS. STANLEY: Oh, dear! . . . June, will you go? . . . What did you say, Richard?

RICHARD (*examining the packages*): One's from New York and one from San Francisco.

MRS. STANLEY: There was something from Alaska early this morning.

JUNE (*at the telephone*): Yes? . . . Yes, that's right.

MRS. STANLEY: Who is it?

(*Before* JUNE *can answer, the double doors are opened again and the* NURSE *appears. The voice calls after her: "Doesn't that bird-brain of yours ever function?"*)

THE NURSE: I—I'll get them right away. . . . He wants some Players Club cigarettes.

MRS. STANLEY: Players Club?

RICHARD: They have 'em at Kitchener's. I'll run down and get 'em.

(*He is off.*)

JUNE (*still at the phone*): Hello. . . . Yes, I'm waiting.

MRS. STANLEY: Tell me, Miss Preen, is he—are they bringing him out soon?

MISS PREEN (*wearily*): We're getting him out of bed now. He'll be out very soon . . . Oh, thank you. (*This last is to* JOHN, *who has descended the stairs with three or four pillows.*)

MRS. STANLEY: Oh, I'm so glad. He must be very happy.

(*And again we hear the invalid's voice as* MISS PREEN *passes into the room.* "*Trapped like a rat in this hell-hole! Take your fish-hooks off me!*")

JUNE (*at the phone*): Hello. . . . Yes, he's here, but he can't come to the phone right now . . . London? (*She covers the transmitter with her hand.*) It's London calling Mr. Whiteside.

MRS. STANLEY: London? My, my!

JUNE: Two o'clock? Yes, I think he could talk then. All right. (*She hangs up.*) Well, who do you think that was? Mr. H. G. Wells.

MRS. STANLEY (*wild-eyed*): H. G. Wells? On our telephone? (*The doorbell again.*)

JUNE: I'll go. This is certainly a busy house.

(*In the meantime* SARAH, *the cook, has come from the dining room with a pitcher of orange juice.*)

MRS. STANLEY (*as* SARAH *knocks on the double doors*): Oh, that's fine, Sarah. Is it fresh?

SARAH: Yes, ma'am.

(*The doors are opened;* SARAH *hands the orange juice to the nurse. The voice roars once more:* "*You have the touch of a sex-starved cobra!*")

SARAH (*beaming*): His voice is just the same as on the radio.

(*She disappears into the dining room as* JUNE *returns from the entrance hall, ushering in two friends of her mother's,* MRS. DEXTER *and* MRS. MCCUTCHEON. *One is carrying a flowering plant, partially wrapped; the other is holding, with some care, what turns out to be a jar of calf's-foot jelly.*)

THE LADIES: Good morning!

MRS. STANLEY: Girls, what do you think? He's getting up and coming out today!

MRS. MCCUTCHEON: You don't mean it!

MRS. DEXTER: Can we stay and see him?

MRS. STANLEY: Why, of course—he'd love it. Girls, do you know what just happened?

JUNE (*departing*): I'll be upstairs, Mother, if you want me.

MRS. STANLEY: What? . . . Oh, yes. June, tell your father he'd better come down, will you? Mr. Whiteside is coming out.

MRS. DEXTER: Is he really coming out today? I brought him a plant— Do you think it's all right if I give it to him?

MRS. STANLEY: Why, I think that would be lovely.

MRS. MCCUTCHEON: And some calf's-foot jelly.

MRS. STANLEY: Why, how nice! Who do you think was on the phone just now? H. G. Wells, from London. And look at those cablegrams. He's had calls and messages from all over this country and Europe. The New York *Times* and Radio City Music Hall—I don't know why *they* called—and Felix Frankfurter, and Dr. Dafoe, the Mount Wilson Observatory—I just can't tell you what's been going on.

MRS. DEXTER: There's a big piece about it in this week's *Time*. Did you see it? (*Drawing it out of her bag.*)

MRS. STANLEY: No—really?

MRS. MCCUTCHEON: Your name's in it too, Daisy. It tells all about the whole thing. Listen: "Portly Sheridan Whiteside, critic, lecturer, wit, radio orator, intimate friend of the great and near great, last week found his celebrated wit no weapon with which to combat a fractured hip. The Falstaffian Mr. Whiteside, trekking across the country on one of his annual lecture tours, met his Waterloo in the shape of a small piece of ice on the doorstep of Mr. and Mrs. Ernest W. Stanley, of Mesalia, Ohio. Result: Cancelled lectures and disappointment to thousands of adoring clubwomen in Omaha, Denver, and points west. Further result: The idol of the air waves rests until further notice in home of surprised Mr. and Mrs. Stanley. Possibility: Christmas may be postponed this year." What's *that* mean?

MRS. STANLEY: Why, what do you think of that?

(*She takes the magazine; reads.*)

"A small piece of ice on the doorstep of Mr. and Mrs. Ernest"— think of it!

MRS. MCCUTCHEON: Of course if it were *my* house, Daisy, I'd have a bronze plate put on the step, right where he fell.

MRS. STANLEY: Well, of course I felt terrible about it. He just never goes to dinner anywhere, and he finally agreed to come here, and then *this* had to happen. Poor Mr. Whiteside! But it's going to be so wonderful having him with us, even for a little while. Just think of it! We'll sit around in the evening and discuss books and plays, all the great people he's known. And he'll talk in that wonderful way of his. He may even read *Good-bye, Mr. Chips* to us.

(MR. STANLEY, *solid, substantial—the American business man—is descending the stairs.*)

STANLEY: Daisy, I can't wait any longer. If—ah, good morning, ladies.

MRS. STANLEY: Ernest, he's coming out any minute, and H. G. Wells telephoned from London, and we're in *Time*. Look!

STANLEY (*taking the magazine*): I don't like this kind of publicity at all, Daisy. When do you suppose he's going to leave?

MRS. STANLEY: Well, he's only getting up this morning—after all, he's had quite a shock, and he's been in bed for two full weeks. He'll certainly have to rest a few days, Ernest.

STANLEY: Well, I'm sure it's a great honor, his being in the house, but it *is* a little upsetting—phone going all the time, bells ringing, messenger boys running in and out—

(*Out of the sick room comes a businesslike-looking young woman about thirty. Her name is* MARGARET CUTLER—MAGGIE *to her friends.*)

MAGGIE: Pardon me, Mrs. Stanley—have the cigarettes come yet?

MRS. STANLEY: They're on the way, Miss Cutler. My son went for them.

MAGGIE: Thank you.

MRS. STANLEY: Ah—this is Miss Cutler, Mr. Whiteside's secretary. (*An exchange of "How do you do's?"*)

MAGGIE: May I move this chair?

MRS. STANLEY (*all eagerness*): You mean he's—coming out now?

MAGGIE (*quietly*): He is indeed.

MRS. STANLEY: Ernest, call June. June! June! Mr. Whiteside is coming out!

(JOHN, *visible in the dining room, summons* SARAH *to attend the excitement. "Sarah! Sarah!"*)

(SARAH *and* JOHN *appear in the dining-room entrance,* JUNE *on the stairs.* MRS. STANLEY *and the two other ladies are keenly expectant; even* MR. STANLEY *is on the qui vive.*)

(*The double doors are opened once more, and* DR. BRADLEY *appears, bag in hand. He has taken a good deal of punishment, and speaks with a rather false heartiness.*)

DR. BRADLEY: Well, here we are, merry and bright. Good morning, good morning. Bring our little patient out, Miss Preen.

(*A moment's pause, and then a wheelchair is rolled through the door. It is full of pillows, blankets, and* SHERIDAN WHITESIDE. SHERIDAN WHITESIDE *is indeed portly and Falstaffian. He is wearing an elaborate velvet smoking jacket and a very loud tie, and he looks like every caricature ever drawn of him.*)

(*There is a hush as the wheelchair rolls into the room. Welcoming smiles break over every face. The chair comes to a halt;* MR. WHITESIDE *looks slowly around, into each and every beaming face. His fingers drum for a moment on the arm of the chair. He looks slowly around once more. And then he speaks.*)

WHITESIDE (*quietly, to* MAGGIE): I may vomit.

MRS. STANLEY (*with a nervous little laugh*): Good morning, Mr. Whiteside. I'm Mrs. Ernest Stanley—remember? And this is Mr. Stanley.

STANLEY: How do you do, Mr. Whiteside? I hope that you are better.

WHITESIDE: Thank you. I am suing you for a hundred and fifty thousand dollars.

STANLEY: How's that? What?

WHITESIDE: I said I am suing you for a hundred and fifty thousand dollars.

MRS. STANLEY: You mean—because you fell on our steps, Mr. Whiteside?

WHITESIDE: Samuel J. Liebowitz will explain it to you in court. . . . Who are those two harpies standing there like the kiss of death?

(MRS. MCCUTCHEON, *with a little gasp, drops the calf's-foot jelly. It smashes on the floor.*)

MRS. MCCUTCHEON: Oh, dear! My calf's-foot jelly.

WHITESIDE: Made from your own foot, I have no doubt. And now, Mrs. Stanley, I have a few small matters to take up with you. Since this corner druggist at my elbow tells me that I shall be confined in this mouldy mortuary for at least another ten days, due entirely to your stupidity and negligence, I shall have to carry on my activities as best I can. I shall require the exclusive use of this room, as well as that drafty sewer which you call the library. I want no one to come in or out while I am in this room.

STANLEY: What do you mean, sir?

MRS. STANLEY (*stunned*): But we have to go up the stairs to get to our rooms, Mr. Whiteside.

WHITESIDE: Isn't there a back entrance?

MRS. STANLEY: Why—yes.

WHITESIDE: Then use that. I shall also require a room for my secretary, Miss Cutler. I shall have a great many incoming and outgoing calls, so please use the telephone as little as possible. I sleep until noon and require quiet through the house until that hour. There will be five for lunch today. Where is the cook?

STANLEY: Mr. Whiteside, if I may interrupt for a moment—

WHITESIDE: You may not, sir. . . . Will you take your clammy hand off my chair? (*This last to the nurse.*) . . . And now will you all leave quietly, or must I ask Miss Cutler to pass among you with a baseball bat?

(MRS. DEXTER *and* MRS. MCCUTCHEON *are beating a hasty retreat, their gifts still in hand.*)

MRS. MCCUTCHEON: Well—good-bye, Daisy. We'll call you—Oh, no, we mustn't use the phone. Well—we'll see you. (*And they are gone.*)

STANLEY (*boldly*): Now look here, Mr. Whiteside—

WHITESIDE: There is nothing to discuss, sir. Considering the damage I have suffered at your hands, I am asking very little. Good day.

STANLEY (*controlling himself*): I'll call you from the office later, Daisy.

WHITESIDE: Not on this phone, please.

(STANLEY *gives him a look, but goes.*)

WHITESIDE: Here is the menu for lunch. (*He extends a slip of paper to* MRS. STANLEY.)

MRS. STANLEY: But—I've already ordered lunch.

WHITESIDE: It will be sent up to you on a tray. I am using the dining room for my guests. . . . Where are those cigarettes?

MRS. STANLEY: Why—my son went for them. I don't know why he— here, Sarah. (*She hands* SARAH *the luncheon slip*.) I'll—have mine upstairs on a tray. (SARAH *and* JOHN *depart*.)

WHITESIDE (*to* JUNE, *who has been posed on the landing during all this*): Young lady, will you either go up those stairs or come down them? I cannot stand indecision.

(JUNE *is about to speak, decides against it, and ascends the stairs with a good deal of spirit*.)

(MRS. STANLEY *is hovering uncertainly on the steps as* RICHARD *returns with the cigarettes*.)

RICHARD: Oh, good morning. I'm sorry I was so long—I had to go to three different stores.

WHITESIDE: How did you travel? By ox-cart?

(RICHARD *is considerably taken aback. His eyes go to his mother who motions to him to come up the stairs. They disappear together their eyes unsteadily on* WHITESIDE.)

WHITESIDE: Is there a man in the world who suffers as I do from the gross inadequacies of the human race! (*To the* NURSE, *who is fussing around the chair again*.) Take those canal boats away from me! (*She obeys, hastily*.) Go in and read the life of Florence Nightingale and learn how unfitted you are for your chosen profession. (MISS PREEN *glares at him, but goes*.)

DR. BRADLEY (*heartily*): Well, I think I can safely leave you in Miss Cutler's capable hands. Shall I look in again this afternoon?

WHITESIDE: If you do, I shall spit right in your eye.

DR. BRADLEY: What a sense of humor you writers have! By the way, it isn't really worth mentioning, but—I've been doing a little writing myself. About my medical experiences.

WHITESIDE (*quietly*): Am I to be spared nothing?

DR. BRADLEY: Would it be too much to ask you to—glance over it while you're here?

WHITESIDE (*eyes half closed, as though the pain were too exquisite to bear*): Trapped.

DR. BRADLEY (*delving into his bag*): I just happen to have a copy with me. (*He brings out a tremendous manuscript*.) "Forty Years an Ohio Doctor. The Story of a Humble Practitioner."

WHITESIDE: I shall drop everything.

DR. BRADLEY: Much obliged, and I hope you like it. Well, see you on the morrow. Keep that hip quiet and don't forget those little pills. (*He goes.*)

WHITESIDE (*handing the manuscript to* MAGGIE): Maggie, will you take *Forty Years Below the Navel* or whatever it's called?

MAGGIE (*surveying him*): I must say you have certainly behaved with all of your accustomed grace and charm.

WHITESIDE: Look here, Puss—I am in no mood to discuss my behavior, good or bad.

MAGGIE: These people have done everything in their power to make you comfortable. And they happen, God knows why, to look upon you with a certain wonder and admiration.

WHITESIDE: If they had looked a little more carefully at their doorstep I would not be troubling them now. I did not wish to cross their cheerless threshold. I was hounded and badgered into it. I now find myself, after two weeks of racking pain, accused of behaving without charm. What would you have me do? Kiss them?

MAGGIE (*giving up*): Very well, Sherry. After ten years I should have known better than to try to do anything about your manners. But when I finally give up this job I may write a book about it all. *Cavalcade of Insult,* or *Through the Years with Prince Charming.*

WHITESIDE: Listen, Repulsive, you are tied to me with an umbilical cord made of piano wire. And now if we may dismiss the subject of my charm, for which, incidentally, I receive fifteen hundred dollars per appearance, possibly we can go to work . . . Oh, no, we can't. Yes?

(*This last is addressed to a wraithlike lady of uncertain years, who has more or less floated into the room. She is carrying a large spray of holly, and her whole manner suggests something not quite of this world.*)

THE LADY (*her voice seems to float, too*): My name is Harriet Stanley. I know you are Sheridan Whiteside. I saw this holly, framed green against the pine trees. I remembered what you had written, about *Tess* and *Jude the Obscure.* It was the nicest present I could bring you. (*She places the holly in his lap, and drifts out of the room again.*)

WHITESIDE (*his eyes following her*): For God's sake, what was that?

MAGGIE: That was Mr. Stanley's sister, Harriet. I've talked to her a few times—she's quite strange.

WHITESIDE: Strange? She's right out of *The Hound of the Baskervilles*. . . . You know, I've seen that face before somewhere.

MAGGIE: Nonsense. You couldn't have.

WHITESIDE (*dismissing it*): Oh, well! Let's get down to work. (*He hands her the armful of holly*.) Here! Press this in the doctor's book. (*He picks up the first of a pile of papers*.) If young men keep asking me how to become dramatic critics—(*He tears up the letter and drops the pieces on the floor*.)

MAGGIE (*who has picked up the little sheaf of messages from the table*): Here are some telegrams.

WHITESIDE (*a letter in his hand*): What date is this?

MAGGIE: December tenth.

WHITESIDE: Send a wire to Columbia Broadcasting. "You can schedule my Christmas Eve broadcast from the New York studio, as I shall return East instead of proceeding to Hollywood. Stop. For special New Year's Eve broadcast will have as my guests Jascha Heifetz, Katharine Cornell, Schiaparelli, the Lunts, and Dr. Alexis Carrel, with Anthony Eden on short wave from England. Whiteside."

MAGGIE: Are you sure you'll be all right by Christmas, Sherry?

WHITESIDE: Of course I will. Send a cable to Sacha Guitry: "Will be in Paris June ninth. Dinner seven-thirty. Whiteside." . . . Wire to *Harper's Magazine:* "Do not worry, Stinky. Copy will arrive. Whiteside." . . . Send a cable to the Maharajah of Jehraput, Bombay: "Dear Boo-Boo: Schedule changed. Can you meet me Calcutta July twelfth? Dinner eight-thirty. Whiteside." . . . Arturo Toscanini. Where *is* he?

MAGGIE: I'll find him.

WHITESIDE: "Counting on you January 4th Metropolitan Opera House my annual benefit Home for Paroled Convicts. As you know this is a very worthy cause and close to my heart. Tibbett, Rethberg, Martinelli and Flagstad have promised me personally to appear. Will you have quiet supper with me and Ethel Barrymore afterwards? Whiteside." (*The telephone rings*.) If that's for Mrs. Stanley tell them she's too drunk to talk.

MAGGIE: Hello . . . Hollywood?

WHITESIDE: If it's Goldwyn, hang up.

MAGGIE: Hello . . . Banjo! (*Her face lights up.*)

WHITESIDE: Banjo! Give me that phone!

MAGGIE: Banjo, you old so-and-so! How are you, darling?

WHITESIDE: Come on—give me that!

MAGGIE: Shut up, Sherry! . . . Are you coming East, Banjo? I miss you . . . No, we're not going to Hollywood . . . Oh, he's going to live.

WHITESIDE: Stop driveling and give me the phone.

MAGGIE: In fact, he's screaming at me now. Here he is.

WHITESIDE (*taking the phone*): How are you, you fawn's behind? And what are you giving me for Christmas? (*He roars with laughter at* BANJO'S *answer.*) What news, Banjo, my boy? How's the picture coming? . . . How are Wacko and Sloppo? . . . No, no, I'm all right. . . . Yes, I'm in very good hands. Dr. Crippen is taking care of me. . . . What about you? Having any fun? . . . Playing any crib-bage? . . . What? (*Again he laughs loudly.*) . . . Well, don't take all his money—leave a little bit for me . . . You're what? . . . Having your portrait painted? By whom? Milt Gross? . . . No, I'm going back to New York from here. I'll be there for twelve days, and then I go to Dartmouth for the Drama Festival. You wouldn't understand . . . Well, I can't waste my time talking to Hollywood riffraff. Kiss Louella Parsons for me. Good-bye. (*He hangs up and turns to* MAGGIE.) He took fourteen hundred dollars from Sam Goldwyn at cribbage last night, and Sam said, "Banjo, I will never play garbage with you again."

MAGGIE: What's all this about his having his portrait painted?

WHITESIDE: Mm. Salvador Dali. That's all that face of his needs—a surrealist to paint it. . . . Now what do *you* want, Miss Bed Pan?

(*This is addressed to the* NURSE, *who has returned somewhat apprehensively to the room.*)

MISS PREEN: It's—it's your pills. One every—forty-five minutes. (*She drops them into his lap and hurries out of the room.*)

WHITESIDE: Now where were we?

MAGGIE (*the messages in her hand*): Here's a cable from that dear friend of yours, Lorraine Sheldon.

WHITESIDE: Let me see it.

MAGGIE (*reading the message in a tone that gives* MISS SHELDON *none the better of it*): "Sherry, my poor sweet lamb, have been in Scotland on a shooting party with Lord and Lady Cunard and only just heard of your poor hip." (MAGGIE *gives a faint raspberry, then reads on.*) "Am down here in Surrey with Lord Bottomley. Sailing Wednesday on the *Normandie* and cannot wait to see my poor sweet Sherry. Your blossom girl, Lorraine." . . . In the words of the master, I may vomit.

WHITESIDE: Don't be bitter, Puss, just because Lorraine is more beautiful than you are.

MAGGIE: Lorraine Sheldon is a very fair example of that small but vicious circle you move in.

WHITESIDE: Pure sex jealousy if ever I saw it . . . Give me the rest of those.

MAGGIE (*mumbling to herself*): Lorraine Sheldon . . . Lord Bottomley . . . My Aunt Fanny.

WHITESIDE (*who has opened the next message*): Ah! It's from Destiny's Tot.

MAGGIE (*peering over his shoulder*): England's little Rover Boy?

WHITESIDE: Um-hm. (*He reads.*) "Treacle Face, what is this I hear about a hip fractured in some bordello brawl? Does this mean our Hollywood Christmas party is off? Finished the new play in Pago-Pago and it's superb. Myself and a ukulele leave Honolulu tomorrow, in that order. By the way, the Sultan of Zanzibar wants to meet Ginger Rogers. Let's face it. Oscar Wilde."

MAGGIE: He does travel, doesn't he? You know, it'd be nice if the world went around Beverly Carlton for a change.

WHITESIDE: Hollywood next week—why couldn't he stop over on his way to New York? Send him a cable: "Beverly Carlton, Royal Hawaiian Hotel, Honolulu—" (*The doorbell rings.* MR. WHITESIDE *is properly annoyed.*) If these people intend to have their friends using the front door—

MAGGIE: What do you want them to use—a rope ladder?

WHITESIDE: I will not have a lot of mildewed pus-bags rushing in and out of this house—

(*He stops as the voice of* JOHN *is heard at the front door.* "Oh, good morning, Mr. Jefferson." *The answering voice of* MR JEFFERSON *is not quite audible.*)

WHITESIDE (*roaring*): There's nobody home! The Stanleys have been arrested for counterfeiting! Go away!

(*But the visitor, meanwhile, has already appeared in the archway.* MR. JEFFERSON *is an interesting-looking young man in his early thirties.*)

JEFFERSON: Good morning, Mr. Whiteside. I'm Jefferson, of the Mesalia *Journal.*

WHITESIDE (*sotto voce, to* MAGGIE): Get rid of him.

MAGGIE (*brusquely*): I'm sorry—Mr. Whiteside is seeing no one.

JEFFERSON: Really?

MAGGIE: So will you please excuse us? Good day.

JEFFERSON (*not giving up*): Mr. Whiteside seems to be sitting up and taking notice.

MAGGIE: I'm afraid he isn't taking notice of the Mesalia *Journal.* Do you mind?

JEFFERSON: You know, if I'm going to be insulted I'd like it to be by Mr. Whiteside himself. I never did like road companies.

WHITESIDE (*looking around, interested*): Mm. Touché if I ever heard one. And in Mesalia too, Maggie dear.

MAGGIE (*still on the job*): Will you please leave?

JEFFERSON (*ignoring her*): How about an interview, Mr. Whiteside?

WHITESIDE: I never give them. Go away.

JEFFERSON: Mr. Whiteside, if I don't get this interview, I lose my job.

WHITESIDE: That would be quite all right with me.

JEFFERSON: Now you don't mean that, Mr. Whiteside. You used to be a newspaper man yourself. You know what editors are like. Well, mine's the toughest one that ever lived.

WHITESIDE: You won't get around me that way. If you don't like him, get off the paper.

JEFFERSON: Yes, but I happen to think it's a good paper. William Allen White could have got out of Emporia, but he didn't.

WHITESIDE: You have the effrontery, in my presence, to compare yourself with William Allen White?

JEFFERSON: Only in the sense that William Allen White stayed in Emporia, and I want to stay here and say what I want to say.

WHITESIDE: Such as what?

JEFFERSON: Well, I can't put it into words, Mr. Whiteside—it'd sound like an awful lot of hooey. But the *Journal* was my father's paper. It's kind of a sentimental point with me, the paper. I'd like to carry on where he left off.

WHITESIDE: Ah—just a minute. Then this terrifying editor, this dread journalistic Apocalypse is—you?

JEFFERSON: Ah—yes, in a word. (WHITESIDE *chuckles with appreciation.*)

MAGGIE (*annoyed*): In the future, Sherry, I wish you would let me know when you don't want to talk to people. I'll usher them right in. (*She goes into the library.*)

WHITESIDE: Young man, that kind of journalist trick went out with Richard Harding Davis . . . Come over here. I suppose you've written that novel?

JEFFERSON: No, I've written that play.

WHITESIDE: Well, I don't want to read it. But you can send me your paper—I'll take a year's subscription. Do you write the editorials, too?

JEFFERSON: Every one of them.

WHITESIDE: I know just what they're like. Ah, me! I'm afraid you're that noble young newspaper man—crusading, idealistic, dull. (*He looks him up and down.*) Very good casting, too.

JEFFERSON: You're not bad casting yourself, Mr. Whiteside.

WHITESIDE: We won't discuss it. . . . Do these old eyes see a box of goodies over there? Hand them to me on your way out.

JEFFERSON (*as he passes over the candy*): The trouble is, Mr. Whiteside, that your being in this town comes under the heading of news. Practically the biggest news since the Armistice.

WHITESIDE (*examining the candy*): Mm. Pecan butternut fudge.

(MISS PREEN, *on her way to the kitchen from the library, stops short as she sees* MR. WHITESIDE *with a piece of candy in his hand.*)

MISS PREEN: Oh, my! You mustn't eat candy, Mr. Whiteside. It's very bad for you.

WHITESIDE (*turning*): My great-aunt Jennifer ate a whole box of candy every day of her life. She lived to be a hundred and two, and when she had been dead three days she looked better than you do now. (*He swings blandly back to his visitor.*) What were you saying, old fellow?

JEFFERSON (*as* MISS PREEN *makes a hasty exit*): I can at least report to my readers that chivalry is not yet dead.

WHITESIDE: We won't discuss it. . . . Well, now that you have won me with your pretty ways, what do you want?

JEFFERSON: Well, how about a brief talk on famous murders? You're an authority on murder as a fine art.

WHITESIDE: My dear boy, when I talk about murder I get paid for it. I have made more money out of the Snyder-Gray case than the lawyers did. So don't expect to get it for nothing.

JEFFERSON: Well, then, what do you think of Mesalia, how long are you going to be here, where are you going, things like that?

WHITESIDE: Very well. (a) Mesalia is a town of irresistible charm, (b) I cannot wait to get out of it, and (c) I am going from here to Crockfield, for my semi-annual visit to the Crockfield Home for Paroled Convicts, for which I have raised over half a million dollars in the last five years. From there I go to New York. . . . Have you ever been to Crockfield, Jefferson?

JEFFERSON: No, I haven't. I always meant to.

WHITESIDE: As a newspaper man you ought to go, instead of wasting your time with me. It's only about seventy-five miles from here. Did you ever hear how Crockfield started?

JEFFERSON: No, I didn't.

WHITESIDE: Ah! Sit down, Jefferson. It is one of the most endearing and touching stories of our generation. One misty St. Valentine's Eve —the year was 1901—a little old lady who had given her name to an era, Victoria, lay dying in Windsor Castle. Maude Adams had not yet caused every young heart to swell as she tripped across the stage as Peter Pan; Irving Berlin had not yet written the first note of a ragtime rigadoon that was to set the nation's feet a-tapping, and Elias P. Crockfield was just emerging from the State penitentiary. Destitute, embittered, cruel of heart, he wandered, on this St. Valentine's Eve, into a little church. But there was no godliness in his heart that night, no prayer upon his lips. In the faltering twilight, Elias P. Crockfield made his way toward the poor box. With callous fingers he ripped open this poignant testimony of a simple people's faith. Greedily he clutched at the few pitiful coins within. And then a child's wavering treble broke the twilight stillness. "Please, Mr. Man," said a little girl's voice, "won't you be my Valentine?" Elias P. Crockfield turned. There stood before him a bewitching little creature of five, her yellow curls cascading over her shoulders like a golden Niagara, in her tiny outstretched hand a humble valentine. In that one crystal moment a sealed door opened in the heart of Elias P. Crockfield, and in his mind was born an idea. Twenty-five years later three thousand ruddy-cheeked convicts were gamboling on the broad lawns of Crockfield Home, frolicking in the cool depths of its swimming pool, broadcasting with their own symphony orchestra from their own radio station. Elias P. Crockfield has long since gone to his Maker, but the little girl of the golden curls, now grown to lovely womanhood, is known as the Angel of Crockfield, for she is the wife of the warden, and in the main hall of Crockfield, between a Rembrandt and an El Greco, there hangs, in a simple little frame, a humble valentine.

MAGGIE (*who has emerged from the library in time to hear the finish of this*): And in the men's washroom, every Christmas Eve, the ghost of Elias P. Crockfield appears in one of the booths . . . Will you sign these, please?

(*The doorbell is heard.*)

WHITESIDE: This aging ingénue, Mr. Jefferson, I retain in my employ only because she is the sole support of her two-headed brother.

JEFFERSON: I understand. . . . Well, thank you very much, Mr. Whiteside—you've been very kind. By the way, I'm a cribbage player, if you need one while you're here.

WHITESIDE: Fine. How much can you afford to lose?

JEFFERSON: I usually win.

WHITESIDE: We won't discuss that. Come back at eight-thirty. We'll play three-handed with Elsie Dinsmore . . . Metz!

(JOHN, *who has answered the doorbell, has ushered in a strange-looking little man in his fifties. His hair runs all over his head and his clothes are too big for him.*)

WHITESIDE: Metz, you incredible beetle-hound! What are you doing here?

METZ (*with a mild Teutonic accent*): I explain, Sherry. First I kiss my little Maggie.

MAGGIE (*embracing him*): Metz darling, what a wonderful surprise!

WHITESIDE: The enchanted Metz! Why aren't you at the university? . . . Jefferson, you are standing in the presence of one of the great men of our time. When you write that inevitable autobiography, be sure to record the day that you met Professor Adolph Metz, the world's greatest authority on insect life. Metz, stop looking at me adoringly and tell me why you're here.

METZ: You are sick, Sherry, so I come to cheer you.

MAGGIE: Metz, you tore yourself away from your little insects and came here? Sherry, you don't deserve it.

WHITESIDE: How are all your little darlings, Metz? Jefferson, would you believe that eight volumes could be written on the mating instinct of the female white ant? He did it.

METZ: Seven on the female, Sherry. One on the male.

WHITESIDE: Lived for two years in a cave with nothing but plant lice. He rates three pages in the *Encyclopaedia Britannica*. Don't you, my little hookworm?

METZ: Please, Sherry, you embarrass me. Look—I have brought you a present to while away the hours. (*He motions to* JOHN, *who comes forward bearing a great box, wrapped in brown paper. He unwraps it as he speaks.*)

METZ: I said to my students: "Boys and girls, I want to give a present to my sick friend, Sheridan Whiteside." So you know what we did? We made for you a community of *Periplaneta Americana,* commonly known as the American cockroach. Behold, Sherry! (*He strips off the paper.*) Roach City! Inside here are ten thousand cockroaches.

JOHN: Ten thousand—(*Heading for the kitchen in great excitement.*) Sarah! Sarah!

METZ: Here in Roach City they play, they make love, they mate, they die. See—here is the graveyard. They even bury their own dead.

MAGGIE: I'm glad of that, or I'd have to do it.

WHITESIDE (*glaring at her*): Ssh!

METZ: You can watch them, Sherry, while they live out their whole lives. It is fascinating. Look! Here is where they store their grain, here is the commissary of the aristocracy, here is the maternity hospital.

WHITESIDE: Magnificent! This is my next piece for the London *Mercury.*

METZ: With these earphones, Sherry, you listen to the mating calls. There are microphones down inside. Listen! (*He puts the earphones over* WHITESIDE'S *head.*)

WHITESIDE (*listening, rapt*): Mm. How long has this been going on?

(MRS. STANLEY *starts timorously to descend the stairs. She tiptoes as far as the landing, then pauses as she sees the group below.*)

(*Meanwhile* PROF. METZ, *his mind on his work, has moved in the direction of the dining room.*)

METZ (*suddenly his face lights up*): Aha! *Periplaneta Americana!* There are cockroaches in this house!

MRS. STANLEY (*shocked into speech*): I beg your pardon! (*The doorbell rings.*) Mr. Whiteside, I don't know who this man is, but I will not stand here and—

WHITESIDE: Then go upstairs. These are probably my luncheon guests. Metz, you're staying for the day, of course? Jefferson, stay for lunch? Maggie, tell 'em there'll be two more. Ah, come right in, Baker. Good morning, gentlemen. (*The gentlemen addressed are three in number—two white, one black. They are convicts, and they look the part. Prison gray, handcuffed together.* BAKER, *in uniform, is a prison guard. He carries a rifle.*) Jefferson, here are the fruits of that humble valentine. These men, now serving the final months of their prison terms, have chosen to enter the ivy-covered walls of Crockfield. They have come here today to learn from me a little of its tradition . . . Gentlemen, I envy you your great adventure.

JOHN (*in the dining-room doorway*): Lunch is ready, Mr. Whiteside.

WHITESIDE: Good! Let's go right in. (*To one of the convicts, as they pass.*) You're Michaelson, aren't you? Butcher-shop murders?

MICHAELSON: Yes, sir.

WHITESIDE: Thought I recognized you. . . . After you, Baker. . . . The other fellow, Jefferson—(*He lowers his tone.*)—is Henderson, the hatchet fiend. Always did it in a bathtub—remember? (*His voice rises as he wheels himself into the dining room.*) We're having chicken livers Tetrazzini, and Cherries Jubilee for dessert. I hope every little tummy is a-flutter with gastric juices. Serve the white wine with the fish, John, and close the doors. I don't want a lot of people prying on their betters.

(*The doors close. Only* MRS. STANLEY *is left outside. She collapses quietly into a chair.*)

THE CURTAIN FALLS

SCENE II

SCENE—*Late afternoon, a week later. Only a single lamp is lit. The room, in the week that has passed, has taken on something of the character of its occupant. Books and papers everywhere. Stacks of books on the tables, some of them just half*

out of their cardboard boxes. Half a dozen or so volumes,
which apparently have not appealed to the Master, have been
thrown onto the floor. A litter of crumpled papers around the
WHITESIDE *wheelchair; an empty candy box has slid off his lap.*
An old pair of pants have been tossed over one chair, a seedy
bathrobe over another. A handsome Chinese vase has been
moved out of its accustomed spot and is doing duty as an ash
receiver.

MR. WHITESIDE *is in his wheelchair, asleep. Roach City is on*
a stand beside him, the earphones, over his head. He has ap-
parently dozed off while listening to the mating calls of
Periplaneta Americana.

For a moment only his rhythmic breathing is heard. Then
MISS PREEN *enters from the library. She brings some medicine*
—a glass filled with a murky mixture. She pauses when she sees
that he is asleep, then, after a good deal of hesitation, gently
touches him on the shoulder. He stirs a little; she musters up
her courage and touches him again.

WHITESIDE (*slowly opening his eyes*): I was dreaming of Lillian Rus-
sell, and I wake to find *you.*

MISS PREEN: Your—your medicine, Mr. Whiteside.

WHITESIDE (*taking the glass*): What time is it?

MISS PREEN: About half-past six.

WHITESIDE: Where is Miss Cutler?

MISS PREEN: She went out.

WHITESIDE: Out?

MISS PREEN: With Mr. Jefferson. (*She goes into the library.*) (JOHN,
meanwhile, has entered from the dining room.)

JOHN: All right if I turn the lights up, Mr. Whiteside?

WHITESIDE: Yes. Go right ahead, John.

JOHN: And Sarah has something for you, Mr. Whiteside. Made it special.

WHITESIDE: She has? Where is she? My Soufflé Queen!

SARAH (*proudly entering with a tray on which reposes her latest delicacy*): Here I am, Mr. Whiteside.

WHITESIDE: She walks in beauty like the night, and in those deft hands
there is the art of Michelangelo. Let me taste the new creation. (*With*

one hand he pours the medicine into the Chinese vase, then swallows at a gulp one of SARAH'S *not so little cakes. An ecstatic expression comes over his face.*) Poetry! Sheer poetry!

SARAH (*beaming*): I put a touch of absinthe in the dough. Do you like it?

WHITESIDE (*rapturously*): Ambrosia!

SARAH: And I got you your terrapin Maryland for dinner.

WHITESIDE: I have known but three great cooks in my time. The Khedive of Egypt had one, my great-aunt Jennifer another, and the third, Sarah, is you.

SARAH: Oh, Mr. Whiteside!

WHITESIDE (*lowering his voice*): How would you like to come to New York and work for me? You and John.

SARAH: Why, Mr. Whiteside!

JOHN: Sarah! . . . It would be wonderful, Mr. Whiteside, but what would we say to Mr. and Mrs. Stanley?

WHITESIDE: Just "good-bye."

SARAH: But—but they'd be awfully mad, wouldn't they? They've been very kind to us.

WHITESIDE (*lightly*): Well, if they ever come to New York we can have them for dinner, if I'm not in town. Now run along and think it over. This is our little secret—just between us. And put plenty of sherry in that terrapin . . . Miss Preen! (SARAH *and* JOHN *withdraw in considerable excitement.* WHITESIDE *raises his voice to a roar.*) Miss Preen!

MISS PREEN (*appearing, breathless*): Yes? Yes?

WHITESIDE: What have you *got* in there, anyway? A sailor?

MISS PREEN: I was—just washing my hands.

WHITESIDE: What time did Miss Cutler go out?

MISS PREEN: A couple of hours ago.

WHITESIDE: Mr. Jefferson called for her?

MISS PREEN: Yes, sir.

WHITESIDE (*impatiently*): All right, all right. Go back to your sex life.

(MISS PREEN *goes.* WHITESIDE *tries to settle down to his book, but his mind is plainly troubled. He shifts a little, looks anxiously toward the outer door.*)

(HARRIET STANLEY *comes softly down the steps. She seems delighted to find* MR. WHITESIDE *alone.*)

HARRIET (*opening an album that she has brought with her*): Dear Mr. Whiteside, may I show you a few mementoes of the past? I somehow feel that you would love them as I do.

WHITESIDE: I'd be delighted. (*Observing her.*) Miss Stanley, haven't we met somewhere before?

HARRIET: Oh, no. I would have remembered. It would have been one of my cherished memories—like these. (*She spreads the portfolio before him.*) Look! Here I am with my first sweetheart, under our lovely beechwood tree. I was eight and he was ten. I have never forgotten him. What happy times we had! What—(*She stops short as she hears footsteps on the stairway.*) There's someone coming! I'll come back! . . . (*She gathers up her album and vanishes into the dining room.*)

   (WHITESIDE *looks after her, puzzled.*)
   (*It is* MR. STANLEY *who comes down the stairs. He is carrying a slip of paper in his hand, and he is obviously at the boiling point.*)
   (*A few steps behind comes* MRS. STANLEY, *apprehensive and nervous.*)

MRS. STANLEY: Now, Ernest, please—

STANLEY: Be quiet, Daisy. . . . Mr. Whiteside, I want to talk to you. I don't care whether you're busy or not. I have stood all that I'm going to stand.

WHITESIDE: Indeed?

STANLEY: This is the last straw. I have just received a bill from the telephone company for seven hundred and eighty-four dollars. (*He reads from the slip in his hand.*) Oklahoma City, Calcutta, Hollywood, Paris, Brussels, Rome, New York, New York, New York, New York, New York, New York— (*His voice trails off in an endless succession of New Yorks.*) Now I realize, Mr. Whiteside, that you are a distinguished man of letters—

MRS. STANLEY: Yes, of course. We both do.

STANLEY: Please . . . But in the past week we have not been able to call our souls our own. We have not had a meal in the dining room *once*. I have to tiptoe out of the house in the mornings.

MRS. STANLEY: Now, Ernest—

STANLEY (*waving her away*): I come home to find convicts sitting at my dinner table—butcher-shop murderers. A man putting cockroaches in the kitchen.

MRS. STANLEY: They just escaped, Ernest.

STANLEY: That's not the point. I don't like coming home to find twenty-two Chinese students using my bathroom. I tell you I won't stand for it, no matter *who* you are.

WHITESIDE: Have you quite finished?

STANLEY: No, I have not. I go down into the cellar this morning and trip over that octopus that William Beebe sent you. I tell you I won't stand for it. Mr. Whiteside, I want you to leave this house as soon as you can and go to a hotel. . . . Stop pawing me, Daisy. . . . That's all I've got to say, Mr. Whiteside.

WHITESIDE: And quite enough, I should say. May I remind you again, Mr. Stanley, that I am not a willing guest in this house? I am informed by my doctor that I must remain quiet for another ten days, at which time I shall get out of here so fast that the wind will knock you over, I hope. If, however, you insist on my leaving before that, thereby causing me to suffer a relapse, I shall sue you for every additional day that I am held inactive, which will amount, I assure you, to a tidy sum.

STANLEY (*to his wife*): This is outrageous. Do we have to—

WHITESIDE: As for the details of your petty complaints, those twenty-two Chinese students came straight from the White House, where I assure you they used the bathroom too.

MRS. STANLEY: Mr. Whiteside, my husband didn't mean—

STANLEY: Yes, I did. I meant every word of it.

WHITESIDE: There is only one point that you make in which I see some slight justice. I do not expect you to pay for my telephone calls, and I shall see to it that restitution is made. Can you provide me with the exact amount?

STANLEY: I certainly can, and I certainly will.

WHITESIDE: Good. I shall instruct my lawyers to deduct it from the hundred and fifty thousand dollars that I am suing you for.

(MR. STANLEY *starts to speak, but simply chokes with rage. Furious, he storms up the steps again,* MRS. STANLEY *following.*)

WHITESIDE (*calling after him*): And I'll thank you not to trip over that octopus, which is very sensitive.

(*Left alone,* MR. WHITESIDE *enjoys his triumph for a moment, then his mind jumps to more important matters. He looks at his watch, considers a second, then wheels himself over to the telephone.*)

WHITESIDE: Give me the Mesalia *Journal,* please. (*He peers at Roach City while waiting.*) Hello, *Journal?* . . . Is Mr. Jefferson there? . . . When do you expect him? . . . No. No message. (*He hangs up, drums impatiently on the arm of his chair. Then he turns sharply at the sound of the outer door opening. But it is the younger* STANLEYS, RICHARD *and* JUNE, *who enter. They are in winter togs, with ice skates under their arms. In addition,* RICHARD *has a camera slung over his shoulder.*)

(*Their attitudes change as they see that* WHITESIDE *is in the room. They slide toward the stairs, obviously trying to be as unobtrusive as possible.*)

WHITESIDE: Come here, you two. . . . Come on, come on. I'm not going to bite you. . . . Now look here. I am by nature a gracious and charming person. If I err at all it is on the side of kindness and amiability. I have been observing you two for this past week, and you seem to me to be extremely likeable young people. I am afraid that when we first met I was definitely unpleasant to you. For that I am sorry, and I wish that in the future you would not treat me like something out of Edgar Allan Poe. How do you like my new tie?

JUNE: Thank you, Mr. Whiteside. This makes things much pleasanter. And I think the tie is very pretty.

RICHARD: Well, now that we're on speaking terms, Mr. Whiteside, I don't mind telling you that I have been admiring all your ties.

WHITESIDE: Do you like this one?

RICHARD: I certainly do.

WHITESIDE: It's yours. (*He takes it off and tosses it to him.*) Really, this curious legend that I am a difficult person is pure fabrication. . . . Ice-skating, eh? Ah, me! I used to cut figure eights myself, arm in arm with Betsy Ross, waving the flag behind us.

JUNE: It was wonderful on the ice today. Miss Cutler and Mr. Jefferson were there.

WHITESIDE: Maggie? Skating?

RICHARD: Yes, and she's good, too. I got a marvelous picture of her.

WHITESIDE: Were they still there when you left?

RICHARD: I think so. Say, Mr. Whiteside, mind if I take a picture of you? I'd love to have one.

WHITESIDE: Very well. Do you want my profile? (*He indicates his stomach.*)

JUNE (*starting up the stairs*): I'm afraid you're done for, Mr. White-side. My brother is a camera fiend.

RICHARD (*clicking his camera*): Thank you, Mr. Whiteside. I got a great one. (*He and* JUNE *go up the stairs as* MAGGIE *enters from the hallway. They call a "Hello, Miss Cutler!" as they disappear.*)

MAGGIE: Hello, there. . . . Good evening, Sherry. Really Sherry, you've got this room looking like an old parrot-cage. . . . Did you nap while I was out? (WHITESIDE *merely glowers at her.*) What's the matter, dear? Cat run away with your tongue? (*She is on her knees, gathering up debris.*)

WHITESIDE (*furious*): Don't look up at me with those great cow-eyes, you sex-ridden hag. Where have you been all afternoon? Alley-catting around with Bert Jefferson?

MAGGIE (*her face aglow*): Sherry—Bert read his play to me this afternoon. It's superb. It isn't just that play written by a newspaper man. It's superb. I want you to read it *tonight*. (*She puts it in his lap.*) It just cries out for Cornell. If you like it, will you send it to her, Sherry? And will you read it tonight?

WHITESIDE: No, I will not read it tonight or any other time. And while we're on the subject of Mr. Jefferson, you might ask him if he wouldn't like to pay your salary, since he takes up all your time.

MAGGIE: Oh, come now, Sherry. It isn't as bad as that.

WHITESIDE: I have not even been able to reach you, not knowing what haylofts you frequent.

MAGGIE: Oh, stop behaving like a spoiled child, Sherry.

WHITESIDE: Don't take that patronizing tone with me, you flea-bitten Cleopatra. I am sick and tired of your sneaking out like some lovesick high-school girl every time my back is turned.

MAGGIE: Well, Sherry—(*She pulls together the library doors and faces* WHITESIDE.)—I'm afraid you've hit the nail on the head. (*With a little flourish, she removes her hat.*)

WHITESIDE: Stop acting like Zasu Pitts and explain yourself.

MAGGIE: I'll make it quick, Sherry. I'm in love.

WHITESIDE: Nonsense. This is merely delayed puberty.

MAGGIE: No, Sherry, I'm afraid this is it. You're going to lose a very excellent secretary.

WHITESIDE: You are out of your mind.

MAGGIE: Yes, I think I am, a little. But I'm a girl who's waited a long time for this to happen, and now it has. Mr. Jefferson doesn't know it yet, but I'm going to try my darnedest to marry him.

WHITESIDE (*as she pauses*): Is that all?

MAGGIE: Yes, except that—well—I suppose this is what might be called my resignation—as soon as you've got someone else.

WHITESIDE (*there is a slight pause*): Now listen to me, Maggie. We have been together for a long time. You are indispensable to me, but I think I am unselfish enough not to let that stand in the way where your happiness is concerned. Because, whether you know it or not, I have a deep affection for you.

MAGGIE: I know that, Sherry.

WHITESIDE: That being the case, I will not stand by and allow you to make a fool of yourself.

MAGGIE: I'm not, Sherry.

WHITESIDE: You are, my dear. You are behaving like a Booth Tarkington heroine. It's—it's incredible. I cannot believe that a girl who for the past ten years has had the great of the world served up on a platter before her—I cannot believe that it is anything but a kind of temporary insanity when you are swept off your feet in seven days by a second-rate, small-town newspaper man.

MAGGIE: Sherry, I can't explain what's happened. I can only tell you that it's so. It's hard for me to believe too, Sherry. Here I am, a hardbitten old cynic, behaving like *True Story Magazine,* and liking it. Discovering the moon, and ice-skating—I keep laughing to myself all the time, but there it is. What can I do about it, Sherry? I'm in love.

WHITESIDE (*with sudden decision*): We're leaving here tomorrow. Hip or no hip, we're leaving here tomorrow. I don't care if I fracture the other one. Get me a train schedule and start packing. *I*'ll pull you out of this, Miss Stardust. *I*'ll get the ants out of those moonlit pants.

MAGGIE: It's no good, Sherry. I'd be back on the next streamlined train.

WHITESIDE: It's completely unbelievable. Can you see yourself, the wife of the editor of the Mesalia *Journal,* having an evening at home for Mr. and Mrs. Stanley, Mr. and Mrs. Poop-Face, and the members of the Book-of-the-Month Club?

MAGGIE: Sherry, I've had ten years of the great figures of our time, and don't think I'm not grateful to you for it. I've loved every minute of it. They've been wonderful years, Sherry. Gay and stimulating—why, I don't think anyone has ever had the fun we've had. But a girl can't laugh all the time, Sherry. There comes a time when she wants—Bert

Jefferson. You don't know Bert, Sherry. He's gentle, and he's unassuming, and—well, I love him, that's all.

WHITESIDE: I see. Well, I remain completely unconvinced. You are drugging yourself into this Joan Crawford fantasy, and before you become completely anesthetized I shall do everything in my power to bring you to your senses.

MAGGIE (*wheeling on him*): Now listen to me, Whiteside. I know you. Lay off. I know what a devil you can be. I've seen you do it to other people, but don't you dare to do it to me. Don't drug *yourself* into the idea that all you're thinking of is my happiness. You're thinking of yourself a little bit, too, and all those months of breaking in somebody new. I've seen you in a passion before when your life has been disrupted, and you couldn't dine in Calcutta on July twelfth with Boo-Boo. Well, that's too bad, but there it is. I'm going to marry Bert if he'll have me, and don't you dare try any of your tricks. I'm on to every one of them. So lay off. That's my message to *you*, Big Lord Fauntleroy. (*And she is up the stairs.*)

(*Left stewing in his own juice,* MR. WHITESIDE *is in a perfect fury. He bangs the arm of his chair, then slaps at the manuscript in his lap. As he does so, the dawn of an idea comes into his mind. He sits perfectly still for a moment, thinking it over. Then, with a slow smile, he takes the manuscript out of its envelope.*

He looks at the title page, ruffles through the script, then stops and thinks again. His face breaks out into one great smile. Then he quickly wheels himself over to the table and hunts hurriedly through a pile of old cablegrams and letters, until he finds the one he wants. With this in his hand, he takes up the telephone receiver.)

WHITESIDE (*in a lowered voice*): Long distance, please. I want to put in a trans-Atlantic call. (*He looks at the cablegram again for confirmation.*) Hello. Trans-Atlantic operator? . . . This is Mesalia one four two. I want to talk to Miss Lorraine Sheldon—S-h-e-l-d-o-n. She's on the *Normandie*. It sailed from Southampton day before yesterday. . . . Will it take long? . . . All right. My name is Whiteside. . . . Thank you. (*He hangs up as the doorbell rings. He goes back to the manuscript again and looks through it.* JOHN *then ushers in* DR. BRADLEY.)

DR. BRADLEY (*hearty, as usual*): Well, well! Good Evening, Mr. Whiteside!

WHITESIDE: Come back tomorrow—I'm busy.

DR. BRADLEY (*turning cute*): Now what would be the best news that I could possibly bring you?

WHITESIDE: You have hydrophobia.

DR. BRADLEY (*laughing it off*): No, no. . . . Mr. Whiteside, you are a well man. You can get up and walk *now*. You can leave here tomorrow.

WHITESIDE: What do you mean?

DR. BRADLEY: Well sir! I looked at those X-rays again this morning, and do you know what? I had been looking at the wrong X-rays. I had been looking at old Mrs. Moffat's X-rays. You are perfectly, absolutely well!

WHITESIDE: Lower your voice, will you?

DR. BRADLEY: What's the matter? Aren't you pleased?

WHITESIDE: Delighted. . . . Naturally. . . . Ah—this is a very unexpected bit of news, however. It comes at a very curious moment. (*He is thinking fast; suddenly he gets an idea. He clears his throat and looks around apprehensively.*) Dr. Bradley, I—ah—I have some good news for you, too. I have been reading your book—ah—*Forty Years*—what is it?

DR. BRADLEY (*eagerly*): *An Ohio Doctor*—yes?

WHITESIDE: I consider it extremely close to being one of the great literary contributions of our time.

DR. BRADLEY: Mr. Whiteside!

WHITESIDE: So strongly do I feel about it, Dr. Bradley, that I have a proposition to make to you. Just here and there the book is a little uneven, a little rough. What I would like to do is to stay here in Mesalia and work with you on it.

DR. BRADLEY (*all choked up*): Mr. Whiteside, I would be so terribly honored—

WHITESIDE: Yes. But there is just one difficulty. You see, if my lecture bureau and my radio sponsors were to learn that I am well, they would insist on my fulfilling my contracts, and I would be forced to leave Mesalia. Therefore, we must not tell anyone—not anyone at all —that I am well.

DR. BRADLEY: I see. I see.

WHITESIDE: Not even Miss Cutler, you understand.

DR. BRADLEY: No, I won't. Not a soul. Not even my wife.

WHITESIDE: That's fine.

DR. BRADLEY: When do we start work—tonight? I've got just one patient that's dying and then I'll be perfectly free.

(*The phone rings.*)

WHITESIDE (*waving him away*): Ah—tomorrow morning. This is a private call—would you forgive me? . . . Hello. . . . Yes, I'm on. (*He turns again to the* DOCTOR.) Tomorrow morning.

DR. BRADLEY: Tomorrow morning it is. Good night. You've made me very proud, Mr. Whiteside. (*He goes.*)

WHITESIDE (*again on the phone*): Yes, yes, this is Mr. Whiteside on the phone. Put them through. . . . Hello. Is this my Blossom Girl? How are you, my lovely? . . . No, no, I'm all right. . . . Yes, still out here. . . . Lorraine dear, when do you land in New York? . . . Tuesday? That's fine. . . . Now listen closely, my pet. I've great news for you. I've discovered a wonderful play with an enchanting part in it for you. Cornell would give her eye teeth to play it, but I think I can get it for you. . . . Now wait, wait. Let me tell you. The author is a young newspaper man in this town. Of course he wants Cornell, but if you jump on a train and get right out here, I think you could swing it, if you play your cards right. . . . No, he's young, and very attractive, and just your dish, my dear. It just takes a little doing, and you're the girl that can do it. Isn't that exciting, my pet? . . . Yes. . . . Yes, that's right. . . . And look. Don't send me any messages. Just get on a train and arrive. . . . Oh, no, don't thank me, my darling. It's perfectly all right. Have a nice trip and hurry out here. Good-bye, my blossom. (*He hangs up and looks guiltily around. Then he straightens up and gleefully rubs his hands together.*)

(MISS PREEN *enters, medicine in hand, and frightened, as usual.*)

WHITESIDE (*jovial as hell*): Hello, Miss Preen. My, you're looking radiant this evening.

MISS PREEN (*staggered*): What?

WHITESIDE: Nothing. Nothing at all. Just said you are ravishing. (*He takes the medicine from her and swallows it at one gulp.* MISS PREEN, *still staggered, retreats into the library, just as* MAGGIE *comes down the stairs. She is dressed for the street.*)

MAGGIE (*pausing on the landing*): Sherry, I'm sorry for what I said before. I'm afraid I was a little unjust.

WHITESIDE (*all nobility*): That's all right, Maggie dear. We all lose our tempers now and then.

MAGGIE: I promised to have dinner with Bert and go to a movie, but we'll come back and play cribbage with you instead.

WHITESIDE: Fine.

MAGGIE: See you soon, Sherry dear. (*She kisses him lightly on the forehead and goes on her way.*)

(WHITESIDE *looks after her until he hears the doors close. Then his face lights up again and he bursts happily into song as he wheels himself into the library.*)

WHITESIDE:

> "I'se des a 'ittle wabbit in the sunshine,
> I'se des a 'ittle wabbit in the wain—"

CURTAIN

ACT TWO

SCENE—*A week later, late afternoon.*

The room is now dominated by a large Christmas tree, set in the curve of the staircase, and hung with the customary Christmas ornaments.

SARAH *and* JOHN *are passing in and out of the library, bringing forth huge packages which they are placing under the tree.* MAGGIE *sits at a little table at one side, going through a pile of correspondence.*

JOHN: Well, I guess that's all there are, Miss Cutler. They're all under the tree.

MAGGIE: Thank you, John.

SARAH: My, I never saw anyone get so many Christmas presents. I can hardly wait to see what's in 'em.

JOHN: When'll Mr. Whiteside open them, Miss Cutler?

MAGGIE: Well, John, you see Christmas is Mr. Whiteside's personal property. He invented it and it belongs to him. First thing tomorrow morning, Mr. Whiteside will open each and every present, and there will be the damnedest fuss you ever saw.

SARAH (*bending over the packages*): My, look who he's got presents from! Shirley Temple, William Lyon Phelps, Billy Rose, Ethel Waters, Somerset Maugham—I can hardly wait for tonight.

(*The doorbell rings.* JOHN *departs for the door.*)

SARAH: My, it certainly is wonderful. And Mr. Whiteside's tree is so beautiful, too. Mr. and Mrs. Stanley had to put theirs in their bedroom, you know. They can hardly undress at night.

(*It is* BERT JEFFERSON *who enters.*)

BERT: Hello, Maggie. Merry Christmas, Sarah.

SARAH: Merry Christmas, Mr. Jefferson (*She and* JOHN *disappear into the dining room.*)

BERT (*observing the pile of packages under the tree*): Say, business is good, isn't it? My, what a little quiet blackmail and a weekly radio hour can get you. What did his sponsors give him?

MAGGIE: They gave him a full year's supply of their product, Cream of Mush.

BERT: Well, he'll give it right back to them over the air.

MAGGIE: Wait until you hear tonight's broadcast, old fellow. It's so sticky I haven't been able to get it off my fingers since I copied it.

BERT: I'll bet . . . Look, I'll come clean. Under the influence of God knows what I have just bought you a Christmas present.

MAGGIE (*surprised*): Why, Mr. Jefferson, sir.

BERT: Only I'd like you to see it before I throw away my hard-earned money. Can you run downtown with me and take a look at it?

MAGGIE: Bert, this is very sweet of you. I'm quite touched. What is it? I can't wait.

BERT: A two years' subscription to *Screen Romances*. . . . Listen, do you think I'm going to tell you? Come down and see.

MAGGIE (*she calls into the library*): Sherry! Sherry, I'm going out for a few minutes. With Horace Greeley. I won't be long. (*She goes into the hallway for her coat and hat.*)

BERT (*raising his voice*): Noël, Noël, Mr. W.! How about some cribbage after your broadcast tonight?

(*The* WHITESIDE *wheelchair is rolling into the room.*)

WHITESIDE: No, I will not play cribbage with you, Klondike Harry. You have been swindling the be-jesus out of me for two weeks. . . . Where are you off to now, Madame Butterfly?

MAGGIE: I'm being given a Christmas present. Anything you want done downtown?

WHITESIDE: 'Es. B'ing baby a lollipop. . . . What are *you* giving me for Christmas, Jefferson? I have enriched your feeble life beyond your capacity to repay me.

BERT: Yes, that's what I figured, so I'm not giving you anything.

WHITESIDE: I see. Well, I was giving you my old truss, but now I shan't. . . . Maggie, what time are those radio men coming?

MAGGIE: About six-thirty—I'll be here. You've got to cut, Sherry. You're four minutes over. Oh, by the way, there was a wire from Beverly. It's there somewhere. He doesn't know what train he can get out of Chicago, but he'll be here some time this evening.

WHITESIDE: Good! Is he staying overnight?

MAGGIE: No, he has to get right out again. He's sailing Friday on the *Queen Mary*.

BERT: Think I could peek in at the window and get a look at him? Beverly Carlton used to be one of my heroes.

WHITESIDE: Used to be, you ink-stained hack? Beverly Carlton is the greatest single talent in the English theatre today. Take this illiterate numbskull out of my sight, Maggie, and don't bring him back.

BERT: Yes, Mr. Whiteside, sir. I won't come back until Beverly Carlton gets here.

MAGGIE (*as they go on their way*): Where are we going, Bert? I want to know what you've bought me—I'm like a ten-year-old kid.

BERT (*laughing a little*): You know, you look like a ten-year-old kid right now, Maggie, at that. (*They are out of earshot by this time.*)

(WHITESIDE *looks after them intently, listens until the door closes. He considers for a second, then wheels himself over to the telephone.*)

WHITESIDE (*on the phone*): Will you give me the Mansion House, please? . . . No, I don't know the number. . . . Hello? Mansion House? . . . Tell me, has a Miss Lorraine Sheldon arrived yet? . . . Yes, that's right—Miss Lorraine Sheldon. From New York. . . . She hasn't, eh? Thank you. (*He hangs up, drums with his fingers on the chair arm, looks at his watch. He slaps his knees impatiently, stretches. Then, vexed at his self-imposed imprisonment, he looks cautiously around the room, peers up the stairs. Then, slowly, he gets out of his chair; standing beside it, he indulges in a few mild calisthenics, looking cautiously around all the while.*)

(*Then the sound of the library doors being opened sends him scurrying back to his chair. It is* MISS PREEN *who emerges.*)

WHITESIDE (*annoyed*): What do you want, coming in like that? Why don't you knock before you come into a room?

MISS PREEN: But—I wasn't coming in. I was coming out.

WHITESIDE: Miss Preen, you are obviously *in* this room. That is true, isn't it?

MISS PREEN: Yes, it is, but—

WHITESIDE: Therefore you came in. Hereafter, please knock.

(*Before* MISS PREEN *can reply, however,* JOHN *enters from the dining room.*)

JOHN (*en route to the front door*): There're some expressmen here with a crate, Mr. Whiteside. I told them to come around the front.

WHITESIDE: Thank you, John. . . . Don't stand there, Miss Preen. You look like a frozen custard. Go away.

MISS PREEN (*controlling herself as best as she can*): Yes, sir. (*She goes.*)

(*At the same time two* EXPRESSMEN, *carrying a crate, enter from the front door.*)

JOHN: Bring it right in here. Careful there—don't scrape the wall. Why, it's some kind of animals.

EXPRESSMAN: I'll say it's animals. We had to feed 'em at seven o'clock this morning.

WHITESIDE: Bring it over here, John. Who's it from?

JOHN (*reading from the top of the crate as they set it down*): Admiral Richard E. Byrd. Say!

WHITESIDE (*peering through the slats*): Why, they're penguins. Two —three—four penguins. Hello, my pretties.

EXPRESSMEN: Directions for feeding are right on top. These two slats are open.

JOHN (*reading*): "To be fed only whale blubber, eels and cracked lobster."

EXPRESSMAN: They got Coca-Cola this morning. And liked it. (*They go.*)

WHITESIDE (*peering through the slats again*): Hello, hello, hello. You know, they make the most entrancing companions, John. Admiral Byrd has one that goes on all his lecture tours. I want these put right in the library with me. Take 'em right in.

JOHN (*picking up the crate*): Yes, sir.

WHITESIDE: Better tell Sarah to order a couple of dozen lobsters. I don't suppose there's any whale blubber in Mesalia.

(*At which point* DR. BRADLEY *obligingly enters from the hall.* MR. WHITESIDE *is equal to the occasion.*)

WHITESIDE (*with just the merest glance at the* DOCTOR): Oh, yes, there is.

DR. BRADLEY: The door was open, so I—Good afternoon, Mr. Whiteside. And Merry Christmas.

WHITESIDE: Merry Christmas, Merry Christmas. Do you happen to know if eels are in season, Doctor?

DR. BRADLEY: How's that?

WHITESIDE: Never mind. I was a fool to ask you.

(JOHN *returns from the library, carefully closing the doors.*)

JOHN: I opened those two slats a little, Mr. Whiteside—they seemed so crowded in there.

WHITESIDE: Thank you, John. (JOHN *goes on his way.*) On your way downtown, Doctor, will you send these air mail? Miss Cutler forgot them. (*He hands him a few letters.*) Good-bye. Sorry you dropped in just now. I have to do my Yogi exercises. (*He fold his arms, leans back and closes his eyes.*)

DR. BRADLEY: But, Mr. Whiteside, it's been a week now. My book, you know—when are we going to start work on the book? (WHITESIDE, *his eyes still closed, places his fingers to his lips, for absolute silence.*) I was hoping that today you'd be—(*He stops short as* MISS PREEN *returns from the dining room.*) Good afternoon, Miss Preen.

MISS PREEN: Good afternoon, Dr. Bradley. (*She opens the doors to enter the library, then freezes in her tracks. She closes the doors again and turns to the* DOCTOR, *glassy-eyed. She raises a trembling hand to her forehead.*) Doctor, perhaps I'm—not well, but—when I opened the doors just now I thought I saw a penguin with a thermometer in its mouth.

WHITESIDE: What's this? Have those penguins got out of their crate?

MISS PREEN: Oh, thank God. I thought perhaps the strain had been too much.

DR. BRADLEY (*incredulous*): Penguins?

WHITESIDE: Yes. Doctor, will you go in and capture them, please, and put them back in their crate? There're four of them.

DR. BRADLEY (*somewhat staggered*): Very well. Do you suppose that later on, Mr. Whiteside, we might—

WHITESIDE: We'll see, we'll see. First catch the penguins. And, Miss Preen, will you amuse them, please, until I come in?

MISS PREEN (*swallowing hard*): Yes, sir.

(*Meanwhile* JOHN *has descended the stairs.*)

JOHN: The Christmas tree just fell on Mr. Stanley. He's got a big bump on his forehead.

WHITESIDE (*brightly*): Why, isn't that too bad? . . . Go ahead, Doctor. Go on, Miss Preen.

(RICHARD *pops in from the hallway.*)

RICHARD: Hello, Mr. Whiteside.

WHITESIDE: Hello, Dickie, my boy.

DR. BRADLEY (*still lingering*): Mr. Whiteside, will you have some time later?

WHITESIDE (*impatient*): I don't know, Doctor. I'm busy now.

DR. BRADLEY: Well, suppose I wait a little while? I'll—I'll wait a little while. (*He goes into the library.*)

WHITESIDE: Dr. Bradley is the greatest living argument for mercy killings. . . . Well, Dickie, would you like a candid camera shot of my left nostril this evening?

RICHARD: I'm sort of stocked up on those. Have you got a minute to look at some new ones I've taken?

WHITESIDE: I certainly have. . . . Why, these are splendid, Richard. There's real artistry in them—they're as good as anything by Margaret Bourke-White. I like all the things you've shown me. This is the essence of photographic journalism.

RICHARD: Say, I didn't know they were as good as that. I just like to take pictures, that's all.

WHITESIDE: Richard, I've been meaning to talk to you about this. You're not just a kid fooling with a camera any more. These are good. This is what you ought to do. You ought to get out of here and do some of the things you were telling me about. Just get on a boat and get off wherever it stops. Galveston, Mexico, Singapore—work your way through and just take pictures—everything.

RICHARD: Say, wouldn't I like to, though! It's what I've been dreaming of for years. If I could do that I'd be the happiest guy in the world.

WHITESIDE: Well, why can't you do it? If I were your age, I'd do it like a shot.

RICHARD: Well, you know why. Dad.

WHITESIDE: Richard, do you really want to do this more than anything else in the world?

RICHARD: I certainly do.

WHITESIDE: Then do it.

(JUNE *comes quietly in from the dining room. Obviously there is something on her mind.*)

JUNE: Hello, Dick. Good afternoon, Mr. Whiteside.

WHITESIDE: Hello, my lovely. . . . So I'm afraid it's up to *you*, Richard.

RICHARD: I guess it is. Well, thank you, Mr. Whiteside. You've been swell and I'll never forget it.

WHITESIDE: Righto, Richard.

RICHARD: June, are you coming upstairs?

JUNE: Ah—in a few minutes, Richard.

RICHARD: Well—knock on my door, will you? I want to talk to you.

JUNE: Yes, I will.

(RICHARD *disappears up the stairs.*)

WHITESIDE (*brightly opening his book*): June, my lamb, you were too young to know about the Elwell murder, weren't you? Completely fascinating. I have about five favorite murders, and the Elwell case is one of them. Would you like to hear about it?

JUNE: Well, Mr. Whiteside, I wanted to talk to you. Would you mind, for a few minutes? It's important.

WHITESIDE: Why, certainly, my dear. I take it this is all about your young Lothario at the factory?

JUNE: Yes. I just can't seem to make Father understand. It's like talking to a blank wall. He won't meet him—he won't even talk about it. What are we going to do, Mr. Whiteside? Sandy and I love each other. I don't know where to turn.

WHITESIDE: My dear, I'd like to meet this young man. I'd like to see him for myself.

JUNE: Would you, Mr. Whiteside? Would you meet him? He's—he's outside now. He's in the kitchen.

WHITESIDE: Good! Bring him in.

JUNE (*hesitating*): Mr. Whiteside, he's—he's a very sensitive boy. You will be nice to him, won't you?

WHITESIDE: God damn it, June, when will you learn that I am *always* kind and courteous! Bring this idiot in!

JUNE (*calling through the dining room in a low voice*): Sandy. . . . Sandy. . . . (*She stands aside as a young man enters. Twenty-three or -four, keen-looking, neatly but simply dressed.*) Here he is, Mr. Whiteside. This is Sandy.

SANDY: How do you do, sir?

WHITESIDE: How do you do? Young man, I've been hearing a good deal about you from June this past week. It seems, if I have been correctly informed, that you two babes in the woods have quietly gone out of your minds.

JUNE: There's another name for it. It's called love.

WHITESIDE: Well, you've come to the right place. Dr. Sheridan Whiteside, Broken Hearts Mended, Brakes Relined, Hamburgers. Go right ahead.

SANDY: Well, if June has told you anything at all, Mr. Whiteside, you know the jam we're in. You see, I work for the union, Mr. Whiteside. I'm an organizer. I've been organizing the men in Mr. Stanley's factory, and Mr. Stanley's pretty sore about it.

WHITESIDE: I'll bet.

SANDY: Did June tell you that?

WHITESIDE: Yes, she did.

SANDY: Well, that being the case, Mr. Whiteside, I don't think I have the right to try to influence June. If she marries me it means a definite break with her family, and I don't like to bring that about. But Mr. Stanley's so stubborn about it, so arbitrary. You know, this is not something I've done just to spite him. We fell in love with each other. But Mr. Stanley behaves as though it were all a big plot—John L. Lewis sent me here just to marry his daughter.

JUNE: He's tried to fire Sandy twice, out at the factory, but he couldn't on account of the Wagner Act, thank God!

SANDY: Yes, he thinks I wrote that, too.

JUNE: If he'd only let me talk to him. If he'd let Sandy talk to him.

SANDY: Well, we've gone over all that, June. Anyway, this morning I got word I'm needed in Chicago. I may have to go on to Frisco from there. So you see the jam we're in.

JUNE: Sandy's leaving tonight, Mr. Whiteside. He'll probably be gone a year. We've simply got to decide. *Now*.

WHITESIDE: My dear, this is absurdly simple. It's no problem at all. Now to my jaundiced eye—(*The telephone rings.*) Oh-h! Hello. . . . Yes. . . . This is Whiteside. . . . Excuse me—it's a trans-Atlantic call. . . . Yes? . . . Yes, I'm on. Who's calling me? (*His tone suddenly becomes one of keen delight.*) All right—put her through. (*He turns to the young pair.*) It's Gertrude Stein, in Paris. . . . Hello. . . . Hello, Gertie! How's my little nightingale? . . . Yes, I hoped you would. How'd you know I was here? . . . I see. Well, it's wonderful of you to call. . . . Yes. Yes, I'm listening. Ten seconds more? (*A quick aside to the others.*) It'll be Christmas in Paris in ten seconds, and every year—yes? . . . Yes, Gertie, I hear them. It's wonderful. As though they were right outside. . . . June! (*He holds the receiver out to* JUNE *for a second.*) Thank you, my dear, and a very Merry Christmas to *you*. Don't forget we're dining on June tenth. . . . Pourquoi ne pas se réunir chez vous après? Tachez d'avoir Picasso, Matisse, Cocteau. Je serai seulement là pour quelques jours et je veux voir tout-le-monde. N'est-ce pas? Ah! Bon! Au revoir—au revoir. (*He hangs up.*) You know what that was you listened to? The bells of Notre Dame.

JUNE: Not really.

WHITESIDE: Miss Stein calls me every Christmas, no matter where I am, so that I can hear them. Two years ago I was walking on the bottom of the ocean in a diving suit with William Beebe, but she got me. . . . Now, where were we? Oh, yes. . . . June, I like your young man. I have an unerring instinct about people—I've never been wrong. That's why I wanted to meet him. My feeling is that you two will be very happy together. Whatever his beliefs are, he's entitled to them, and you shouldn't let anything stand in your way. As I see it, it's no problem at all. Stripped of its externals, what does it come down to? Your father. The possibility of making him unhappy. Is that right?

JUNE: *Very* unhappy.

WHITESIDE: That isn't the point. Suppose your parents *are* unhappy— it's good for them. Develops their characters. Look at me. I left home at the age of four and haven't been back since. They hear me on the radio and that's enough for them.

SANDY: Then—your advice is to go ahead, Mr. Whiteside?

WHITESIDE: It is. Marry him tonight, June.

JUNE (*almost afraid to make the leap*): You—you mean that, Mr. Whiteside?

WHITESIDE (*bellowing*): No, I mean you should marry Senator Borah. If I didn't mean it I wouldn't say it. What do you want me to do— say it all over again? My own opinion is—

(*The voice of* MR. STANLEY *is heard at the head of the stairs.* "Come on, Daisy—stop dawdling.")

(JUNE *quickly pushes her young man out of the room, as* MR. *and* MRS. STANLEY *descend the stairs.*)

STANLEY (*with deep sarcasm*): Forgive us for trespassing, Mr. Whiteside.

WHITESIDE: Not at all, old fellow—not at all. It's Christmas, you know. Merry Christmas, Merry Christmas.

MRS. STANLEY (*nervously*): Ah—yes. Merry Christmas. . . . Would you like to come along with us, June? We're taking some presents over to the Dexters.

JUNE: No—no, thank you, Mother. I—I have to write some letters. (*She hurries up the stairs.*)

STANLEY (*who has been donning his coat*): Come along, Daisy. (*Turning, he reveals a great patch of court plaster on his head.*)

WHITESIDE (*entirely too sweetly*): Why, Mr. Stanley, what happened to your forehead? Did you have an accident?

STANLEY (*just as sweetly*): No, Mr. Whiteside. I'm taking boxing lessons. . . . Come, Daisy. (*They go.*)

(HARRIET, *who has been hovering at the head of the stairs, hurries down as the* STANLEYS *depart. She is carrying a little Christmas package.*)

HARRIET: Dear Mr. Whiteside, I've been trying all day to see you. To give you—*this.*

WHITESIDE: Why, Miss Stanley. A Christmas gift for me?

HARRIET: It's only a trifle, but I wanted you to have it. It's a picture of me as I used to be. It was taken on another Christmas Eve, many years ago. Don't open it till the stroke of midnight, will you? (*The doorbell rings.* HARRIET *looks apprehensively over her shoulder.*) Merry Christmas, dear Mr. Whiteside. Merry Christmas.

WHITESIDE: Merry Christmas to you, Miss Stanley, and thank you. (*She glides out of the room.*)

(*In the hallway, as* JOHN *opens the door, we hear a woman's voice, liquid and melting.* "This is the Stanley residence, isn't it?" "Yes, it is." "I've come to see Mr. Whiteside. Will you tell him Miss Sheldon is here?")

WHITESIDE: Lorraine! My Blossom Girl!

LORRAINE (*coming into view*): Sherry, my sweet!

(*And quite a view it is.* LORRAINE SHELDON *is known as the most chic actress on the New York or London stage, and justly so. She glitters as she walks. She is beautiful, and even, God save the word, glamorous. . . . Her rank as one of the Ten Best-Dressed Women of the World is richly deserved. She is, in short, a siren of no mean talents, and knows it.*)

LORRAINE (*wasting no time*): Oh, darling, look at that poor sweet tortured face! Let me kiss it! You poor darling, your eyes have a kind of gallant compassion. How drawn you are! Sherry, my sweet, I want to cry.

WHITESIDE: All right, all right. You've made a very nice entrance. Now relax, dear.

LORRAINE: But, Sherry, darling, I've been so worried. And now seeing you in that chair . . .

WHITESIDE: This chair fits my fanny as nothing else ever has. I feel better than I have in years, and my only concern is news of the outside world. So take that skunk off and tell me everything. How are you, my dear?

LORRAINE (*removing a cascade of silver fox from her shoulders*): Darling, I'm so relieved. You look perfectly wonderful—I never saw you look better. My dear, do I look a wreck? I just dashed through New York. Didn't do a thing about Christmas. Hattie Carnegie and had my hair done, and got right on the train. And the *Normandie* coming back was simply hectic. Fun, you know, but simply exhausting. Jock Whitney, and Cary Grant, and Dorothy di Frasso—it was *too* exhausting. And of course London before that was so magnificent, my dear—well, I simply never got to bed at all. Darling, I've so much to tell you I don't know where to start.

WHITESIDE: Well, start with the dirt first, dear—that's what I want to hear.

LORRAINE: Let me see. . . . Well, Sybil Cartwright got thrown right out of Ciro's—it was the night before I sailed. She was wearing one of those new cellophane dresses, and you could absolutely see Trafalgar Square. And, oh, yes—Sir Harry Montrose—the painter, *you* know—is suing his mother for disorderly conduct. It's just shocked *every*one. Oh, and before I forget—Anthony Eden told me he's going to be on your New Year's broadcast, and he gave me a message for you. He said for God's sake not to introduce him again as the English Grover Whalen.

WHITESIDE: Nonsense. . . . Now come, dear, what about *you?* What about your love life? I don't believe for one moment that you never got to bed at all, if you'll pardon the expression.

LORRAINE: Sherry dear, you're dreadful.

WHITESIDE: What about that splendid bit of English mutton, Lord Bottomley? Haven't you hooked him yet?

LORRAINE: Sherry, please. Cedric is a very dear friend of mine.

WHITESIDE: Now, Blossom Girl, this is Sherry. Don't try to pull the bed clothes over *my* eyes. Don't tell *me* you wouldn't like to be Lady Bottomley, with a hundred thousand pounds a year and twelve castles. By the way, has he had his teeth fixed yet? Every time I order Roquefort cheese I think of those teeth.

LORRAINE: Sherry, really! . . . Cedric may not be brilliant, but he's rather sweet, poor lamb, and he's very fond of me, and he does represent a kind of English way of living that I like. Surrey, and London for the season—shooting box in Scotland—that lovely old castle in Wales. You were there, Sherry—you know what I mean.

WHITESIDE: Mm. I do indeed.

LORRAINE: Well, really, Sherry, why not? If I can marry Cedric I don't know why I shouldn't. Shall I tell you something, Sherry? I think, from something he said just before I sailed, that he's finally coming around to it. It wasn't definite, mind you, but—don't be surprised if I *am* Lady Bottomley before very long.

WHITESIDE: Lady Bottomley! Won't Kansas City be surprised! However, I shall be a flower girl and give the groom an iron toothpick as a wedding present. Come ahead, my blossom—let's hear some more of your skullduggery.

(*The library doors are quietly opened at this point and the* DOCTOR's *head appears.*)

DR. BRADLEY (*in a heavy whisper*): Mr. Whiteside.

WHITESIDE: What? No, no—not now. I'm busy. (*The* DOCTOR *disappears.*)

LORRAINE: Who's that?

WHITESIDE: He's fixing the plumbing. . . . Now come on, come on—I want more news.

LORRAINE: But, Sherry, what about this play? After all, I've come all the way from New York—even on Christmas Eve—I've been so excited ever since your phone call. Where is it? When can I read it?

WHITESIDE: Well, here's the situation. This young author—his name is Bert Jefferson—brought me the play with the understanding that I send it to Kit Cornell. It's a magnificent part, and God knows I feel disloyal to Kit, but there you are. Now *I've* done *this* much—the rest is up to you. He's young and attractive—now, just how you'll go about persuading him, I'm sure you know more about that than I do.

LORRAINE: Darling, how can I ever thank you? Does he know I'm coming—Mr. Jefferson, I mean?

WHITESIDE: No, no. You're just out here visiting me. You'll meet him, and that's that. Get him to take you to dinner, and work around to the play. Good God, I don't have to tell you how to do these things. How did you get all those other parts?

LORRAINE: Sherry! . . . Well, I'll go back to the hotel and get into something more attractive. I just dumped my bags and rushed right over here. Darling, you're wonderful. (*Lightly kissing him.*)

WHITESIDE: All right—run along and get into your working clothes. Then come right back here and spend Christmas Eve with Sherry and I'll have Mr. Jefferson on tap. By the way, I've got a little surprise for you. Who do you think's paying me a flying visit tonight? None other than your old friend and fellow actor, Beverly Carlton.

LORRAINE (*not too delighted*): Really? Beverly? I thought he was being glamorous again on a tramp steamer.

WHITESIDE: Come, come, dear—mustn't be bitter because he got better notices than you did.

LORRAINE: Don't be silly, Sherry. I never read notices. I simply wouldn't care to act with him again, that's all. He's not staying here, is he? I *hope* not!

WHITESIDE: Temper, temper, temper. No, he's not. . . . Where'd you get that diamond clip, dear? That's a new bit of loot, isn't it?

LORRAINE: Haven't you seen this before? Cedric gave it to me for his mother's birthday. . . . Look, darling, I've got a taxi outside. If I'm going to get back here—

(*At this point the voice of* MAGGIE *is heard in the hallway.*)

MAGGIE: Sherry, what do you think? I've just been given the most beautiful . . . (*She stops short and comes to a dead halt as she sees* LORRAINE.)

LORRAINE: Oh, hello, Maggie. I knew you must be around somewhere. How are you, my dear?

WHITESIDE: Santa's been at work, my pet. Blossom Girl just dropped in out of the blue and surprised us.

MAGGIE (*quietly*): Hello, Lorraine.

WHITESIDE (*as* JEFFERSON *appears*): Who's that—Bert? This is Mr. Bert Jefferson, Lorraine. Young newspaper man. Miss Lorraine Sheldon.

BERT: How do you do, Miss Sheldon?

LORRAINE: How do you do? I didn't quite catch the name—Jefferson?

WHITESIDE (*sweetly*): That's right, Pet.

LORRAINE (*full steam ahead*): Why, Mr. Jefferson, you don't look like a newspaper man. You don't look like a newspaper man at all.

BERT: Really? I thought it was written all over me in neon lights.

LORRAINE: Oh, no, not at all. I should have said you were—oh, I don't know—an aviator or an explorer or something. They have that same kind of dash about them. I'm simply enchanted with your town, Mr. Jefferson. It gives one such a warm, gracious feeling. Tell me—have you lived here all your life?

BERT: Practically.

WHITESIDE: If you wish to hear the story of his life, Lorraine, kindly do so on your own time. Maggie and I have work to do. Get out of here, Jefferson. On your way, Blossom.

LORRAINE: He's the world's rudest man, isn't he? Can I drop you, Mr. Jefferson? I'm going down to the—Mansion House, I think it's called.

BERT: Thank you, but I've got my car. Suppose I drop you?

LORRAINE: Oh, would you? That'd be lovely—we'll send the taxi off. See you in a little while, Sherry. 'Bye, Maggie.

BERT: Good-bye, Miss C. (*He turns to* WHITESIDE.) I'm invited back for dinner, am I not?

WHITESIDE: Yes—yes, you are. At Christmas I always feed the needy. Now please stop oozing out—*get* out.

LORRAINE: Come on, Mr. Jefferson. I want to hear more about this charming little town. And I want to know a good deal about you, too.

(*And they are gone.*)
(*There is a slight but pregnant pause after they go.* MAGGIE *simply stands looking at* WHITESIDE, *waiting for what may come forth.*)

WHITESIDE (*as though nothing had happened*): Now let's see, have you got a copy of that broadcast? How much did you say they wanted out—four minutes?

MAGGIE: That's right—four minutes. . . . She's looking very well, isn't she?

WHITESIDE (*busy with his manuscript*): What's that? Who?

MAGGIE: The Countess di Pushover. . . . Quite a surprise, wasn't it—her dropping in?

WHITESIDE: Yes—yes, it was. Now come on, Maggie, come on. Get to work.

MAGGIE: Why, she must have gone through New York like a dose of salts. How long's she going to stay?

WHITESIDE (*completely absorbed*): What? Oh, I don't know—a few days . . . (*He reads from his manuscript.*) "At this joyous season of the year, when in the hearts of men—" I can't cut that.

MAGGIE: Isn't it curious? There was Lorraine, snug as a bug in some-body's bed on the *Normandie*—

WHITESIDE (*so busy*): "Ere the Yuletide season pass—"

MAGGIE (*quietly taking the manuscript out of his hands*): Now, Sherry dear, we will talk a bit.

WHITESIDE: Now look here, Maggie. Just because a friend of mine hap-pens to come out to spend Christmas with me—(*The doorbell rings.*) I have a hunch that's Beverly. Maggie, see if it is. Go ahead—run! Run!

(MAGGIE *looks at him—right through him, in fact. Then she goes slowly toward the door.*)

(*We hear her voice at the door:* "Beverly!" *Then, in clipped Eng-lish tones:* "Magpie! A large, moist, incestuous kiss for my Magpie!")

WHITESIDE (*roaring*): Come in here, you Piccadilly penpusher, and gaze upon a soul in agony.

(BEVERLY CARLTON *enters, arm in arm with* MAGGIE. *Very confident, very British, very Beverly Carlton.*)

BEVERLY: Don't tell me how you are, Sherry dear. I want none of the tiresome details. I have only a little time, so the conversation will be entirely about *me,* and I shall love it. Shall I tell you how I glittered through the South Seas like a silver scimitar, or would you rather hear how I frolicked through Zambesia, raping the Major General's daughter and finishing a three-act play at the same time? . . . Magpie dear, you are the moonflower of my middle age, and I love you very much. Say something beautiful to me. Sherry dear, without going into mountainous waves of self-pity, how are you?

WHITESIDE: I'm fine, you presumptuous Cockney. . . . Now, how was the trip, wonderful?

BEVERLY: Fabulous. I did a fantastic amount of work. By the way, did I glimpse that little boudoir butterfly, La Sheldon, in a motor-car as I came up the driveway?

MAGGIE: You did indeed. She's paying us a Christmas visit.

BEVERLY: Dear girl! They do say she set fire to her mother, but I don't believe it. . . . Sherry, my evil one, not only have I written the finest comedy since Molière, but also the best revue since my last one and an operetta that frightens me—it's so good. I shall play it for eight weeks in London and six in New York—that's all. No matinees. Then I am off to the Grecian Islands. . . . Magpie, why don't you come along? Why don't you desert this cannon ball of fluff and come with me?

MAGGIE: Beverly dear, be careful. You're catching me at a good moment.

WHITESIDE (*changing the subject*): Tell me, did you have a good time in Hollywood? How long were you there?

BEVERLY: Three unbelievable days. I saw everyone from Adrian to Zanuck. They came, poor dears, as to a shrine. I was insufferably charming and ruthlessly firm in refusing seven million dollars for two minutes' work.

WHITESIDE: What about Banjo? Did you see my wonderful Banjo in Hollywood?

BEVERLY: I did. He gave a dinner for me. I arrived, in white tie and tails, to be met at the door by two bewigged flunkies, who quietly proceeded to take my trousers off. I was then ushered, in my lemon silk drawers, into a room full of Norma Shearer, Claudette Colbert, and Aldous Huxley, among others. Dear, sweet, incomparable Banjo.

WHITESIDE: I'll never forget that summer at Antibes, when Banjo put a microphone in Lorraine's mattress, and then played the record the next day at lunch.

BEVERLY: I remember it indeed. Lorraine left Antibes by the next boat.

MAGGIE (*half to herself*): I wish Banjo were here now.

BEVERLY: What's the matter, Magpie? Is Lorraine being her own sweet sick-making self?

MAGGIE: You wouldn't take her to the Grecian Islands with you, would you, Beverly? Just for me?

WHITESIDE: Now, now. Lorraine is a charming person who has gallantly given up her own Christmas to spend it with me.

BEVERLY: Oh, I knew I had a bit of dirt for us all to nibble on. (*He draws a letter out of his pocket.*)

(*Again the library doors are opened and the* DOCTOR's *head comes through.*)

DR. BRADLEY: Mr. Whiteside.

WHITESIDE: No, no, not now. Go away.

(*The* DOCTOR *withdraws.*)

BEVERLY: Have you kidnapped someone, Sherry?

WHITESIDE: Yes, that was Charley Ross . . . Go ahead. Is this something juicy?

BEVERLY: Juicy as a pomegranate. It is the latest report from London on the winter maneuvers of Miss Lorraine Sheldon against the left flank—in fact, all flanks—of Lord Cedric Bottomley. Listen: "Lorraine has just left us in a cloud of Chanel Number Five. Since September, in her relentless pursuit of His Lordship, she has paused only to change girdles and check her oil. She has chased him, panting, from castle to castle, till he finally took refuge, for several week-ends, in the gentlemen's lavatory of the House of Lords. Practically no one is betting on the Derby this year; we are all making book on Lorraine. She is sailing tomorrow on the *Normandie,* but would return on the *Yankee Clipper* if Bottomley so much as belches in her direction." Have you ever met Lord Bottomley, Magpie dear? (*He goes immediately into an impersonation of His Lordship. Very British, very full of teeth, stuttering.*)

"No v-v-very good shooting today, blast it. Only s-s-six partridges, f-f-four grouse, and the D-D-Duke of Sutherland."

WHITESIDE (*chuckling*): My God, that's Bottomley to the very bottom.

BEVERLY (*still in character*): "R-r-ripping debate in the House today. Old Basil spoke for th-th-three hours. D-d-dropped dead at the end of it. Ripping."

MAGGIE: You're making it up, Beverly. No one sounds like that.

WHITESIDE: It's so good it's uncanny. . . . Damn it, Beverly, why must you race right out of here? I never see enough of you, you ungrateful moppet.

BEVERLY: Sherry darling, I can only tell you that my love for you is so great that I changed trains at Chicago to spend ten minutes with you and wish you a Merry Christmas. Merry Christmas, my lad. My little Magpie. (*A look at his watch.*) And now I have just time for one magnificent number, to give you a taste of how brilliant the whole thing is. It's the second number in the revue. (*He strikes a chord on the piano, but before he can go further the telephone rings.*)

WHITESIDE: Oh, damn! Get rid of them, Maggie.

MAGGIE: Hello . . . Oh, hello, Bert . . . Oh! well, just a minute. . . . Beverly, would you talk to a newspaper man for just two minutes? I kind of promised him.

BEVERLY: Won't have time, Magpie, unless he's under the piano.

MAGGIE: Oh! (*Into the phone.*) Wait a minute. (*To* BEVERLY *again.*) Would you see him at the station, just for a minute before the train goes? (BEVERLY *nods.*) Bert, go to the station and wait for him. He'll be there in a few minutes. . . . 'Bye.

WHITESIDE: The stalls are impatient, Beverly. Let's have this second-rate masterpiece.

BEVERLY (*his fingers rippling over the keys*): It's called: "What Am I to Do?"

> "Oft in the nightfall
>   I think I might fall
>   Down from my perilous height;
>   Deep in the heart of me,
>   Always a part of me,
>   Quivering, shivering light.
>   Run, little lady,
>   Ere the shady
>   Shafts of time
>   Barb you with their winged desire,
>   Singe you with their sultry fire.
>   Softly a fluid
>   Druid
>   Meets me,
>   Olden
>   and golden
>   the dawn that greets me;
>   Cherishing,
>   Perishing,
>   Up to the stars
>   I climb.

> "What am I to do
>   Toward ending this madness,
>   This sadness,
>   That's rending me through?
>   The flowers of yesteryear
>   Are haunting me,
>   Taunting me,
>   Darling, for wanting you.
>   What am I to say
>   To warnings of sorrow

When morning's tomorrow
Greets the dew?
   Will I see the cosmic Ritz
   Shattered and scattered to bits?
What *not* am I to do?"

(*As he swings into the chorus for a second time the doorbell rings, and* JOHN *is glimpsed as he goes to the door.*)

(*It is a trio of* RADIO MEN *who appear in the doorway, their arms filled with equipment for* MR. WHITESIDE'S *broadcast.*)

WHITESIDE: Oh, come in, Westcott. . . . Beverly, it's superb. The best thing you've ever written. It'll be played by every ragtag orchestra from Salem to Singapore.

BEVERLY: Please! Let *me* say that . . . Ah, the air waves, eh? Well, I shan't have to hear you, thank God. I shall be on the train.

MAGGIE: Come on, Whiteside, say good-bye. Mr. Westcott, he's still four minutes over—you'll have to chisel it out.

WHITESIDE (*as* MAGGIE *starts to wheel him into the library*): Stop this nonsense. Beverly, my lamb—

MAGGIE: You can kiss Beverly in London on July twelfth. (*Then to the technicians.*) The microphone set-up is right there, gentlemen, and you can connect up outside. John, show them where it is.

WHITESIDE: Maggie, what the hell are you—

BEVERLY (*calling after the fast-disappearing* WHITESIDE): Au revoir, Sherry. Merry Christmas. Magpie, come get a kiss.

MAGGIE (*emerging from the library and closing the doors behind her*): Beverly, I want one minute, I must have it. You'll make the train. The station's a minute and a half from here.

BEVERLY: Why, what's the matter, Magpie?

(*At which the library doors are opened and the* DOCTOR *emerges, rather apologetically. He is sped on his way by* MR. WHITESIDE'S *roaring voice—"Oh, get out of here!"*)

DR. BRADLEY: I'm—I'm just waiting in the kitchen until Mr. Whiteside is—Excuse me. (*He darts out through the dining room.*)

BEVERLY: Who *is* that man?

MAGGIE: Never mind . . . Beverly, I'm in great trouble.

BEVERLY: Why, Magpie dear, what's the matter?

MAGGIE: I've fallen in love. For the first time in my life. Beverly, I'm in love. I can't tell you about it—there isn't time. But Sherry is trying to break it up. In his own fiendish way he's doing everything he can to break it up.

BEVERLY: Why, the old devil! What's he doing?

MAGGIE: Lorraine. He's brought Lorraine here to smash it.

BEVERLY: Oh, it's somebody *here?* In this town?

MAGGIE (*nodding*): He's a newspaper man—the one you're going to see at the station—and he's written a play, and I know Sherry must be using that as bait. You know Lorraine—she'll eat him up alive. You've got to help me, Beverly.

BEVERLY: Of course I will, Magpie. What do you want me to do?

MAGGIE: I've got to get Lorraine out of here—the farther away the better—and you can do it for me.

BEVERLY: But how? How can I? I'm leaving.

(*The library doors are opened and* WESTCOTT, *the radio man, emerges.*)

WESTCOTT: Have you a carbon copy of the broadcast, Miss Cutler?

MAGGIE: It's on that table.

WESTCOTT: Thank you. One of those penguins ate the original.

(*The voice of* WHITESIDE *is now heard calling from his room.*)

WHITESIDE: Beverly, are you still there?

MAGGIE: No, he's gone, Sherry. (*She lowers her voice.*) Come out here.

(*Maneuvering him into the hall, we see her whisper to him; his head bobs up and down quickly in assent. Then he lets out a shriek of laughter.*)

BEVERLY: I'd love it. I'd absolutely love it. (MAGGIE *puts a quick finger to his lips, peers toward the* WHITESIDE *room. But* MR. WESTCOTT *has gone in; the doors are closed.*) It's simply enchanting, and bitches Sherry and Lorraine at the same time. It's pure heaven! I adore it, and I shall do it up brown. (*He embraces her.*)

MAGGIE: Darling, the first baby will be named Beverly. You're wonderful.

BEVERLY: Of course I am. Come to Chislewick for your honeymoon and I'll put you up. Good-bye, my lovely. I adore you. (*And he is gone.*)

(MAGGIE *comes back into the room, highly pleased with herself. She even sings a fragment of* BEVERLY'S *song. "What am I to do? Tra-la-la-la-la-la."*)
(JOHN, *entering from the dining room, breaks the song.*)

JOHN: Shall I straighten up the room for the broadcast, Miss Cutler?

MAGGIE: No, John, it isn't television, thank God. They only *hear* that liquid voice.

JOHN: He's really wonderful, isn't he? The things he finds time to do.

MAGGIE: Yes, he certainly sticks his nose into everything, John. (*She goes into the library.*)

(JOHN *is putting the room in order when suddenly* JUNE *comes quietly down the stairs. She is dressed for the street and is carrying a suitcase.*)

JOHN: Why, Miss June, are you going away?

JUNE: Why—no, John. No. I'm just—Mr. Whiteside is inside, I suppose?

JOHN: Yes, he's getting ready to go on the radio.

JUNE: Oh! Well, look, John—

(*And then* RICHARD *darts down the stairs. A light bag, two cameras slung over his shoulder.*)

RICHARD (*to* JUNE, *in a heavy whisper*): Where's Mr. Whiteside? In there?

JUNE: Yes, he is.

RICHARD: Oh! Well, maybe we ought to—

(*The doorbell rings.* RICHARD *and* JUNE *exchange looks, then scurry out quickly through the dining room.*)
(JOHN *looks after them for a second, puzzled, then goes to the door.*)
(*It is* LORRAINE *who comes in, resplendent now in evening dress and wrap, straight from Paris. At the same time* MAGGIE *emerges from the library and* JOHN *goes on his way.*)

LORRAINE: Hello, dear. Where's Sherry?

MAGGIE: Inside, working—he's broadcasting very soon.

LORRAINE: Oh, of course—Christmas Eve. What a wonderful man Sheridan Whiteside is! You know, my dear, it must be such an utter joy to be secretary to somebody like Sherry.

MAGGIE: Yes, you meet such interesting people. . . . That's quite a gown, Lorraine. Going anywhere?

LORRAINE: This? Oh, I just threw on anything at all. Aren't you dressing for dinner?

MAGGIE: No, just what meets the eye. (*She has occasion to carry a few papers across the room at this point.* LORRAINE'S *eye watches her narrowly.*)

LORRAINE: Who does your hair, Maggie?

MAGGIE: A little French woman named Maggie Cutler comes in every morning.

LORRAINE: You know, every time I see you I keep thinking your hair could be so lovely. I always want to get my hands on it.

MAGGIE (*quietly*): I've always wanted to get mine on yours, Lorraine.

LORRAINE (*absently*): What, dear?

(*One of the radio men drifts into the room, plugs into the control board, drifts out again.* LORRAINE'S *eyes follow him idly. Then she turns to* MAGGIE *again.*)

By the way, what time does Beverly get here? I'm not over-anxious to meet him.

MAGGIE: He's been and gone, Lorraine.

LORRAINE: Really? Well, I'm very glad. . . . Of course you're great friends, aren't you—you and Beverly?

MAGGIE: Yes, we are. I think he's a wonderful person.

LORRAINE: Oh, I suppose so. But when I finished acting with him I was a perfect wreck. All during that tender love scene that the critics thought was so magnificent he kept dropping peanut shells down my dress. I wouldn't act with him again if I were starving.

MAGGIE (*casually*): Tell me, Lorraine, have you found a new play yet?

LORRAINE (*at once on guard*): No. No, I haven't. There was a pile of manuscripts waiting in New York for me, but I hurried right out here to Sherry.

MAGGIE: Yes, it was wonderful of you, Lorraine—to drop everything that way and rush to Sherry's wheelchair.

LORRAINE: Well, after all, Maggie dear, what else has one in this world but friends? . . . How long will Sherry be in there, I wonder?

MAGGIE: Not long. . . . Did you know that Mr. Jefferson has written quite a good play? The young man that drove you to the hotel.

LORRAINE: Really? No, I didn't. Isn't that interesting?

MAGGIE: Yes, isn't it?

(*There is a considerable pause. The ladies smile at each other.*)

LORRAINE (*evading* MAGGIE's *eyes*): They've put a polish on my nails I simply loathe. I don't suppose Elizabeth Arden has a branch in this town.

MAGGIE (*busy with her papers*): Not if she has any sense.

LORRAINE: Oh, well, I'll just bear it, but it does depress me. (*She rises, wanders aimlessly for a moment, picks up a book from the table.*) Have you read this, Maggie? Everybody was reading it on the boat. I hear you simply can't put it down.

MAGGIE: *I* put it down—right there.

(LORRAINE *casually strikes a note or two on the piano.*)
(*The telephone rings.*)

MAGGIE (*taking up the receiver a little too casually*): Hello . . . Yes . . . Yes . . . Miss Lorraine Sheldon? Yes, she's here . . . There's a trans-Atlantic call coming through for you, Lorraine.

LORRAINE: Trans-Atlantic—for me? Here? Why, what in the world—

MAGGIE (*as she hands over the receiver*): It's London.

LORRAINE: London? . . . Hello. (*Then in a louder tone.*) Hello . . . Cedric! Cedric, is this you? . . . Why, Cedric, you darling! Why, what a surprise! How'd you know I was here? . . . Darling, don't talk so fast and you won't stutter so . . . That's better . . . Yes, now I can hear you . . . Yes, very clearly. It's as though you were just around the corner. . . . I see . . . What? . . . Darling! Cedric, dearest, would you wait just one moment? (*She turns to* MAGGIE.) Maggie, would you mind? It's Lord Bottomley—a *very* personal call. Would you mind?

MAGGIE: Oh, not at all. (*She goes into the dining room; almost does a little waltz step as she goes.*)

LORRAINE: Yes, my dearest—now tell me . . . Cedric, please don't stutter so. Don't be nervous. (*She listens for a moment again.*) Oh, my darling. Oh, my sweet. You don't know how I've prayed for this, every night on the boat . . . Darling, yes! YES, a thousand times Yes! . . . I'll take a plane right out of here and catch the next boat. Oh, my sweet, we're going to be the happiest people in the world. I wish I were there now in your arms, Cedric . . . What? . . . Cedric, don't stutter so . . . Yes, and I love *you,* my darling—oh, so much! . . . Oh, my dear sweet. My darling, my darling. . . . Yes, yes! I will, I will, darling! I'll be thinking of you every moment . . . You've made me the happiest girl in the world . . . Good-bye, good-bye, darling. Good-bye. (*Bursting with her news, she throws open the library doors.*) Sherry, Sherry! Do you know what's happened? Cedric just called from London—He's asked me to marry him. Sherry, think of it! At last! I've got to get right out of here and catch the next boat. How far are we from Chicago? I can get a plane from there.

MAGGIE (*emerging, mouse-like, from the dining room*): May I come in?

LORRAINE: Maggie dear, can I get a plane out of here right away? Or I'll even take a train to Chicago and fly from there. I've simply got to get the next boat for England. When is it—do you know? Is there a newspaper here?

MAGGIE: The *Queen Mary* sails Friday. Why, what's all the excitement, Lorraine? What's happened?

LORRAINE: Maggie, the most wonderful thing in the world has happened. Lord Bottomley has asked me to marry him . . . Oh, Maggie! (*And in her exuberance she throws her arms around her.*)

MAGGIE: Really? Well, what do you know?

LORRAINE: Isn't it wonderful? I'm so excited I can hardly think. Maggie dear, you must help me get out of here.

MAGGIE: I'd be delighted to, Lorraine.

LORRAINE: Oh, thank you, thank you. Will you look things up right away?

MAGGIE: Yes, I've a time-table right here. And don't worry, because if there's no train I'll drive you to Toledo and you can catch the plane from there.

LORRAINE: Maggie darling, you're wonderful. . . . Sherry, what's the matter with you? You haven't said a word. You haven't even congratulated me.

WHITESIDE (*who has been sitting through this like a thundercloud*): Let me understand this, Lorraine. Am I to gather from your girlish squeals that you are about to toss your career into the ashcan?

LORRAINE: Oh, not at all. Of course I may not be able to play this season, but there'll be other seasons, Sherry.

WHITESIDE: I see. And everything goes into the ashcan with it—Is that right?

LORRAINE: But, Sherry, you couldn't expect me to—

WHITESIDE (*icily*): Don't explain, Lorraine. I understand only too well. And I also understand why Cornell remains the First Actress of our theatre.

MAGGIE (*busy with her time-tables*): Oh, this is wonderful! We're in luck, Lorraine. You can get a plane out of Toledo at ten-three. It takes about an hour to get there. Why, it all works out wonderfully, doesn't it, Sherry?

WHITESIDE (*through his teeth*): Peachy!

LORRAINE (*heading for the phone*): Maggie, what's the number of that hotel I'm at? I've got to get my maid started packing.

MAGGIE: Mesalia three two.

LORRAINE (*into the phone*): Mesalia three two, please . . . Let's see— I sail Friday, five-day boat, that means I ought to be in London Wednesday night. . . . Hello. This is Miss Sheldon. . . . That's right. Connect me with my maid.

MAGGIE (*at the window*): Oh, look, Sherry, it's starting to snow. Isn't that wonderful, Sherry? Oh, I never felt more like Christmas in my life. Don't you, Sherry dear?

WHITESIDE: Shut your nasty little face!

LORRAINE (*on the phone*): Cosette? . . . Now listen carefully, Cosette. Have you got a pencil? . . . We're leaving here tonight by plane and sailing Friday on the *Queen Mary*. Start packing immediately and I'll call for you in about an hour . . . Yes, that's right . . . Now I want you to send these cables for me . . . Ready? . . . The first one goes to Lord and Lady Cunard—you'll find all these addresses in my little book. It's in my dressing case. "Lord and Lady Cunard. My darlings. Returning Friday *Queen Mary*. Cedric and I being married immediately on arrival. Wanted you to be the first to know. Love.—Lorraine." . . . Now send the same message—what? . . . Oh, thank you, Cosette. Thank you very much . . . Send the same message to Lady Astor, Lord Beaverbrook, and the Duchess of Sutherland . . . Got that? . . . And send a cable to Molyneaux, in Paris. "Please meet me Claridge's Thursday of next week with sketches of bridal gown and trousseau.—Lorraine Sheldon." And then send one to Monsieur Pierre Cartier, Cartier's, Paris: "Can you bring over to London the triple string of pearls I picked out in October? Cable me *Queen Mary*.—Lorraine Sheldon." . . . Have you got all that straight, Cosette? . . . That's fine. Now you'll have to rush, my dear —I'll be at the hotel in about an hour, so be ready. . . . Good-bye. (*She hangs up.*) Thank goodness for Cosette—I'd die without her. She's the most wonderful maid in the world. . . . Well! Life is really just full of surprises, isn't it? Who'd have thought an hour ago that I'd be on my way to London?

MAGGIE: An *hour* ago? No, I certainly wouldn't have thought it an hour ago.

WHITESIDE (*beside himself with temper*): Will you both stop this female drooling? I have a violent headache.

MAGGIE (*all solicitude*): Oh, Sherry! Can I get you something?

LORRAINE: Look here, Sherry, I'm sorry if I've offended you, but after all my life is my own and I'm not going to—(*She stops as* BERT JEFFERSON *comes in from the outside.*)

BERT: Hello, everybody. Say, do you know it's snowing out? Going to have a real old-fashioned Christmas.

WHITESIDE: Why don't you telephone your scoop to the New York *Times*?

MAGGIE: Bert, Miss Sheldon has to catch a plane tonight, from Toledo. Can we drive her over, you and I?

BERT: Why, certainly. Sorry you have to go, Miss Sheldon. No bad news, I hope?

LORRAINE: Oh, on the contrary—very good news. Wonderful news.

MAGGIE: Yes, indeed—calls for a drink, I think. You're not being a very good host, Sherry. How about a bottle of champagne?

BERT: Oh, I can do better than that—let me mix you something. It's a Jefferson Special. Okay, Mr. Whiteside?

WHITESIDE: Yes, yes, yes, yes, yes. Mix anything. Only stop driveling.

BERT (*on his way to the dining room*): Anybody admired my Christmas present yet, Maggie?

MAGGIE: Oh, dear, I forgot. (*She raises her arm, revealing a bracelet.*) Look, everybody! From Mr. Jefferson to me.

LORRAINE: Oh, it's charming. Let me see it. Oh! Why, it's inscribed, too. "To Maggie. Long may she wave. Bert." Maggie, it's a lovely Christmas present. Isn't it sweet, Sherry?

WHITESIDE (*glowering*): Ducky!

MAGGIE: I told you it was beautiful, Bert. See?

BERT: Well, shows what you get if you save your coupons.

LORRAINE (*looking from* BERT *to* MAGGIE): Well, what's going on between you two, anyhow? Maggie, are you hiding something from us?

WHITESIDE (*a hand to his head*): Great God, will this drivel never stop? My head is bursting.

BERT: A Jefferson Special will cure anything. . . . By the way, I got a two-minute interview with Beverly Carlton at the station. You were right, Mr. Whiteside—He's quite something.

MAGGIE (*uneasily*): Go ahead, Bert—mix the drinks.

BERT: I was lucky to get even two minutes. He was in a telephone booth most of the time. Couldn't hear what he was saying, but from the faces he was making it looked like a scene from one of his plays.

MAGGIE (*hiding her frenzy*): Bert, mix those drinks, will you?

WHITESIDE (*suddenly galvanized*): Just a minute, if you please, Jefferson. Mr. Carlton was in a telephone booth at the station?

BERT: Certainly was—I thought he'd never come out. Kept talking and making the damnedest faces for about five minutes.

MAGGIE (*tensely*): Bert, for goodness sake, will you—

WHITESIDE (*ever so sweetly*): Bert, my boy, I have an idea I shall love the Jefferson Special. Make me a double one, will you? My headache has gone with the wind.

BERT: Okay. (*He goes.*)

(WHITESIDE, *his eyes gleaming, immediately whirls his wheelchair across the room to the telephone.*)

WHITESIDE (*a finger to his lips*): Sssh! Philo Vance is now at work.

LORRAINE: What?

WHITESIDE: Sssh! (*He picks up the telephone. His voice is absolutely musical.*) Operator! Has there been a call from England over this telephone within the past half hour? . . . Yes, I'll wait.

LORRAINE: Sherry, what *is* all this?

WHITESIDE: What's that? There have been no calls from England for the past three days? Thank you . . . Now, will you repeat that please? . . . Blossom Girl. (*He beckons to* LORRAINE, *then puts the receiver to her ear.*) Hear it, dear? (*Then, again to the operator.*)

Thank you, and a Merry Christmas. (*He hangs up.*) Yes, indeed, it seems we're going to have a real old-fashioned Christmas.

LORRAINE (*stunned*): Sherry, what is all this? What's going on? What does this mean?

WHITESIDE: My dear, you have just played the greatest love scene of your career with your old friend, Beverly Carlton.

LORRAINE: Why—why, that's not true. I was talking to Cedric. What do you mean?

WHITESIDE: I mean, my blossom, that that was Beverly you poured out your girlish heart to, not Lord Bottomley. Ah, me, who'd have thought five minutes ago that you would not be going to London!

LORRAINE: Sherry, stop it! What is this? I want this explained.

WHITESIDE: Explained? You heard the operator, my dear. All I can tell you is that Beverly was indulging in one of his famous bits of mimicry, that's all. You've heard him do Lord Bottomley before, haven't you?

LORRAINE (*as it dawns on her*): Yes . . . of course . . . But—but why would he want to do such a thing! This is one of the most dreadful— oh, my God! Those cables! (*In one bound she is at the telephone.*) Give me the hotel—whatever it's called—I want the hotel—I'll pay him off for this if it's the last thing that I—Why, the cad! The absolute unutterable cad! The dirty rotten—Mansion House? Connect me with my maid . . . What? . . . Who the hell do you *think* it is? Miss Sheldon, of course . . . Oh, God! Those cables! If only Cosette hasn't—Cosette! Cosette! Did you send those cables? . . . Oh, God! Oh, God! . . . Now listen, Cosette, I want you to send another cable to every one of those people, and tell them somebody has been using my name, and to disregard anything and everything they hear from me—except this, of course . . . Don't ask questions—do as you're told . . . Don't argue with me, you French bitch—God damn it, do as you're told . . . And unpack—we're not going! (*She hangs up.*)

WHITESIDE: Now steady, my blossom. Take it easy.

LORRAINE (*in a white rage*): What do you mean take it easy? Do you realize I'll be the laughingstock of England? Why, I won't dare show my face! I always knew Beverly Carlton was low, but not this low. Why? WHY? It isn't even funny. Why would he do it, that's what I'd like to know. Why would he do it! Why would anyone in the world want to play a silly trick like this? I can't understand it. Do you, Sherry? Do you, Maggie? You both saw him this afternoon. Why would he walk out of here, go right to a phone booth, and try to ship me over to England on a fool's errand! There must have been some reason—there must have. It doesn't make sense otherwise. Why would Beverly Carlton, or anybody else for that matter, want me to—(*She stops as a dim light begins to dawn.*) Oh! Oh! (*Her eye, which has been on* MAGGIE, *goes momentarily to the dining room, where* BERT *has disappeared. Then her gaze returns to* MAGGIE *again.*) I—I think I begin to—of course! Of course! That's it. Of course that's it. Yes, and that's a very charming bracelet that Mr. Jefferson gave you—isn't it, Maggie dear? Of course. It makes complete sense now. And to think that I nearly—well! Wild horses couldn't get me out of here *now*, Maggie. And if I were you I'd hang onto that bracelet, dear. It'll be something to remember him by!

(*Out of the library comes* MR. WESTCOTT, *his hands full of papers. At the same time the two technicians emerge from the dining room and go to the control board.*)

WESTCOTT (*his eyes on his watch*): All right, Mr. Whiteside. Almost time. Here's your new copy. Hook her up, boys. Start testing.

WHITESIDE: How much time?

WESTCOTT (*bringing him a microphone*): Couple of minutes.

(*One of the radio technicians is talking into a microphone, testing:* "One, two, three, four, one, two, three, four. How are we coming in, New York? . . . A, B, C, A, B, C. Mary had a little lamb, Mary had a little lamb.")

(MR. *and* MRS. STANLEY, *having delivered their Christmas presents, enter from the hallway and start up the stairs.* MRS. STANLEY *looks hungrily at the radio goings-on, but* MR. STANLEY *delivers a stern* "Come, Daisy," *and she follows him up the stairs.*)

(*The voices of the technicians drone on:* "One, two, three, four, one, two, three, four. O.K., New York. Waiting." MR. WESTCOTT *stands with watch in hand.*)

(*From the dining room comes* BERT JEFFERSON, *a tray of drinks in hand.*)

BERT: Here comes the Jefferson Special . . . Oh! Have we time?

LORRAINE: Oh, I'm sure we have. Mr. Jefferson, I'm not leaving after all. My plans are changed.

BERT: Really? Oh, that's good.

LORRAINE: And I hear you've written a simply marvelous play, Mr. Jefferson. I want you to read it to me—tonight. Will you? We'll go back to the Mansion House right after dinner, and you'll read me your play.

BERT: Why—why, I should say so. I'd be delighted. . . . Maggie, did you hear that? I'll bet *you* did this. You arranged the whole thing. Well, it's the finest Christmas present you could have given me.

(MAGGIE *looks at him for one anguished moment. Then, without a word, she dashes into the hall, grabs her coat and flings herself out of the house.*)

(BERT, *bewildered, stands looking after her.* MR. *and* MRS. STANLEY *come pellmell down the stairs. Each clutches a letter, and they are wild-eyed.*)

STANLEY: *Mr.* Whiteside! My son has run off on a freighter and my daughter is marrying an anarchist! They say *you* told them to do it!

MRS. STANLEY: My poor June! My poor Richard! This is the most awful—

WESTCOTT: Quiet! Quiet, please! We're going on the air.

STANLEY: How dare you! This is the most outrageous—

WESTCOTT (*raising his voice*): Please! Please! Quiet! We're going on the air.

(STANLEY *chokes and looks with fury.* MRS. STANLEY *is softly crying.*)

(*In this moment of stillness,* DR. BRADLEY *emerges from the dining room.*)

DR. BRADLEY: Oh! I see you're still busy.

STANLEY (*bursting forth*): Mr. Whiteside, you are the—

WESTCOTT (*yelling*): *Quiet!* For God's sake, quiet! QUIET! . . . All right, boys!

(*From the hallway come six* CHOIR BOYS, *dressed in their robes. They take their places by the microphone as the voice of the technician completes the hook-up.*)

TECHNICIAN: O.K., New York. (*He raises his arm, waiting to give the signal.* WESTCOTT *is watching him. There is a dead pause of about five seconds.* JOHN *and* SARAH *are on tiptoe in the dining room. Then the arm drops.*)

WESTCOTT (*into the microphone*): Good evening, everybody. Cream of Mush brings you Sheridan Whiteside.

(*The* LEADER *gestures to the* CHOIR BOYS, *and they raise their lovely voices in* "Heilige Nacht." *Another gesture from* WESTCOTT, *and* WHITESIDE *begins to speak, with the boys singing as a background.*)

WHITESIDE: This is Whiteside speaking. On this eve of eves, when my own heart is overflowing with peace and kindness, I think it is most fitting to tell once again the story of that still and lustrous night, nigh onto two thousand years ago, when first the star of Bethlehem was glimpsed in a wondrous sky . . .

(*The famous* WHITESIDE *voice goes out over the air to the listening millions as—*

THE CURTAIN FALLS

ACT THREE

SCENE—*Christmas morning.*
The bright December sunlight streams in through the window.
But the Christmas calm is quickly broken. From the library comes the roaring voice of MR. WHITESIDE. "*Miss Preen! Miss Preen!*"
MISS PREEN, *who is just coming through the dining room, rushes to open the library doors.*

MISS PREEN (*nervously*): Yes, sir. Yes, sir.

(MR. WHITESIDE, *in a mood, rolls himself into the room.*)

WHITESIDE: Where *do* you disappear to all the time, My Lady Nausea?
MISS PREEN (*firmly*): Mr. Whiteside, I can only be in one place at a time.

WHITESIDE: That's very fortunate for this community. . . . Go away, Miss Preen. You remind me of last week's laundry.

(MISS PREEN *goes indignantly into the library and slams the doors after her.*)
(JOHN *emerges from the dining room.*)

JOHN: Good morning, Mr. Whiteside. Merry Christmas.

WHITESIDE (*testily*): Merry Christmas, John. Merry Christmas.

JOHN: And Sarah and I want to thank you for the wonderful present.

WHITESIDE: That's quite all right, John.

JOHN: Are you ready for your breakfast, Mr. Whiteside?

WHITESIDE: No, I don't think I want any breakfast. . . . Has Miss Cutler come down yet?

JOHN: No, sir, not yet.

WHITESIDE: Is she in her room, do you know?

JOHN: Yes, sir, I think she is. Shall I call her?

WHITESIDE: No, no. That's all, John.

JOHN: Yes, sir.

(MAGGIE *comes down the stairs. She wears a traveling suit, and carries a bag.* WHITESIDE *waits for her to speak.*)

MAGGIE: I'm taking the one o'clock train, Sherry. I'm leaving.

WHITESIDE: You're doing nothing of the kind!

MAGGIE: Here are your keys—your driving license. The key to the safe-deposit vault is in the apartment in New York. I'll go in here now and clear things up. (*She opens the library doors.*)

WHITESIDE: Just a moment, Mrs. Siddons! Where *were* you until three o'clock this morning? I sat up half the night in this station wagon, worrying about you. You heard me calling to you when you came in. Why didn't you answer me?

MAGGIE: Look, Sherry, it's over, and you've won. I don't want to talk about it.

WHITESIDE: Oh, come, come, come, come, come. What are you trying to do—make me feel like a naughty, naughty boy? Honestly, Maggie, sometimes you can be very annoying.

MAGGIE (*looking at him in wonder*): You know, you're quite wonderful, Sherry, in a way. *You're* annoyed. I wish there was a laugh left in me. Shall I tell you something, Sherry? I think you are a selfish, petty egomaniac who would see his mother burned at the stake if that was the only way he could light his cigarette. I think you'd sacrifice your best friend without a moment's hesitation if he disturbed the sacred routine of your self-centered, paltry little life. I think you are incapable of any human emotion that goes higher up than your stomach, and I was the fool of the world for ever thinking I could trust you.

WHITESIDE (*pretty indignant at this*): Well, as long as I live, I shall never do anyone a good turn again. I won't ask you to apologize, Maggie, but six months from now you will be thanking me instead of berating me.

MAGGIE: In six months, Sherry, I expect to be so far away from you— (*She is halted by a loud voice from the hallway, as the door bangs. "Hello—hello—hello!" It is* BERT JEFFERSON *who enters, full of Christmas cheer.*)

BERT: Merry Christmas, everybody! Merry Christmas! I'm a little high, but I can explain everything. Hi, Maggie! Hi, Mr. Whiteside! Shake hands with a successful playwright. Maggie, why'd you run away last night? Where were you? Miss Sheldon thinks the play is wonderful. I read her the play and she thinks it's wonderful. Isn't that wonderful?

MAGGIE: Yes, that's fine, Bert.

BERT: Isn't that wonderful, Mr. Whiteside?

WHITESIDE: Jefferson, I think you ought to go home, don't you?

BERT: What? No—biggest day of my life. I know I'm a little drunk, but this is a big day. We've been sitting over in Billy's Tavern all night. Never realized it was daylight until it was daylight. . . . Listen, Maggie—Miss Sheldon says the play needs just a little bit of fixing—do it in three weeks. She's going to take me to a little place she's got in Lake Placid—just for three weeks. Going to work on the play together. Isn't it wonderful? Why don't you say something, Maggie?

WHITESIDE: Look, Bert, I suggest you tell us all about this later. Now, why don't you—(*He stops as* DR. BRADLEY *enters from the hallway.*)

DR. BRADLEY: Oh, excuse me! Merry Christmas, everybody. Merry Christmas.

BERT: God bless us all, and Tiny Tim.

DR. BRADLEY: Yes. . . . Mr. Whiteside, I thought perhaps if I came very early—

BERT: You know what, Doc? I'm going to Lake Placid for three weeks

—isn't that wonderful? Ever hear of Lorraine Sheldon, the famous actress? Well, we're going to Lake Placid for three weeks.

WHITESIDE: Dr. Bradley, would you do me a favor? I think Mr. Jefferson would like some black coffee and a little breakfast. Would you take care of him, please?

DR. BRADLEY (*none too pleased*): Yes, yes, of course.

BERT: Dr. Bradley, I'm going to buy breakfast for *you*—biggest breakfast you ever had.

DR. BRADLEY: Yes, yes. Come along, Jefferson.

BERT: You know what, Doctor? Let's climb down a couple of chimneys. I got a friend doesn't believe in Santa Claus—let's climb down his chimney and frighten the hell out of him. (*He goes out with the* DOCTOR.)

WHITESIDE (*in a burst of magnanimity*): Now listen to me, Maggie. I am willing to forgive your tawdry outburst and talk about this calmly.

MAGGIE (*now crying openly*): I love him so terribly. Oh, Sherry, Sherry, why did you do it? Why did you do it? (*She goes stumblingly into the library.*)

(WHITESIDE, *left alone, looks at his watch; heaves a long sigh. Then* HARRIET *comes down the steps, dressed for the street.*)

HARRIET: Merry Christmas, Mr. Whiteside.

WHITESIDE: Oh! . . . Merry Christmas, Miss Stanley.

HARRIET (*nervously*): I'm afraid I shouldn't be seen talking to you, Mr. Whiteside—my brother is terribly angry. I just couldn't resist asking —did you like my Christmas present?

WHITESIDE: I'm very sorry, Miss Stanley—I haven't opened it. I haven't opened any of my presents yet.

HARRIET: Oh, dear. I was so anxious to—it's right here, Mr. Whiteside. (*She goes to the tree.*) Won't you open it now?

WHITESIDE (*as he undoes the string*): I appreciate your thinking of me, Miss Stanley. This is very thoughtful of you. (*He takes out the gift.*) Why, it's lovely. I'm very fond of these old photographs. Thank you very much.

HARRIET: I was twenty-two when that was taken. That was my favorite dress. . . . Do you really like it?

WHITESIDE: I do indeed. When I get back to town I shall send *you* a little gift.

HARRIET: Will you? Oh, thank you, Mr. Whiteside. I shall treasure it. . . . Well, I shall be late for church. Good-bye. Good-bye.

WHITESIDE: Good-bye, Miss Stanley.

(*As she goes out the front door,* WHITESIDE'S *eyes return to the gift. He puzzles over it for a second, shakes his head. Mumbles to himself—"What is there about that woman?" Shakes his head again in perplexity.*)

(JOHN *comes from the dining room, en route to the second floor with* MRS. STANLEY'S *tray.*)

JOHN: Sarah's got a little surprise for you, Mr. Whiteside. She's just taking it out of the oven.

WHITESIDE: Thank you, John.

(JOHN *disappears up the stairs.*)

(*Then suddenly there is a great ringing of the doorbell. It stops for a second, then picks up violently again—rhythmically, this time. It continues until the door is opened.*)

WHITESIDE: Miss Preen! Miss Preen!

(MISS PREEN *comes hurrying from the library.*)

MISS PREEN: Yes, sir. Yes, sir.

WHITESIDE: Answer the door, will you? John is upstairs.

(MISS PREEN, *obviously annoyed, hurries to the door.*)

(*We hear her voice from the hallway: "Who is it?" An answering male voice: "Polly Adler's?" Then a little shriek from* MISS PREEN *and in a moment we see the reason why. She is carried into the room in the arms of a pixie-like gentleman, who is kissing her over and over.*)

THE GENTLEMAN CARRYING MISS PREEN: I love you madly—madly! Did you hear what I said—madly! Kiss me! Again! Don't be afraid of my passion. Kiss me! I can feel the hot blood pounding through your varicose veins.

MISS PREEN (*through all this*): Put me down! Put me down, do you hear! Don't you dare kiss me! Who are you! Put me down or I'll scream. Mr. Whiteside! Mr. Whiteside!

WHITESIDE: Banjo! Banjo, for God's sake!

BANJO (*quite calmly*): Hello, Whiteside. Will you sign for this package, please?

WHITESIDE: Banjo, put that woman down. That is my nurse, you mental delinquent.

BANJO (*Putting* MISS PREEN *on her feet*): Come to my room in half an hour and bring some rye bread. (*And for good measure he slaps* MISS PREEN *right on the fanny.*)

MISS PREEN (*outraged*): Really, Mr. Whiteside! (*She adjusts her clothes with a quick jerk and marches into the library.*)

BANJO: Whiteside, I'm here to spend Christmas with you. Give me a kiss! (*He starts to embrace him.*)

WHITESIDE: Get away from me, you reform-school fugitive. How did you get here anyway?

BANJO: Darryl Zanuck loaned me his reindeer. . . . Whiteside, we finished shooting the picture yesterday and I'm on my way to Nova Scotia. Flew here in twelve hours—borrowed an airplane from Howard Hughes. Whiteside, I brought you a wonderful Christmas present. (*He produces a little tissue-wrapped package.*) This brassière was once worn by Hedy Lamarr.

WHITESIDE: Listen, you idiot, how long can you stay?

BANJO: Just long enough to take a bath. I'm on my way to Nova Scotia. Where's Maggie?

WHITESIDE: Nova Scotia? What are you going to Nova Scotia for?

BANJO: I'm sick of Hollywood and there's a dame in New York I don't want to see. So I figured I'd go to Nova Scotia and get some good salmon. . . . Where the hell's Maggie? I want to see her. . . . What's the matter with you? Where is she?

WHITESIDE: Banjo, I'm glad you're here. I'm very annoyed at Maggie. Very!

BANJO: What's the matter? . . . (*To his considerable surprise, at this point, he sees* WHITESIDE *get up out of his chair and start to pace up and down the room.*) Say, what *is* this? I thought you couldn't walk.

WHITESIDE: Oh, I've been all right for weeks. That isn't the point. I'm furious at Maggie. She's turned on me like a viper. You know how fond I am of her. Well, after all these years she's repaying my affection by behaving like a fishwife.

BANJO: What are you talking about?

WHITESIDE: But I never believed for a moment she was really in love with him.

BANJO: In love with *who?* I just got here—remember.

WHITESIDE: Great God, I'm telling you, you Hollywood nitwit. A young newspaper man here in town.

BANJO (*surprised and pleased*): Maggie finally fell—well, what do you know? What kind of a guy is he?

WHITESIDE: Oh, shut up and listen, will you?

BANJO: Well, go on. What happened?

WHITESIDE: Well, Lorraine Sheldon happened to come out here and visit me.

BANJO: Old Hot-pants—here?

WHITESIDE: Now listen! He'd written a play—this young fellow. You can guess the rest. He's going away with Lorraine this afternoon. To "rewrite." So there you are. Maggie's in there now, crying her eyes out.

BANJO: Gee! . . . (*Thinking it over.*) Say, wait a minute. What do you mean Lorraine Sheldon *happened* to come out here? I smell a rat, Sherry—a rat with a beard.

(*And it might be well to add, at this point, that* MR. SHERIDAN WHITESIDE *wears a beard.*)

WHITESIDE: Well, all right, all right. But I did it for Maggie—because I thought it was the right thing for her.

BANJO: Oh, sure. You haven't thought of yourself in years. . . . Gee, poor kid. Can I go in and talk to her?

WHITESIDE: No—no. Leave her alone.

BANJO: Any way I could help, Sherry? Where's this guy live—this guy she likes? Can we get hold of him?

WHITESIDE: Now, wait a minute, Banjo. We don't want any phony warrants, or you pretending to be J. Edgar Hoover. I've been through all that with you before. (*He paces again.*) I got Lorraine out here and I've got to get her away.

BANJO: It's got to be good, Sherry. Lorraine's no dope. . . . Now, there must be *some*thing that would get her out of here like a bat out of hell. . . . Say! I think I've got it! That fellow she's so crazy about over in England—Lord Fanny or whatever it is. Bottomley—that's it!

WHITESIDE (*with a pained expression*): No, Banjo. No.

BANJO: Wait a minute—you don't catch on. We send Lorraine a cablegram from Lord Bottomley—

WHITESIDE: I catch on, Banjo. Lorraine caught on, too. It's been tried.

BANJO: Oh! . . . I told you she was no dope. . . . (*Seeing* WHITESIDE'S *chair, he sits in it and leans back with a good deal of pleasure.*) Well, you've got a tough proposition on your hands.

WHITESIDE: The trouble is there's so damned little time. . . . Get out of my chair! (WHITESIDE *gets back into it.*) Lorraine's taking him away with her this afternoon. Oh, damn, damn, damn. There must be some way out. The trouble is I've done this job too well. Hell and damnation.

BANJO (*pacing*): Stuck, huh?

WHITESIDE: In the words of one of our greatest lyric poets, you said it.

BANJO: Yeh. . . . Gee, I'm hungry. We'll think of something, Sherry—you watch. We'll get Lorraine out of here if I have to do it one piece at a time.

(SARAH *enters from the dining room bearing a tray on which reposes the culinary surprise that* JOHN *has mentioned. She holds it behind her back.*)

SARAH: Merry Christmas, Mr. Whiteside. . . . Excuse me. (*This last is to* BANJO.) I've got something for you. . . .

(BANJO *blandly lifts the latest delicacy and proceeds to eat it as* SARAH *presents the empty plate to* WHITESIDE.)

SARAH (*almost in tears*): But, Mr. Whiteside, it was for you.

WHITESIDE: Never mind, Sarah. He's quite mad.

BANJO: Come, Petrouchka, we will dance in the snow until all St. Petersburg is aflame with jealousy. (*He clutches* SARAH *and waltzes her toward the kitchen, loudly humming the Merry Widow waltz.*)

SARAH (*as she is borne away*): Mr. Whiteside! Mr. Whiteside!

WHITESIDE: Just give him some breakfast, Sarah. He's harmless.

(MR. WHITESIDE *barely has a moment in which to collect his thoughts before the library doors are opened and* MISS PREEN *emerges. It is* MISS PREEN *in street clothes this time, and with a suitcase in her hand.*)

(*She plants herself squarely in front of* WHITESIDE, *puts down her bag and starts drawing on a pair of gloves.*)

WHITESIDE: And just what does this mean?

MISS PREEN: It means, Mr. Whiteside, that I am leaving. My address is on the desk inside; you can send me a check.

WHITESIDE: You realize, Miss Preen, that this is completely unprofessional.

MISS PREEN: I do indeed. I am not only walking out on this case, Mr. Whiteside—I am leaving the nursing profession. I became a nurse because all my life, ever since I was a little girl, I was filled with the idea of serving a suffering humanity. After one month with you, Mr. Whiteside, I am going to work in a munitions factory. From now on anything that I can do to help exterminate the human race will fill me with the greatest of pleasure. If Florence Nightingale had ever nursed *you*, Mr. Whiteside, she would have married Jack the Ripper instead of founding the Red Cross. Good day. (*And she sails out.*)

(*Before* WHITESIDE *has time to digest this little bouquet*, MRS. STANLEY, *in a state of great fluttery excitement, rushes down the stairs.*)

MRS. STANLEY: Mr. Stanley is here with June. He's brought June back. Thank goodness, thank goodness. (*We hear her at the door.*) June, June, thank God you're back. You're not married, are you?

JUNE (*from the hallway*): No, Mother, I'm not. And please don't be hysterical.

(MRS. STANLEY *comes into view, her arms around a rebellious* JUNE. *Behind them looms* MR. STANLEY, *every inch the stern father.*)

MRS. STANLEY: Oh, June, if it had been anyone but that awful boy. You know how your father and I felt. . . . Ernest, thank goodness you stopped it. How did you do it?

STANLEY: Never mind that, Daisy. Just take June upstairs. I have something to say to Mr. Whiteside.

MRS. STANLEY: What about Richard? Is there any news?

STANLEY: It's all right, Daisy—all under control. Just take June upstairs.

JUNE: Father, haven't we had enough melodrama? I don't have to be taken upstairs—I'll go upstairs. . . . Merry Christmas, Mr. Whiteside. It looks bad for John L. Lewis. Come on, Mother—lock me in my room.

MRS. STANLEY: Now, June, you'll feel much better after you've had a hot bath, I know. Have you had anything to eat? (*She follows her daughter up the stairs.*)

(STANLEY *turns to* MR. WHITESIDE.)

STANLEY: I am pleased to inform you, sir, that your plans for my daughter seem to have gone a trifle awry. She is not, nor will she ever be, married to that labor agitator that you so kindly picked out for her. As for my son, he has been apprehended in Toledo, and will be brought back home within the hour. Not having your gift for invective, I cannot tell you what I think of your obnoxious interference in my affairs, but I have now arranged that you will interfere no longer. (*He turns toward the hallway.*) Come in, gentlemen. (*Two burly* MEN *come into view and stand in the archway.*) Mr. Whiteside, these gentlemen are deputy sheriffs. They have a warrant by which I am enabled to put you out of this house, and I need hardly add that it will be the greatest moment of my life. Mr. Whiteside—(*He looks at his watch.*)—I am giving you fifteen minutes in which to pack up and get out. If you are not gone in fifteen minutes, Mr. Whiteside, these gentlemen will forcibly eject you. (*He turns to the deputies.*) Thank you, gentlemen. Will you wait outside, please? (*The* TWO MEN *file out.*) Fifteen minutes, Mr. Whiteside—and that means bag, baggage, wheelchair, penguins, octopus and cockroaches. I am now going upstairs to smash our radio, so that not even accidentally will I ever hear your voice again.

WHITESIDE: Sure you don't want my autograph, old fellow?

STANLEY: Fifteen minutes, Mr. Whiteside. (*And he goes.*)

(BANJO, *still eating, returns from the kitchen.*)

BANJO: Well, Whiteside, I didn't get an idea. Any news from the front?

WHITESIDE: Yes. The enemy is at my rear, and nibbling.

BANJO: Where'd you say Maggie was? In there?

WHITESIDE: It's no use, Banjo. She's taking the one o'clock train out.

BANJO: No kidding? You didn't tell me that. You mean she's quitting you, after all these years? She's really leaving?

WHITESIDE: She is!

BANJO: That means you've only got till one o'clock to do something?

WHITESIDE: No, dear. I have exactly fifteen minutes—(*He looks at his watch.*)—ah—fourteen minutes in which to pull out of my hat the God-damnedest rabbit you have ever seen.

BANJO: What do you mean fifteen minutes?

WHITESIDE: In exactly fifteen minutes Baby's rosy little body is being tossed into the snow. My host has sworn out a warrant. I am being kicked out.

BANJO: What? I never heard of such a thing. What would he do a thing like that for?

WHITESIDE: Never mind, never mind. The point is, I have only fifteen minutes. Banjo dear, the master is growing a little desperate.

BANJO (*paces a moment*): What about laying your cards on the table with Lorraine?

WHITESIDE: Now, Banjo. You know Dream Girl as well as I do. What do *you* think?

BANJO: You're right. . . . Say! If I knew where she was I could get a car and run her over. It wouldn't hurt her much.

WHITESIDE (*wearily*): Banjo, for God's sake. Go in and talk to Maggie for a minute—right in there. I want to think.

BANJO: Could we get a doctor to say Lorraine has smallpox?

WHITESIDE: Please, Banjo. I've got to think.

BANJO (*opening the library doors*): Pardon me, miss, is this the Y.M.C.A.?

(*The doors close.*)

(WHITESIDE *is alone again. He leans back, concentrating intensely. He shakes his head as, one after another, he discards a couple of ideas.*)

(*We hear the outer door open and close, and from the hallway comes* RICHARD. *Immediately behind him is a stalwart-looking* MAN *with an air of authority.*)

THE MAN (*to* RICHARD, *as he indicates* WHITESIDE): Is this your father?

RICHARD: No, you idiot. . . . Hello, Mr. Whiteside. I didn't get very far. Any suggestions?

WHITESIDE: I'm very sorry, Richard—very sorry indeed. I wish I were in position—

STANLEY (*descending the stairs*): Well, you're *not* in position. . . . Thank you very much, officer. Here's a little something for your trouble.

THE MAN: Thank you, sir. Good day. (*He goes.*)

STANLEY: Will you go upstairs please, Richard?

> (RICHARD *hesitates for a second. Looks at his father, then at* WHITESIDE; *silently goes up the steps.*)
> (MR. STANLEY *follows him, but pauses on the landing.*)

STANLEY: *Ten* minutes, Mr. Whiteside. (*And he goes.*)

> (JOHN *enters from the dining room, bringing a glass of orange juice.*)

JOHN: Here you are, Mr. Whiteside. Feeling any better?

WHITESIDE: Superb. Any cyanide in this orange juice, John? (*The doorbell rings.*) Open the door, John. It's probably some mustard gas from an old friend.

JOHN (*en route to the door*): Yes, sir. . . . Say, that crazy fellow made a great hit with Sarah. He wants to give her a screen test.

> *At the outer door we hear* LORRAINE'S *voice: "Good morning! Is Mr. Whiteside up yet?"* JOHN'S *answer: "Yes, he is, Miss Sheldon— he's right here."*)
> (WHITESIDE *groans as he hears her voice.*)

LORRAINE (*entering, in a very smart Christmas morning costume*): Merry Christmas, darling! Merry Christmas! I've come to have Christmas breakfast with you, my dear. May I? (*She kisses him.*)

WHITESIDE (*nothing matters any more*): Of course, my sprite. John, a tray for Miss Sheldon—better make it one-minute eggs.

LORRAINE: Sherry, it's the most perfect Christmas morning—the snow is absolutely glistening. Too bad you can't get out.

WHITESIDE: Oh, I'll probably see a bit of it. . . . I hear you're off for Lake Placid, my blossom. What time are you going?

LORRAINE: Oh, Sherry, how did you know? Is Bert here?

WHITESIDE: No, he rolled in a little while ago. Worked rather fast, didn't you, dear?

LORRAINE: Darling, I was just swept off my feet by the play—it's fantastically good. Sherry, it's the kind of part that only comes along once in ten years. I'm so grateful to you, darling. Really, Sherry, sometimes I think that you're the only friend I have in the world.

WHITESIDE (*dryly*): Thank you, dear. What time did you say you were leaving—you and Jefferson?

LORRAINE: Oh, I don't know—I think it's four o'clock. You know, quite apart from anything else, Sherry, Bert is really a very attractive man. It makes it rather a pleasure, squaring accounts with little Miss Vitriol. In fact, it's all worked out beautifully. . . . Sherry lamb, I want to give you the most beautiful Christmas present you've ever had in your life. Now, what do you want? Anything! I'm deliriously happy that—(*A bellowing laugh comes from the library. She stops, lips compressed.*) That sounds like Banjo. Is he here?

WHITESIDE: He is, my dear. Just the family circle gathering at Christmas. (*A look at his watch.*) My, how time flies when you're having fun.

(BANJO *emerges from the library.*)

BANJO: Why, hello, Sweetie Pants! How are you?

LORRAINE (*not over-cordial*): Very well, thank you. And you, Banjo?

BANJO: I'm fine, fine. How's the mattress business, Lorraine?

LORRAINE: *Very* funny. It's too bad, Banjo, that your pictures aren't as funny as you seem to think *you* are.

BANJO: You've got me there, mama. Say, you look in the pink, Lorraine. . . . Anything in the wind, Whiteside?

WHITESIDE: Not a glimmer.

BANJO: What time does the boat sail?

WHITESIDE: Ten minutes.

LORRAINE: What boat is this?

BANJO: The good ship Up the Creek. . . . Oh, well! You feel fine, huh, Lorraine?

LORRAINE: What? Yes, of course I do. . . . Where's that breakfast, Sherry?

(MAGGIE *emerges from the library, a sheaf of papers in her hand. She stops imperceptibly as she sees* LORRAINE.)

MAGGIE: I've listed everything except the New Year's Eve broadcast. Wasn't there a schedule on that?

WHITESIDE (*uneasily*): I think it's on the table there, some place.

MAGGIE: Thank you. (*She turns to the papers on the table.*)

LORRAINE (*obviously for* MAGGIE'S *ears*): New Year's Eve? Oh, Bert and I'll hear it in Lake Placid. You were at my cottage up there once, weren't you, Sherry? It's lovely, isn't it? Away from everything. Just snow and clear, cold nights. (*The doorbell rings.*) Oh, that's probably Bert. I told him to meet me here. (MAGGIE, *as though she had not heard a word, goes quietly into the library.* LORRAINE *relaxes.*) You know, I'm looking forward to Lake Placid. Bert's the kind of man who will do all winter sports beautifully.

BANJO (*gently*): Will he get time?

(*Voices are heard from the hallway. "Whiteside?" "Yes, sir." "American Express."* JOHN *backs into the room, obviously directing a major operation.*)

JOHN: All right—come ahead. Care now—careful—right in here. It's for you, Mr. Whiteside.

LORRAINE: Why, Sherry, what's this?

(*Into view come two* EXPRESSMEN, *groaning and grunting under the weight of nothing more or less than an Egyptian mummy case. It seems that* MR. WHITESIDE'S *friends are liable to think of anything.*)

EXPRESSMAN: Where do you want this put?

JOHN: Right there.

WHITESIDE: Dear God, if there was one thing I needed right now it was an Egyptian mummy.

BANJO (*reading from a tag*): "Merry Christmas from the Khedive of Egypt." What did you send *him*? Grant's Tomb?

(MR. STANLEY, *drawn by the voices of the* EXPRESSMEN, *has descended the stairs in time to witness this newest hue and cry.*)

STANLEY (*surveying the scene*): *Five* minutes, Mr. Whiteside! (*He indicates the mummy case.*) Including *that.* (*And up the stairs again.*)

LORRAINE: Why, what was all that about? Who is that man?

WHITESIDE: He announces the time every few minutes. I pay him a small sum.

LORRAINE: But what on earth for, Sherry?

WHITESIDE (*violently*): I lost my watch!

(*From the hallway a familiar figure peeps in.*)

DR. BRADLEY: Oh, excuse me, Mr. Whiteside. Are you busy?

WHITESIDE (*closing his eyes*): Good God!

DR. BRADLEY (*coming into the room*): I've written a new chapter on the left kidney. Suppose I—(*He smiles apologetically at* LORRAINE *and* BANJO.) Pardon me. (*Goes into the library.*)

LORRAINE: Is that the plumber again, Sherry? . . . Oh, dear, I wonder where Bert is. . . . Darling, you're not very Christmasy—you're usually bubbling over on Christmas morning. . . . *Who* sent this to you, Sherry—the Khedive of Egypt? You know, I think it's rather beautiful. I must go to Egypt some day—I really must. I know I'd love it. The first time I went to Pompeii I cried all night. All those people—all those lives. Where are they now? Sherry! Don't you ever think about that? I do. Here was a woman—like myself—a woman who once lived and loved, full of the same passions, fears, jealousies, hates. And what remains of any of it now? Just this, and nothing more. (*She opens the case, then, with a sudden impulse, steps into it and folds her arms, mummy-fashion.*) A span of four thousand years —a mere atom in the eternity of time—and here am I, another woman living out her life. I want to cry. (*She closes her eyes, and as she stands there, immobilized, the eyes of* BANJO *and* WHITESIDE *meet. The same idea has leaped into their minds.* BANJO, *rising slowly from the couch, starts to approach the mummy case, casually whistling "Dixie." But just before he reaches it* LORRAINE *steps blandly out.*)

LORRAINE: Oh, I mustn't talk this way today. It's Christmas, it's Christmas!

(BANJO *puts on a great act of unconcern.*)

WHITESIDE (*rising to the occasion, and dripping pure charm*): Lorraine dear, have you ever played Saint Joan?

LORRAINE: No, I haven't, Sherry. What makes you ask that?

WHITESIDE: There was something about your expression as you stood in that case—there was an absolute halo about you.

LORRAINE: Why, Sherry, how sweet!

WHITESIDE: It transcended any mortal expression I've ever seen. Step into it again, dear.

LORRAINE: Sherry, you're joshing me—aren't you?

WHITESIDE: My dear, I don't make light of these things. I was deeply moved. There was a strange beauty about you, Lorraine—pure da Vinci. Please do it again.

LORRAINE: Well, I don't know exactly what it was that I did, but I'll— (*She starts to step into the case again, then changes her mind.*) Oh, I feel too silly, Sherry.

(BANJO'S *eyes are fixed somewhere on the ceiling, but he is somewhat less innocent than he seems.*)

WHITESIDE (*returning to the battle*): Lorraine dear, in that single moment you approached the epitome of your art, and you should not be ashamed of it. You asked me a little while ago what I wanted for a Christmas present. All that I want, Lorraine, is the memory of you in that mummy case.

LORRAINE: Why, darling, I'm—all choked up. (*Crossing her arms, she takes a moment or two to throw herself in the mood, then steps reverently into the case.*) "Dust thou art, and dust to dust—"

(*Bang!* BANJO *has closed the case and fastened it.* WHITESIDE *leaps out of the chair.*)

WHITESIDE: Eureka!

BANJO: There's service for you!

WHITESIDE: Will she be all right in there?

BANJO: Sure—she can breathe easy. I'll let her out as soon as we get on the plane. . . . What are we going to do now? How do we get this out of here?

WHITESIDE: One thing at a time—that's the next step.

BANJO: Think fast, Captain. Think fast.

(*And* MAGGIE *enters from the library, papers in hand.* WHITESIDE *scrambles back into his chair;* BANJO *is again the little innocent.*)

MAGGIE: This is everything, Sherry—I'm leaving three carbons. Is there anything out here? (*She inspects a small basket fastened to his chair.*) What's in this basket?

WHITESIDE (*eager to be rid of her*): Nothing at all. Thank you, thank you.

MAGGIE: Shall I file these letters? Do you want this picture?

WHITESIDE: No—throw everything away. Wait—give me the picture. I want the picture.

MAGGIE: The only thing I haven't done is to put all your broadcasts in order. Do you want me to do that?

WHITESIDE (*a flash of recollection has come to him as he takes* HARRIET's *photograph in his hand, but he contrives to smother his excitement*): What? . . . Ah—do that, will you? Do it right away —it's very important. Right away, Maggie.

MAGGIE: I'll see you before I go, Banjo. (*She goes into the library again, closing the doors.*)

WHITESIDE (*watching her out, then jumping up in great excitement*): I've got it!

BANJO: What?

WHITESIDE: I knew I'd seen this face before! I knew it! Now I know how to get this out of here.

BANJO: What face? How?

(*And, at that instant,* MR. STANLEY *comes down the stairs, watch in hand.*)

STANLEY (*vastly enjoying himself*): The time is up, Mr. Whiteside. Fifteen minutes.

WHITESIDE: Ah, yes, Mr. Stanley. Fifteen minutes. But just one favor before I go. I would like you to summon those two officers and ask them to help this gentleman down to the airport with this mummy case. Would you be good enough to do that, Mr. Stanley?

STANLEY: I will do nothing of the kind.

WHITESIDE (*ever so sweetly*): Oh, I think you will, Mr. Stanley. Or shall I inform my radio audience, on my next broadcast, that your sister, Harriet Stanley, is none other than the famous Harriet Sedley, who murdered her mother and father with an axe twenty-five years ago in Gloucester, Massachusetts. . . . (*At which* MR. STANLEY *quietly collapses into a chair.*) Come, Mr. Stanley, it's a very small favor. Or would you rather have the good folk of Mesalia repeating at your very doorstep that once popular little jingle:

> "Harriet Sedley took an axe
> And gave her mother forty whacks,
> And when the job was nicely done,
> She gave her father forty-one."

Remember, Mr. Stanley, I too am giving up something. It would make a hell of a broadcast. . . . Well?

STANLEY (*licked at last*): Mr. Whiteside, you are the damnedest person I have ever met.

WHITESIDE: I often think so myself, old fellow. . . . Officers, will you come in here, please?

BANJO: Whiteside, you're a great man. (*He places a reverent kiss on the mummy case.*)

WHITESIDE (*as the* DEPUTIES *enter*): Come right in, officers. Mr. Stanley would like you to help this gentleman down to the airport with this mummy case. He is sending it to a friend in Nova Scotia.

BANJO: Collect.

WHITESIDE: Right, Mr. Stanley?

STANLEY (*weakly*): Yes. . . . Yes.

WHITESIDE: Thank you, gentlemen—handle it carefully. . . . Banjo, my love, you're wonderful and I may write a book about you.

BANJO: Don't bother—I can't read. (*To* MAGGIE, *as she enters from library.*) Good-bye, Maggie—love conquers all. . . . Don't drop that case, boys—it contains an antique. (*And out he goes with the mummy case, to say nothing of* MISS LORRAINE SHELDON.)

MAGGIE (*catching on to what has happened*): Sherry! Sherry, was that—?

WHITESIDE: It was indeed. The field is clear and you have my blessing.

MAGGIE: Sherry! Sherry, you old reprobate!

WHITESIDE: Just send me a necktie some time. My hat and coat, Maggie, and also your railroad ticket. I am leaving for New York.

MAGGIE: You're leaving, Sherry?

WHITESIDE: Don't argue, Rat Girl—Do as you're told.

MAGGIE: Yes, Mr. Whiteside. (*She goes happily into the library, just as* BERT *returns.*)

BERT: Mr. Whiteside, I want to apologize for—

WHITESIDE: Don't give it a thought, Bert. There's been a slight change of plan. Miss Sheldon is off on a world cruise—I am taking your play to Katharine Cornell. Miss Cutler will explain everything. (MAGGIE *brings* WHITESIDE'S *coat, hat, cane.*) Oh, thank you, Maggie, my darling.

(*And just then the* DOCTOR *comes out of the library. Still trying.*)

DR. BRADLEY: Mr. Whiteside, are you very busy?

WHITESIDE: Ah, yes, Doctor. *Very* busy. But if you ever get to New York, Doctor, try and find me. (*He takes* MAGGIE *in his arms.*) Good-bye, my lamb. I love you very much.

MAGGIE: Sherry, you're wonderful.

WHITESIDE: Nonsense. . . . Good-bye, Jefferson. You'll never know the trouble you've caused.

BERT: Good-bye, Mr. Whiteside.

WHITESIDE: Good-bye, Mr. Stanley. I would like to hear, in the near future, that your daughter has married her young man and that your son has been permitted to follow his own bent. OR ELSE. . . . Merry Christmas, everybody! (*And out he strolls.*)

(*But the worst is yet to come. There is a loud crash on the porch, followed by an anguished yell.* MAGGIE *gives a little shriek and rushes out.* BERT *and the* DOCTOR *rush after her. Down the stairs come* MRS. STANLEY, JUNE *and* RICHARD. *From the dining room* JOHN *and* SARAH *come running.* "*What's happened?*" "*What is it?*")

(*And then we see. Into view come* BERT *and the* DOCTOR, *carrying* MR. WHITESIDE *between them. He is screaming his head off.*)

WHITESIDE: Miss Preen! Miss Preen! I want Miss Preen back! . . . Mr. Stanley, I am suing you for *three* hundred and fifty thousand dollars!

(MR. STANLEY *throws up his hands in despair.* MRS. STANLEY *simply faints away.*)

CURTAIN

Life With Father

HOWARD LINDSAY
and
RUSSEL CROUSE

Why our respondents liked

 LIFE WITH FATHER

"A perfect recreation of Clarence Day's perfect recreation of his wonderfully irascible and loveable father."

GEORGE OPPENHEIMER

"Clarence Day was created by the Lord for the theatre."

DORE SCHARY

"Charming, human, elegant and uproarious."

JOSHUA LOGAN

Life With Father has the distinction of being the second longest-running play in Broadway history. Howard Lindsay, with his previous writing, acting, and directing credits, and Russel Crouse, formerly a newspaper columnist, worked on the script for the play for two years. Prior to this success, they had jointly produced a series of musical comedy librettos. *Life With Father* was adapted from the late Clarence Day's humorous autobiographical sketches which had appeared in magazine and newspaper articles. Originally, he and his wife were reluctant to permit the stories to be adapted into a play. Mr. Day felt that most books about real people were either about glamorous life-styles or unusual or unique situations, whereas he felt his own family was rather conventional. Eventually, the family's opposition subsided, and Mrs. Day served as a consultant in bringing these stories to the stage. From the beginning the play was tremendously popular, with audiences taking great delight in looking in on life with the Day family in the New York of the 1880s. *Life With Father*'s first production was staged in a summer theatre in Maine with Howard Lindsay and his wife Dorothy Stickney in the lead roles of Clarence and Vinnie Day. The play then moved to Broadway on November 8, 1939, and didn't close until July 12, 1947, having achieved the world's longest unbroken run of a play and establishing itself as a much-loved classic of the American people.

Life With Father was presented by Oscar Serlin on November 8, 1939, at the Empire Theatre, New York City. The play was adapted by Howard Lindsay and Russel Crouse from a book and essays by Clarence Day. The cast was as follows:

Vinnie	Dorothy Stickney
Annie	Katherine Bard
Clarence	John Drew Devereaux
John	Richard Simon
Whitney	Raymond Roe
Harlan	Larry Robinson
Father	Howard Lindsay
Margaret	Dorothy Bernard
Cora	Ruth Hammond
Mary	Teresa Wright
The Rev. Dr. Lloyd	Richard Sterling
Delia	Portia Morrow
Nora	Nellie Burt
Dr. Humphreys	A. H. Van Buren
Dr. Somers	John C. King
Maggie	Timothy Kearse

Staged by Bretaigne Windust
Setting and costumes by Stewart Chaney

*The entire action of the play takes place in the Morning Room
of the Day house on Madison Avenue, New York City, 1880.*

ACT ONE

SCENE 1: *Breakfast time. An early summer afternoon.*
SCENE 2: *Tea time. The same day.*

ACT TWO

SCENE 1: *Sunday, after church. A week later.*
SCENE 2: *Breakfast time. Two days later.*
*(During Scene 2 the curtain is lowered to denote
a lapse of three hours.)*

ACT THREE

SCENE 1: *Mid-afternoon. A month later.*
SCENE 2: *Breakfast time. The next morning.*

ACT ONE

SCENE I

The Morning Room of the Day home at 420 Madison Avenue. In the custom of the Victorian period, this was the room where the family gathered for breakfast, and because it was often the most comfortable room in the house, it served also as a living-room for the family and their intimates.

There is a large arch in the center of the upstage wall of the room, through which we can see the hall and the stairs leading to the second floor, and below them the rail of the stairwell leading to the basement. The room can be closed off from the hall by sliding doors in the archway. The front door of the house, which is stage right, can't be seen, but frequently is heard to slam.

In the Morning Room the sunshine streams through the large window at the right which looks out on Madison Avenue. The room itself is furnished with the somewhat less than comfortable furniture of the period, which is the late 1880's. The general color scheme in drapes and upholstery is green. Below the window is a large comfortable chair where Father generally sits to read his paper. Right of center is the table which serves as a living-room table, with its proper table cover and fruit bowl; but now, expanded by extra leaves, it is doing service as a breakfast table. Against the back wall, either side of the arch, are two console tables which are used by the maid as serving tables. Left of center is a sofa, with a table just above its right end holding a lamp, framed photographs, and other ornaments. In the left wall is a fireplace, its mantel draped with a lambrequin. On the mantel are a clock and other ornaments, and above the mantel is a large mirror in a Victorian frame. The room is cluttered with the minutiæ of the period, including the inevitable rubber plant, and looking down from the walls are the Day ancestors in painted portraits. The room has the warm quality that comes only from having been lived in by a family which enjoys each other's company—a family of considerable means.

As the curtain rises, ANNIE, *the new maid, a young Irish girl, is finishing setting the table for breakfast. After an uncertain look at the result she crosses over to her tray on the console table.* VINNIE *comes down the stairs and into the room.* VINNIE *is a charming, lovable, and spirited woman of forty. She has a lively mind which darts quickly away from any practical matter. She has red hair.*

ANNIE: Good morning, ma'am.

VINNIE: Good morning, Annie. How are you getting along?

ANNIE: All right, ma'am, I hope.

VINNIE: Now, don't be worried just because this is your first day. Everything's going to be all right—but I do hope nothing goes wrong (*Goes to the table.*) Now, let's see, is the table all set? (ANNIE *follows her.*) The cream and the sugar go down at this end.

ANNIE (*placing them where* VINNIE *has indicated*): I thought in the center, ma'am; everyone could reach them easier.

VINNIE: Mr. Day sits here.

ANNIE (*gets a tray of napkins, neatly rolled and in their rings, from the console table*): I didn't know where to place the napkins, ma'am.

VINNIE: You can tell which go where by the rings. (*Takes them from the tray and puts them down as she goes around the table.* ANNIE *follows her.*) This one belongs to Whitney—it has his initial on it, "W" that one with the little dog on it is Harlan's, of course. He's the baby. This "J" is for John and the "C" is for Clarence. This narrow plain one is mine. And this is Mr. Day's. It's just like mine—except that it got bent one morning. And that reminds me—always be sure Mr. Day's coffee is piping hot.

ANNIE: Ah, your man has coffee instead of tea of a morning?

VINNIE: We all have coffee except the two youngest boys. They have their milk. And, Annie, always speak of my husband as Mr. Day.

ANNIE: I will that.

VINNIE (*correcting her*): "Yes, ma'am," Annie.

ANNIE: Yes, ma'am.

VINNIE: And if Mr. Day speaks to you, just say: "Yes, sir." Don't be nervous—you'll get used to him.

(CLARENCE, *the eldest son, about seventeen, comes down the stairs and into the room. He is a manly, serious, good-looking boy. Because he is starting at Yale next year, he thinks he is grown-up. He is red-headed.*)

CLARENCE: Good morning, Mother. (*He kisses her.*)

VINNIE: Good morning, Clarence.

CLARENCE: Did you sleep well, Mother?

VINNIE: Yes, thank you, dear. (CLARENCE *goes to* FATHER'S *chair and picks up the morning paper.*) (*To* ANNIE.) We always start with fruit, except the two young boys, who have porridge. (ANNIE *brings the fruit and porridge to the table.* CLARENCE, *looking at the paper, makes a whistling sound.*)

CLARENCE: Jiminy! Another wreck on the New Haven. That always disturbs the market. Father won't like that.

VINNIE: I do wish that New Haven would stop having wrecks. If they knew how it upset your father—(*Sees that* CLARENCE'S *coat has been torn and mended.*) My soul and body, Clarence, what's happened to your coat?

CLARENCE: I tore it. Margaret mended it for me.

VINNIE: It looks terrible. Why don't you wear your blue suit?

CLARENCE: That looks worse than this one. You know. I burnt that hole in it.

VINNIE: Oh, yes—well, you can't go around looking like that. I'll have to speak to your father. Oh, dear!

(JOHN, *who is about fifteen, comes down the stairs and into the room.* JOHN *is gangly and a little overgrown. He is red-headed.*)

JOHN: Good morning, Mother. (*He kisses her.*)

VINNIE: Good morning, John.

JOHN (*to* CLARENCE): Who won?

CLARENCE: I haven't looked yet.

JOHN: Let me see. (*He tries to take the paper away from* CLARENCE.)

CLARENCE: Be careful!

VINNIE: Boys, don't wrinkle that paper before your father's looked at it.

CLARENCE (*to* JOHN): Yes!

(VINNIE *turns to* ANNIE.)

VINNIE: You'd better get things started. We want everything ready when Mr. Day comes down. (ANNIE *exits.*) Clarence, right after breakfast I want you and John to move the small bureau from my room into yours.

CLARENCE: What for? Is somebody coming to visit us?

JOHN: Who's coming?

VINNIE: I haven't said anyone was coming. And don't you say anything about it. I want it to be a surprise.

CLARENCE: Oh! Father doesn't know yet?

VINNIE: No. And I'd better speak to him about a new suit for you before he finds out he's being surprised by visitors.

(ANNIE *enters with a tray on which are two glasses of milk, which she puts at* HARLAN'S *and* WHITNEY'S *places at the table.*)

(WHITNEY *comes down the stairs and rushes into the room. He is about thirteen. Suiting his age, he is a lively active boy. He is red-headed.*)

WHITNEY: Morning. (*He kisses his mother quickly, then runs to* CLARENCE *and* JOHN.) Who won?

JOHN: The Giants, 7 to 3. Buck Ewing hit a home run.

WHITNEY: Let me see!

(HARLAN *comes sliding down the banister. He enters the room, runs to his mother, and kisses her.* HARLAN *is a roly-poly, lovable, good-natured youngster of six. He is red-headed.*)

VINNIE: How's your finger, darling?

HARLAN: It itches.

VINNIE (*kissing the finger*): That's a sign it's getting better. Now don't scratch it. Sit down, boys. Get in your chair, darling. (*The boys move to the table and take their places.* CLARENCE *puts the newspaper beside his father's plate.* JOHN *stands waiting to place* VINNIE'S *chair when she sits.*) Now, Annie, watch Mr. Day, and as soon as he finishes his fruit—(*Leaves the admonition hanging in mid-air as the sound of* FATHER'S *voice booms from upstaris.*)

FATHER'S VOICE: Vinnie! Vinnie!

(*All eyes turn toward the staircase.* VINNIE *rushes to the foot of the stairs, speaking as she goes.*)

VINNIE: What's the matter, Clare?

FATHER'S VOICE: Where's my necktie?

VINNIE: Which necktie?

FATHER'S VOICE: The one I gave you yesterday.

VINNIE: It isn't pressed yet. I forgot to give it to Margaret.

FATHER'S VOICE: I told you distinctly I wanted to wear that necktie today.

VINNIE: You've got plenty of neckties. Put on another one right away and come down to breakfast.

FATHER'S VOICE: Oh, damn! Damnation!

(VINNIE *goes to her place at the table.* JOHN *places her chair for her, then sits.* WHITNEY *has started eating.*)

CLARENCE: Whitney!

VINNIE: Wait for your father, Whitney.

WHITNEY: Oh, and I'm in a hurry! John, can I borrow your glove today? I'm going to pitch.

JOHN: If I don't play myself.

WHITNEY: Look, if you need it, we're playing in that big field at the corner of Fifty-seventh and Madison.

VINNIE: 'Way up there!

WHITNEY: They're building a house on that vacant lot on Fiftieth Street.

VINNIE: My! My! My! Here we move to Forty-eighth Street just to get out of the city!

WHITNEY: Can't I start breakfast, Mother? I promised to be there by eight o'clock.

VINNIE: After breakfast, Whitney, you have to study your catechism.

WHITNEY: Mother, can't I do that this afternoon?

VINNIE: Whitney, you have to learn five questions every morning before you leave the house.

WHITNEY: Aw, Mother—

VINNIE: You weren't very sure of yourself when I heard you last night.

WHITNEY: I know them now.

VINNIE: Let's see. (WHITNEY *rises and faces his mother.*) "What is your name?"

WHITNEY: Whitney Benjamin.

VINNIE: "Who gave you this name?"

WHITNEY: "My sponsors in baptism, wherein I was made a member of Christ, the child of God and an inheritor of the Kingdom of Heaven." Mother, if I hadn't been baptized wouldn't I have a name?

VINNIE: Not in the sight of the Church. "What did your sponsors then for you?"

WHITNEY: "They did promise and vow three things in my name—"

(FATHER *makes his appearance on the stairway and comes down into the room.* FATHER *is in his forties, distinguished in appearance, with great charm and vitality, extremely well dressed in a conservative way. He is red-headed.*)

FATHER (*heartily*): Good morning, boys. (*They rise and answer him.*) Good morning, Vinnie. (*He goes to her and kisses her.*) Have a good night?

VINNIE: Yes, thank you, Clare.

FATHER: Good! Sit down, boys.

(*The doorbell rings and a postman's whistle is heard.*)

VINNIE: That's the doorbell, Annie. (ANNIE *exits.*) Clare, that new suit looks very nice.

FATHER: Too damn tight! (*He sits in his place at the head of the table.*) What's the matter with those fellows over in London? I wrote them a year ago they were making my clothes too tight!

VINNIE: You've put on a little weight, Clare.

FATHER: I weigh just the same as I always have. (*Attacks his orange. The boys dive into their breakfasts.* ANNIE *enters with the mail, starts to take it to* VINNIE. FATHER *sees her.*) What's that? The mail? That goes to me.

(ANNIE *gives the mail to* FATHER *and exits with her tray.*)

VINNIE: Well, Clarence has just managed to tear the only decent suit of clothes he has.

FATHER (*looking through the mail*): Here's one for you, Vinnie. John, hand that to your mother. (*He passes the letter on.*)

VINNIE: Clare dear, I'm sorry, but I'm afraid Clarence is going to have to have a new suit of clothes.

FATHER: Vinnie, Clarence has to learn not to be so hard on his clothes.

CLARENCE: Father, I thought—

FATHER: Clarence, when you start in Yale in the fall, I'm going to set aside a thousand dollars just to outfit you, but you'll get no new clothes this summer.

CLARENCE: Can't I have one of your old suits cut down for me?

FATHER: Every suit I own still has plenty of wear in it. I wear my clothes until they're worn out.

VINNIE: Well, if you want your clothes worn out, Clarence can wear them out much faster than you can.

CLARENCE: Yes, and, Father, you don't get a chance to wear them out. Every time you get a new batch of clothes, Mother sends the old ones to the missionary barrel. I guess I'm just as good as any old missionary.

(ANNIE *returns with a platter of bacon and eggs and a pot of coffee.*)

VINNIE: Clarence, before you compare yourself to a missionary, remember the sacrifices they make.

FATHER (*chuckling*): I don't know, Vinnie, I think my clothes would look better on Clarence than on some Hottentot. (*To* CLARENCE.) Have that black suit of mine cut down to fit you before your mother gets her hands on it.

(ANNIE *clears the fruit.*)

CLARENCE: Thank you, Father. (*To John.*) One of Father's suits! Thank you, sir!

FATHER: Whitney, don't eat so fast.

WHITNEY: Well, Father, I'm going to pitch today and I promised to get there early, but before I go I have to study my catechism.

FATHER: What do you bother with that for?

VINNIE (*with spirit*): Because if he doesn't know his catechism he can't be confirmed!

WHITNEY (*pleading*): But I'm going to pitch today.

FATHER: Vinnie, Whitney's going to pitch today and he can be confirmed any old time.

VINNIE: Clare, sometimes it seems to me that you don't care whether your children get to Heaven or not.

FATHER: Oh, Whitney'll get to Heaven all right. (*To* WHITNEY.) I'll be there before you are, Whitney; I'll see that you get in.

VINNIE: What makes you so sure they'll let you in?

FATHER: Well, if they don't I'll certainly raise a devil of a row.

(ANNIE *is at* FATHER'S *side with the platter of bacon and eggs, ready to serve him, and draws back at this astounding declaration, raising the platter.*)

VINNIE (*with shocked awe*): Clare, I do hope you'll behave when you get to Heaven.

(FATHER *has turned to serve himself from the platter, but* ANNIE, *not yet recovered from the picture of* FATHER *raising a row at the gates of Heaven, is holding it too high for him.*)

FATHER (*storming*): Vinnie, how many times have I asked you not to engage a maid who doesn't even know how to serve properly?

VINNIE: Clare, can't you see she's new and doing her best?

FATHER: How can I serve myself when she's holding that platter over my head?

VINNIE: Annie, why don't you hold it lower?

(ANNIE *lowers the platter.* FATHER *serves himself, but goes on talking.*)

FATHER: Where'd she come from anyway? What became of the one we had yesterday? I don't see why you can't keep a maid.

VINNIE: Oh, you don't!

FATHER: All I want is service. (ANNIE *serves the others nervously. So far as* FATHER *is concerned, however, the storm has passed, and he turns genially to* WHITNEY.) Whitney, when we get to Heaven we'll organize a baseball team of our own.

(*The boys laugh.*)

VINNIE: It would be just like you to try to run things up there.

FATHER: Well, from all I've heard about Heaven, it seems to be a pretty unbusinesslike place. They could probably use a good man like me. (*Stamps on the floor three times. It is his traditional signal to summon* MARGARET, *the cook, from the kitchen below.*)

VINNIE: What do you want Margaret for? What's wrong?

(ANNIE *has reached the sideboard and is sniffling audibly.*)

FATHER (*distracted*): What's that damn noise?

VINNIE: Shhh—it's Annie.

FATHER: Annie? Who's Annie?

VINNIE: The maid. (ANNIE, *seeing that she has attracted attention, hurries out into the hall where she can't be seen or heard.*) Clare, aren't you ashamed of yourself?

FATHER (*surprised*): What have I done now?

VINNIE: You made her cry—speaking to her the way you did.

FATHER: I never said a word to her—I was addressing myself to you.

VINNIE: I do wish you'd be more careful. It's hard enough to keep a maid—and the uniforms just fit this one.

(MARGARET, *the cook, a small Irishwoman of about fifty, hurries into the room.*)

MARGARET: What's wanting?

FATHER: Margaret, this bacon is *good*. (MARGARET *beams and gestures deprecatingly.*) It's *good*. It's done just right!

MARGARET: Yes, sir!

(*She smiles and exits.* ANNIE *returns, recovered, and starts serving the coffee.* VINNIE *has opened her letter and glanced through it.*)

VINNIE: Clare, this letter gives me a good idea. I've decided that next winter I won't give a series of dinners.

FATHER: I should hope not.

VINNIE: I'll give a big musicale instead.

FATHER: You'll give a what?

VINNIE: A musicale.

FATHER (*peremptorily*): Vinnie, I won't have my peaceful home turned into a Roman arena with a lot of hairy fiddlers prancing about.

VINNIE: I didn't say a word about hairy fiddlers. Mrs. Spiller has written me about this lovely young girl who will come for very little.

FATHER: What instrument does this inexpensive paragon play?

VINNIE: She doesn't play, Clare, she whistles.

FATHER: Whistles? Good God!

VINNIE: She whistles sixteen different pieces. All for twenty-five dollars.

FATHER (*stormily*): I won't pay twenty-five dollars to any human peanut stand.

(*He tastes his coffee, grimaces, and again stamps three times on the floor.*)

VINNIE: Clare, I can arrange this so it won't cost you a penny. If I invite fifty people and charge them fifty cents apiece, there's the twenty-five dollars right there!

FATHER: You can't invite people to your own house and charge them admission.

VINNIE: I can if the money's for the missionary fund.

FATHER: Then where will you get the twenty-five dollars to pay that poor girl for her whistling?

VINNIE: Now, Clare, let's not cross that bridge until we come to it.

FATHER: And if we do cross it, it will cost me twenty-five dollars. Vinnie, I'm putting my foot down about this musicale, just as I've had to put my foot down about your keeping this house full of visiting relatives. Why can't we live here by ourselves in peace and comfort?

(MARGARET *comes dashing into the room.*)

MARGARET: What's wanting?

FATHER (*sternly*): Margaret, what is this? (*He holds up his coffee cup and points at it.*)

MARGARET: It's coffee, sir.

FATHER: It is not coffee! You couldn't possibly take water and coffee beans and arrive at that! It's slops, that's what it is—slops! Take it away! Take it away, I tell you!

(MARGARET *takes* FATHER'S *cup and dashes out.* ANNIE *starts to take* VINNIE'S *cup.*)

VINNIE: Leave my coffee there, Annie! It's perfectly all right!

(ANNIE *leaves the room.*)

FATHER (*angrily*): It is not! I swear I can't imagine how she concocts such an atrocity. I come down to this table every morning hungry—

VINNIE: Well, if you're hungry, Clare, why aren't you eating your breakfast?

FATHER: What?

VINNIE: If you're hungry, why aren't you eating your breakfast?

FATHER (*thrown out of bounds*): I am. (*He takes a mouthful of bacon and munches it happily, his eyes falling on* HARLAN.) Harlan, how's that finger? Come over here and let me see it. (HARLAN *goes to his father's side. He shows his finger.*) Well, that's healing nicely. Now don't pick that scab or it will leave a scar, and we don't want scars on our fingers, do we? (*He chuckles.*) I guess you'll remember after this that cats don't like to be hugged. It's all right to stroke them, but don't squeeze them. Now go back and finish your oatmeal.

HARLAN: I don't like oatmeal.

FATHER (*kindly*): It's good for you. Go back and eat it.

HARLAN: But I don't like it.

FATHER (*quietly, but firmly*): I'll tell you what you like and what you don't like. You're not old enough to know about such things. You've no business not to like oatmeal. It's good.

HARLAN: I hate it.

FATHER (*firmly, but not quietly*): That's enough! We won't discuss it! Eat that oatmeal at once!

(*In contrast to* HARLAN, WHITNEY *has been eating his oatmeal at a terrific rate of speed. He pauses and puts down his spoon.*)

WHITNEY: I've finished *my* oatmeal. May I be excused?

FATHER: Yes, Whitney, you may go. (WHITNEY *slides off his chair and hurries to the stairs.*) Pitch a good game.

VINNIE: Whitney!

WHITNEY: I'm going upstairs to study my catechism.

VINNIE: Oh, that's all right. Run along.

WHITNEY (*on the way up*): Harlan, you'd better hurry up and finish your oatmeal if you want to go with me.

(*Throughout breakfast* FATHER *has been opening and glancing through his mail. He has just reached one letter, however, that bewilders him.*)

FATHER: I don't understand why I'm always getting damn fool letters like this!

VINNIE: What is it, Clare?

FATHER: "Dear Friend Day: We are assigning you the exclusive rights for Staten Island for selling the Gem Home Popper for popcorn—"

CLARENCE: I think that's for me, Father.

FATHER: Then why isn't it addressed to Clarence Day, Jr.? (*He looks at the envelope.*) Oh, it is. Well, I'm sorry. I didn't mean to open your mail.

(MARGARET *returns and slips a cup of coffee to the table beside* FATHER.)

FATHER: I wouldn't get mixed up in that, Clarence. People like popcorn, but they won't go all the way to Staten Island to buy it.

(FATHER *has picked up the paper and is reading it. He drinks his coffee absentmindedly.*)

FATHER: Chauncey Depew's having another birthday.

VINNIE: How nice.

FATHER: He's always having birthdays. Two or three a year. Damn! Another wreck on the New Haven!

VINNIE: Yes. Oh, that reminds me. Mrs. Bailey dropped in yesterday.

FATHER: Was she in the wreck?

VINNIE: No. But she was born in New Haven. Clarence, you're having tea with Edith Bailey Thursday afternoon.

CLARENCE: Oh, Mother, do I have to?

JOHN (*singing*): "I like coffee, I like tea. I like the girls and the girls like me."

CLARENCE: Well, the girls don't like me and I don't like them.

VINNIE: Edith Bailey's a very nice girl, isn't she, Clare?

FATHER: Edith Bailey? Don't like her. Don't blame Clarence.

(FATHER *goes to his chair by the window and sits down with his newspaper and a cigar. The others rise.* HARLAN *runs upstairs.* ANNIE *starts clearing the table and exits with the tray of dishes a little later.* VINNIE *speaks in a guarded tone to the two boys.*)

VINNIE: Clarence, you and John go upstairs and do—what I asked you to.

JOHN: You said the small bureau, Mother?

VINNIE: Shh! Run along.

(*The boys go upstairs, somewhat unwillingly.* MARGARET *enters.*)

MARGARET: If you please, ma'am, there's a package been delivered with a dollar due on it. Some kitchen knives.

VINNIE: Oh, yes, those knives from Lewis & Conger's. (*She gets her purse from the drawer in the console table and gives* MARGARET *a dollar.*) Here, give this dollar to the man, Margaret.

FATHER: Make a memorandum of that, Vinnie. One dollar and whatever it was for.

VINNIE (*looking into purse*): Clare, dear, I'm afraid I'm going to need some more money.

FATHER: What for?

VINNIE: You were complaining of the coffee this morning. Well, that nice French drip coffee pot is broken—and you know how it got broken.

FATHER (*taking out his wallet*): Never mind that, Vinnie. As I remember, that coffee pot cost five dollars and something. Here's six dollars. (*He gives her six dollars.*) And when you get it, enter the exact amount in the ledger downstairs.

VINNIE: Thank you, Clare.

FATHER: We can't go on month after month having the household accounts in such a mess.

VINNIE (*she sits on the arm of* FATHER'S *chair*): No, and I've thought of a system that will make my bookkeeping perfect.

FATHER: I'm certainly relieved to hear that. What is it?

VINNIE: Well, Clare dear, you never make half the fuss over how much I've spent as you do over my not being able to remember what I've spent it for.

FATHER: Exactly. This house must be run on a business basis. That's why I insist on your keeping books.

VINNIE: That's the whole point, Clare. All we have to do is open charge accounts everywhere and the stores will do my bookkeeping for me.

FATHER: Wait a minute, Vinnie—

VINNIE: Then when the bills come in you'd know exactly where your money had gone.

FATHER: I certainly would. Vinnie, I get enough bills as it is.

VINNIE: Yes, and those bills always help. They show you just where I spent the money. Now if we had charge accounts everywhere—

FATHER: Now, Vinnie, I don't know about that.

VINNIE: Clare dear, don't you hate those arguments we have every month? I certainly do. Not to have those I should think would be worth something to you.

FATHER: Well, I'll open an account at Lewis & Conger's—and one at McCreery's to start with—we'll see how it works out. (*He shakes his head doubtfully. Her victory gained,* VINNIE *moves away.*)

VINNIE: Thank you, Clare. Oh—the rector's coming to tea today.

FATHER: The rector? I'm glad you warned me. I'll go to the club. Don't expect me home until dinner time.

VINNIE: I do wish you'd take a little more interest in the church. (*Goes behind* FATHER'S *chair and looks down at him with concern.*)

FATHER: Vinnie, getting me into Heaven's your job. If there's anything wrong with my ticket when I get there, you can fix it up. Everybody loves you so much—I'm sure God must, too.

VINNIE: I'll do my best, Clare. It wouldn't be Heaven without you.

FATHER: If you're there, Vinnie, I'll manage to get in some way, even if I have to climb the fence.

JOHN (*from upstairs*): Mother, we've moved it. Is there anything else?

FATHER: What's being moved?

VINNIE: Never mind, Clare. I'll come right up, John. (*She goes to the arch, stops. Looks back at* FATHER.) Oh, Clare, it's eight-thirty. You don't want to be late at the office.

FATHER: Plenty of time. (VINNIE *looks nervously toward the door, then goes upstairs.* FATHER *returns to his newspaper.* VINNIE *has barely disappeared when something in the paper arouses* FATHER's *indignation.*) Oh, God!

(VINNIE *comes running downstairs.*)

VINNIE: What's the matter, Clare? What's wrong?

FATHER: Why did God make so many damn fools and Democrats?

VINNIE (*relieved*): Oh, politics. (*She goes upstairs again.*)

FATHER (*shouting after her*): Yes, but it's taking the bread out of our mouths. It's robbery, that's what it is, highway robbery! Honest Hugh Grant! Honest! Bah! A fine mayor you've turned out to be. (FATHER *launches into a vigorous denunciation of Mayor Hugh Grant, addressing that gentleman as though he were present in the room, called upon the Day carpet to listen to* FATHER's *opinion of Tammany's latest attack on his pocketbook.*) If you can't run this city without raising taxes every five minutes, you'd better get out and let someone who can. Let me tell you, sir, that the real-estate owners of New York City are not going to tolerate these conditions any longer. Tell me this—are these increased taxes going into public improvements or are they going into graft—answer me that, honestly, if you can, Mr. Honest Hugh Grant. You can't! I thought so. Bah! (ANNIE *enters with her tray. Hearing* FATHER *talking, she curtsies and backs into the hall, as if uncertain whether to intrude on* FATHER *and the Mayor.* VINNIE *comes downstairs.*) If you don't stop your plundering of the pocketbooks of the good citizens of New York, we're going to throw you and your boodle Board of Aldermen out of office.

VINNIE: Annie, why aren't you clearing the table?

ANNIE: Mr. Day's got a visitor.

FATHER: I'm warning you for the last time.

VINNIE: Oh, nonsense, he's just reading his paper, Annie. Clear the table.

(VINNIE *goes off through the arch.* ANNIE *comes in timidly and starts to clear the table.*)

FATHER (*still lecturing Mayor Grant*): We pay you a good round sum to watch after our interests, and all we get is inefficiency! (ANNIE *looks around trying to see the Mayor and, finding the room empty, assumes* FATHER's *remarks are directed at her.*) I know you're a nincompoop and I strongly suspect you of being a scalawag. (ANNIE *stands petrified.* WHITNEY *comes downstairs.*) It's graft—that's what it is—Tammany graft—and if you're not getting it, somebody else is.

WHITNEY (*to* FATHER): Where's John? Do you know where John is?

FATHER: Dick Croker's running this town and you're just his cat's-paw.

(VINNIE *comes in from downstairs, and* HARLAN *comes down from upstairs.* FATHER *goes on talking. The others carry on their conversation simultaneously, ignoring* FATHER *and his imaginary visitor.*)

HARLAN: Mother, where's John?

VINNIE: He's upstairs, dear.

FATHER: And as for you, Richard Croker—don't think, just because you're hiding behind these minions you've put in public office, that you're going to escape your legal responsibilities.

WHITNEY (*calling upstairs*): John, I'm going to take your glove!

JOHN (*from upstairs*): Don't you lose it! And don't let anybody else have it either!

VINNIE: Annie, you should have cleared the table long ago.

(ANNIE *loads her tray feverishly, eager to escape.*)

FATHER (*rising and slamming down the paper in his chair*): *Legal* responsibilities—by gad, sir, I mean *criminal* responsibilities.

(*The boys start toward the front door.*)

VINNIE (*starting upstairs*): Now you watch Harlan, Whitney. Don't let him be anywhere the ball can hit him. Do what Whitney says, Harlan. And don't be late for lunch.

(FATHER *has reached the arch on his way out of the room, where he pauses for a final shot at Mayor Grant.*)

FATHER: Don't forget what happened to William Marcy Tweed—and if you put our taxes up once more, we'll put you in jail!

(*He goes out of the archway to the left. A few seconds later he is seen passing the arch toward the outer door wearing his square derby and carrying his stick and gloves. The door is heard to slam loudly.*)

(ANNIE *seizes her tray of dishes and runs out of the arch to the left toward the basement stairs. A second later there is a scream from* ANNIE *and a tremendous crash.*)

(JOHN *and* CLARENCE *come rushing down and look over the rail of the stairs below.* VINNIE *follows them almost immediately.*)

VINNIE: What is it? What happened?

CLARENCE: The maid fell downstairs.

VINNIE: I don't wonder, with your Father getting her so upset. Why couldn't she have finished with the table before she fell downstairs?

JOHN: I don't think she hurt herself.

VINNIE: And today of all days! Boys, will you finish the table? And, Clarence, don't leave the house until I talk to you. (*She goes downstairs.*)

(*During the following scene* CLARENCE *and* JOHN *remove* VINNIE'S *best breakfast tablecloth and cram it carelessly into the drawer of the console table, then take out the extra leaves from the table, push it together, and replace the living-room table cover and the bowl of fruit.*)

JOHN: What do you suppose Mother wants to talk to you about?

CLARENCE: Oh, probably about Edith Bailey.

JOHN: What do you talk about when you have tea alone with a girl?

CLARENCE: We don't talk about anything. I say: 'Isn't it a nice day?' and she says: 'Yes,' and I say: 'I think it's a little warmer than yesterday,' and she says: 'Yes, I like warm weather, don't you?' and I say: 'Yes,' and then we wait for the tea to come in. And then she says: 'How many lumps?' and I say: 'Two, thank you,' and she says 'You must have a sweet tooth,' and I can't say: 'Yes' and I can't say: 'No,' so we just sit there and look at each other for half an hour. Then I say: 'Well, it's time I was going,' and she says: 'Must you?' and I say: 'I've enjoyed seeing you very much,' and she says: 'You must come again,' and I say 'I will,' and get out.

JOHN (*shaking his head*): Some fellows like girls.

CLARENCE: I don't.

JOHN: And did you ever notice fellows, when they get sweet on a girl— the silly things a girl can make them do? And they don't even seem to know they're acting silly.

CLARENCE: Well, not for Yours Truly!

(VINNIE *returns from downstairs.*)

VINNIE: I declare I don't see how anyone could be so clumsy.

CLARENCE: Did she hurt herself?

VINNIE: No, she's not hurt—she's just hysterical! She doesn't make sense. Your father may have raised his voice; and if she doesn't know how to hold a platter properly, she deserved it—but I know he didn't threaten to put her in jail. Oh, well! Clarence, I want you to move your things into the front room. You'll have to sleep with the other boys for a night or two.

CLARENCE: You haven't told us who's coming.

VINNIE (*happily*): Cousin Cora. Isn't that nice?

CLARENCE: It's not nice for me. I can't get any sleep in there with those children.

JOHN: Wait'll Father finds out she's here! There'll be a rumpus.

VINNIE: John, don't criticize your father. He's very hospitable after he gets used to the idea.

(*The doorbell rings.* JOHN *and* VINNIE *go to the window.*)

JOHN: Yes, it's Cousin Cora. Look, there's somebody with her.

VINNIE (*looking out*): She wrote me she was bringing a friend of hers. They're both going to stay here. (*A limping* ANNIE *passes through the hall.*) Finish with the room, boys.

CLARENCE: Do I have to sleep with the other boys and have tea with Edith Bailey all in the same week?

VINNIE: Yes, and you'd better take your father's suit to the tailor's right away, so it will be ready for Thursday.

(VINNIE *goes down the hall to greet* CORA *and* MARY. CLARENCE *hurries off, carrying the table leaves.*)

VINNIE'S VOICE (*in the hall*): Cora dear—

CORA'S VOICE: Cousin Vinnie, I'm so glad to see you! This is Mary Skinner.

VINNIE'S VOICE: Ed Skinner's daughter! I'm so glad to see you. Leave your bags in the hall and come right upstairs.

(VINNIE *enters, going toward the stairs.* CORA *follows her, but, seeing* JOHN, *enters the room and goes to him.* MARY *follows* CORA *in timidly.* CORA *is an attractive country cousin of about thirty.* MARY *is a refreshingly pretty small-town girl of sixteen.*)

CORA (*seeing* JOHN): Well, Clarence, it's so good to see you!

VINNIE (*coming into the room*): Oh, no, that's John.

CORA: John! Why, how you've grown! You'll be a man before your mother! (*She laughs herself at this time-worn quip.*) John, this is Mary Skinner. (*They exchange greetings.*) Vinnie, I have so much to tell you. We wrote you Aunt Carrie broke her hip. That was the night Robert Ingersoll lectured. Of course she couldn't get there; and it was a good thing for Mr. Ingersoll she didn't. (CLARENCE *enters.*) And Grandpa Ebbetts hasn't been at all well.

CLARENCE: How do you do, Cousin Cora? I'm glad to see you.

CORA: This can't be Clarence!

VINNIE: Yes, it is.

CORA: My goodness, every time I see you boys you've grown another foot. Let's see—you're going to St. Paul's now, aren't you?

CLARENCE (*with pained dignity*): St. Paul's! I was through with St. Paul's long ago. I'm starting in Yale this fall.

MARY: Yale!

CORA: Oh, Mary, this is Clarence—Mary Skinner. (MARY *smiles, and* CLARENCE, *the woman-hater, nods politely and walks away.*) This is Mary's first trip to New York. She was so excited when she saw a horse car.

VINNIE: We'll have to show Mary around. I'll tell you—I'll have Mr. Day take us all to Delmonico's for dinner tonight.

MARY: Delmonico's!

CORA: Oh, that's marvelous! Think of that, Mary—Delmonico's! And Cousin Clare's such a wonderful host.

VINNIE: I know you girls want to freshen up. So come upstairs. Clarence, I'll let the girls use your room now, and when they've finished you can move, and bring up their bags. They're out in the hall. (*Starts upstairs with* CORA.) I've given you girls Clarence's room, but he didn't know about it until this morning and he hasn't moved out yet.

(VINNIE *and* CORA *disappear upstairs.*)

(MARY *follows more slowly and on the second step stops and looks* *back.* CLARENCE *has gone into the hall with his back toward* MARY *and stares morosely in the direction of their luggage.*)

CLARENCE: John, get their old bags.

(JOHN *disappears toward the front door. The voices of* VINNIE *and* CORA *have trailed off into the upper reaches of the house.* CLARENCE *turns to scowl in their direction and finds himself looking full into the face of* MARY.)

MARY: Cora didn't tell me about you. I never met a Yale man before.

(*She gives him a devastating smile and with an audible whinny of girlish excitement she runs upstairs.* CLARENCE *stares after her a few seconds, then turns toward the audience with a look of "What happened to me just then?" Suddenly, however, his face breaks into a smile which indicates that, whatever has happened, he likes it.*)

CURTAIN

SCENE II

The same day. Tea time.

VINNIE *and the* RECTOR *are having tea.* THE REVEREND DR. LLOYD *is a plump, bustling man, very good-hearted and pleasant.* VINNIE *and* DR. LLOYD *have one strong point in common: their devotion to the Church and its rituals.* VINNIE'S *devotion comes from her natural piety;* DR. LLOYD'S *is a little more professional.*

At rise, DR. LLOYD *is seated with a cup of tea.* VINNIE *is also seated and* WHITNEY *is standing next to her, stiffly erect in the manner of a boy reciting.* HARLAN *is seated next to his mother, watching* WHITNEY'S *performance.*

WHITNEY (*reciting*): "—to worship Him, to give Him thanks; to put my whole trust in Him, to call upon Him—" (*He hesitates.*)

VINNIE (*prompting*): "—to honor—"

WHITNEY: "—to honor His Holy Name and His word and to serve Him truly all the days of my life."

DR. LLOYD: "What is thy duty toward thy neighbour?"

WHITNEY: Whew! (*He pulls himself together and makes a brave start.*) "My duty toward my neighbor is to love him as myself, and to do to all men as I would they should do unto me; to love, honor, and succor my father and my mother; to honor and obey—"

VINNIE: "—civil authorities."

WHITNEY: "—civil authorities. To—to—to—"

VINNIE (*to* DR. LLOYD): He really knows it.

WHITNEY: I know most of the others.

DR. LLOYD: Well, he's done very well for so young a boy. I'm sure if he applies himself between now and Sunday I could hear him again with the others.

VINNIE: There, Whitney, you'll have to study very hard if you want Dr. Lloyd to send your name in to Bishop Potter next Sunday. I must confess to you, Dr. Lloyd, it's really my fault. Instead of hearing Whitney say his catechism this morning I let him play baseball.

WHITNEY: We won, too; 35 to 27.

DR. LLOYD: That's splendid, my child. I'm glad your side won. But winning over your catechism is a richer and fuller victory.

WHITNEY: Can I go now?

VINNIE: Yes, darling. Thank Dr. Lloyd for hearing you and run along.

WHITNEY: Thank you, Dr. Lloyd.

DR. LLOYD: Not at all, my little man.

(WHITNEY *starts out, turns back, takes a piece of cake and runs out.*)

VINNIE: Little Harlan is very apt at learning things by heart.

HARLAN (*scrambling to his feet*): I can spell Constantinople. Want to hear me? (DR. LLOYD *smiles his assent.*) C-o-enna-conny—annaconny—sissaconny—tan-tan-tee—and a nople and a pople and a Constantinople!

DR. LLOYD: Very well done, my child.

VINNIE (*handing him a cake from the tea-tray*): That's nice, darling. This is what you get for saying it so well.

(HARLAN *quickly looks at the cake and back to* DR. LLOYD.)

HARLAN: Want me to say it again for you?

VINNIE: No, darling. One cake is enough. You run along and play with Whitney.

HARLAN: I can spell "huckleberry pie."

VINNIE: Run along, dear.

(HARLAN *goes out, skipping in rhythm to his recitation.*)

HARLAN: H-a-huckle—b-a-buckle—h-a-huckle-high. H-a-huckle—b-a-buckle—huckleberry pie!

DR. LLOYD (*amused*): You and Mr. Day must be very proud of your children. (VINNIE *beams.*) I was hoping I'd find Mr. Day at home this afternoon.

VINNIE (*evasively*): Well, he's usually home from the office by this time.

DR. LLOYD: Perhaps he's gone for a gallop in the park—it's such a fine day. He's very fond of horseback riding, I believe.

VINNIE: Oh, yes.

DR. LLOYD: Tell me—has he ever been thrown from a horse?

VINNIE: Oh, no! No horse would throw Mr. Day.

DR. LLOYD: I've wondered. I thought he might have had an accident. I notice he never kneels in church.

VINNIE: Oh, that's no accident! But I don't want you to think he doesn't pray. He does. Why, sometimes you can hear him pray all over the house. But he never kneels.

DR. LLOYD: Never kneels! Dear me! I was hoping to have the opportunity to tell you and Mr. Day about our plans for the new edifice.

VINNIE: I'm so glad we're going to have a new church.

DR. LLOYD: I'm happy to announce that we're now ready to proceed. The only thing left to do is raise the money.

VINNIE: No one should hesitate about contributing to that.

(*The front door slams.*)

DR. LLOYD: Perhaps that's Mr. Day now.

VINNIE: Oh, no, I hardly think so. (FATHER *appears in the archway.*) Why, it is!

FATHER: Oh, damn! I forgot.

VINNIE: Clare, you're just in time. Dr. Lloyd's here for tea.

FATHER: I'll be right in. (*He disappears the other side of the archway.*)

VINNIE: I'll send for some fresh tea. (*She goes to the bell-pull and rings for the maid.*)

DR. LLOYD: Now we can tell Mr. Day about our plans for the new edifice.

VINNIE (*knowing her man*): After he's had his tea.

(FATHER *comes back into the room.* DR. LLOYD *rises.*)

FATHER: How are you, Dr. Lloyd?

(CLARENCE *comes down the stairs and eagerly looks around for* MARY).

CLARENCE: Oh, it was Father.

DR. LLOYD: Very well, thank you. (*They shake hands.*)

CLARENCE (*to* VINNIE): They're not back yet?

VINNIE: No! Clarence, no!

(CLARENCE *turns, disappointed, and goes back upstairs.*)

DR. LLOYD: It's a great pleasure to have a visit with you, Mr. Day. Except for a fleeting glimpse on the Sabbath, I don't see much of you.

(FATHER *grunts and sits down.* DELIA, *a new maid, enters.*)

DELIA: Yes, ma'am.

VINNIE: Some fresh tea and a cup for Mr. Day. (DELIA *exits and* VINNIE *hurries down to the tea table to start the conversation.*) Well, Clare, did you have a busy day at the office?

FATHER: Damn busy.

VINNIE: Clare!

FATHER: Very busy day. Tired out.

VINNIE: I've ordered some fresh tea. (*To* DR. LLOYD.) Poor Clare, he must work very hard. He always comes home tired. Although how a man can get tired just sitting at his desk all day, I don't know. I suppose Wall Street is just as much a mystery to you as it is to me, Dr. Lloyd.

DR. LLOYD: No, no, it's all very clear to me. My mind often goes to the business man. The picture I'm most fond of is when I envision him at the close of the day's work. There he sits—this hardheaded man of affairs—surrounded by the ledgers that he has been studying closely and harshly for hours. I see him pausing in his toil—and by chance he raises his eyes and looks out of the window at the light in God's sky and it comes over him that money and ledgers are dross. (FATHER *stares at* DR. LLOYD *with some amazement.*) He realizes that all those figures of profit and loss are without importance or consequence—vanity and dust. And I see this troubled man bow his head and with streaming eyes resolve to devote his life to far higher things.

FATHER: Well, I'll be damned!

(*At this moment* DELIA *returns with the fresh tea for* FATHER.)

VINNIE: Here's your tea, Clare.

(FATHER *notices the new maid.*)

FATHER: Who's this?

VINNIE (*quietly*): The new maid.

FATHER: Where's the one we had this morning?

VINNIE: Never mind, Clare.

FATHER: The one we had this morning was prettier. (DELIA, *with a slight resentment, exits.* FATHER *attacks the tea and cakes with relish.*) Vinnie, these cakes are *good.*

DR. LLOYD: Delicious!

VINNIE: Dr. Lloyd wants to tell us about the plans for the new edifice.

FATHER: The new what?

VINNIE: The new church—Clare, you knew we were planning to build a new church.

DR. LLOYD: Of course, we're going to have to raise a large sum of money.

FATHER (*alive to the danger*): Well, personally I'm against the church hop-skipping-and-jumping all over the town. And it so happens that during the last year I've suffered heavy losses in the market—damned heavy losses—

VINNIE: Clare!

FATHER: —so any contribution I make will have to be a small one.

VINNIE: But, Clare, for so worthy a cause!

FATHER: —and if your Finance Committee thinks it's too small they can blame the rascals that are running the New Haven Railroad!

DR. LLOYD: The amount everyone is to subscribe has already been decided.

FATHER (*bristling*): Who decided it?

DR. LLOYD: After considerable thought we've found a formula which we believe is fair and equitable. It apportions the burden lightly on those least able to carry it and justly on those whose shoulders we know are stronger. We've voted that our supporting members should each contribute a sum equal to the cost of their pews.

(FATHER'S *jaw drops*.)

FATHER: I paid five thousand dollars for my pew!

VINNIE: Yes, Clare. That makes our contribution five thousand dollars.

FATHER: That's robbery! Do you know what that pew is worth today? Three thousand dollars. That's what the last one sold for. I've taken a dead loss of two thousand dollars on that pew already. Frank Baggs sold me that pew when the market was at its peak. He knew when to get out. (*He turns to* VINNIE.) And I'm warning you now that if the market ever goes up I'm going to unload that pew.

VINNIE: Clarence Day! How can you speak of the Lord's temple as though it were something to be bought and sold on Wall Street!

FATHER: Vinnie, this is a matter of dollars and cents, and that's something you don't know anything about!

VINNIE: Your talking of religion in the terms of dollars and cents seems to me pretty close to blasphemy.

DR. LLOYD (*soothingly*): Now, Mrs. Day, your husband is a business man and he has a practical approach toward this problem. We've had to be practical about it too—we have all the facts and figures.

FATHER: Oh, really! What's the new piece of property going to cost you?

DR. LLOYD: I think the figure I've heard mentioned is eighty-five thousand dollars—or was it a hundred and eighty-five thousand dollars?

FATHER: What's the property worth where we are now?

DR. LLOYD: Well, there's quite a difference of opinion about that.

FATHER: How much do you have to raise to build the new church?

DR. LLOYD: Now, I've seen those figures—let me see—I know it depends somewhat upon the amount of the mortgage.

FATHER: Mortgage, eh? What are the terms of the amortization?

DR. LLOYD: Amortization? That's not a word I'm familiar with.

FATHER: It all seems pretty vague and unsound to me. I certainly wouldn't let any customer of mine invest on what I've heard.

(*The doorbell rings.*)

DR. LLOYD: We've given it a great deal of thought. I don't see how you can call it vague.

(DELIA *passes along the hall toward the front door.*)

FATHER: Dr. Lloyd, you preach that some day we'll all have to answer to God.

DR. LLOYD: We shall indeed!

FATHER: Well, I hope God doesn't ask you any questions with figures in them.

(CORA'S *voice is heard in the hall, thanking* DELIA. VINNIE *goes to the arch just in time to meet* CORA *and* MARY *as they enter, heavily laden with packages, which they put down.* FATHER *and* DR. LLOYD *rise.*)

CORA: Oh, Vinnie, what a day! We've been to every shop in town and —(*She sees* FATHER.) Cousin Clare!

FATHER (*cordially*): Cora, what are you doing in New York?

CORA: We're just passing through on our way to Springfield.

FATHER: We?

(CLARENCE *comes downstairs into the room with eyes only for* MARY.)

VINNIE: Oh, Dr. Lloyd, this is my favorite cousin, Miss Cartwright, and her friend, Mary Skinner. (*They exchange mutual how-do-you-do's.*)

DR. LLOYD: This seems to be a family reunion. I'll just run along.

FATHER (*promptly*): Goodbye, Dr. Lloyd.

DR. LLOYD: Goodbye, Miss Cartwright. Goodbye, Miss—er—

VINNIE: Clarence, you haven't said how-do-you-do to Dr. Lloyd.

CLARENCE: Goodbye, Dr. Lloyd.

VINNIE (*to* DR. LLOYD): I'll go the door with you. (DR. LLOYD *and* VINNIE *go out, talking.*)

FATHER: Cora, you're as welcome as the flowers in May! Have some tea with us. (*To* DELIA.) Bring some fresh tea—and some more of those cakes.

CORA: Oh, we've had tea! We were so tired shopping we had tea downtown. (*With a gesture* FATHER *countermands his order to* DELIA, *who removes the tea table and exits.*)

MARY: At the Fifth Avenue Hotel.

FATHER: At the Fifth Avenue Hotel, eh? Who'd you say this pretty little girl was?

CORA: She's Ed Skinner's daughter. Well, Mary, at last you've met Mr. Day. I've told Mary so much about you, Cousin Clare, that she's just been dying to meet you.

FATHER: Well, sit down! Sit down! Even if you have had tea you can stop and visit for a while. As a matter of fact, why don't you both stay to dinner?

(VINNIE *enters just in time to hear this and cuts in quickly.*)

VINNIE: That's all arranged, Clare. Cora and Mary are going to have dinner with us.

FATHER: That's fine! That's fine!

CORA: Cousin Clare, I don't know how to thank you and Vinnie for your hospitality.

MARY: Yes, Mr. Day.

FATHER: Well, you'll just have to take pot luck.

CORA: No, I mean—

(VINNIE *speaks quickly to postpone the revelation that* FATHER *has house guests.*)

VINNIE: Clare, did you know the girls are going to visit Aunt Judith in Springfield for a whole month?

FATHER: That's fine. How long are you going to be in New York, Cora?

CORA: All week.

FATHER: Splendid. We'll hope to see something of you, eh, Vinnie?

(CORA *looks bewildered and is about to speak.*)

VINNIE: Did you find anything you wanted in the shops?

CORA: Just everything.

VINNIE: I want to see what you got.

CORA: I just can't wait to show you. (*She goes coyly to* FATHER.) But I'm afraid some of the packages can't be opened in front of Cousin Clare.

FATHER: Shall I leave the room? (*Laughs at his own joke.*)

CORA: Clarence, do you mind taking the packages up to our room—or should I say your room? (*To* FATHER.) Wasn't it nice of Clarence to give up his room to us for a whole week?

FATHER (*with a sudden drop in temperature*): Vinnie!

VINNIE: Come on, Cora, I just can't wait to see what's in those packages.

(CORA, MARY, *and* VINNIE *start out.* CLARENCE *is gathering up the packages.*)

FATHER (*ominously*): Vinnie, I wish to speak to you before you go upstairs.

VINNIE: I'll be down in just a minute, Clare.

FATHER: I wish to speak to you now! (*The girls have disappeared upstairs.*)

VINNIE: I'll be up in just a minute, Cora. (*We hear a faint* "All right" *from upstairs.*)

FATHER (*his voice is low but stern*): Are those two women encamped in this house?

VINNIE: Now, Clare!

FATHER (*much louder*): Answer me, Vinnie!

VINNIE: Just a minute—control yourself, Clare. (VINNIE, *sensing the coming storm, hurries to the sliding doors.* CLARENCE *has reached the hall with his packages and he, too, has recognized the danger signal and as* VINNIE *closes one door he closes the other, leaving himself out in the hall and* FATHER *and* VINNIE *facing each other in the room.*) (*Persuasively.*) Now, Clare, you know you've always liked Cora.

FATHER (*exploding*): What has that got to do with her planking herself down in my house and bringing hordes of strangers with her?

VINNIE (*reproachfully*): How can you call that sweet little girl a horde of strangers?

FATHER: Why don't they go to a hotel? New York is full of hotels built for the express purpose of housing such nuisances.

VINNIE: Clare! Two girls alone in a hotel! Who knows what might happen to them?

FATHER: All right. Then put 'em on the next train. If they want to roam —the damned gypsies—lend 'em a hand! Keep 'em roaming!

VINNIE: What have we got a home for if we can't show a little hospitality?

FATHER: I didn't buy this home to show hospitality—I bought it for my own comfort!

VINNIE: Well, how much are they going to interfere with your comfort living in that little room of Clarence's?

FATHER: The trouble is, damn it, they don't live there. They live in the bathroom! Every time I want to take my bath it's full of giggling females—washing their hair. From the time they take, you'd think it was the Seven Sutherland Sisters. I tell you, I won't have it! Send 'em to a hotel. I'll pay the bill gladly, but get them out of here!

(CLARENCE *puts his head through the sliding door.*)

CLARENCE: Father, I'm afraid they can hear you upstairs.

FATHER: Then keep those doors closed!

VINNIE (*with decision*): Clarence, you open those doors—open them all the way! (CLARENCE *does so.*)

VINNIE (*to* FATHER, *lowering her voice, but maintaining her spirit*): Now, Clare, you behave yourself! (FATHER *glares at her angrily.*) They're here and they're going to stay here.

FATHER: That's enough, Vinnie! I want no more of this argument. (*He goes to his chair by the window, muttering.*) Damnation!

CLARENCE (*to* VINNIE): Mother, Cousin Cora's waiting for you.

FATHER: What I don't understand is why this swarm of locusts always descends on us without any warning. (*He sits down.* VINNIE *looks at him; then, convinced of her victory, she goes upstairs.*) Damn! Damnation! Damn! (*He follows her upstairs with his eyes; he remembers he is very fond of her.*) Vinnie! Dear Vinnie! (*He remembers he is very angry at her.*) Damn!

CLARENCE: Father, can't I go along with the rest of you to Delmonico's tonight?

FATHER: What's that? Delmonico's?

CLARENCE: You're taking Mother, Cora, and Mary to Delmonico's for dinner.

FATHER (*exploding*): Oh, God! (*At this sound from* FATHER, VINNIE *comes flying downstairs again.*) I won't have it. I won't have it. (FATHER *stamps angrily across the room.*)

VINNIE (*on the way down*): Clarence, the doors!

FATHER: I won't stand it, by God! I won't stand it! (VINNIE *and* CLARENCE *hurriedly close the sliding doors again.*)

VINNIE: Clare! What's the matter now?

FATHER (*with the calm of anger that has turned to ice*): Do I understand that I can't have dinner in my own home?

VINNIE: It'll do us both good to get out of this house. You need a little change. It'll make you feel better.

FATHER: I have a home to have dinner in. Any time I can't have dinner at home this house is for sale!

VINNIE: Well, you can't have dinner here tonight because it isn't ordered.

FATHER: Let me tell you I'm ready to sell this place this very minute if I can't live here in peace. And we can all go and sit under a palm tree and live on breadfruit and pickles.

VINNIE: But, Clare, Cora and Mary want to see something of New York.

FATHER: Oh, that's it! Well, that's no affair of mine! I am not a guide to Chinatown and the Bowery. (*Drawing himself up, he stalks out, throwing open the sliding doors. As he reaches the foot of the stairs,* MARY *comes tripping down.*)

MARY: I love your house, Mr. Day. I could just live here forever. (FATHER *utters a bark of disgust and continues on upstairs.* MARY *comes into the room a little wide-eyed.*) Cora's waiting for you, Mrs. Day.

VINNIE: Oh, yes, I'll run right up. (*She goes upstairs.*)

CLARENCE: I'm glad you like our house.

MARY: Oh, yes, I like it very much. I like green.

CLARENCE: I like green myself. (*She looks up at his red hair.*)

MARY: Red's my favorite color.

(*Embarrassed,* CLARENCE *suddenly hears himself talking about something he has never thought about.*)

CLARENCE: It's an interesting thing about colors. Red's a nice color in a house, too; but outside, too much red would be bad. I mean, for instance, if all the trees and the grass were red. Outside, green is the best color.

MARY (*impressed*): That's right! I've never thought of it that way—but when you do think of it, it's quite a thought! I'll bet you'll make your mark at Yale.

CLARENCE (*pleased, but modest*): Oh!

(*The outer door is heard to slam.*)

MARY: My mother wants me to go to college. Do you believe in girls going to college?

CLARENCE: I guess it's all right if they want to waste that much time— before they get married, I mean.

(JOHN *comes in, bringing* The Youth's Companion.)

JOHN: Oh, hello! Look! A new *Youth's Companion!*

(*They say* "Hello" *to him.*)

CLARENCE (*from a mature height*): John enjoys *The Youth's Companion.* (JOHN *sits right down and starts to read.* CLARENCE *is worried by this.*) John! (JOHN *looks at him non-plussed.* CLARENCE *glances toward* MARY. JOHN *remembers his manners and stands.* CLARENCE *speaks formally to* MARY.) Won't you sit down?

MARY: Oh, thank you!

(*She sits.* JOHN *sits down again quickly and dives back into* The Youth's Companion. CLARENCE *sits beside* MARY.)

CLARENCE: As I was saying—I think it's all right for a girl to go to college if she goes to a girls' college.

MARY: Well, Mother wants me to go to Ohio Wesleyan—because it's Methodist. (*Then almost as a confession.*) You see, we're Methodists.

CLARENCE: Oh, that's too bad! I don't mean it's too bad that you're a Methodist. Anybody's got a right to be anything they want. But what I mean is—we're Episcopalians.

MARY: Yes, I know. I've known ever since I saw your minister—and his collar. (*She looks pretty sad for a minute and then her face brightens.*) Oh, I just remembered—my father was an Episcopalian.

He was baptized an Episcopalian. He was an Episcopalian right up to the time he married my mother. *She* was the Methodist.

(MARY'S *tone would have surprised her mother—and even* MARY, *if she had been listening.*)

CLARENCE: I'll bet your father's a nice man.

MARY: Yes, he is. He owns the livery stable.

CLARENCE: He does? Well, then you must like horses.

MARY: Oh, I love horses! (*They are happily united again in their common love of horses.*)

CLARENCE: They're my favorite animal. Father and I both think there's nothing like a horse!

(FATHER *comes down the stairs and into the room. The children all stand.*)

MARY: Oh, Mr. Day, I'm having such a lovely time here!

FATHER: Clarence is keeping you entertained, eh?

MARY: Oh, yes, sir. We've been talking about everything—colors and horses and religion.

FATHER: Oh! (*To* JOHN.) Has the evening paper come yet?

JOHN: No, sir.

FATHER: What are you reading?

JOHN: *The Youth's Companion,* sir.

(WHITNEY *and* HARLAN *enter from the hall,* WHITNEY *carrying a small box.*)

WHITNEY: Look what we've got!

FATHER: What is it?

WHITNEY: Tiddle-dy-winks. We put our money together and bought it.

FATHER: That's a nice game. Do you know how to play it?

WHITNEY: I've played it lots of times.

HARLAN: Show me how to play it.

FATHER: Here, I'll show you. (*Opens the box and arranges the glass and disks.*)

MARY (*hopefully to* CLARENCE): Are you going out to dinner with us tonight?

CLARENCE (*looking at* FATHER): I don't know yet—but it's beginning to look as though I might.

FATHER: It's easy, Harlan. You press down like this and snap the little fellow into the glass. Now watch me— (*He snaps it and it goes off the table.*) The table isn't quite large enough. You boys better play it on the floor.

WHITNEY: Come on, Harlan, I'll take the reds, and you take the yellows.

FATHER: John, have you practiced your piano today?

JOHN: I was going to practice this evening.

FATHER: Better do it now. Music is a delight in the home.

(JOHN *exits, passing* CORA *and* VINNIE *as they enter, coming downstairs.*)

VINNIE: Clare, what do you think Cora just told me? She and Clyde are going to be married this fall!

FATHER: Oh, you finally landed him, eh? (*Everybody laughs.*) Well, he's a very lucky man. Cora, being married is the only way to live.

CORA: If we can be half as happy as you and Cousin Vinnie—

VINNIE (*who has gone to the children*): Boys, shouldn't you be playing that on the table?

WHITNEY: The table isn't big enough. Father told us to play on the floor.

VINNIE: My soul and body! Look at your hands! Delia will have your supper ready in a few minutes. Go wash your hands right away and come back and show Mother they're clean.

(*The boys pick up the tiddle-dy-winks and depart reluctantly. From the next room we hear* JOHN *playing "The Happy Farmer."*)

FATHER (*sitting down on the sofa with* MARY): Vinnie, this young lady looks about the same age you were when I came out to Pleasantville to rescue you.

VINNIE: Rescue me! You came out there to talk me into marrying you.

FATHER: It worked out just the same. I saved you from spending the rest of your life in that one-horse town.

VINNIE: Cora, the other day I came across a tin-type of Clare taken in Pleasantville. I want to show it to you. You'll see who needed rescuing. (*She goes to the table and starts to rummage around in its drawer.*)

FATHER: There isn't time for that, Vinnie. If we're going to Delmonico's for dinner hadn't we all better be getting ready? It's after six now.

CORA: Gracious! I'll have to start. If I'm going to dine in public with a prominent citizen like you, Cousin Clare—I'll have to look my best. (*She goes to the arch.*)

MARY: I've changed already.

CORA: Yes, I know, but I'm afraid I'll have to ask you to come along and hook me up, Mary.

MARY: Of course.

CORA: It won't take a minute and then you can come right back.

(FATHER *rises.* MARY *crosses in front of* FATHER *and starts toward the hall, then turns and looks back at him.*)

MARY: Mr. Day, were you always an Episcopalian?

FATHER: What?

MARY: Were you always an Episcopalian?

FATHER: I've always gone to the Episcopal church, yes.

MARY: But you weren't baptized a Methodist or anything, were you? You were baptized an Episcopalian?

FATHER: Come to think of it, I don't believe I was ever baptized at all.

MARY: Oh!

VINNIE: Clare, that's not very funny, joking about a subject like that.

FATHER: I'm not joking—I remember now—I never was baptized.

VINNIE: Clare, that's ridiculous, everyone's baptized.

FATHER (*sitting down complacently*): Well, I'm not.

VINNIE: Why, no one would keep a little baby from being baptized.

FATHER: You know Father and Mother—free-thinkers, both of them— believed their children should decide those things for themselves.

VINNIE: But, Clare—

FATHER: I remember when I was ten or twelve years old, Mother said I ought to give some thought to it. I suppose I thought about it, but I never got around to having it done to me.

(*The shock to* VINNIE *is as great as if* FATHER *had calmly an-*

nounced himself guilty of murder. She walks to FATHER *staring at him in horror.* CORA *and* MARY, *sensing the coming battle, withdraw to the neutral shelter of the hall.*)

VINNIE: Clare, do you know what you're saying?

FATHER: I'm saying I've never been baptized.

VINNIE (*in a sudden panic*): Then something has to be done about it right away.

FATHER (*not the least concerned*): Now, Vinnie, don't get excited over nothing.

VINNIE: Nothing! (*Then as only a woman can ask such a question.*) Clare, why haven't you ever told me?

FATHER: What difference does it make?

VINNIE (*the panic returning*): I've never heard of anyone who wasn't baptized. Even the savages in darkest Africa—

FATHER: It's all right for savages and children. But if an oversight was made in my case it's too late to correct it now.

VINNIE: But if you're not baptized you're not a Christian!

FATHER (*rising in wrath*): Why, confound it, of course I'm a Christian! A damn good Christian, too! (FATHER'S *voice tells* CLARENCE *a major engagement has begun. He hurriedly springs to the sliding doors and closes them, removing himself,* MARY, *and* CORA *from the scene of action.*) A lot better Christian than those psalm-singing donkeys in church!

VINNIE: You can't be if you won't be baptized.

FATHER: I won't be baptized and I will be a Christian! I beg to inform you I'll be a Christian in my own way.

VINNIE: Clare, don't you want to meet us all in Heaven?

FATHER: Of course! And I'm going to!

VINNIE: But you can't go to Heaven if you're not baptized!

FATHER: That's a lot of folderol!

VINNIE: Clarence Day, don't you blaspheme like that! You're coming to church with me before you go to the office in the morning and be baptized then and there!

FATHER: Vinnie, don't be ridiculous! If you think I'm going to stand there and have some minister splash water on me at my age, you're mistaken!

VINNIE: But, Clare—

FATHER: That's enough of this, Vinnie. I'm hungry. (*Draws himself up and starts for the door. He does not realize that he and* VINNIE *are now engaged in a battle to the death.*) I'm dressing for dinner. (*Throws open the doors, revealing* WHITNEY *and* HARLAN, *who obviously have been eavesdropping and have heard the awful revelation of* FATHER'S *paganism.* FATHER *stalks past them upstairs. The two boys come down into the room staring at their mother, who has been standing, too shocked at* FATHER'S *callous impiety to speak or move.*)

WHITNEY: Mother, if Father hasn't been baptized he hasn't any name. In the sight of the Church he hasn't any name.

VINNIE: That's right! (*To herself.*) Maybe we're not even married!

(*This awful thought takes possession of* VINNIE. *Her eyes turn slowly toward the children and she suddenly realizes their doubtful status. Her hand goes to her mouth to cover a quick gasp of horror as the curtain falls.*)

CURTAIN

ACT TWO

SCENE I

The same.

The following Sunday. After church.

The stage is empty as the curtain rises. VINNIE *comes into the archway from the street door, dressed in her Sunday best, carrying her prayer book, hymnal, and a cold indignation. As soon as she is in the room,* FATHER *passes across the hall in his Sunday cutaway and silk hat, carrying gloves and cane.* VINNIE *looks over her shoulder at him as he disappears.* CORA, WHITNEY, *and* HARLAN *come into the room,* CORA *glancing after* FATHER *and then toward* VINNIE. *All three walk as though the sound of a footfall might cause an explosion, and speak in subdued tones.*

HARLAN: Cousin Cora, will you play a game of tiddle-dy-winks with me before you go?

CORA: I'm going to be busy packing until it's time to leave.

WHITNEY: We can't play games on Sunday. (*We hear the door close and* JOHN *enters and looks into the room apprehensively.*)

CORA: John, where are Clarence and Mary?

JOHN: They dropped behind—'way behind! (*He goes upstairs.* WHITNEY *takes* HARLAN'S *hat from him and starts toward the arch.*)

VINNIE: Whitney, don't hang up your hat. I want you to go over to Sherry's for the ice-cream for dinner. Tell Mr. Sherry strawberry—if he has it. And take Harlan with you.

WHITNEY: All right, Mother. (*He and* HARLAN, *trained in the good manners of the period, bow and exit.*)

CORA: Oh, Vinnie, I hate to leave. We've had such a lovely week.

VINNIE (*voice quivers in a tone of scandalized apology*): Cora, what must you think of Clare, making such a scene on his way out of church today?

CORA: Cousin Clare probably thinks that you put the rector up to preaching that sermon.

VINNIE (*tone changes from apology to self-defense with overtones of guilt*): Well, I had to go to see Dr. Lloyd to find out whether we were really married. The sermon on baptism was his own idea. If Clare just hadn't *shouted* so—now the whole congregation knows he's never been baptized! But he's going to be, Cora—you mark my words—he's going to be! I just couldn't go to Heaven without Clare. Why, I get lonesome for him when I go to Ohio.

(FATHER *enters holding his watch. He's also holding his temper. He speaks quietly.*)

FATHER: Vinnie, I went to the dining-room and the table isn't set for dinner yet.

VINNIE: We're having dinner late today.

FATHER: Why can't I have my meals on time?

VINNIE: The girls' train leaves at one-thirty. Their cab's coming at one o'clock.

FATHER: Cab? The horse cars go right past our door.

VINNIE: They have those heavy bags.

FATHER: Clarence and John could have gone along to carry their bags. Cabs are just a waste of money. Why didn't we have an early dinner?

VINNIE: There wasn't time for an early dinner and church, too.

FATHER: As far as I'm concerned this would have been a good day to miss church.

VINNIE (*spiritedly*): I wish we had!

FATHER (*flaring*): I'll bet you put him up to preaching that sermon!

VINNIE: I've never been so mortified in all my life! You stamping up the aisle roaring your head off at the top of your voice!

FATHER: That Lloyd needn't preach at me as though I were some damn criminal! I wanted him to know it, and as far as I'm concerned the whole congregation can know it, too!

VINNIE: They certainly know it now!

FATHER: That suits me!

VINNIE (*pleading*): Clare, you don't seem to understand what the church is for.

FATHER (*laying down a new Commandment*): Vinnie, if there's one place the church should leave alone, it's a man's soul!

VINNIE: Clare, dear, don't you believe what it says in the Bible?

FATHER: A man has to use his common sense about the Bible, Vinnie, if he has any. For instance, you'd be in a pretty fix if I gave all my money to the poor.

VINNIE: Well, that's just silly!

FATHER: Speaking of money—where are this month's bills?

VINNIE: Clare, it isn't fair to go over the household accounts while you're hungry.

FATHER: Where are those bills, Vinnie?

VINNIE: They're downstairs on your desk. (FATHER *exits almost eagerly. Figures are something he understands better than he does women.*) Of all times! (*To* CORA.) It's awfully hard on a woman to love a man like Clare so much.

CORA: Yes, men can be aggravating. Clyde gets me so provoked! We kept company for six years, but the minute he proposed—the moment I said "Yes"—he began to take me for granted.

VINNIE: You have to expect that, Cora. I don't believe Clare has come right out and told me he loves me since we've been married. Of course I know he does, because I keep reminding him of it. You have to keep reminding them, Cora.

(*The door slams.*)

CORA: That must be Mary and Clarence.

(*There's a moment's pause. The two women look toward the hall —then at each other with a knowing sort of smile.* CORA *rises, goes up to the arch, peeks out—then faces front and innocently asks:*) Is that you, Mary?

MARY (*dashing in*): Yes!

(CLARENCE *crosses the arch to hang up his hat.*)

CORA: We have to change our clothes and finish our packing. (*Goes upstairs.*)

(CLARENCE *returns as* MARY *starts up the stairs.*)

MARY (*to* CLARENCE): It won't take me long.

CLARENCE: Can I help you pack?

VINNIE (*shocked*): Clarence! (MARY *runs upstairs.* CLARENCE *drifts into the living-room, somewhat abashed.* VINNIE *collects her hat and gloves, starts out, stops to look at* CLARENCE, *then comes down to him.*) Clarence, why didn't you kneel in church today?

CLARENCE: What, Mother?

VINNIE: Why didn't you kneel in church today?

CLARENCE (*troubled*): I just couldn't.

VINNIE: Has it anything to do with Mary? I know she's a Methodist.

CLARENCE: Oh, no, Mother! Methodists kneel. Mary told me. They don't get up and down so much, but they stay down longer.

VINNIE: If it's because your father doesn't kneel—you must remember he wasn't brought up to kneel in church. But you were—you always have—and, Clarence, you want to, don't you?

CLARENCE: Oh, yes! I wanted to today! I started to—you saw me start —but I just couldn't.

VINNIE: Is that suit of your father's too tight for you?

CLARENCE: No, it's not too *tight*. It fits fine. But it *is* the suit. Very peculiar things have happened to me since I started to wear it. I haven't been myself since I put it on.

VINNIE: In what way, Clarence? How do you mean?

(CLARENCE *pauses, then blurts out his problem.*)

CLARENCE: Mother, I can't seem to make these clothes do anything Father wouldn't do!

VINNIE: That's nonsense, Clarence—and not to kneel in church is a sacrilege.

CLARENCE: But making Father's trousers kneel seemed more of a sacrilege.

VINNIE: Clarence!

CLARENCE: No! Remember the first time I wore this? It was at Dora Wakefield's party for Mary. Do you know what happened? We were playing musical chairs and Dora Wakefield sat down suddenly right in my lap. I jumped up so fast she almost got hurt.

VINNIE: But it was all perfectly innocent.

CLARENCE: It wasn't that Dora was sitting on my lap—she was sitting on Father's trousers. Mother, I've got to have a suit of my own. (CLARENCE'S *metaphysical problem is one that* VINNIE *can't cope with at this particular minute.*)

VINNIE: My soul and body! Clarence, you have a talk with your father about it. I'm sure if you approach him the right way—you know— tactfully—he'll see—

(MARY *comes downstairs and hesitates at the arch.*)

MARY: Oh, excuse me.

VINNIE: Gracious! Have you finished your packing?

MARY: Practically. I never put my comb and brush in until I'm ready to close my bag.

VINNIE: I must see Margaret about your box lunch for the train. I'll leave you two together. Remember, it's Sunday. (*She goes downstairs.*)

CLARENCE: I was hoping we could have a few minutes together before you left.

MARY (*not to admit her eagerness*): Cora had so much to do I wanted to get out of her way.

CLARENCE: Well, didn't you want to see me?

MARY (*self-consciously*): I did want to tell you how much I've enjoyed our friendship.

CLARENCE: You're going to write me when you get to Springfield, aren't you?

MARY: Of course, if you write me first.

CLARENCE: But you'll have something to write about—your trip—and

THE IMPORTANCE OF BEING EARNEST—John Gielgud, Pamela Brown, Jane Baxter, Robert Flemyng, in the play's 1947 revival at the Royale Theatre.

THE MAN WHO CAME TO DINNER—Monty Woolley, Edith Atwater, LeRoi Operti, George Probert, Theodore Newton.

PRIVATE LIVES—Noel Coward, Gertrude Lawrence.

THE MAN WHO CAME TO DINNER—George Kaufman and Moss
Hart acted the parts of Sheridan Whiteside and Beverly Carlton
at the Bucks County Playhouse, New Hope, Pa.

LIFE WITH FATHER—(Clockwise) Howard Lindsay as Father, Katharine Bard, John Drew Devereaux, Richard Simon, Dorothy Bernard, Dorothy Stickney as Mother, Larry Robinson, Raymond Roe.

LIFE WITH FATHER—Howard Lindsay, Virginia Dunning.

Aunt Judith—and how things are in Springfield. You write me as soon as you get there.

MARY: Maybe I'll be too busy. Maybe I won't have time. (*She sits on the sofa.*)

CLARENCE (*with the authority of* FATHER'S *trousers*): You find the time! Let's not have any nonsense about that! You'll write me first— and you'll do it right away, the first day! (*Sits beside her.*)

MARY: How do you know I'll take orders from you?

CLARENCE: I'll show you. (*He takes a quick glance toward the hall.*) Give me your hand!

MARY: Why should I?

CLARENCE: Give me your hand, confound it!

(MARY *gives it to him.*)

MARY: What do you want with my hand?

CLARENCE: I just wanted it. (*Holding her hand, he melts a little and smiles at her. She melts, too. Their hands, clasped together, are resting on* CLARENCE'S *knee and they relax happily.*) What are you thinking about?

MARY: I was just thinking.

CLARENCE: About what?

MARY: Well, when we were talking about writing each other I was hoping you'd write me first because that would mean you liked me.

CLARENCE (*with the logic of the male*): What's writing first got to do with my liking you?

MARY: Oh, you *do* like me?

CLARENCE: Of course I do. I like you better than any girl I ever met.

MARY (*with the logic of the female*): But you don't like me well enough to write first?

CLARENCE: I don't see how one thing's got anything to do with the other.

MARY: But a girl can't write first—because she's a *girl*.

CLARENCE: That doesn't make sense. If a girl has something to write about and a fellow hasn't, there's no reason why she shouldn't write first.

MARY (*starting a flanking movement*): You know, the first few days I was here you'd do anything for me and then you changed. You used to be a lot of fun—and then all of a sudden you turned into an old sober-sides.

CLARENCE: When did I?

MARY: The first time I noticed it was when we walked home from Dora Wakefield's party. My, you were on your dignity! You've been that way ever since. You even dress like an old sober-sides.

(CLARENCE'S *face changes as* FATHER'S *pants rise to haunt him. Then he notices that their clasped hands are resting on these very pants, and he lifts them off. Agony obviously is setting in.* MARY *sees the expression on his face.*) What's the matter?

CLARENCE: I just happened to remember something.

MARY: What? (CLARENCE *doesn't answer, but his face does.*) Oh, I know. This is the last time we'll be together. (*She puts her hand on his shoulder. He draws away.*)

CLARENCE: Mary, please!

MARY: But, Clarence! We'll see each other in a month. And we'll be writing each other, too. I hope we will. (*She gets up.*) Oh, Clarence, please write me first, because it will show me how much you like me. Please! I'll show you how much I like you! (*She throws herself on his lap and buries her head on his shoulder.* CLARENCE *stiffens in agony.*)

CLARENCE (*hoarsely*): Get up! Get up! (*She pulls back her head and looks at him, then springs from his lap and runs away, covering her face and sobbing.* CLARENCE *goes to her.*) Don't do that, Mary! Please don't do that!

MARY: Now you'll think I'm just a bold and forward girl.

CLARENCE: Oh, no!

MARY: Yes, you will—you'll think I'm bold.

CLARENCE: Oh, no—it's not that.

MARY (*hopefully*): Was it because it's Sunday?

CLARENCE (*in despair*): No, it would be the same any day— (*He is about to explain, but* MARY *flares.*)

MARY: Oh, it's just because you didn't want me sitting on your lap.

CLARENCE: It was nice of you to do it.

MARY: It was nice of me! So you told me to get up! You just couldn't bear to have me sit there. Well, you needn't write me first. You needn't write me any letters at all, because I'll tear them up without opening them! (FATHER *enters the archway, a sheath of bills in his hand and his account book under his arm.*) I guess I know now you don't like me! I never want to see you again. I—I—

(*She breaks and starts to run toward the stairs. At the sight of* FA-THER *she stops, but only for a gasp, then continues on upstairs, unable to control her sobs.* CLARENCE, *who has been standing in unhappy indecision, turns to follow her, but stops short at the sight of* FATHER, *who is standing in the arch looking at him with some amazement.* FATHER *looks from* CLARENCE *toward the vanished* MARY, *then back to* CLARENCE.)

FATHER: Clarence, that young girl is crying—she's in tears. What's the meaning of this?

CLARENCE: I'm sorry, Father, it's all my fault.

FATHER: Nonsense! What's that girl trying to do to you?

CLARENCE: What? No, she wasn't—it was—I—how long have you been here?

FATHER: Well, whatever the quarrel was about, Clarence, I'm glad you held your own. Where's your mother?

CLARENCE (*desperately*): I have to have a new suit of clothes—you've *got* to give me the money for it.

(FATHER'S *account book reaches the table with a sharp bang as he stares at* CLARENCE *in astonishment.*)

FATHER: Young man, do you realize you're addressing your father?

(CLARENCE *wilts miserably and sinks into a chair.*)

CLARENCE: I'm sorry, Father—I apologize—but you don't know how important this is to me. (CLARENCE'S *tone of misery gives* FATHER *pause.*)

FATHER: A suit of clothes is so—? Now, why should a—? (*Something dawns on* FATHER *and he looks up in the direction in which* MARY *has disappeared, then looks back at* CLARENCE.) Has your need for a suit of clothes anything to do with that young lady?

CLARENCE: Yes, Father.

FATHER: Why, Clarence! (*Suddenly realizes that women have come into* CLARENCE'S *emotional life and there comes a yearning to protect this inexperienced and defenseless member of his own sex.*) This comes as quite a shock to me.

CLARENCE: What does, Father?

FATHER: Your being so grown up! Still, I might have known that if you're going to college this fall—yes, you're at an age when you'll be meeting girls. Clarence, there are things about women that I think you ought to know! (*He goes up and closes the doors, then comes down and sits beside* CLARENCE, *hesitating for a moment before he speaks.*) Yes, I think it's better for you to hear this from me than to have to learn it for yourself. Clarence, women aren't the angels that you think they are! Well, now—first, let me explain this to you. You see, Clarence, we men have to run this world and it's not an easy job. It takes work, and it takes thinking. A man has to be sure of his facts and figures. He has to reason things out. Now, you take a woman—a woman thinks—no I'm wrong right there—a woman doesn't think at all! She gets stirred up! And she gets stirred up over the damnedest things! Now, I love my wife just as much as any man, but that doesn't mean I should stand for a lot of folderol! By God! I won't stand for it! (*Looks around toward the spot where he had his last clash with* VINNIE.)

CLARENCE: Stand for what, Father?

FATHER (*to himself*): That's the one thing I will not submit myself to. (*Has ceased explaining women to* CLARENCE *and is now explaining himself.*) Clarence, if a man thinks a certain thing is the wrong thing to do he shouldn't do it. If he thinks a thing is right he should do it. Now that has nothing to do with whether he loves his wife or not.

CLARENCE: Who says it has, Father?

FATHER: They do!

CLARENCE: Who, sir?

FATHER: Women! They get stirred up and then they try to get you stirred up, too. If you can keep reason and logic in the argument, a man can hold his own, of course. But if they can *switch* you—pretty soon the argument's about whether you love them or not. I swear I don't know how they do it! Don't you let 'em, Clarence! Don't you let 'em!

CLARENCE: I see what you mean so far, Father. If you don't watch yourself, love can make you do a lot of things you don't want to do.

FATHER: Exactly!

CLARENCE: But if you do watch out and know just how to handle women—

FATHER: Then you'll be all right. All a man has to do is be firm. You know how sometimes I have to be firm with your mother. Just now about this month's household accounts—

CLARENCE: Yes, but what can you do when they cry?

FATHER (*he gives this a moment's thought*): Well, that's quite a question. You just have to make them understand that what you're doing is for their good.

CLARENCE: I see.

FATHER (*rising*): Now, Clarence, you know all about women. (*Goes to the table and sits down in front of his account book, opening it. CLARENCE rises and looks at him.*)

CLARENCE: But, Father—

FATHER: Yes, Clarence.

CLARENCE: I thought you were going to tell me about—

FATHER: About what?

CLARENCE: About women.

(FATHER *realizes with some shock that* CLARENCE *expected him to be more specific.*)

FATHER: Clarence, there are some things gentlemen don't discuss! I've told you all you need to know. The thing for you to remember is—be firm. (CLARENCE *turns away. There is a knock at the sliding doors.*) Yes, come in.

(MARY *opens the doors.*)

MARY: Excuse me!

(MARY *enters.* FATHER *turns his attention to the household accounts.* MARY *goes to the couch and picks up her handkerchief and continues around the couch.* CLARENCE *crosses to meet her above the couch, determined to be firm.* MARY *passes him without a glance.* CLARENCE *wilts, then again assuming firmness, turns up into the arch in an attempt to quail* MARY *with a look.* MARY *marches upstairs ignoring him.* CLARENCE *turns back into the room defeated. He looks down at his clothes unhappily, then decides to be firm with his father. He straightens up and steps toward him. At this moment* FATHER, *staring at a bill, emits his cry of rage.*)

FATHER: Oh, God!

(CLARENCE *retreats.* FATHER *rises and holds the bill in question between thumb and forefinger as though it were too repulsive to touch.* VINNIE *comes rushing down the stairs.*)

VINNIE: What's the matter, Clare? What's wrong?

FATHER: I will *not* send this person a check!

(VINNIE *looks at it.*)

VINNIE: Why, Clare, that's the only hat I've bought since March and it was reduced from forty dollars.

FATHER: I don't question your buying the hat or what you paid for it, but the person from whom you bought it—this Mademoiselle Mimi —isn't fit to be in the hat business or any other.

VINNIE: I never went there before, but it's a very nice place and I don't see why you object to it.

FATHER (*exasperated*): I object to it because this confounded person doesn't put her name on her bills! Mimi what? Mimi O'Brien? Mimi Jones? Mimi Weinstein?

VINNIE: How do I know? It's just Mimi.

FATHER: It isn't just Mimi. She must have some other name, damn it! Now, I wouldn't make out a check payable to Charley or to Jimmy, and I won't make out a check payable to Mimi. Find out what her last name is, and I'll pay her the money.

VINNIE: All right. All right. (*She starts out.*)

FATHER: Just a minute, Vinnie, that isn't all.

VINNIE: But Cora will be leaving any minute, Clare, and it isn't polite for me—

FATHER: Never mind Cora. Sit down. (CLARENCE *goes into the hall, looks upstairs, wanders up and down the hall restlessly.* VINNIE *reluctantly sits down opposite* FATHER *at the table.*) Vinnie, you know I like to live well, and I want my family to live well. But this house must be run on a business basis. I must know how much money I'm spending and what for. For instance, if you recall, two weeks ago I gave you six dollars to buy a new coffee pot—

VINNIE: Yes, because you broke the old one. You threw it right on the floor.

FATHER: I'm not talking about that. I'm simply endeavoring—

VINNIE: But it was so silly to break that nice coffee pot, Clare, and there was nothing the matter with the coffee that morning. It was made just the same as always.

FATHER: It was not! It was made in a damned barbaric manner!

VINNIE: I couldn't get another imported one. That little shop has stopped selling them. They said the tariff wouldn't let them. And that's your fault, Clare, because you're always voting to raise the tariff.

FATHER: The tariff protects America against cheap foreign labor. (*He sounds as though he is quoting.*) Now I find that—

VINNIE: The tariff does nothing but put up the prices and that's hard on everybody, especially the farmer. (*She sounds as though she is quoting back.*)

FATHER (*annoyed*): I wish to God you wouldn't talk about matters you don't know a damn thing about!

VINNIE: I do too know about them. Miss Gulick says every intelligent woman should have some opinion—

FATHER: Who, may I ask, is Miss Gulick?

VINNIE: Why, she's that current-events woman I told you about and the tickets are a dollar every Tuesday.

FATHER: Do you mean to tell me that a pack of idle-minded females pay a dollar apiece to hear another female gabble about the events of the day? Listen to me if you want to know anything about the events of the day!

VINNIE: But you get so excited, Clare, and besides, Miss Gulick says that our President, whom you're always belittling, prays to God for guidance and—

FATHER (*having had enough of Miss Gulick*): Vinnie, what happened to that six dollars?

VINNIE: What six dollars?

FATHER: I gave you six dollars to buy a new coffee pot and now I find that you apparently got one at Lewis & Conger's and charged it. Here's their bill: "One coffee pot—five dollars."

VINNIE: So you owe me a dollar and you can hand it right over. (*She holds out her hand for it.*)

FATHER: I'll do nothing of the kind! What did you do with that six dollars?

VINNIE: Why, Clare, I can't tell you now, dear. Why didn't you ask me at the time?

FATHER: Oh, my God!

VINNIE: Wait a moment! I spent four dollars and a half for that new umbrella I told you I wanted and you said I didn't need, but I did, very much.

(FATHER *takes his pencil and writes in the account book.*)

FATHER: Now we're getting somewhere. One umbrella—four dollars and a half.

VINNIE: And that must have been the week I paid Mrs. Tobin for two extra days' washing.

FATHER (*entering the item*): Mrs. Tobin.

VINNIE: So that was two dollars more.

FATHER: Two dollars.

VINNIE: That makes six dollars and fifty cents. And that's another fifty cents you owe me.

FATHER: I don't owe you anything. (*Stung by* VINNIE's *tactics into a determination to pin her butterfly mind down.*) What you owe me is an explanation of where my money's gone! We're going over this account book item by item. (*Starts to sort the bills for the purposes of cross-examination, but the butterfly takes wing again.*)

VINNIE: I do the very best I can to keep down expenses. And you know yourself that Cousin Phoebe spends twice as much as we do.

FATHER: Damn Cousin Phoebe!—I don't wish to be told how she throws her money around.

VINNIE: Oh, Clare, how can you? And I thought you were so fond of Cousin Phoebe.

FATHER: All right, I am fond of Cousin Phoebe, but I can get along without hearing so much about her.

VINNIE: You talk about your own relatives enough.

FATHER (*hurt*): That's not fair, Vinnie. When I talk about my relatives I criticize them.

VINNIE: If I can't even speak of Cousin Phoebe—

FATHER: You can speak of her all you want to—but I won't have Cousin Phoebe or anyone else dictating to me how to run my house. Now this month's total—

VINNIE (*righteously*): I didn't say a word about her dictating, Clare— she isn't that kind!

FATHER (*dazed*): I don't know what you said, now. You never stick to the point. I endeavor to show you how to run this house on a business basis and you wind up by jibbering and jabbering about everything under the sun. If you'll just explain to me—

(*Finally cornered,* VINNIE *realizes the time has come for tears. Quietly she turns them on.*)

VINNIE: I don't know what you expect of me. I tire myself out chasing up and down those stairs all day long—trying to look after your comfort—to bring up our children—I do the mending and the marketing and as if that isn't enough, you want me to be an expert bookkeeper, too.

FATHER (*touched where* VINNIE *has hoped to touch him*): Vinnie, I want to be reasonable; but can't you understand?—I'm doing all this for your own good. (VINNIE *rises with a moan.* FATHER *sighs with resignation.*) I suppose I'll have to go ahead just paying the bills and hoping I've got enough money in the bank to meet them. But it's all very discouraging.

VINNIE: I'll try to do better, Clare.

(FATHER *looks up into her tearful face and melts.*)

FATHER: That's all I'm asking. (*She goes to him and puts her arm around his shoulder.*) I'll go down and make out the checks and sign them. (VINNIE *doesn't seem entirely consoled, so he attempts a lighter note to cheer her up.*) Oh, Vinnie, maybe I haven't any right to sign those checks, since in the sight of the Lord I haven't any name at all. Do you suppose the bank will feel that way about it too —or do you think they'll take a chance?

(*He should not have said this.*)

VINNIE: That's right! Clare, to make those checks good you'll have to be baptized right away.

FATHER (*retreating angrily*): Vinnie, the bank doesn't care whether I've been baptized or not!

VINNIE: Well, I care! And no matter what Dr. Lloyd says, I'm not sure we're really married.

FATHER: Damn it, Vinnie, we have four children! If we're not married now we never will be!

VINNIE: Oh, Clare, don't you see how serious this is? You've got to do something about it.

FATHER: Well, just now I've got to do something about these damn bills you've run up. (*Sternly.*) I'm going downstairs.

VINNIE: Not before you give me that dollar and a half!

FATHER: What dollar and a half?

VINNIE: The dollar and a half you owe me!

FATHER (*thoroughly enraged*): I don't owe you any dollar and a half! I gave you money to buy a coffee pot for me and somehow it turned into an umbrella for you.

VINNIE: Clarence Day, what kind of a man are you? Quibbling about a dollar and a half when your immortal soul is in danger! And what's more—

FATHER: All right. All right. All right. (*He takes the dollar and a half from his change purse and gives it to her.*)

VINNIE (*smiling*): Thank you, Clare.

(VINNIE *turns and leaves the room. Her progress upstairs is a one-woman march of triumph.*)

(FATHER *puts his purse back, gathers up his papers and his dignity, and starts out.* CLARENCE *waylays him in the arch.*)

CLARENCE: Father—you never did tell me—can I have a new suit of clothes?

FATHER: No, Clarence! I'm sorry, but I have to be firm with you, too!

(*He stalks off.* JOHN *comes down the stairs carrying a traveling bag, which he takes out toward the front door. He returns empty-handed and starts up the stairs again.*)

CLARENCE: John, come here a minute.

JOHN (*coming into the room*): What do you want?

CLARENCE: John, have you got any money you could lend me?

JOHN: With this week's allowance, I'll have about three dollars.

CLARENCE: That's no good. I've got to have enough to buy a new suit of clothes.

JOHN: Why don't you earn some money? That's what I'm going to do. I'm going to buy a bicycle—one of those new low kind, with both wheels the same size—you know, a safety.

CLARENCE: How are you going to earn that much money?

JOHN: I've got a job practically. Look, I found this ad in the paper. (*He hands* CLARENCE *a clipping from his pocket.*)

CLARENCE (*reading*): "Wanted, an energetic young man to handle household necessity that sells on sight. Liberal commissions. Apply 312 West Fourteenth Street, Tuesday from eight to twelve." Listen, John, let me have that job.

JOHN: Why should I give you my job? They're hard to get.

CLARENCE: But I've got to have a new suit of clothes.

JOHN: Maybe I could get a job for both of us. (*The doorbell rings.*) I'll tell you what I'll do, I'll ask the man.

FATHER (*hurrying to the foot of the stairs*): Vinnie! Cora! The cab's here. Hurry up! (*Goes through the arch toward the front door.*)

CLARENCE: We've both got to get down there early Tuesday—the first thing.

JOHN: Oh, no you don't—I'm going alone. But I'll put in a good word with the boss about you.

FATHER (*off*): They'll be right out. Vinnie! Cora! (*He comes back to the foot of the stairs and calls up.*) Are you coming? The cab's waiting!

VINNIE (*from upstairs*): We heard you, Clare. We'll be down in a minute.

(FATHER *comes into the room.*)

FATHER: John, go upstairs and hurry them down.

(JOHN *goes upstairs.* FATHER *crosses to the window and looks out, then consults his watch.*)

FATHER: What's the matter with those women? Don't they know cabs cost money? Clarence, go see what's causing this infernal delay!

(CLARENCE *goes out to the hall.*)

CLARENCE: Here they come, Father.

(MARY *comes sedately downstairs. She passes* CLARENCE *without a glance and goes to* FATHER.)

MARY: Goodbye, Mr. Day. I can't tell you how much I appreciate your hospitality.

FATHER: Not at all! Not at all!

(VINNIE *and* CORA *appear at top of stairs and come down.* JOHN *follows with the bags and takes them out.*)

CORA: Goodbye, Clarence. (*She starts into the room.*)

FATHER: Cora, we can say goodbye to you on the sidewalk.

VINNIE: There's no hurry. Their train doesn't go until one-thirty.

FATHER: Cabs cost money. If they have any waiting to do they ought to do it at the Grand Central Depot. They've got a waiting-room there just *for* that.

VINNIE (*to* MARY): If there's one thing Mr. Day can't stand it's to keep a cab waiting.

CORA: It's been so nice seeing you again, Clarence. (*She kisses him.*)

(MARGARET *enters with a box of lunch.*)

MARGARET: Here's the lunch.

FATHER: All right. All right. Give it to me. Let's get started.

(MARGARET *gives it to him and exits.*)

CORA: Where's John?

FATHER: He's outside. Come on. (*Leads the way.* CORA *and* VINNIE *follow.* MARY *starts.*)

CLARENCE: Mary, aren't you going even to shake hands with me?

MARY: I don't think I'd better. You may remember that when I get too close to you you feel contaminated. (*Starts out.* CLARENCE *follows her.*)

CLARENCE: Mary! (*She stops in the arch. He goes to her.*) You're going to write me, aren't you?

MARY: Are you going to write first?

CLARENCE (*resolutely*): No, Mary. There are times when a man has to be firm.

(JOHN *enters.*)

JOHN: Mary, Mother says you'd better hurry out before Father starts yelling. It's Sunday.

MARY: Goodbye, John. I'm very happy to have made *your* acquaintance.

(*She walks out. We hear the door close.* JOHN *goes out.* CLARENCE *takes a step toward the door, stops, suffers a moment, then turns to the writing desk, takes paper and pen and ink to the table, and sits down to write a letter.*)

CLARENCE (*writing*): Dear Mary—

CURTAIN

SCENE II

The same.

Two days later. The breakfast table.

HARLAN *and* WHITNEY *are at the table, ready to start breakfast.* CLARENCE *is near the window reading the paper. The places of* JOHN *and* VINNIE *and* FATHER *are empty.* NORA, *a new maid, is serving the fruit and cereal.* NORA *is heavily built and along toward middle age. The doorbell rings and we hear the postman's whistle.* CLARENCE *drops the paper and looks out the window toward the door.* NORA *starts toward the arch.*

CLARENCE: Never mind, Nora. It's the postman. I'll go. (*He runs out through the arch.*)

WHITNEY (*to* NORA): You forgot the sugar. It goes here between me and Father.

(CLARENCE *comes back with three or four letters which he sorts eagerly. Then his face falls in utter dejection.* FATHER *comes down the stairs.*)

FATHER: Good morning, boys! John late? (*He shouts.*) John! John! Hurry down to your breakfast.

CLARENCE: John had his breakfast early, Father, and went out to see about something.

FATHER: See about what?

CLARENCE: John and I thought we'd work this summer and earn some money.

FATHER: Good! Sit down boys. (*Goes to his chair.*)

CLARENCE: We saw an ad in the paper and John went down to see about it.

FATHER: Why didn't you go, too?

CLARENCE: I was expecting an answer to a letter I wrote, but it didn't come. Here's the mail. (*He seems depressed.*)

FATHER (*sitting*): What kind of work is this you're planning to do?

CLARENCE: Sort of salesman, the ad said.

FATHER: Um-hum. Well, work never hurt anybody. It's good for them. But if you're going to work, work hard. King Solomon had the right idea about work. "Whatever thy hand findeth to do," Solomon said, "do thy damnedest!" Where's your mother?

NORA: If you please, sir, Mrs. Day doesn't want any breakfast. She isn't feeling well, so she went back upstairs to lie down again.

FATHER (*uneasily*): Now, why does your mother do that to me? She knows it just upsets my day when she doesn't come down to breakfast. Clarence, go tell your mother I'll be up to see her before I start for the office.

CLARENCE: Yes, sir. (*He goes upstairs.*)

HARLAN: What's the matter with Mother?

FATHER: There's nothing the matter with your mother. Perfectly healthy woman. She gets an ache or a twinge and instead of being firm about it, she just gives in to it. (*The postman whistles. Then the doorbell rings.* NORA *answers it.*) Boys, after breakfast you find out what your mother wants you to do today. Whitney, you take care of Harlan.

(NORA *comes back with a special-delivery letter.*)

NORA: It's a special delivery.

(*She hands it to* FATHER, *who tears it open at once.* CLARENCE *comes rushing down the stairs.*)

CLARENCE: Was that the postman again?

WHITNEY: It was a special delivery.

CLARENCE: Yes? Where is it?

WHITNEY: It was for Father.

CLARENCE (*again disappointed*): Oh— (*He sits at the table.*)

(FATHER *has opened the letter and is reading it. Bewildered, he turns it over and looks at the signature.*)

FATHER: I don't understand this at all. Here's a letter from some woman I never even heard of.

(FATHER *tackles the letter again.* CLARENCE *sees the envelope, picks it up, looks at the postmark, worried.*)

CLARENCE: Father!

FATHER: Oh, God!

CLARENCE: What is it, Father?

FATHER: This is the damnedest nonsense I ever read! As far as I can make out this woman claims that she sat on my lap and I didn't like it. (CLARENCE *begins to turn red.* FATHER *goes on reading a little further and then holds the letter over in front of* CLARENCE.) Can you make out what that word is? (CLARENCE *begins feverishly to read as much as possible, but* FATHER *cuts in.*) No, that word right there. (*He points.*)

CLARENCE: It looks like—"curiosity."

(FATHER *withdraws the letter,* CLARENCE'S *eyes following it hungrily.*)

FATHER (*reads*): "I only opened your letter as a matter of curiosity." (*Breaks off reading aloud as he turns the page.*)

CLARENCE: Yes? Go on.

FATHER: Why, this gets worse and worse! It just turns into a lot of sentimental lovey-dovey mush. (*Crushes the letter, stalks across the room, and throws it into the fireplace,* CLARENCE *watching him with dismay.*) Is this someone's idea of a practical joke? Why must I be the butt—

(VINNIE *comes hurrying down the stairs. Her hair is down in two braids over her shoulder. She is wearing a lacy combing jacket over her corset cover, and a striped petticoat.*)

VINNIE: What's the matter, Clare? What's wrong?

FATHER (*going to her*): Nothing wrong—just a damn fool letter. How are you, Vinnie?

VINNIE (*weakly*): I don't feel well. I thought you needed me, but if you don't I'll go back to bed.

FATHER: No, now that you're here, sit down with us. (*He moves out her chair.*) Get some food in your stomach. Do you good.

VINNIE (*protesting*): I don't feel like eating anything, Clare.

(NORA *enters with a tray of bacon and eggs, stops at the serving table.*)

FATHER (*heartily*): That's all the more reason why you should eat. Build up your strength! (*He forces* VINNIE *into her chair and turns to speak to* NORA, *who has her back to him.*) Here— (*Then to* CLARENCE.) What's this one's name?

CLARENCE: Nora.

FATHER: Nora! Give Mrs. Day some of the bacon and eggs.

VINNIE: No, Clare! (NORA, *however, has gone to* VINNIE'S *side with the platter.*) No, take it away, Nora. I don't even want to smell it.

(*The maid retreats, and serves* FATHER; *then* CLARENCE; *then serves coffee and exits.*)

FATHER: Vinnie, it's just weak to give in to an ailment. Any disease can be cured by firmness. What you need is strength of character.

VINNIE: I don't know why you object to my complaining a little. I notice when you have a headache you yell and groan and swear enough.

FATHER: Of course I yell! That's to prove to the headache that I'm stronger than it is. I can usually swear it right out of my system.

VINNIE: This isn't a headache. I think I've caught some kind of a germ. There's a lot of sickness around. Several of my friends have had to send for the doctor. I may have the same thing.

FATHER: I'll bet this is all your imagination, Vinnie. You hear a lot of other people having some disease and then you get scared and think you have it yourself. So you go to bed and send for the doctor. The doctor—all poppycock!

VINNIE: I didn't say anything about my sending for the doctor.

FATHER: I should hope not. Doctors think they know a damn lot, but they don't.

VINNIE: But Clare, dear, when people are seriously ill you have to do something.

FATHER: Certainly you have to do something! Cheer 'em up—that's the way to cure 'em!

VINNIE (*with slight irony*): How would you go about cheering them up?

FATHER: I? I'd tell 'em—bah! (VINNIE, *out of exasperation and weakness, begins to cry.* FATHER *looks at her amazed.*) What have I done now?

VINNIE: Oh, Clare—hush up! (*She moves from the table to the sofa, where she tries to control her crying.* HARLAN *slides out of his chair and runs over to her.*) Harlan dear, keep away from Mother. You might catch what she's got. Whitney, if you've finished your breakfast—

WHITNEY (*rising*): Yes, Mother.

VINNIE: I promised Mrs. Whitehead to send over Margaret's recipe for floating-island pudding. Margaret has it all written out. And take Harlan with you.

WHITNEY: All right, Mother. I hope you feel better.

(WHITNEY *and* HARLAN *exit.* FATHER *goes over and sits beside* VINNIE *on the sofa.*)

FATHER: Vinnie. (*Contritely.*) I didn't mean to upset you. I was just trying to help. (*He pats her hand.*) When you take to your bed I have a damned lonely time around here. So when I see you getting it into your head that you're sick, I want to do something about it. (*He continues to pat her hand vigorously with what he thinks is reassurance.*) Just because some of your friends have given in to this is no reason why you should imagine you're sick, Vinnie.

VINNIE (*snatching her hand away*): Oh, stop, Clare!—get out of this house and go to your office!

(FATHER *is a little bewildered and somewhat indignant at this rebuff to his tenderness. He gets up and goes out into the hall, comes back with his hat and stick, and marches out of the house, slamming the door.* VINNIE *rises and starts toward the stairs.*)

CLARENCE: I'm sorry you're not feeling well, Mother.

VINNIE: Oh, I'll be all right, Clarence. Remember last fall I had a touch of this and I was all right the next morning.

CLARENCE: Are you sure you don't want the doctor?

VINNIE: Oh, no. I really don't need him—and besides doctors worry your father. I don't want him to be upset.

CLARENCE: Is there anything I can do for you?

VINNIE: Ask Margaret to send me up a cup of tea. I'll try to drink it. I'm going back to bed.

CLARENCE: Do you mind if John and I go out today or will you need us?

VINNIE: You run right along. I just want to be left alone.

(*She exits up the stairs.* CLARENCE *starts for the fireplace eager to retrieve Mary's letter.* NORA *enters. He stops.*)

CLARENCE: Oh!—Nora—will you take a cup of tea up to Mrs. Day in her room?

NORA: Yes, sir. (*Exits.*)

(CLARENCE *hurries around the table, gets the crumpled letter, and starts to read it feverishly. He reads quickly to the end, then draws a deep, happy breath. The door slams. He puts the letter in his pocket.* JOHN *enters, carrying two heavy packages.*)

CLARENCE: Did you get the job?

JOHN: Yes, for both of us. Look, I've got it with me.

CLARENCE: What is it?

JOHN: Medicine.

CLARENCE (*dismayed*): Medicine! You took a job for us to go out and sell medicine!

JOHN: But it's wonderful medicine. (*Gets a bottle out of the package and reads from the label.*) "Bartlett's Beneficent Balm—A Boon to Mankind." Look what it cures! (*He hands the bottle to* CLARENCE.)

CLARENCE (*reading*): "A sovereign cure for colds, coughs, catarrh, asthma, quincy, and sore throat; poor digestion, summer complaint, colic, dyspepsia, heartburn, and shortness of breath; lumbago, rheumatism, heart disease, giddiness, and women's complaints; nervous prostration, St. Vitus' dance, jaundice, and la grippe; proud flesh, pink eye, seasickness, and pimples."

(*As* CLARENCE *has read off the list he has become more and more impressed.*)

JOHN: See?

CLARENCE: Say, that sounds all right!

JOHN: It's made "from a secret formula known only to Dr. Bartlett."

CLARENCE: He must be quite a doctor!

JOHN (*enthusiastically*): It sells for a dollar a bottle and we get twenty-five cents commission on every bottle.

CLARENCE: Well, where does he want us to sell it?

JOHN: He's given us the territory of all Manhattan Island.

CLARENCE: That's bully! Anybody that's sick at all ought to need a bottle of this. Let's start by calling on friends of Father and Mother.

JOHN: That's a good idea. But wait a minute. Suppose they ask us if we use it at our house?

CLARENCE (*a little worried*): Oh, yes. It would be better if we could say we did.

JOHN: But we can't because we haven't had it here long enough.

(NORA *enters with a tray with a cup of tea. She goes to the table and puts the sugar bowl and cream pitcher on it.*)

CLARENCE: Is that the tea for Mrs. Day?

NORA: Yes.

(*The suspicion of a good idea dawns on* CLARENCE.)

CLARENCE: I'll take it up to her. You needn't bother.

NORA: Thank you. Take it up right away while it's hot. (*She exits.* CLARENCE *watches her out.*)

CLARENCE (*eyeing* JOHN): Mother wasn't feeling well this morning.

JOHN: What was the matter with her?

CLARENCE: I don't know—she was just complaining.

JOHN (*getting the idea immediately and consulting the bottle*): Well, it says here it's good for women's complaints.

(*They look at each other.* CLARENCE *opens the bottle and smells its contents.* JOHN *leans over and takes a sniff, too. Then he nods to* CLARENCE, *who quickly reaches for a spoon and measures out a teaspoonful, which he puts into the tea.* JOHN, *wanting to be sure* MOTHER *has enough to cure her, pours still more into the tea from the bottle as the curtain falls.*)

(THE CURTAIN *remains down for a few seconds to denote a lapse of three hours.*)

(*When the curtain rises again, the breakfast things have been cleared and the room is in order.* HARLAN *is kneeling on* FATHER'S *chair looking out the window as if watching for someone.* MARGARET *comes down from upstairs.*)

MARGARET: Has your father come yet?

HARLAN: Not yet.

(NORA *enters from downstairs with a steaming tea-kettle and a towel and meets* MARGARET *in the hall.*)

MARGARET: Hurry that upstairs. The doctor's waiting for it. I've got to go out.

NORA: Where are you going?

MARGARET: I have to go and get the minister. (NORA *goes upstairs.*)

HARLAN: There's a cab coming up the street.

MARGARET: Well, I hope it's him, poor man—but a cab doesn't sound like your father. (*She hurries downstairs.*)

(HARLAN *sees something through the window, then rushes to the stairwell and shouts down to* MARGARET.)

HARLAN: Yes, it's Father. Whitney got him all right. (*Runs back to the window. The front door slams and* FATHER *crosses the arch and hurries upstairs.* WHITNEY *comes into the room.*) What took you so long?

WHITNEY: Long? I wasn't long. I went right down on the elevated and got Father right away and we came all the way back in a *cab.*

HARLAN: I thought you were never coming.

WHITNEY: Well, the horse didn't go very fast at first. The cabby whipped him and swore at him and still he wouldn't gallop. Then Father spoke to the horse personally—How is Mother?

HARLAN: I don't know. The doctor's up there now.

WHITNEY: Well, she'd better be good and sick or Father may be mad at me for getting him up here—'specially in a cab.

(FATHER *comes down the stairs muttering to himself.*)

FATHER (*indignantly*): Well, huh!—It seems to me I ought to be shown a little consideration. I guess I've got some feelings, too!

WHITNEY (*hopefully*): Mother's awfully sick, isn't she?

FATHER: How do I know? I wasn't allowed to stay in the same room with her.

WHITNEY: Did the doctor put you out?

FATHER: No, it was your mother, damn it! (*He goes out and hangs up his hat and stick, then returns.* FATHER *may be annoyed, but he is also worried.*) You boys keep quiet around here today.

WHITNEY: She must be pretty sick.

FATHER: She must be, Whitney! I don't know! Nobody ever tells me anything in this house. Not a damn thing!

   (DR. HUMPHREYS *comes down the stairs. He's the family-doctor type of the period, with just enough whiskers to make him impressive. He carries his satchel.*)

DR. HUMPHREYS: Mrs. Day is quieter now.

FATHER: How sick is she? What's the matter with her?

DR. HUMPHREYS: She's a pretty sick woman, Mr. Day. I had given her a sedative just before you came—and after you left the room I had to give her another. Have you a telephone?

FATHER: A telephone! No—I don't believe in them. Why?

DR. HUMPHREYS: Well, it would only have saved me a few steps. I'll be back in ten minutes. (*He turns to go.*)

FATHER: Wait a minute—I think I'm entitled to know what's the matter with my wife.

   (DR. HUMPHREYS *turns back.*)

DR. HUMPHREYS: What did Mrs. Day have for breakfast this morning?

FATHER: She didn't eat anything—not a thing.

DR. HUMPHREYS: Are you sure?

FATHER: I tried to get her to eat something, but she wouldn't.

DR. HUMPHREYS (*almost to himself*): I can't understand it.

FATHER: Understand what?

DR. HUMPHREYS: These violent attacks of nausea. It's almost as though she were poisoned.

FATHER: Poisoned!

DR. HUMPHREYS: I'll try not to be gone more than ten or fifteen minutes. (*He exits.*)

FATHER (*trying to reassure himself*): Damn doctors! They never know what's the matter with anybody. Well, he'd better get your mother well, and damn soon or he'll hear from me.

WHITNEY: Mother's going to get well, isn't she?

(FATHER *looks at* WHITNEY *sharply as though he is a little angry at anyone even raising the question.*)

FATHER: Of course she's going to get well!

HARLAN (*running to* FATHER): I hope she gets well soon. When Mamma stays in bed it's lonesome.

FATHER: Yes, it is, Harlan. It's lonesome. (*He looks around the room and finds it pretty empty.*) What were you boys supposed to do today?

WHITNEY: I was to learn the rest of my catechism.

FATHER: Well, if that's what your mother wanted you to do, you'd better do it.

WHITNEY: I know it—I think.

FATHER: You'd better be sure.

WHITNEY: I can't be sure unless somebody hears me. Will you hear me?

FATHER (*with sudden willingness to be useful*): All right. I'll hear you, Whitney.

(WHITNEY *goes to the mantel and gets* VINNIE'S *prayer book.* FATHER *sits on the sofa.* HARLAN *climbs up beside him.*)

HARLAN: If Mamma's still sick will you read to me tonight?

FATHER: Of course I'll read to you.

(WHITNEY *opens the prayer book and hands it to* FATHER.)

WHITNEY: Here it is, Father. Just the end of it. Mother knows I know the rest. Look, start here. (*He points.*)

FATHER: All right. (*Reading.*) "How many parts are there in a Sacrament?"

WHITNEY (*reciting*): "Two; the outward visible sign, and the inward spiritual grace."

(FATHER *nods in approval.*)

FATHER: "What is the outward visible sign or form in Baptism?"

WHITNEY: "Water; wherein the person is baptized, in the name of the Father, and of the Son, and of the Holy Ghost." You haven't been baptized, Father, have you?

FATHER (*ignoring it*): "What is the inward and spiritual grace?"

WHITNEY: If you don't have to be baptized, why do I have to be confirmed?

FATHER (*ignoring this even more*): "What is the inward and spiritual grace?"

WHITNEY: "A death unto sin, and a new birth unto righteousness; for being by nature born in sin, and the children of wrath, we are hereby made the children of grace." Is that why you get mad so much, Father—because you're a child of wrath?

FATHER: Whitney, mind your manners! You're not supposed to ask questions of your elders! "What is required of persons to be baptized?"

WHITNEY: "Repentance, whereby—whereby—" (*He pauses.*)

FATHER (*quickly shutting the book and handing it to* WHITNEY): You don't know it well enough, Whitney. You'd better study it some more.

WHITNEY: Now?

FATHER (*softening*): No, you don't have to do it now. Let's see, now, what can we do?

WHITNEY: Well, I was working with my tool chest out in the back yard. (*Edges toward the arch.*)

FATHER: Better not do any hammering with your mother sick upstairs. You'd better stay here.

WHITNEY: I wasn't hammering—I was doing wood-carving.

FATHER: Well, Harlan—how about you? Shall we play some tiddle-dy-winks?

HARLAN (*edging toward* WHITNEY): I was helping Whitney.

FATHER: Oh—all right. (*The boys go out.* FATHER *goes to the stairwell.*) Boys, don't do any shouting. We all have to be very quiet around here. (*He stands in the hall and looks up toward* VINNIE, *worried. Then he tiptoes across the room and stares gloomily out of the window. Then he tiptoes back into the hall and goes to the rail of the basement stairs, and calls quietly.*) Margaret! (*There is no an-*

swer and he raises his voice a little.) Margaret! (*There is still no answer and he lets loose.*) Margaret! Why don't you answer when you hear me calling?

(*At this moment* MARGARET, *hat on, appears in the arch from the right, having come through the front door.*)

MARGARET: Sh—sh—

(FATHER *turns quickly and sees* MARGARET.)

FATHER: Oh, there you are!

MARGARET (*reprovingly*): We must all be quiet, Mr. Day—Mrs. Day is very sick.

FATHER (*testily*): I know she's sick. That's what I wanted you for. You go up and wait outside her door in case she needs anything. (MARGARET *starts upstairs.*) And what were you doing out of the house, anyway?

MARGARET: I was sent for the minister.

FATHER (*startled*): The minister!

MARGARET: Yes, he'll be right in. He's paying off the cab.

(MARGARET *continues upstairs. The door slams.* THE REVEREND DR. LLOYD *appears in the archway and meets* FATHER *in the hall.*)

DR. LLOYD: I was deeply shocked to hear of Mrs. Day's illness. I hope I can be of some service. Will you take me up to her?

FATHER (*with a trace of hostility*): She's resting now. She can't be disturbed.

DR. LLOYD: But I've been summoned.

FATHER: The doctor will be back in a few minutes and we'll see what he has to say about it. You'd better come in and wait.

DR. LLOYD: Thank you. (*Comes into the room.* FATHER *follows him reluctantly.*) Mrs. Day has been a tower of strength in the parish. Everyone liked her so much. Yes, she was a fine woman.

FATHER: I wish to God you wouldn't talk about Mrs. Day if she were dead.

(NORA *comes down the stairs and looks into the room.*)

NORA: Is the doctor back yet?

FATHER: No. Does she need him?

NORA: She's kinda' restless. She's talking in her sleep and twisting and turning.

(*She goes downstairs.* FATHER *looks up toward* VINNIE'S *room, worried, then looks angrily toward the front door.*)

FATHER: That doctor said he'd be right back. (*He goes to the window.*)

MARGARET (*coming downstairs*): Here comes the doctor. I was watching for him out the window. (*She goes to the front door. A moment later* DR. HUMPHREYS *enters.*)

FATHER: Well, doctor—seems to me that was a pretty long ten minutes.

DR. HUMPHREYS (*indignantly*): See here, Mr. Day, if I'm to be responsible for Mrs. Day's health, I must be allowed to handle this case in my own way.

FATHER: Well, you can't handle it if you're out of the house.

DR. HUMPHREYS (*flaring*): I left this house because—(DR. SOMERS, *an imposing medical figure, enters and stops at* DR. HUMPHREYS'S *side.*) This is Dr. Somers.

DR. SOMERS: How do you do?

DR. HUMPHREYS: I felt that Mrs. Day's condition warranted my getting Dr. Somers here as soon as possible for consultation. I hope that meets with your approval.

FATHER (*a little awed*): Why, yes, of course. Anything that can be done.

DR. HUMPHREYS: Upstairs, doctor! (*The two doctors go upstairs.* FATHER *turns back into the room, obviously shaken.*)

DR. LLOYD: Mrs. Day is in good hands now, Mr. Day. There's nothing you and I can do at the moment to help.

(*After a moment's consideration* FATHER *decides there is something that can be done to help. He goes to* DR. LLOYD. FATHER *indicates the seat in front of the table to* DR. LLOYD *and they both sit.*)

FATHER: Dr. Lloyd, there's something that's troubling Mrs. Day's mind. I think you know what I refer to.

DR. LLOYD: Yes, you mean the fact that you've never been baptized.

FATHER: I gathered you knew about it from your sermon last Sunday.

(*Looks at him a second with indignant memory*.) But let's not ge
angry. I think something had better be done about it.

DR. LLOYD: Yes, Mr. Day.

FATHER: When the doctors get through up there I want you to talk to
Mrs. Day. I want you to tell her something.

DR. LLOYD (*eagerly*): Yes, I'll be glad to.

FATHER: You're just the man to do it! She shouldn't be upset about this
—I want you to tell her that my being baptized would just be a lot o
damn nonsense.

 (*This isn't what* DR. LLOYD *has expected and it is hardly his idea o
how to help* MRS. DAY.)

DR. LLOYD: But, Mr. Day!

FATHER: No, she'd take your word on a thing like that—and we've go
to do everything we can to help her now.

DR. LLOYD (*rising*): But baptism is one of the sacraments of the
Church—

FATHER (*rising*): You're her minister and you're supposed to bring her
comfort and peace of mind.

DR. LLOYD: But the solution is so simple. It would take only your consent to be baptized.

FATHER: That's out of the question! And I'm surprised that a grown
man like you should suggest such a thing.

DR. LLOYD: If you're really concerned about Mrs. Day's peace of mind
don't you think—

FATHER: Now see here—if you're just going to keep her stirred up
about this, I'm not going to let you see her at all. (*He turns away*. DR.
LLOYD *follows him*.)

DR. LLOYD: Now, Mr. Day, as you said, we must do everything we can
—(*The doctors come downstairs*. FATHER *sees them*.)

FATHER: Well, doctor, how is she? What have you decided?

DR. HUMPHREYS: We've just left Mrs. Day. Is there a room we could
use for our consultation?

FATHER: Of course. (MARGARET *starts downstairs*.) Margaret, you go
back upstairs! I don't want Mrs. Day left alone!

MARGARET: I have to do something for the doctor. I'll go back up as
soon as I get it started.

FATHER: Well, hurry. And, Margaret, show these gentlemen downstairs to the billiard room.

MARGARET: Yes, sir. This way, doctor—downstairs. (*Exits, followed by* DR. SOMERS. FATHER *delays* DR. HUMPHREYS.)

FATHER: Dr. Humphreys, you know now, don't you—this isn't serious, is it?

DR. HUMPHREYS: After we've had our consultation we'll talk to you, Mr. Day.

FATHER: But surely you must—

DR. HUMPHREYS: Just rest assured that Dr. Somers will do everything that is humanly possible.

FATHER: Why, you don't mean—

DR. HUMPHREYS: We'll try not to be long. (*Exits.* FATHER *turns and looks at* DR. LLOYD. *He is obviously frightened.*)

FATHER: This Dr. Somers—I've heard his name often—he's very well thought of, isn't he?

DR. LLOYD: Oh, yes indeed.

FATHER: If Vinnie's really—if anyone could help her, he could—don't you think?

DR. LLOYD: A very fine physician. But there's a greater Help, ever present in the hour of need. Let us turn to Him in prayer. Let us kneel and pray. (FATHER *looks at him, straightens, then walks to the other side of the room.*) Let us kneel and pray. (FATHER *finally bows his head.* DR. LLOYD *looks at him and, not kneeling himself, raises his head and speaks simply in prayer.*) Oh, Lord, look down from Heaven—behold, visit, and relieve this Thy servant who is grieved with sickness, and extend to her Thy accustomed goodness. We know she has sinned against Thee in thought, word, and deed. Have mercy on her, O Lord, have mercy on this miserable sinner. Forgive her—

FATHER: She's not a miserable sinner and you know it! (*Then* FATHER *speaks directly to the Deity.*) O God! You know Vinnie's not a miserable sinner. She's a damn fine woman! She shouldn't be made to suffer. It's got to stop, I tell You, it's got to stop!

(VINNIE *appears on the stairway in her nightgown.*)

VINNIE: What's the matter, Clare? What's wrong?

FATHER (*not hearing her*): Have mercy, I say, have mercy, damn it!

VINNIE: What's the matter Clare? What's wrong?

(FATHER *turns, sees* VINNIE, *and rushes to her.*)

FATHER: Vinnie, what are you doing down here? You shouldn't be out of bed. You get right back upstairs. (*He now has his arms around her.*)

VINNIE: Oh, Clare, I heard you call. Do you need me?

FATHER (*deeply moved*): Vinnie—I know now how much I need you. Get well, Vinnie. I'll be baptized. I promise. I'll be baptized.

VINNIE: You will? Oh, Clare!

FATHER: I'll do anything. We'll go to Europe, just we two—you won't have to worry about the children or the household accounts— (VINNIE *faints against* FATHER'S *shoulder.*) Vinnie! (*He stoops to lift her.*)

DR. LLOYD: I'll get the doctor. But don't worry, Mr. Day—she'll be all right now. (FATHER *lifts* VINNIE *up in his arms.*) Bless you for what you've done, Mr. Day.

FATHER: What did I do?

DR. LLOYD: You promised to be baptized!

FATHER (*aghast*): I did? (*With horror* FATHER *realizes he has been betrayed—and by himself.*) *OH, GOD!*

CURTAIN

ACT THREE

SCENE I

The same.
> *A month later. Mid-afternoon.*
> VINNIE *is seated on the sofa embroidering petit point.* MARGARET *enters, as usual uncomfortable at being upstairs.*

MARGARET: You wanted to speak to me, ma'am?

VINNIE: Yes, Margaret, about tomorrow morning's breakfast—we must plan it very carefully.

MARGARET (*puzzled*): Mr. Day hasn't complained to me about his breakfasts lately. As a matter of fact, I've been blessing my luck!

VINNIE: Oh, no, it's not that. But tomorrow morning I'd like something for his breakfast that would surprise him.

MARGARET (*doubtfully*): Surprising Mr. Day is always a bit of a risk, ma'am. My motto with him has always been "Let well enough alone."

VINNIE: But if we think of something he especially likes, Margaret— what would you say to kippers?

MARGARET: Well, I've served him kippers, but I don't recall his ever saying he liked them.

VINNIE: He's never said he didn't like them, has he?

MARGARET: They've never got a stamp on the floor out of him one way or the other.

VINNIE: If Mr. Day doesn't say he doesn't like a thing you can assume that he does. Let's take a chance on kippers, Margaret.

MARGARET: Very well, ma'am. (*She starts out.*)

VINNIE (*innocently*): And, Margaret, you'd better have enough breakfast for two extra places.

MARGARET (*knowingly*): Oh—so that's it! We're going to have company again.

VINNIE: Yes, my cousin, Miss Cartwright, and her friend are coming back from Springfield. I'm afraid they'll get here just about breakfast time.

MARGARET: Well, in that case I'd better make some of my Sunday morning hot biscuits, too.

VINNIE: Yes. We *know* Mr. Day likes those.

MARGARET: I've been getting him to church with them for the last fifteen years. (*The door slams.* MARGARET *goes to the arch and looks.*) Oh, it's Mr. Clarence, ma'am. (*Goes off downstairs and* CLARENCE *enters with a large package.*)

CLARENCE: Here it is, Mother. (*He puts it on the table.*)

VINNIE: Oh, it was still in the store! They hadn't sold it! I'm so thrilled. Didn't you admire it, Clarence? (*She hurries over to the table.*)

CLARENCE: Well, it's unusual.

VINNIE (*unwrapping the package*): You know, I saw this down there the day before I got sick. I was walking through the bric-a-brac section and it caught my eye. I was so tempted to buy it! And all the time I lay ill I just couldn't get it out of my head. I can't understand how it could stay in the store all this time without somebody snatching it up. (*She takes it out of the box. It is a large china pug dog.*) Isn't that the darlingest thing you ever saw! It does need a ribbon, though. I've got the very thing somewhere. Oh, yes, I know. (*Goes to the side table and gets a red ribbon out of the drawer.*)

CLARENCE: Isn't John home yet?

VINNIE: I haven't seen him. Why?

CLARENCE: Well, you know we've been working, and John went down to collect our money.

VINNIE: That's fine. (*She ties the ribbon around the dog's neck.*) Oh, Clarence, I have a secret for just the two of us; who do you think is coming to visit us tomorrow?—Cousin Cora and Mary.

CLARENCE: Yes, I know.

VINNIE: How did you know?

CLARENCE: I happened to get a letter.

(JOHN *enters, carrying two packages of medicine.*)

VINNIE: John, did you ever see anything so sweet?

JOHN: What is it?

VINNIE: It's a pug dog. Your father would never let me have a real one, but he can't object to one made of china. This ribbon needs pressing. I'll take it down and have Margaret do it right away. (*Exits with the beribboned pug dog.*)

CLARENCE: What did you bring home more medicine for? (*Then, with sudden fright.*) Dr. Bartlett paid us off, didn't he?

JOHN: Oh, yes!

CLARENCE (*heaving a great sigh of relief*): You had me scared for a minute. When I went down to McCreery's to get that pug dog for Mother, I ordered the daisiest suit you ever saw. Dr. Bartlett owed us sixteen dollars apiece, and the suit was only fifteen. Wasn't that lucky? Come on, give me my money.

JOHN: Clarence, Dr. Bartlett paid us off in medicine.

CLARENCE: You let him pay us off with that old Beneficent Balm!

JOHN: Well, he thanked us, too, for our services to mankind.

CLARENCE (*in agony*): But my suit!

JOHN: You'll just have to wait for your suit.

CLARENCE: I can't wait! I've got to have it tomorrow—and besides they're making the alterations. I've got to pay for it this afternoon! Fifteen dollars!

JOHN (*helpfully*): Why don't you offer them fifteen bottles of medicine?

(CLARENCE *gives it a little desperate thought.*)

CLARENCE: They wouldn't take it. McCreery's don't sell medicine.

(JOHN *is by the window and looks out.*)

JOHN: That's too bad. Here comes Father.

CLARENCE: I'll have to brace him for that fifteen dollars. I hate to do it, but I've got to—that's all—I've got to.

JOHN: I'm not going to be here when you do. I'd better hide this somewhere, anyway. (*Takes the packages and hurries upstairs. The door slams.* FATHER *enters and looks into the room.*)

CLARENCE: Good afternoon, sir.

FATHER: How's your mother, Clarence? Where is she?

CLARENCE: She's all right. She's downstairs with Margaret. Oh, Father—

(FATHER *goes off down the hall and we hear him calling downstairs.*)

FATHER: Vinnie! Vinnie! I'm home. (*Comes back into the room, carrying his newspaper.*)

CLARENCE: Father, Mother will be well enough to go to church with us next Sunday.

FATHER: That's fine, Clarence. That's fine.

CLARENCE: Father, have you noticed that I haven't been kneeling down in church lately?

FATHER: Clarence, don't let your mother catch you at it.

CLARENCE: Then I've got to have a new suit of clothes right away!

FATHER (*after a puzzled look*): Clarence, you're not even making sense!

CLARENCE: But a fellow doesn't feel right in cut-down clothes—especially your clothes. That's why I can't kneel down in church—I can't do anything in them you wouldn't do.

FATHER: Well, that's a damn good thing! If my old clothes make you behave yourself I don't think you ought to wear anything else.

CLARENCE (*desperately*): *Oh, no!* You're you and I'm me! I want to be myself! Besides, you're older and there are things I've got to do that I wouldn't do at your age.

FATHER: Clarence, you should never do anything I wouldn't do.

CLARENCE: Oh, yes,—look, for instance: Suppose I should want to kneel down in front of a girl?

FATHER: Why in Heaven's name should you want to do a thing like that?

CLARENCE: Well, I've got to get married *sometime.* I've got to propose to a girl *sometime.*

FATHER (*exasperated*): Before you're married, you'll be earning your own clothes, I hope. Don't get the idea into your head, I'm going to support you and a wife, too. Besides, at your age, Clarence—

CLARENCE (*hastily*): Oh, I'm not going to be married right away, but for fifteen dollars I can get a good suit of clothes.

FATHER (*bewildered and irritated*): Clarence! (*He stares at him. At this second,* VINNIE *comes through the arch.*) Why, you're beginning to talk as crazy as your mother. (*He sees her.*) Oh, hello, Vinnie. How're you feeling today?

VINNIE: I'm fine, Clare. (*They kiss.*) You don't have to hurry home from the office every day like this.

(CLARENCE *throws himself in the chair by the window, sick with disappointment.*)

FATHER: Business the way it is, no use going to the office at all.

VINNIE: But you haven't been to your club for weeks.

FATHER: Can't stand the damn place. You do look better, Vinnie. What did you do today? (*Drops on the sofa.* VINNIE *stands behind the sofa. Her chatter does not succeed in diverting* FATHER *from his newspaper.*)

VINNIE: I took a long walk and dropped in to call on old Mrs. Whitehead.

FATHER: Well, that's fine.

VINNIE: And, Clare, it was the most fortunate thing that ever happened. I've got wonderful news for you! Who do you think was there? Mr. Morley!

FATHER (*not placing him*): Morley?

VINNIE: You remember—that nice young minister who substituted for Dr. Lloyd one Sunday?

FATHER: Oh, yes! Bright young fellow preached a good sensible sermon.

VINNIE: It was the only time I ever saw you put five dollars in the plate!

FATHER: Ought to be more ministers like him. I could get along with that young man without any trouble at all.

VINNIE: Well, Clare, his parish is in Audubon—you know, 'way up above Harlem.

FATHER: Is that so?

VINNIE: Isn't that wonderful? Nobody knows you up there. You'll be perfectly safe!

FATHER: Safe? Vinnie, what the devil are you talking about?

VINNIE: I've been all over everything with Mr. Morley and he's agreed to baptize you.

FATHER: Oh, he has—the young whipper-snapper! Damn nice of him!

VINNIE: We can go up there any morning, Clare—we don't even have to make an appointment.

FATHER: Vinnie, you're just making a lot of plans for nothing. Who said I was going to be baptized at all?

VINNIE (aghast): Why, Clare! You did!

FATHER: Now, Vinnie!—

VINNIE: You gave me your promise—your Sacred Promise. You stood right on that spot and said: "I'll be baptized. I promise—I'll be baptized."

FATHER: What if I did?

VINNIE (amazed, she comes down and faces him): Aren't you a man of your word?

FATHER (rising): Vinnie, that was under entirely different circumstances. We all thought you were dying, so naturally I said that to make you feel better. As a matter of fact, the doctor told me that's what cured you. So it seems to me pretty ungrateful of you to press this matter any further.

VINNIE: Clarence Day, you gave me your Sacred Promise!

FATHER (getting annoyed): Vinnie, you were sick when I said that. Now you're well again.

(MARGARET enters with the pug dog, which now has the freshly pressed ribbon tied around its neck. She puts it on the table.)

MARGARET: Is that all right, Mrs. Day?

VINNIE (*dismissingly*): That's fine, Margaret, thank you. (MARGARET *exits*.) My being well has nothing to do with it. You gave me your word! You gave the Lord your word. If you had seen how eager Mr. Morley was to bring you into the fold. (FATHER, *trying to escape, has been moving toward the arch when suddenly the pug dog catches his eye and he stares at it fascinated*.) And you're going to march yourself up to his church some morning before you go to the office and be christened. If you think for one minute that I'm going to—

FATHER: What in the name of Heaven is that?

VINNIE: If you think I'm going to let you add the sin of breaking your Solemn and Sacred Promise—

FATHER: I demand to know what that repulsive object is!

VINNIE (*exasperated in her turn*): It's perfectly plain what it is—it's a pug dog!

FATHER: What's it doing in this house?

VINNIE (*defiantly*): I wanted it and I bought it.

FATHER: You spent good money for that?

VINNIE: Clare, we're not talking about that! We're talking about you. Don't try to change the subject!

FATHER: How much did you pay for that atrocity?

VINNIE: I don't know. I sent Clarence down for it. Listen to me, Clare—

FATHER: Clarence, what did you pay for that?

CLARENCE: I didn't pay anything. I charged it.

FATHER (*looking at* VINNIE): Charged it! I might have known. (*To* CLARENCE.) How much was it?

CLARENCE: Fifteen dollars.

FATHER: Fifteen dollars for that eyesore?

VINNIE (*to the rescue of the pug dog*): Don't you call that lovely work of art an eyesore! That will look beautiful sitting on a red cushion by the fireplace in the parlor.

FATHER: If that sits in the parlor, I won't! Furthermore, I don't even want it in the same house with me. Get it out of here!

(*He starts for the stairs.*)

VINNIE: You're just using that for an excuse. You're not going to get out of this room until you set a date for your baptism.

(FATHER *turns at the foot of the stairs.*)

FATHER: I'll tell you one thing! I'll never be baptized while that hideous monstrosity is in this house. (*He stalks upstairs.*)

VINNIE (*calling after him*): All right! (*She goes to the pug dog.*) All right! It goes back this afternoon and he's christened first thing in the morning.

CLARENCE: But, Mother—

VINNIE: Clarence, you heard him say that he'd be baptized as soon as I got this pug dog out of the house. You hurry right back to McCreery's with it—and be sure they credit us with fifteen dollars.

(*The fifteen dollars rings a bell in* CLARENCE'S *mind.*)

CLARENCE: Oh, say, Mother, while I was at McCreery's, I happened to see a suit I would like very much and the suit was only fifteen dollars.

VINNIE (*regretfully*): Well, Clarence, I think your suit will have to wait until after I get your father christened.

CLARENCE (*hopefully*): No. I meant that since the suit cost just the same as the pug dog, if I exchange the pug dog for the suit—

VINNIE: Why, yes! Then your suit wouldn't cost Father anything! Why, how bright of you, Clarence, to think of that!

CLARENCE (*quickly*): I'd better start right away before McCreery's closes. (*They have collected the box, wrapper, and tissue paper.*)

VINNIE: Yes. Let's see. If we're going to take your father all the way up to Audubon—Clarence, you stop at Ryerson & Brown's on your way back and tell them to have a cab here at eight o'clock tomorrow morning.

CLARENCE: Mother, a cab! Do you think you ought to do that?

VINNIE: Well, we can't walk to Audubon.

CLARENCE (*warningly*): But you know what a cab does to Father!

VINNIE: This is an important occasion.

CLARENCE (*with a shrug*): All right! A brougham or a Victoria?

VINNIE: Get one of their best cabs—the kind they use at funerals.

CLARENCE: Those cost two dollars an hour! And if Father gets mad—

VINNIE: Well, if your father starts to argue in the morning, you remember—

CLARENCE (*remembering his suit*): Oh, he agreed to it! We both heard him!

(VINNIE *has removed the ribbon and is about to put the pug dog back in the box.*)

VINNIE (*regretfully*): I did have my heart set on this. (*An idea comes to her.*) Still—if they didn't sell him in all that time, he might be safe there for a few more weeks. (*She gives the dog a reassuring pat and puts him in the box. She begins to sing "Sweet Marie" happily.* FATHER *comes down the stairs.* CLARENCE *takes his hat and the box and goes happily and quickly out.* FATHER *watches him.*) I hope you notice that Clarence is returning the pug dog.

FATHER: That's a sign you're getting your faculties back. (VINNIE *is singing quietly to herself in a satisfied way.*) Good to hear you singing again, Vinnie. (*Suddenly remembering something.*) Oh!—on my way uptown I stopped in at Tiffany's and bought you a little something. Thought you might like it. (*He takes out of his pocket a small ring-box and holds it out to her. She takes it.*)

VINNIE: Oh, Clare. (*She opens it eagerly.*) What a beautiful ring! (*She takes the ring out, puts it on her finger, and admires it.*)

FATHER: Glad if it pleases you. (*He settles down to his newspaper on the sofa.*)

VINNIE: I don't know how to thank you. (*She kisses him.*)

FATHER: It's thanks enough for me to have you up and around again. When you're sick, Vinnie, this house is like a tomb. There's no excitement.

VINNIE (*sitting beside him*): Clare, this is the loveliest ring you ever bought me. Now that I have this, you needn't buy me any more rings.

FATHER: Well, if you don't want any more.

VINNIE: What I'd really like now is a nice diamond necklace.

FATHER (*alarmed*): Vinnie, do you know how much a diamond necklace costs?

VINNIE: I know, Clare, but don't you see?—your giving me this ring shows that I mean a little something to you. Now, a diamond necklace—

FATHER: Good God, if you don't know by this time how I feel about you! We've been married for twenty years and I've loved you every minute of it.

VINNIE: What did you say? (*Her eyes well with tears at* FATHER'S *definite statement of his love.*)

FATHER: I said we'd been married twenty years and I've loved you every minute of it. But if I have to buy out jewelry stores to prove it

—if I haven't shown it to you in my words and actions, I might as well—(*He turns and sees* VINNIE *dabbing her eyes and speaks with resignation.*) What have I done now?

VINNIE: It's all right, Clare—I'm just so happy.

FATHER: Happy!

VINNIE: You said you loved me! And this beautiful ring—that's something else I didn't expect. Oh, Clare, I love surprises.

(*She nestles against him.*)

FATHER: That's another thing I can't understand about you, Vinnie. Now, *I* like to know what to expect. Then I'm prepared to meet it.

VINNIE (*putting her head on his shoulder*): Yes, I know. But, Clare, life would be pretty dull if we always knew what was coming.

FATHER: Well, it's certainly not dull around here. In this house you never know what's going to hit you tomorrow.

VINNIE (*to herself*): Tomorrow! (*She starts to sing,* FATHER *listening to her happily.*)

> "Every daisy in the dell,
>   Knows my secret, knows it well,
>   And yet I dare not tell,
>   Sweet Marie!"

CURTAIN

SCENE II

The same.
    The next morning. Breakfast. All the family except JOHN *and* VINNIE *are at the table and in good spirits.*

JOHN (*entering*): Mother says she'll be right down. (*He sits at the table.*)

(MAGGIE, *the new maid, enters with a plate of hot biscuits and serves* FATHER. *As* FATHER *takes a biscuit, he glances up at her and shows some little surprise.*)

FATHER: Who are you? What's your name?

MAGGIE: Margaret, sir.

FATHER: Can't be Margaret. We've got one Margaret in the house.

MAGGIE: At home they call me Maggie, sir.

FATHER (*genially*): All right, Maggie. (MAGGIE *continues serving the biscuits.*) Boys, if her name's Margaret, that's a good sign. Maybe she'll stay awhile. You know, boys, your mother used to be just the same about cooks as she is about maids. Never could keep them for some reason. Well, one day about fifteen years ago—yes, it was right after you were born, John—my, you were a homely baby. (*They all laugh at* JOHN's *expense.*) I came home that night all tired out and what did I find—no dinner, because the cook had left. Well, I decided I'd had just about enough of that, so I just marched over to the employment agency on Sixth Avenue and said to the woman in charge: "Where do you keep the cooks?" She tried to hold me up with a lot of red-tape folderol, but I just walked into the room where the girls were waiting, looked 'em over, saw Margaret, pointed at her, and said: "I'll take that one." I walked her home, she cooked dinner that night, and she's been cooking for us ever since. Damn good cook, too. (*He stamps on the floor three times.*)

(VINNIE *comes down the stairs dressed in white. Somehow she almost has the appearance of a bride going to her wedding.*)

VINNIE: Good morning, Clare. Good morning, boys.

(*The boys and* FATHER *rise.* VINNIE *takes her bonnet and gloves and lays them on the chair below the fireplace.* FATHER *goes to* VINNIE's *chair and holds it out for her, glancing at her holiday appearance.* VINNIE *sits.*)

FATHER: Sit down, boys. (*As* FATHER *returns to his own chair, he notices that all of the boys are dressed in their Sunday best.*) Everyone's dressed up this morning. What's on the program for this fine day? (VINNIE, *who always postpones crises in the hope some miracle will aid her, postpones this one.*)

VINNIE: Well, this afternoon May Lewis's mother is giving a party for everyone in May's dancing class. Harlan's going to that.

HARLAN: I don't want to go, Mamma.

VINNIE: Why, Harlan, don't you want to go to a party and get ice cream and cake?

HARLAN: May Lewis always tries to kiss me.

(*This is greeted with family laughter.*)

FATHER (*genially*): When you get a little older, you won't object to girls' wanting to kiss you, will he, Clarence?

(MARGARET *comes hurrying in.*)

MARGARET: What's wanting?

FATHER: Margaret, these kippers are *good*. (MARGARET *makes her usual deprecatory gesture toward him.*) Haven't had kippers for a long time. I'm glad you remembered I like them.

MARGARET: Yes, sir.

(MARGARET *and* VINNIE *exchange knowing looks.* MARGARET *goes out happy.*)

FATHER: What's got into Margaret this morning? Hot biscuits, too!

VINNIE: She knows you're fond of them. (*The doorbell rings.* MAGGIE *goes to answer it.* VINNIE *stirs nervously in her chair.*) Who can that be? It can't be the mail man because he's been here.

FATHER (*with sly humor*): Clarence has been getting a good many special deliveries lately. Is that business deal going through, Clarence?

(*The family has a laugh at* CLARENCE. MAGGIE *comes back into the arch with a suit box.*)

MAGGIE: This is for you, Mr. Day. Where shall I put it?

CLARENCE (*hastily*): Oh, that's for me, I think. Take it upstairs, Maggie.

FATHER: Wait a minute, Maggie, bring it here. Let's see it.

(CLARENCE *takes the box from* MAGGIE, *who exits. He holds it toward his father.*)

CLARENCE: See, it's for me, Father—Clarence Day, Jr.

FATHER: Let me look. Why, that's from McCreery's and it's marked "Charge." What is it?

VINNIE: It's all right, Clare. It's nothing for you to worry about.

FATHER: Well, at least I think I should know what's being charged to me. What is it?

VINNIE: Now, Clare, stop your fussing. It's a new suit of clothes for Clarence and it's not costing you a penny.

FATHER: It's marked "Charge fifteen dollars"—it's costing me fifteen dollars. And I told Clarence—

VINNIE: Clare, can't you take my word it isn't costing you a penny?

FATHER: I'd like to have you explain why it isn't.

VINNIE (*triumphantly*): Because Clarence took the pug dog back and got the suit instead.

FATHER: Of course, and they'll charge me fifteen dollars for the suit.

VINNIE: Nonsense, Clare. We gave them the pug dog for the suit. Don't you see?

FATHER: Then they'll charge me fifteen dollars for the pug dog.

VINNIE: But, Clare, they can't! We haven't got the pug dog. We sent that back.

FATHER (*bewildered, but not convinced*): Now wait a minute, Vinnie. There's something wrong with your reasoning.

VINNIE: I'm surprised, Clare, and you're supposed to be so good at figures. Why, it's perfectly clear to me.

FATHER: Vinnie! They're going to charge me for one thing or the other.

VINNIE: Don't you let them!

(FATHER *gets up and throws his napkin on the table.*)

FATHER: Well, McCreery's aren't giving away suits and they aren't giving away pug dogs. (*He walks over to the window in his irritation.*) Can't you get it through your—(*Looking out the window.*) Oh, God!

VINNIE: What is it, Clare? What's wrong?

FATHER: Don't anybody answer the door.

VINNIE: Who is it? Who's coming?

FATHER: Those damn women are back!

WHITNEY: What women?

FATHER: Cora and that little idiot. (CLARENCE *dashes madly up the stairs clutching the box containing his new suit.*) They're moving in on us again, bag and baggage! (*The doorbell rings.*) Don't let them in!

VINNIE: Clarence Day, as if we could turn our own relatives away!

FATHER: Tell them to get back in that cab and drive right on to Ohio. If they're extravagant enough to take cabs when horse cars run right by our door—

(MAGGIE *crosses the hall to answer the doorbell.*)

VINNIE: Now, Clare—you be quiet and behave yourself. They're here and there's nothing you can do about it. (*She starts toward the hall.*)

FATHER (*shouting after her*): Well, why do they always pounce on us without warning?—the damn gypsies!

VINNIE (*from the arch*): Shhh!—Clare! (*Then in her best welcoming tone.*) Cora! Mary! It's so nice to have you back again.

CORA: How are you, Vinnie? We've been so worried about you.

VINNIE: Oh, I'm fine now!

(CORA *and* MARY *and* VINNIE *enter and* CORA *sweeps right down into the room.*)

CORA: Hello, Harlan! Whitney! Well, Cousin Clare. Here we are again! (*Kisses* FATHER *on the cheek. He draws back sternly.* MARY *looks quickly around the room for* CLARENCE, *then greets and is greeted by the other boys.*) And John! Where's Clarence?

MARY: Yes, where is Clarence?

VINNIE: John, go find Clarence and tell him that Cora and Mary are here.

JOHN: Yes, Mother. (*Goes upstairs.*)

VINNIE: You got here just in time to have breakfast with us.

CORA: We had breakfast at the depot.

VINNIE: Well, as a matter of fact, we'd just finished.

FATHER (*with cold dignity*): *I* haven't finished my breakfast!

VINNIE: Well, then sit down, Clare. (*To* CORA *and* MARY.) Margaret gave us kippers this morning and Clare's so fond of kippers. Why don't we all sit down? (*Indicates the empty places and the girls sit.* FATHER *resumes his chair and breakfast in stony silence.* MAGGIE *has come into the room to await orders.*) Maggie, clear those things away. (*She indicates the dishes in front of the girls, and* MAGGIE *removes them.* FATHER *takes a letter from his stack of morning mail and opens it.*) Clare, don't let your kippers get cold. (*To* CORA.) Now—tell us all about Springfield.

CORA: We had a wonderful month—but tell us about you, Cousin Vinnie. You must have had a terrible time.

VINNIE: Yes, I was pretty sick, but I'm all right again now.

CORA: What was it?

VINNIE: Well, the doctors don't know exactly, but they did say this—that they'd never seen anything like it before, whatever it was.

CORA: You certainly look well enough now. Doesn't she, Clare?

(*Whatever is in the letter* FATHER *has been reading comes to him as a shock.*)

FATHER: Oh, God!

VINNIE: What's the matter, Clare? What's wrong?

FATHER: John! John!

(JOHN *is seen halfway up the stairs with the girls' bags. He comes running down the stairs, going to* FATHER.)

JOHN: Yes, Father?

FATHER: Have you been going around this town selling medicine?

JOHN (*a little frightened*): Yes, Father.

FATHER: Dog medicine?

JOHN (*indignantly*): No, Father, not dog medicine!

FATHER: It must have been dog medicine!

JOHN: It wasn't dog medicine, Father—

FATHER: This letter from Mrs. Sprague says you sold her a bottle of this medicine and that her little boy gave some of it to their dog and it killed him! Now she wants ten dollars from me for a new dog.

JOHN: Well, he shouldn't have given it to a dog. It's for humans! Why, it's Bartlett's Beneficent Balm—"Made from a secret formula!"

FATHER: Have you been going around among our friends and neighbors selling some damned Dr. Munyon patent nostrum?

JOHN: But it's good medicine, Father. I can prove it by Mother.

FATHER: Vinnie, what do you know about this?

VINNIE: Nothing, Clare, but I'm sure that John—

JOHN: No, I mean that day Mother—

FATHER: That's enough! You're going to every house where you sold a bottle of that concoction and buy it all back.

JOHN (*dismayed*): But it's a dollar a bottle!

FATHER: I don't care how much it is. How many bottles did you sell?

JOHN: A hundred and twenty-eight.

FATHER (*roaring*): A hundred and twenty-eight!

VINNIE: Clare, I always told you John would make a good business man.

FATHER (*calmly*): Young man, I'll give you the money to buy it back —a hundred and twenty-eight dollars. And ten more for Mrs. Sprague. That's a hundred and thirty-eight dollars. But it's coming out of your allowance! That means you'll not get another penny until that hundred and thirty-eight dollars is all paid up.

(JOHN *starts toward the hall, counting on his fingers, then turns and addresses his father in dismay.*)

JOHN: I'll be twenty-one years old!

(FATHER *glares at him.* JOHN *turns and goes on up the stairs, with the bags.*)

VINNIE (*persuasively*): Clare, you know you've always encouraged the boys to earn their own money.

FATHER: Vinnie, I'll handle this. (*There is a pause. He buries himself in his newspaper.*)

CORA (*breaking through the constraint*): Of course, Aunt Judith sent her love to all of you—

VINNIE: I haven't seen Judith for years. You'd think living so close to Springfield—maybe I could run up there before the summer's over.

CORA: Oh, she'll be leaving for Pleasantville any day now. Grandpa Ebbetts has been failing very fast and that's why I have to hurry back.

VINNIE: Hurry back? Well, you and Mary can stay with us a few days at least.

CORA: No, I hate to break the news to you, Vinnie, but we can't even stay overnight. We're leaving on the five o'clock train this afternoon.

VINNIE (*disappointed*): Oh, what a pity!

(FATHER *lowers the paper.*)

FATHER (*heartily*): Well, Cora, it certainly is good to see you again. (*To* MARY.) Young lady, I think you've been enjoying yourself—you look prettier than ever.

(MARY *laughs and blushes.*)

WHITNEY: I'll bet Clarence will think so.

(*The doorbell rings.* MAGGIE *crosses to answer it.*)

FATHER: That can't be another special delivery for Clarence. (*To* MARY, *slyly.*) While you were in Springfield our postman was kept pretty busy. Sure you girls don't want any breakfast?

MARY: No, thank you. (*Rises and goes to the arch and stands looking upstairs, watching for* CLARENCE.)

CORA: Oh, no, thank you, Cousin Clare, we've had our breakfast.

FATHER: At least you ought to have a cup of coffee with us. Vinnie, you might have thought to order some coffee for the girls.

CORA: No, no, thank you, Cousin Clare.

(MAGGIE *appears again in the arch.*)

MAGGIE: It's the cab, ma'am. (*Exits.*)

FATHER: The cab! What cab?

VINNIE: The cab that's to take us to Audubon.

FATHER: Who's going to Audubon?

VINNIE: We all are. Cora, the most wonderful thing has happened!

CORA: What, Cousin Vinnie?

VINNIE (*happily*): Clare's going to be baptized this morning.

FATHER (*not believing his ears*): Vinnie—what are you saying?

VINNIE (*with determination*): I'm saying you're going to be baptized this morning!

FATHER: I am not going to be baptized this morning or any other morning!

VINNIE: You promised yesterday that as soon as I sent that pug dog back you'd be baptized.

FATHER: I promised no such thing!

VINNIE: You certainly did!

FATHER: I never said anything remotely like that!

VINNIE: Clarence was right here and heard it. You ask him!

FATHER: Clarence be damned! I know what I said! I don't remember exactly, but it wasn't that!

VINNIE: Well, I remember. That's why I ordered the cab!

FATHER (*suddenly remembering*): The cab! Oh, my God, that cab! (*He rises and glares out the window at the cab, then turns back and speaks peremptorily.*) Vinnie! You send that right back!

VINNIE: I'll do nothing of the kind. I'm going to see that you get to Heaven.

FATHER: I can't go to Heaven in a cab!

VINNIE: Well, you can start in a cab! I'm not sure whether they'll ever let you into Heaven or not, but I know they won't unless you're baptized.

FATHER: They can't keep me out of Heaven on a technicality.

VINNIE: Clare, stop quibbling! You might as well face it—you've got to make your peace with God.

FATHER: I never had any trouble with God until you stirred Him up!

(MARY *is tired of waiting for* CLARENCE *and chooses this moment to interrupt.*)

MARY: Mrs. Day?

(VINNIE *answers her quickly, as if expecting* MARY *to supply her with an added argument.*)

VINNIE: Yes, Mary?

MARY: Where do you suppose Clarence is?

FATHER: You keep out of this, young lady! If it hadn't been for you, no one would have known whether I was baptized or not. (MARY *breaks into tears.*) Damn! Damnation!

VINNIE: Harlan! Whitney! Get your Sunday hats. (*Calls upstairs.*) John! Clarence!

(HARLAN *and* WHITNEY *start out, but stop as* FATHER *speaks.*)

FATHER (*blazing with new fire*): Vinnie, are you mad? Was it your plan that my own children should witness this indignity?

VINNIE: Why, Clare, they'll be proud of you!

FATHER: I suppose Harlan is to be my godfather! (*With determination.*) Vinnie, it's no use. I can't go through with this thing and I won't. That's final.

VINNIE: Why, Clare dear, if you feel that way about it—

FATHER: I do!

VINNIE: —the children don't have to go.

(JOHN *enters.*)

JOHN: Yes, Mother?

(FATHER *sees* JOHN *and an avenue of escape opens up.*)

FATHER: Oh, John! Vinnie, I can't do anything like that this morning. I've got to take John down to the office and give him the money to buy back that medicine. (*To* JOHN.) When I think of you going around this town selling dog medicine!—

JOHN (*insistently*): It wasn't dog medicine, Father.

FATHER: John, we're starting downtown this minute!

VINNIE: You're doing no such thing! You gave me your Sacred Promise that day I almost died—

JOHN: Yes, and she would have died if we hadn't given her some of that medicine. That proves it's good medicine!

FATHER (*aghast*): You gave your mother some of that dog medicine!

VINNIE: Oh, no, John, you didn't! (*Sinks weakly into the chair below the fireplace.*)

JOHN: Yes, we did, Mother. We put some in your tea that morning.

FATHER: You did what? Without her knowing it? Do you realize you might have killed your mother? You did kill Mrs. Sprague's dog. (*After a solemn pause.*) John, you've done a very serious thing. I'll have to give considerable thought as to how you're going to be punished for this.

VINNIE: But, Clare—

FATHER: No, Vinnie. When I think of that day—with the house full of doctors—why, Cora, we even sent for the minister. Why, we might have lost you! (*He goes to* VINNIE, *really moved, and puts his hand on her shoulder.*) It's all right now, Vinnie, thank God. You're well again. But what I went through that afternoon—the way I felt—I'll never forget it.

VINNIE: Don't talk that way, Clare. You've forgotten it already.

FATHER: What do you mean?

VINNIE: That was the day you gave me your Sacred Promise.

FATHER: But I wouldn't have promised if I hadn't thought you were dying—and you wouldn't have almost died if John hadn't given you that medicine. Don't you see? The whole thing's illegal!

VINNIE: Suppose I had died! It wouldn't make any difference to you. You don't care whether we meet in Heaven or not—you don't care whether you ever see me and the children again.

(*She almost succeeds in crying.* HARLAN *and* WHITNEY *go to her in sympathy, putting their arms around her.*)

FATHER (*distressed*): Now, Vinnie, you're not being fair to me.

VINNIE: It's all right, Clare. If you don't love us enough there's nothing we can do about it.

(*Hurt,* FATHER *walks away to the other side of the room.*)

FATHER: That's got nothing to do with it! I love my family as much as any man. There's nothing within reason I wouldn't do for you, and you know it! All these years I've struggled and worked just to prove —(*He has reached the window and looks out.*) There's that damn cab! Vinnie, you're not well enough to go all the way up to Audubon.

VINNIE (*perkily*): I'm well enough if we ride.

FATHER: But that trip would take all morning. And those cabs cost a dollar an hour.

VINNIE (*with smug complacence*): That's one of their best cabs. That costs two dollars an hour.

(FATHER *stares at her a second, horrified—then explodes.*)

FATHER: Then why aren't you ready? Get your hat on! Damn! Damnation! Amen!

(*Exits for his hat and stick.* VINNIE *is stunned for a moment by this sudden surrender, then hastily puts on her bonnet.*)

WHITNEY: Let's watch them start! Come on, Cousin Cora, let's watch them start!

CORA: I wouldn't miss it!

(WHITNEY, HARLAN, *and* CORA *hurry out.* VINNIE *starts, but* JOHN *stops her in the arch.*)

JOHN (*contritely*): Mother, I didn't mean to almost kill you.

VINNIE: Now, don't you worry about what your father said. (*Ten-*

derly.) It's all right, dear. (*She kisses him.*) It worked out fine! (*She exits.* JOHN *looks upstairs, then at* MARY, *who has gone to the window.*)

JOHN: Mary! Here comes Clarence!

(JOHN *exits.* MARY *sits in* FATHER'S *chair.* CLARENCE *comes down the stairs in his new suit. He goes into the room and right to* MARY. *Without saying a word he kneels in front of her. They both are starry-eyed.*)

(FATHER, *with hat and stick, comes into the arch on his way out. He sees* CLARENCE *kneeling at* MARY'S *feet.*)

FATHER: *Oh, God!*

(CLARENCE *springs up in embarrassment.* VINNIE *re-enters hurriedly.*)

VINNIE: What's the matter? What's wrong?

CLARENCE: Nothing's wrong, Mother— (*Then, for want of something to say.*) Going to the office, Father?

FATHER: No! I'm going to be baptized, damn it!

(*He slams his hat on angrily and stalks out.* VINNIE *gives a triumphant nod and follows him. The curtain starts down, and as it falls,* CLARENCE *again kneels at* MARY'S *feet.*)

CURTAIN

Arsenic and Old Lace

JOSEPH KESSELRING

Why our respondents liked

 ARSENIC AND OLD LACE

"Have played it twice on TV and enjoyed every minute."
HELEN HAYES

"Unique. Arsenic and Old Lace *is not the stuff of which comedies are generally made. Murder! Not slapdash, accidental murder! But real purposeful murder!"*

ABE BURROWS

"Yes yes yes yes yes. Perhaps the blackest comedy ever written."
JOSHUA LOGAN

"Beautifully constructed."
RICHARD RODGERS

"A jolly gothic! There's never been anything like it."
HEYWOOD HALE BROUN

Arsenic and Old Lace is a most unusual comedy—about the elderly Brewster sisters who have killed thirteen gentlemen friends—and in the beginning there was some misunderstanding about how it should be produced, as well as mixed reaction to it from audiences. Abe Burrows, in talking to Howard Lindsay and Russel Crouse, the producers, learned that when Joseph Kesselring sent them his play, "he thought he had written a very serious, chilling murder mystery." (Kesselring originally entitled his script *Bodies in Our Cellar*.) "Lindsay and Crouse read the play, and thought it was very funny. They put it on and treated it as a comedy." One of the special touches to the play came as a climax to the show, when final bows were taken. The thirteen murdered elderly men would come up from the cellar and march across the stage to join the rest of the cast. When *Arsenic and Old Lace* opened in 1941, the audience thought the play was hilarious. Even a certain vocal minority who couldn't see any humor in references to homicide and insanity couldn't stop the play from becoming a legendary hit, with a long run on Broadway of 1,444 performances.

Arsenic and Old Lace was presented by Howard Lindsay and Russel Crouse on January 10, 1941, at the Fulton Theatre, New York City. The cast was as follows:

Abby Brewster	Josephine Hull
The Rev. Dr. Harper	Wyrley Birch
Teddy Brewster	John Alexander
Officer Brophy	John Quigg
Officer Klein	Bruce Gordon
Martha Brewster	Jean Adair
Elaine Harper	Helen Brooks
Mortimer Brewster	Allyn Joslyn
Mr. Gibbs	Henry Herbert
Jonathan Brewster	Boris Karloff
Dr. Einstein	Edgar Stehli
Officer O'Hara	Anthony Ross
Lieutenant Rooney	Victor Sutherland
Mr. Witherspoon	William Parke

Staged by Bretaigne Windust
Setting by Raymond Sovey

The entire action of the play takes place in the living room of the Brewster home in Brooklyn.

ACT ONE

An afternoon in September

ACT TWO

The same night

ACT THREE

Scene 1: *Later that night*
Scene 2: *Early the next morning*

ACT ONE

TIME: *Late afternoon. September. Present.*

PLACE: *The living-room of the old Brewster home in Brooklyn, N.Y. It is just as Victorian as the two sisters* ABBY *and* MARTHA BREWSTER, *who occupy the house with their nephew,* TEDDY.

Down stage right is the front door of the house, a large door with frosted glass panels in the upper half, beyond which, when it is open, can be seen the front porch and the lawn and shrubbery of the front garden of the Brewster house. On either side of the door are narrow windows of small panes of glass, curtained. The remainder of the right wall is taken up by the first flight of stairs leading to the upper floors. In the up-stage corner is a landing where the stairs turn to continue along the back wall of the room. At the top of the stairs, along the back wall, is another landing, from which a door leads into the second-floor bedrooms, and an arch at the left end of this landing suggests the stairs leading to the third floor.

On stage level under this landing is a door which leads to the cellar. To the left of this door is a recess which contains a sideboard, on the top of which at either end are two small cabinets, where the sisters keep, among other things, bottles of elderberry wine. To the left of the recess is the door leading to the kitchen.

In the left wall of the room, there is a large window looking out over the cemetery of the neighboring Episcopal Church. This window has the usual lace curtains and thick drapes, which open and close by the use of a heavy curtain cord. Below the window is a large window seat. When this lid is raised, the hinges creak audibly.

At the left of the foot of the stairs is a small desk, on which stands a dial telephone, and by this desk is a stool. Along the back wall, to the right of the cellar door, is an old-fashioned sofa. Left center in the room is a round table. There is a small chair right of this table and behind it, to the left of the table, a larger, comfortable armchair. On the walls are the usual pictures, including several portraits of the rather eccentric Brewster ancestors.

As the curtain rises, ABBY BREWSTER, *a plump little darling in her late sixties, is presiding at tea. She is sitting behind the table in front of a high silver tea service. At her left, in the comfortable armchair, is the* REVEREND DR. HARPER, *the elderly rector of the near-by church. Standing, stage center, thoughtfully sipping a cup of tea, is her nephew,* TEDDY, *in a frock coat, and wearing pince-nez attached to a black ribbon.* TEDDY *is in his forties and has a large mustache.*

ABBY: Yes indeed, my sister Martha and I have been talking all week about your sermon last Sunday. It's really wonderful, Dr. Harper—in only two short years you've taken on the spirit of Brooklyn.

HARPER: That's very gratifying, Miss Brewster.

ABBY: You see, living here next to the church all our lives, we've seen so many ministers come and go. The spirit of Brooklyn we always say is friendliness—and your sermons are not so much sermons as friendly talks.

TEDDY: Personally, I've always enjoyed my talks with Cardinal Gibbons —or have I met him yet?

ABBY: No, dear, not yet. (*Changing the subject.*) Are the biscuits good?

TEDDY (*he sits on sofa*): Bully!

ABBY: Won't you have another biscuit, Dr. Harper?

HARPER: Oh, no, I'm afraid I'll have no appetite for dinner now. I always eat too many of your biscuits just to taste that lovely jam.

ABBY: But you haven't tried the quince. We always put a little apple in with it to take the tartness out.

HARPER: No, thank you.

ABBY: We'll send you over a jar.

HARPER: No, no. You keep it here so I can be sure of having your biscuits with it.

ABBY: I do hope they don't make us use that imitation flour again. I mean with this war trouble. It may not be very charitable of me, but

I've almost come to the conclusion that this Mr. Hitler isn't a Christian.

HARPER (*with a sigh*): If only Europe were on another planet!

TEDDY (*sharply*): Europe, sir?

HARPER: Yes, Teddy.

TEDDY: Point your gun the other way!

HARPER: Gun?

ABBY (*trying to calm him*): Teddy.

TEDDY: To the West! There's your danger! There's your enemy! Japan!

HARPER: Why, yes—yes, of course.

ABBY: Teddy!

TEDDY: No, Aunt Abby! Not so much talk about Europe and more about the canal!

ABBY: Well, let's not talk about war. Will you have another cup of tea, dear?

TEDDY: No, thank you, Aunt Abby.

ABBY: Dr. Harper?

HARPER: No, thank you. I must admit, Miss Abby, that war and violence seem far removed from these surroundings.

ABBY: It is peaceful here, isn't it?

HARPER: Yes—peaceful. The virtues of another day—they're all here in this house. The gentle virtues that went out with candlelight and good manners and low taxes.

ABBY (*glancing about her contentedly*): It's one of the oldest houses in Brooklyn. It's just as it was when Grandfather Brewster built and furnished it—except for the electricity—and we use it as little as possible. It was Mortimer who persuaded us to put it in.

HARPER (*beginning to freeze*): Yes, I can understand that. Your nephew Mortimer seems to live only by electric light.

ABBY: The poor boy has to work so late. I understand he's taking Elaine with him to the theatre again tonight. Teddy, your brother Mortimer will be here a little later.

TEDDY (*baring his teeth in a broad grin*): Dee-lighted!

ABBY (*to* HARPER): We're so happy it's Elaine Mortimer takes to the theatre with him.

HARPER: Well, it's a new experience for me to wait up until three o'clock in the morning for my daughter to be brought home.

ABBY: Oh, Dr. Harper, I hope you don't disapprove of Mortimer.

HARPER: Well—

ABBY: We'd feel so guilty if you did—sister Martha and I. I mean since it was here in our home that your daughter met Mortimer.

HARPER: Of course, Miss Abby. And so I'll say immediately that I believe Mortimer himself to be quite a worthy gentleman. But I must also admit that I have watched the growing intimacy between him and my daughter with some trepidation. For one reason, Miss Abby.

ABBY: You mean his stomach, Dr. Harper?

HARPER: Stomach?

ABBY: His dyspepsia—he's bothered with it so, poor boy.

HARPER: No, Miss Abby, I'll be frank with you. I'm speaking of your nephew's unfortunate connection with the theatre.

ABBY: The theatre! Oh, no, Dr. Harper! Mortimer writes for a New York newspaper.

HARPER: I know, Miss Abby, I know. But a dramatic critic is constantly exposed to the theatre, and I don't doubt but what some of them do develop an interest in it.

ABBY: Well, not Mortimer. You need have no fear of that. Why, Mortimer hates the theatre.

HARPER: Really?

ABBY: Oh, yes! He writes awful things about the theatre. But you can't blame him, poor boy. He was so happy writing about real estate, which he really knew something about, and then they just made him take this terrible night position.

HARPER: My! My!

ABBY: But, as he says, the theatre can't last much longer anyway and in the meantime it's a living. (*Complacently.*) Yes, I think if we give the theatre another year or two, perhaps ... (*A knock on door.*) Well, now, who do you suppose that is? (*They all rise as* ABBY *goes to door.* TEDDY *starts for door at same time, but* ABBY *stops him.*) No, thank you, Teddy. I'll go. (*She opens door to admit two cops,* OFFICERS BROPHY *and* KLEIN.) Come in, Mr. Brophy.

BROPHY: Hello, Miss Brewster.

ABBY: How are you, Mr. Klein?

KLEIN: Very well, Miss Brewster.

(*The* COPS *cross to* TEDDY *who is standing near desk, and salute him.* TEDDY *returns salute.*)

TEDDY: What news have you brought me?

BROPHY: Colonel, we have nothing to report.

TEDDY: Splendid! Thank you, gentlemen! At ease!

(COPS *relax.* ABBEY *has closed door, and turns to* COPS.)

ABBY: You know Dr. Harper.

KLEIN: Sure! Hello, Dr. Harper.

BROPHY (*turns to* ABBY, *doffing cap*): We've come for the toys for the Christmas Fund.

ABBY: Oh, yes.

HARPER (*standing below table*): That's a splendid work you men do—fixing up discarded toys to give poor children a happier Christmas.

KLEIN: It gives us something to do when we have to sit around the station. You get tired playing cards and then you start cleaning your gun, and the first thing you know you've shot yourself in the foot.

ABBY (*crossing to* TEDDY): Teddy, go upstairs and get that big box from your Aunt Martha's room. (TEDDY *crosses upstage toward stairs.* ABBY *speaks to* BROPHY.) How is Mrs. Brophy today? Mrs. Brophy has been quite ill, Dr. Harper.

BROPHY (*to* HARPER): Pneumonia!

HARPER: I'm sorry to hear that.

(TEDDY *has reached first landing on stairs where he stops and draws an imaginary sword.*)

TEDDY (*shouting*): CHARGE! (*He charges up stairs and exits off balcony. The others pay no attention to this.*)

BROPHY: Oh, she's better now. A little weak still—

ABBY (*starting toward kitchen*): I'm going to get you some beef broth to take to her.

BROPHY: Don't bother, Miss Abby! You've done so much for her already.

ABBY (*at kitchen door*): We made it this morning. Sister Martha is taking some to poor Mr. Benitzky right now. I won't be a minute. Sit down and be comfortable, all of you. (*She exits into kitchen.*)

(HARPER *sits again.* BROPHY *crosses to table and addresses the other two.*)

BROPHY: She shouldn't go to all that trouble.

KLEIN: Listen, try to stop her or her sister from doing something nice—and for nothing! They don't even care how you vote. (*He sits on window-seat.*)

HARPER: When I received my call to Brooklyn and moved next door my wife wasn't well. When she died and for months before—well, if I know what pure kindness and absolute generosity are, it's because I've known the Brewster sisters.

(*At this moment* TEDDY *steps out on balcony and blows a bugle call. They all look.*)

BROPHY: Colonel, you promised not to do that.

TEDDY: But I have to call a Cabinet meeting to get the release of those supplies. (TEDDY *wheels and exits.*)

BROPHY: He used to do that in the middle of the night. The neighbors raised cain with us. They're a little afraid of him, anyway.

HARPER: Oh, he's quite harmless.

KLEIN: Suppose he does think he's Teddy Roosevelt. There's a lot worse people he could think he was.

BROPHY: Damn shame—a nice family like this hatching a cuckoo.

KLEIN: Well, his father—the old girls' brother, was some sort of a genius, wasn't he? And their father—Teddy's grandfather—seems to me I've heard he was a little crazy too.

BROPHY: Yeah—he was crazy like a fox. He made a million dollars.

HARPER: Really? Here in Brooklyn?

BROPHY: Yeah. Patent medicine. He was a kind of a quack of some sort. Old Sergeant Edwards remembers him. He used the house here as a sort of a clinic—tried 'em out on people.

KLEIN: Yeah, I hear he used to make mistakes occasionally, too.

BROPHY: The department never bothered him much because he was pretty useful on autopsies sometimes. Especially poison cases.

KLEIN: Well, whatever he did he left his daughters fixed for life. Thank God for that——

BROPHY: Not that they ever spend any of it on themselves.

HARPER: Yes, I'm well acquainted with their charities.

KLEIN: You don't know a tenth of it. When I was with the Missing Persons Bureau I was trying to trace an old man that we never did find (*Rises.*)—do you know there's a renting agency that's got this house down on its list for furnished rooms? They don't rent rooms—but you can bet that anybody who comes here lookin' for a room goes away with a good meal and probably a few dollars in their kick.

BROPHY: It's just their way of digging up people to do some good to.

(MARTHA BREWSTER *enters.* MARTHA *is also a sweet elderly woman with Victorian charm. She is dressed in the old-fashioned manner of* ABBY, *but with a high lace collar that covers her neck.* MEN *all on feet.*)

MARTHA (*at door*): Well, now, isn't this nice? (*Closes door.*)

BROPHY (*crosses to* MARTHA): Good afternoon, Miss Brewster.

MARTHA: How do you do, Mr. Brophy? Dr. Harper. Mr. Klein.

KLEIN: How are you, Miss Brewster? We dropped in to get the Christmas toys.

MARTHA: Oh, yes, Teddy's Army and Navy. They wear out. They're all packed. (*She turns to stairs.* BROPHY *stops her.*)

BROPHY: The Colonel's upstairs after them—it seems the Cabinet has to O.K. it.

MARTHA: Yes, of course. I hope Mrs. Brophy's better?

BROPHY: She's doin' fine, ma'am. Your sister's getting some soup for me to take to her.

MARTHA: Oh, yes, we made it this morning. I just took some to a poor man who broke ever so many bones.

(ABBY *enters from kitchen carrying a covered pail.*)

ABBY: Oh, you're back, Martha. How was Mr. Benitzky?

MARTHA: Well, dear, it's pretty serious, I'm afraid. The doctor was there. He's going to amputate in the morning.

ABBY (*hopefully*): Can we be present?

MARTHA (*disappointment*): No. I asked him but he says it's against the rules of the hospital. (MARTHA *crosses to sideboard, puts pail down. Then puts cape and hat on small table.*)

(TEDDY *enters on balcony with large cardboard box and comes downstairs to desk, putting box on stool.* KLEIN *crosses to toy box.* HARPER *speaks through this.*)

HARPER: You couldn't be of any service—and you must spare yourselves something.

ABBY (*to* BROPHY): Here's the broth, Mr. Brophy. Be sure it's good and hot.

BROPHY: Yes, ma'am.

KLEIN: This is fine—it'll make a lot of kids happy. (*Lifts out toy soldier.*) That O'Malley boy is nuts about soldiers.

TEDDY: That's General Miles. I've retired him. (KLEIN *removes ship.*) What's this! The Oregon!

MARTHA: Teddy, dear, put it back.

TEDDY: But the Oregon goes to Australia.

ABBY: Now, Teddy—

TEDDY: No, I've given my word to Fighting Bob Evans.

MARTHA: But, Teddy—

KLEIN: What's the difference what kid gets it—Bobby Evans, Izzy Cohen? (*Crosses to door with box, opens door.* BROPHY *follows.*) We'll run along, ma'am, and thank you very much.

ABBY: Not at all. (*The* COPS *stop in doorway, salute* TEDDY *and exit.* ABBY *crosses and shuts door as she speaks.* TEDDY *starts upstairs.*) Good-bye.

HARPER (*crosses to sofa, gets hat*): I must be getting home.

ABBY: Before you go, Dr. Harper—

> (TEDDY *has reached stair landing.*)

TEDDY: CHARGE! (*He dashes upstairs. At top he stops and with a sweeping gesture over the balcony rail, invites all to follow him as he speaks.*) Charge the blockhouse! (*He dashes through door, closing it after him.*)

HARPER: The blockhouse?

MARTHA: The stairs are always San Juan Hill.

HARPER: Have you ever tried to persuade him that he wasn't Teddy Roosevelt?

ABBY: Oh, no!

MARTHA: He's so happy being Teddy Roosevelt.

ABBY: Once, a long time ago—(*She crosses below to* MARTHA.) remember, Martha? We thought if he would be George Washington it might be a change for him—

MARTHA: But he stayed under his bed for days and just wouldn't be anybody.

ABBY: And we'd so much rather he'd be Mr. Roosevelt than nobody.

HARPER: Well, if he's happy—and what's more important you're happy—(*He takes blue-backed legal paper from inside pocket.*) You'll see that he signs these.

MARTHA: What are they?

ABBY: Dr. Harper has made all arrangements for Teddy to go to Happy Dale Sanitarium after we pass on.

MARTHA: But why should Teddy sign any papers now?

HARPER: It's better to have it all settled. If the Lord should take you away suddenly perhaps we couldn't persuade Teddy to commit himself and that would mean an unpleasant legal procedure. Mr. Witherspoon understands they're to be filed away until the times comes to use them.

MARTHA: Mr. Witherspoon? Who's he?

HARPER: He's the Superintendent of Happy Dale.

ABBY (*to* MARTHA): Dr. Harper has arranged for him to drop in tomorrow or the next day to meet Teddy.

HARPER (*crossing to door and opening it*): I'd better be running along or Elaine will be over here looking for me.

(ABBY *crosses to door and calls out after him.*)

ABBY: Give our love to Elaine—and Dr. Harper, please don't think harshly of Mortimer because he's a dramatic critic. Somebody has to do those things. (ABBY *closes door, comes back into room.*)

(MARTHA *crosses to sideboard, puts legal papers on it . . . notices tea things on table.*)

MARTHA: Did you just have tea? Isn't it rather late?

ABBY (*as one who has a secret*): Yes—and dinner's going to be late too.

(TEDDY *enters on balcony, starts downstairs to first landing.* MARTHA *steps to* ABBY.)

MARTHA: So? Why?

ABBY: Teddy! (TEDDY *stops on landing.*) Good news for you. You're going to Panama and dig another lock for the canal.

TEDDY: Dee-lighted! That's bully! Just bully! I shall prepare at once for the journey. (*He turns to go upstairs, stops as if puzzled, hurries back to landing, cries CHARGE!, and rushes up and off.*)

MARTHA (*elated*): Abby! While I was out?

ABBY (*taking* MARTHA'S *hand*): Yes, dear! I just couldn't wait for you. I didn't know when you'd be back and Dr. Harper was coming.

MARTHA: But all by yourself?

ABBY: Oh, I got along fine!

MARTHA: I'll run right downstairs and see.

(*She starts happily for cellar door.*)

ABBY: Oh, no, there wasn't time, and I was all alone.

(MARTHA *looks around room toward kitchen.*)

MARTHA: Well—

ABBY (*coyly*): Martha—just look in the window-seat. (MARTHA *almost skips to window-seat, and just as she gets there a knock is heard on door. She stops. They both look toward door.* ABBY *hurries to door and opens it.* ELAINE HARPER *enters.* ELAINE *is an attractive girl in her twenties; she looks surprisingly smart for a minister's daughter.*) Oh, it's Elaine. (*Opens door.*) Come in, dear.

ELAINE: Good afternoon, Miss Abby. Good afternoon, Miss Martha. I thought Father was here.

MARTHA: He just this minute left. Didn't you meet him?

ELAINE: No, I took the short cut through the cemetery. Mortimer hasn't come yet?

ABBY: No, dear.

ELAINE: Oh? He asked me to meet him here. Do you mind if I wait?

MARTHA: Not at all.

ABBY: Why don't you sit down, dear?

MARTHA: But we really must speak to Mortimer about doing this to you.

ELAINE: Doing what?

MARTHA: Well, he was brought up to know better. When a gentleman is taking a young lady out he should call for her at her house.

ELAINE (*to both*): Oh, there's something about calling for a girl at a parsonage that discourages any man who doesn't embroider.

ABBY: He's done this too often—we're going to speak to him.

ELAINE: Oh, please don't. After young men whose idea of night life was to take me to prayer meeting, it's wonderful to go to the theatre almost every night of my life.

MARTHA: It's comforting for us, too, because if Mortimer has to see some of those plays he has to see—at least he's sitting next to a minister's daughter. (MARTHA *steps to back of table.*)

(ABBY *crosses to back of table, starts putting tea things on tray.* ELAINE *and* MARTHA *help.*)

ABBY: My goodness, Elaine, what must you think of us—not having tea cleared away by this time. (*She picks up tray and exits to kitchen.*)

(MARTHA *blows out one candle and takes it to sideboard.* ELAINE *blows out other, takes to sideboard.*)

MARTHA (*as* ABBY *exits*): Now don't bother with anything in the kitchen until Mortimer comes, and then I'll help you. (*To* ELAINE.) Mortimer will be here any minute now.

ELAINE: Yes. Father must have been surprised not to find me at home. I'd better run over and say good night to him.

MARTHA: It's a shame you missed him, dear.

ELAINE (*opening door*): If Mortimer comes you tell him I'll be right back. (*She has opened door, but sees* MORTIMER *just outside.*) Hello, Mort!

(MORTIMER BREWSTER *walks in. He is a dramatic critic.*)

MORTIMER: Hello, Elaine. (*As he passes her going toward* MARTHA, *thus placing himself between* ELAINE *and* MARTHA, *he reaches back and pats* ELAINE *on the fanny . . . then embraces* MARTHA.) Hello, Aunt Martha.

(MARTHA *exits to kitchen, calling as she goes.*)

MARTHA: Abby, Mortimer's here!

(ELAINE *slowly closes door.*)

MORTIMER: Were you going somewhere?

ELAINE: I was just going over to tell Father not to wait up for me.

MORTIMER: I didn't know that was still being done, even in Brooklyn. (*He throws his hat on sofa.*)

(ABBY *enters from kitchen.* MARTHA *follows.*)

ABBY (*crosses to* MORTIMER): Hello, Mortimer.

MORTIMER (*embraces and kisses her*): Hello, Aunt Abby.

ABBY: How are you, dear?

MORTIMER: All right. And you look well. You haven't changed much since yesterday.

ABBY: Oh, my goodness, it was yesterday, wasn't it? We're seeing a great deal of you lately. (*She crosses and starts to sit in chair above table.*) Well, come, sit down. Sit down.

(MARTHA *stops her from sitting.*)

MARTHA: Abby—haven't we something to do in the kitchen?

ABBY: Huh?

MARTHA: You know—the tea things.

ABBY (*suddenly seeing* MORTIMER *and* ELAINE, *and catching on*): Oh, yes! Yes! The tea things—(*She backs toward kitchen.*) Well—you two just make yourselves at home. Just—

MARTHA: —make yourselves at home.

(*They exit kitchen door,* ABBY *closing door.*)

ELAINE (*stepping to* MORTIMER *ready to be kissed*): Well, can't you take a hint?

MORTIMER (*complaining*): No . . . that was pretty obvious. A lack of inventiveness, I should say.

ELAINE (*only slightly annoyed as she crosses to table, and puts handbag on it*): Yes—that's exactly what you'd say.

MORTIMER (*he is at desk, fishing various pieces of notepaper from his pockets, and separating dollar bills that are mixed in with papers*): Where do you want to go for dinner?

ELAINE (*opening bag, looking in hand mirror*): I don't care. I'm not very hungry.

MORTIMER: Well, I just had breakfast. Suppose we wait until after the show?

ELAINE: But that'll make it pretty late, won't it?

MORTIMER: Not with the little stinker we're seeing tonight. From what I've heard about it we'll be at Blake's by ten o'clock.

ELAINE: You ought to be fair to these plays.

MORTIMER: Are these plays fair to me?

ELAINE: *I've* never seen you walk out on a musical.

MORTIMER: That musical isn't opening tonight.

ELAINE (*disappointed*): No?

MORTIMER: Darling, you'll have to learn the rules. With a musical there are always four changes of title and three postponements. They liked it in New Haven but it needs a lot of work.

ELAINE: Oh, I was hoping it was a musical.

MORTIMER: You have such a light mind.

ELAINE: Not a bit. Musicals somehow have a humanizing effect on you. (*He gives her a look.*) After a serious play we join the proletariat in the subway and I listen to a lecture on the drama. After a musical you bring me home in a taxi, (*Turning away.*) and you make a few passes.

MORTIMER: Now wait a minute, darling, that's a very inaccurate piece of reporting.

ELAINE: Oh, I will admit that after the Behrman play you told me I had authentic beauty—and that's a hell of a thing to say to a girl. It wasn't until after our first musical you told me I had nice legs. And I have too.

(MORTIMER *stares at her legs a moment, then walks over and kisses her.*)

MORTIMER: For a minister's daughter you know a lot about life. Where'd you learn it?

ELAINE (*casually*): In the choir loft.

MORTIMER: I'll explain that to you some time, darling—the close connection between eroticism and religion.

ELAINE: Religion never gets as high as the choir loft. (*Crosses below table, gathers up bag.*) Which reminds me, I'd better tell Father please not to wait up for me tonight.

MORTIMER (*almost to himself*): I've never been able to rationalize it.

ELAINE: What?

MORTIMER: My falling in love with a girl who lives in Brooklyn.

ELAINE: Falling in love? You're not stooping to the articulate, are you?

MORTIMER (*ignoring this*): The only way I can regain my self-respect is to keep you in New York.

ELAINE (*few steps toward him*): Did you say keep?

MORTIMER: No, no. I've come to the conclusion that you're holding out for the legalities.

ELAINE: (*crossing to him as he backs away*): I can afford to be a good girl for quite a few years yet.

MORTIMER (*stops and embraces her*): And I can't wait that long. Where could we be married in a hurry—say tonight?

ELAINE: I'm afraid Father will insist on officiating.

MORTIMER (*turning away from her*): Oh, God; I'll bet your father could make even the marriage service sound pedestrian.

ELAINE: Are you by any chance writing a review of it?

MORTIMER: Forgive me, darling. It's an occupational disease. (*She smiles at him lovingly and walks toward him. He meets her halfway and they forget themselves for a moment in a sentimental embrace and kiss. When they come out of it, he turns away from her quickly.*) I may give that play tonight a good notice.

ELAINE: Now, darling, don't pretend you love me that much.

MORTIMER (*looks at her with polite lechery, then starts toward her*): Be sure to tell your father not to wait up tonight.

ELAINE: I think tonight I'd better tell him to wait up.

MORTIMER (*following her*): I'll telephone Winchell to publish the banns.

ELAINE: Nevertheless—

MORTIMER: All right, everything formal and legal. But not later than next month.

ELAINE (*runs into his arms*): Darling! I'll talk it over with Father and set the date.

MORTIMER: No—we'll have to see what's in rehearsal. There'll be a lot of other first nights in October.

(TEDDY *enters from balcony and comes downstairs dressed in tropical clothes and a solar topee. At foot of stairs he sees* MORTIMER, *crosses to him and shakes hands.*)

TEDDY: Hello, Mortimer!

MORTIMER (*gravely*): How are you, Mr. President?

TEDDY: Bully, thank you. Just bully! What news have you brought me?

MORTIMER: Just this, Mr. President—the country is squarely behind you.

TEDDY (*beaming*): Yes, I know. Isn't it wonderful? (*He shakes* MORTIMER'S *hand again.*) Well, good-bye. (*He crosses to* ELAINE *and shakes hands with her.*) Good-bye. (*He goes to cellar door.*)

ELAINE: Where are you off to, Teddy?

TEDDY: Panama. (*He exits through cellar door, shutting it.* ELAINE *looks at* MORTIMER *inquiringly.*)

MORTIMER: Panama's the cellar. He digs locks for the canal down there.

ELAINE: You're so sweet with him—and he's very fond of you.

MORTIMER: Well, Teddy was always my favorite brother.

ELAINE (*stopping and turning to him*): Favorite? Were there more of you?

MORTIMER: There's another brother—Jonathan.

ELAINE: I never heard of him. Your aunts never mention him.

MORTIMER: No, we don't like to talk about Jonathan. He left Brooklyn very early—by request. Jonathan was the kind of boy who liked to cut worms in two—with his teeth.

ELAINE: What became of him?

MORTIMER: I don't know. He wanted to become a surgeon like Grandfather but he wouldn't go to medical school first and his practice got him into trouble.

(ABBY *enters from kitchen.*)

ABBY: Aren't you two going to be late for the theatre?

MORTIMER: We're skipping dinner. We won't have to start for half an hour.

ABBY: Well, then I'll leave you two alone together again.

ELAINE: Don't bother, darling. I'm going to run over to speak to Father. (*To* MORTIMER.) Before I go out with you he likes to pray over me a little. (*She runs to door and opens it.*) I'll be right back—I'll cut through the cemetery.

MORTIMER (*crossing to her, puts his hand on hers*): If the prayer isn't too long, I'd have time to lead you beside distilled waters.

(ELAINE *laughs and exits.* MORTIMER *shuts door.*)

ABBY: Mortimer, that's the first time I've ever heard you quote the Bible. We knew Elaine would be a good influence for you.

MORTIMER (*laughs*): Oh, by the way—I'm going to marry her.

ABBY: What? Oh, darling! (*She runs and embraces him. Then she dashes toward kitchen door as* MORTIMER *crosses to window and looks out.*) Martha! Martha! (MARTHA *enters from kitchen.*) Come right in here. I've got the most wonderful news for you—Mortimer and Elaine are going to be married.

MARTHA: Married? Oh, Mortimer! (*She runs over to* MORTIMER, *who is looking out window, embraces and kisses him.*)

ABBY: We hoped it would happen just like this.

MARTHA: Well, Elaine must be the happiest girl in the world.

MORTIMER (*pulls curtain back, looks out window*): Happy! Just look at her leaping over those gravestones. (*As he looks out window* MORTIMER'S *attention is suddenly drawn to something.*) Say! What's that?

MARTHA: What's what, dear?

MORTIMER: See that statue there. That's horundinida carnina.

MARTHA: Oh, no, dear—that's Emma B. Stout ascending to heaven.

MORTIMER: No, no,—standing on Mrs. Stout's left ear. That bird— that's a red-crested swallow. I've only seen one of those before in my life.

ABBY: I don't know how you can be thinking about a bird now—what with Elaine and the engagement and everything.

MORTIMER: It's a vanishing species. (*He turns away from window.*) Thoreau was very fond of them. (*As he crosses to desk to look through various drawers and papers.*) By the way, I left a large envelope around here last week. It was one of the chapters of my book on Thoreau. Have you seen it?

MARTHA (*pushing armchair into table*): Well, if you left it here it must be here somewhere.

ABBY: When are you going to be married? What are your plans? There must be something more you can tell us about Elaine.

MORTIMER: Elaine? Oh, yes, Elaine thought it was brilliant. (*He crosses to sideboard, looks through cupboards and drawers.*)

MARTHA: What was, dear?

MORTIMER: My chapter on Thoreau. (*He finds a bundle of papers (script) in drawer and takes them to table and looks through them.*)

ABBY: Well, when Elaine comes back I think we ought to have a little celebration. We must drink to your happiness. Martha, isn't there some of that Lady Baltimore cake left?

(*During last few speeches* MARTHA *has picked up pail from sideboard and her cape, hat and gloves from table.*)

MARTHA: Oh, yes!

ABBY: And I'll open a bottle of wine.

MARTHA (*as she exits to kitchen*): Oh, and to think it happened in this room!

MORTIMER (*has finished looking through papers, is gazing around room*): Now where could I have put that?

ABBY: Well, with your fiancée sitting beside you tonight, I do hope the play will be something you can enjoy for once. It may be something romantic. What's the name of it?

MORTIMER: "Murder Will Out."

ABBY: Oh dear! (*She disappears into kitchen as* MORTIMER *goes on talking.*)

MORTIMER: When the curtain goes up the first thing you'll see will be a dead body.

(*He lifts window-seat and sees one. Not believing it, he drops window-seat again and starts downstage. He suddenly stops with a "take," then goes back, throws window-seat open and stares in. He goes slightly mad for a moment. He backs away, then hears* ABBY *humming on her way into the room. He drops window-seat again and holds it down, staring around the room.* ABBY *enters carrying a silencer and table cloth which she puts on armchair, then picks up bundle of papers and returns them to drawer in sideboard.*)

MORTIMER (*speaks in a somewhat strained voice*): Aunt Abby!

ABBY (*at sideboard*): Yes, dear?

MORTIMER: You were going to make plans for Teddy to go to that . . . sanitarium—Happy Dale—

ABBY (*bringing legal papers from sideboard to* MORTIMER): Yes, dear, it's all arranged. Dr. Harper was here today and brought the papers for Teddy to sign. Here they are.

(*He takes them from her.*)

MORTIMER: He's got to sign them right away.

ABBY (*arranging silencer on table.* MARTHA *enters from kitchen door with table silver and plates on a tray. She sets tray on sideboard. Goes to table*): That's what Dr. Harper thinks. Then there won't be any legal difficulties after we pass on.

MORTIMER: He's got to sign them this minute! He's down in the cellar —get him up here right away.

MARTHA (*unfolding tablecloth*): There's no such hurry as that.

ABBY: No. When Teddy starts working on the canal you can't get his mind on anything else.

MORTIMER: Teddy's got to go to Happy Dale now—tonight.

MARTHA: Oh, no, dear, that's not until after we're gone.

MORTIMER: Right away, I tell you!—right away!

ABBY (*turning to* MORTIMER): Why, Mortimer, how can you say such a thing? Why, as long as we live we'll never be separated from Teddy.

MORTIMER (*trying to be calm*): Listen, darlings, I'm frightfully sorry, but I've got some shocking news for you. (*The* AUNTS *stop work and look at him with some interest.*) Now we've all got to try and keep our heads. You know we've sort of humored Teddy because we thought he was harmless.

MARTHA: Why he *is* harmless!

MORTIMER: He *was* harmless. That's why he has to go to Happy Dale. Why he has to be confined.

ABBY (*stepping to* MORTIMER): Mortimer, why have you suddenly turned against Teddy?—your own brother?

MORTIMER: You've got to know sometime. It might as well be now, Teddy's—killed a man!

MARTHA: Nonsense, dear.

(MORTIMER *rises and points to window-seat.*)

MORTIMER: There's a body in the window-seat!

ABBY: Yes, dear, we know.

(MORTIMER *"takes" as* ABBY *and* MARTHA *busy themselves again at table.*)

MORTIMER: You *know?*

MARTHA: Of course, dear, but it has nothing to do with Teddy. (*Gets tray from sideboard—arranges silver and plates on table.*)

ABBY: Now, Mortimer, just forget about it—forget you ever saw the gentleman.

MORTIMER: *Forget?*

ABBY: We never dreamed you'd peek.

MORTIMER: But who is he?

ABBY: His name's Hoskins—Adam Hoskins. That's really all I know about him—except that he's a Methodist.

MORTIMER: That's all you know about him? Well, what's he doing here? What happened to him?

MARTHA: He died.

MORTIMER: Aunt Martha, men don't just get into window-seats and die.

ABBY (*silly boy*): No, he died first.

MORTIMER: Well, how?

ABBY: Oh, Mortimer, don't be so inquisitive. The gentleman died because he drank some wine with poison in it.

MORTIMER: How did the poison get in the wine?

MARTHA: Well, we put it in wine because it's less noticeable—when it's in tea it has a distinct odor.

MORTIMER: *You* put it in the wine?

ABBY: Yes. And I put Mr. Hoskins in the window-seat because Dr. Harper was coming.

MORTIMER: So you knew what you'd done! You didn't want Dr. Harper to see the body!

ABBY: Well, not at tea—that wouldn't have been very nice. Now, Mortimer, you know the whole thing, just forget about it. I do think Martha and I have the right to our own little secrets. (*She crosses to sideboard to get two goblets from cupboard as* MARTHA *comes to table from sideboard with salt dish and pepper shaker.*)

MARTHA: And don't you tell Elaine! (*She gets third goblet from sideboard, then turns to* ABBY *who takes tray from sideboard.*) Oh, Abby, while I was out I dropped in on Mrs. Schultz. She's much better but she would like us to take Junior to the movies again.

ABBY: Well, we must do that tomorrow or next day.

MARTHA: Yes, but this time we'll go where we want to go. (*She starts for kitchen door.* ABBY *follows.*) Junior's not going to drag me into another one of those scary pictures. (*They exit into kitchen as* MORTIMER *wheels around and looks after them.* ABBY *shuts door.*)

MORTIMER (*dazed, looks around the room. His eyes come to rest on phone on desk; he crosses to it and dials a number. Into phone*): City desk! (*There is a pause.*) Hello, Al. Do you know who this is? (*Pause.*) That's right. Say, Al, when I left the office, I told you where I was going, remember?—Well, where did I say? (*Pause.*) Uh-huh. Well, it would take me about half an hour to get to Brooklyn. What time have you got? (*He looks at his watch.*) That's right. I must be here. (*He hangs up, sits for a moment, then suddenly leaps off stool toward kitchen.*) Aunt Abby! Aunt Martha! Come in here! (*He backs to* c. *stage as the two* AUNTS *bustle in.* MARTHA *has tray with plates, cups, saucers and soup cups.*) What are we going to do? What are we going to do?

MARTHA: What are we going to do about what, dear?

MORTIMER (*pointing to window-seat*): There's a body in there.

ABBY: Yes—Mr. Hoskins.

MORTIMER: Well, good heavens, I can't turn you over to the police! But what am I going to do?

MARTHA: Well, for one thing, dear, stop being so excited.

ABBY: And for pity's sake stop worrying. We told you to forget the whole thing.

MORTIMER: Forget! My dear Aunt Abby, can't I make you realize that something has to be done?

ABBY (*a little sharply*): Now, Mortimer, you behave yourself. You're too old to be flying off the handle like this.

MORTIMER: But Mr. Hotchkiss—

(ABBY, *on her way to sideboard, stops and turns to* MORTIMER.)

ABBY: Hoskins, dear. (*She continues on her way to sideboard and gets napkins and rings from drawer.* MARTHA *puts her tray, with cups, plates, etc., on table.* MORTIMER *continues speaking through this.*)

MORTIMER: Well, whatever his name is, you can't leave him there.

MARTHA: We don't intend to dear.

ABBY (*crossing to table with napkins and rings*): No, Teddy's down in the cellar now digging the lock.

MORTIMER: You mean you're going to bury Mr. Hotchkiss in the cellar?

MARTHA (*stepping to him*): Oh, yes, dear,—that's what we did with the others.

MORTIMER (*walking away*): No! You can't bury Mr.—(*Double take. Turns back to them*)—others?

ABBY: The other gentlemen.

MORTIMER: When you say others—do you mean—others? More than one others?

MARTHA: Oh, yes, dear. Let me see, this is eleven. Isn't it, Abby?

ABBY: No, dear, this makes twelve.

(MORTIMER *backs away from them, stunned, toward phone stool at desk.*)

MARTHA: Oh, I think you're wrong, Abby. This is only eleven.

ABBY: No, dear, because I remember when Mr. Hoskins first came in, it occurred to me that he would make just an even dozen.

MARTHA: Well, you really shouldn't count the first one.

ABBY: Oh, *I* was counting the first one. So that makes it twelve.

(*Phone rings.* MORTIMER, *in a daze, turns toward it and without picking up receiver, speaks.*)

MORTIMER: Hello! (*He comes to, picks up receiver.*) Hello. Oh, hello, Al. My, it's good to hear your voice.

(ABBY, *at table is still holding out for a "twelve" count.*)

ABBY: Well, anyway, they're all down in the cellar—

MORTIMER (*to* AUNTS): Ssshhh—(*Into phone, as* AUNTS *cross to sideboard and put candelabras from top to bottom shelf.*) Oh, no, Al, I'm sober as a lark. I just called you because I was feeling a little Pirandello—Piran—you wouldn't know, Al. Look, I'm glad you called. Get hold of George right away. He's got to review the play tonight. I can't make it. No, Al, you're wrong. I'll tell you all about it tomorrow. Well, George has got to cover the play tonight! This is my department and I'm running it! You get ahold of George! (*He hangs up and sits a moment trying to collect himself.*) Now let's see, where were we? (*He suddenly leaps from stool.*) TWELVE!

MARTHA: Yes, Abby thinks we ought to count the first one and that makes twelve. (*She goes back to sideboard.*)

(MORTIMER *takes* MARTHA *by the hand, leads her to chair and sets her in it.*)

MORTIMER: All right—now—who was the first one?

ABBY (*crossing from above table to* MORTIMER): Mr. Midgely. He was a Baptist.

MARTHA: Of course, I still think we can't claim full credit for him because he just died.

ABBY: Martha means without any help from us. You see, Mr. Midgely came here looking for a room—

MARTHA: It was right after you moved to New York.

ABBY: —And it didn't seem right for that lovely room to be going to waste when there were so many people who needed it—

MARTHA: —He was such a lonely old man. . . .

ABBY: All his kith and kin were dead and it left him so forlorn and unhappy—

MARTHA: —We felt so sorry for him.

ABBY: And then when his heart attack came—and he sat dead in that chair (*Pointing to armchair.*) looking so peaceful—remember, Martha—we made up our minds then and there that if we could help other lonely old men to that same peace—we would!

MORTIMER (*all ears*): He dropped dead right in that chair! How awful for you!

MARTHA: Oh, no, dear. Why, it was rather like old times. Your grandfather always used to have a cadaver or two around the house. You see, Teddy had been digging in Panama and he thought Mr. Midgely was a Yellow Fever victim.

ABBY: That meant he had to be buried immediately.

MARTHA: So we all took him down to Panama and put him in the lock. (*She rises, puts her arm around* ABBY.) Now that's why we told you not to worry about it because we know exactly what's to be done.

MORTIMER: And that's how all this started—that man walking in here and dropping dead.

ABBY: Of course, we realized we couldn't depend on that happening again. So—

MARTHA (*crosses to* MORTIMER): You remember those jars of poison that have been up on the shelves in Grandfather's laboratory all these years—?

ABBY: You know your Aunt Martha's knack for mixing things. You've eaten enough of her piccalilli.

MARTHA: Well, dear, for a gallon of elderberry wine I take one teaspoonful of arsenic, then add a half teaspoonful of strychnine and then just a pinch of cyanide.

MORTIMER (*appraisingly*): Should have quite a kick.

ABBY: Yes! As a matter of fact one of our gentlemen found time to say "How delicious!"

MARTHA: Well, I'll have to get things started in the kitchen.

ABBY (*to* MORTIMER): I wish you could stay for dinner.

MARTHA: I'm trying out a new recipe.

MORTIMER: I couldn't eat a thing.

(MARTHA *goes out to kitchen.*)

ABBY (*calling after* MARTHA): I'll come and help you, dear. (*She pushes chair into table.*) Well, I feel so much better now. Oh, you have to wait for Elaine, don't you? (*She smiles.*) How happy you must be. (*She goes to kitchen doorway.*) Well, dear, I'll leave you alone with your thoughts. (*She exits, shutting door.*)

(*The shutting of the door wakes* MORTIMER *from his trance. He crosses to window-seat, kneels down, raises cover, looks in. Not believing, he lowers cover, rubs his eyes, raises cover again. This time he really sees Mr. Hoskins. Closes window-seat hastily, rises, steps back. Runs over and closes drapes over window. Backs up to above table. Sees water glass on table, picks it up, raises it to lips, suddenly remembers that poisoned wine comes in glasses, puts it down quickly. Crosses to cellar door, opens it.* ELAINE *enters, he closes cellar door with a bang. As* ELAINE *puts her bag on top of desk he looks at her, and it dawns on him that he knows her. He speaks with faint surprise.*)

MORTIMER: Oh, it's you. (ELAINE *crosses to him, takes his hand.*)

ELAINE: Don't be cross, darling! Father could see that I was excited—so I told him about us and that made it hard for me to get away. But listen, darling—he's not going to wait up for me tonight.

MORTIMER (*looking at window-seat*): You run along home, Elaine, and I'll call you up tomorrow.

ELAINE: Tomorrow!

MORTIMER (*irritated*): You know I always call you up every day or two.

ELAINE: But we're going to the theatre tonight.

MORTIMER: No—no we're not!

ELAINE: Well, why not?

MORTIMER (*turning to her*): Elaine, something's come up.

ELAINE: What, darling? Mortimer—you've lost your job!

MORTIMER: No—no—I haven't lost my job. I'm just not covering that play tonight. (*Pushing her.*) Now you run along home, Elaine.

ELAINE: But I've got to know what's happened. Certainly you can tell me.

MORTIMER: No, dear, I can't.

ELAINE: But if we're going to be married—

MORTIMER: Married?

ELAINE: Have you forgotten that not fifteen minutes ago you proposed to me?

MORTIMER (*vaguely*): I did? Oh—yes! Well, as far as I know that's still on. Now you run along home, Elaine. I've got to do something.

ELAINE: Listen, you can't propose to me one minute and throw me out of the house the next.

MORTIMER (*pleading*): I'm not throwing you out of the house, darling. Will you get out of here?

ELAINE: No. I won't get out of here. (MORTIMER *crosses toward kitchen.* ELAINE *crosses below to window-seat.*) Not until I've had some kind of explanation. (ELAINE *is about to sit on window-seat.* MORTIMER *grabs her by the hand. Phone rings.*)

MORTIMER: Elaine! (*He goes to phone, dragging* ELAINE *with him.*) Hello! Oh, hello, Al. Hold on a minute, will you?— All right, it's important! But it can wait a minute, can't it? Hold on! (*He puts receiver on desk. Takes* ELAINE's *bag from top of desk and hands it to her. Then takes her by hand and leads her to door and opens it.*) Look, Elaine, you're a sweet girl and I love you. But I have something on my mind now and I want you to go home and wait until I call you.

ELAINE (*in doorway*): Don't try to be masterful.

MORTIMER (*annoyed to the point of being literate*): When we're married and I have problems to face I hope you're less tedious and uninspired!

ELAINE: And when we're married *if* we're married—I hope I find you adequate! (*She exits.* MORTIMER *does take, then runs out on porch after her, calling*—)

MORTIMER: Elaine! Elaine! (*He runs back in, shutting door, crosses and kneels on window-seat to open window. Suddenly remembers contents of window-seat and leaps off it. Dashes into kitchen but remembers Al is on phone, re-enters immediately and crosses to phone.*) Hello, Al? Hello . . . hello. . . . (*He pushes hook down and starts to dial when doorbell rings. He thinks it's the phone.* ABBY *enters from kitchen.*) Hello. Hello, Al?

ABBY (*crossing to door and opening it*): That's the doorbell, dear, not the telephone. (MORTIMER *pushes hook down . . . dials.* MR. GIBBS *steps in doorway.*) How do you do? Come in.

GIBBS: I understand you have a room to rent.

(MARTHA *enters from kitchen. Puts "Lazy Susan" on sideboard.*)

ABBY: Yes. Won't you step in?

GIBBS (*stepping into room*): Are you the lady of the house?

ABBY: Yes, I'm Miss Brewster. And this is my sister, another Miss Brewster.

GIBBS: My name is Gibbs.

ABBY (*easing him to chair*): Oh, won't you sit down? I'm sorry we were just setting the table for dinner.

MORTIMER (*into phone*): Hello—let me talk to Al again. City desk. (*Loud.*) AL!! CITY DESK! WHAT? I'm sorry, wrong number. (*He hangs up and starts dialling again as* GIBBS *looks at him.* GIBBS *turns to* ABBY.)

GIBBS: May I see the room?

MARTHA: Why don't you sit down a minute and let's get acquainted.

GIBBS: That won't do much good if I don't like the room.

ABBY: Is Brooklyn your home?

GIBBS: Haven't got a home. Live in a hotel. Don't like it.

MORTIMER (*into phone*): Hello. City desk.

MARTHA: Are your family Brooklyn people?

GIBBS: Haven't got any family.

ABBY (*another victim*): All alone in the world?

GIBBS: Yep.

ABBY: Well, Martha—(MARTHA *goes happily to sideboard, gets bottle of wine from cupboard, and a wine glass, and sets them on table.* ABBY *eases* GIBBS *into chair and continues speaking to him, then to above table.*) Well, you've come to just the right house. Do sit down.

MORTIMER (*into phone*): Hello, Al? Mort. We got cut off. Al, I can't cover the play tonight—that's all there is to it, I can't!

MARTHA: What church do you go to? There's an Episcopal church practically next door. (*Her gesture toward window brings her to window-seat and she sits.*)

GIBBS: I'm Presbyterian. Used to be.

MORTIMER (*into phone*): What's George doing in Bermuda? (*Rises and gets loud.*) Certainly I told him he could go to Bermuda—it's my department, isn't it? Well, you've got to get somebody. Who else is there around the office? (*He sits on second chair.*)

GIBBS (*annoyed. Rises and crosses below table*): Is there always this much noise?

MARTHA: Oh, he doesn't live with us.

(ABBY *sits above table.*)

MORTIMER (*into phone*): There must be somebody around the place. Look, Al, how about the office boy? You know the bright one—the one we don't like? Well, you look around the office, I'll hold on.

GIBBS: I'd really like to see the room.

ABBY (*after seating* GIBBS *she has sat in chair above table*): It's upstairs. Won't you try a glass of our wine before we start up?

GIBBS: Never touch it.

MARTHA: We make this ourselves. It's elderberry wine.

GIBBS (*to* MARTHA): Elderberry wine. Hmmph. Haven't tasted elderberry wine since I was a boy. Thank you. (*He pulls armchair around and sits as* ABBY *uncorks bottle and starts to pour wine.*)

MORTIMER (*into phone*): Well, there must be some printers around. Look, Al, the fellow who sets my copy. He ought to know about what I'd write. His name is Joe. He's the third machine from the left. But, Al, he might turn out to be another Burns Mantle!

GIBBS (*to* MARTHA): Do you have your own elderberry bushes?

MARTHA: No, but the cemetery is full of them.

MORTIMER (*rising*): No, I'm not drinking, but I'm going to start now.

GIBBS: Do you serve meals?

ABBY: We might, but first just see whether you like our wine.

(MORTIMER *hangs up, puts phone on top of desk. He sees wine on table. Goes to sideboard, gets glass, brings it to table and pours drink.* GIBBS *has his glass in hand and is getting ready to drink.*)

MARTHA (*sees* MORTIMER *pouring wine*): Mortimer! Eh eh eh eh! (GIBBS *stops and looks at* MARTHA. MORTIMER *pays no attention.*) Eh eh eh eh!

(*As* MORTIMER *raises glass to lips,* ABBY *reaches up and pulls his arm down.*)

ABBY: Mortimer. Not that. (MORTIMER, *still dumb, puts his glass down on table. Then he suddenly sees* GIBBS *who has just got glass to his lips and is about to drink. He points across table at* GIBBS *and gives a wild cry.* GIBBS *looks at him, putting his glass down.* MORTIMER, *still pointing at* GIBBS, *goes around above table toward him.* GIBBS, *seeing a madman, rises slowly, then turns and runs,* MORTIMER *following him.* GIBBS *opens door and* MORTIMER *pushes him out, closing door after him. Then he turns and leans on door in exhausted relief.*)

ABBY (*great disappointment*): Now you've spoiled everything. (*She goes to sofa and sits.*)

(MARTHA *sits in armchair.* MORTIMER *looks from one to the other . . . then speaks to* ABBY.)

MORTIMER: You can't do things like that. I don't know how to explain this to you, but it's not only against the law. It's wrong! (*To* MARTHA.) It's not a nice thing to do. (MARTHA *turns away from him as* ABBY *has done in his lines to her.*) People wouldn't understand. (*Points to door after* GIBBS.) *He* wouldn't understand.

MARTHA: Abby, we shouldn't have told Mortimer!

MORTIMER: What I mean is—well, this has developed into a very bad habit.

ABBY (*rises*): Mortimer, we don't try to stop you from doing things you like to do. I don't see why you should interfere with us.

(*Phone rings.* MORTIMER *answers.* MARTHA *rises to below table.*)

MORTIMER: Hello? (*It's Al again.*) All right, I'll see the first act and I'll pan the hell out of it. But look, Al, you've got to do something for me. Get hold of O'Brien—our lawyer, the head of our legal department. Have him meet me at the theatre. Now, don't let me down. O.K. I'm starting now. (*He hangs up and turns to* AUNTS.) Look, I've got to go to the theatre. I can't get out of it. But before I go will you promise me something?

MARTHA: We'd have to know what it was first.

MORTIMER: I love you very much and I know you love me. You know I'd do anything in the world for you and I want you to do just this little thing for me.

ABBY: What do you want us to do?

MORTIMER: Don't *do* anything. I mean don't do *anything*. Don't let anyone in this house—and leave Mr. Hoskins right where he is.

MARTHA: Why?

MORTIMER: I want time to think—and I've got quite a little to think about. You know I wouldn't want anything to happen to you.

ABBY: Well, what on earth could happen to us?

MORTIMER (*beside himself*): Anyway—you'll do this for me, won't you?

MARTHA: Well—we were planning on holding services before dinner.

MORTIMER: Services!

MARTHA (*a little indignant*): Certainly. You don't think we'd bury Mr. Hoskins without a full Methodist service, do you? Why he was a Methodist.

MORTIMER: But can't that wait until I get back?

ABBY: Oh, then you could join us.

MORTIMER (*going crazy himself*): Yes! Yes!

ABBY: Oh, Mortimer, you'll enjoy the services—especially the hymns. (*To* MARTHA.) Remember how beautifully Mortimer used to sing in the choir before his voice changed?

MORTIMER: And remember, you're not going to let anyone in this house while I'm gone—it's a promise!

MARTHA: Well—

ABBY: Oh, Martha, we can do that now that Mortimer's cooperating with us. (*To* MORTIMER.) Well, all right, Mortimer.

(MORTIMER *heaves a sigh of relief. Crosses to sofa and gets his hat.*)

MORTIMER: Have you got some paper? I'll get back just as soon as I can. (*Taking legal papers from coat pocket as he crosses.*) There's a man I've got to see.

(ABBY *has gone to desk for stationery. She hands it to* MORTIMER.)

ABBY: Here's some stationery. Will this do?

MORTIMER (*taking stationery*): That'll be fine. I can save time if I write my review on the way to the theatre. (*He exists.*)

(*The* AUNTS *stare after him.* MARTHA *crosses and closes door.* ABBY *goes to sideboard and brings two candelabras to table. Then gets matches from sideboard—lights candles during lines.*)

MARTHA: Mortimer didn't seem quite himself today.

ABBY (*lighting candles*): Well, that's only natural—I think I know why.

MARTHA (*lighting floor lamp*): Why?

ABBY: He's just become engaged to be married. I suppose that always makes a man nervous.

MARTHA (*during this speech she goes to first landing and closes drapes over window, then comes downstairs and turns off remote switch*): Well, I'm so happy for Elaine—and their honeymoon ought to give Mortimer a real vacation. I don't think he got much rest this summer.

ABBY: Well, at least he didn't go kiting off to China or Spain.

MARTHA: I could never understand why he wanted to go to those places.

ABBY: Well, I think to Mortimer the theatre has always seemed pretty small potatoes. He needs something big to criticize—something like the human race.

MARTHA: Oh, Abby, if Mortimer's coming back for the services for Mr. Hoskins, we'll need another hymnal. There's one in my room. (*She starts upstairs to first landing.*)

ABBY: You know, dear, it's really my turn to read the services, but since you weren't here when Mr. Hoskins came I want you to do it.

MARTHA (*pleased*): That's very nice of you, dear—but, are you sure you want me to?

ABBY: It's only fair.

MARTHA: Well, I think I'll wear my black bombazine and Mother's old brooch. (*She starts up again when doorbell rings.*)

ABBY (*crossing as far as desk*): I'll go, dear.

MARTHA (*hushed*): We promised Mortimer we wouldn't let anyone in.

ABBY (*trying to peer through curtained window in door*): Who do you suppose it is?

MARTHA: Wait a minute, I'll look. (*She turns to landing window and peeks out the curtains.*) It's two men—and I've never seen them before.

ABBY: Are you sure?

MARTHA: There's a car at the curb—they must have come in that.

ABBY: Let me look! (*She hurries up stairs. There is a knock on door.* ABBY *peeks out the curtains.*)

MARTHA: Do you recognize them?

ABBY: They're strangers to me.

MARTHA: We'll just have to pretend we're not at home. (*The two of them huddle back in corner of landing.*)

(*Another knock at the door, the knob is turned, and door swings slowly open. A tall* MAN *walks in with assurance and ease as though the room were familiar to him—in every direction but that of the stairs. There is something sinister about the man—something that brings a slight chill in his presence. It is in his walk, his bearing, and his strange resemblance to Boris Karloff. From stair-landing* ABBY *and* MARTHA *watch him, almost afraid to speak. Having completed his survey of the room, the* MAN *turns and addresses someone outside the front door.*)

JONATHAN: Come in, Doctor. (DR. EINSTEIN *enters. He is somewhat ratty in appearance. His face wears the benevolent smirk of a man who lives in a pleasant haze of alcohol. There is something about him that suggests the unfrocked priest. He stands just inside the door, timid but expectant.*) This is the home of my youth. As a boy I couldn't wait to escape from this place—now I'm glad to escape back into it.

EINSTEIN (*shutting door. His back to* AUNTS): Yah, Chonny, it's a fine hideout.

JONATHAN: The family must still live here. There's something so unmistakably Brewster about the Brewsters. I hope there's a fatted calf awaiting the return of the prodigal.

EINSTEIN: Yah, I'm hungry. (*He suddenly sees the fatted calf in the form of the two glasses of wine on table.*) Look, Chonny, drinks! (*He runs over below to table.* JONATHAN *crosses to above side.*)

JONATHAN: As though we were expected. A good omen.

(They raise glasses to their lips as ABBY *steps down a couple of stairs and speaks.)*

ABBY: Who are you? What are you doing here?

(They both put glasses down. EINSTEIN *picks up his hat from armchair, ready to run for it.* JONATHAN *turns to* ABBY.)

JONATHAN: Why, Aunt Abby! Aunt Martha! It's Jonathan.

MARTHA *(frightened)*: You get out of here.

JONATHAN *(crossing to* AUNTS): I'm Jonathan—your nephew, Jonathan.

ABBY: Oh, no, you're not. You're nothing like Jonathan, so don't pretend you are! You just get out of here!

JONATHAN *(crossing closer)*: But I am Jonathan. And this *(Indicating* EINSTEIN.) is Dr. Einstein.

ABBY: And he's not Dr. Einstein either.

JONATHAN: Not Dr. Albert Einstein—Dr. Herman Einstein.

ABBY *(down another step)*: Who are you? You're not our nephew, Jonathan.

JONATHAN *(peering at* ABBY'S *outstretched hand)*: I see you're still wearing the lovely garnet ring that Grandma Brewster bought in England. (ABBY *gasps, looks at ring.)* And you, Aunt Martha, still the high collar—to hide the scar where Grandfather's acid burned you.

*(*MARTHA'S *hand goes to her throat. The* AUNTS *look at* JONATHAN. MARTHA *comes down a few steps to behind* ABBY.)

MARTHA: His voice is like Jonathan's.

ABBY *(stepping down to stage floor)*: Have you been in an accident?

JONATHAN *(his hand goes to side of his face)*: No—*(He clouds.)* —my face—Dr. Einstein is responsible for that. He's a plastic surgeon. He changes people's faces.

MARTHA *(comes down to* ABBY): But I've seen that face before. *(To* ABBY.) Abby, remember when we took the little Schultz boy to the movies and I was so frightened? It was that face!

*(*JONATHAN *grows tense and looks toward* EINSTEIN. EINSTEIN *addresses* AUNTS.)

EINSTEIN: Easy, Chonny—easy! (*To* AUNTS.) Don't worry, ladies. The last five years I give Chonny three new faces. I give him another one right away. This last face—well, I saw that picture too—just before I operate. And I was intoxicated.

JONATHAN (*with a growing and dangerous intensity as he walks toward* EINSTEIN): You see, Doctor—you see what you've done to me. Even my own family—

EINSTEIN: Chonny—you're home—in this lovely house—(*To* AUNTS.) How often he tells me about Brooklyn—about this house—about his aunts that he lofes so much. (*To* JONATHAN.) They know you, Chonny. (*To* ABBY *as he leads her toward* JONATHAN.) You know it's Jonathan. Speak to him. Tell him so.

ABBY: Well—Jonathan—it's been a long time—what have you been doing all these years?

MARTHA: Yes, Jonathan, where have you been?

JONATHAN (*recovering his composure*): Oh, England, South Africa, Australia,—the last five years Chicago. Dr. Einstein and I were in business there together

ABBY: Oh, we were in Chicago for the World's Fair.

MARTHA (*for want of something to say*): Yes—we found Chicago awfully warm.

EINSTEIN: Yah—it got hot for us too.

JONATHAN (*turning on the charm as he crosses above* ABBY, *placing himself between the* AUNTS): Well, it's wonderful to be in Brooklyn again. And you—Abby—Martha you don't look a day older. Just as I remembered you—sweet—charming—hospitable. (The AUNTS *don't react too well to this charm.*) And dear Teddy—(*He indicates with his hand a lad of eight or ten.*)—did he get into politics? (*He turns to* EINSTEIN.) My little brother, Doctor, was determined to become President.

ABBY: Oh, Teddy's fine! Just fine! And Mortimer's well too.

JONATHAN (*a bit of a sneer*): I know about Mortimer. I've seen his picture at the head of his column. He's evidently fulfilled all the promise of his early nasty nature.

ABBY (*defensively*): We're very fond of Mortimer.

(*There is a slight pause. Then* MARTHA *speaks uneasily as she gestures toward door.*)

MARTHA: Well, Jonathan, it's very nice to have seen you again.

JONATHAN (*expanding*): Bless you, Aunt Martha. It's good to be home again.

(*The* AUNTS *look at each other with dismay.*)

ABBY: Well, Martha, we mustn't let what's on the stove boil over. (*She starts to kitchen, then sees* MARTHA *isn't following. She crosses back and tugs at* MARTHA, *then crosses toward kitchen again.*)

MARTHA: Yes. If you'll excuse us for a minute, Jonathan. Unless you're in a hurry to go somewhere.

(JONATHAN *looks at her balefully.* MARTHA *crosses around above table, takes bottle of wine and puts it back in sideboard, then exits with* ABBY. ABBY, *who has been waiting in kitchen doorway for* MARTHA, *closes door after them.*

EINSTEIN: Well, Chonny, where do we go from here? We got to think fast. The police. The police have got pictures of that face. I got to operate on you right away. We got to find some place for that—and we got to find a place for Mr. Spenalzo too.

JONATHAN: Don't waste any worry on that rat.

EINSTEIN: But, Chonny, we got a hot stiff on our hands.

JONATHAN (*flinging hat onto sofa*): Forget Mr. Spenalzo.

EINSTEIN: But you can't leave a dead body in the rumble seat. You shouldn't have killed him, Chonny. He's a nice fellow—he gives us a lift—and what happens?

JONATHAN (*remembering bitterly*): He said I looked like Boris Karloff! (*He starts for* EINSTEIN.) That's your work, Doctor. You did that to me!

EINSTEIN: Now, Chonny—we find a place somewhere—I fix you up quick!

JONATHAN: Tonight!

EINSTEIN: Chonny—I got to eat first. I'm hungry—I'm weak.

(*The* AUNTS *enter from kitchen.* MARTHA *remains in kitchen doorway.*)

ABBY: Jonathan—we're glad that you remembered us and took the trouble to come in and say "Hello." But you were never happy in this house and we were never happy while you were in it—so, we've just come in to say good-bye.

JONATHAN (*takes a menacing step toward* ABBY. *Then decides to try the "charm" again*): Aunt Abby, I can't say that your feelings toward me come as a surprise. I've spent a great many hours regretting the many heartaches I must have given you as a boy.

ABBY: You were quite a trial to us, Jonathan.

JONATHAN: But my great disappointment is for Dr. Einstein. (EINSTEIN *is a little surprised*.) I promised him that no matter how rushed we were in passing through Brooklyn, I'd take the time to bring him here for one of Aunt Martha's home-cooked dinners.

MARTHA: Oh . . .

ABBY: I'm sorry. I'm afraid there wouldn't be enough.

MARTHA: Abby, it's a pretty good-sized pot roast.

JONATHAN (*how wonderful*): Pot roast!

MARTHA: I think the least we can do is to—

JONATHAN: Thank you, Aunt Martha! We'll stay to dinner.

ABBY (*backing to kitchen door and not at all pleased*): Well, we'll hurry it along.

MARTHA: Yes! (*She exits into kitchen.*)

ABBY (*stopping in doorway*): Oh, Jonathan, if you want to freshen up —why don't you use the washroom in Grandfather's old laboratory?

JONATHAN (*crossing to her*): Is that still there?

ABBY: Oh, yes. Just as he left it. Well, I'll help Martha get things started —since we're all in a hurry. (*She exits into kitchen.*)

EINSTEIN: Well, we get a meal anyway.

JONATHAN (*above table*): Grandfather's laboratory! (*Looks upstairs.*) And just as it was. Doctor, a perfect operating room.

EINSTEIN: Too bad we can't use it.

JONATHAN: After you've finished with me—Why, we could make a fortune here. The laboratory—that large ward in the attic—ten beds, Doctor—and Brooklyn is crying for your talents.

EINSTEIN: Vy vork yourself up, Chonny? Anyway, for Brooklyn I think we're a year too late.

JONATHAN: You don't know this town, Doctor. Practically everybody in Brooklyn needs a new face.

EINSTEIN: But so many of the old faces are locked up.

JONATHAN: A very small percentage—and the boys in Brooklyn are famous for paying generously to stay out of jail.

EINSTEIN: Take it easy, Chonny. Your aunts—they don't want us here.

JONATHAN: We're here for dinner, aren't we?

EINSTEIN: Yah—but after dinner?

JONATHAN (*crossing up to sofa*): Leave it to me, Doctor. I'll handle it. Why, this house'll be our headquarters for years.

EINSTEIN (*a pretty picture*): Oh, that would be beautiful, Chonny! This nice quiet house. Those aunts of yours—what sweet ladies. I love them already. I get the bags, yah?

JONATHAN (*stopping him*): Doctor! We must wait until we're invited.

EINSTEIN: But you chust said that—

JONATHAN: We'll be invited.

EINSTEIN: And if they say no—?

JONATHAN: Doctor—two helpless old women? (*He sits on sofa.*)

EINSTEIN (*takes bottle flask from hip pocket and unscrews cork as he crosses to window-seat*): It's like comes true a beautiful dream— Only I hope you're not dreaming. (*He stretches out on window-seat, taking a swig from bottle.*) It's so peaceful.

JONATHAN (*stretched out on sofa*): That's what makes this house so perfect for us—it's so peaceful.

(TEDDY *enters from cellar, blows a terrific blast on his bugle, as* JONATHAN *backs up.* TEDDY *marches to stairs and on up to first landing, as the two* MEN *look at his tropical garb with some astonishment.*)

TEDDY: CHARGE! (*He rushes up the stairs and off.*)

(JONATHAN *watches him from foot of stairs.* EINSTEIN, *sitting on window-seat, takes a hasty swig from his flask as the curtain comes down on the word CHARGE!*)

ACT TWO

SCENE: *The same. Later that night.*

JONATHAN, *with an after-dinner cigar, is occupying armchair completely at his ease.* ABBY *and* MARTHA, *seated on window-seat, are giving him a nervous attention in the attitude of peo-*

ple who wish their guests would go home. EINSTEIN *is relaxed and happy. Dinner dishes have been cleared. There is a red cloth on table, with a saucer to serve as ash-tray for* JONATHAN. *The room is in order. All doors are closed, as are drapes over windows.*

JONTHAN: Yes, Aunties, those five years in Chicago were amongst the busiest and happiest of my life.

EINSTEIN: And from Chicago we go to South Bend, Indiana. (*He shakes his head as though he wishes they hadn't.*)

(JONATHAN *gives him a look.*)

JONATHAN: They wouldn't be interested in our experience in Indiana.

ABBY: Well, Jonathan, you've led a very interesting life, I'm sure—but we really shouldn't have allowed you to talk so late.

(*She starts to rise.* JONATHAN *seats her just by the tone of his voice.*)

JONATHAN: My meeting Dr. Einstein in London, I might say, changed the whole course of my life. You remember I had been in South Africa, in the diamond business—then Amsterdam, the diamond market. I wanted to go back to South Africa—and Dr. Einstein made it possible for me.

EINSTEIN: A good job, Chonny. (*To* AUNTS.) When we take off the bandages—his face look so different, the nurse had to introduce me.

JONATHAN: I loved that face. I still carry the picture with me. (*He produces snapshot-size picture from inside coat pocket, looks at it a moment, then hands it to* MARTHA. *She looks at it and hands it to* ABBY.)

ABBY: This looks more the way you used to look, but still I wouldn't know you.

JONATHAN: I think we'll go back to that face, Doctor.

EINSTEIN: Yah, it's safe now.

ABBY (*rising*): Well, I know you both want to get to—where you're going.

JONATHAN (*relaxing even more*): My dear aunts—I'm so full of that delicious dinner I'm unable to move a muscle.

EINSTEIN (*relaxing too*): Yah, it's nice here.

MARTHA (*rises*): After all—it's very late and—

(TEDDY *enters on balcony wearing his solar topee, carrying a book, open, and another topee.*)

TEDDY (*descending stairs*): I found it! I found it!

JONATHAN: What did you find, Teddy?

TEDDY: The story of my life—my biography. Here's the picture I was telling you about, General. (*He lays open book on table showing picture to* EINSTEIN.) Here we are, both of us. "President Roosevelt and General Goethals at Culebra Cut." That's me, General, and that's you.

(EINSTEIN *looks at picture.*)

EINSTEIN: My, how I've changed.

(TEDDY *looks at* EINSTEIN, *a little puzzled but makes adjustment.*)

TEDDY: Well, you see that picture hasn't been taken yet. We haven't even started work on Culebra Cut. We're still digging locks. And now, General, we will both go to Panama and inspect the new lock.

ABBY: No, Teddy—not to Panama.

EINSTEIN: We go some other time. Panama's a long way off.

TEDDY: Nonsense, it's just down in the cellar.

JONATHAN: The cellar?

MARTHA: We let him dig the Panama Canal in the cellar.

TEDDY (*severely*): General Goethals, as President of the United States, Commander-in-Chief of the Army and Navy and the man who gave you this job, I demand that you accompany me on the inspection of this new lock.

JONATHAN: Teddy! I think it's time you went to bed.

TEDDY: I beg your pardon! (*He puts on his pince-nez as he crosses.*) Who are you?

JONATHAN: I'm Woodrow Wilson. Go to bed.

TEDDY: No—you're not Wilson. But your face is familiar. Let me see— You're not anyone I know now. Perhaps later—on my hunting trip to Africa—yes, you look like someone I might meet in the jungle.

(JONATHAN *stiffens.* ABBY *crosses in front of* TEDDY, *getting between him and* JONATHAN.)

ABBY: It's your brother, Jonathan, dear.

MARTHA (*rising*): He's had his face changed.

TEDDY: So that's it—a nature faker!

ABBY: And perhaps you had better go to bed, Teddy—Jonathan and his friend have to go back to their hotel.

JONATHAN (*rising*): General Goethals, (*To* EINSTEIN.) inspect the canal.

EINSTEIN (*rising*): All right, Mr. President. We go to Panama.

TEDDY: Bully! Bully! (*He crosses to cellar door, opens it.*) Follow me, General. (TEDDY *taps solar topee in* EINSTEIN'S *hand, then taps his own head.*) It's down south you know. (*He exits downstairs.*)

(EINSTEIN *puts on topee, which is too large for him. Then turns in cellar doorway and speaks.*)

EINSTEIN: Well—bon voyage. (*He exits, closing door.*)

JONATHAN: Aunt Abby, I must correct your misapprehension. You spoke of our hotel. We have no hotel. We came directly here—

MARTHA: Well, there's a very nice little hotel just three blocks down the—

JONATHAN (*cutting her off*): Aunt Martha, this is my home.

ABBY: But, Jonathan, you can't stay here. We need our rooms.

JONATHAN: You need them?

ABBY: Yes, for our lodgers.

JONATHAN (*alarmed*): Are there lodgers in this house?

MARTHA: Well, not just now, but we plan to have some.

JONATHAN (*cutting her off again*): Then my old room is still free.

ABBY: But Jonathan, there's no place for Dr. Einstein.

JONATHAN (*crosses below table, drops cigar ashes into saucer*): He'll share the room with me.

ABBY: No, Jonathan, I'm afraid you can't stay here.

(JONATHAN *is below table. He grinds cigar out in saucer, then starts toward* AUNTS.)

JONATHAN: Dr. Einstein and I need a place to sleep. You remembered, this afternoon, that as a boy I could be disagreeable. It wouldn't be very pleasant for any of us if—

MARTHA: Perhaps we'd better let them stay here tonight—

ABBY: Well, just overnight, Jonathan.

JONATHAN: That's settled. Now, if you'll get my room ready—

MARTHA (*starting upstairs,* ABBY *following*): It only needs airing out.

ABBY: We keep it ready to show our lodgers. I think you and Dr. Einstein will find it comfortable.

(JONATHAN *follows them to first landing and leans on newel-post.* AUNTS *are on balcony.*)

JONATHAN: You have a most distinguished guest in Dr. Einstein. I'm afraid you don't appreciate his skill. But you will. In a few weeks you'll see me looking like a very different Jonathan.

MARTHA: He can't operate on you here.

JONATHAN (*ignoring*): When Dr. Einstein and I get organized—when we resume practice—Oh, I forgot to tell you. We're turning Grandfather's laboratory into an operating room. We expect to be quite busy.

ABBY: Jonathan, we will not let you turn this house into a hospital.

JONATHAN (*laughing*): A hospital—heavens no! It will be a beauty parlor.

(EINSTEIN *enters excitedly from cellar.*)

EINSTEIN: Hey, Chonny, down in the cellar—(*He sees* AUNTS *and stops.*)

JONATHAN: Dr. Einstein—my dear aunts have invited us to live with them.

EINSTEIN: Oh, you fixed it?

ABBY: Well, you're sleeping here tonight.

JONATHAN: Please get our room ready immediately.

MARTHA: Well—

ABBY: For tonight.

(*They exit through arch.* JONATHAN *comes to foot of stairs.*)

EINSTEIN: Chonny, when I go down in the cellar, what do you think I find?

JONATHAN: What?

EINSTEIN: The Panama Canal.

JONATHAN: The Panama Canal.

EINSTEIN: It just fits Mr. Spenalzo. It's a hole Teddy dug. Six feet long and four feet wide.

JONATHAN (*gets the idea. Opens cellar door and looks down*): Down there!

EINSTEIN: You'd think they knew we were bringing Mr. Spenalzo along. That's hospitality.

JONATHAN (*closing cellar door*): Rather a good joke on my aunts— their living in a house with a body buried in the cellar.

EINSTEIN: How do we get him in?

JONATHAN: Yes. We can't just walk him through the door. We'll drive the car up between the house and the cemetery—then when they've gone to *bed*, we'll bring Mr. Spenalzo in through the window.

EINSTEIN (*taking out bottle flask*): Bed! Just think, we've got a bed to-night! (*He starts swigging.*)

JONATHAN (*grabbing his arm*): Easy, Doctor. Remember you're operating tomorrow. And this time you'd better be sober.

EINSTEIN: I fix you up beautiful.

JONATHAN: And if you don't—(*Gives* EINSTEIN *shove to door.*)

ABBY (*she and* MARTHA *enter on balcony*): Jonathan! Your room is ready.

JONATHAN: Then you can go to bed. We're moving the car up behind the house.

MARTHA: It's all right where it is—until morning.

JONATHAN (EINSTEIN *has opened door*): I don't want to leave it in the street—that might be against the law. (*He exits.*)

(EINSTEIN *follows him out, closing door.* ABBY *and* MARTHA *start downstairs and reach below table.*)

MARTHA: Abby, what we going to do?

ABBY: Well, we're not going to let them stay more than one night in this house for one thing. What would the neighbors think? People coming in here with one face and going out with another.

MARTHA: What are we going to do about Mr. Hoskins?

ABBY (*crosses to window-seat.* MARTHA *follows*): Oh, Mr. Hoskins. It can't be very comfortable for him in there. And he's been so patient, the poor dear. Well, I think Teddy had better get Mr. Hoskins downstairs right away.

MARTHA (*adamant*): Abby—I will not invite Jonathan to the funeral services.

ABBY: Oh, no. We'll wait until they've gone to bed and then come down and hold the services.

(TEDDY *enters from cellar*.)

TEDDY: General Goethals was very pleased. He says the Canal is just the right size.

ABBY: Teddy! Teddy, there's been another Yellow Fever victim.

TEDDY (*takes off pince-nez*): Dear me—this will be a shock to the General.

MARTHA: Then we mustn't tell about it.

TEDDY (*crosses below* ABBY *to* MARTHA): But it's his department.

ABBY: No, we mustn't tell him, Teddy. It would just spoil his visit.

TEDDY: I'm sorry, Aunt Abby. It's out of my hands—he'll have to be told. Army regulations, you know.

ABBY: No, Teddy, we *must* keep it a secret.

MARTHA: Yes!

TEDDY (*he loves them*): A state secret?

ABBY: Yes, a state secret.

MARTHA: Promise?

TEDDY (*what a silly request*): You have the word of the President of the United States. Cross my heart and hope to die. (*He spits.*) Now let's see—(*Puts pince-nez on, then puts arms around both* AUNTS.) How are we going to keep it a secret?

ABBY: Well, Teddy, you go back down in the cellar and when I turn out the lights—when it's all dark—you come up and take the poor man down to the Canal. (*Urging him to cellar door, which he opens.*) Now go along, Teddy.

MARTHA: And we'll come down later and hold services.

TEDDY (*in doorway*): You may announce the President will say a few words. (*He starts, then turns back.*) Where is the poor devil?

MARTHA: He's in the window-seat.

TEDDY: It seems to be spreading. We've never had Yellow Fever there before. (*He exits, closing door.*)

ABBY: Martha, when Jonathan and Dr. Einstein come back, let's see if we can get them to go to bed right away.

MARTHA: Yes. Then by the time they're asleep, we'll be dressed for the funeral. (*Sudden thought.*) Abby, I've never even seen Mr. Hoskins.

ABBY: Oh, my goodness, that's right—you were out. Well, you just come right over and see him now. (*They go to window-seat,* ABBY *first.*) He's really very nice looking—considering he's a Methodist. (*As they go to lift window-seat,* JONATHAN *throws window open from outside with a bang.* AUNTS *scream and draw back.* JONATHAN *puts his head in through drapes.*)

JONATHAN: We're bringing—the luggage through here.

ABBY: Jonathan, your room's waiting for you. You can go right up.

(*Two dusty bags and a large instrument case are passed through window by* EINSTEIN. JONATHAN *puts them on floor.*)

JONATHAN: I'm afraid we don't keep Brooklyn hours—but you two run along to bed.

ABBY: Now, you must be very tired, both of you—and we don't go to bed this early.

JONATHAN: Well, you should. It's time I came home to take care of you.

MARTHA: We weren't planning to go until—

JONATHAN (*the master*): Aunt Martha, did you hear me say go to bed! (AUNT MARTHA *starts upstairs as* EINSTEIN *comes in through window and picks up two bags.* JONATHAN *takes instrument case and puts it near window-seat.*) The instruments can go to the laboratory in the morning. (EINSTEIN *starts upstairs.* JONATHAN *closes window.* MARTHA *is partway upstairs as* EINSTEIN *passes her.*) Now, then, we're all going to bed.

ABBY: I'll wait till you're up, then turn out the lights.

(JONATHAN, *going upstairs, sees* EINSTEIN *pausing at balcony door.* MARTHA *is almost up to balcony.*)

JONATHAN: Another flight, Doctor. (*To* MARTHA.) Run along, Aunt Martha. (MARTHA *hurries into doorway.* EINSTEIN *goes through arch to third floor.*) All right, Aunt Abby.

ABBY (*stalling. Looks toward cellar door*): I'll be right up.

JONATHAN: Now, Aunt Abby. (*Definite.*) Turn out the lights!

(ABBY *turns switch, plunging stage into darkness except for spot shining down stairway from arch.* ABBY *goes up stairs to her door where* MARTHA *is waiting. She takes a last frightened look at* JONATHAN *and exits.* MARTHA *closes door.* JONATHAN *goes off through arch, closing that door, blotting out the spot.* TEDDY *opens cellar door, then turns on cellar light, outlining him in the doorway. He crosses to window-seat and opens it—the window-seat cover giving out its usual rusty squeak. He reaches in and pulls Mr. Hoskins over his shoulder and, leaving window-seat open, crosses to cellar door and goes down into cellar with Mr. Hoskins. Closes door.* JONATHAN *and* EINSTEIN *come through arch. It is dark. They light matches and listen at the* AUNTS' *door for a moment.* EINSTEIN *speaks.*)

EINSTEIN: All right, Chonny.

(*The matches go out.* JONATHAN *lights another and they come down to foot of stairs.*)

JONATHAN: I'll get the window open. You go around and hand him through.

EINSTEIN: No, he's too heavy for me. You go outside and push—I stay here and pull. Then together we get him down to Panama.

JONATHAN: All right. (*He blows out match, crosses and opens door.*) I'll take a look around outside the house. When I tap on the glass, you open the window.

EINSTEIN: All right. (JONATHAN *exits, closing door.* EINSTEIN *lights match. He bumps into table and match goes out. He feels his way from there. We hear ejaculations and noise.* EINSTEIN *has fallen into window-seat. In window-seat he lights another match and slowly rises up to a sitting position and looks around. He blows out match and hauls himself out of window-seat, speaking.*) Who left dis open? Dummkopf! (*We hear the creak of the cover as he closes it. In the darkness we hear a tap on the window.* EINSTEIN *opens it. Then in a hushed voice.*) Chonny? O.K. Allez Oop. Wait—wait a minute. You lost a leg somewhere.—Ach—now I got him. Come on—ugh—(*He falls on floor and there is a crash of a body and the sound of a "Sshhhh" from outside.*) That was me, Chonny. I schlipped.

JONATHAN (*voice*): Be more careful.

(*Pause.*)

EINSTEIN: Well, his shoe came off. (*Pause.*) All right, Chonny. I got

him! (*There is a knock at the door.*) Chonny! Somebody at the door!
Go quick. NO. I manage here—go quick!

(*A second knock at door. A moment's silence and we hear the
creak of window-seat as* EINSTEIN *puts Mr. Spenalzo in Mr. Hoskins'
place. A third knock, as* EINSTEIN *struggles with body. A fourth
knock and then the creak of the window-seat as* EINSTEIN *closes it.
He scurries around to beside desk, keeping low to avoid being seen
through door.* ELAINE *enters, calling softly.*)

ELAINE: Miss Abby! Miss Martha! (*In the dim path of light she comes,
calling toward balcony.*) Miss Abby! Miss Martha! (*Suddenly*
JONATHAN *steps through door and closes it. The noise swings* ELAINE
around and she gasps.) Uhhh! Who is it? Is that you, Teddy? (*JON-
ATHAN comes toward her as she backs into chair.*) Who *are* you?

JONATHAN: Who are *you*?

ELAINE: I'm Elaine Harper—I live next door!

JONATHAN: Then what are you doing here?

ELAINE: I came over to see Miss Abby and Miss Martha.

JONATHAN (*to* EINSTEIN, *without turning.* EINSTEIN *has crept to light-
switch after* JONATHAN'S *cross*): Turn on the lights, Doctor. (*The
lights go on.* ELAINE *gasps as she sees* JONATHAN *and sits in chair.*
JONATHAN *looks at her for a moment.*) You chose rather an untimely
moment for a social call. (*He crosses toward window-seat, looking
for Spenalzo, but doesn't see him. He looks up, behind table. Looks
out window, then comes back into the room.*)

ELAINE (*trying to summon courage*): I think you'd better explain what
you're doing here.

JONATHAN: We happen to live here.

ELAINE:You *don't* live here. I'm in this house every day and I've never
seen you before. (*Frightened.*) Where are Miss Abby and Miss
Martha? What have you done to them?

JONATHAN (*a step to below table*): Perhaps we'd better introduce ourselves. This—(*Indicating.*)—is Dr. Einstein.

ELAINE (*looks at* EINSTEIN): Dr. Einstein? (*She turns back to*
JONATHAN. EINSTEIN, *behind her back, is gesturing to* JONATHAN *the
whereabouts of Spenalzo.*)

JONATHAN: A surgeon of great distinction—(*He looks under table for
Spenalzo, and not finding him*—)—and something of a magician.

ELAINE: And I suppose you're going to tell me you're Boris Kar—

JONATHAN: I'm Jonathan Brewster.

ELAINE (*drawing back almost with fright*): Oh—you're Jonathan!

JONATHAN: I see you've heard of me.

(EINSTEIN *drifts to front of sofa.*)

ELAINE: Yes—just this afternoon for the first time.

JONATHAN (*stepping toward her*): And what did they say about me?

ELAINE: Only that there was another brother named Jonathan—that's all that was said. (*Calming.*) Well, that explains everything. Now that I know who you are—(*Running to door.*) I'll be running along back home. (*The door is locked. She turns to* JONATHAN.) If you'll kindly unlock the door.

(JONATHAN *crosses to her, then, before reaching her, he unlocks door.* EINSTEIN *drifts down to chair. As* JONATHAN *opens door partway,* ELAINE *starts toward it. He turns and stops her with a gesture.*)

JONATHAN: "That explains everything?" Just what did you mean by that? Why did you come here at this time of night?

ELAINE: I thought I saw someone prowling around the house. I suppose it was you.

(JONATHAN *closes door and locks it, leaving key in lock.*)

JONATHAN: You thought you saw someone prowling around the house?

ELAINE: Yes—weren't you outside? Isn't that your car?

JONATHAN: You saw someone at the car?

ELAINE: Yes.

JONATHAN: What else did you see?

ELAINE: Just that—that's all. That's why I came over here. I wanted to tell Miss Abby to call the police. But if it was you, and that's your car, I don't need to bother Miss Abby. I'll be running along. (*She takes a step toward door above* JONATHAN. *He steps in her path.*)

JONATHAN: What was the man doing at the car?

ELAINE (*excited*): I don't know. You see I was on my way over here.

JONATHAN: I think you're lying.

EINSTEIN: I think she tells the truth, Chonny. We let her go now, huh?

JONATHAN: I think she's lying. Breaking into a house this time of night. I think she's dangerous. She shouldn't be allowed around loose.

(*He seizes* ELAINE'S *arm. She screams.*)

ELAINE: Take your hands off me—
JONATHAN: Doctor—

(TEDDY *enters from cellar, shutting door.*)

TEDDY (*simply*): It's going to be a private funeral. (*He goes up stairs to first landing.* ELAINE *crosses to desk, dragging* JONATHAN *with her.*)

ELAINE: Teddy! Teddy! Tell these men who I am.

(TEDDY *turns and looks at her.*)

TEDDY: That's my daughter—Alice. (*He cries "CHARGE!" Dashes up stairs and exits.*)

ELAINE (*struggling to get away from* JONATHAN): No! No! Teddy!

(JONATHAN *has* ELAINE'S *arm twisted in back of her, his other hand is over her mouth.*)

JONATHAN: Doctor! Your handkerchief! (*As* EINSTEIN *hands him a handkerchief,* JONATHAN *releases his hand from* ELAINE'S *mouth to take it. She screams. He puts his hand over her mouth again. Spies the cellar door and speaks to* EINSTEIN.) The cellar!

(EINSTEIN *runs and opens cellar door. Then he runs back and turns off lightswitch, putting stage in darkness.* JONATHAN *pushes* ELAINE *through cellar doorway.* EINSTEIN *runs back and down cellar stairs with* ELAINE. JONATHAN *shuts door, remaining on stage as the* AUNTS *enter on balcony above in their mourning clothes. Everything is in complete darkness except for street lamp.*)

ABBY: What's the matter?
MARTHA: What's happening down there?

(MARTHA *shuts her door and* ABBY *puts on lights from switch on balcony. They look down at the room a moment, then come downstairs, speaking as they come.*)

ABBY: What's the matter? (*Reaching foot of stairs as she sees* JONATHAN.) What are you doing?

JONATHAN: We caught a burglar—a sneak thief. Go back to your room.

ABBY: We'll call the police.

JONATHAN: We've called the police. We'll handle this. Go back to your room. Do you hear me?

(*The doorbell rings, followed by several knocks.* ABBY *runs and opens door.* MORTIMER *enters with suitcase. At the same time,* ELAINE *runs out of cellar and into* MORTIMER'S *arms.* JONATHAN *makes a grab for* ELAINE *but misses.* EINSTEIN *sneaks behind* JONATHAN.)

ELAINE: Mortimer! (*He drops suitcase.*) Where have you been?

MORTIMER: To the Nora Bayes Theatre and I should have known better. (*He sees* JONATHAN.) My God!—I'm still there.

ABBY: This is your brother Jonathan—and this is Dr. Einstein.

(MORTIMER *surveys his* AUNTS *all dressed in black.*)

MORTIMER: I know this isn't a nightmare, but what is it?

JONATHAN: I've come back home, Mortimer.

MORTIMER (*looking at him, and then to* ABBY): Who did you say this was?

ABBY: It's your brother Jonathan. He's had his face changed. Dr. Einstein performed the operation.

MORTIMER (*taking a closer look at* JONATHAN): Jonathan! Jonathan, you always were a horror, but do you have to look like one?

(JONATHAN *takes a step toward him.* EINSTEIN *pulls on his sleeve.* ELAINE *and* MARTHA *draw back to desk.*)

EINSTEIN: Easy, Chonny! Easy.

JONATHAN: Mortimer, have you forgotten the things I used to do to you when we were boys? Remember the time you were tied to the bedpost—the needles under your fingernails—?

MORTIMER: By God, it is Jonathan.—Yes, I remember. I remember you as the most detestable, vicious, venomous form of animal life I ever knew.

(JONATHAN *grows tense.* ABBY *steps between them.*)

ABBY: Now don't you two boys start quarrelling again the minute you've seen each other.

MORTIMER (*crosses to door, open it*): There won't be any fight, Aunt Abby. Jonathan, you're not wanted here—get out!

JONATHAN: Dr. Einstein and I have been invited to stay.

MORTIMER: Not in this house.

ABBY: Just for tonight.

MORTIMER: I don't want him anywhere near me.

ABBY: But we did invite them for tonight, and it wouldn't be very nice to go back on our word.

MORTIMER (*unwillingly*): All right, tonight. But the first thing in the morning—out! (*He picks up his suitcase.*) Where are they sleeping?

ABBY: We put them in Jonathan's old room.

MORTIMER: That's my old room. (*Starts upstairs.*) I'm sleeping in that room. I'm here to stay.

MARTHA: Oh, Mortimer, I'm so glad.

EINSTEIN: Chonny, we sleep down here.

MORTIMER: You bet your life you sleep down here.

EINSTEIN (*to* JONATHAN): You sleep on the sofa and I sleep on the window-seat.

(*At the mention of window-seat,* MORTIMER *has reached the landing; after hanging his hat on hall tree, he turns and comes slowly downstairs, speaking as he reaches the floor and crossing over to window-seat.*)

MORTIMER: The window-seat! Oh, well, let's not argue about it. That window-seat's good enough for me for tonight. I'll sleep on the window-seat. (*As* MORTIMER *crosses above table,* EINSTEIN *makes a gesture as though to stop him from going to window-seat, but he's too late. He turns to* JONATHAN *as* MORTIMER *sits on window-seat.*)

EINSTEIN: You know, Chonny—all this argument—it makes me think of Mr. Spenalzo.

JONATHAN: Spenalzo! (*He looks around for Spenalzo again. Realizing it would be best for them to remain downstairs, he speaks to* MORTIMER.) Well, now, Mortimer—It really isn't necessary to inconvenience you like this—we'll sleep down here.

MORTIMER (*rising*): Jonathan, your sudden consideration for me is very unconvincing.

EINSTEIN (*goes upstairs to landing*): Come along, Chonny. We get our things out of the room, eh?

MORTIMER: Don't bother, Doctor!

JONATHAN: By the way, Doctor, I've completely lost track of Mr. Spenalzo.

MORTIMER: Who's this Mr. Spenalzo?

EINSTEIN (*from landing*): Just a friend of ours Chonny's been looking for.

MORTIMER: Well, don't bring anyone else in here!

EINSTEIN: It's all right, Chonny. While we pack I tell you all about it. (*He goes up and through arch.* JONATHAN *starts upstairs.*)

ABBY: Mortimer, you don't have to sleep down here. I can go in with Martha and you can take my room.

JONATHAN (*he has reached the balcony*): No trouble at all, Aunt Abby. We'll be packed in a few minutes. And then you can have the room, Mortimer. (*He exits through arch.*)

(MORTIMER *crosses up to sofa.* MARTHA *crosses to armchair and as* MORTIMER *speaks she picks up sport shoe belonging to Spenalzo, that* EINSTEIN *put there in blackout scene, unnoticed by anyone. She pretends to dust hem of her dress.*)

MORTIMER: You're just wasting your time—I told you I'm sleeping down here.

(ELAINE *leaps up from stool into* MORTIMER'S *arms.*)

ELAINE: Mortimer!

MORTIMER: What's the matter with you, dear?

ELAINE (*semi-hysterical*): I've almost been killed.

MORTIMER: You've almost been—(*He looks quickly at the* AUNTS.) Abby! Martha!

MARTHA: No! It was Jonathan.

ABBY: He mistook her for a sneak-thief.

ELAINE: No, it was more than that. He's some kind of maniac. Mortimer, I'm afraid of him.

MORTIMER: Why, darling, you're trembling. (*Seats her on sofa. To* AUNTS.) Have you got any smelling salts?

MARTHA: No, but do you think some hot tea, or coffee—?

MORTIMER: Coffee. Make some for me, too—and some sandwiches. I haven't had any dinner.

MARTHA: We'll make something for both of you.

(MORTIMER *starts to question* ELAINE *as* ABBY *takes off her hat and gloves and puts them on sideboard. Talking to* MARTHA *at the same time.*)

ABBY: Martha, we can leave our hats downstairs here, now.

MORTIMER: You weren't going out somewhere, were you? Do you know what time it is? It's after twelve. (*The word twelve rings a bell.*) TWELVE! (*He turns to* ELAINE.) Elaine, you've got to go home!

ELAINE: Whaa-t?

ABBY: Why, you wanted some sandwiches for you both. It won't take a minute. (*She exits into kitchen.*)

(MORTIMER *is looking at* ELAINE *with his back to* MARTHA. MARTHA *crosses to him with shoe in hand.*)

MARTHA: Why, don't you remember—we wanted to celebrate your engagement? (*She punctuates the word "engagement" by pointing the shoe at* MORTIMER'S *back. She looks at the shoe in wonderment. Wondering how that shoe ever got in her hand. She stares at it a moment* (*the other two do not see it, of course*), *then puts it on top of the table. Finally dismissing it she turns to* MORTIMER *again.*) That's what we'll do, dear. We'll make a nice supper for both of you. (*She starts out kitchen door, then turns back.*) And we'll open a bottle of wine! (*She exits kitchen door.*)

MORTIMER (*vaguely*): All right. (*Suddenly changes his mind and runs to kitchen door.*) No WINE! (*He closes the door as* ELAINE *rises from the sofa to him. She is still very upset.*)

ELAINE: Mortimer! What's going on in this house?

MORTIMER (*suspicious*): What do you mean—what's going on in this house?

ELAINE: You were supposed to take me to dinner and the theatre tonight—you called it off. You asked me to marry you—I said I would—and five minutes later you threw me out of the house. To-night, just after your brother tries to strangle me, you want to chase me home. Now, listen, Mr. Brewster—before I go home, I want to know where I stand. Do you love me?

MORTIMER (*taking her hands*): I love you very much, Elaine. In fact I love you so much I can't marry you.

ELAINE: Have you suddenly gone crazy?

MORTIMER: I don't think so but it's just a matter of time. (*They both sit on sofa as* MORTIMER *begins to explain.*) You see, insanity runs in my family. (*He looks upstairs and toward kitchen.*) It practically gallops. That's why I can't marry you, dear.

ELAINE: Now wait a minute, you've got to do better than that.

MORTIMER: No, dear—there's a strange taint in the Brewster blood. If you really knew my family it's—well—it's what you'd expect if Strindberg had written *Hellzapoppin*.

ELAINE: Now just because Teddy is a little—

MORTIMER: No, it goes way back. The first Brewster—the one who came over on the Mayflower. You know in those days the Indians used to scalp the settlers—he used to scalp the Indians.

ELAINE: Mortimer, that's ancient history—

MORTIMER: No, the whole family . . . (*He rises and points to a picture of Grandfather over the sideboard.*) Take my grandfather—he tried his patent medicines out on dead people to be sure he wouldn't kill them.

ELAINE: He wasn't so crazy. He made a million dollars.

MORTIMER: And then there's Jonathan. You just said he was a maniac —he tried to kill you.

ELAINE (*rises, crosses to him*): But he's your brother, not you. I'm in love with you.

MORTIMER: And there's Teddy, too. You *know* Teddy. He thinks he's Roosevelt. No, dear, no Brewster should marry. I realize now that if I'd met my father in time I'd have stopped him.

ELAINE: Now, darling, all this doesn't prove *you're* crazy. Look at your aunts—they're Brewsters, aren't they?—and the sanest, sweetest people I've ever known.

(MORTIMER *crosses above table to window-seat, speaking as he goes.*)

MORTIMER: Well, even they have their peculiarities.

ELAINE: Yes, but what lovely peculiarities!—Kindness, generosity—
human sympathy—

(MORTIMER *sees* ELAINE'S *back is to him. He lifts window-seat to
take a peek, and sees Mr. Spenalzo instead of Mr. Hoskins. He puts
window-seat down again and staggers to table, and leans on it.*)

MORTIMER (*to himself*): There's another one!

ELAINE (*turning to* MORTIMER): Oh, Mortimer, there are plenty of
others. You can't tell me anything about your aunts.

MORTIMER: I'm not going to. (*Crossing to her.*) Look, Elaine, you've
got to go home. Something very important has just come up.

ELAINE: Up, from where? We're here alone together.

MORTIMER: I know I'm acting irrationally, but just put it down to the
fact that I'm a mad Brewster.

ELAINE: If you think you're going to get out of this by pretending
you're insane—you're crazy. Maybe you're not going to marry me,
but I'm going to marry you. I love you, you dope.

MORTIMER: Well, if you love me will you get the hell out of here!

ELAINE: Well, at least take me home, won't you, I'm afraid.

MORTIMER: Afraid! A little walk through the cemetery?

(ELAINE *crosses to door, then changing tactics, turns to*
MORTIMER.)

ELAINE: Mortimer, will you kiss me good night?

MORTIMER (*holding out arms*): Of course, dear. (*What* MORTIMER
plans to be a desultory peck, ELAINE *turns into a production number.
He comes out of it with no less of poise.*) Good night, dear. I'll call
you up in a day or two.

ELAINE (*turns to* MORTIMER): You—you critic! (*She slams door after
her.*)

(MORTIMER *looks at the door helplessly then turns and stalks to
the kitchen door.*)

MORTIMER (*in doorway*): Aunt Abby! Aunt Martha! Come in here!

ABBY (*offstage*): We'll be in a minute, dear.

MORTIMER: Come in here now!

(ABBY *enters from kitchen.*)

ABBY: Yes, dear, what is it? Where's Elaine?

MORTIMER: I thought you promised me not to let anyone in this house while I was gone!

(*The following speeches overlap.*)

ABBY: Well, Jonathan just walked in—

MORTIMER: I don't mean Jonathan—

ABBY: And Dr. Einstein was with him—

MORTIMER: I don't mean Dr. Einstein. Who's that in the window-seat?

ABBY: We told you—Mr. Hoskins.

(MORTIMER *throws open the window-seat.*)

MORTIMER: It is *not* Mr. Hoskins.

(ABBY, *a little puzzled, walks to window-seat and looks in, then speaks very simply.*)

ABBY: Who can that be?

MORTIMER: Are you trying to tell me you've never seen this man before?

ABBY: I certainly am. Why, this is a fine how do you do! It's getting so anybody thinks he can walk into this house.

MORTIMER: Now Aunt Abby, don't you try to get out of this. That's another one of your gentlemen!

ABBY: Mortimer, how can you say such a thing! That man's an impostor! And if he came here to be buried in our cellar he's mistaken.

MORTIMER: Oh, Aunt Abby, you admitted to me that you put Mr. Hoskins in the window-seat.

ABBY: Yes, I did.

MORTIMER: Well, this man couldn't have just got the idea from Mr. Hoskins. By the way—where is Mr. Hoskins? (*He looks toward cellar door.*)

(ABBY *crosses above table.*)

ABBY: He must have gone to Panama.

MORTIMER: Oh, you buried him?

ABBY: No, not yet. He's just down there waiting for the services, poor dear. We haven't had a minute what with Jonathan in the house. (*At the mention of* JONATHAN'S *name,* MORTIMER *closes the window-seat.*) Oh, dear. We've always wanted to hold a double funeral, (*Crossing to kitchen door.*) but I will not read services over a total stranger.

MORTIMER (*going up to her*): A stranger! Aunt Abby, how can I believe you? There are twelve men in the cellar and you admit you poisoned them.

ABBY: Yes, I did. But you don't think I'd stoop to telling a fib. Martha! (*She exits into kitchen.*)

(*At the same time* JONATHAN *enters through the arch onto balcony and comes down quickly to foot of stairs.*)

JONATHAN: Oh, Mortimer—I'd like to have a word with you.

MORTIMER (*standing up to him*): A word's about all you'll have time for, Jonathan, because I've decided you and your Doctor friend are going to have to get out of this house just as quickly as possible.

JONATHAN (*smoothly*): I'm glad you recognize the fact you and I can't live under the same roof—but you've arrived at the wrong solution. Take your suitcase and get out! (*He starts to cross above* MORTIMER, *anxious to get to the window-seat, but* MORTIMER *makes big sweep around above table and comes back to him.*)

MORTIMER: Jonathan!—You're beginning to bore me. You've played your one night stand in Brooklyn—move on!

JONATHAN: My dear Mortimer, just because you've graduated from the back fence to the typewriter, don't think you've grown up. . . . (*He takes a sudden step around* MORTIMER *and gets to the window-seat and sits.*) I'm staying, and you're leaving—and I mean now!

MORTIMER (*crossing to him*): If you think I can be frightened—if you think there's anything I fear—

JONATHAN (*he rises, they stand facing each other*): I've lived a strange life, Mortimer. But it's taught me one thing—to be afraid of nothing! (*They glare at each other with equal courage when* ABBY *marches in from the kitchen, followed by* MARTHA.)

ABBY: Martha, just look and see what's in that window-seat.

(*Both* MEN *throw themselves on the window-seat simultaneously.*

MORTIMER *and* JONATHAN: Now, Aunt Abby!

(MORTIMER *turns his head slowly to* JONATHAN, *light dawning on his face. He rises with smiling assurance.*)

MORTIMER: Jonathan, let Aunt Martha see what's in the window-seat (JONATHAN *freezes dangerously.* MORTIMER *crosses below table up to* ABBY.) Aunt Abby, I owe you an apology. (*He kisses her on forehead.*) I have very good news for you. Jonathan is leaving. He's taking Dr. Einstein and their cold companion with him. (JONATHAN *rises but holds his ground.*) Jonathan, you're my brother. You're a Brewster. I'm going to give you a chance to get away and take the evidence with you—you can't ask for more than that. (JONATHAN *doesn't move.*) Very well,—in that case I'll have to call the police. (MORTIMER *crosses to phone and picks it up.*)

JONATHAN: Don't reach for that telephone. Are you still giving me orders after seeing what's happened to Mr. Spenalzo?

MARTHA (*she's above table*): Spenalzo?

ABBY: I knew he was a foreigner.

JONATHAN: Remember what happened to Mr. Spenalzo can happen to you too.

(*There is a knock on door.* ABBY *crosses and opens it and* OFFICER O'HARA *sticks his head in.*)

O'HARA: Hello, Miss Abby.

ABBY: Oh, Officer O'Hara. Is there something we can do for you?

(MORTIMER *puts phone down and drifts down close to* O'HARA.)

O'HARA: I saw your lights on and thought there might be sickness in the house. (*He sees* MORTIMER.) Oh, you got company—I'm sorry I disturbed you.

MORTIMER (*taking* O'HARA *by the arm*): No, no, come in.

ABBY: Yes, come in.

MARTHA (*crossing to door*): Come right in, Officer O'Hara. (MORTIMER *leads* O'HARA *in a couple of steps and shuts door.*) This is our nephew, Mortimer.

O'HARA: Pleased to meet you.

(JONATHAN *starts toward kitchen.*)

ABBY (*stopping* JONATHAN): And this is another nephew, Jonathan.

O'HARA (*crosses below* MORTIMER *and gestures to* JONATHAN *with his night stick*): Pleased to make your acquaintance. (JONATHAN ignores *him.* O'HARA *speaks to* AUNTS.) Well, it must be nice havin' your nephews visitin' you. Are they going to stay with you for a bit?

MORTIMER: I'm staying. My brother Jonathan is just leaving.

(JONATHAN *starts for stairs.* O'HARA *stops him.*)

O'HARA: I've met you here before, haven't I?

ABBY: I'm afraid not. Jonathan hasn't been home for years.

O'HARA: Your face looks familiar to me. Maybe I seen a picture of you somewheres.

JONATHAN: I don't think so. (*He hurries up stairs.*)

MORTIMER: Yes, Jonathan, I'd hurry if I were you. Your things are all packed anyway, aren't they?

O'HARA: Well, you'll be wanting to say your good-byes. I'll be running along.

MORTIMER: What's the rush? I'd like to have you stick around until my brother goes.

(JONATHAN *exits through arch.*)

O'HARA: I just dropped in to make sure everything was all right.

MORTIMER: We're going to have some coffee in a minute. Won't you join us?

ABBY: Oh, I forgot the coffee. (*She goes out to kitchen.*)

MARTHA (*crossing to kitchen door*): Well, I'd better make some more sandwiches. I ought to know your appetite by this time, Officer O'Hara. (*She goes out to kitchen.*)

O'HARA: Don't bother. I'm due to ring in in a few minutes.

MORTIMER: You can have a cup of coffee with us. My brother will be gone soon. (*He leads* O'HARA *below table to armchair.*) Sit down.

O'HARA: Say—ain't I seen a photograph of your brother around here some place?

MORTIMER: I don't think so.

O'HARA: He certainly reminds me of somebody.

MORTIMER: He looks like somebody you've probably seen in the movies.

O'HARA: I never go to the movies. I hate 'em! My mother says the movies is a bastard art.

MORTIMER: Yes, it's full of them.—Your, er, mother said that?

O'HARA: Yeah. My mother was an actress—a stage actress. Perhaps you heard of her—Peaches Latour.

MORTIMER: It sounds like a name I've seen on a program. What did she play?

O'HARA: Well, her big hit was "Mutt and Jeff." Played it for three years. I was born on tour—the third season.

MORTIMER: You were?

O'HARA: Yep. Sioux City, Iowa. I was born in the dressing room at the end of the second act, and Mother made the finale.

MORTIMER: What a trouper! There must be a good story in your mother—you know, I write about the theatre.

O'HARA: You do? Say!—you're not Mortimer Brewster, the dramatic critic!

MORTIMER: Yes.

O'HARA: Well, I certainly am glad to meet you. (*He moves his hat and stick preparatory to shaking hands with* MORTIMER. *He also picks up the sport shoe which* MARTHA *has left on the table. He looks at it just for a split second and puts it on the table.* MORTIMER *sees it and stares at it.*) Say, Mr. Brewster—we're in the same line of business.

MORTIMER (*still intent on shoe*): We are?

O'HARA: Yeah. I'm a playwright. Oh, this being on the police force is just temporary.

MORTIMER: How long have you been on the force?

O'HARA: Twelve years. I'm collecting material for a play.

MORTIMER: I'll bet it's a honey.

O'HARA: Well, it ought to be. With all the drama I see being a cop. Mr. Brewster—you got no idea what goes on in Brooklyn.

MORTIMER: I think I have. (*He puts the shoe under his chair, then looks at his watch, then looks toward balcony.*)

O'HARA: Say, what time you got?

MORTIMER: Ten after one.

O'HARA: Gee, I gotta ring in. (*He starts for door but* MORTIMER *stops him.*)

MORTIMER: Wait a minute, O'Hara. On that play of yours—I may be able to help you. (*Sits him in chair.*)

O'HARA (*ecstasy*): You would! (*Rises.*) Say, it was fate my walking in here tonight. Look—I'll tell you the plot!

(*At this point* JONATHAN *enters on the balcony followed by* DR. EINSTEIN. *They each have a bag. At the same moment* ABBY *enters from the kitchen. Helpful as the cop has been,* MORTIMER *does not want to listen to his plot. As he backs away from him he speaks to* JONATHAN *as they come down stairs.*)

MORTIMER: Oh, you're on your way, eh? Good! You haven't got much time, you know.

ABBY: Well, everything's just about ready. (*Sees* JONATHAN *and* EINSTEIN *at foot of stairs.*) Oh, you leaving now, Jonathan? Good-bye. Good-bye, Dr. Einstein. (*She sees instrument case above window-seat.*) Oh, docsn't this case belong to you?

(*This reminds* MORTIMER *of Mr. Spenalzo, also.*)

MORTIMER: Yes, Jonathan—you can't go without *all* your things. (*Now to get rid of* O'HARA. *He turns to him.*) Well, O'Hara, it was nice meeting you. I'll see you again and we'll talk about your play.

O'HARA (*refusing to leave*): Oh, I'm not leaving now, Mr. Brewster.

MORTIMER: Why not?

O'HARA: Well, you just offered to help me with my play, didn't you? You and me are going to write my play together.

MORTIMER: I can't do that, O'Hara—I'm not a creative writer.

O'HARA: I'll do the creating. You just put the words to it.

MORTIMER: But O'Hara—

HARA: No, sir, Mr. Brewster. I ain't leaving this house till I tell you the plot.

(*He crosses and sits on window-seat.*)

JONTHAN: In that case, Mortimer . . . we'll be running along.

MORTIMER: Don't try that. You can't go yet. You've got to take *every-thing* with you, you know. (*He turns and sees* O'HARA *on window-seat and runs to him.*) Look, O'Hara, you run along now, eh? My brother's just going—

O'HARA: I can wait. I've been waiting twelve years.

(MARTHA *enters from kitchen with a tray of coffee and sand-wiches.*)

MARTHA: I'm sorry I was so long.

MORTIMER: Don't bring that in here. O'Hara, would you join us for a bite in the kitchen?

MARTHA: The kitchen?

ABBY (*to* MARTHA): Jonathan's leaving.

MARTHA: Oh. Well, that's nice. Come along, Officer O'Hara. (*She exits to kitchen.*)

(O'HARA *gets to kitchen doorway as* ABBY *speaks.*)

ABBY: Sure you don't mind eating in the kitchen, Mr. O'Hara?

O'HARA: And where else would you eat?

ABBY: Good-bye, Jonathan, nice to have seen you again.

(O'HARA *exits to kitchen, followed by* ABBY. MORTIMER *crosses to kitchen doorway and shuts door, then turns to* JONATHAN.

MORTIMER: I'm glad you came back to Brooklyn, Jonathan, because it gives me a chance to throw you out—and the first one out is your boy friend, Mr. Spenalzo. (*He lifts up window-seat. As he does so,* O'HARA, *sandwich in hand, enters from kitchen.* MORTIMER *drops window-seat.*)

O'HARA: Look, Mr. Brewster, we can talk in here.

MORTIMER (*pushing him into kitchen*): Coming right out.

JONATHAN: I might have known you'd grow up to write a play with a policeman.

MORTIMER (*from kitchen doorway*): Get going now—all three of you. (*He exits, shutting door.*)

(JONATHAN *puts bag down and crosses to window-seat.*)

JONATHAN: Doctor, this affair between my brother and me has got to be settled.

EINSTEIN (*crossing to window-seat for instrument case and bringing it back to foot of stairs*): Now, Chonny, we got trouble enough. Your brother gives us a chance to get away—what more could you ask?

JONATHAN: You don't understand. (*He lifts window-seat.*) This goes back a good many years.

EINSTEIN (*foot of stairs*): Now, Chonny, let's get going.

JONATHAN (*harshly*): We're not going. We're going to sleep right here tonight.

EINSTEIN: With a cop in the kitchen and Mr. Spenalzo in the window-seat.

JONATHAN: That's all he's got on us. (*Puts window-seat down.*) We'll take Mr. Spenalzo down and dump him in the bay, and come right back here.—Then if he tries to interfere—

EINSTEIN: Now, Chonny.

JONATHAN: Doctor, you know when I make up my mind—

EINSTEIN: Yeah—when you make up your mind, you lose your head. Brooklyn ain't a good place for you.

JONATHAN (*peremptorily*): Doctor!

EINSTEIN: O.K. We got to stick together. (*He crosses to bags.*) Some day we get stuck together. If we're coming back here do we got to take these with us?

JONATHAN: No. Leave them here. Hide them in the cellar. Move fast! (*He moves to bags as* EINSTEIN *goes down cellar with instrument case.*) Spenalzo can go out the same way he came in! (*He kneels on window-seat and looks out. Then as he starts to lift window-seat,* EINSTEIN *comes in from the cellar with some excitement.*)

EINSTEIN: Hey, Chonny, come quick!

JONATHAN (*crossing to him*): What's the matter?

EINSTEIN: You know that hole in the cellar?

JONATHAN: Yes.

EINSTEIN: We got an *ace* in the hole. Come on I show you. (*They both exit into cellar.* JONATHAN *shuts door.*)

(MORTIMER *enters from kitchen, sees their bags still there. He opens window-seat and sees Spenalzo. Then he puts his head out window and yells.*)

MORTIMER: Jonathan! Jonathan! (JONATHAN *comes through cellar door unnoticed by* MORTIMER *and crosses to back of him.* EINSTEIN *comes down.*) Jonathan!

JONATHAN (*quietly*): Yes, Mortimer.

MORTIMER (*leaping backwards to below table*): Where have you two been? I thought I told you to get—

JONATHAN: We're not going.

MORTIMER: Oh, you're not? You think I'm not serious about this, eh? Do you want O'Hara to know what's in that window-seat?

JONATHAN: We're staying here.

MORTIMER (*crossing around above table to kitchen door*): All right! You asked for it. This gets me rid of you and Officer O'Hara at the same time. (*Opens kitchen door, yells out.*) Officer O'Hara, come in here!

JONATHAN: If you tell O'Hara what's in the window-seat, I'll tell him what's down in the cellar.

(MORTIMER *closes kitchen door quickly.*)

MORTIMER: The cellar?

JONATHAN: There's an elderly gentleman down there who seems to be very dead.

MORTIMER: What were you doing down in the cellar?

EINSTEIN: What's *he* doing down in the cellar?

(O'HARA'S *voice is heard offstage.*)

O'HARA: No, thanks, ma'am. They were fine. I've had plenty.

JONATHAN: Now what are you going to say to O'Hara?

(O'HARA *walks in kitchen door.*)

O'HARA: Say, Mr. Brewster, your aunts want to hear it too. Shall I get them in here?

MORTIMER: No, O'Hara, you can't do that now. You've got to ring in.

(O'HARA *stops as* MORTIMER *opens the door.*)

O'HARA: The hell with ringing in. I'll get your aunts in here and tell you the plot.

(*He starts for kitchen door.*)

MORTIMER (*grabbing him*): No, O'Hara, not in front of all these people. We'll get together alone, some place later.

O'HARA: How about the back room at Kelly's?

MORTIMER: Fine! You go ring in, and I'll meet you at Kelly's.

JONATHAN (*at window-seat*): Why don't you two go down in the cellar?

MORTIMER (*grabbing him again, pushing toward door*): Nooo! We'll go to Kelly's. But you're going to ring in on the way.

O'HARA (*as he exits*): All right, that'll only take a couple of minutes. (*He's gone.*) (MORTIMER *takes his hat from hall tree and crosses to open door.*)

MORTIMER: I'll ditch this guy and be back in five minutes. I'll expect to find you gone. (*Changes his mind.*) Wait for me.

(*He exits.*)

JONATHAN: We'll wait for him, Doctor. I've waited a great many years for a chance like this.

EINSTEIN: We got him right where we want him. Did he look guilty!

JONATHAN (*rising*): Take the bags back up to our room, Doctor.

(EINSTEIN *gets bags and reaches foot of stairs with them.* ABBY *and* MARTHA *enter from kitchen.* ABBY *speaks as she enters.*)

ABBY: Have they gone? (*Sees* JONATHAN *and* EINSTEIN.) Oh—we thought we heard somebody leave.

JONATHAN: Just Mortimer, and he'll be back in a few minutes. Is there any food left in the kitchen? I think Dr. Einstein and I would enjoy a bite.

MARTHA: But you won't have time.

ABBY: No, if you're still here when Mortimer gets back he won't like it.

EINSTEIN: He'll like it. He's gotta like it.

JONATHAN: Get something for us to eat while we bury Mr. Spenalzo in the cellar.

MARTHA (*crossing to below table*): Oh no!

ABBY: He can't stay in our cellar. No, Jonathan, you've got to take him with you.

JONATHAN: There's a friend of Mortimer's downstairs waiting for him.

ABBY: A friend of Mortimer's?

JONATHAN: He and Mr. Spenalzo will get along fine together. They're both dead.

MARTHA: They must mean Mr. Hoskins.

EINSTEIN: Mr. Hoskins?

JONATHAN: You know about what's downstairs?

ABBY: Of course we do, and he's no friend of Mortimer's. He's one of our gentlemen.

EINSTEIN: Your chentlemen?

MARTHA: And we won't have any strangers buried in our cellar.

JONATHAN (*noncomprehending*): But Mr. Hoskins—

MARTHA: Mr. Hoskins isn't a stranger.

ABBY: Besides, there's no room for Mr. Spenalzo. The cellar's crowded already.

JONATHAN: Crowded? With what?

ABBY: There are twelve graves down there now.

(*The two* MEN *draw back in amazement.*)

JONATHAN: Twelve graves!

ABBY: That leaves very little room and we're going to need it.

JONATHAN: You mean you and Aunt Martha have murdered—?

ABBY: Murdered! Certainly not. It's one of our charities.

MARTHA (*indignantly*): Why, what we've been doing is a mercy.

ABBY (*gesturing outside*): So you just take your Mr. Spenalzo out of here.

JONATHAN (*still unable to believe*): You've done that—here in this house—(*Points to floor*) and you've buried them down there!

EINSTEIN: Chonny—we've been chased all over the world—they stay right here in Brooklyn and do just as good as you do.

JONATHAN (*facing him*): What?

EINSTEIN: You've got twelve and they've got twelve.

JONATHAN (*slowly*): I've got thirteen.

EINSTEIN: No, Chonny, twelve.

JONATHAN: Thirteen! (*Counting on fingers.*) There's Mr. Spenalzo. Then the first one in London—two in Johannesburg—one in Sydney —one in Melbourne—two in San Francisco—one in Phoenix, Arizona—

EINSTEIN: Phoenix?

JONATHAN: The filling station. The three in Chicago and the one in South Bend. That makes thirteen!

EINSTEIN: But you can't count the one in South Bend. He died of pneumonia.

JONATHAN: He wouldn't have got pneumonia if I hadn't shot him.

EINSTEIN (*adamant*): No, Chonny, he died of pneumonia. He don't count.

JONATHAN: He counts with me. I say thirteen.

EINSTEIN: No, Chonny. You got twelve and they got twelve. (*Crossing to* AUNTS.) The old ladies are just as good as you are. (*The two* AUNTS *smile at each other happily.* JONATHAN *turns, facing the three of them and speaks menacingly.*)

JONATHAN: Oh, they are, are they? Well, that's easily taken care of. All I need is one more, that's all—just one more.

(MORTIMER *enters, closing door behind him, and turns to them with a nervous smile.*)

MORTIMER: Well, here I am!

(JONATHAN *turns and looks at him with the widening eyes of someone who has just solved a problem, as the curtain falls.*)

ACT THREE

SCENE I

The scene is the same. Still later that night. The curtain rises on an empty stage. The window-seat is open and we see that it's empty. The drapes over the windows are closed. All doors except cellar are closed. ABBY'S *hymnal and black gloves are on sideboard.* MARTHA'S *hymnal and gloves are on table. Otherwise the room is the same. As the curtain rises we hear a row from the cellar, through the open door. The speeches overlap in excitement and anger until the* AUNTS *appear on the stage, from cellar door.*

MARTHA: You stop doing that!

ABBY: This is our house and this is our cellar and you can't do that.

EINSTEIN: Ladies! Please!—Go back upstairs where you belong.

JONATHAN: Abby! Martha! Go upstairs!

MARTHA: There's no use your doing what you're doing because it will just have to be undone.

ABBY: I tell you we won't have it and you'd better stop it right now.

MARTHA (*entering from cellar*): All right! You'll find out. You'll find out whose house this is. (*She crosses to door, opens it and looks out. Then closes it.*)

ABBY (*entering*): I'm warning you! You'd better stop it! (*To* MARTHA.) Hasn't Mortimer come back yet?

MARTHA: No.

ABBY: It's a terrible thing to do—to bury a good Methodist with a foreigner. (*She crosses to window-seat.*)

MARTHA (*crossing to cellar door*): I will not have our cellar desecrated!

ABBY (*drops window-seat*): And we promised Mr. Hoskins a full Christian funeral. Where do you suppose Mortimer went?

MARTHA: I don't know, but he must be doing something—because he said to Jonathan, "You just wait, I'll settle this."

ABBY (*crossing up to sideboard*): Well, he can't very well settle it while he's out of the house. That's all we want settled—what's going on down there.

(MORTIMER *enters, closes door.*)

MORTIMER (*as one who has everything settled*): All right. Now, where's Teddy?

(*The* AUNTS *are very much annoyed with* MORTIMER.)

ABBY: Mortimer, where have you been?

MORTIMER: I've been over to Dr. Gilchrist's. I've got his signature on Teddy's commitment papers.

MARTHA: Mortimer, what is the matter with you?

ABBY (*to below table*): Running around getting papers signed at a time like this!

MARTHA: Do you know what Jonathan's doing?

ABBY: He's putting Mr. Hoskins and Mr. Spenalzo in together.

MORTIMER (*to cellar door*): Oh, he is, is he? Well, let him. (*He shuts cellar door.*) Is Teddy in his room?

MARTHA: Teddy won't be any help.

MORTIMER: When he signs these commitment papers I can tackle Jonathan.

ABBY: What have they got to do with it?

MORTIMER: You had to go and tell Jonathan about those twelve graves. If I can make Teddy responsible for those I can protect you, don't you see?

ABBY: No, I don't see. And we pay taxes to have the police protect us.

MORTIMER (*going upstairs*): I'll be back down in a minute.

ABBY (*takes gloves and hymnal from table*): Come, Martha. We're going for the police.

(MARTHA *gets her gloves and hymnal from sideboard. They both start toward the door.*)

MORTIMER (*on landing*): All right. (*He turns and rushes downstairs to door before they can reach it.*) The police. You can't go for the police.

MARTHA: Why can't we?

MORTIMER: Because if you tell the police about Mr. Spenalzo they'd find Mr. Hoskins, too, (*Crosses to* MARTHA.) and that might make them curious, and they'd find out about the other twelve gentlemen.

ABBY: Mortimer, we know the police better than you do. I don't think they'd pry into our private affairs if we asked them not to.

MORTIMER: But if they found your twelve gentlemen they'd have to report to headquarters.

MARTHA (*pulling on her gloves*): I'm not so sure they'd bother. They'd have to make out a very long report—and if there's one thing a policeman hates to do, it's to write.

MORTIMER: You can't depend on that. It might leak out!—and you couldn't expect a judge and jury to understand.

MARTHA: Oh, Judge Cullman would.

ABBY (*drawing on her gloves*): We know him very well.

MARTHA: He always comes to church to pray—just before election.

ABBY: And he's coming here to tea some day. He promised.

MARTHA: Oh, Abby, we must speak to him again about that. (*To*

MORTIMER.) His wife died a few years ago and it's left him very lonely.

ABBY: Well, come along, Martha. (*She starts toward door.* MORTIMER *gets there first.*)

MORTIMER: No! You can't do this. I won't let you. You can't leave this house, and you can't have Judge Cullman to tea.

ABBY: Well, if you're not going to do something about Mr. Spenalzo, we are.

MORTIMER: I am going to do something. We may have to call the police in later, but if we do, I want to be ready for them.

MARTHA: You've got to get Jonathan out of this house!

ABBY: And Mr. Spenalzo, too!

MORTIMER: Will you please let me do this my own way? (*He starts upstairs.*) I've got to see Teddy.

ABBY (*facing* MORTIMER *on stairs*): If they're not out of here by morning, Mortimer, we're going to call the police.

MORTIMER (*on balcony*): They'll be out, I promise you that! Go to bed, will you? And for God's sake get out of those clothes—you look like Judith Anderson. (*He exits into hall, closing door.*)

(*The* AUNTS *watch him off.* MARTHA *turns to* ABBY.)

MARTHA: Well, Abby, that's a relief, isn't it?

ABBY: Yes—if Mortimer's going to do something at last, it just means Jonathan's going to a lot of unnecessary trouble. We'd better tell him. (ABBY *starts to cellar door as* JONATHAN *comes in. His clothes are dirty.*) Oh, Jonathan—you might as well stop what you're doing.

JONATHAN: *It's all done.* Did I hear Mortimer?

ABBY: Well, it will just have to be undone. You're all going to be out of this house by morning. Mortimer's promised.

JONATHAN: Oh, are we? In that case, you and Aunt Martha can go to bed and have a pleasant night's sleep.

MARTHA (*always a little frightened by* JONATHAN, *starts upstairs*): Yes. Come, Abby.

(ABBY *follows* MARTHA *upstairs.*)

JONATHAN: Good night, Aunties.

ABBY: Not good night, Jonathan. Good-bye. By the time we get up you'll be out of this house. Mortimer's promised.

MARTHA (*on balcony*): And he has a way of doing it too!

JONATHAN: Then Mortimer is back?

ABBY: Oh, yes, he's up here talking to Teddy.

MARTHA: Good-bye, Jonathan.

ABBY: Good-bye, Jonathan.

JONATHAN: Perhaps you'd better say good-bye to Mortimer.

ABBY: Oh, you'll see Mortimer.

JONATHAN (*sitting on stool*): Yes—I'll see Mortimer.

(ABBY *and* MARTHA *exit.* JONATHAN *sits without moving. There is murder in his thought.* EINSTEIN *enters from cellar. He dusts off his trouser cuffs, lifting his leg, and we see he is wearing Spenalzo's sport shoes.*)

EINSTEIN: Whew! That's all fixed up. Smooth like a lake. Nobody'd ever know they were down there. (JONATHAN *still sits without moving.*) That bed feels good already. Forty-eight hours we didn't sleep. (*Crossing to second chair.*) Come on, Chonny, let's go up, yes?

JONATHAN: You're forgetting, Doctor.

EINSTEIN: Vat?

JONATHAN: My brother Mortimer.

EINSTEIN: Chonny—tonight? We do that tomorrow or the next day.

JONATHAN (*just able to control himself*): No, tonight! Now!

EINSTEIN (*down to floor*): Chonny, please—I'm tired—and tomorrow I got to operate.

JONATHAN: Yes, you're operating tomorrow, Doctor. But tonight we take care of Mortimer.

EINSTEIN (*kneeling in front of* JONATHAN, *trying to passify him*): But, Chonny, not tonight—we go to bed, eh?

JONATHAN (*rising.* EINSTEIN *straightens up too.*): Doctor, look at me. You can see it's going to be done, can't you?

EINSTEIN (*retreating*): Ach, Chonny—I can see. I know dat look!

JONATHAN: It's a little too late for us to dissolve our partnership.

EINSTEIN: O.K., we do it. But the quick way. The quick twist like in London. (*He gives that London neck another twist with his hands and makes a noise suggesting strangulation.*)

JONATHAN: No, Doctor, I think this calls for something special. I think perhaps the Melbourne method.

EINSTEIN: Chonny—no—not that. Two hours! And when it was all over, what? The fellow in London was just as dead as the fellow in Melbourne.

JONATHAN: We had to work too fast in London. There was no esthetic satisfaction in it—but Melbourne, ah, there was something to remember.

EINSTEIN: Remember! (*He shivers.*) I vish I didn't. No, Chonny—not Melbourne—not me!

JONATHAN: Yes, Doctor. Where are the instruments?

EINSTEIN: I won't do it, Chonny—I won't do it.

JONATHAN (*advancing on him*): Get your instruments!

EINSTEIN: No, Chonny!

JONATHAN: Where are they? Oh, yes—you hid them in the cellar. Where?

EINSTEIN: I won't tell you.

JONATHAN (*going to cellar door*): I'll find them, Doctor. (*He exits to cellar, closing door.*)

(TEDDY *enters on balcony and lifts his bugle to blow.* MORTIMER *dashes out and grabs his arm.* EINSTEIN *has rushed to cellar door. He stands there as* MORTIMER *and* TEDDY *speak.*)

MORTIMER: Don't do that, Mr. President.

TEDDY: I cannot sign any proclamation without consulting my cabinet.

MORTIMER: But this must be a secret.

TEDDY: A secret proclamation? How unusual.

MORTIMER: Japan mustn't know until it's signed.

TEDDY: Japan! Those yellow devils. I'll sign it right away. (*Taking legal paper from* MORTIMER.) You have my word for it. I can let the cabinet know later.

MORTIMER: Yes, let's go and sign it.

TEDDY: You wait here. A secret proclamation has to be signed in secret.

MORTIMER: But at once, Mr. President.

TEDDY: I'll have to put on my signing clothes. (TEDDY *exits.*)

(MORTIMER *comes downstairs.* EINSTEIN *crosses and takes* MORTIMER'S *hat off of hall tree and hands it to him.*)

EINSTEIN (*anxious to get* MORTIMER *out of the house*): Ah, you go now, eh?

MORTIMER (*takes hat and puts it on desk*): No, Doctor, I'm waiting for something. Something important.

EINSTEIN: Please—you go now!

MORTIMER: Dr. Einstein, I have nothing against you personally. You seem to be a nice fellow. Take my advice and get out of this house and get just as far away as possible.

EINSTEIN: Trouble, yah! You get out.

MORTIMER: All right, don't say I didn't warn you.

EINSTEIN: I'm warning you—get away quick.

MORTIMER: Things are going to start popping around here any minute.

EINSTEIN: Listen—Chonny's in a bad mood. When he's like dis, he's a madman—things happen—terrible things.

MORTIMER: Jonathan doesn't worry me now.

EINSTEIN: Ach, himmel—don't those plays you see teach you anything?

MORTIMER: About what?

EINSTEIN: Vell, at least people in plays act like they got sense—that's more than you do.

MORTIMER (*interested in this observation*): Oh, you think so, do you? You think people in plays act intelligently. I wish you had to sit through some of the ones I have to sit through. Take the little opus I saw tonight for instance. In this play, there's a man—he's supposed to be bright . . . (JONATHAN *enters from cellar with instrument case, stands in doorway and listens to* MORTIMER.)—he knows he's in a house with murderers—he ought to know he's in danger—he's even been warned to get out of the house—but does he go? No, he stays there. Now I ask you, Doctor, is that what an intelligent person would do?

EINSTEIN: You're asking me?

MORTIMER: He didn't even have sense enough to be frightened, to be on guard. For instance, the murderer invites him to sit down.

EINSTEIN (*he moves so as to keep* MORTIMER *from seeing* JONATHAN): You mean—"Won't you sit down?"

MORTIMER (*reaches out and pulls armchair to him without turning his head from* EINSTEIN): Believe it or not, that one was in there too.

EINSTEIN: And what did he do?

MORTIMER (*sitting in armchair*): He sat down. Now mind you, this fellow's supposed to be bright. There he sits—just waiting to be trussed up. And what do you think they used to tie him with.

EINSTEIN: Vat?

MORTIMER: The curtain cord.

(JONATHAN *spies curtain cords on either side of window. He crosses, stands on window-seat and cuts cords with penknife.*)

EINSTEIN: Vell, why not? A good idea. Very convenient.

MORTIMER: A little too convenient. When are playwrights going to use some imagination! The curtain cord!

(JONATHAN *has got the curtain cord and is moving in slowly behind* MORTIMER.)

EINSTEIN: He didn't see him get it?

MORTIMER: See him? He sat there with his back to him. That's the kind of stuff we have to suffer through night after night. And they say the critics are killing the theatre—it's the playwrights who are killing the theatre. So there he sits—the big dope—this fellow who's supposed to be bright—just waiting to be trussed up and gagged.

(JONATHAN *drops loop of curtain cord over* MORTIMER'S *shoulder and draws it taut. At the same time he throws other loop of cord on floor beside* EINSTEIN. *Simultaneously,* EINSTEIN *leaps to* MORTIMER *and gags him with handkerchief, then takes his curtain cord and ties* MORTIMER'S *legs to chair.*)

EINSTEIN (*finishing up the tying*): You're right about dat fella—he vasn't very bright.

JONATHAN: Now, Mortimer, if you don't mind—we'll finish the story. (*He goes to sideboard and brings two candelabras to table and speaks as he lights them.* EINSTEIN *remains kneeling beside* MORTIMER.) Mortimer, I've been away for twenty years, but never once in all that time—my dear brother—were you out of my mind. In Melbourne one night, I dreamed of you—when I landed in San Francisco I felt a strange satisfaction—once more I was in the same country with you. (JONATHAN *has finished lighting candles. He crosses and flips light-switch, darkening stage. As he crosses,* EINSTEIN *gets up and crosses to window-seat.* JONATHAN *picks up instrument case at cellar doorway and sets it on table between candela-*

bras and opens it, revealing various surgical instruments both in the bottom of case and on the inside of cover.) Now, Doctor, we go to work! (*He removes an instrument from the case and fingers it lovingly,* EINSTEIN *crosses and kneels on chair. He is not too happy about all this.*)

EINSTEIN: Please, Chonny, for me, the quick way!

JONATHAN: Doctor! This must really be an artistic achievement. After all, we're performing before a very distinguished critic.

EINSTEIN: Chonny!

JONATHAN (*flaring*): Doctor!

EINSTEIN (*beaten*): All right. Let's get it over. (*He closes drapes tightly and sits on window-seat.* JONATHAN *takes three or four more instruments out of the case and fingers them. At last, having the necessary equipment laid out on the towel he begins to put on a pair of rubber gloves.*)

JONATHAN: All ready for you, Doctor!

EINSTEIN: I gotta have a drink. I can't do this without a drink.

(*He takes the bottle from pocket. Drinks. Finds it empty. Rises.*)

JONATHAN: Pull yourself together, Doctor.

EINSTEIN: I gotta have a drink. Ven ve valked in here this afternoon there was wine here—remember? Vere did she put that? (*He looks at sideboard and remembers. He goes to it, opens cupboard and brings bottle and two wine glasses to end of table top.*) Look, Chonny, we got a drink. (*He pours wine into the two glasses, emptying the bottle.* MORTIMER *watches him.*) Dat's all dere is. I split it with you. We both need a drink. (*He hands one glass to* JONATHAN, *then raises his own glass to his lips.* JONATHAN *stops him.*)

JONATHAN: One moment, Doctor—please. Where are your manners? Yes, Mortimer, I realize now it was you who brought me back to Brooklyn. . . . (*He looks at wine, then draws it back and forth under his nose smelling it. He decides that it's all right apparently for he raises his glass—*) Doctor—to my dear dead brother—

(*As they get the glasses to their lips,* TEDDY *steps out on the balcony and blows a terrific call on his bugle.* EINSTEIN *and* JONATHAN *drop their glasses, spilling the wine.* TEDDY *turns and exits.*)

EINSTEIN: Ach Gott!

JONATHAN: Damn that idiot! (*He starts for stairs.* EINSTEIN *rushes over and intercepts him.*) He goes next ! That's all—he goes next!

EINSTEIN: No, Chonny, not Teddy—that's where I shtop—not Teddy!

JONATHAN: We get to Teddy later!

JONATHAN: Now we've got to work fast!

EINSTEIN: We don't get to him at all.

EINSTEIN: Yah, the quick way—eh, Chonny?

JONATHAN: Yes, Doctor, the quick way! (*He pulls a large silk handkerchief from his inside pocket and drops it around* MORTIMER'S *neck.*)

(*At this point the door bursts open and* OFFICER O'HARA *comes in, very excited.*)

O'HARA: Hey! The Colonel's gotta quit blowing that horn!

JONATHAN (*he and* EINSTEIN *are standing in front of* MORTIMER, *hiding him from* O'HARA): It's all right, Officer. We're taking the bugle away from him.

O'HARA: There's going to be hell to pay in the morning. We promised the neighbors he wouldn't do that any more.

JONATHAN: It won't happen again, Officer. Good night.

O'HARA: I'd better speak to him myself. Where are the lights? (O'HARA *puts on lights and goes upstairs to landing, when he sees* MORTIMER.) Hey! You stood me up. I waited an hour at Kelly's for you. (*He comes downstairs and over to* MORTIMER *and looks at him, then speaks to* JONATHAN *and* EINSTEIN.) What happened to him?

EINSTEIN (*thinking fast*): He was explaining the play he saw tonight— that's what happened to the fella in the play.

O'HARA: Did they have that in the play you saw tonight? (MORTIMER *nods his head—yes.*) Gee, they practically stole that from the second act of my play—(*He starts to explain.*) Why, in my second act, just before the—(*He turns back to* MORTIMER.) I'd better begin at the beginning. It opens in my mother's dressing room where I was born —only I ain't born yet—(MORTIMER *rubs his shoes together to attract* O'HARA'S *attention.*) Huh? Oh, yeah. (O'HARA *starts to remove the gag from* MORTIMER'S *mouth and then decides not to.*) No! You've got to hear the plot. (*He gets stool and sits, continuing on with his "plot" as the curtain falls.*) Well, she's sitting there making up, see—when all of a sudden through the door—a man with a black mustache walks in—turns to my mother and says—"Miss Latour, will you marry me?" He doesn't know she's pregnant.

CURTAIN

SCENE II

Scene is the same. Early the next morning. When the curtain rises again, daylight is streaming through the windows. All doors closed. All drapes open. MORTIMER *is still tied in his chair and seems to be in a semi-conscious state.* JONATHAN *is asleep on sofa.* EINSTEIN, *pleasantly intoxicated, is seated, his head resting on table top.* O'HARA, *with his coat off and his collar loosened, is standing over the stool which is between him and* MORTIMER. *He has progressed to the most exciting scene of his play. There is a bottle of whiskey and a water tumbler on the table along with a plate full of cigarette butts.*

O'HARA: —there she is lying unconscious across the table in her lingerie —the Chink is standing over her with a hatchet—(*He takes the pose.*)—I'm tied up in a chair just like you are—the place is an inferno of flames—it's on fire—when all of a sudden—through the window—in comes Mayor LaGuardia. (EINSTEIN *raises his head and looks out the window. Not seeing anyone he reaches for the bottle and pours himself another drink.* O'HARA *crosses above to him and takes the bottle.*) Hey, remember who paid for that—go easy on it.

EINSTEIN: Vell, I'm listening, ain't I? (*He crosses to* JONATHAN *on the sofa.*)

O'HARA: How do you like it so far?

EINSTEIN: Vell, it put Chonny to sleep.

(O'HARA *has just finished a swig from the bottle.*)

O'HARA: Let him alone. If he ain't got no more interest than that—he don't get a drink. (EINSTEIN *takes his glass and sits on bottom stair. At the same time* O'HARA *crosses, puts stool under desk and whiskey bottle on top of desk, then comes back to center and goes on with his play—*) All right. It's three days later—I been transferred and I'm under charges—that's because somebody stole my badge. (*He panto-*

mimes through following lines.) All right. I'm walking my beat on Staten Island—forty-sixth precinct—when a guy I'm following, it turns out—is really following me. (*There is a knock on door.* EINSTEIN *goes up and looks out landing window. Leaves glass behind drape.*) Don't let anybody in.—So I figure I'll outsmart him. There's a vacant house on the corner. I goes in.

EINSTEIN: It's cops!

O'HARA: I stands there in the dark and I see the door handle turn.

EINSTEIN (*rushing downstairs, shakes* JONATHAN *by the shoulder*): Chonny! It's cops! Cops! (JONATHAN *doesn't move.* EINSTEIN *rushes upstairs and off through the arch.*)

(O'HARA *is going on with his story without a stop.*)

O'HARA: I pulls my guns—braces myself against the wall—and I says— "Come in." (OFFICERS BROPHY *and* KLEIN *walk in, see* O'HARA *with gun pointed at them and raise their hands. Then, recognizing their fellow officer, lower them.*) Hello, boys.

BROPHY: What the hell is going on here?

O'HARA (*goes to* BROPHY): Hey, Pat, whaddya know? This is Mortimer Brewster! He's going to write my play with me. I'm just tellin' him the story.

KLEIN (*crossing to* MORTIMER *and untying him*): Did you have to tie him up to make him listen?

BROPHY: Joe, you better report in at the station. The whole force is out looking for ya.

O'HARA: Did they send you here for me?

KLEIN: We didn't know you was here.

BROPHY: We came to warn the old ladies that there's hell to pay. The Colonel blew that bugle again in the middle of the night.

KLEIN: From the way the neighbors have been calling in about it you'd think the Germans had dropped a bomb on Flatbush Avenue.

(*He has finished untying* MORTIMER. *Puts cords on sideboard.*)

BROPHY: The Lieutenant's on the warpath. He says the Colonel's got to be put away some place.

MORTIMER (*staggers to feet*): Yes! Yes!

O'HARA (*going to* MORTIMER): Gee, Mr. Brewster, I got to get away, so I'll just run through the third act quick.

MORTIMER (*staggering*): Get away from me.

(BROPHY *gives* KLEIN *a look, goes to phone and dials.*)

KLEIN: Say, do you know what time it is? It's after eight o'clock in the morning.

O'HARA: It is? (*He follows* MORTIMER *to stairs.*) Gee, Mr. Brewster, them first two acts run a little long, but I don't see anything we can leave out.

MORTIMER (*almost to landing*): You can leave it *all* out.

(BROPHY *sees* JONATHAN *on sofa.*)

BROPHY: Who the hell is this guy?

MORTIMER (*hanging on railing, almost to balcony*): That's my brother.

BROPHY: Oh, the one that ran away? So he came back.

MORTIMER: Yes, he came back!

(JONATHAN *stirs as if to get up.*)

BROPHY (*into phone*): This is Brophy. Get me Mac. (*To* O'HARA, *sitting on bottom stair.*) I'd better let them know we found you, Joe. (*Into phone.*) Mac? Tell the Lieutenant he can call off the big manhunt—we got him. In the Brewster house. (JONATHAN *hears this and suddenly becomes very much awake, looking up to see* KLEIN *and* BROPHY.) Do you want us to bring him in? Oh—all right, we'll hold him right here. (*He hangs up.*) The Lieutenant's on his way over.

JONATHAN (*rising*): So I've been turned in, eh? (BROPHY *and* KLEIN *look at him with some interest.*) All right, you've got me! (*Turning to* MORTIMER, *who is on balcony looking down.*) And I suppose you and that stool-pigeon brother of mine will split the reward?

KLEIN: Reward?

(*Instinctively* KLEIN *and* BROPHY *both grab* JONATHAN *by an arm.*)

JONATHAN (*dragging*): Now I'll do some turning in! You think my aunts are sweet charming old ladies, don't you? Well, there are thirteen bodies buried in their cellar.

MORTIMER (*as he rushes off to see* TEDDY): Teddy! Teddy! Teddy!

KLEIN: What the hell are you talking about?

BROPHY: You'd better be careful what you're saying about your aunts— they happen to be friends of ours.

JONATHAN (*raving as he drags them toward the cellar door*): I'll show you! I'll prove it to you! You come to the cellar with me!

KLEIN: Wait a minute! Wait a minute!

JONATHAN: Thirteen bodies! I'll show you where they're buried.

KLEIN (*refusing to be kidded*): Oh, yeah?

JONATHAN: You don't want to see what's down in the cellar?

BROPHY (*releases* JONATHAN'S *arm, then to* KLEIN): Go on down in the cellar with him, Abe.

KLEIN (*drops* JONATHAN'S *arm and looks at him*): I'm not so sure I want to be down in the cellar with him. Look at that puss. He looks like Boris Karloff. (JONATHAN, *at mention of Karloff, grabs* KLEIN *by the throat, starts choking him.*) Hey—what the hell—Hey, Pat! Get him off me.

(BROPHY *takes out rubber blackjack.*)

BROPHY: Here, what do you think you're doing! (*He socks* JONATHAN *on head.* JONATHAN *falls unconscious, face down.*) (KLEIN, *throwing* JONATHAN'S *weight to floor, backs away, rubbing his throat.*)

KLEIN: Well what do you know about that?

(*There is a knock on door.*)

O'HARA: Come in.

(LIEUTENANT ROONEY *bursts in, slamming door after him. He is a very tough, driving, dominating officer.*)

ROONEY: What the hell are you men doing here? I told you *I* was going to handle this.

KLEIN: Well, sir, we was just about to—(KLEIN'S *eyes go to* JONATHAN *and* ROONEY *sees him.*)

ROONEY: What happened? Did he put up a fight?

BROPHY: This ain't the guy that blows the bugle. This is his brother. He tried to kill Klein.

KLEIN (*feeling his throat*): All I said was he looked like Boris Karloff.

ROONEY (*his face lights up*): Turn him over.

(*The two* COPS *turn* JONATHAN *over on his back.* KLEIN *steps back.* ROONEY *crosses front of* BROPHY *to take a look at* JONATHAN.)

BROPHY: We kinda think he's wanted somewhere.

ROONEY: Oh, you kinda *think* he's wanted somewhere? If you guys don't look at the circulars we hang up in the station, at least you could read *True Detective*. Certainly he's wanted. In Indiana! Escaped from the prison for the Criminal Insane! He's a lifer. For God's sake that's how he was described—he *looked* like Karloff!

KLEIN: Was there a reward mentioned?

ROONEY: Yeah—and *I'm* claiming it.

BROPHY: He was trying to get us down in the cellar.

KLEIN: He said there was thirteen bodies buried down there.

ROONEY (*suspicious*): Thirteen bodies buried in the cellar? (*Deciding it's ridiculous.*) And that didn't tip you off he came out of a nuthouse!

O'HARA: I thought all along he talked kinda crazy.

(ROONEY *sees* O'HARA *for the first time. Turns to him.*)

ROONEY: Oh, it's Shakespeare! (*Crossing to him.*) Where have you been all night? And you needn't bother to tell me.

O'HARA: I've been right here, sir. Writing a play with Mortimer Brewster.

ROONEY (*tough*): Yeah? Well, you're gonna have plenty of time to write that play. You're suspended! Now get back and report in!

(O'HARA *takes his coat, night stick, and cap from top of desk. Goes to door and opens it. Then turns to* ROONEY.)

O'HARA: Can I come over sometime and use the station typewriter?

ROONEY: No!—Get out of here. (O'HARA *runs out.* ROONEY *closes door and turns to the* COPS. TEDDY *enters on balcony and comes downstairs unnoticed and stands at* ROONEY'S *back.* ROONEY, *to* COPS.) Take that guy somewhere else and bring him to. (*The* COPS *bend down to pick up* JONATHAN.) See what you can find out about his accomplice. (*The* COPS *stand up again in a questioning attitude.* ROONEY *explains.*) The guy that helped him escape. He's wanted too.

No wonder Brooklyn's in the shape it's in, with the police force full of flatheads like you—falling for that kind of a story—thirteen bodies in the cellar!

TEDDY: But there are thirteen bodies in the cellar.

ROONEY (*turning on him*): Who are you?

TEDDY: I'm President Roosevelt.

ROONEY: What the hell is this?

BROPHY: He's the fellow that blows the bugle.

KLEIN: Good morning, Colonel.

(*They salute* TEDDY, *who returns it.* ROONEY *finds himself saluting* TEDDY *also. He pulls his hand down in disgust.*)

ROONEY: Well, Colonel, you've blown your last bugle.

TEDDY (*seeing* JONATHAN *on floor*): Dear me—another Yellow Fever victim?

ROONEY: What-at?

TEDDY: All the bodies in the cellar are Yellow Fever victims.

(ROONEY *crosses exasperatedly to door.*)

BROPHY: No, Colonel, this is a spy we caught in the White House.

ROONEY (*pointing to* JONATHAN): Will you get that guy out of here!

(COPS *pick up* JONATHAN *and drag him to kitchen.* TEDDY *follows them.* MORTIMER *enters, comes down stairs.*)

TEDDY (*turning back to* ROONEY): If there's any questioning of spies, that's my department!

ROONEY: You keep out of this!

TEDDY: You're forgetting! As President, I am also head of the Secret Service.

(BROPHY *and* KLEIN *exit with* JONATHAN *into kitchen.* TEDDY *follows them briskly.*)

MORTIMER: Captain—I'm Mortimer Brewster.

ROONEY: Are you sure?

MORTIMER: I'd like to talk to you about my brother Teddy—the one who blew the bugle.

ROONEY: Mr. Brewster, we ain't going to talk about that—he's got to be put away!

MORTIMER: I quite agree with you. In fact, it's all arranged for. I had these commitment papers signed by Dr. Gilchrist, our family physician. Teddy has signed them himself, you see—and I've signed them as next of kin.

ROONEY: Where's he going?

MORTIMER: Happy Dale.

ROONEY: All right, I don't care where he goes as long as he goes!

MORTIMER: Oh, he's going all right. But I want you to know that everything that's happened around here Teddy's responsible for. Now, those thirteen bodies in the cellar—

ROONEY (*he's had enough of those thirteen*): Yeah—yeah—those thirteen bodies in the cellar! It ain't enough that the neighbors are all afraid of him, and his disturbing the peace with that bugle—but can you imagine what would happen if that cock-eyed story about thirteen bodies in the cellar got around? And now he's starting a Yellow Fever scare. Cute, ain't it?

MORTIMER (*greatly relieved, with an embarrassed laugh*): Thirteen bodies. Do you think anybody would believe that story?

ROONEY: Well, you can't tell. Some people are just dumb enough. You don't know what to believe sometimes. About a year ago a crazy guy starts a murder rumor over in Greenpoint, and I had to dig up a half acre lot, just to prove that—

(*There is a knock on door.*)

MORTIMER: Will you excuse me? (*He goes to door and admits* ELAINE *and* MR. WITHERSPOON, *an elderly, tight-lipped disciplinarian. He is carrying a brief case.*)

ELAINE (*briskly*): Good morning, Mortimer.

MORTIMER (*not knowing what to expect*): Good morning, dear.

ELAINE: This is Mr. Witherspoon. He's come to meet Teddy.

MORTIMER: To meet Teddy?

ELAINE: Mr. Witherspoon's the superintendent of Happy Dale.

MORTIMER (*eagerly*): Oh, come right in. (*They shake hands.* MORTIMER *indicates* ROONEY.) This is Captain—

ROONEY: *Lieutenant* Rooney. I'm glad you're here, Super, because you're taking him back with you today!

WITHERSPOON: Today? I didn't know that—

ELAINE: (*cutting in*): Not today!

MORTIMER: Look, Elaine, I've got a lot of business to attend to, so you run along home and I'll call you up.

ELAINE: Nuts! (*She crosses to window-seat and sits.*)

WITHERSPOON: I had no idea it was this immediate.

ROONEY: The papers are all signed, he goes today!

(TEDDY *backs into room from kitchen, speaking sharply in the direction whence he's come.*)

TEDDY: Complete insubordination! You men will find out I'm no mollycoddle. (*He slams door and comes down to below table.*) When the President of the United States is treated like that—what's this country coming to?

ROONEY: There's your man, Super.

MORTIMER: Just a minute! (*He crosses to* TEDDY *and speaks to him as to a child.*) Mr. President, I have very good news for you. Your term of office is over.

TEDDY: Is this March the Fourth?

MORTIMER: Practically.

TEDDY (*thinking*): Let's see—OH!—Now I go on my hunting trip to Africa! Well, I must get started immediately. (*He starts across the room and almost bumps into* WITHERSPOON. *He looks at him then steps back to* MORTIMER.) Is he trying to move into the White House before I've moved out?

MORTIMER: Who, Teddy?

TEDDY (*indicating* WITHERSPOON): Taft!

MORTIMER: This isn't Mr. Taft, Teddy. This is Mr. Witherspoon—he's to be your guide in Africa.

TEDDY (*shakes hands with* WITHERSPOON *enthusiastically*): Bully! Bully! I'll bring down my equipment. (*He crosses to stairs.* MARTHA *and* ABBY *have entered on balcony during last speech and are coming downstairs.*) When the safari comes, tell them to wait. (*As he passes the* AUNTS *on his way to landing, he shakes hands with each, without stopping his walk.*) Good-bye, Aunt Abby. Good-bye, Aunt Martha. I'm on my way to Africa—isn't it wonderful? (*He has reached the landing.*) CHARGE!

(*He charges up the stairs and off.*)

(*The* AUNTS *are at foot of stairs.*)

MORTIMER (*crossing to aunts*): Good morning, darlings.

MARTHA: Oh, we have visitors.

MORTIMER: This is Lieutenant Rooney.

ABBY (*crossing, shakes hands with him*): How do you do, Lieutenant? My, you don't look like the fussbudget the policemen say you are.

MORTIMER: Why the Lieutenant is here—You know, Teddy blew his bugle again last night.

MARTHA: Yes, we're going to speak to Teddy about that.

ROONEY: It's a little more serious than that, Miss Brewster.

MORTIMER (*easing* AUNTS *to* WITHERSPOON *who is above table where he has opened his brief case and extracted some papers*): And you haven't met Mr. Witherspoon. He's the Superintendent of Happy Dale.

ABBY: Oh, Mr. Witherspoon—how do you do?

MARTHA: You've come to meet Teddy.

ROONEY (*somewhat harshly*): He's come to *take* him.

(*The* AUNTS *turn to* ROONEY *questioningly.*)

MORTIMER (*making it as easy as possible*): Aunties—the police want Teddy to go there, today.

ABBY: Oh—no!

MARTHA (*behind* ABBY): Not while we're alive!

ROONEY: I'm sorry, Miss Brewster, but it has to be done. The papers are all signed and he's going along with the Superintendent.

ABBY: We won't permit it. We'll promise to take the bugle away from him.

MARTHA: We won't be separated from Teddy.

ROONEY: I'm sorry, ladies, but the law's the law! He's committed himself and he's going!

ABBY: Well, if he goes, we're going too.

MARTHA: Yes, you'll have to take us with him.

MORTIMER (*has an idea. Crosses to* WITHERSPOON): Well, why not?

WITHERSPOON (*to* MORTIMER): Well, that's sweet of them to want to, but it's impossible. You see, we can't take *sane* people at Happy Dale.

MARTHA (*turning to* WITHERSPOON): Mr. Witherspoon, if you'll let us live there with Teddy, we'll see that Happy Dale is in our will—and for a very generous amount.

WITHERSPOON: Well, the Lord knows we could use the money, but— I'm afraid—

ROONEY: Now, let's be sensible about this, ladies. For instance, here I am wasting my morning when I've got serious work to do. You know there are still *murders* to be solved in Brooklyn.

MORTIMER: Yes! (*Covering.*) Oh, are there?

ROONEY: It ain't only his bugle blowing and the neighbors all afraid of him, but things would just get worse. Sooner or later we'd be put to the trouble of digging up your cellar.

ABBY: Our cellar?

ROONEY: Yeah.—Your nephew's been telling around that there are thirteen bodies in your cellar.

ABBY: But there are thirteen bodies in our cellar.

(ROONEY *looks disgusted.* MORTIMER *drifts quietly to front of cellar door.*)

MARTHA: If that's why you think Teddy has to go away—you come down to the cellar with us and we'll prove it to you.

ABBY: There's one—Mr. Spenalzo—who doesn't belong here and who will have to leave—but the other twelve are our gentlemen.

MORTIMER: I don't think the Lieutenant wants to go down in the cellar. He was telling me that only last year he had to dig up a half-acre lot —weren't you, Lieutenant?

ROONEY: That's right.

ABBY (*to* ROONEY): Oh, you wouldn't have to dig here. The graves are all marked. We put flowers on them every Sunday.

ROONEY: Flowers? (*He steps up toward* ABBY, *then turns to* WITHERSPOON, *indicating the* AUNTS *as he speaks.*) Superintendent—don't you think you can find room for these ladies?

WITHERSPOON: Well, I—

ABBY (*to* ROONEY): You come along with us, and we'll show you the graves.

ROONEY: I'll take your word for it, lady—I'm a busy man. How about it, Super?

WITHERSPOON: Well, they'd have to be committed.

MORTIMER: Teddy committed himself. Can't they commit themselves? Can't they sign the papers?

WITHERSPOON: Why, certainly.

MARTHA (*sits in chair as* WITHERSPOON *draws it out for her*): Oh, if we can go with Teddy, we'll sign the papers. Where are they?

ABBY: Yes, where are they?

(WITHERSPOON *opens brief case for more papers.* KLEIN *enters from kitchen.*)

KLEIN: He's coming around, Lieutenant.

ABBY: Good morning, Mr. Klein.

MARTHA: Good morning, Mr. Klein. Are you here too?

KLEIN: Yeah. Brophy and me have got your other nephew out in the kitchen.

ROONEY: Well, sign 'em up, Superintendent. I want to get this all cleaned up. (*He crosses to kitchen door, shaking his head as he exits and saying:*) Thirteen bodies.

(KLEIN *follows him out.* MORTIMER *has fountain pen in hand.* WITHERSPOON *also has a pen.*)

WITHERSPOON (*handing* MARTHA *pen*): If you'll sign right here.

(MARTHA *signs.*)

MORTIMER: And you here, Aunt Abby.

(ABBY *signs.*)

ABBY (*signing*): I'm really looking forward to going—the neighborhood here has changed so.

MARTHA: Just think, a front lawn again.

(EINSTEIN *enters through arch and comes down stairs to door carrying suitcase. He picks hat from hall tree on way down.*)

WITHERSPOON: Oh, we're overlooking something.

MARTHA: What?

WITHERSPOON: Well, we're going to need the signature of a doctor.

MORTIMER: Oh! (*He sees* EINSTEIN *about to disappear through the door.*) Dr. Einstein! Will you come over here—we'd like you to sign some papers.

EINSTEIN: Please, I must—

MORTIMER (*crosses to him*): Just come right over, Doctor. At one time last night, I thought the Doctor was going to operate on me. (EINSTEIN *puts down suitcase and his hat just inside the door.*) Just come right over, Doctor. Just sign right here, Doctor.

(*The* DOCTOR *signs* ABBY'S *paper and* MARTHA'S *paper.* ROONEY *and* KLEIN *enter from kitchen.* ROONEY *crosses to desk and dials phone.* KLEIN *stands near kitchen door.*)

ABBY: Were you leaving, Doctor?

EINSTEIN (*signing papers*): I think I must go.

MARTHA: Aren't you going to wait for Jonathan?

EINSTEIN: I don't think we're going to the same place.

(MORTIMER *sees* ELAINE *on window-seat and crosses to her.*)

MORTIMER: Hello, Elaine. I'm glad to see you. Stick around, huh?

ELAINE: Don't worry, I'm going to.

(MORTIMER *stands back of* MARTHA'S *chair.* ROONEY *speaks into phone.*)

ROONEY: Hello, Mac. Rooney. We've picked up that guy that's wanted in Indiana. Now there's a description of his accomplice—it's right on the desk there—read it to me. (EINSTEIN *sees* ROONEY *at phone. He starts toward kitchen and sees* KLEIN *standing there. He comes back and stands there dejectedly waiting for the pinch.* ROONEY *repeats the description given him over phone, looking blankly at* EINSTEIN *the while.*) Yeah—about fifty-four—five foot six—hundred and forty pounds—blue eyes—talks with a German accent. Poses as a doctor. Thanks, Mac. (*He hangs up as* WITHERSPOON *crosses to him with papers in hand.*)

WITHERSPOON. It's all right, Lieutenant. The Doctor here has just completed the signatures.

(ROONEY *goes to* EINSTEIN *and shakes his hand.*)

ROONEY: Thanks, Doc. You're really doing Brooklyn a service.

(ROONEY *and* KLEIN *exit to kitchen.*)

(EINSTEIN *stands amazed for a moment then grabs up his hat and suitcase and disappears through door. The* AUNTS *rise and cross over, looking out after him.* ABBY *shuts the door and they stand there.*)

WITHERSPOON (*above table*): Mr. Brewster, you sign now as next of kin.

(*The* AUNTS *whisper to each other as* MORTIMER *signs.*)

MORTIMER: Yes, of course. Right here?
WITHERSPOON: That's fine.
MORTIMER: That makes everything complete—everything legal?
WITHERSPOON: Oh, yes.
MORTIMER (*with relief*): Well, Aunties, now you're safe.
WITHERSPOON (*to* AUNTS): When do you think you'll be ready to start?
ABBY: Well, Mr. Witherspoon, why don't you go upstairs and tell Teddy just what he can take along?
WITHERSPOON: Upstairs?
MORTIMER: I'll show you.
ABBY (*stopping him*): No, Mortimer, you stay here. We want to talk to you. (*To* WITHERSPOON.) Yes, Mr. Witherspoon, just upstairs and turn to the left.

(WITHERSPOON *puts his brief case on sofa and goes upstairs, the* AUNTS *keeping an eye on him while talking to* MORTIMER.)

MARTHA: Well, Mortimer now that we're moving, this house really is yours.
ABBY: Yes, dear, we want you to live here now.
MORTIMER (*below table*): No, Aunt Abby, this house is too full of memories.

MARTHA: But you'll need a home when you and Elaine are married.

MORTIMER: Darlings, that's very indefinite.

ELAINE (*rises and crosses*): It's nothing of the kind—we're going to be married right away.

(WITHERSPOON *has exited off balcony.*)

ABBY: Mortimer—Mortimer, we're really very worried about something.

MORTIMER: Now, darlings, you're going to love it at Happy Dale.

MARTHA: Oh, yes, we're very happy about the whole thing. That's just it—we don't want anything to go wrong.

ABBY: Will they investigate those signatures?

MORTIMER: Don't worry, they're not going to look up Dr. Einstein.

MARTHA: It's not his signature, dear, it's yours.

ABBY: You see, you signed as next of kin.

MORTIMER: Of course. Why not?

MARTHA: Well, dear, it's something we never wanted to tell you. But now you're a man—and it's something Elaine should know too. You see, dear—you're not really a Brewster.

(MORTIMER *stares as does* ELAINE.)

ABBY: Your mother came to us as a cook—and you were born about three months afterward. But she was such a sweet woman—and such a good cook we didn't want to lose her—so brother married her.

MORTIMER: I'm—not—really—a—Brewster?

MARTHA: Now, don't feel badly about it, dear.

ABBY: And Elaine, it won't make any difference to you?

MORTIMER (*turning slowly to face* ELAINE. *His voice rising*): Elaine! Did you hear? Do you understand? I'm a bastard!

(ELAINE *leaps into his arms. The two* AUNTS *watch them.*)

MARTHA: Well, now I really must see about breakfast.

ELAINE (*leading* MORTIMER *to door; opening door*): Mortimer's coming over to my house. Father's gone to Philadelphia, and Mortimer and I are going to have breakfast together.

MORTIMER: Yes, I need some coffee—I've had quite a night.

ABBY: In that case I should think you'd want to get to bed.

MORTIMER (*with a sidelong glance at* ELAINE): I do. (*They exit, closing door.*)

(WITHERSPOON *enters on balcony, carrying two canteens. He starts downstairs when* TEDDY *enters carrying large canoe paddle. He is dressed in Panama outfit with pack on his back.*)

TEDDY: One moment, Witherspoon. Take this with you! (*He exits off balcony again as* WITHERSPOON *comes on downstairs to sofa. He puts canteens on sofa and leans paddle against wall.*)

(*At the same time* ROONEY *and the two cops with* JONATHAN *between them enter. The* COPS *have twisters around* JONATHAN'S *wrists.* ROONEY *enters first.*)

ROONEY: We won't need the wagon. My car's out front.

MARTHA: Oh, you leaving now, Jonathan?

ROONEY: Yeah—he's going back to Indiana. There's some people there want to take care of him for the rest of his life. Come on.

(ROONEY *opens door as the two* COPS *and* JONATHAN *cross.*)

ABBY: Well, Jonathan, it's nice to know you have some place to go.

MARTHA: We're leaving too.

ABBY: Yes, we're going to Happy Dale.

JONATHAN: Then this house is seeing the last of the Brewsters.

MARTHA: Unless Mortimer wants to live here.

JONATHAN: I have a suggestion to make. Why don't you turn this property over to the church?

ABBY: Well, we never thought of that.

JONATHAN: After all, it *should* be part of the cemetery.

ROONEY: All right, get going, I'm a busy man.

JONATHAN (*holding his ground for his one last word*): Good-bye, Aunties. Well, I can't better my record now but neither can you—at least I have that satisfaction. The score stands even, *twelve* to *twelve*.

(JONATHAN *and the* COPS *exit, as the* AUNTS *look out after them.*)

(WITHERSPOON *crosses above to window-seat and stands quietly looking out the window. His back is to the* AUNTS.)

MARTHA (*starting toward door to close it*): Jonathan always was a mean boy. Never could stand to see anyone get ahead of him. (*She closes door.*)

ABBY (*turning slowly around as she speaks*): I wish we could show him he isn't so smart! (*Her eyes fall on* WITHERSPOON. *She studies him.* MARTHA *turns from door and sees* ABBY'S *contemplation.* ABBY *speaks sweetly.*) Mr. Witherspoon? (WITHERSPOON *turns around facing them.*) Does your family live with you at Happy Dale?

WITHERSPOON: I have no family.

ABBY: Oh—

MARTHA (*stepping into room*): Well, I suppose you consider everyone at Happy Dale your family?

WITHERSPOON: I'm afraid you don't quite understand. As head of the institution, I have to keep quite aloof.

ABBY: That must make it very lonely for you.

WITHERSPOON: It does. But my duty is my duty.

ABBY (*turning to* MARTHA): Well, Martha—(MARTHA *takes her cue and goes to sideboard for bottle of wine. Bottle in cupboard is empty. She puts it back and takes out full bottle from cupboard. She brings bottle and wine-glass to table.* ABBY *continues talking.*) If Mr. Witherspoon won't join us for breakfast, I think at least we should offer him a glass of elderberry wine.

WITHERSPOON (*severely*): Elderberry wine?

MARTHA: We make it ourselves.

WITHERSPOON (*melting slightly*): Why, yes . . . (*Severely again.*) Of course, at Happy Dale our relationship will be more formal—but here—(*He sits in chair as* MARTHA *pours wine.* ABBY *is beside* MARTHA.) You don't see much elderberry wine nowadays—I thought I'd had my last glass of it.

ABBY: Oh, no—

MARTHA (*handing him glass of wine*): No, here it is.

(WITHERSPOON *toasts the ladies and lifts glass to his lips, but the curtain falls before he does. . . .*)

CURTAIN

Harvey

MARY CHASE

Why our respondents liked

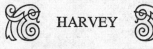 HARVEY

"The play I think made me believe in pookas, as I know I believe in Mary Chase."

WALTER KERR

" 'What did you have in mind?' was a great line—or was it because Frank Fay delivered it so well?"

EARL WILSON

"A classic as far as I'm concerned. Comedy without malice."

HELEN HAYES

Harvey, the Pulitzer Prize winner of the 1944–45 Broadway season, was written by Mary Coyle Chase, a Denver newspaper reporter before she began writing plays at home in her spare time. The script was originally submitted to Brock Pemberton to produce, since he had worked on a previous play of hers back in 1936 entitled *Now You've Done It.* Despite some discouragement from friends and colleagues, Pemberton persisted in his support of bringing this new play about Elwood P. Dowd and his six foot one and a half inch rabbit companion to the stage. After much correspondence between him and Mrs. Chase and over a dozen revisions of the script, the play was ready for production. Having undergone several name changes—*The Pooka* (referring to a Celtic fairy spirit, otherwise known as Harvey), *The White Rabbit*—the play became known to theatre audiences as simply *Harvey.* Frank Fay, a former vaudeville and nightclub performer, was selected for the starring role of Elwood P. Dowd and Josephine Hull was cast as his sister. Later actors in the role of Elwood were James Stewart, Joe E. Brown, James Dunn, Jack Buchanan, producer Brock Pemberton, and Bert Wheeler. During its tryout in Boston, the play was performed with an actor dressed in a rabbit suit for the part of Harvey, but the author and producer quickly decided that it would be much more effective if Harvey was invisible. On November 1, 1944, *Harvey* opened to excellent reviews and the next day tickets were already being sold for three months in advance. The play would run 1,775 performances on Broadway. This comic fantasy, even upon recent revival, continues to delight and endear itself to theatre audiences.

Harvey was presented by Brock Pemberton on November 1, 1944, at the Forty-Eighth Street Theatre, New York City. The cast was as follows:

Myrtle Mae Simmons	Jane Van Duser
Veta Louise Simmons	Josephine Hull
Elwood P. Dowd	Frank Fay
Miss Johnson	Eloise Sheldon
Mrs. Ethel Chauvenet	Frederica Going
Ruth Kelly, R.N.	Janet Tyler
Duane Wilson	Jesse White
Lyman Sanderson, M.D.	Tom Seidel
William R. Chumley, M.D.	Fred Irving Lewis
Betty Chumley	Dora Clement
Judge Omar Gaffney	John Kirk
E. J. Lofgren	Robert Gist

Staged by Antoinette Perry
Settings by John Root

The action of the play takes place in a city in the Far West in the library of the old Dowd family mansion and the reception room of Chumley's Rest.

ACT ONE

Scene 1: *The library, late afternoon*
Scene 2: *Chumley's Rest, an hour later*

ACT TWO

Scene 1: *The library, an hour later*
Scene 2: *Chumley's Rest, four hours later*

ACT THREE

Chumley's Rest, a few minutes later

ACT ONE

SCENE I

TIME: *Mid-afternoon of a spring day. The present.*

SCENE: *The library of the old Dowd family mansion—a room lined with books and set with heavy, old-fashioned furniture of a faded grandeur. The most conspicuous item in the room is an oil painting over a black marble Victorian mantelpiece. This is the portrait of a lantern-jawed older woman. Double doors, now pulled apart, lead to the hallway and across to the parlor, which is not seen. Telephone is on small table. This afternoon there is a festive look to the room—silver bowls with spring flowers set about. From the parlor comes the sound of a bad female voice saying, "I'm Called Little Buttercup."*

AT RISE: MYRTLE MAE *is discovered coming through door and as telephone rings, she goes to it.*

MYRTLE: Mrs. Simmons? Mrs. Simmons is my mother, but she has guests this afternoon. Who wants her? (*Respectful change in tone after she hears who it is.*) Oh—wait just a minute. Hang on just a minute. (*Goes to doorway and calls.*) Psst—Mother! (*Cranes her neck more.*) Psst—Mother! (*Crooks her finger insistently several times. Singing continues.*)

VETA (*enters humming "Buttercup"*): Yes, dear?

MYRTLE: Telephone.

VETA (*turning to go out again*): Oh, no, dear. Not with all of them in there. Say I'm busy.

MYRTLE: But, Mother. It's the Society Editor of the Evening News Bee—

VETA (*turning*): Oh—the Society Editor. She's very important. (*She fixes her hair and goes to phone. Her voice is very sweet. She throws out chest and assumes dignified pose.*) Good afternoon, Miss Ellerbe. This is Veta Simmons. Yes—a tea and reception for the members of the Wednesday Forum. You might say—program tea. My mother, you know—(*Waves hand toward portrait*) the late Marcella Pinney Dowd, pioneer cultural leader—she came here by ox-team as a child and she founded the Wednesday Forum. (MYRTLE *is watching out door.*) Myrtle—how many would you say?

MYRTLE: Seventy-five, at least. Say a hundred.

VETA (*on phone*): Seventy-five. Miss Tewksbury is the soloist, accompanied by Wilda McCurdy, accompanist.

MYRTLE: Come on! Miss Tewksbury is almost finished with her number.

VETA: She'll do an encore.

MYRTLE: What if they don't give her a lot of applause?

VETA: I've known her for years. She'll do an encore. (MYRTLE *again starts to leave.*) You might say that I am entertaining, assisted by my daughter, Miss Myrtle Mae Simmons. (*To* MYRTLE—*indicates her dress.*) What color would you call that?

MYRTLE: Rancho Rose, they told me.

VETA (*into phone*): Miss Myrtle Mae Simmons looked charming in a modish Rancho Rose toned crepe, picked up at the girdle with a touch of magenta on emerald. I wish you could see her, Miss Ellerbe.

MYRTLE (*Looks through door*): Mother—please—she's almost finished and where's the cateress?

VETA (*to* MYRTLE): Everything's ready. The minute she's finished singing we open the dining-room doors and we begin pouring. (*Into phone.*) The parlors and halls are festooned with smilax. Yes, festooned. (*Makes motion in air with finger.*) That's right. Yes, Miss Ellerbe, this is the first party we've had in years. There's a reason but I don't want it in the papers. We all have our troubles, Miss Ellerbe. The guest list? Oh, yes—

MYRTLE: Mother—come.

VETA: If you'll excuse me now, Miss Ellerbe. I'll call you later. (*Hangs up.*)

MYRTLE: Mother—Mrs. Chauvenet just came in!

VETA (*arranging flowers on phone table*): Mrs. Eugene Chauvenet Senior! Her father was a scout with Buffalo Bill.

MYRTLE: So that's where she got that hat!

VETA (*as she and* MYRTLE *start to exit*): Myrtle, you must be nice to Mrs. Chauvenet. She has a grandson about your age.

MYRTLE: But what difference will it make, with Uncle Elwood?—Mae!

VETA: Myrtle—remember! We agreed not to talk about that this afternoon. The point of this whole party is to get you started. We work through those older women to the younger group.

MYRTLE: We can't have anyone here in the evenings, and that's when men come to see you—in the evenings. The only reason we can even have a party this afternoon is because Uncle Elwood is playing pinochle at the Fourth Avenue Firehouse. Thank God for the firehouse!

VETA: I know—but they'll just have to invite you out and it won't hurt them one bit. Oh, Myrtle—you've got so much to offer. I don't care what anyone says, there's something sweet about every girl. And a man takes that sweetness, and look what he does with it! (*Crosses to mantel with flowers.*) But you've got to meet somebody, Myrtle. That's all there is to it.

MYRTLE: If I do they say, That's Myrtle Mae Simmons! Her uncle is Elwood P. Dowd—the biggest screwball in town. Elwood P. Dowd and his pal—

VETA (*puts hand on her mouth*): You promised.

MYRTLE (*crossing above table, sighs*): All right—let's get them into the dining-room.

VETA: Now when the members come in here and you make your little welcome speech on behalf of your grandmother—be sure to do this. (*Gestures toward portrait on mantel.*)

MYRTLE (*in fine disgust*): And then after that, I mention my Uncle Elwood and say a few words about his pal Harvey. Damn Harvey! (*In front of table, as she squats.*)

VETA (*the effect on her is electric. She runs over and closes doors*): Myrtle Mae—that's right! Let everybody in the Wednesday Forum hear you. You said that name. You promised you wouldn't say that name and you said it.

MYRTLE (*rising*): I'm sorry, Mother. But how do you know Uncle Elwood won't come in and introduce Harvey to everybody? (*To mantel. Places flowers on it.*)

VETA: This is unkind of you, Myrtle Mae. Elwood is the biggest heartache I have. Even if people do call him peculiar he's still my brother, and he won't be home this afternoon.

MYRTLE: Are you sure?

VETA: Of course I'm sure.

MYRTLE: But Mother, why can't we live like other people?

VETA: Must I remind you again? Elwood is not living with us—we are living with him.

MYRTLE: Living with him and Harvey! Did Grandmother know about Harvey?

VETA: I've wondered and wondered about that. She never wrote me if she did.

MYRTLE: Why did she have to leave all her property to Uncle Elwood?

VETA: Well, I suppose it was because she died in his arms. People are sentimental about things like that.

MYRTLE: You always say that and it doesn't make sense. She couldn't make out her will after she died, could she?

VETA: Don't be didactic, Myrtle Mae. It's not becoming in a young girl, and men loathe it. Now don't forget to wave your hand.

MYRTLE: I'll do my best. (*Opens door.*)

VETA: Oh, dear—Miss Tewksbury's voice is certainly fading!

MYRTLE: But not fast enough. (*She exits.*)

VETA (*exits through door, clapping hands, pulling down girdle*): Lovely, Miss Tewksbury—perfectly lovely. I loved it.

(*Through door enters* ELWOOD P. DOWD. *He is a man about 47 years old with a dignified bearing, and yet a dreamy expression in his eyes. His expression is benign, yet serious to the point of gravity. He wears an overcoat and a battered old hat. This hat, reminiscent of the Joe College era, sits on the top of his head. Over his arm he carries another hat and coat. As he enters, although he is alone, he seems to be ushering and bowing someone else in with him. He bows the invisible person over to a chair. His step is light, his movements quiet and his voice low-pitched.*)

ELWOOD (*to invisible person*): Excuse me a moment. I have to answer the phone. Make yourself comfortable, Harvey. (*Phone rings.*) Hello. Oh, you've got the wrong number. But how are you, anyway? This is Elwood P. Dowd speaking. I'll do? Well, thank you. And what is your name, my dear? Miss Elsie Greenawalt? (*To chair.*) Harvey, it's a Miss Elsie Greenawalt. How are you today, Miss Greenawalt? That's fine. Yes, my dear. I would be happy to join your club. I belong to several clubs now—the University Club, the Country Club and the Pinochle Club at the Fourth Avenue Firehouse. I spend a good deal of my time there, or at Charlie's Place, or over at Eddie's Bar. And what is your club, Miss Greenawalt? (*He listens— then turns to empty chair.*) Harvey, I get the Ladies Home Journal, Good Housekeeping and the Open Road for Boys for two years for six twenty-five. (*Back to phone.*) It sounds fine to me. I'll join it. (*To chair.*) How does it sound to you, Harvey? (*Back to phone.*) Harvey says it sounds fine to him also, Miss Greenawalt. He says he will join, too. Yes—two subscriptions. Mail everything to this address. . . . I hope I will have the pleasure of meeting you some time, my dear. Harvey, she says she would like to meet me. When? When would you like to meet me, Miss Greenawalt? Why not right now? My sister seems to be having a few friends in and we would consider it an honor if you would come and join us. My sister will be delighted. 343 Temple Drive—I hope to see you in a very few minutes. Good-by, my dear. (*Hangs up.*) She's coming right over. (*Moves to* HARVEY.) Harvey, don't you think we'd better freshen up? Yes, so do I. (*He takes up hats and coats and exits.*)

VETA (*enters, followed by* MAID): I can't seem to remember where I put that guest list. I must read it to Miss Ellerbe. . . . Have you seen it, Miss Johnson?

MAID: No, I haven't, Mrs. Simmons.

VETA: Look on my dresser. (MAID *exits.*)

MYRTLE (*enters*): Mother—Mrs. Chauvenet—she's asking for you. (*Turning—speaking in oh-so-sweet tone to someone in hall.*) Here's Mother, Mrs. Chauvenet. Here she is. (*Enter* MRS. CHAUVENET. *She is a woman of about 65—heavy, dressed with the casual sumptuousness of a wealthy Western society woman—in silvery gold and plush, and mink scarf even though it is a spring day. She rushes over to* VETA.)

MRS. CHAUVENET: Veta Louise Simmons! I thought you were dead. (*Gets to her and takes hold of her.*)

VETA (*rushing to her, they kiss*): Aunt Ethel! (*Motioning to* MYRTLE *to come forward and meet the great lady.*) Oh, no—I'm very much alive—thank you—

MRS. CHAUVENET (*turning to* MYRTLE):—and this full-grown girl is your daughter—I've known you since you were a baby.

MYRTLE: I know.

MRS. CHAUVENET: What's your name, dear?

VETA (*proudly*): This is Myrtle—Aunt Ethel. Myrtle Mae—for the two sisters of her father. He's dead. That's what confused you.

MRS. CHAUVENET: Where's Elwood?

VETA (*with a nervous glance at* MYRTLE MAE): He couldn't be here, Aunt Ethel—now let me get you some tea.

MRS. CHAUVENET: Elwood isn't here?

VETA: No—

MRS. CHAUVENET: Oh, shame on him. That was the main reason I came. (*Takes off scarf—puts it on chair.*) I want to see Elwood.

VETA: Come—there are loads of people anxious to speak to you.

MRS. CHAUVENET: Do you realize, Veta, it's been years since I've seen Elwood?

VETA: No—where does the time go?

MRS. CHAUVENET: But I don't understand it. I was saying to Mr. Chauvenet only the other night—what on earth do you suppose has happened to Elwood Dowd? He never comes to the club dances any more. I haven't seen him at a horse show in years. Does Elwood see anybody these days?

VETA (*and* MYRTLE *glance at each other*): Oh, yes—Aunt Ethel. Elwood sees somebody.

MYRTLE: Oh, yes.

MRS. CHAUVENET (*to* MYRTLE): Your Uncle Elwood, child, is one of my favorite people. (VETA *rises and crosses around chair.*) Always has been.

VETA: Yes, I remember.

MRS. CHAUVENET: Is Elwood happy, Veta?

VETA: Elwood's very happy, Aunt Ethel. You don't need to worry about Elwood——(*Looks through doorway. She is anxious to get the subject on something else.*) Why, there's Mrs. Frank Cummings— just came in. Don't you want to speak to her?

MRS. CHAUVENET (*crosses above chair to peer out*): My—but she looks ghastly! Hasn't she failed though?

VETA: If you think she looks badly—you should see him!

MRS. CHAUVENET: Is that so? I must have them over. (*Looks again.*) She looks frightful. I thought she was dead.

VETA: Oh, no.

MRS. CHAUVENET: Now—what about tea, Veta?

VETA: Certainly—(*Starts forward to lead the way.*) If you will forgive me, I will precede you——(ELWOOD *enters.* MRS. CHAUVENET *turns back to pick up her scarf from chair, and sees him.*)

MRS. CHAUVENET (*rushing forward*): Elwood! Elwood Dowd! Bless your heart.

ELWOOD (*coming forward and bowing as he takes her hand*): Aunt Ethel! What a pleasure to come in and find a beautiful woman waiting for me!

MRS. CHAUVENET (*looking at him fondly*): Elwood—you haven't changed.

VETA (*moves forward quickly, takes hold of her*): Come along, Aunt Ethel—you mustn't miss the party.

MYRTLE: There's punch if you don't like tea.

MRS. CHAUVENET: But I do like tea. Stop pulling at me, you two. Elwood, what night next week can you come to dinner?

ELWOOD: Any night. Any night at all, Aunt Ethel—I would be delighted.

VETA: Elwood, there's some mail for you today. I took it up to your room.

ELWOOD: Did you, Veta? That was nice of you. Aunt Ethel—I want you to meet Harvey. As you can see he's a Pooka. (*Turns toward air beside him.*) Harvey, you've heard me speak of Mrs. Chauvenet? We always called her Aunt Ethel. She is one of my oldest and dearest friends. (*Inclines head toward space and goes "Hmm!" and then listens as though not hearing first time. Nods as though having heard someone next to him speak.*) Yes—yes—that's right. She's the one. This is the one. (*To* MRS. CHAUVENET.) He says he would have known you anywhere. (*Then as a confused, bewildered look comes over* MRS. CHAUVENET'S *face and as she looks to left and right of* ELWOOD *and cranes her neck to see behind him*—ELWOOD, *not seeing her expression, crosses her toward* VETA *and* MYRTLE MAE.) You both look lovely. (*Turns to the air next to him.*) Come in with me, Harvey—We must say hello to all of our friends——(*Bows to* MRS. CHAUVENET.) I beg your pardon, Aunt Ethel. If you'll excuse me for one moment—(*Puts his hand gently on her arm, trying to turn her.*)

MRS. CHAUVENET: What?

ELWOOD: You are standing in his way—(SHE *gives a little—her eyes wide on him.*) Come along, Harvey. *He watches the invisible Harvey cross to door, then stops him.*) Uh-uh! (ELWOOD *goes over to door. He turns and pantomimes as he arranges the tie and brushes off the head of the invisible Harvey. Then he does the same thing to his own tie. They are all watching him,* MRS. CHAUVENET *in horrified fascination. The heads of* VETA *and* MYRTLE, *bowed in agony.*) Go right on in, Harvey. I'll join you in a minute. (*He pantomimes as though slapping him on the back, and ushers him out. Then turns and comes back to* MRS. CHAUVENET.) Aunt Ethel, I can see you are disturbed about Harvey. Please don't be. He stares like that at everybody. It's his way. But he liked you. I could tell. He liked you very much. (*Pats her arm reassuringly, smiles at her, then calmly and confidently goes on out. After his exit,* MRS. CHAUVENET, MYRTLE *and* VETA *are silent. Finally* VETA—*with a resigned tone—clears her throat.*)

VETA (*looking at* MRS. CHAUVENET): Some tea—perhaps—?

MRS. CHAUVENET: Why, I—not right now—I—well—I think I'll be running along. (*Crosses back of table.*)

MYRTLE: But—

VETA (*putting a hand over hers to quiet her*): I'm so sorry—

MRS. CHAUVENET: I'll—I'll be talking to you soon. Good-by—good-by —(*She exits quickly.* VETA *stands stiffly—her anger paralyzing her.* MYRTLE *finally tiptoes over and closes one side of door—peeking over, but keeping herself out of sight.*)

MYRTLE: Oh, God—(*Starts to run for doorway.*) Oh, my God!

VETA: Myrtle—where are you going?

MYRTLE: Up to my room. He's introducing Harvey to everybody. I can't face those people now. I wish I were dead.

VETA: Come back here. Stay with me. We'll get him out of there and upstairs to his room.

MYRTLE: I won't do it. I can't. I can't.

VETA: Myrtle Mae! (MYRTLE *stops.* VETA *goes over to her and pulls her directly in line with doorway.*) Now—pretend I'm fixing your corsage.

MYRTLE (*covering her face with her hands in shame*): Oh, Mother!

VETA: We've got to. Pretend we're having a gay little chat. Keep looking. When you catch his eye, tell me. He always comes when I call him. Now, then—do you see him yet?

MYRTLE: No—not yet. How do you do, Mrs. Cummings.

VETA: Smile, can't you? Have you no pride? I'm smiling—(*Laughs.*) and he's my own brother!

MYRTLE: Oh, Mother—people get run over by trucks every day. Why can't something like that happen to Uncle Elwood?

VETA: Myrtle Mae Simmons, I'm ashamed of you. This thing is not your uncle's fault. (*Phone rings.*)

MYRTLE: Ouch! You're sticking me with that pin!

VETA: That's Miss Ellerbe. Keep looking. Keep smiling. (*She goes to phone.*)

MYRTLE: Mrs. Cummings is leaving. Uncle Elwood must have told her what Harvey is. Oh, God!

VETA (*on phone*): Hello—this is Mrs. Simmons. Should you come in the clothes you have on—What have you on? Who is this? But I don't know any Miss Greenawalt. Should you what?—May I ask who invited you? Mr. Dowd! Thank you just the same, but I believe there has been a mistake.—Well, I never!

MYRTLE: Never what?

VETA: One of your Uncle Elwood's friends. She asked me if she should bring a quart of gin to the Wednesday Forum!

MYRTLE: There he is—he's talking to Mrs. Halsey.

VETA: Is Harvey with him?

MYRTLE: What a thing to ask! How can I tell? How can anybody tell but Uncle Elwood?

VETA (*calls*): Oh, Elwood, could I see you a moment, dear? (*To* MYRTLE.) I promise you your Uncle Elwood has disgraced us for the last time in this house. I'm going to do something I've never done before.

MYRTLE: What did you mean just now when you said this was not Uncle Elwood's fault? If it's not his fault, whose fault is it?

VETA: Never you mind. I know whose fault it is. Now lift up your head and smile and go back in as though nothing had happened.

MYRTLE: You're no match for Uncle Elwood.

VETA: You'll see. (ELWOOD *is coming.*)

MYRTLE (*as they pass at door*): Mother's waiting for you. (*She exits.*)

VETA: Elwood! Could I see you for a moment, dear?

ELWOOD: Yes, sister. Excuse me, Harvey. (VETA *steps quickly over and pulls double doors together.*)

VETA: Elwood, would you mind sitting down in here and waiting for me until the party is over? I want to talk to you. It's very important.

ELWOOD (*crossing*): Of course, sister. I happen to have a little free time right now and you're welcome to all of it, Veta. Do you want Harvey to wait too?

VETA (*quite seriously—not in a pampering, humoring tone at all*): Yes, Elwood. I certainly do. (*She steals out—watching him as she crosses through door. After she has gone out we see doors being*

pulled together from the outside and hear the click of a lock. ELWOOD
*goes calmly over to bookcase, peruses it carefully, and then when he
has found the book he wants, takes it out and from behind it pulls a
half-filled pint bottle of liquor.*)

ELWOOD (*looking at book he holds in one hand*): Ah—Jane Austen.
(*He gets one chair, pulls it down, facing front. Gets chair and pulls it
right alongside. Sits down, sets bottle on floor between chairs.*) Sit
down, Harvey. Veta wants to talk to us. She said it was important. I
think she wants to congratulate us on the impression we made at her
party. (*Reads. Turns to Harvey. Inclines head and listens, then looks
at back of book and answers as though Harvey had asked what edition it is, who published it and what are those names on the fly leaf;
turning head toward empty chair each time and twice saying
"Hmm?"*) Jane Austen—De Luxe Edition—Limited—Grosset and
Dunlap—The usual acknowledgements. Chapter One—

AND THE CURTAIN FALLS

SCENE II

SCENE: *The office in the main building of Chumley's Rest—a
sanitarium for mental patients. The wall at back is half plaster
and half glass. Through a center door we can see the corridor
of the sanitarium itself. In the right wall is a door which is
lettered "Dr. Chumley." Above wall is a bookcase, a small
filing-case on top of it. Across the room is another door lettered "Dr. Sanderson." Down left is the door leading from the
outside. There is a big desk at right angles with footlights, with
a chair at either side of the desk. At right is a table with chairs
on either side.*

TIME: *An hour after the curtain of Scene I.*

AT RISE: MISS RUTH KELLY, *head nurse at Chumley's Rest, is
seated, taking notes as she talks to* VETA SIMMONS. MISS KELLY
*is a very pretty young woman of about twenty-four. She is wear-
ing a starched white uniform and cap. As she talks to Veta she
writes on a slip of paper with a pencil.*

KELLY (*writing*): Mrs. O. R. Simmons, 343 Temple Drive, is that
right?

VETA (*nodding, taking handkerchief from handbag*): We were born and raised there. It's old but we love it. It's our home. (*Crosses to table, puts down handbag.*)

KELLY: And you wish to enter your brother here at the sanitarium for treatment. Your brother's name?

VETA (*coming back to desk—raising handkerchief to eyes and dabbing*): It's—oh—

KELLY: Mrs. Simmons, what is your brother's name?

VETA: I'm sorry. Life is not easy for any of us. I'll have to hold my head up and go on just the same. That's what I keep telling Myrtle and that's what Myrtle Mae keeps telling me. She's heart-broken about her Uncle Elwood—Elwood P. Dowd. That's it. (*Sits.*)

KELLY (*writing*): Elwood P. Dowd. His age?

VETA: Forty-seven the 24th of last April. He's Taurus—Taurus—the bull. I'm Leo, and Myrtle is on a cusp.

KELLY: Forty-seven. Is he married?

VETA: No, Elwood has never married. He stayed with Mother. He was always a great home boy. He loved his home.

KELLY: You have him with you now?

VETA: He's in a taxicab down in the driveway. (KELLY *rings buzzer.*) I gave the driver a dollar to watch him, but I didn't tell the man why. You can't tell these things to perfect strangers. (*Enter* WILSON. *He is the sanitarium strongarm. He is a big burly attendant, black-browed, about 28.* KELLY *crosses in front of desk toward bookcase.*)

KELLY: Mr. Wilson, would you step down to a taxi in the driveway and ask a Mr. Dowd if he would be good enough to step up to Room number 24—South Wing G?

WILSON: *Ask* him?

KELLY (*with a warning glance toward* VETA): This is his sister, Mrs. Simmons. (KELLY *crosses to cabinet for card.*)

WILSON (*with a feeble grin*): How do—why, certainly—be glad to *escort* him. (*Exits.*)

VETA: Thank you.

KELLY (*handing* VETA *her printed slip*): The rates here, Mrs. Simmons —you'll find them printed on this card.

VETA (*waving it away*): That will all be taken care of by my mother's estate. The late Marcella Pinney Dowd. Judge Gaffney is our attorney.

KELLY: Now I'll see if Dr. Sanderson can see you. (*Starts toward office.*)

VETA: Dr. Sanderson? I want to see Dr. Chumley himself.

KELLY (*backs down*): Oh, Mrs. Simmons, Dr. Sanderson is the one who sees everybody. Dr. Chumley sees no one.

VETA: He's still head of this institution, isn't he? He's still a psychiatrist, isn't he?

KELLY (*shocked at such heresy*): Still a psychiatrist! Dr. Chumley is more than that. He is a psychiatrist with a national reputation. Whenever people have mental breakdowns they at once think of Dr. Chumley.

VETA (*pointing*): That's his office, isn't it? Well, you march right in and tell him I want to see him. If he knows who's in here he'll come out here.

KELLY: I wouldn't dare disturb him, Mrs. Simmons. I would be discharged if I did.

VETA: Well, I don't like to be pushed off onto any second fiddle.

KELLY: Dr. Sanderson is nobody's second fiddle. (*Crosses to back of desk, her eyes aglow.*) He's young, of course, and he hasn't been out of medical school very long, but Dr. Chumley tried out twelve and kept Dr. Sanderson. He's really wonderful—(*Catches herself*) to the patients.

VETA: Very well. Tell him I'm here.

KELLY (*straightens her cap. As she exits she primps*): Right away. (VETA *rises, takes off coat—puts it on back of chair, sighs.*) Oh dear—oh dear (*And crosses to table.* WILSON *and* ELWOOD *appear in corridor.* ELWOOD *pulls over a little from* WILSON *and sees* VETA.)

ELWOOD: Veta—isn't this wonderful!

(WILSON *takes him forcefully off upstairs.* VETA *is still jumpy and nervous from the surprise, and her back is to door as* DR. SANDERSON *enters.* LYMAN SANDERSON *is a good-looking man of 27 or 28. He is wearing a starched white coat over dark trousers. His eyes follow* MISS KELLY, *who has walked out before him and gone out, closing doors. Then he sees* VETA, *pulls down his jacket, and gets a professional bearing.* VETA *has not heard him come in. She is busy with her compact.*)

SANDERSON (*looking at slip in his hand*): Mrs. Simmons?

VETA (*startled—she jumps*): Oh—oh dear—I didn't hear you come in. You startled me. You're Dr. Sanderson?

SANDERSON (*he nods*): Yes. Will you be seated, please?

VETA (*sits*): Thank you. I hope you don't think I'm jumpy like that all the time, but I—

SANDERSON (*crossing in front of table*): Of course not. Miss Kelly tells me you are concerned about your brother. Dowd, is it? Elwood P. Dowd?

VETA: Yes, Doctor—he's—this isn't easy for me, Doctor.

SANDERSON (*kindly*): Naturally these things aren't easy for the families of patients. I understand.

VETA (*twisting her handkerchief nervously*): It's what Elwood's doing to himself, Doctor—that's the thing. Myrtle Mae has a right to nice friends. She's young and her whole life is before her. That's my daughter.

SANDERSON (*sits*): Your daughter. How long has it been since you began to notice any peculiarity in your brother's actions?

VETA: I noticed it right away when Mother died, and Myrtle Mae and I came back home from Des Moines to live with Elwood. I could see that he—that he—(*Twists handkerchief—looks pleadingly at* SANDERSON.)

SANDERSON: That he—what? Take your time, Mrs. Simmons. Don't strain. Let it come. I'll wait for it.

VETA: Doctor—everything I say to you is confidential? Isn't it?

SANDERSON: That's understood.

VETA: Because it's a slap in the face to everything we've stood for in this community the way Elwood is acting now.

SANDERSON: I am not a gossip, Mrs. Simmons. I am a psychiatrist.

VETA: Well—for one thing—he drinks.

SANDERSON: To excess?

VETA: To excess? Well—don't you call it excess when a man never lets a day go by without stepping into one of those cheap taverns, sitting around with riff-raff and people you never heard of? Inviting them to the house—playing cards with them—giving them food and money. And here I am trying to get Myrtle Mae started with a nice group of young people. If that isn't excess I'm sure I don't know what excess is.

SANDERSON: I didn't doubt your statement, Mrs. Simmons. I merely asked if your brother drinks.

VETA: Well, yes, I say definitely Elwood drinks and I want him committed out here permanently, because I cannot stand another day of that Harvey. Myrtle and I have to set a place at the table for Harvey. We have to move over on the sofa and make room for Harvey. We have to answer the telephone when Elwood calls and asks to speak to Harvey. Then at the party this afternoon with Mrs. Chauvenet there— We didn't even know anything about Harvey until we came back here. Doctor, don't you think it would have been a little bit kinder of Mother to have written and told me about Harvey? Be honest, now— don't you?

SANDERSON: I really couldn't answer that question, because I——

VETA: I can. Yes—it certainly would have.

SANDERSON: This person you call Harvey—who is he?

VETA: He's a rabbit.

SANDERSON: Perhaps—but just who is he? Some companion—someone your brother has picked up in these bars, of whom you disapprove?

VETA (*patiently*): Doctor—I've been telling you. Harvey is a rabbit—a big white rabbit—six feet high—or is it six feet and a half? Heaven knows I ought to know. He's been around the house long enough.

SANDERSON (*regarding her narrowly*): Now, Mrs. Simmons, let me understand this—you say—

VETA (*impatient*): Doctor—do I have to keep repeating myself? My brother insists that his closest friend is this big white rabbit. This rabbit is named Harvey. Harvey lives at our house. Don't you understand? He and Elwood go every place together. Elwood buys railroad tickets, theater tickets, for both of them. As I told Myrtle Mae—if your uncle was so lonesome he had to bring something home—why couldn't he bring home something human? He has me, doesn't he? He has Myrtle Mae, doesn't he? (*She leans forward.*) Doctor—(*She rises to him. He inclines toward her.*) I'm going to tell you something I've never told anybody in the world before. (*Puts her hand on his shoulder.*) Every once in a while I see that big white rabbit myself. Now isn't that terrible? I've never even told that to Myrtle Mae.

SANDERSON (*now convinced. Starts to rise*): Mrs. Simmons—

VETA (*straightening*): And what's more—he's every bit as big as Elwood says he is. Now don't ever tell that to anybody, Doctor. I'm ashamed of it.

SANDERSON (*crosses to* VETA): I can see that you have been under a great nervous strain recently.

VETA: Well—I certainly have.

SANDERSON: Grief over your mother's death depressed you considerably?

VETA (*sits*): Nobody knows how much.

SANDERSON: Been losing sleep?

VETA: How could anybody sleep with that going on?

SANDERSON (*crosses to back of desk*): Short-tempered over trifles?

VETA: You just try living with those two and see how your temper holds up.

SANDERSON (*presses buzzer*): Loss of appetite?

VETA: No one could eat at a table with my brother and a big white rabbit. Well, I'm finished with it. I'll sell the house—be appointed conservator of Elwood's estate, and Myrtle Mae and I will be able to entertain our friends in peace. It's too much, Doctor. I just can't stand it.

SANDERSON (*has been repeatedly pressing a buzzer on his desk. He looks with annoyance toward hall door. His answer now to* VETA *is gentle*): Of course, Mrs. Simmons. Of course it is. You're tired.

VETA (*she nods*): Oh, yes I am.

SANDERSON: You've been worrying a great deal.

VETA (*nods*): Yes, I have. I can't help it.

SANDERSON: And now I'm going to help you.

VETA: Oh, Doctor . . .

SANDERSON (*goes cautiously to door—watching her*): Just sit there quietly, Mrs. Simmons. I'll be right back. (*He exits.*)

VETA (*sighing with relief, rises and calls out as she takes coat*): I'll just go down to the cab and get Elwood's things. (*She exits.* SANDERSON, KELLY, *and* WILSON *come from center stage.*)

SANDERSON: Why didn't someone answer the buzzer?

KELLY: I didn't hear you, Doctor—

SANDERSON: I rang and rang. (*Looks into his office. It is empty.*) Mrs. Simmons—(*Looks out door, shuts it, comes back.*) Sound the gong, Wilson. That poor woman must not leave the grounds.

WILSON: She's made with a getaway, huh, Doc? (WILSON *presses a button on the wall and we hear a loud gong sounding.*)

SANDERSON: Her condition is serious. Go after her. (WILSON *exits.*)

KELLY: I can't believe it. (SANDERSON *sits and picks up phone.*)

SANDERSON: Main gate. Henry, Dr. Sanderson. Allow no one out of the main gate. We're looking for a patient. (*Hangs up.*) I shouldn't have left her alone, but no one answered the buzzer.

KELLY: Wilson was in South, Doctor.

SANDERSON (*making out papers*): What have we available, Miss Kelly?

KELLY: Number 13, upper West R., is ready, Doctor.

SANDERSON: Have her taken there immediately, and I will prescribe preliminary treatment. I must contact her brother. Dowd is the name. Elwood P. Dowd. Get him on the telephone for me, will you please, Miss Kelly?

KELLY: But Doctor—I didn't know it was the woman who needed the treatment. She said it was for her brother.

SANDERSON: Of course she did. It's the oldest dodge in the world—always used by a cunning type of psychopath. She apparently knew her brother was about to commit her, so she came out to discredit him. Get him on the telephone, please.

KELLY: But, Doctor—I thought the woman was all right, so I had Wilson take the brother up to No. 24 South Wing G. He's there now.

SANDERSON (*staring at her with horror*): You had Wilson take the brother in? No gags, please, Kelly. You're not serious, are you?

KELLY: Oh, I did, Doctor. I did. Oh, Doctor, I'm terribly sorry.

SANDERSON: Oh, well then, if you're sorry, that fixes everything. (*He starts to pick up house phone and finishes the curse under his breath.*) Oh—no! (*Buries his head in his hands.*)

KELLY: I'll do it, Doctor. I'll do it. (*She takes phone.*) Miss Dunphy—will you please unlock the door to Number 24—and give Mr. Dowd his clothes and——? (*Looks at* SANDERSON *for direction.*)

SANDERSON: Ask him to step down to the office right away.

KELLY (*into phone*): Ask him to step down to the office right away. There's been a terrible mistake and Dr. Sanderson wants to explain—

SANDERSON (*crosses below table*): Explain? Apologize!

KELLY (*hanging up*): Thank heaven they hadn't put him into a hydro tub yet. She'll let him out.

SANDERSON (*staring at her*): Beautiful—and dumb, too. It's almost too good to be true.

KELLY: Doctor—I feel terrible. I didn't know. Judge Gaffney called and said Mrs. Simmons and her brother would be out here, and when she came in here—you don't have to be sarcastic.

SANDERSON: Oh, don't I? Stop worrying. We'll squirm out of it some way. (*Thinking—starts toward right.*)

KELLY: Where are you going?

SANDERSON: I've got to tell the chief about it, Kelly. He may want to handle this himself.

KELLY: He'll be furious. I know he will. He'll die. And then he'll terminate me.

SANDERSON (*below table, catches her shoulders*): The responsibility is all mine, Kelly.

KELLY: Oh, no—tell him it was all my fault, Doctor.

SANDERSON: I never mention your name. (*Crossing to door.*) Except in my sleep.

KELLY: But this man Dowd——(*Kneels on chair.*)

SANDERSON: Don't let him get away. I'll be right back.

KELLY: But what shall I say to him? What shall I do? He'll be furious.

SANDERSON: Look, Kelly—he'll probably be fit to be tied—but he's a man, isn't he?

KELLY: I guess so—his name is Mister. (*Off chair.*)

SANDERSON (*across chair from her*): Go into your old routine—you know—the eyes—the swish—the works. I'm immune—but I've seen it work with some people—some of the patients out here. Keep him here, Kelly—if you have to do a strip tease. (*He exits.*)

KELLY (*very angry. Speaks to closed door*): Well, of all the—oh— you're wonderful, Dr. Sanderson! You're just about the most wonderful person I ever met in my life. (*Kicks chair.*)

WILSON (*has entered in time to hear last sentence*): Yeah—but how about giving me a lift here just the same?

KELLY: What?

WILSON: That Simmons dame.

KELLY (*crosses to* WILSON): Did you catch her?

WILSON: Slick as a whistle. She was comin' along the path hummin' a little tune. I jumped out at her from behind a tree. I says "Sister— there's a man wants to see you." Shoulda heard her yell! She's whacky, all right.

KELLY: Take her to No. 13 upper West R. (*Crosses* WILSON *to back of desk.*)

WILSON: She's there now. Brought her in through the diet kitchen. She's screamin' and kickin' like hell. I'll hold her if you'll come and undress her.

KELLY: Just a second, Wilson. Dr. Sanderson told me to stay here till her brother comes down—(*Round back of desk.*)

WILSON: Make it snappy—(*Goes out.* ELWOOD *enters.* KELLY *rises.*)

KELLY: You're Mr. Dowd?

ELWOOD (*carrying another hat and coat over his arm. He bows*): Elwood P.

KELLY: I'm Miss Kelly.

ELWOOD: Let me give you one of my cards. (*Fishes in vest pocket—pulls out card.*) If you should want to call me—call me at this number. Don't call me at that one.

KELLY: Thank you.

ELWOOD: Perfectly all right, and if you lose it—don't worry, my dear. I have plenty more.

KELLY: Won't you have a chair, please, Mr. Dowd?

ELWOOD: Thank you. I'll have two. Allow me. (*He brings another chair. Puts extra hat and coat on table. Motions Harvey to sit in chair. He stands waiting.*)

KELLY: Dr. Sanderson is very anxious to talk to you. He'll be here in a minute. Please be seated.

ELWOOD (*waving her toward chair*): After you, my dear.

KELLY: Oh, I really can't, thank you. I'm in and out all the time. But you mustn't mind me. Please sit down.

ELWOOD (*bowing*): After you.

KELLY (*she sits. He sits on chair he has just put in place*): Could I get you a magazine to look at?

ELWOOD: I would much rather look at you, Miss Kelly, if you don't mind. You really are very lovely.

KELLY: Oh—well. Thank you. Some people don't seem to think so.

ELWOOD: Some people are blind. That is often brought to my attention. And now, Miss Kelly—I would like to have you meet—(*Enter* SANDERSON. MISS KELLY *rises and backs up to below desk.* ELWOOD *rises when she does, and he makes a motion to the invisible Harvey to rise, too.*)

SANDERSON (*going to him, extending hand*): Mr. Dowd?

ELWOOD: Elwood P. Let me give you one of my cards. If you should want—

SANDERSON: Mr. Dowd—I am Dr. Lyman Sanderson, Dr. Chumley's assistant out here.

ELWOOD: Well, good for you! I'm happy to know you. How are you, Doctor?

SANDERSON: That's going to depend on you, I'm afraid. Please sit down. You've met Miss Kelly, Mr. Dowd?

ELWOOD: I have had that pleasure, and I want both of you to meet a very dear friend of mine—

SANDERSON: Later on—be glad to. Won't you be seated, because first I want to say—

ELWOOD: After Miss Kelly—

SANDERSON: Sit down, Kelly—(*She sits, as does* ELWOOD—*who indicates to Harvey to sit also.*) Is that chair quite comfortable, Mr. Dowd?

ELWOOD: Yes, thank you. Would you care to try it? (*He takes out a cigarette.*)

SANDERSON: No, thank you. How about an ash tray there? Could we give Mr. Dowd an ash tray? (KELLY *gets up—gets it from wall.* ELWOOD *and Harvey rise also.* ELWOOD *beams as he turns and watches her.* KELLY *puts ash tray by* DOWD, *who moves it to share with Harvey.*) Is it too warm in here for you, Mr. Dowd? Would you like me to open a window? (ELWOOD *hasn't heard. He is watching* MISS KELLY.)

KELLY (*turning, smiling at him*): Mr. Dowd—Dr. Sanderson wants to know if he should open a window?

ELWOOD: That's entirely up to him. I wouldn't presume to live his life for him. (*During this dialogue* SANDERSON *is near window.* KELLY *has her eyes on his face.* ELWOOD *smiles at Harvey fondly.* KELLY *sits.*)

SANDERSON: Now then, Mr. Dowd, I can see that you're not the type of person to be taken in by any high-flown phrases or beating about the bush. (*Sits on corner of desk.*)

ELWOOD (*politely*): Is that so, Doctor?

SANDERSON: You have us at a disadvantage here. You know it. We know it. Let's lay the cards on the table.

ELWOOD: That certainly appeals to me, Doctor.

SANDERSON: Best way in the long run. People are people, no matter where you go.

ELWOOD: That is very often the case.

SANDERSON: And being human are therefore liable to mistakes. Miss Kelly and I have made a mistake here this afternoon, Mr. Dowd, and we'd like to explain it to you.

KELLY: It wasn't Doctor Sanderson's fault, Mr. Dowd. It was mine.

SANDERSON: A human failing—as I said.

ELWOOD: I find it very interesting, nevertheless. You and Miss Kelly here? (*They nod.*) This afternoon—you say? (*They nod.* ELWOOD *gives Harvey a knowing look.*)

KELLY: We do hope you'll understand, Mr. Dowd.

ELWOOD: Oh, yes. Yes. These things are often the basis of a long and warm friendship.

SANDERSON: And the responsibility is, of course, not hers—but mine.

ELWOOD: Your attitude may be old-fashioned, Doctor—but I like it.

SANDERSON: Now, if I had seen your sister first—that would have been an entirely different story.

ELWOOD: Now there you surprise me. I think the world and all of Veta —but I had supposed she had seen her day. (KELLY *sits*.)

SANDERSON: You must not attach any blame to her. She is a very sick woman. Came in here insisting you were in need of treatment. That's perfectly ridiculous.

ELWOOD: Veta shouldn't be upset about me. I get along fine.

SANDERSON: Exactly—but your sister had already talked to Miss Kelly, and there had been a call from your family lawyer, Judge Gaffney.

ELWOOD: Oh, yes, I know him. Know his wife, too. Nice people. (*He turns to Harvey, takes cigarette; he needs a match.*)

SANDERSON: Is there something I can get for you, Mr. Dowd?

ELWOOD: What did you have in mind?

SANDERSON: A light—here—let me give you a light. (*Crosses to* DOWD, *lights his cigarette.* ELWOOD *brushes smoke away from the rabbit.*) Your sister was extremely nervous and plunged right away into a heated tirade on your drinking. (*Crosses back to sit on chair.*)

ELWOOD: That was Veta.

SANDERSON: She became hysterical.

ELWOOD: I tell Veta not to worry about that. I'll take care of that.

SANDERSON: Exactly. Oh, I suppose you take a drink now and then— the same as the rest of us?

ELWOOD: Yes, I do. As a matter of fact, I would like one right now.

SANDERSON: Matter of fact, so would I, but your sister's reaction to the whole matter of drinking was entirely too intense. Does your sister drink, Mr. Dowd?

ELWOOD: Oh, no, Doctor. No. I don't believe Veta has ever taken a drink.

SANDERSON: Well, I'm going to surprise you. I think she has and does —constantly.

ELWOOD: I am certainly surprised.

SANDERSON: But it's not her alcoholism that's going to be the basis for my diagnosis of her case. It's much more serious than that. It was when she began talking so emotionally about this big white rabbit—Harvey—yes, I believe she called him Harvey—

ELWOOD (*nodding*): Harvey is his name.

SANDERSON: She claimed you were persecuting her with this Harvey.

ELWOOD: I haven't been persecuting her with Harvey. Veta shouldn't feel that way. And now, Doctor, before we go any further I must insist you let me introduce—(*He starts to rise.*)

SANDERSON: Let me make my point first, Mr. Dowd. This trouble of your sister's didn't spring up overnight. Her condition stems from trauma.

ELWOOD (*sits down again*): From what?

SANDERSON: From trauma spelled T-R-A-U-M-A. It means shock. Nothing unusual about it. There is the birth trauma. The shock to the act of being born.

ELWOOD (*nodding*): That's the one we never get over—

SANDERSON: You have a nice sense of humor, Dowd—hasn't he, Miss Kelly?

KELLY: Oh, yes, Doctor.

ELWOOD: May I say the same about both of you?

SANDERSON: To sum it all up—your sister's condition is serious, but I can help her. She must however remain out here temporarily.

ELWOOD: I've always wanted Veta to have everything she needs.

SANDERSON: Exactly.

ELWOOD: But I wouldn't want Veta to stay out here unless she liked it out here and wanted to stay here.

SANDERSON: Of course. (*To* KELLY.) Did Wilson get what he went after? (KELLY *nods.*)

KELLY: Yes, Doctor. (*She rises.*)

SANDERSON: What was Mrs. Simmons' attitude, Miss Kelly?

KELLY (*crosses above desk to file cabinet*): Not unusual, Doctor.

SANDERSON (*rising*): Mr. Dowd, if this were an ordinary delusion—something reflected on the memory picture—in other words, if she were seeing something she had seen once—that would be one thing. But this is more serious. It stands to reason nobody has ever seen a white rabbit six feet high.

ELWOOD (*smiles at* HARVEY): Not very often, Doctor.

SANDERSON: I like you, Dowd.

ELWOOD: I like you, too, Doctor. And Miss Kelly here. (*Looks for* MISS KELLY, *who is just crossing in front of window seat.* ELWOOD *springs to his feet.* KELLY *sits quickly.* ELWOOD *motions Harvey down and sits, himself.*) I like her, too.

SANDERSON: So she must be committed here temporarily. Under these circumstances I would commit my own grandmother.

ELWOOD: Does your grandmother drink, too?

SANDERSON: It's just an expression. (*Leans over desk.*) Now will you sign these temporary commitment papers as next-of-kin—just a formality?

ELWOOD (*rises*): You'd better have Veta do that, Doctor. She always does all the signing and managing for the family. She's good at it. (*Pushes chair under desk.*)

SANDERSON: We can't disturb her now. (*Sits.*)

ELWOOD: Perhaps I'd better talk it over with Judge Gaffney?

SANDERSON: You can explain it all to him later. Tell him I advised it. And it isn't as if you couldn't drop in here any time and make inquiries. Glad to have you. I'll make out a full visitor's pass for you. When would you like to come back? Wednesday, say? Friday, say?

ELWOOD: You and Miss Kelly have been so pleasant I can come back right after dinner. About an hour.

SANDERSON (*taken aback*): Well—we're pretty busy around here, but I guess that's all right.

ELWOOD: I don't really have to go now. I'm not very hungry.

SANDERSON: Delighted to have you stay—but Miss Kelly and I have to get on upstairs now. Plenty of work to do. But I tell you what you might like to do.

ELWOOD: What might I like to do?

SANDERSON: We don't usually do this—but just to make sure in your mind that your sister is in good hands why don't you look around here? If you go through that door—(*Rises—points beyond stairway*) and turn right just beyond the stairway you'll find the occupational therapy room down the hall, and beyond that the conservatory, the library, and the diet kitchen.

ELWOOD: For Veta's sake I believe I'd better do that, Doctor.

SANDERSON: Very well, then. (*He is now anxious to terminate the interview. Rises, shakes hands.*) It's been a great pleasure to have this little talk with you, Mr. Dowd. (*Gives him pass.*)

ELWOOD (*walking toward her*): I've enjoyed it too, Doctor—meeting you and Miss Kelly.

SANDERSON: And I will say that for a layman you show an unusually acute perception into psychiatric problems.

ELWOOD: Is that a fact? I never thought I knew anything about it. Nobody does, do you think?

SANDERSON: Well—the good psychiatrist is not found under every bush.

ELWOOD: You have to pick the right bush. Since we all seem to have enjoyed this so much, let us keep right on. I would like to invite you to come with me now down to Charlie's Place and have a drink. When I enjoy people I like to stay right with them.

SANDERSON: Sorry—we're on duty now. Give us a rain check. Some other time be glad to.

ELWOOD: When?

SANDERSON: Oh—can't say right now. Miss Kelly and I don't go off duty till ten o'clock at night.

ELWOOD: Let us go to Charlie's at ten o'clock tonight.

SANDERSON: Well—

ELWOOD: And you, Miss Kelly?

KELLY: I—(*Looks at* SANDERSON.)

SANDERSON: Dr. Chumley doesn't approve of members of the staff fraternizing, but since you've been so understanding perhaps we could manage it.

ELWOOD: I'll pick you up out here in a cab at ten o'clock tonight and the four of us will spend a happy evening. I want you both to become friends with a very dear friend of mine. You said later on—so later on it will be. Good-by, now. (*Motions good-by to Harvey. Tips hat, exits.*)

KELLY (*places chair and ash tray against back wall*): Whew—now I can breathe again!

SANDERSON: Boy, that was a close shave all right, but he seemed to be a pretty reasonable sort of fellow. That man is proud—what he has to be proud of I don't know. I played up to that pride. You can get to almost anybody if you want to. Now I must look in on that Simmons woman. (*Crosses below desk.*)

KELLY: Dr. Sanderson—! (SANDERSON *turns.*) You say you can get to anybody if you want to. How can you do that?

SANDERSON: Takes study, Kelly. Years of specialized training. There's only one thing I don't like about this Dowd business.

KELLY: What's that?

SANDERSON: Having to make that date with him. Of course the man has left here as a good friend and booster of this sanitarium—so I guess I'll have to go with him tonight—but you don't have to go.

KELLY: Oh!

SANDERSON: No point in it. I'll have a drink with him, pat him on the back and leave. I've got a date tonight, anyway.

KELLY (*freezing*): Oh, yes—by all means. I didn't intend to go, anyway. The idea bored me stiff. I wouldn't go if I never went anywhere again. I wouldn't go if my life depended on it.

SANDERSON (*stepping back to her*): What's the matter with you, Kelly? What are you getting so emotional about?

KELLY: He may be a peculiar man with funny clothes, but he knows how to act. His manners were perfect.

SANDERSON: I saw you giving him the doll-puss stare. I didn't miss that.

KELLY: He wouldn't sit down till I sat down. He told me I was lovely and he called me dear. I'd go to have a drink with him if you weren't going.

SANDERSON: Sure you would. And look at him! All he does is hang around bars. He doesn't work. All that corny bowing and getting up out of his chair every time a woman makes a move. Why, he's as outdated as a cast-iron deer. But you'd sit with him in a bar and let him flatter you—You're a wonderful girl, Kelly.

KELLY: Now let me tell you something—you—(*Enter* DR. WILLIAM CHUMLEY. DR. CHUMLEY *is a large, handsome man of about 57. He has gray hair and wears rimless glasses, which he removes now and then to tap on his hand for emphasis. He is smartly dressed. His manner is confident, pompous, and lordly. He is good and he knows it.*)

CHUMLEY (*enters with book*): Dr. Sanderson! Miss Kelly! (*They break apart and jump to attention like two buck privates before a C.O.*)

KELLY AND SANDERSON: Yes, Doctor?

CHUMLEY: Tell the gardener to prune more carefully around my prize dahlias along the fence by the main road. They'll be ready for cutting next week. (*At upper corner of bookcase.*) The difficulty of the woman who has the big white rabbit—has it been smoothed over?

SANDERSON: Yes, Doctor. I spoke to her brother and he was quite reasonable.

CHUMLEY: While I have had many patients out here who saw animals, I have never before had a patient with an animal that large. (*Puts book in bookcase.*)

SANDERSON: Yes, Doctor. She called him Harvey.

CHUMLEY: Harvey. Unusual name for an animal of any kind. Harvey is a man's name. I have known several men in my day named Harvey, but I have never heard of any type of animal whatsoever with that name. The case has an interesting phase, Doctor. (*Finishes straightening books.*)

SANDERSON: Yes, Doctor.

CHUMLEY: I will now go upstairs with you and look in on this woman. It may be that we can use my formula 977 on her. I will give you my advice in prescribing the treatment, Doctor. (*Crosses to below table.*)

SANDERSON: Thank you, Doctor.

CHUMLEY: (*Starts to move across stage and stops, draws himself up sternly.*) And now—may I ask—what is that hat and coat doing on that table? Whose is it?

SANDERSON: I don't know. Do you know, Miss Kelly? Was it Dowd's?

KELLY (*above table, picking up hat and coat*): He had his hat on, Doctor. Perhaps it belongs to a relative of one of the patients.

CHUMLEY: Hand me the hat. (KELLY *hands it. Looking inside:*) There may be some kind of identification—Here—what's this—what's this? (*Pushes two fingers up through the holes.*) Two holes cut in the crown of this hat. See!

KELLY: That's strange!

CHUMLEY: Some new fad—put them away. Hang them up—get them out of here. (KELLY *takes them into office.* CHUMLEY *starts crossing to table.* KELLY *has come out.* WILSON *comes in.*)

WILSON (*very impressed with* DR. CHUMLEY *and very fond of him*): Hello, Dr. Chumley.

CHUMLEY: Oh, there you are.

WILSON: How is every little old thing? (DR. CHUMLEY *picks up pad of notes;* KELLY *re-enters from upper left.*)

CHUMLEY: Fair, thank you, Wilson, fair.

WILSON (*top of desk*): Look—somebody's gonna have to give me a hand with this Simmons dame—order a restraining jacket or something. She's terrible. (*To* KELLY.) Forgot me, didn't you? Well, I got her corset off all by myself.

CHUMLEY: We're going up to see this patient right now, Wilson.

WILSON: She's in a hydro tub now—my God—I left the water running on her! (*Runs off upstairs, followed by* KELLY.) (BETTY CHUMLEY, *the Doctor's wife, enters. She is a good-natured, gay, bustling woman of about 55.*)

BETTY: Willie—remember your promise—Hello, Dr. Sanderson. Willie, you haven't forgotten Dr. McClure's cocktail party? We promised them faithfully. (*Sits.*)

CHUMLEY: That's right. I have to go upstairs now and look in on a patient. Be down shortly—(*Exits upstairs.*)

BETTY (*calling after him; she sits, fixes her shoe*): Give a little quick diagnosis, Willie—we don't want to be late to the party. I'm dying to see the inside of that house. (*Enter* ELWOOD. *He doesn't see* BETTY *at first. He looks around the room carefully.*) Good evening.

ELWOOD (*removing his hat and bowing*): Good evening. (*Puts hat on desk. Walks over to her.*)

BETTY: I am Mrs. Chumley. Doctor Chumley's wife.

ELWOOD: I'm happy to know that. Dowd is my name. Elwood P. Let me give you one of my cards. (*Gives her one.*) If you should want to call me—call me at this one. Don't call me at that one, because that's —(*Points at card*) the old one. (*Starts one step. Looking.*)

BETTY: Thank you. Is there something I can do for you?

ELWOOD (*turns to her*): What did you have in mind?

BETTY: You seem to be looking for someone.

ELWOOD (*walking*): Yes, I am. I'm looking for Harvey. I went off without him.

BETTY: Harvey? Is he a patient here?

ELWOOD (*turns*): Oh, no. Nothing like that. (*Cross to door.*)

BETTY: Does he work here?

ELWOOD (*looking out*): Oh, no. He is what you might call my best friend. He is also a pooka. He came out here with me and Veta this afternoon.

BETTY: Where was he when you last saw him?

ELWOOD: In that chair there—with his hat and coat on the table.

BETTY: There doesn't seem to be any hat and coat around here now. Perhaps he left?

ELWOOD: Apparently. I don't see him anywhere. (*Looks in* SANDERSON'S *office.*)

BETTY: What was that word you just said—pooka?

ELWOOD (*crosses, he is looking in hallway*): Yes—that's it.

BETTY: Is that something new? (*Looks in hallway.*)

ELWOOD (*coming down*): Oh, no. As I understand it, that's something very old.

BETTY: Oh, really? I had never happened to hear it before.

ELWOOD: I'm not too surprised at that. I hadn't myself, until I met him. I do hope you get an opportunity to meet him. I'm sure he would be quite taken with you.

BETTY: Oh, really? Well, that's very nice of you to say so, I'm sure.

ELWOOD: Not at all. If Harvey happens to take a liking to people he expresses himself quite definitely. If he's not particularly interested, he sits there like an empty chair or an empty space on the floor. Harvey takes his time making his mind up about people. Choosey, you see.

BETTY: That's not such a bad way to be in this day and age.

ELWOOD: Harvey is fond of my sister, Veta. That's because he is fond of me, and Veta and I come from the same family. Now you'd think that feeling would be mutual, wouldn't you? (*Looks in office.*) But Veta doesn't seem to care for Harvey. Don't you think that's rather too bad, Mrs. Chumley?

BETTY: Oh, I don't know, Mr. Dowd. I gave up a long time ago expecting my family to like my friends. It's useless.

ELWOOD: But we must keep on trying. (*Sits.*)

BETTY: Well, there's no harm in trying, I suppose.

ELWOOD: Because if Harvey has said to me once he has said a million times—"Mr. Dowd, I would do anything for you." Mrs. Chumley—

BETTY: Yes—

ELWOOD: Did you know that Mrs. McElhinney's Aunt Rose is going to drop in on her unexpectedly tonight from Cleveland?

BETTY: Why, no I didn't—

ELWOOD: Neither does she. That puts you both in the same boat, doesn't it?

BETTY: Well, I don't know anybody named—Mrs.—

ELWOOD: Mrs. McElhinney? Lives next door to us. She is a wonderful woman. Harvey told me about her Aunt Rose. That's an interesting little news item, and you are perfectly free to pass it around.

BETTY: Well, I—

ELWOOD: Would you care to come downtown with me now, my dear? I would be glad to buy you a drink.

BETTY: Thank you very much, but I am waiting for Dr. Chumley and if he came down and found me gone he would be liable to raise—he would be irritated!

ELWOOD: We wouldn't want that, would we? Some other time, maybe? (*He rises.*)

BETTY: I'll tell you what I'll do, however.

ELWOOD: What will you do, however? I'm interested.

BETTY: If your friend comes in while I'm here I'd be glad to give him a message for you.

ELWOOD (*gratefully*): Would you do that? I'd certainly appreciate that. (*Goes to top of desk for his hat.*)

BETTY: No trouble at all. I'll write it down on the back of this. (*Holds up card. Takes pencil from purse.*) What would you like me to tell him if he comes in while I'm still here?

ELWOOD: Ask him to meet me downtown—if he has no other plans.

BETTY (*writing*): Meet Mr. Dowd downtown. Any particular place downtown?

ELWOOD: He knows where. Harvey knows this town like a book.

BETTY (*writing*): Harvey—you know where. Harvey what?

ELWOOD: Just Harvey.

BETTY (*rises—crosses to desk*): I'll tell you what.

ELWOOD: What?

BETTY: Doctor and I are going right downtown—to 12th and Montview. Dr. McClure is having a cocktail party.

ELWOOD (*he writes that down on pad on desk*): A cocktail party at 12th and Montview.

BETTY: We're driving there in a few minutes. We could give your friend a lift into town.

ELWOOD: I hate to impose on you—but I would certainly appreciate that.

BETTY: No trouble at all. Dr. McClure is having this party for his sister from Wichita.

ELWOOD: I didn't know Dr. McClure had a sister in Wichita.

BETTY: Oh—you *know* Dr. McClure?

ELWOOD: No.

BETTY (*puts Elwood's card down on desk*): But——(*Sits.*)

ELWOOD: You're quite sure you haven't time to come into town with me and have a drink?

BETTY: I really couldn't—but thank you just the same.

ELWOOD: Some other time, perhaps?

BETTY: Thank you.

ELWOOD: It's been very pleasant to meet you, and I hope to see you again.

BETTY: Yes, so do I.

ELWOOD: Good-night, my dear. (*Tips hat—bows—goes to door, turns.*) You can't miss Harvey. He's very tall—(*Shows with hands.*) Like that—(*Exits.* CHUMLEY *enters, followed by* SANDERSON *and* KELLY.)

CHUMLEY (*working with pen on desk-pad*): That Simmons woman is unco-operative, Doctor. She refused to admit to me that she has this big rabbit. Insists it's her brother. Give her two of these at nine—another at ten—if she continues to be so restless. Another trip to the hydro-room at eight, and one in the morning at seven. Then we'll see if she won't co-operate tomorrow, won't we, Doctor?

SANDERSON: Yes, Doctor.

CHUMLEY (*putting pen away*): You know where to call me if you need me. Ready, pet?

BETTY: Yes, Willie—and oh, Willie—

CHUMLEY: Yes—

BETTY: There was a man in here—a man named—let me see—(*picks up card from desk.*) Oh, here is his card—Dowd—Elwood P. Dowd. (KELLY *enters. She has Dr. Chumley's hat.*)

SANDERSON: That's Mrs. Simmons' brother, Doctor. I told him he could look around, and I gave him full visiting privileges.

CHUMLEY: She mustn't see anyone tonight. Not anyone at all. Tell him that.

SANDERSON: Yes, Doctor.

BETTY: He didn't ask to see her. He was asking for someone—some friend of his.

CHUMLEY: Who could that be, Dr. Sanderson?

SANDERSON: I don't know, Doctor.

BETTY: He said it was someone he came out here with this afternoon.

SANDERSON: Was there anyone with Dowd when you saw him, Miss Kelly?

KELLY: No, Doctor—not when I saw him.

BETTY: Well, he said there was. He said he last saw his friend sitting

right in that chair there with his hat and coat. He seemed quite disappointed.

KELLY (*at top of table—a funny look is crossing her face*): Dr. Sanderson—

BETTY: I told him if we located his friend we'd give him a lift into town.
He could ride in the back seat. Was that all right, Willie?

CHUMLEY: Of course—of course—

BETTY: Oh here it is. I wrote it down on the back of this card. His
friend's name was Harvey.

KELLY: Harvey!

BETTY: He didn't give me his last name. He mentioned something else
about him—pooka—but I didn't quite get what that was.

SANDERSON AND CHUMLEY: Harvey!

BETTY (*rises*): He said his friend was very tall—Well, why are you
looking like that, Willie? This man was a very nice, polite man, and
he merely asked that we give his friend a lift into town, and if we
can't do a favor for someone, why are we living?

SANDERSON (*gasping*): Where—where did he go, Mrs. Chumley? How
long ago was he in here?

CHUMLEY (*thundering*): Get me that hat! By George, we'll find out
about this! (KELLY *goes out.*)

BETTY: I don't know where he went. Just a second ago. (SANDERSON,
his face drawn, sits, and picks up house phone. CHUMLEY, *with a terrible look on his face, has started to thumb through phone book.*)

SANDERSON (*on the phone*): Main gate—Henry—Dr. Sanderson—

CHUMLEY (*thumbing through book*): Gaffney—Judge Gaffney—

SANDERSON: Henry—did a man in a brown suit go through the gate a
minute ago? He did? He's gone? (*Hangs up and looks stricken.*
KELLY *enters with hat.*)

CHUMLEY (*has been dialing*): Judge Gaffney—this is Dr. William
Chumley—the psychiatrist. I'm making a routine checkup on the
spelling of a name before entering it into our records. Judge—you
telephoned out here this afternoon about having a client of yours
committed? How is that name spelled? With a W, not a U—Mr. Elwood P. Dowd. Thank you, Judge—(*Hangs up—rises—pushes chair
in to desk—takes hat from* KELLY. *Stands silently for a moment, con-
templating* SANDERSON.) Dr. Sanderson—I believe your name is Sanderson?

SANDERSON: Yes, Doctor.

CHUMLEY: You know that much, do you? You went to medical school —you specialized in the study of psychiatry? You graduated—you went forth. (*Holds up hat and runs two fingers up through holes in it.*) Perhaps they neglected to tell you that a rabbit has large pointed ears! That a hat for a rabbit would have to be perforated to make room for those ears?

SANDERSON: Dowd seemed reasonable enough this afternoon, Doctor.

CHUMLEY: Doctor—the function of a psychiatrist is to tell the difference between those who are reasonable, and those who merely talk and act reasonably. (*Presses buzzer. Flings hat on desk.*) Do you realize what you have done to me? You don't answer. I'll tell you. You have permitted a psychopathic case to walk off these grounds and roam around with an overgrown white rabbit. You have subjected me—a psychiatrist—to the humiliation of having to call— of all things—a lawyer to find out who came out here to be commit- ted—and who came out here to commit! (WILSON *enters.*)

SANDERSON: Dr. Chumley—I—

CHUMLEY: Just a minute, Wilson—I want you. (*Back to* SANDERSON.) I will now have to do something I haven't done in fifteen years. I will have to go out after this patient, Elwood P. Dowd, and I will have to bring him back, and when I do bring him back, your connection with this institution is ended—as of that moment! (*Turns to* WILSON— *others are standing frightened.*) Wilson, get the car. (*To* BETTY.) Pet, call the McClures and say we can't make it. Miss Kelly—come upstairs with me and we'll get that woman out of the tub—(*Starts upstairs on the run.*)

KELLY (*follows him upstairs*): Yes—Doctor—

(SANDERSON *turns on his heel, goes into his office.* WILSON *is get- ting into a coat in hall.*)

BETTY: I'll have to tell the cook we'll be home for dinner. She'll be furi- ous. (*She turns.*) Wilson—

WILSON: Yes, ma'am.

BETTY: What is a pooka?

WILSON: A what?

BETTY: A pooka.

WILSON: You can search me, Mrs. Chumley.

BETTY: I wonder if it would be in the Encyclopedia here? (*Goes to bookcase and takes out book.*) They have everything here. I wonder if it is a lodge, or what it is! (*Starts to look in it, then puts it on table open.*) Oh, I don't dare to stop to do this now. Dr. Chumley won't want to find me still here when he comes down. He'll raise—I mean —oh, dear! (*She exits.*)

WILSON (*goes above tables, picks up book, looks in it. Runs forefinger under words*): P-o-o-k-a. "Pooka. From old Celtic mythology. A fairy spirit in animal form. Always very large. The pooka appears here and there, now and then, to this one and that one at his own caprice. A wise but mischievous creature. Very fond of rum-pots, crackpots," and how are you, Mr. Wilson. (*Looks at book startled— looks at doorway fearfully—then back to book.*) How are you, Mr. Wilson? (*Shakes book, looks at it in surprise.*) Who in the encyclopedia wants to know? (*Looks at book again, drops it on table.*) Oh —to hell with it! (*He exits quickly.*)

CURTAIN

ACT TWO

SCENE I

SCENE: *The Dowd library again.*

TIME: *About an hour after the curtain of Act One.*

AT RISE: *Doobell is ringing and* MYRTLE *enters. She calls behind her.*

MYRTLE (*calling*): That's right. The stairs at the end of the hall. It goes to the third floor. Go right up. I'll be with you in a minute. (JUDGE OMAR GAFFNEY *enters, an elderly white-haired man. He looks displeased.*)

JUDGE (*entering and looking around*): Well, where is she? (*Back of table.*)

MYRTLE: Where is who? Whom do you mean, Judge Gaffney? Sit down, won't you?

JUDGE: I mean your mother. Where's Veta Louise? (*Crosses in front of chair.*)

MYRTLE: Why Judge Gaffney! You know where she is. She took Uncle Elwood out to the sanitarium.

JUDGE: I know that. But why was I called at the club with a lot of hysteria? Couldn't even get what she was talking about. Carrying on something fierce. (*Sits.*)

MYRTLE: Mother carrying on! What about?

JUDGE: I don't know. She was hysterical.

MYRTLE: That's strange! She took Uncle Elwood out to the sanitarium. All she had to do was put him in. (*Opens door and looks through, calling.*) Did you find it? I'll be right up. (*Waits. Turns to him.*) They found it.

JUDGE: Who? Found what? What are you talking about?

MYRTLE: When Mother left the house with Uncle Elwood I went over to the real estate office to put the house on the market. And what do you think I found there? (*She sits.*)

JUDGE: I'm not a quiz kid.

MYRTLE: Well, I found a man there who was looking for an old house just like this to cut up into buffet apartments. He's going through it now.

JUDGE: Now see here, Myrtle Mae. This house doesn't belong to you. It belongs to your Uncle Elwood.

MYRTLE: But now that Elwood is locked up, mother controls the property, doesn't she?

JUDGE: Where is your mother? Where is Veta Louise?

MYRTLE: Judge, she went out to Chumley's Rest to tell them about Harvey and put Uncle Elwood in.

JUDGE: Why did she call me at the club when I was in the middle of a game, and scream at me to meet her here about something important?

MYRTLE: I don't know. I simply don't know. Have you got the deed to this house?

JUDGE: Certainly, it's in my safe. Myrtle, I feel pretty bad about this thing of locking Elwood up.

MYRTLE: Mother and I will be able to take a long trip now—out to Pasadena.

JUDGE: I always liked that boy. He could have done anything—been anything—made a place for himself in this community.

MYRTLE: And all he did was get a big rabbit.

JUDGE: He had everything. Brains, personality, friends. Men liked him. Women liked him. I liked him.

MYRTLE: Are you telling me that once Uncle Elwood was like other men—that women actually liked him—I mean in that way?

JUDGE: Oh, not since he started running around with this big rabbit. But they did once. Once that mailbox of your grandmother's was full of those little blue-scented envelopes for Elwood.

MYRTLE: I can't believe it.

JUDGE: Of course there was always something different about Elwood.

MYRTLE: I don't doubt that.

JUDGE: Yes—he was always so calm about any sudden change in plans. I used to admire it. I should have been suspicious. Take your average man looking up and seeing a big white rabbit. He'd do something about it. But not Elwood. He took that calmly, too. And look where it got him!

MYRTLE: You don't dream how far overboard he's gone on this rabbit.

JUDGE: Oh, yes I do. He's had that rabbit in my office many's the time. I'm old but I don't miss much. (*Noise from upstairs.*) What's that noise?

MYRTLE: The prospective buyer on the third floor. (*Looks up.* VETA *is standing in doorway, looking like something the cat dragged in. Shakes her head sadly; looks into the room and sighs; her hat is crooked.* MYRTLE *jumps up.*) Mother! Look, Judge—

JUDGE (*rising*): Veta Louise—what's wrong, girl?

VETA (*shaking her head*): I never thought I'd see either of you again. (MYRTLE *and* JUDGE *take* VETA *to chair.*)

MYRTLE: Take hold of her, Judge. She looks like she's going to faint. (JUDGE *gets hold of her on one side and* MYRTLE *on the other. They start to bring her into the room.*) Now, Mother—you're all right. You're going to be perfectly all right.

JUDGE: Steady—steady, girl, steady.

VETA: Please—not so fast.

JUDGE: Don't rush her, Myrtle—ease her in.

VETA: Let me sit down. Only get me some place where I can sit down.

JUDGE (*guiding her to a big chair*): Here you are, girl. Easy, Myrtle—easy. (VETA *is about to lower herself into chair. She sighs. But before she can complete the lowering,* MYRTLE MAE *lets out a yelp and* VETA *straightens up quickly.*)

MYRTLE: Oh—(*She picks up envelope off chair. Holds it up.*) The gas bill.

VETA (*hand at head*): Oh—oh, my—(*Sits.*)

JUDGE: Get her some tea, Myrtle. Do you want some tea, Veta?

MYRTLE: I'll get you some tea, Mother. Get her coat off, Judge.

JUDGE: Let Myrtle get your coat off, Veta. Get her coat off, Myrtle.

VETA: Leave me alone. Let me sit here. Let me get my breath.

MYRTLE: Let her get her breath, Judge.

VETA: Let me sit here a minute and then let me get upstairs to my own bed where I can let go.

MYRTLE: What happened to you, Mother?

VETA: Omar, I want you to sue them. They put me in and let Elwood out.

JUDGE: What's this?

MYRTLE: Mother!

VETA (*taking off hat*): Just look at my hair.

MYRTLE: But why? What did you say? What did you do? (*Kneels at* VETA's *feet.*) You must have done something.

VETA: I didn't do one thing. I simply told them about Elwood and Harvey.

JUDGE: Then how could it happen to you? I don't understand it. (*Sits.*)

VETA: I told them about Elwood, and then I went down to the cab to get his things. As I was walking along the path—this awful man stepped out. He was a white slaver. I know he was. He had on one of those white suits. That's how they advertise.

MYRTLE: A man—what did he do, Mother?

VETA: What did he do? He took hold of me and took me in there and then he—(*Bows her head.* MYRTLE *and* JUDGE *exchange a look.*)

JUDGE (*softly*): Go on, Veta Louise. Go on, girl.

MYRTLE (*goes over, takes her hand*): Poor Mother—was he a young man?

JUDGE: Myrtle Mae—perhaps you'd better leave the room.

MYRTLE: Now? I should say not! Go on, Mother.

JUDGE (*edging closer*): What did he do, Veta?

VETA: He took me upstairs and tore my clothes off.

MYRTLE (*shrieking*): Oh—did you hear that, Judge! Go on, Mother. (*She is all ears.*)

JUDGE: By God—I'll sue them for this!

VETA: And then he sat me down in a tub of water.

MYRTLE (*disappointed*): Oh! For heaven's sake! (*Rises.*)

VETA: I always thought that what you were, showed on your face. Don't you believe it, Judge! Don't you believe it, Myrtle. This man took hold of me like I was a woman of the streets—but I fought. I always said if a man jumped at me—I'd fight. Haven't I always said that, Myrtle?

MYRTLE: She's always said that, Judge. That's what Mother always told me to do.

VETA: And then he hustled me into that sanitarium and set me down in that tub of water and began treating me like I was a—

MYRTLE: A what—?

VETA: A crazy woman—but he did that just for spite.

JUDGE: Well, I'll be damned!

VETA: And those doctors came upstairs and asked me a lot of questions —all about sex-urges—and all that filthy stuff. That place ought to be cleaned up, Omar. You better get the authorities to clean it up. Myrtle, don't you ever go out there. You hear me?

JUDGE: This stinks to high heaven, Veta. By God, it stinks!

VETA: You've got to do something about it, Judge. You've got to sue them.

JUDGE: I will, girl. By God, I will! If Chumley thinks he can run an unsavory place like this on the outskirts of town he'll be publicly chastised. By God, I'll run him out of the state!

VETA: Tell me, Judge. Is that all those doctors do at places like that—think about sex?

JUDGE: I don't know.

VETA: Because if it is they ought to be ashamed—of themselves. It's all in their head anyway. Why don't they get out and go for long walks in the fresh air? (*To* MYRTLE.) Judge Gaffney walked everywhere for years—didn't you, Judge?

JUDGE: Now let me take some notes on this. (MYRTLE *goes to back of table.*) You said—these doctors came up to talk to you—Dr. Chumley and—What was the other doctor's name?

VETA: Sanderson—(*Sits up straight, glances covertly at them, and becomes very alert.*) But, Judge, don't you pay any attention to anything he tells you. He's a liar. Close-set eyes. They're always liars. Besides—I told him something in strictest confidence and he blabbed it.

MYRTLE: What did you tell him, Mother? (*She is back of table.*)

VETA: Oh, what difference does it make? Let's forget. I don't even want to talk about it. (*Rises—crosses to back of chair.*) You can't trust anybody.

JUDGE: Anything you told this Dr. Sanderson you can tell us, Veta Louise. This is your daughter and I am your lawyer.

VETA: I know which is which. I don't want to talk about it. I want to sue them and I want to get into my own bed. (JUDGE *rises.*)

MYRTLE: But, Mother—this is the important thing, anyway. Where is Uncle Elwood?

VETA (*to herself*): I should have known better than to try to do anything about him. Something protects him—that awful Pooka—

MYRTLE: Where is Uncle Elwood? Answer me.

VETA (*trying to be casual*): How should I know? They let him go. They're not interested in men at places like that. Don't act so naïve, Myrtle Mae. (*Noise from upstairs.*) What's that noise?

MYRTLE: I've found a buyer for the house.

VETA: What?

MYRTLE: Listen, Mother, we've got to find Uncle Elwood—no matter who jumped at you, we've still got to lock up Uncle Elwood.

VETA: I don't know where he is. The next time *you* take him, Judge. Wait until Elwood hears what they did to me. He won't stand for it. Don't forget to sue them, Judge—Myrtle Mae, all I hope is that never, never as long as you live a man pulls the clothes off you and dumps you down into a tub of water. (*She exits.*)

MYRTLE (*turning to* JUDGE): Now, see—Mother muffed everything. No matter what happened out there—Uncle Elwood's still wandering around with Harvey.

JUDGE (*pondering*): The thing for me to do is take some more notes.

MYRTLE: It's all Uncle Elwood's fault. He found out what she was up to—and he had her put in. Then he ran.

JUDGE: Oh, no—don't talk like that. (*Crosses up to back of chair.*) Your uncle thinks the world and all of your mother. Ever since he was a little boy he always wanted to share everything he had with her.

MYRTLE: I'm not giving up. We'll get detectives. We'll find him. And, besides—you'd better save some of that sympathy for me and Mother —you don't realize what we have to put up with. Wait till I show you something he brought home about six months ago, and we hid it out in the garage. You just wait—

JUDGE: I'm going up to talk to Veta. There's more in this than she's telling. I sense that.

MYRTLE (*as she exits*): Wait till I show you, Judge.

JUDGE: All right. I'll wait. (WILSON *enters.*)

WILSON: Okay—is he here?

JUDGE: What? What's this?

WILSON: That crackpot with the rabbit. Is he here?

JUDGE: No—and who, may I ask, are you?

WILSON (*stepping into hallway, calling*): Not here, Doctor—okay— (*To* JUDGE.) Doctor Chumley's comin' in, anyway. What's your name?

JUDGE: Chumley—well, well, well—I've got something to say to him! (*Sits.*)

WILSON: What's your name? Let's have it.

JUDGE: I am Judge Gaffney—where is Chumley?

WILSON: The reason I asked your name is the Doctor always likes to know who he's talkin' to. (*Enter* CHUMLEY.) This guy says his name is Judge Gaffney, Doctor.

JUDGE: Well, well, Chumley—

CHUMLEY: Good evening, Judge. Let's not waste time. Has he been here?

JUDGE: Who? Elwood—no—but see here, Doctor—

WILSON: Sure he ain't been here? He's wise now. He's hidin'. It'll be an awful job to smoke him out.

CHUMLEY: It will be more difficult, but I'll do it. They're sly. They're cunning. But I get them. I always get them. Have you got the list of the places we've been, Wilson? (*Crosses to* WILSON.)

WILSON (*pulling paper out of his pocket*): Right here, Doctor.

CHUMLEY (*sits*): Read it.

WILSON (*crosses to* CHUMLEY): We've been to seventeen bars, Eddie's Place, Charlie's Place, Bessie's Barn-dance, The Fourth Avenue Firehouse, the Tenth and Twelfth and Ninth Avenue firehouses, just to make sure. The Union Station, the grain elevator—say, why does this guy go down to a grain elevator?

JUDGE: The foreman is a friend of his. He has many friends—many places.

CHUMLEY: I have stopped by here to ask Mrs. Simmons if she has any other suggestions as to where we might look for him.

JUDGE: Doctor Chumley, I have to inform you that Mrs. Simmons has retained me to file suit against you—

DR. CHUMLEY: What?

JUDGE: —for what happened to her at the sanitarium this afternoon . . .

CHUMLEY: A suit!

JUDGE: And while we're on that subject—

WILSON (*crosses to back of table*): That's pretty, ain't it, Doctor? After us draggin' your tail all over town trying to find that guy.

CHUMLEY: What happened this afternoon was an unfortunate mistake. I've discharged my assistant who made it. And I am prepared to take charge of this man's case personally. It interests me. And my interest in a case is something no amount of money can buy. You can ask any of them.

JUDGE: But this business this afternoon, Doctor—

CHUMLEY: Water under the dam. This is how I see this thing. I see it this way—(MYRTLE *has come into the room. She is carrying a big flat parcel, wrapped in brown paper. Stands it up against wall and listens.*) The important item now is to get this man and take him out to the sanitarium where he belongs.

MYRTLE (*coming forward*): That's right, Judge—that's just what I think—

JUDGE: Let me introduce Miss Myrtle Mae Simmons, Mr. Dowd's niece, Mrs. Simmons' daughter. (CHUMLEY *rises.*)

MYRTLE: How do you do, Dr. Chumley.

CHUMLEY: (*giving her the careful scrutiny he gives all women*): How do you do, Miss Simmons.

WILSON: Hello, Myrtle—

MYRTLE (*now seeing him and looking at him with a mixture of horror and intense curiosity*): What? Oh—

CHUMLEY: Now, then, let me talk to Mrs. Simmons.

MYRTLE: Mother won't come down, Doctor. I know she won't. (*To* JUDGE.) You try to get Mother to talk to him, Judge. (*Puts package down.*)

JUDGE: But, see here—your mother was manhandled. She was—God knows what she was—the man's approach to her was not professional, it was personal. (*Looks at* WILSON.)

CHUMLEY: Wilson—this is a serious charge.

WILSON: Dr. Chumley, I've been with you for ten years. Are you gonna believe—what's your name again?

JUDGE: Gaffney. Judge Omar Gaffney.

WILSON: Thanks. You take the word of this old blister Gaffney—

CHUMLEY: Wilson!

WILSON: Me! Me and a dame who sees a rabbit!

JUDGE: It's not Mrs. Simmons who sees a rabbit. It's her brother.

MYRTLE: Yes, it's Uncle Elwood.

JUDGE: If you'll come with me, Doctor—

CHUMLEY: Very well, Judge. Wilson, I have a situation here. Wait for me. (*He and* JUDGE *exit.*)

WILSON: OK, Doctor. (MYRTLE MAE *is fascinated by* WILSON. *She lingers and looks at him. He comes over to her, grinning.*)

WILSON: So your name's Myrtle Mae?

MYRTLE: What? Oh—yes—(*She backs up. He follows.*)

WILSON: If we grab your uncle you're liable to be comin' out to the sanitarium on visiting days?

MYRTLE: Oh, I don't really know—I—

WILSON: Well, if you do, I'll be there.

MYRTLE: You will? Oh—

WILSON: And if you don't see me right away—don't give up. Stick around. I'll show up.

MYRTLE: You will? Oh—

WILSON: Sure. (*He is still following her.*) You heard Dr. Chumley tell me to wait?

MYRTLE: Yeah—

WILSON: Tell you what—while I'm waiting I sure could use a sandwich and a cup of coffee.

MYRTLE: Certainly. If you'll forgive me I'll precede you into the kitchen. (*She tries to go. He traps her.*)

WILSON: Yessir—you're all right, Myrtle.

MYRTLE: What?

WILSON: Doctor Chumley noticed it right away. He don't miss a trick. (*Crowds closer; raises finger and pokes her arm for emphasis.*) Tell you somethin' else, Myrtle—

MYRTLE: What?

WILSON: You not only got a nice build—but, kid, you got something else, too.

MYRTLE: What?

WILSON: You got the screwiest uncle that ever stuck his puss inside our nuthouse. (MYRTLE *starts to exit in a huff, and* WILSON *raises hand to give her a spank, but she turns and so he puts up raised hand to his hair. They exit. The stage is empty for a half-second, and then* ELWOOD *comes in, goes to phone, dials a number.*)

ELWOOD: Hello, Chumley's Rest? Is Doctor Chumley there? Oh—it's Mrs. Chumley! This is Elwood P. Dowd speaking. How are you to-night? Tell me, Mrs. Chumley, were you able to locate Harvey?— Don't worry about it. I'll find him. I'm sorry I missed you at the McClure cocktail party. The people were all charming and I was able to leave quite a few of my cards. I waited until you phoned and said you couldn't come because a patient had escaped. Where am I? I'm here. But I'm leaving right away. I must find Harvey. Well, good-by, Mrs. Chumley. My regards to you and anybody else you happen to run into. Good-by. (*Hangs up, then he sees the big flat parcel against wall. He gets an "Ah, there it is!" expression on his face, goes over, and takes off paper. We see revealed a very strange thing. It is an oil painting of Elwood seated on a chair while behind him stands a large white rabbit, in a blue polka-dot collar and red necktie.* ELWOOD *holds it away from him and surveys it proudly. Then looks around for a place to put it. Takes it over and sets it on mantel. It obscures the picture of Marcella Pinney Dowd completely. He gathers up wrapping paper, admires the rabbit again, tips his hat to it, and exits. Phone rings and* VETA *enters, followed by* DR. CHUMLEY.)

VETA: Doctor, you might as well go home and wait. I'm suing you for fifty thousand dollars and that's final. (*Crosses to phone—her back is to mantel, she hasn't looked up.*)

CHUMLEY (*follows her to chair*): Mrs. Simmons—

VETA (*into phone*): Yes—Well, all right.

CHUMLEY: This picture over your mantel.

VETA: That portrait happens to be the pride of this house.

CHUMLEY (*looking at her*): Who painted it?

VETA: Oh, some man. I forget his name. He was around here for the sittings, and then we paid him and he went away. Hello—yes—No. This is Dexter 1567. (*Hangs up.*)

CHUMLEY: I suppose if you have the money to pay people, you can per-suade them to do anything.

VETA: Well, Dr. Chumley—(*Walks over and faces him.*) When you helped me out of that tub at your place, what did I say to you?

CHUMLEY: You expressed yourself. I don't remember the words.

VETA: I said, "Dr. Chumley, this is a belated civility." Isn't that what I said?

CHUMLEY: You said something of the sort—

VETA: You brought this up; you may as well learn something quick. I took a course in art this last winter. The difference between a fine oil painting and a mechanical thing like a photograph is simply this: a photograph shows only the reality; a painting shows not only the reality but the dream behind it—It's our dreams that keep us going. That separate us from the beasts. I wouldn't even want to live if I thought it was all just eating and sleeping and taking off my clothes. Well—putting them on again—(*Turns—sees picture—screams—totters—falls back.*) Oh—Doctor—oh—hold me—oh—

CHUMLEY (*taking hold of her*): Steady now—steady—don't get excited. Everything's all right. (*Seats her in chair.*) Now—what's the matter?

VETA (*pointing*): Doctor—that is *not* my mother!

CHUMLEY: I'm glad to hear that.

VETA: Oh, Doctor. Elwood's been here. He's been here.

CHUMLEY: Better be quiet. (*Phone rings.*) I'll take it. (*He answers it.*) Hello. Yes, yes—who's calling? (*Drops his hands over mouthpiece quickly.*) Here he is. Mrs. Simmons, it's your brother!

VETA (*getting up. Weak no longer*): Oh—let me talk to him!

CHUMLEY: Don't tell him I'm here. Be casual.

VETA: Hello, Elwood—(*Laughs.*) Where are you? What? Oh—just a minute. (*Covers phone.*) He won't say where he is. He wants to know if Harvey is here.

CHUMLEY: Tell him Harvey *is* here.

VETA: But he isn't.

CHUMLEY: Tell him. That will bring him here, perhaps. Humor him. We have to humor them.

VETA: Yes—Elwood. Yes, dear. Harvey is here. Why don't you come home? Oh, oh, oh—well—all right. (*Looks around uncomfortably. Covers phone again.*) It won't work. He says for me to call Harvey to the telephone.

CHUMLEY: Say Harvey is here, but can't come to the telephone. Say— he—say—he's in the bathtub.

VETA: Bathtub?

CHUMLEY: Say he's in the bathtub, and you'll send him over there. That way we'll find out where he is.

VETA: Oh, Doctor!

CHUMLEY: Now, you've got to do it, Mrs. Simmons.

VETA: Hello, Elwood. Yes, dear. Harvey is here but he can't come to the telephone, he's in the bathtub. I'll send him over as soon as he's dry. Where are you? Elwood? (*Bangs phone.*)

CHUMLEY: Did he hang up?

VETA: Harvey just walked in the door! He told me to look in the bathtub—it must be a stranger. But I know where he is. He's at Charlie's Place. That's a bar over at 12th and Main.

CHUMLEY (*picking up his hat from table*): 12th and Main. That's two blocks down and one over, isn't it?

VETA: Doctor—where are you going?

CHUMLEY: I'm going over there to get your brother and take him out to the sanitarium, where he belongs.

VETA: Oh, Dr. Chumley—don't do that. Send one of your attendants. I'm warning you.

CHUMLEY: But, Mrs. Simmons, if I am to help your brother—

VETA: He can't be helped. (*Looks at picture.*) There is no help for him. He must be picked up and locked up and left.

CHUMLEY: You consider your brother a dangerous man?

VETA: Dangerous!

CHUMLEY: Why?

VETA: I won't tell you why, but if I didn't, why would I be asking for a permanent commitment for him?

CHUMLEY: Then I must observe this man. I must watch the expression on his face as he talks to this rabbit. He does talk to the rabbit, you say?

VETA: They tell each other everything.

CHUMLEY: What's that?

VETA: I said, of course he talks to him. But don't go after him, Doctor. You'll regret it if you do.

CHUMLEY: Nonsense—you underestimate me, Mrs. Simmons.

VETA: Oh, no, Doctor. You underestimate my brother.

CHUMLEY: Not at all. Don't worry now. I can handle him! (*He exits.*)

VETA (*after he has gone*): You can handle him? That's what you think! (*Calls.*) Myrtle Mae! See who's in the bathtub. OH!

CURTAIN

SCENE II

SCENE: *The main office at* CHUMLEY'S REST *again.*
　TIME: *Four hours after the curtain of Scene I, Act Two.*
　AT RISE: KELLY *is on the phone.* WILSON *is helping*
SANDERSON *carry boxes of books out of his office and onto*
table.

KELLY: Thank you. I may call later. (*Hangs up.*)

WILSON: How about the stuff in your room, Doctor—upstairs?

SANDERSON (*to table, puts box on it*): All packed—thanks Wilson.

WILSON: Tough your gettin' bounced. I had you pegged for the one who'd make the grade.

SANDERSON: Those are the breaks.

WILSON: When you takin' off?

SANDERSON: As soon as Dr. Chumley gets back.

WILSON (*to* KELLY): Did you get a report back yet from the desk sergeant in the police accident bureau?

KELLY: Not yet. I just talked to the downtown dispensary. They haven't seen him.

WILSON: It's beginning to smell awful funny to me. Four hours he's been gone and not a word from him. (*Goes to* SANDERSON—*extends hand.*) I may not see you again, Doctor, so I want to say I wish you a lot of luck and I'm mighty sorry you got a kick in the atpray.

SANDERSON: Thanks, Wilson—good luck to you, too—

WILSON (*starts to exit, but stops at door, turns toward* KELLY): Look, Kelly, let me know when you hear from the desk sergeant again. If there's no sign of the doctor, I'm goin' into town and look for him. He should know better'n to go after a psycho without me.

SANDERSON: I'd like to help look for the doctor, too, Wilson.

WILSON: That's swell of you, Doctor, right after he give you the brush.

SANDERSON: I've no resentment against Dr. Chumley. He was right. I was wrong. (*He rises.*) Chumley is the biggest man in his field. It's my loss not to be able to work with him. (*Crosses up to bookcase.*)

WILSON: You're not so small yourself, Doctor—

SANDERSON: Thanks, Wilson.

WILSON: Don't mention it. (*Exits.*)

KELLY (*taking deep breath and standing above desk*): Dr. Sanderson—

SANDERSON (*without looking up*): Yes—

KELLY (*plunging in*): Well, Doctor—(*Takes another deep breath.*) I'd like to say that I wish you a lot of luck, too, and I'm sorry to see you leave.

SANDERSON (*going on with his work*): Are you sure you can spare these good wishes, Miss Kelly?

KELLY (*she flushes*): On second thought—I guess I can't. Forget it. (*Starts for below desk.*)

SANDERSON (*now looking up*): Miss Kelly—(*To back of table.*) This is for nothing—just a little advice. I'd be a little careful if I were you about the kind of company I kept.

KELLY: I beg your pardon, Doctor?

SANDERSON: You don't have to. I told you it was free. I saw you Saturday night—dancing with that drip in the Rose Room down at the Frontier Hotel.

KELLY (*putting books on desk*): Oh, did you? I didn't notice you.

SANDERSON: I'd be a little careful of him, Kelly. He looked to me like a schizophrenic all the way across the floor.

KELLY: You really shouldn't have given him a thought, Doctor. He was my date—not yours. (*Hands book to* SANDERSON.)

SANDERSON: That was his mentality. The rest of him—well—(*Puts book in box front of table.*)

KELLY: But she was beautiful, though—

SANDERSON: Who?

KELLY: That girl you were with—

SANDERSON: I thought you didn't notice?

KELLY: You bumped into us twice. How could I help it?

SANDERSON: Not that it makes any difference to you, but that girl is a charming little lady. *She* has a sweet kind disposition and *she* knows how to conduct herself.

KELLY: Funny she couldn't rate a better date on a Saturday night!

SANDERSON: And she has an excellent mind.

KELLY: Why doesn't she use it?

SANDERSON (*crossing toward* KELLY): Oh, I don't suppose you're to be censured for the flippant hard shell you have. You're probably compensating for something.

KELLY: I am not, and don't you use any of your psychiatry on me.

SANDERSON: Oh—if I could try something else on you—just once! Just to see if you'd melt under any circumstances. I doubt it.

KELLY: You'll never know, Doctor.

SANDERSON: Because you interest me as a case history—that's all. I'd like to know where you get that inflated ego—(*Goes back of desk.*)

KELLY (*now close to tears*): If you aren't the meanest person—inflated ego—case history! (*Turns and starts out.*)

SANDERSON: Don't run away. Let's finish it. (*Phone rings.*)

KELLY: Oh, leave me alone. (*Goes to answer it.*)

SANDERSON: Gladly. (*Exits.*)

KELLY (*in angry, loud voice*): Chumley's Rest. Yes—Sergeant. No accident report on him either in town or the suburbs. Look, Sergeant—maybe we better—(*Looks up as door opens and* ELWOOD *enters. He is carrying a bouquet of dahlias.*) Oh, never mind, Sergeant. They're here now. (*Hangs up. Goes toward* ELWOOD.) Mr. Dowd!

ELWOOD: (*handing her flowers*): Good evening, my dear. These are for you.

KELLY: For me—oh, thank you!

ELWOOD: They're quite fresh, too. I just picked them outside.

KELLY: I hope Dr. Chumley didn't see you. They're his prize dahlias. Did he go upstairs? (*Backing up.*)

ELWOOD: Not knowing, I cannot state. Those colors are lovely against your hair.

KELLY: I've never worn burnt orange. It's such a trying color.

ELWOOD: You would improve any color, my dear.

KELLY: Thank you. Did Dr. Chumley go over to his house?

ELWOOD: I don't know. Where is Dr. Sanderson?

KELLY: In his office there—I think. (*Crosses back to desk.*)

ELWOOD (*going over to door and knocking*): Thank you.

SANDERSON (*enters*): Dowd! There you are!

ELWOOD: I have a cab outside, if it's possible for you and Miss Kelly to get away now.

SANDERSON: Where is Dr. Chumley?

ELWOOD: Is he coming with us? That's nice.

KELLY (*answering question on* SANDERSON'S *face*): I don't know, Doctor.

ELWOOD: I must apologize for being a few seconds late. I thought Miss

Kelly should have some flowers. (*Crosses to table.*) After what happened out here this afternoon, the flowers really should be from you, Doctor. As you grow older and pretty women pass you by, you will think with deep gratitude of these generous girls of your youth. Shall we go now? (KELLY *exits.*)

SANDERSON (*pressing buzzer*): Just a moment, Dowd—The situation has changed since we met this afternoon. But I urge you to have no resentments. Dr. Chumley is your friend. He only wants to help you.

ELWOOD: That's very nice of him. I would like to help him, too. (*At table.*)

SANDERSON: If you'll begin by taking a co-operative attitude—that's half the battle. We all have to face reality, Dowd—sooner or later.

ELWOOD: Doctor, I wrestled with reality for forty years, and I am happy to state that I finally won out over it. (KELLY *enters.*) Won't you and Miss Kelly join me—down at Charlie's? (*Enter* WILSON.)

WILSON: Here you are! (*Goes over to* ELWOOD.) Upstairs, buddy— we're going upstairs. Is the doctor O.K.? (*He asks* SANDERSON *this.*)

ELWOOD: There must be some mistake. Miss Kelly and Dr. Sanderson and I are going downtown for a drink. I'd be glad to have you come with us, Mr. ———

WILSON: Wilson.

ELWOOD: —Wilson. They have a wonderful floor show.

WILSON: Yeah? Well—wait'll you see the floor show we've got—Upstairs, buddy!

SANDERSON: Just a minute, Wilson. Where did you say Dr. Chumley went, Dowd?

ELWOOD: As I said, he did not confide his plans in me.

WILSON: You mean the doctor ain't showed up yet? (*Crosses to desk.*)

KELLY: Not yet.

WILSON: Where is he?

SANDERSON: That's what we're trying to find out.

KELLY: Mr. Dowd walked in here by himself.

WILSON: Oh, he did, eh? Listen, you—talk fast or I'm workin' you over!

ELWOOD: I'd rather you didn't do that, and I'd rather you didn't even mention such a thing in the presence of a lovely young lady like Miss Kelly—

SANDERSON: Mr. Dowd, Dr. Chumley went into town to pick you up. That was four hours ago.

ELWOOD: Where has the evening gone to?

WILSON: Listen to that! Smart, eh?

SANDERSON: Just a minute, Wilson. Did you see Dr. Chumley tonight, Dowd?

ELWOOD: Yes, I did. He came into Charlie's Place at dinnertime. It is a cozy spot. Let's all go there and talk it over with a tall one.

WILSON: We're going no place—(*Crosses between* ELWOOD *and* SANDERSON.) Now I'm askin' you a question, and if you don't button up your lip and give me some straight answers I'm gonna beat it out of you!

ELWOOD: What you suggest is impossible.

WILSON: What's that?

ELWOOD: You suggest that I button up my lip and give you some straight answers. It can't be done. (*Sits.*)

SANDERSON: Let me handle this, Wilson.

WILSON: Well, handle it, then. But find out where the doctor is. (*Back of desk.*)

SANDERSON: Dr. Chumley *did* come into Charlie's Place, you say?

ELWOOD: He did, and I was very glad to see him.

WILSON: Go on—

ELWOOD: He had asked for me, and naturally the proprietor brought him over and left him. We exchanged the conventional greetings. I said, "How do you do, Dr. Chumley," and he said, "How do you do, Mr. Dowd." I believe we said that at least once.

WILSON: Okay—okay—

ELWOOD: I am trying to be factual. I then introduced him to Harvey.

WILSON: To who?

KELLY: A white rabbit. Six feet tall.

WILSON: Six feet!

ELWOOD: Six feet one and a half!

WILSON: Okay—fool around with him, and the doctor is probably some place bleedin' to death in a ditch.

ELWOOD: If those were his plans for the evening he did not tell me.

SANDERSON: Go on, Dowd.

ELWOOD: Dr. Chumley sat down in the booth with us. I was sitting on the outside like this. (*Shows.*) Harvey was on the inside near the wall, and Dr. Chumley was seated directly across from Harvey where he could look at him.

WILSON: That's right. Spend all night on the seatin' arrangements!

ELWOOD: Harvey then suggested that I buy him a drink. Knowing that he does not like to drink alone, I suggested to Dr. Chumley that we join him.

WILSON: And so?

ELWOOD: We joined him.

WILSON: Go on—go on.

ELWOOD: We joined him again.

WILSON: Then what?

ELWOOD: We kept right on joining him.

WILSON: Oh, skip all the joining!

ELWOOD: You are asking me to skip a large portion of the evening—

WILSON: Tell us what happened—come on—please—

ELWOOD: Dr. Chumley and Harvey got into a conversation—quietly at first. Later it became rather heated and Dr. Chumley raised his voice.

WILSON: Yeah—why?

ELWOOD: Harvey seemed to feel that Dr. Chumley should assume part of the financial responsibility of the joining, but Dr. Chumley didn't seem to want to do that.

KELLY (*it breaks out from her*): I can believe *that* part of it!

WILSON: Let him talk. See how far he'll go. This guy's got guts.

ELWOOD: I agreed to take the whole thing because I did not want any trouble. We go down to Charlie's quite often—Harvey and I—and the proprietor is a fine man with an interesting approach to life. Then the other matter came up.

WILSON: Cut the damned double-talk and get on with it!

ELWOOD: Mr. Wilson, you are a sincere type of person, but I must ask you not to use that language in the presence of Miss Kelly. (*He makes a short bow to her.*)

SANDERSON: You're right, Dowd, and we're sorry. You say—the other matter came up?

ELWOOD: There was a beautiful blonde woman—a Mrs. Smethills—and her escort seated in the booth across from us. Dr. Chumley went over to sit next to her, explaining to her that they had once met. In Chicago. Her escort escorted Dr. Chumley back to me and Harvey and tried to point out that it would be better for Dr. Chumley to mind his own affairs. Does he have any?

WILSON: Does he have any what?

ELWOOD: Does he have any affairs?

WILSON: How would I know?

KELLY: Please hurry, Mr. Dowd—we're all so worried.

ELWOOD: Dr. Chumley then urged Harvey to go with him over to Blondie's Chicken Inn. Harvey wanted to go to Eddie's instead. While they were arguing about it I went to the bar to order another drink, and when I came back they were gone.

WILSON: Where did they go? I mean where did the doctor go?

ELWOOD: I don't know—I had a date out here with Dr. Sanderson and Miss Kelly, and I came out to pick them up—hoping that later on we might run into Harvey and the doctor and make a party of it.

WILSON: So you satisfied? You got his story—(*Goes over to* ELWOOD, *fists clenched.*) O.K. You're lyin' and we know it!

ELWOOD: I never lie, Mr. Wilson.

WILSON: You've done somethin' with the doctor and I'm findin' out what it is—

SANDERSON (*moving after him*): Don't touch him, Wilson—

KELLY: Maybe he isn't lying, Wilson—

WILSON (*turning on them. Furiously*): That's all this guy is, a bunch of lies! You two don't believe this story he tells about the doctor sittin' there talkin' to a big white rabbit, do you?

KELLY: Maybe Dr. Chumley *did* go to Charlie's Place.

WILSON: And saw a big rabbit, I suppose.

ELWOOD: And why not? Harvey was there. At first the doctor seemed a little frightened of Harvey, but that gave way to admiration as the evening wore on—The evening wore on! That's a nice expression. With your permission I'll say it again. The evening wore on.

WILSON (*lunging at him*): With your permission I'm gonna knock your teeth down your throat!

ELWOOD (*not moving an inch*): Mr. Wilson—haven't you some old friends you can go play with? (SANDERSON *has grabbed* WILSON *and is struggling with him.*)

WILSON (*he is being held. Glares fiercely at* ELWOOD. KELLY *dials phone*): The nerve of this guy! He couldn't come out here with an ordinary case of D.T.'s. No. He has to come out with a six-foot rabbit.

ELWOOD (*rises—goes toward desk*): Stimulating as all this is, I really must be getting downtown.

KELLY (*on phone*): Charlie's Place? Is Dr. Chumley anywhere around there? He was there with Mr. Dowd earlier in the evening. What?

Well, don't bite my head off! (*Hangs up.*) My, that man was mad. He said Mr. Dowd was welcome any time, but his friend was not.

ELWOOD: That's Mr. McNulty the bartender. He thinks a lot of me. Now let's all go down and have a drink.

WILSON: Wait a minute—

KELLY: Mr. Dowd—(*Goes over to him.*)

ELWOOD: Yes, my dear—may I hold your hand?

KELLY: Yes—if you want to. (ELWOOD *does.*) Poor Mrs. Chumley is so worried. Something must have happened to the doctor. Won't you please try and remember something—something else that might help her? Please—

ELWOOD: For you I would do anything. I would almost be willing to live my life over again. Almost. But I've told it all.

KELLY: You're sure?

ELWOOD: Quite sure—but ask me again, anyway, won't you? I liked that warm tone you had in your voice just then.

SANDERSON (*without realizing he is saying it*): So did I. (*Looks at* KELLY.)

WILSON: Oh, nuts!

ELWOOD: What?

WILSON: Nuts!

ELWOOD: Oh! I must be going. I have things to do.

KELLY: Mr. Dowd, what is it you do?

ELWOOD (*sits*): Harvey and I sit in the bars and we have a drink or two and play the jukebox. Soon the faces of the other people turn toward mine and smile. They are saying: "We don't know your name, Mister, but you're a lovely fellow." Harvey and I warm ourselves in all these golden moments. We have entered as strangers—soon we have friends. They come over. They sit with us. They drink with us. They talk to us. They tell about the big terrible things they have done. The big wonderful things they *will* do. Their hopes, their regrets, their loves, their hates. All very large because nobody ever brings anything small into a bar. Then I introduce them to Harvey. And he is bigger and grander than anything they offer me. When they leave, they leave impressed. The same people seldom come back— but that's envy, my dear. There's a little bit of envy in the best of us —too bad, isn't?

SANDERSON (*leaning forward*): How did you happen to call him Harvey?

ELWOOD: Harvey is his name.

SANDERSON: How do you know that?

ELWOOD: That was rather an interesting coincidence, Doctor. One night several years ago I was walking early in the evening along Fairfax Street—between 18th and 19th. You know that block?

SANDERSON: Yes, yes.

ELWOOD: I had just helped Ed Hickey into a taxi. Ed had been mixing his rye with his gin, and I felt he needed conveying. I started to walk down the street when I heard a voice saying: "Good evening, Mr. Dowd." I turned, and there was this great white rabbit leaning against a lamp-post. Well, I thought nothing of that, because when you have lived in a town as long as I have lived in this one, you get used to the fact that everybody knows your name. Naturally, I went over to chat with him. He said to me: "Ed Hickey is a little spiffed this evening, or could I be mistaken?" Well, of course he was not mistaken. I think the world and all of Ed, but he was spiffed. Well, anyway, we stood there and talked, and finally I said—"You have the advantage of me. You know my name and I don't know yours." Right back at me he said: "What name do you like?" Well, I didn't even have to think a minute: Harvey has always been my favorite name. So I said, "Harvey," and this is the interesting part of the whole thing. He said— "What a coincidence! My name happens to be Harvey."

SANDERSON (*crossing above desk*): What was your father's name, Dowd?

ELWOOD: John. John Frederick.

SANDERSON: Dowd, when you were a child you had a playmate, didn't you? Someone you were very fond of—with whom you spent many happy, carefree hours?

ELWOOD: Oh, yes, Doctor. Didn't you?

SANDERSON: What was his name?

ELWOOD: Verne. Verne McElhinney. Did you ever know the McElhinneys, Doctor?

SANDERSON: No.

ELWOOD: Too bad. There were a lot of them, and they circulated. Wonderful people.

SANDERSON: Think carefully, Dowd. Wasn't there someone, somewhere, sometime, whom you knew—by the name of Harvey? Didn't you ever know anybody by that name?

ELWOOD: No, Doctor. No one. Maybe that's why I always had such hopes for it.

SANDERSON: Come on, Wilson, we'll take Mr. Dowd upstairs now.

WILSON: I'm taking him nowhere. You've made this your show—now run it. Lettin' him sit here—forgettin' all about Dr. Chumley! O.K. It's your show—you run it.

SANDERSON: Come on, Dowd—(*Pause. Putting out his hand.*) Come on, Elwood—

ELWOOD (*rises*): Very well, Lyman. (SANDERSON *and* KELLY *take him to door.*) But I'm afraid I won't be able to visit with you for long. I have promised Harvey I will take him to the floor-show. (*They exit.* WILSON *is alone. Sits at desk, looks at his watch.*)

WILSON: Oh, boy! (*Puts head in arms on desk.* DR. CHUMLEY *enters.*)

WILSON (*jumping up, going to him*): Dr. Chumley—Are you all right?

CHUMLEY: All right? Of course I'm all right. I'm being followed. Lock that door.

WILSON (*goes to door, locks it*): Who's following you?

CHUMLEY: None of your business. (*Exits into office, locks door behind him.*)

(WILSON *stands a moment perplexed, then shrugs shoulders, turns off lights and exits. The stage is dimly lit. Then from door comes the rattle of the doorknob. Door opens and shuts, and we hear locks opening and closing, and see light from hall on stage. The invisible Harvey has come in. There is a count of eight while he crosses the stage, then door of* CHUMLEY'S *office opens and closes, with sound of locks clicking. Harvey has gone in—and then—*)

CURTAIN

ACT THREE

SCENE: *The sanitarium office at Chumley's Rest.*

TIME: *A few minutes after the curtain of Act Two.*

AT RISE: *Lights are still dim as at preceding curtain. There is a loud knocking and the sound of* CHUMLEY'S *voice calling,* "Wilson! Wilson!"

WILSON (*enters, opens door.* CHUMLEY *enters, whitefaced*): How didja get out here, Doctor? I just say you go in there.

CHUMLEY: I went out through my window. Wilson—don't leave me!

WILSON: No, Doctor.

CHUMLEY: Get that man Dowd out of here.

WILSON: Yes, Doctor. (*Starts to exit.*)

CHUMLEY: No—don't leave me!

WILSON (*turning back—confused*): But you said—

CHUMLEY: Dumphy—on the telephone.

WILSON: Yes, Doctor. (*Crosses to phone.*) Dumphy—give that guy Dowd his clothes and get him down here right away. (*A knock on the door.*)

CHUMLEY: Don't leave me!

WILSON: Just a minute, Doctor. (*Crosses up and turns on lights. Crosses down and opens door.*) Judge Gaffney.

JUDGE: I want to see Dr. Chumley. (*Enter* JUDGE *and* MYRTLE MAE.)

WILSON: Hiya, Myrtle.

MYRTLE: Hello.

JUDGE: Chumley, we've got to talk to you. This thing is serious.

MYRTLE: It certainly is.

GAFFNEY: More serious than you suspect. Where can we go to talk? (*Moves toward* CHUMLEY'S *office.*)

CHUMLEY (*blocking door*): Not in there.

WILSON: The doctor doesn't want you in his office.

CHUMLEY: No, sir.

JUDGE: Then sit down, Dr. Chumley. Sit down, Myrtle Mae.

CHUMLEY (*dazed*): Sit down, Dr. Chumley. Sit down, Myrtle Mae. Don't go, Wilson. Don't leave me.

JUDGE: Now, Chumley, here are my notes—the facts. Can anybody hear me?

WILSON: Yeah, we can all hear you. Is that good?

JUDGE (*gives* WILSON *a look of reproof*): Now, Chumley, has it ever occurred to you that possibly there might *be* something like this rabbit Harvey?

MYRTLE: Of course there isn't. And anybody who thinks so is crazy. (CHUMLEY *stares at her.*) Well, don't look at me like that. There's nothing funny about me. I'm like my father's family, they're all dead.

JUDGE: Now, then, my client, the plaintiff, Mrs. Veta Louise Simmons, under oath, swears that on the morning of November second while standing in the kitchen of her home, hearing her name called, she turned and saw this great white rabbit, Harvey. He was staring at her. Resenting the intrusion, the plaintiff made certain remarks and drove the creature from the room. He went.

CHUMLEY: What did she say to him?

JUDGE: She was emphatic. The remarks are not important.

CHUMLEY: I want to know how she got this creature out of her sanitarium—I mean—her home.

MYRTLE: I hate to have to tell him, Judge. It isn't a bit like Mother.

WILSON: Quit stalling. Let's have it.

GAFFNEY: She looked him right in the eye and exclaimed in the heat of anger—"To hell with you!"

CHUMLEY (*looking at door*): "To hell with you!" He left?

JUDGE: Yes, he left. But that's beside the point. The point is—is it perjury or is it something we can cope with? I ask for your opinion. (KELLY *enters from stairs.* SANDERSON *comes from diet kitchen.*)

SANDERSON: Ruthie! I've been looking all over for you.

CHUMLEY: Dr. Sanderson, disregard what I said this afternoon. I want you on my staff. You are a very astute young man.

KELLY: Oh, Lyman! Did you hear?

SANDERSON: Oh, baby!

KELLY: See you later. (*Exits, blowing him a kiss.* SANDERSON *exits into his office.*)

MYRTLE: You've just got to keep Uncle Elwood out here, Doctor. (JUDGE *crosses to desk.*)

CHUMLEY: No. I want this sanitarium the way it was before that man came out here this afternoon.

MYRTLE: I know what you mean.

CHUMLEY: You do?

MYRTLE: Well, it certainly gets on anyone's nerves the way Uncle Elwood knows what's going to happen before it happens. This morning, for instance, he told us that Harvey told him Mrs. McElhinney's Aunt Rose would drop in on her unexpectedly tonight from Cleveland.

CHUMLEY: And did she?

MYRTLE: Did she what?

CHUMLEY: Aunt Rose—did she come just as Harvey said she would?

MYRTLE: Oh, yes. Those things always turn out the way Uncle Elwood says they will—but what of it? What do we care about the McElhinneys?

CHUMLEY: You say this sort of thing happens often?

MYRTLE: Yes, and isn't it silly? Uncle Elwood says Harvey tells him everything. Harvey knows everything. How could he when there is no such thing as Harvey?

CHUMLEY (*goes over, tries lock at door*): Fly-specks. I've been spending my life among fly-specks while miracles have been leaning on lamp-posts on 18th and Fairfax.

VETA (*enters. Looks around cautiously. Sighs with relief*): Good. Nobody here but people.

MYRTLE: Oh, Mother! You promised you wouldn't come out here.

VETA: Well, good evening. Now, Myrtle Mae, I brought Elwood's bathrobe. Well, why are you all just sitting here? I thought you'd be committing him.

JUDGE: Sit down there, girl. (*Motioning to chair near* WILSON).

VETA: I will not sit down there. (*Sits.*)

WILSON: How about you and me stepping out Saturday night, Myrtle Mae?

VETA: Certainly not. Myrtle Mae, come here.

MYRTLE: I'm sorry. (*Goes down to* VETA.)

VETA: Is everything settled?

CHUMLEY: It will be.

SANDERSON (*enters from his office.*): Doctor, may I give an opinion?

CHUMLEY: Yes, do. By all means.

VETA (*sniffing*): His opinion! Omar—he's the doctor I told you about. The eyes!

SANDERSON: It's my opinion that Elwood P. Dowd is suffering from a third degree hallucination and the—(*Pointing at* VETA's *back.*) other party concerned is the victim of autosuggestion. I recommend shock formula number 977 for him and bed-rest at home for—(*Points again.*)

CHUMLEY: You do?

SANDERSON: That's my diagnosis, Doctor. (*To* VETA.) Mr. Dowd will not see this rabbit any more after this injection. We've used it in hundreds of psychopathic cases.

VETA: Don't you call my brother a psychopathic case! There's never been anything like that in our family.

MYRTLE: If you didn't think Uncle Elwood was psychopathic, why did you bring him out here?

VETA: Where else could I take him? I couldn't take him to jail, could I? Besides, this is not your uncle's fault. Why did Harvey have to speak to him in the first place? With the town full of people, why did he have to bother Elwood?

JUDGE: Stop putting your oar in. Keep your oar out. If this shock formula brings people back to reality, give it to him. That's where we want Elwood.

CHUMLEY: I'm not sure that it would work in a case of this kind, Doctor.

SANDERSON: It always has.

VETA: Harvey always follows Elwood home.

CHUMLEY: He does?

VETA: Yes. But if you give him the formula and Elwood doesn't see Harvey, he won't let him in. Then when he comes to the door, I'll deal with him.

MYRTLE: Mother, won't you stop talking about Harvey as if there was such a thing?

VETA: Myrtle Mae, you've got a lot to learn and I hope you never learn it. (*She starts up toward* WILSON.)

(ELWOOD *is heard offstage, humming.*)

JUDGE: Sh! Here he is.

ELWOOD (*enters*): Good evening, everybody.

(*All nod.*)

VETA: Good evening, Elwood. I've brought you your bathrobe.

ELWOOD: Thank you, Veta.

JUDGE: Well, Chumley, what do we do? We've got to do something.

VETA: Oh, yes, we must.

MYRTLE: I should say so.

CHUMLEY (*looking at door*): Yes, it's imperative.

ELWOOD: Well, while you're making up your minds, why don't we all go down to Charlie's and have a drink?

VETA: You're not going anywhere, Elwood. You're staying here.

MYRTLE: Yes, Uncle Elwood.

JUDGE: Stay here, son.

ELWOOD: I plan to leave. You want me to stay. An element of conflict in any discussion is a good thing. It means everybody is taking part and nobody is left out. I like that. Oh—how did you get along with Harvey, Doctor?

CHUMLEY: Sh-h!

JUDGE: We're waiting for your answer, Doctor.

CHUMLEY: What?

JUDGE: What is your decision?

CHUMLEY: I must be alone with this man. Will you all step into the other room? (MYRTLE *exits.*) I'll have my diagnosis in a moment.

VETA: Do hurry, Doctor.

CHUMLEY: I will.

VETA: You stay here, Elwood. (*She and* JUDGE GAFFNEY *exit.*)

CHUMLEY: Here, Mr. Dowd. Let me give you this chair. (*Indicates chair.*) Let me give you a cigar. (*Does so.*) Is there anything else I can get you?

ELWOOD (*seated in chair*): What did you have in mind?

CHUMLEY: Mr. Dowd (*Lowers voice, looks toward office.*) What kind of a man are you? Where do you come from?

ELWOOD (*getting out card*): Didn't I give you one of my cards?

CHUMLEY: And where on the face of this tired old earth did you find a thing like him?

ELWOOD: Harvey the Pooka?

CHUMLEY (*sits*): Is it true that he has a function—that he—

ELWOOD: Gets advance notice? I'm happy to say it is. Harvey is versatile. Harvey can stop clocks.

DR. CHUMLEY: What?

ELWOOD: You've heard that expression, "His face would stop a clock?"

CHUMLEY: Yes. But why? To what purpose?

ELWOOD: Harvey says that he can look at your clock and stop it and you can go away as long as you like with whomever you like and go as far as you like. And when you come back not one minute will have ticked by.

CHUMLEY: You mean that he actually—(*Looks toward office.*)

ELWOOD: Einstein has overcome time and space. Harvey has overcome not only time and space—but any objections.

CHUMLEY: And does he do this for you?

ELWOOD: He is willing to at any time, but so far I've never been able to think of any place I'd rather be. I always have a wonderful time just where I am, whomever I'm with. I'm having a fine time right now with you, Doctor. (*Holds up cigar.*) Corona-Corona.

CHUMLEY: I know where I'd go.

ELWOOD: Where?

CHUMLEY: I'd go to Akron.

ELWOOD: Akron?

CHUMLEY: There's a cottage camp outside Akron in a grove of maple trees, cool, green, beautiful.

ELWOOD: My favorite tree.

CHUMLEY: I would go there with a pretty young woman, a strange woman, a quiet woman.

ELWOOD: Under a tree?

CHUMLEY: I wouldn't even want to know her name. I would be—just Mr. Brown.

ELWOOD: Why wouldn't you want to know her name? You might be acquainted with the same people.

CHUMLEY: I would send out for cold beer. I would talk to her. I would tell her things I have never told anyone—things that are locked in here. (*Beats his breast.* ELWOOD *looks over at his chest with interest.*) And then I would send out for more cold beer.

ELWOOD: No whiskey?

CHUMLEY: Beer is better.

ELWOOD: Maybe under a tree. But she might like a highball.

CHUMLEY: I wouldn't let her talk to me, but as I talked I would want her to reach out a soft white hand and stroke my head and say, "Poor thing! Oh, you poor, poor thing!"

ELWOOD: How long would you like that to go on?

CHUMLEY: Two weeks.

ELWOOD: Wouldn't that get monotonous? Just Akron, beer, and "poor, poor thing" for two weeks?

CHUMLEY: No. No, it would not. It would be wonderful.

ELWOOD: I can't help but feel you're making a mistake in not allowing that woman to talk. If she gets around at all, she may have picked up some very interesting little news items. And I'm sure you're making a mistake with all that beer and no whiskey. But it's your two weeks.

CHUMLEY (*dreamily*): Cold beer at Akron and one last fling! God, man!

ELWOOD: Do you think you'd like to lie down for awhile?

CHUMLEY: No. No. Tell me Mr. Dowd, could he—would he do this for me?

ELWOOD: He could and he might. I have never heard Harvey say a word against Akron. By the way, Doctor, where is Harvey?

CHUMLEY (*rising. Very cautiously*): Why, don't you know?

ELWOOD: The last time I saw him he was with you.

CHUMLEY: Ah!

ELWOOD: Oh! He's probably waiting for me down at Charlie's.

CHUMLEY (*with a look of cunning toward his office*): That's it! He's down at Charlie's.

ELWOOD: Excuse me, Doctor. (*Rises, starts upstage.*)

CHUMLEY: No, no, Mr. Dowd. Not in there.

ELWOOD: I couldn't leave without saying good-night to my friend, Dr. Sanderson.

CHUMLEY: Mr. Dowd, Dr. Sanderson is not your friend. None of those people are your friends. *I* am your friend.

ELWOOD: Thank you, Doctor. And I'm yours.

CHUMLEY: And this sister of yours—she is at the bottom of this conspiracy against you. She's trying to persuade me to lock you up. Today she had commitment papers drawn up. She's got your power of attorney and the key to your safety box. She brought you out here.

ELWOOD: My sister did all that in one afternoon? Veta is certainly a whirlwind.

CHUMLEY (*moving down below desk*): God, man, haven't you any righteous indignation?

ELWOOD: Dr. Chumley, my mother used to say to me, "In this world, Elwood"—she always called me Elwood—she'd say, "In this world, Elwood, you must be oh, so smart or oh, so pleasant." For years I was smart. I recommend pleasant. You may quote me.

CHUMLEY: Just the same, I will protect you if I have to commit her. Would you like me to do that?

ELWOOD: No, Doctor, not unless Veta wanted it that way. Oh, not that you don't have a nice place out here, but I think Veta would be happier at home with me and Harvey and Myrtle Mae. (KELLY *enters with flower in hair, goes to put magazines on table.* ELWOOD *turns to her.*) Miss Kelly! "Diviner grace has never brightened this enchanting face!" (*To* CHUMLEY.) Ovid's Fifth Elegy. (*To* MISS KELLY.) My dear, you will never look lovelier!

KELLY: I'll never feel happier, Mr. Dowd. I know it. (*Kisses him.*)

CHUMLEY: Well!

KELLY: Yes, Doctor. (*Exits.*)

(WILSON *enters hall in time to see the kiss.*)

ELWOOD: I wonder if I would be able to remember any more of that poem?

WILSON: Say, maybe this rabbit gag is a good one. Kelly never kissed me.

ELWOOD (*looking at* WILSON): Ovid has always been my favorite poet.

WILSON: O.K., pal—You're discharged. This way out—(*Takes him by arm downstage.*)

CHUMLEY: Wilson! Take your hands off that man!

WILSON: What?

CHUMLEY: Apologize to Mr. Dowd.

WILSON: Apologize to him—this guy with the rabbit?

CHUMLEY (*looking toward his office*): Apologize! Apologize—

WILSON: I apologize. This is the door.

ELWOOD: If I leave, I'll remember. (WILSON *exits.*)

CHUMLEY: Wait a minute, Dowd. Do women often come up to you and kiss you like Miss Kelly did just now?

ELWOOD: Every once in a while.

CHUMLEY: Yes?

ELWOOD: I encourage it, too.

CHUMLEY (*to himself*): To hell with decency! I've got to have that rabbit! Go ahead and knock. (ELWOOD *starts for* SANDERSON'S *door just as* SANDERSON *comes out.*)

ELWOOD: Dr. Sanderson, I couldn't leave without—

SANDERSON: Just a minute, Dowd—(*To* CHUMLEY.) Doctor, do you agree with my diagnosis?

CHUMLEY: Yes, yes! Call them all in.

SANDERSON: Thank you, Doctor. Mrs. Simmons—Judge Gaffney—will you step in here for a minute, please?

VETA (*enters*): Is it settled? (MYRTLE *and* JUDGE *enter.*)

CHUMLEY: I find I concur with Dr. Sanderson!

SANDERSON: Thank you, Doctor.

MYRTLE: Oh, that's wonderful! What a relief!

JUDGE: Good boy!

ELWOOD: Well, let's celebrate—(*Takes little book out of his pocket.*) I've got some new bars listed in the back of this book.

CHUMLEY (*speaking to others in low tone*): This injection carries a violent reaction. We can't give it to him without his consent. Will he give it?

VETA: Of course he will, if I ask him.

CHUMLEY: To give up this rabbit—I doubt it.

MYRTLE: Don't ask him. Just give it to him.

ELWOOD: "Bessie's Barn Dance. Blondie's Chicken Inn. Better Late Than Never—Bennie's Drive In"—

VETA: Elwood!

ELWOOD: We'll go to Bennie's Drive In—We should telephone for a table. How many of us will there be, Veta?

VETA (*starting to count, then catching herself*): Oh—Elwood!

CHUMLEY: Mr. Dowd, I have a formula—977—that will be good for you. Will you take it?

JUDGE: Elwood, you won't see this rabbit any more.

SANDERSON: But you will see your responsibilities, your duties—

ELWOOD: I'm sure if you thought of it, Doctor, it must be a very fine thing. And if I happen to run into anyone who needs it, I'll be glad to recommend it. For myself, I wouldn't care for it.

VETA: Hear that, Judge! Hear that, Doctor! That's what we have to put up with.

ELWOOD (*turning to look at her*): Veta, do you want me to take this?

VETA: Elwood, I'm only thinking of you. You're my brother and I've known you for years. I'd do anything for you. That Harvey wouldn't do anything for you. He's making a fool out of you, Elwood. Don't be a fool.

ELWOOD: Oh, I won't.

VETA: Why, you could amount to something. You could be sitting on the Western Slope Water Board right now if you'd only go over and ask them.

ELWOOD: All right, Veta. If that's what you want, Harvey and I will go over and ask them tomorrow.

VETA: Tomorrow! I never want to see another tomorrow. Not if Myrtle Mae and I have to live in the house with that rabbit. Our friends never come to see us—we have no social life; we have no life at all.

We're both miserable. I wish I were dead—but maybe you don't care!

ELWOOD (*slowly*): I've always felt that Veta should have everything she wants. Veta, are you sure? (VETA *nods.*) I'll take it. Where do I go, Doctor?

CHUMLEY: In Dr. Sanderson's office, Dowd.

ELWOOD: Say good-by to the old fellow for me, won't you? (*Exits.* CHUMLEY *exits.*)

JUDGE: How long will this take, Doctor?

SANDERSON: Only a few minutes. Why don't you wait? (*Exits.*)

JUDGE: We'll wait. (*Sits.*)

VETA (*sighs*): Dr. Sanderson said it wouldn't take long.

MYRTLE: Now, Mother, don't fidget.

VETA: Oh, how can I help it?

MYRTLE (*picks up edge of draperies*): How stunning! Mother, could you see me in a housecoat of this material.

VETA (*to* MYRTLE—*first looking at draperies. Sighs again*): Yes, dear, but let me get a good night's sleep first. (*Loud knocking at door.*)

JUDGE: Come in. (*Enter* CAB DRIVER.)

JUDGE: What do you want?

CAB DRIVER: I'm lookin' for a little, short—(*Seeing* VETA.) Oh, there you are! Lady, you jumped outta the cab without payin' me.

VETA: Oh, yes. I forgot. How much is it?

CAB DRIVER: All the way out here from town? $2.75.

VETA (*looking in purse*): $2.75! I could have sworn I brought my coin purse—where is it? (*Gets up, goes to table, turns pocketbook upside down, in full view of audience. Nothing comes out of it but a compact and a handkerchief.*) Myrtle, do you have any money?

MYRTLE: I spent that money Uncle Elwood gave me for my new hair-do for the party.

VETA: Judge, do you have $2.75 I could give this man?

JUDGE: Sorry. Nothing but a check.

CAB DRIVER: We don't take checks.

JUDGE: I know.

VETA: Dr. Chumley, do you happen to have $2.75 I could borrow to pay this cab driver?

CHUMLEY (*He has just entered, now wearing white starched jacket*):

Haven't got my wallet. No time to get it now. Have to get on with this injection. Sorry. (*Exits.*)

VETA: Well, I'll get it for you from my brother, but I can't get it right now. He's in there to get an injection. It won't be long. You'll have to wait.

CAB DRIVER: You're gonna get my money from your brother and he's in there to get some of that stuff they shoot out here?

VETA: Yes, it won't be but a few minutes.

CAB DRIVER: Lady, I want my money now.

VETA: But I told you it would only be a few minutes. I want you to drive us back to town, anyway.

CAB DRIVER: And I told you I want my money now or I'm nosin' the cab back to town, and you can wait for the bus—at six in the morning.

VETA: Well, of all the pig-headed, stubborn things!

MYRTLE: I should say so.

JUDGE: What's the matter with you?

CAB DRIVER: Nothin' that $2.75 won't fix. You heard me. Take it or leave it.

VETA (*getting up*): I never heard of anything so unreasonable in my life. (*Knocks.*) Dr. Chumley, will you let Elwood step out here a minute. This cab driver won't wait.

CHUMLEY: Don't be too long. (*Enter* ELWOOD. CHUMLEY *follows.*)

VETA: Elwood, I came off without my coin purse. Will you give this man $2.75? But don't give him any more. He's been very rude.

ELWOOD (*extending his hand*): How do you do? Dowd is my name. Elwood P.

CAB DRIVER: Lofgren's mine. E. J.

ELWOOD: I'm glad to meet you, Mr. Lofgren. This is my sister, Mrs. Simmons. My charming litle niece, Myrtle Mae Simmons. Judge Gaffney and Dr. Chumley. (*All bow coldly.*)

CAB DRIVER: Hi—

ELWOOD: Have you lived around here long, Mr. Lofgren?

CAB DRIVER: Yeah, I've lived around here all my life.

ELWOOD: Do you enjoy your work?

CAB DRIVER: It's O.K. I been with the Apex Cabs fifteen years and my brother Joe's been drivin' for Brown Cabs pretty near twelve.

ELWOOD: You drive for Apex and your brother Joe for Brown's? That's interesting, isn't it, Veta? (VETA *reacts with a sniff*.) Mr. Lofgren—let me give you one of my cards. (*Gives him one.*)

CHUMLEY: Better get on with this, Mr. Dowd.

ELWOOD: Certainly. One minute. My sister and my charming little niece live here with me at this address. Won't you and your brother come and have dinner wih us some time?

CABBY: Sure—be glad to.

ELWOOD: When—when would you be glad to?

CABBY: I couldn't come any night but Tuesday. I'm on duty all the rest of the week.

ELWOOD: You must come on Tuesday, then. We'll expect you and be delighted to see you, won't we, Veta?

VETA: Oh, Elwood, I'm sure this man has friends of his own.

ELWOOD: Veta, one can't have too many friends.

VETA: Elwood, don't keep Dr. Chumley waiting—that's rude.

ELWOOD: Of course. (*Gives him bill.*) Here you are—keep the change. I'm glad to have met you and I'll expect you Tuesday with your brother. Will you excuse me now?

LOFGREN: Sure. (ELWOOD *exits.* CHUMLEY *follows.*)

CAB DRIVER: A sweet guy.

VETA: Certainly. You could just as well have waited.

CAB DRIVER: Oh, no. Listen, lady. I've been drivin' this route fifteen years. I've brought 'em out here to get that stuff and drove 'em back after they had it. It changes 'em. (*Crosses to desk.*)

VETA: Well, I certainly hope so.

CAB DRIVER: And you ain't kiddin'. On the way out here they sit back and enjoy the ride. They talk to me. Sometimes we stop and watch the sunsets and look at the birds flyin'. Sometimes we stop and watch the birds when there ain't no birds and look at the sunsets when it's rainin'. We have a swell time and I always get a big tip. But afterward—oh—oh—(*Starts to exit again.*)

VETA: Afterwards—oh—oh! What do you mean afterwards—oh—oh?

CAB DRIVER: They crab, crab, crab. They yell at me to watch the lights, watch the brakes, watch the intersections. They scream at me to hurry. They got no faith—in me or my buggy—yet it's the same cab —the same driver—and we're goin' back over the very same road. It's no fun—and no tips—(*Turns to door.*)

VETA: But my brother would have tipped you, anyway. He's very generous. Always has been.

CAB DRIVER: Not after this he won't be. Lady, after this, he'll be a perfectly normal human being and you know what bastards they are! Glad I met you. I'll wait. (*Exits.*)

VETA (*starts to run for door*): Oh, Judge Gaffney—Myrtle Mae! Stop it—stop it—don't give it to him! Elwood, come out of there.

JUDGE: You can't do that. Dr. Chumley is giving the injection.

MYRTLE: Mother—stop this—

VETA (*pounding on door*): I don't want Elwood to have it! I don't want Elwood that way. I don't like people like that.

MYRTLE: Do something with her, Judge. Mother, stop it—

VETA (*turning on her*): You shut up! I've lived longer than you have. I remember my father. I remember your father. I remember—

CHUMLEY (*opens door*): What's this? What's all this commotion?

WILSON (*enters*): What's the trouble, Doctor? She soundin' off again?

JUDGE: She wants to stop the injection.

VETA: You haven't—you haven't already given it to him, have you?

CHUMLEY: No, but we're ready. Take Mrs. Simmons away, Wilson.

VETA: Leave me alone. Take your hands off me, you whiteslaver!

JUDGE: You don't know what you want. You didn't want that rabbit, either.

VETA: And what's wrong with Harvey? If Elwood and Myrtle Mae and I want to live with Harvey it's nothing to you! You don't even have to come around. It's our business. Elwood—Elwood! (ELWOOD *enters. She throws herself weepingly into his arms. He pats her shoulder.*)

ELWOOD: There, there, Veta. (*To others.*) Veta is all tired out. She's done a lot today.

JUDGE: Have it your own way. I'm not giving up my game at the club again, no matter how big the animal is. (*He exits.*)

VETA (*crossing* ELWOOD *to desk*): Come on, Elwood—let's get out of here. I hate this place. I wish I'd never seen it!

CHUMLEY: But—see—here—

ELWOOD: It's whatever Veta says, Doctor.

VETA: Why, look at this! That's funny. (*It's her coin purse.*) It must have been there all the time. I could have paid that cab driver myself. Harvey!

VETA: Come on, Myrtle Mae. Come on, Elwood. Hurry up. (*She exits down left.* MYRTLE *follows.*)

ELWOOD: Good night, Doctor Chumley. Good night, Mr. Wilson.

VETA (*offstage*): Come along, Elwood.

ELWOOD: Doctor, for years I've known what my family thinks of Harvey. But I've often wondered what Harvey's family thinks of me. (*He looks beyond* CHUMLEY *to the door of his office.*) Oh—there you are! Doctor—do you mind? (*Gestures for him to step back.*) You're standing in his way. (*There is the sound of a lock clicking open and the door of* CHUMLEY'S *office opens wide. The invisible Harvey crosses to him and as they exit together:*) Where've you been? I've been looking all over for you—

CURTAIN

Born Yesterday

GARSON KANIN

Why our respondents liked

 BORN YESTERDAY

"Probably the best of the American comedies, perfectly structured, damn funny, and about something important."
HAL PRINCE

"Everything a comedy has to have."
DORE SCHARY

"Funny and touching."
RICHARD RODGERS

Born Yesterday began its highly acclaimed appearance on Broadway in February 1946. It was the first play authored by Garson Kanin—distinguished director, author, and actor—who was also responsible for its staging. Mr. Kanin's past credits had included acting on the Broadway stage and assisting director George Abbott on a number of successful comedies, including *Three Men on a Horse, Brother Rat,* and *Room Service.* In addition to his being a prolific director of films and plays—among them *The Diary of Anne Frank, A Hole in the Head, Do Re Mi, Funny Girl*—Mr. Kanin has written the screenplays for such noted films as *Adam's Rib* and *Pat and Mike* (both co-authored with his wife Ruth Gordon), *It Should Happen to You,* and *The Rat Race.* In recent years his writings—fiction and nonfiction—have included *One Hell of an Actor, Hollywood, A Thousand Summers,* and *Tracy and Hepburn.*

Originally, the part of Billie Jean in *Born Yesterday* was to be played by well-known actress Jean Arthur. However, during the play's tryout she became ill and Judy Holliday was chosen to be her replacement. Miss Holliday had appeared primarily in nightclubs and her role in *Born Yesterday* was to launch her career as a popular comedienne. The play also served as a fine vehicle for the talented stage and screen actor Paul Douglas, featured in the role of Harry Brock. Garson Kanin's outstanding script, teamed with a fine cast, proved to be a surefire hit on Broadway.

Born Yesterday was presented by Max Gordon on February 4, 1946, at the Lyceum Theatre, New York City. The cast was as follows:

Billie Dawn	Judy Holliday
Harry Brock	Paul Douglas
Paul Verrall	Gary Merrill
Ed Devery	Otto Hulett
Senator Norval Hedges	Larry Oliver
Mrs. Hedges	Mona Bruns
Eddie Brock	Frank Otto
The Assistant Manager	Carroll Ashburn
Helen	Ellen Hall
A Bellhop	William Harmon
Another Bellhop	Rex King
A Barber	Ted Mayer
A Manicurist	Mary Laslo
A Bootblack	Parris Morgan
A Waiter	C. L. Burke

Staged by Garson Kanin
Assistant to Mr. Kanin, Hal Gerson
Setting by Donald Oenslager
Miss Holliday's costumes by Mainbocher
Costumes (other than Miss Holliday's) by Ruth Kanin
Production Stage Manager, David M. Pardoll
Stage Manager, William Harmon

The scene is Washington, D.C.

ACT ONE

September, 1945

ACT TWO

Two months later

ACT THREE

Late that night

ACT ONE

SCENE: This happens in the sitting room of Suite 67D, a large part of the best hotel in Washington, D.C. 67D is so called because it is a duplex apartment on the sixth and seventh floors of the hotel. It is a masterpiece of offensive good taste, colorful and lush and rich. There are mops and brooms in the doorway when the curtain rises and in the room a chambermaid's cleaning unit. The main door is open and the telephone bell is ringing. A maid comes down the staircase which leads from the bedrooms, carrying a large vase of yellow roses. She sets them down, and goes off to the service wing, paying the phone no mind. It rings some more. In a moment, the maid returns and tends to a few more chores in the room. The phone stops. A man walks by the open door. He looks in, but passes. A moment later he returns and stands in the doorway. This is PAUL VERRALL, *of the* New Republic's Washington *staff.* VERRALL *is in his middle thirties, handsome, alert, and energetic. There is nothing wrong with him at all, in fact, with the possible exception of a tendency to take things, and himself, too seriously. He knows this. He is carrying several books, magazines, and newspapers. He wears eyeglasses. He lights a cigarette and leans in the doorway.*

PAUL: Who's coming in here, Helen, do you know?

HELEN: Hello, Mr. Verrall. No, I don't.

PAUL: A Harry Brock, by any chance?

HELEN: I'm not the room clerk, please.

PAUL: I'm supposed to meet this guy, that's all. I wondered if maybe he was coming in here.

(HELEN *looks at the card stuck in among the roses.*)

HELEN: Brock. (*She goes about her work.*)

PAUL (*looking around*): I figured. (*He steps into the room.*)

HELEN: Who's Brock?

PAUL: *Harry* Brock.

HELEN: Never heard of him.

PAUL: You will, Helen. Big man. Ran a little junk yard into fifty million bucks, with no help from anyone or anything—except maybe World War II.

HELEN: Anybody checks into 67D I got no desire to meet. Believe me.

PAUL: Why not?

HELEN: Listen, you know what they charge for this layout? (*She is about to continue, impressively, when* PAUL *interrupts.*)

PAUL: Two hundred and thirty-five a day.

HELEN: Who told you?

PAUL: Frank.

HELEN: Oh.

PAUL: What about it?

HELEN: Listen, anybody's got two hundred and thirty-five dollars a day to spend on a hotel room there ought to be a law.

PAUL: Too many laws already.

HELEN: While I'm getting eighteen a week I don't see why anybody should spend two hundred and thirty-five a day.

PAUL: For a hotel room.

HELEN: That's what I say.

PAUL (*smiling*): I know some people who'd call you a communist.

HELEN (*darkly*): Tell them I'm thinking about it. Seriously.

(PAUL *is at the window, looking out over the city.*)

HELEN: Changed much, do you think?

PAUL: What?

HELEN: Washington?

PAUL: Not enough. I could stand a little more change. The idea of the war wasn't to leave everything the same, you know.

HELEN: The trouble with you, Mr. Verrall, you think too much. Most fellows your age get more—

(*She breaks off as a bellhop enters, carrying a large leather box and several brief cases. He is followed by* EDDIE BROCK, *who is* HARRY BROCK'S *cousin—and servant.*)

EDDIE: This stays down. The rest goes up.

THE BELLHOP: Yes, sir.

(HELEN *picks up her paraphernalia and goes.* PAUL *is on his way out. So is the* BELLHOP. *As they reach the door, however, they step aside.* HARRY BROCK *stamps in, followed by the* ASSISTANT MANAGER. *Then* BILLIE DAWN *appears wearing a mink coat and carrying another.* BROCK *is a huge man in his late thirties. Gross is the word for him.* BILLIE *is breathtakingly beautiful and breathtakingly stupid. The* BELLHOP *leaves.*)

THE ASSISTANT MANAGER (*a Rotarian*): Here we are.

(BROCK *and* BILLIE *are looking around.* BROCK *is impressed by the room, but tries not to show it. As he looks around he sees* PAUL, *but doesn't particularly notice him.*)

BROCK (*without enthusiasm*): It's all right.

THE ASSISTANT MANAGER (*pointing*): Service wing. Terrace. (*Going toward the staircase.*) And the bedchambers are right this way.

(*He goes up.* BILLIE *follows.* EDDIE *is unpacking bottles of liquor from the leather box and putting them on a side table.* BROCK *sits on a large modern sofa, the principal piece of furniture in the room, and removes his shoes.* PAUL *comes down to him.*)

PAUL (*extending his hand*): Hello, Mr. Brock.

BROCK (*brusquely, ignoring* PAUL'S *hand*): How are you? (*He turns away.* PAUL *thinks a moment, then leaves*).

BROCK: Who the hell was that?

EDDIE: Search me.

BROCK: What kind of a joint is this—people in and out of your place all the time?

(*The* ASSISTANT MANAGER *returns.*)

THE ASSISTANT MANAGER: Mrs. Brock seems delighted with the bed-chambers.

BROCK: It's not Mrs. Brock.

THE ASSISTANT MANAGER (*gulping*): I see.

BROCK: All right. Just don't get nosey.

THE ASSISTANT MANAGER: Not at all.

BROCK: There ain't no Mrs. Brock, except my mother. And she's dead.

THE ASSISTANT MANAGER: I see.

BROCK (*snapping his fingers*): Eddie! Take care of him. (EDDIE *comes over, reaches into his pocket, and takes out a roll of bills. He looks at* BROCK. *They reach a swift, silent, understanding as to how much.* EDDIE *hands the* ASSISTANT MANAGER *two ten-dollar bills.*)

THE ASSISTANT MANAGER (*to Eddie*): Thank you. (*Then, to* BROCK.) That is, thank *you*. So much.

BROCK: All right, all right. Just listen. Anybody works in this room just tell 'em to do it good and do it quick and nobody'll get hurt. I'm a big tipper, tell 'em, and I don't like a lot of people around all the time and I don't like to wait for nothin'. I ain't used to it.

THE ASSISTANT MANAGER: I'm sure everything will be just that, Mr. Brock.

BROCK (*with a wave*): Okay. Knock off.

THE ASSISTANT MANAGER: Thank you *very* much, Mr. Brock. (*He leaves.*)

BROCK (*rising and shouting*): Billie!!

BILLIE (*appearing on the balcony*): What?

BROCK (*indicating the room*): Not bad, huh?

BILLIE (*without enthusiasm*): It's all right.

(*The door buzzer sounds.* EDDIE *goes to answer it.*)

BROCK (*sore*): All right, she says. You know what this place costs a day?

BILLIE: Two hundred and thirty-five. You told me.

(*She leaves, with a bored wave of her hips.* EDDIE *opens the door.* ED DEVERY *comes in, slightly drunk.*)

DEVERY: Hello, Eddie.

EDDIE: Hello.

(About ED DEVERY. *Thirty years ago, when he was secretary to a great Supreme Court Justice, he was known as a young man destined for greatness. The white star shone clearly on his forehead. Fifteen years later, he was still so known—except to himself. He knew then that he had lost his way. Now everyone knows. They speak of his past brilliance in law and charitably forget that he now has but one client,* HARRY BROCK, *who might have difficulty in finding a reputable lawyer to serve him. But* ED DEVERY *is past caring.* BROCK *represents over $100,000 a year, which buys plenty of the best available Scotch.)*

DEVERY: Welcome to our city.

BROCK: Yeah.

EDDIE: Say I got this ticket to be fixed.

(He reaches into his pocket, searching for it.)

DEVERY *(annoyed)*: What's it about?

EDDIE: Ah, some louse just as we blew into town. Here. *(He hands over a pink traffic summons.)*

DEVERY *(loud and mean)*: I should like to impress one thing on your nonexistent intellect . . . the fact that I am a lawyer does not mean that I own the law.

EDDIE: What'd *I* do? What'd I *do?*

DEVERY: All right. I'll see what I can manage. *(He takes a deep, weary breath.)*

BROCK: You plastered again?

DEVERY: Still.

BROCK: I told you I got a couple things can't wait.

DEVERY: Don't worry about me, massa, I can see a loophole at twenty paces.

BROCK: How'd we make out?

DEVERY: It's going to be all right. May cost slightly more than we estimated, but there is no cause for alarm.

BROCK: How much more?

DEVERY: It's negligible.

BROCK: Why more?

DEVERY: Supply and demand, Harry. A crook is becoming a rare item in these parts. Therefore, he comes high. Don't worry.

BROCK: What do you mean, "don't worry?" This kind of stuff ain't deductible, you know.

DEVERY: I'm not sure. Perhaps we should make a trial issue of it. (*Dictating.*) To the Collector of Internal Revenue. Herewith additional deduction for Tax Return now on file, one bribe, $80,000.

BROCK (*outraged*): Eighty?

(*The phone rings.*)

DEVERY: What's the matter?

BROCK: You said—uh—negligible.

DEVERY: We figured fifty, didn't we?

EDDIE (*answering phone*): Yeah?

BROCK (*to* DEVERY): You're very handy with *my* dough, you know it?

EDDIE (*on the phone*): . . . Yes, he is. Who wants him? Wait a second. (*To* DEVERY.) Some guy for *you*. Verrall.

DEVERY (*going to phone*): Thanks. (*Into phone.*) How are you, Paul? . . . Good. . . . How's the crusade business? . . . Sure, any time now. Sooner the better. Fine. . . . See you. . . . (*He hangs up*).

BROCK: What's all that?

DEVERY: Paul Verrall. I told you about him.

BROCK: I don't remember no Verrall.

DEVERY: He's a writer. *New Republic*. Wants an interview. Smart boy. He's just back from a long time in the service with lots of ideas and lots of energy.

BROCK: I don't want to talk to no writers. I got to get shaved.

DEVERY: I think you'd better talk to this one.

BROCK: What's so important?

DEVERY: Just do it.

BROCK: Why?

DEVERY: This is one of the few fellows in Washington to look out for. Thing to do is take him in. Then he doesn't go poking.

BROCK (*loudly*): Eddie!

DEVERY: How's Billie?

BROCK: She's all right. Upstairs. (EDDIE *comes in.*) Get me a shave up here.

EDDIE: Right.

DEVERY: Harry—

BROCK: What?

EDDIE (*on the phone*): Barber shop.

DEVERY: Tell Billie to wear something nice and plain for the Senator. He may be bringing his wife.

BROCK: Tell her yourself. You ain't pregnant.

EDDIE (*on the phone*): This is Harry Brock's apartment. Send up a barber and a manicure. Right away. . . . Harry Brock. . . . That's right. . . . Okay, make it snappy.

BROCK (*yelling*): And a shine!

EDDIE (*echoing him*): And a shine! (*He hangs up.*) Be right up.

DEVERY: Eddie, how would you like to save my life?

EDDIE: Soda or plain water?

DEVERY: Neat.

EDDIE: Right! (*He goes to work with the liquor.*)

BROCK (*removing his jacket and tie*): Don't worry about Billie. One thing, she knows how to dress. You know what it costs me for clothes for her?

DEVERY: That's not all I'm worried about, Harry.

BROCK: What?

DEVERY: Well, did you *have* to bring Billie?

BROCK: I may be here God knows how long.

DEVERY: Trouble is, this is a city of few secrets and much chat.

BROCK: Anybody chats me I'll bust 'em in half.

DEVERY: Fine. That'll get you right where you want to go. Up with the dress-for-dinner bunch.

BROCK: What do I care?

DEVERY: I don't know. What *do* you care? (EDDIE *hands him a drink.*) Thanks. (*Sitting down beside* BROCK.) Listen, Harry, you've got a chance to be one of the men who runs this country. Better than that. You can run the men who run it. It takes power. You've got some. It takes money. You've got plenty. Above all, it takes judgment and intelligence. (*A pause.*) That's why you pay me a hundred thousand a year.

BROCK: What's all the excitement?

DEVERY: Nothing. I'm just trying to make it clear where I fit in.

BROCK: You don't have to holler.

DEVERY: All right.

BROCK: Honest to God, I thought I done somethin' wrong. (*He rises and moves away.*)

DEVERY: When Verrall gets here, be friendly. Treat him nicely. Don't bull him. Just be yourself. Treat him like a woman you're trying to make.

BROCK: Wait a minute!

(*The buzzer sounds.*)

DEVERY: I'll leave you alone with him. Better that way. I want to see Billie, anyway. (DEVERY *opens the door and admits* VERRALL.) Hello, Paul.

PAUL: Ed. (*They shake hands.*)

DEVERY: Harry Brock, Paul Verrall.

PAUL: How do you do, sir? (*He bows, slightly and sharply. A habit.*)

BROCK: How are you? (*He looks at* PAUL, *quizzically.*) Ain't I seen you some place before? (PAUL *just smiles at him.*) Excuse me for my coat off. I have to get shaved and so forth. I hope you don't mind.

PAUL (*to* DEVERY): What have you been telling this guy about me?

DEVERY: If you gentlemen will excuse me—

(*He goes upstairs.*)

BROCK: Sit down. What'll you drink?

(PAUL *sits.*)

PAUL: Scotch, please—if you've got it.

BROCK (*with a short laugh*): If I've got it. (*He calls out, loudly.*) Eddie!! (*To* PAUL.) I got everything. Where do you think you are? (EDDIE *appears.*) Stick around, willya, for Christ's sake, and give the man a Scotch and— (*To* PAUL.) soda?

PAUL: Plain water.

BROCK (*to* EDDIE): Plain water.

EDDIE: Right. Rye ginger ale for you?

BROCK: Right. (*To* PAUL, *happily.*) He always knows what I feel to drink. Yeah. He's worked for me I don't know how many years. Also, he's my cousin. He knows me insides out. (*To* EDDIE.) Right?

EDDIE: That's right.

PAUL: Maybe I should be interviewing Eddie. (*A great howl of laughter from* BROCK.)

BROCK: Hey, you maybe got somethin' there. That's pretty good. What's it gonna be, pal? A plug or a pan?

PAUL: Why—

BROCK: I like to know these things. Then I know how to talk, if I know your angle.

PAUL: No angle. Just, well—just the facts.

BROCK: Oh, a pan! (*He laughs, confident of his boorish charm.* EDDIE *brings their drinks.*)

PAUL: Not exactly. (*Taking the drink.*) Thanks.

(EDDIE *pads around the room, placing cigarettes, matches, and cigars in the right places.*)

BROCK: It's okay! Don't worry. Write what you want. See, the way I look at it is like this. You can't hurt me and you can't help me. Nobody can. (*They drink.*) I'm only talkin' with you because Ed Devery asked me. What the hell, I pay a guy a hundred grand a year for advice so I'm a sucker if I don't take it. Right?

EDDIE (*from a remote part of the room, answers automatically*): That's right.

BROCK (*screaming at him*): Butt out, willya? (EDDIE *looks up, confused and hurt, then goes on with his activity.*) Devery likes it when I get wrote about.

(*He goes to a newly placed humidor.*)

PAUL: Well, of course, in Washington, Mr. Brock, there's a certain amount of value in the right kind of—

BROCK (*getting out a magnificently boxed cigar and bringing it to* PAUL): Cut it out, willya? You're breakin' my heart. Washington! I licked every town I ever decided, so what's different? Have a cigar!

PAUL (*taking it*): Thanks. (*He looks at it carefully.*) I'll give it to a Congressman.

BROCK: Five bucks apiece they cost me. From Cuba someplace.

PAUL: Well, in that case, I'll give it to a Senator. (*He puts it in his pocket.*)

BROCK (*thoughtfully*): Senators are pretty big stuff around here, huh?

PAUL (*hardly knowing how to answer this*): Yes.

BROCK (*in disgust*): Christ!

PAUL: Why? Shouldn't they be?

BROCK: Listen, you know what a Senator is to me? A guy who makes a hundred and fifty bucks a week.

(PAUL *smiles, then takes a few sheets of folded note paper from his breast pocket, a pencil from another pocket, and makes a note.*)

BROCK: What are you puttin' in?

PAUL (*writing*): Your little joke.

BROCK (*delighted*): You like it, huh?

PAUL: First class.

BROCK: Maybe I oughta be on the radio.

PAUL: Maybe.

BROCK: How much you wanna bet I make more money than Amos and Andy?

PAUL: No bet.

(EDDIE *carries a bottle of Poland Water upstairs.* BROCK *lights a cigarette and stretches out on the sofa, happily. He feels he is doing well. He puts his feet up.*)

BROCK (*expansively*): Well, fella, what do you wanna know?

PAUL (*suddenly*): How much money have you got?

BROCK (*startled*): What?

PAUL: How much money have you got?

BROCK: How should I know? What am I, an accountant?

PAUL (*moving to him*): You don't know?

BROCK: Not exactly.

PAUL: Fifty million?

BROCK: I'll tell you the truth. I don't know.

PAUL: Ten million?

BROCK: Maybe.

PAUL: One million?

BROCK: More.

PAUL (*pressing*): How much?

BROCK: Plenty.

(PAUL *gives up, turns away, and crosses back to his chair*.)

PAUL: Okay.

BROCK: And listen. I made every nickel. Nobody ever give me nothin'.

PAUL: Nice work. (*He sits*.)

BROCK (*putting out his cigarette and rising*): I can tell already. You're gonna give me the business.

PAUL (*trying to charm him*): Wait a minute—

BROCK: Go ahead! I like it.

PAUL: —you've got me wrong.

BROCK: Go ahead. Work for me. I got more people workin' for me than knows it. (*He moves away*.)

PAUL (*after a pause*): What do you think about—?

BROCK (*turning violently*): Go ahead! Pan me. Tell how I'm a mugg and a roughneck. You'll do me good.

PAUL: Listen, Mr. Brock—

BROCK: Lemme tell you about Cleveland. In 1937 there's a big dump there, see? And the city wants to get rid of it. High class scrap. So I go out there to look it over myself. There's a lot of other guys there, too. From Bethlehem even and like that. I didn't have a chance and I knew it. I figure I'm out of my class on the deal and I'm ready to pull out when all of a sudden the God-damnedest thing comes out there in one of the papers. About me. A big write-up. It says my name and about how come the city is gonna do business with hoodlums. Mind you, I was out of my class. I didn't have the kind of buttons a guy needs for a deal like that. So the next day—again. This time they got a picture of me. Next thing you know, a guy calls me up. A guy from the Municipal Commission. He comes up to see me and he says they don't want no trouble. So I naturally string him along and I get busy on the phone and I raise some dough with a couple of boys from *De*troit. Then comes the big pan. On the front page. Next day I close the deal and in a week, I'm cartin'.

(EDDIE *comes downstairs*.)

PAUL (*after a pause*): What's your point?

BROCK: My point is you can't do me no harm if you make me out to be a mugg. Maybe you'll help me. Everybody gets scared, and for me that's good. Everybody scares easy.

PAUL: Well, not everybody.

BROCK: Well, enough. You can't hurt me. All you can do is build me up or shut up. Have a drink. (*He snaps his fingers at* EDDIE.)

(EDDIE *picks up* PAUL'S *glass.*)

PAUL (*to* EDDIE): No, thanks. Really.

(EDDIE *puts the glass down and starts to turn away.*)

BROCK (*to* EDDIE): Do what I'm tellin' you! Who the hell pays you around here? (EDDIE *picks up the glass again, quickly, and does as he is told.*) When I'm home, he shaves me in the mornin'. I've got my own barber chair. (*To* EDDIE.) Right?

EDDIE: That's right.

BROCK (*moving back to the sofa*): Well, go ahead, pal. I thought you wanted to interview me.

(*There is a pause.*)

PAUL: Where were you born?

BROCK (*settling back again*): Jersey. Plainfield, New Jersey. 1907. I went to work when I was twelve years old and I been workin' ever since. I'll tell you my first job. A paper route. I bought a kid out with a swift kick in the keester.

PAUL (*writing*): And you've been working ever since.

BROCK (*missing the point*): Right. I'll tell you how I'm the top man in my racket. I been in it over twenty-five years. In the same racket.

PAUL: Steel.

BROCK: Junk. Not steel. *Junk.*

PAUL: Oh.

BROCK: Look, don't butter me up. I'm a junk man. I ain't ashamed to say it.

PAUL: All right.

BROCK: Lemme give you some advice, sonny boy. Never crap a crapper. I can sling it with the best of 'em.

(EDDIE *goes upstairs.*)

PAUL: Twenty-five years, you say?

BROCK: I'll tell you. I'm a kid with a paper route. I've got this little

wagon. So on my way home nights, I come through the alleys pickin'
up stuff. I'm not the only one. All the kids are doin' it. The only
difference is, they keep it. Not me. I sell it. First thing you know, I'm
makin' seven, eight bucks a week from that. Three bucks from
papers. So I figure out right off which is the right racket. I'm just a
kid, mind you, but I could see that. Pretty soon, the guy I'm sellin' to
is handin' me anywheres from fifteen to twenty a week. So he offers
me a job for ten. Dumb jerk. I'd be sellin' this guy his own stuff back
half the time and he never knew.

PAUL: How do you mean?

BROCK (*relishing the memory*): Well, in the night, see, I'm under the
fence and I drag it out and load up. In the mornin', I bring it in the
front way and collect.

PAUL: Twelve years old, you were?

BROCK: Somethin' like that.

PAUL: So pretty soon you owned the whole yard.

BROCK: Damn right! This guy, the jerk? He works for me now. And
you know who else works for me? The kid whose paper route I
swiped. I figure I owe him. That's how I am.

PAUL: Pretty good years for the—junk business, these last few.

BROCK (*with a mysterious grin*): I ain't kickin'.

PAUL: Do you anticipate a decline now?

BROCK (*frowning suddenly*): Talk plain, pal.

(*The buzzer sounds.*)

PAUL: Is it still going to be good, do you think?

BROCK (*darkly*): We'll make it good.

PAUL (*quickly*): Who's we?

(*A pause. BROCK senses he is being cornered.*)

BROCK: We is me, that's who.

PAUL: I see.

BROCK: Fancy talk don't go with me.

(EDDIE *opens the door for the barber, the manicurist, and the
bootblack.*)

THE BARBER: Good evening. In here, sir?

BROCK: Yeah. (*He removes his shirt and hands it to* EDDIE.)

PAUL (*rising*): Well, I'll get out of your—

BROCK: Don't go. Sit down. Sit down.

(*The* BARBER *and* MANICURIST *go about their work.* PAUL *sits down.* BROCK *looks at him and smiles.*)

BROCK: Sit down—I like you. You play your cards right, I'll put you on the payroll. You know what I mean?

PAUL: Sure.

BROOK (*to the barber*): Once over easy and no talkin'. (*To the* MANICURIST.) Just brush 'em up. I get a manicure every day.

THE MANICURIST: Yes, sir.

(*The* BOOTBLACK *gets into position, then notices that* BROCK *is not wearing shoes. He looks up, confused.*)

BROCK: Over there someplace.

(*The* BOOTBLACK *moves his equipment, finds the shoes, and works on them.*)

BROCK (*to* PAUL): Keep goin'. It's okay.

PAUL: I've been wondering what you're doing in Washington.

BROCK (*genially*): None of your God damn business.

PAUL: Sure it is.

BROCK: How come?

PAUL: You're a big man, Mr. Brock.

(*The* BARBER *is putting a towel around* BROCK'S *neck.*)

BROCK (*for no reason*): Not so tight!

THE BARBER: Sorry, sir.

BROCK (*to* PAUL): Sightseein'. That's what I'm in Washington for. Sightseein'.

PAUL: All right.

BROCK: Put that in the write-up, then nobody'll be scared.

PAUL: How long do you think you'll be around?

BROCK: Depends on how many sights I got to see.

PAUL: There's some talk you may be around for a long, long time.

BROCK: Where'd you get that?

PAUL: Around.

BROCK: Bull. What the hell do I care about politics? I got trouble enough in my own racket. I don't know nothin' about the politics racket.

PAUL: I hear you've come to find out.

BROCK: Listen, pal, so far I been nice to you. Don't pump me.

PAUL: My life's work.

BROCK: Well, don't work on me. I like to be friends with you.

(DEVERY *appears on the balcony and starts downstairs.*)

DEVERY (*to* PAUL): How are you getting on with the monarch of all he surveys?

PAUL: Great. I found out he was born in Plainfield, New Jersey. He sure is a tough man to dig.

(*A grunt from* BROCK, *as the* BARBER *works on his face. A* BELLHOP *knocks and enters, carrying a freshly pressed suit. He gives it to* EDDIE, *who takes it upstairs.*)

DEVERY: I can't believe that. He loves to talk.

PAUL: Not to me.

BROCK: Why, I told you the story of my life, practically.

(BILLIE *comes down.*)

PAUL (*to* DEVERY): He wouldn't even tell me how much money he's got.

BROCK: I don't know, I'm tellin' you.

(BILLIE *goes to the liquor table and selects a bottle.*)

PAUL (*to* DEVERY): And he wouldn't tell me what he was doing in Washington.

BROCK: Because it's none of your business.

DEVERY: No secret. Just a little tax stuff. I told you.

PAUL: Yes, I know, but I didn't believe you.

(BILLIE *starts back upstairs carrying the bottle.*)

DEVERY: Oh, Billie, this is my friend Paul Verrall. (*To* PAUL.) Billie Dawn.

PAUL (*making his bow*): How do you do?

(BILLIE *nods and continues to move.*)

BROCK: Wait a minute.

BILLIE (*slightly scared*): What's the matter?

BROCK: Where do you think you're goin' with that?

BILLIE: Upstairs.

BROCK: Put it back.

BILLIE: I just wanted—

BROCK: I know what you wanted. Put it back.

BILLIE: Why can't I—?

BROCK (*mean*): Because I say you can't, that's why. We got somebody comin'. Somebody important. I don't want you stinkin'.

BILLIE: Well, can't I just have—?

BROCK: No! Now put it back and go upstairs and change your clothes and don't give me no trouble.

(BILLIE *stands motionless, humiliated.*)

BROCK (*too loud*): Do what I'm tellin' you!!

(BILLIE *obeys.* PAUL *and* DEVERY *have half turned away in embarrassment.* BROCK *settles back in his chair to let the* BARBER *continue.* BILLIE *goes back upstairs. There is silence in the room. Nobody watches her go. About halfway up, she turns and regards* PAUL *with strange interest, but continues her move. If you were close enough, you might even recognize the faint beginnings of a smile. She goes into her room.* EDDIE *returns.*)

DEVERY: Barber, what'll you take to cut his throat?

(BROCK *sits up so suddenly that the barber almost does so.*)

BROCK (*in a fury*): There's some kind of jokes I don't like, Ed.

DEVERY: Don't get excited.

BROCK: Don't tell me what to do!

(*He strides over to* DEVERY *and pushes his face, hard.* DEVERY *is thrown off balance, but* PAUL *keeps him from falling.*)

DEVERY (*weakly*): Jesus, Harry. It was just a joke.

BROCK (*to the barber*): That's all.

BARBER: Not quite finished, sir.

BROCK: That's all, I told you. Beat it.

BARBER: Very good, sir.

BROCK (*to the* MANICURIST): You too. (*To* EDDIE, *indicating the help.*) Eddie, take care of 'em.

(*The* BARBER, *the* MANICURIST, *and the* BOOTBLACK *prepare to leave.*)

PAUL: I guess I'd better be—

(EDDIE *is attending to the tips.*)

BROCK: Don't go.

PAUL: I really should. I've got some work.

BROCK: Stick around, can't you? Looks like you're about the only friend I got left around here.

PAUL: Well, I'm not far. If anyone starts beating you, just scream and I'll come running.

(BROCK *laughs. The* BARBER, *the* MANICURIST, *and the* BOOTBLACK *leave.* EDDIE *picks up the shoes and takes them upstairs.*)

BROCK: You live in the hotel here?

PAUL: Right down the hall.

BROCK: Fine.

(*They shake hands.*)

PAUL: Other side of the tracks, of course.

BROCK: Say, don't kid me. I hear you do fine.

PAUL (*to* DEVERY): Good night, Ed.

DEVERY (*quietly*): Night.

(*He walks to the liquor table and pours himself a stiff drink.*)

BROCK (*to* PAUL): See you soon.

PAUL (*as he leaves*): Good night. Thanks for everything.

BROCK: Don't mention it.

DEVERY (*getting his brief case*): I need Billie's signature on a few things. Eddie, too.

BROCK: Sure. (*Yells.*) Billie!

BILLIE'S VOICE: What?

BROCK: Come on down here. Right away. (*To* DEVERY.) What are you sore about?

DEVERY: Not sore, Harry.

BROCK: You look funny.

DEVERY: I know.

BROCK: Don't you feel good? You want an aspirin?

DEVERY: No, no. I'm fine. In fact, considering that I have been dead for sixteen years, I am in remarkable health.

(BILLIE *comes down, wearing her most dignified dress.*)

BROCK (*to* DEVERY): Swear to God, sometimes I don't understand you at all.

DEVERY (*smiling*): Sometimes?

BILLIE: What do you want?

BROCK: Ed.

DEVERY: A few things I want you to sign, honey.

BILLIE: That's all I do around here is sign.

BROCK: Too bad about you. (*To* DEVERY.) When is he comin'? This Senator guy?

DEVERY: Any time now.

BROCK: I better get fixed up, huh?

(*Still in his undershirt, and shoeless, he picks up his jacket and tie and starts up. He glances at* BILLIE, *stops, and moves to examine every detail of her get-up.*)

BROCK: She look all right to you?

BILLIE: Look who's talkin'!

DEVERY: Perfect.

BROCK: You *sure* now?

BILLIE (*in a prideful whine*): What's the matter with me?

(BROCK *pays no attention to her.*)

BROCK: Tell me if somethin's wrong. I don't want to start off on no left foot.

DEVERY: Don't worry.

(BROCK *leaves.* DEVERY *brings out a sheaf of legal papers and spreads them out for* BILLIE *to sign. He hands her his fountain pen.*)

BILLIE: What's got into *him?*

DEVERY: Nothing. He just wants to make a good impression.

BILLIE: So let him.

DEVERY (*pointing out a line*): Two places on this one, please.

(EDDIE *enters and goes upstairs.*)

BILLIE (*signing, her head quite close to the paper*): What happened to all that stuff I signed last week?

DEVERY (*smiling*): All used up.

BILLIE: I bet I've signed about a million of these.

DEVERY: What you get for being a multiple corporate officer.

BILLIE: I *am?* (DEVERY *nods.*) What do you know?

DEVERY: You've come a long way from the chorus all right.

BILLIE: I wasn't only in the chorus. In *Anything Goes* I spoke lines.

DEVERY: Really?

BILLIE: Of course.

DEVERY: How many?

BILLIE: How many what?

DEVERY (*blotting*): Lines did you speak?

BILLIE: Five.

DEVERY: I never knew that.

BILLIE: Ask anybody.

DEVERY: I believe you.

BILLIE (*signing*): I could of been a star probably. If I'd of stuck to it.

DEVERY: Why didn't you?

BILLIE (*signing*): Harry didn't want me being in the show. He likes to get to bed early.

DEVERY: I see.

BILLIE: He's changed, Harry. Don't you think so?

DEVERY: How?

BILLIE: I don't know. He used to be like more satisfied. Now he's always runnin' around. Like this. What did he have to come to Washington, D.C., for?

DEVERY (*blotting*): Long story.

BILLIE: Well, don't tell it to me, I don't care where he goes. I just wish he'd settle down.

DEVERY: Ambitious.

BILLIE (*signing*): I know. He *talks* all the time now. He never used to. Now he's got me up half the night tellin' me what a big man he is. And how he's gonna be bigger. Run everything.

DEVERY: He may, at that.

BILLIE: Personally, I don't care one way or another.

DEVERY: Very few people do, that's why he may get to do it. The curse of civilization. Don't-care-ism. Satan's key to success.

BILLIE: What kind of talk is that? You drunk or sump'n?

DEVERY (*blotting*): I'm drunk *and* "sump'n."

BILLIE: All right. I give up. (*She goes to the liquor table.*)

DEVERY (*without looking at her*): Take it easy.

BILLIE: Look now, don't *you* start.

DEVERY: Better if you drink later, Billie, after they've gone.

BILLIE: What's the deal, anyway?

DEVERY: No deal. Just important people, that's all.

BILLIE: Who? This Senator guy?

DEVERY: And *Mrs*. Hedges.

BILLIE: Harry told me this fellow works for him.

DEVERY: In a way.

BILLIE: So what's he puttin' it on for?

DEVERY: I suppose he wants him to *keep* working for him.

BILLIE: Too deep for me.

(*The buzzer sounds.* EDDIE *comes downstairs and goes to the door.*)

DEVERY (*dropping his voice*): All you have to do is be nice and no rough language.

BILLIE: I won't open my mush.

DEVERY: I didn't mean that.

BILLIE: I don't have to be down here, at all, you know. I *could* go upstairs. (*She starts out.*) In fact, I think I will.

(DEVERY *moves to her.*)

DEVERY: I'm telling you, Billie. Harry wouldn't like it.

BILLIE (*making a violent about-face*): All right all right all right! (*She moves to the sofa and sits.*)

(EDDIE *opens the door to admit* SENATOR NORVAL HEDGES *and* MRS. HEDGES. DEVERY *moves to greet them.*)

DEVERY: How are you, Norval?

HEDGES: Can't complain.

DEVERY (*to* MRS. HEDGES): Haven't seen you for a long time, Anna.

MRS. HEDGES: No, you haven't.

DEVERY: Come on in.

(SENATOR HEDGES *is a worried man of sixty—thin, pale, and worn.* MRS. HEDGES *bears out Fanny Dixwell Holmes's comment that Washington is a city filled with great men and the women they married when they were very young. Except that the Senator is not a great man. He just looks like a great man.*)

HEDGES (*to* BILLIE): Good evening.

BILLIE: Good evening.

DEVERY: Senator, you ought to remember this little lady. A great first-nighter like you. She used to be Billie Dawn?

HEDGES (*vaguely*): Oh yes . . . Yes, indeed.

DEVERY: Billie, this is Senator Norval Hedges I've told you so much about.

(HEDGES *offers his hand.* BILLIE *takes it.*)

HEDGES: How do you do?

BILLIE: How do you do?

DEVERY: And this is Mrs. Hedges, Billie.

MRS. HEDGES: Glad to meet you.

BILLIE: Glad to meet you.

(MRS. HEDGES *seats herself beside* BILLIE. *There is an awkward pause.* MRS. HEDGES *suddenly extends her hand.* BILLIE *takes it.*)

DEVERY: What do you say to a drink?

MRS. HEDGES: Love one.

HEDGES: Sounds all right to me.

DEVERY: Whiskey?

HEDGES: Be fine.

DEVERY (*to* EDDIE): Whiskey all around, Eddie.

EDDIE: Right. (*He goes to work on the drinks.*)

HEDGES: That's going to hit the spot just fine. (*He sits down.*)

MRS. HEDGES (*to* BILLIE): He's awfully tired.

DEVERY (*to* HEDGES): What have you been doing? Standing over a hot resolution all day?

HEDGES: Just about.

MRS. HEDGES: How do you like Washington, Mrs. Brock?

(*There is a tiny pause.* BILLIE, *turned slightly away, does not realize for an instant that she is being addressed.* DEVERY, *having taken such pains to avoid identifying her too exactly during the course of the introductions, is afraid* BILLIE *may now correct* MRS. HEDGES *and ruin his careful diplomacy.* BILLIE *catches his eye.*)

BILLIE: I haven't seen it yet.

MRS. HEDGES: You mean to say this is the very first time you've been here?

BILLIE: That's what I mean. I never went on the road.

HEDGES: Well, we must show you around. Beautiful city.

MRS. HEDGES: Too bad the Supreme Court isn't in session. You'd love that.

(*A pause.*)

BILLIE: What is it?

(MRS. HEDGES *doesn't know what to make of this. She looks over at the* SENATOR *to see if he has any ideas.* DEVERY *saves the moment by bursting into laughter.*)

DEVERY: Lots of people would like to know the answer to that one, Billie.

(*The* SENATOR *and* MRS. HEDGES *now settle for* BILLIE'S *remark as a brand of metropolitan humor which they have never been able to get, quite. They join in the laughter.* EDDIE *serves the drinks.*)

DEVERY: What's this jam Wallace has gotten himself into?

HEDGES: Give him enough rope. I've said so from the start.

DEVERY: I know.

HEDGES: Trouble with these professional do-gooders is they never seem to— (*He stops as* BROCK *enters from above, carefully brushed and dressed.*)

BROCK: Hello, everybody!

DEVERY: Here we are.

(*The* SENATOR *rises. For some reason,* MRS. HEDGES *rises, too.*)

DEVERY: Senator Hedges, Harry Brock.

BROCK (*very hearty*): Say, it's about time us two got together, Senator. (*He shakes hands with* HEDGES *using both hands.*)

HEDGES: About time.

BROCK (*moving across the room*): And I suppose this is Mrs. Hedges.

MRS. HEDGES: That's right.

(*They shake hands, and* BROCK *nearly knocks her down with cordiality.*)

BROCK: I certainly am happy to make your acquaintance. Sit down. (*To* HEDGES.) Senator, sit down.

(SENATOR *and* MRS. HEDGES *sit.*)

HEDGES: Have a good trip down?

BROCK: Oh, sure. I come down in my own car. I came. Had to stop in Baltimore on the way down. I got a yard there, you know. A junk yard.

HEDGES: Is that so?

BROCK: Yeah. Just a *little* racket. Tell you the truth, it ain't worth the trouble it takes to run it, but I like it. It was the second yard I picked up. Before that I only had one yard.

MRS. HEDGES: How many do you have now?

BROCK: Hell, I don't know.

(*He stops abruptly, then addresses a blushing apology to* MRS. HEDGES.)

BROCK: *Excuse me.*

MRS. HEDGES (*being big about it*): Oh, that's all right.

BROCK (*to* HEDGES): I don't know why I like that little Baltimore outfit. I just always get kind of a feelin' from it. You know what I mean?

HEDGES: Sentimental.

BROCK: That's it! I'm sentimental. Like you say.

MRS. HEDGES: I think we're *all* a bit sentimental.

(*There is a pause. It seems* BILLIE'S *turn to speak.*)

BILLIE: Well—(*They all look at her.*) It's a free country.

BROCK (*covering quickly*): How's things with you, Senator?

HEDGES: Same old grind.

BROCK: Lemme tell you something, Senator. You got one job I don't never wanna be. Everybody pesterin' you all the time, probably.

HEDGES: Part of the job.

MRS. HEDGES: Do you play bridge, Mrs. Brock?

BILLIE: No. Only gin.

MRS. HEDGES: I beg your pardon?

BILLIE: Gin rummy.

MRS. HEDGES: Oh, yes, of course. I was going to ask you to join us. A few of the girls? We meet now and then.

BILLIE: Yuh. Well, I don't play bridge.

BROCK (*to* BILLIE): You could learn to if you wanted.

BILLIE: I don't think so.

BROCK: Sure you could. (*To* MRS. HEDGES.) She couldn't play gin till I learned her. Now she beats my brains out.

DEVERY: How are you fixed for time tomorrow, Norval?

HEDGES: Pretty tight, I'm afraid.

DEVERY: Oh. I wanted to bring Harry over on a few things.

HEDGES: Ten o'clock all right?

DEVERY: How's that for you, Harry?

BROCK: In the mornin'?

HEDGES: Yes.

BROCK: Pretty early for me.

BILLIE: I'll say.

(BROCK *throws her a look.*)

HEDGES: Eleven?

BROCK: Okay.

DEVERY: Where'll you be?

HEDGES (*awkwardly*): Well, I can drop by here if that's all right.

DEVERY: Sure.

HEDGES (*lamely*): It's right on my way.

(*There is a pause.* BILLIE *rises and speaks to* MRS. HEDGES.)

BILLIE: You wanna wash your hands or anything, honey?

MRS. HEDGES (*so shocked that her reply is inaudible*): No, thank you.

(BILLIE *moves upstairs, through an atmosphere of tense embarrassment.*)

DEVERY (*to* HEDGES): I hope you're free on Friday night.

HEDGES: I think so. Are we, dear?

MRS. HEDGES: Well, we *can* be.

BROCK: Atta girl! (*He moves to sit beside her and puts his arm on the back of the sofa just behind her.*)

DEVERY: Fine. I'm doing a little dinner. Few people I want Harry to meet.

HEDGES: And who want to meet *him,* I'm sure.

BROCK (*coyly*): Say, listen, Senator. I'm just a junk man.

HEDGES: That's no disgrace in America.

DEVERY (*almost sardonic*): No—not if you're a *big* junk man.

(*A pause.* SENATOR HEDGES *rises and moves to* BROCK.)

HEDGES (*softly*): I want to thank you, Mr. Brock. For everything.

BROCK: Call me Harry, Senator, willya?

HEDGES: I haven't written you about it, Harry. Not considered good form. But I want you to know that I'm grateful for all you've done. For your support.

BROCK: Don't mention it. Just tit for tat. (*He stops, confused, then turns to* MRS. HEDGES.) Excuse *me!*

MRS. HEDGES (*at sea*): Quite all right.

BROCK: You see, Senator, what I think is—there's a certain kind of people ought to stick together.

HEDGES: My feeling.

BROCK: You know what I'm interested in. Scrap iron. I wanna buy it—I wanna move it—and I wanna sell it. And I don't want a lot of buttin' in with rules and regulations at no stage of the game.

HEDGES: Obviously.

BROCK (*rising*): I ain't talkin' about peanuts, mind you. All this junk I been sellin' for the last fifteen years—well, it's junk again. And I can sell it again once I lay my hands on it. Do you know how much scrap iron is layin' around all over Europe? Where the war's been?

HEDGES: No, I don't.

BROCK: Well, I don't either. Nobody knows. Nobody ever *will* know. It's more than you can think of. Well, I want to pick it up and bring it back where it belongs. Where it came from. Where I can use it. Who does it belong to anyway?

MRS. HEDGES: Why—isn't that interesting?

HEDGES: I have a copy for you of the preliminary survey made by—

BROCK (*sitting opposite* HEDGES): Boil it down and give it to me fast. I didn't come down here to have to do a lot of paper work. See, the way I work is like this. It's every man for himself—like dog eat dog. Like you gotta get the other guy before he gets you.

HEDGES: Exactly.

BROCK: What I got in mind is an operatin' combo—all over the world. There's enough in it for everybody—if they're *in,* that is. Up to now, I'm doin' fine. Everybody's lined up, everybody understands everybody. I want to get movin', see?—that's all. Only thing is, Ed here comes up with some new trouble every day. *This* law, *that* law, tariffs, taxes, State Department, *this* department, *that* department—

DEVERY: I'm sure you understand, Norval, that in an operation of this kind—

BROCK: Listen, all that stuff is just a lot of hot air to me. There's a way to do anything. That's all I know. It's up to you guys to find out how.

DEVERY: Norval's been working along those lines.

HEDGES: Yes. The Hedges-Keller Amendment, for example, guarantees no interference with free enterprise—foreign or domestic. We're doing everything we can to get it through quickly.

BROCK: Well, see that you do, 'cause that's why I'm here, to see that I get what I paid for.

DEVERY (*picking up the* SENATOR'S *glass*): One more?

HEDGES: I think not.

BROCK: One for the road.

HEDGES: All right.

(DEVERY *hands the glass to* EDDIE.)

BROCK: How do things look to you, Senator?

HEDGES: Generally?

BROCK: Yeah, generally.

HEDGES: Well, not too bad. Just a question of staying on the alert. Too many crackpots around with their foot in the White House door.

BROCK: Tellin' me.

HEDGES (*confidentially*): He listens to everything, you know.

BROCK: Sure.

HEDGES: I said to Sam only last week, "This country will soon have to decide if the people are going to run the government or the government is going to run the people."

BROCK: You said it. (EDDIE *distributes fresh drinks.*) You know where I'd be if I had to start my business today? Up the creek. (*He looks at* MRS. HEDGES.) Excuse me.

(*This time she simply nods.*)

DEVERY: That's good sound thinking, Norval.

HEDGES: Thank you.

DEVERY: Worthy of Holmes.

HEDGES: Great man, Holmes.

DEVERY: My personal god.

BROCK: Who?

DEVERY: Oliver Wendell Holmes, Junior.

HEDGES: A wonderful man.

BROCK: Is he comin' Friday night?

(*An awkward pause.*)

DEVERY (*quietly*): I don't think so.

BROCK: Oh.

HEDGES: Well, we mustn't keep you.

MRS. HEDGES: No, we mustn't.

(*They rise and prepare to leave.*)

BROCK: Don't go. We stay up all the time.

HEDGES: Well, don't think of this as a proper visit. We just wanted to say hello. We'll be seeing a lot of each other, I'm sure.

BROCK: Right. Wait a second! (*He moves quickly to the cigar box and takes out a handful.*) Brought them down special.

(*He hands them to* HEDGES.)

HEDGES (*taking them*): Very kind of you.

BROCK: Don't mention it.

HEDGES: Good night, Harry.

(*They shake hands.* BILLIE *returns.*)

BROCK: Senator, it's a pleasure.

MRS. HEDGES: Good night, Mrs. Brock.

BILLIE: Good night.

MRS. HEDGES (*to* BROCK): Good night and thank you so much.

BROCK: For what? Wait till I get settled down here. I'll show you somethin' to thank me for.

MRS. HEDGES: Good night. Good night, Ed.

DEVERY: See you tomorrow, Norval.

HEDGES: That's right. Good night.

BILLIE: Good night, all.

(*The* HEDGES *leave.* EDDIE *picks up the empty glasses.*)

BROCK: Okay, Eddie. Knock off.

EDDIE: Right.

(EDDIE *starts out.*)

DEVERY: Wait a minute.

(EDDIE *stops.* DEVERY *goes to his brief case and gets out some papers which* EDDIE *signs during the following.*)

BILLIE: Drips.

BROCK: What?

BILLIE: I said they're drips.

BROCK: Who the hell are you to say?

BILLIE (*stretching out on the sofa*): I'm myself, that's who.

BROCK: Well, shut up. Nobody asked you.

(*He sits down and removes his shoes.*)

BILLIE: Pardon me for living.

BROCK: Get upstairs.

BILLIE: Not yet.

BROCK (*rising*): Get upstairs, I told you.

(BILLIE *goes, quietly, attempting to retain her little dignity by giving him a look of contempt.*)

EDDIE (*signing*): Here too?

DEVERY: Yes.

EDDIE: Since when I'm only Vice-President?

DEVERY: You're slipping.

BROCK (*worried*): She's gonna be in the way, that dame.

DEVERY: What are you going to do about it?

BROCK (*sitting*): I don't know. Right now I feel like to give her the brush.

DEVERY: Pretty complicated.

BROCK: I know.

DEVERY: At the moment, she owns more of you than *you* do. On paper.

BROCK: Your idea.

DEVERY: Yes, and a damned good one, too. Keeps you in the clear and you know what it saves you?

BROCK: I know, I know. You told me a million times.

DEVERY: Sorry.

BROCK: You better think somethin' up. She's gonna louse me up all the way down the line. God-damn dumb broad.

DEVERY: Send her home.

BROCK: No.

DEVERY: Why not?

BROCK (*softly*): I'm nuts about her.

(DEVERY *looks at him quickly, in surprise.*)

DEVERY (*turning away*): Can't have your cake and eat it.

BROCK: What?

DEVERY: Just a saying.

BROCK: It don't make sense.

DEVERY: All right.

(*There is a long, long pause.*)

BROCK: What's cakes got to do with it?

DEVERY: Nothing, Harry.

(EDDIE *finishes signing.*)

EDDIE: Okay?

(DEVERY *picks up the papers and looks them over.*)

DEVERY: Okay.

(EDDIE *leaves.*)

BROCK: Must be a way to smarten her up a little. Ain't there?

DEVERY: I suppose so.

BROCK: Some kinda school we could send her to, maybe?

DEVERY: I doubt that.

BROCK: Then what?

DEVERY: Well, we might be able to find someone who could smooth the rough edges off.

BROCK: How?

DEVERY: Let me think about it. And while I'm thinking about that, Harry, there's something you might be turning over in *your* mind.

BROCK: Yeah, what?

DEVERY: Well, if you've got to have her around you—the possibility of getting married.

BROCK: Not me.

DEVERY: Why not?

BROCK: I *been* married. I don't like it.

DEVERY: How long have you—you know—been with Billie?

BROCK: I don't know. Eight, nine years. Why?

DEVERY: Well, what the hell?

BROCK: It gets different when you get married.

DEVERY: Why should it?

BROCK: How do I know why should it? It just does, that's all.

DEVERY: All right.

BROCK: This way, I give her somethin', I'm a hell of a fella. We get married, she's got it comin', she thinks.

DEVERY: Billie's not like that.

BROCK: A broad's a broad.

DEVERY: Time may come you'll be sorry.

BROCK (*rising*): Listen, don't shove me.

DEVERY: All right. (*He gives* BROCK *a patronizing look, and pours a drink.*)

BROCK (*irritated*): Don't make out like I'm some kind of a dope. I know what I'm doin.'

DEVERY: Sure you do.

BROCK: All right. So don't make them Harvard College expressions on your face. So far you still work for me.

DEVERY: That's right, Harry.

BROCK: Okay. Just tell me what you think. If I feel like it, I'll do it. If not, no. And don't give me them looks down your nose.

(DEVERY *nods, quietly.* BROCK *slumps into a chair and sulks for a moment.*)

BROCK: What's so important I should get married all of a sudden?

DEVERY: You're moving up, Harry. Bigger places. Bigger people. No matter what goes on underneath, these people make sure of their respectable fronts.

BROCK: The hell with 'em.

DEVERY: That's just talk. You're in the Big League now, and there are certain rules.

BROCK: Like what? Like you got to be married?

DEVERY: No. Like you can't expect to just pass off a setup like this. There's such a thing as being *too* colorful.

BROCK: All right. I'll let you know. But if I do or if I don't we got to do somethin' with her. She just don't fit in. Do you think so?

DEVERY: You're right.

BROCK: Every time she opened her kisser tonight, somethin' wrong come out.

DEVERY: The hell of it is she doesn't realize.

BROCK (*desperately*): Ed, couldn't you have a talk with her?

DEVERY: Take more than a talk, I'm afraid.

BROCK: Then what?

DEVERY: It's a big job, Harry. It's not easy to make a person over. Maybe impossible. She has to have a great many things explained to her. I won't be around enough, and even if I were, I couldn't do it. No patience, too old, and I don't know enough myself. Not the kind of things she—

(BROCK *has been thinking hard. Now he cuts in, suddenly.*)

BROCK: Wait a minute!

DEVERY: What?

(BROCK *doesn't get ideas often. When he does, he thrills to the sensation.*)

BROCK (*very quietly*): The guy from down the hall?

DEVERY: Who?

BROCK: The interview guy. There's a smart little cookie.

DEVERY: Well—

BROCK (*selling it*): Knows the town. Knows the angles. Very classy, with that bowing. (*He illustrates, in an imitation of Paul's mannerism.*)

DEVERY: He could do it, probably, but he won't.

BROCK: Why not?

DEVERY: Well, he's not—

BROCK: I'll pay him, whatever he wants.

DEVERY: I don't think so.

BROCK: Make you a bet. (*He goes to the phone.*) What's his name again?

DEVERY: Wait a minute, Harry.

BROCK: What?

DEVERY: Verrall. Paul Verrall. Harry, I'm not sure—

BROCK: I like it. (*Into the phone*): Give me Verrall. . . . Yeah . . . Mr. Verrall.

DEVERY (*losing his temper*): I wish you wouldn't sail into things.

BROCK: Shut up. (*Into phone.*) Hello, pal. . . . Harry Brock. . . . You got a minute? I wanna have a little talk. . . . Got a proposition to make you. . . . What? No, no. Nothin' like that. . . . This is all right. . . . Absolutely legitimate. . . . Do that, will you? . . . Fine. . . . I'll be right here. (*He hangs up.*) I like that guy.

DEVERY: Well enough to have him around with Billie all the time?

BROCK: Are you kiddin'? With them glasses? Listen, this is all right. I can feel it. I might even tap him for a little dope myself once in a while.

DEVERY: What about Billie? She may not care for the idea.

BROCK: She'll do what I tell her.

DEVERY: That's not the point, Harry. People don't learn anything unless they want to.

BROCK: She knows what's good for her, she'll want to.

DEVERY: You know best.

BROCK: Damn right. Listen, what do you think I ought to give him?

DEVERY: Seems to me you ought to try just putting it on a friendly basis.

BROCK: I don't believe in nothin' on no friendly basis.

(*The buzzer sounds.*)

DEVERY: I know this fellow.

BROCK: I know lots of fellas. Money talks. I don't want nobody doing me no favors.

DEVERY: Why not talk it over with him and see what—?

(BROCK *goes to the door and opens it.* PAUL *comes in.*)

BROCK (*heartily*): Come on in, pal. Come on in.

PAUL: Thanks.

BROCK: Have a drink.

PAUL: No, thanks. I'm just in the middle of something.

BROCK: Sit down, I want to ask you somethin'.

(PAUL *sits.*)

PAUL: Sure.

BROCK: How much do you make a week?

PAUL: How should I know? What am I, an accountant?

(BROCK *is delighted to hear himself quoted. He laughs.*)

BROCK (*to* DEVERY): I love this guy. (*To* PAUL, *as he sits down beside him.*) What's your name again?

PAUL: Verrall.

BROCK: No, I mean your regular name.

PAUL: Paul.

BROCK: Listen, Paul. Here's the layout. I got a friend. Nice kid. I think you probably seen her in here before. Billie?

PAUL: Oh, yes.

BROCK: Well, she's a good kid, see? Only to tell you the truth, a little on the stupid side. Not her fault, you understand. I got her out of the chorus. For the chorus she was smart enough, but I'm scared she's gonna be unhappy in this town. She's never been around with such kind of people, you know what I mean?

PAUL: No.

BROCK: Well, I figure a guy like you could help her out. And me, too.

PAUL: How?

BROCK: Show her the ropes, sort of. Explain her what goes on and all like that. In your spare time. What do you say?

PAUL: No, I don't think I could handle it, Mr. Brock.

BROCK: Means a lot to me. I'll give you two hundred bucks a week.

PAUL: All right, I'll do it.

(BROCK *looks at* DEVERY *and laughs again.*)

BROCK: I'm tellin' you. I love this guy.

PAUL: When do I start?

BROCK: Right now. Why not right now?

PAUL: Fine.

BROCK: Let me introduce you like and you take it from there.

PAUL: Good.

BROCK (*getting up and calling loudly*): Billie!

BILLIE'S VOICE: What?

BROCK: Come on down here a minute. (*To* PAUL.) She's a hell of a good kid. You'll like her.

(BILLIE *comes out onto the landing, brushing her hair. She is wearing a negligee that does all the proper things.* PAUL *rises.*)

BILLIE (*as she sees* PAUL): I'm not dressed.

BROCK: It's all right. It's all right. He's a friend of the family. (BILLIE *hesitates.*) Come on, I'm tellin' you! (BILLIE *comes down into the room.*) Honey, this is Paul Verrall.

BILLIE: Yes, I know.

BROCK: He wants to talk to you.

BILLIE: What about?

BROCK: You'll find out. Sit down. (BILLIE *sits.*) Come on up a minute, willya, Ed?

DEVERY: Sure.

BROCK: Bring the stuff.

(DEVERY *picks up his brief case and follows* BROCK *out of the room. There is a pause when they have gone. Finally,* PAUL *smiles at* BILLIE. *No response. He stops smiling.*)

PAUL: Your—friend, Mr. Brock, has an idea he'd like us to spend a lit-tle time together. You and me, that is.

BILLIE: You don't say.

PAUL: Yes.

BILLIE: What are you? Some kind of gigolo?

PAUL: Not exactly.

BILLIE: What's the idea?

PAUL: Nothing special. (*He sits on the sofa, some distance from* BILLIE.) He just wants me to put you wise to a few things. Show you the ropes. Answer any questions.

BILLIE: I got no questions.

PAUL: I'll give you some.

BILLIE: Thanks.

PAUL: Might be fun for you, in a way. There's a lot to see down here. I'd be glad you show you around.

BILLIE: You know this Supreme Court?

PAUL: Yes.

BILLIE: I'd like to take that in.

PAUL: Sure. We're on, then?

BILLIE: How do you mean?

PAUL: The arrangement.

BILLIE: I don't mind. I got nothin' much to do.

PAUL: Good.

BILLIE: What's he payin' you?

PAUL: Two hundred.

BILLIE: You're a sucker. You could of got more. He's got plenty.

PAUL: I'd have done it for nothing. (BILLIE *looks at him with rare dis-belief and gives a mirthless little laugh.*) I would.

BILLIE: Why?

PAUL: This isn't work. I like it.

(BILLIE *smiles.*)

BILLIE: He thinks I'm too stupid, huh?

PAUL: Why, no—

BILLIE: He's right. I'm stupid and I like it.

PAUL: You do?

BILLIE: Sure. I'm happy. I got everything I want. Two mink coats. Everything. If there's somethin' I want, I ask. And if he don't come across—I don't come across. (*This candor has* PAUL *off balance.*) If you know what I mean.

PAUL (*with a gulp*): Yes, I do.

BILLIE: So as long as I know how to get what I want, that's all I want to know.

PAUL: As long as you know what you want.

BILLIE: Sure. What?

PAUL: As long as you know what you want.

BILLIE: You tryin' to mix me up?

PAUL: No.

(*A pause.*)

BILLIE: I'll tell you what I *would* like.

PAUL: Yes?

BILLIE: I'd like to learn how to talk good.

PAUL: All right.

BILLIE: Is it hard to learn?

PAUL: I don't think so.

BILLIE: What do I have to do?

PAUL: Well, I might give you a few books to start with. Then, if you don't mind, I'll correct you now and then.

BILLIE: Go ahead.

PAUL: When *I* know, that is. I don't—talk so good myself.

BILLIE: You'll do.

PAUL: Fine.

BILLIE: I never say "ain't." Did you notice that? Never.

PAUL: I do.

BILLIE: Well, I'll correct *you* then.

PAUL: Do that.

BILLIE: Since I was very small, I never say it. We had this teacher. She used to slug you if you did it.

PAUL: Did what?

BILLIE: Said ain't.

PAUL: Oh.

BILLIE: So I got out of the habit.

PAUL: I wonder if it was worth the slugging.

BILLIE: Well, not hard.

PAUL: It's the principle of the thing. There's too much slugging. I don't believe in it.

BILLIE: All right, I don't believe in it either.

PAUL: Good.

BILLIE: I learn pretty fast, don't I?

PAUL (*smiling*): You're great, Miss Dawn.

BILLIE: Billie.

PAUL: Billie. (*A tiny pause.*) Sort of an odd name, isn't it?

BILLIE: What are you talkin'? Half the kids I know are named it. Anyway, it's not my real name.

PAUL: What is?

(*She has to think a moment before she can answer.*)

BILLIE: My God! Emma.

PAUL: What's the matter?

BILLIE: Do I look to you like an Emma?

PAUL: No. You don't look like a Billie, either.

BILLIE: So what do I look like?

PAUL: To me?

BILLIE: Yuh, to you.

PAUL: You look like a little angel.

(*A pause.*)

BILLIE: Lemme ask you. Are you one these talkers, or would be interested in a little action?

PAUL (*stunned*): Huh?

BILLIE: I got a yen for you right off.

PAUL: Do you get many?

BILLIE: Now and then.

PAUL: What do you do about them?

BILLIE: Stick around. You'll find out.

PAUL: All right, I will.

BILLIE: And if you want a tip, I'll tell you. Sweet-talk me. I like it. Like that angel line. (PAUL *looks upstairs with a frown.*) Don't worry about him. He don't see a thing. He's too dizzy from being a big man.

PAUL (*rising and moving away*): This is going to be a little different than I thought.

BILLIE: You mind?

PAUL: No.

BILLIE: It's only fair. We'll educate each other.

PAUL (*in a weak attempt to get on safer ground*): Now, about those books.

BILLIE: Yes?

PAUL: I'll get them for you tomorrow. I'll look around my place, too. If there's anything interesting, I'll drop it by later.

BILLIE: All right.

PAUL: We can figure out time every day the day before.

(BILLIE *beckons.* PAUL *comes to her. She reaches up, takes his lapel, and brings his ear close.*)

BILLIE: Or the night.

PAUL (*straightening*): Sure.

(BROCK *and* DEVERY *come down.* BROCK *now wears a silk lounging jacket.*)

BROCK: Well! You two gonna get together?

PAUL: I think we're all set.

BROCK: Great, great!

(DEVERY *picks up his hat.*)

PAUL: Well, if you'll excuse me—

BROCK: Have a drink.

PAUL: No, thanks.

DEVERY: See you tomorrow, Harry.

BROCK: Right.

DEVERY: Good night, Billie.

BILLIE: So long.

(DEVERY *leaves.*)

PAUL (*to* BILLIE): Good night.

BILLIE: Good night.

BROCK (*taking* PAUL *to the door*): So long, kid. Appreciate it.

PAUL (*with a look at* BILLIE): So do I.

(*He leaves.* BROCK, *beaming satisfaction, comes back into the room. He stops, looks at* BILLIE, *and takes a deck of cards out of his pocket. He moves over to the table and starts to shuffle the cards.* BILLIE *falls automatically into this nightly routine. She brings a box of cigarettes to the table. They cut the cards. He wins. He sits down and begins to deal.* BILLIE *mixes two drinks and brings them to the table. She sits down, takes up her hand, and arranges her cards with flourish. The game begins. They play swiftly, professionally, with no sense of enjoyment. She takes three of his discards in quick succession. He grows tenser and tenser.*)

BILLIE (*laying down her hand*): Gin.

BROCK: Forty-one.

(BILLIE *shoves the cards to him and picks up the score pad.*)

BILLIE: Forty-one?

BROCK: Forty-one.

(*She marks the score, after computing it by drumming her fingers on her temple. He shuffles, cuts, and hands her the pack. She deals. They pick up their cards and play again.*

BROCK: If you pay attention, that Verrall guy can do you some good.

BILLIE: All right.

BROCK: You're in the Big League now. I want you to watch your step.

BILLIE: All right.

BROCK: You got to learn to fit in. If not, I can't have you around, and that's no bull. (*A pause, as they play.*) You got to be careful what you do. (*He draws a card, looks at it, discards it.*) And—what you say. (*She picks it up and lays down her hand.*)

BILLIE: Three!

BROCK: Twenty-eight.

BILLIE: Twenty-eight?

BROCK: Twenty-eight.

(*She scores. He shuffles, cuts. She deals. They play again.*)

BILLIE: You could use a little education yourself, if you ask me.

BROCK: Who asked you?

BILLIE: Nobody.

BROCK: So shut up.

BILLIE: Can't I talk?

BROCK: Play your cards.

(*A pause.*)

BILLIE (*mumbling*): It's a free country.

BROCK: That's what *you* think. (*They play.* BILLIE *starts to hum "Anything Goes."* BROCK'S *nerves are further shaken.*) Do you mind?!!

BILLIE (*laying down her hand*): Gin.

BROCK: Thirty-four.

BILLIE: Thirty-four?

BROCK: Thirty-four.

(*He shuffles the cards as she scores.*)

BILLIE: Schneider.

BROCK: Where do you get the schneid?

(BILLIE *hands him the score.*)

BILLIE: Fifty-five dollars. And sixty cents.

BROCK: All right, that's all!

(BROCK *throws down the cards and rises. He crosses and pours a drink.*)

BILLIE: Pay me now.

BROCK (*yelling*): What the hell's the matter? Don't you trust me?

BILLIE: What are you hollerin' for? You always make *me* pay.

BROCK: Christ's sake!

BILLIE (*taunting him*): Sore loser.

BROCK: Shut up!

BILLIE: Fifty-five dollars. And sixty cents.

(He brings a large roll of bills from his pocket, peels off a few, and puts them on the table. BILLIE *looks at him, hard, until he provides the sixty cents.)*

BILLIE: Thanks.

*(*BROCK *starts for the staircase.)*

BROCK: Come on up.
BILLIE: In a minute.
BROCK: Now.
BILLIE: In a minute, I told you.

(This is the one moment of the day of which BILLIE *is boss.* BROCK *goes up quietly and shuts the door.* BILLIE *lays out a hand of solitaire. As she plays, she sings, softly, and interpolates little orchestral figures.)*

"In olden days a glimpse of stocking
Was looked on as something shocking,
But now Lord knows (tyah dah)
Anything goes. (tata tata—tata tata—tzing!)

Good authors, too, who once—"

(The door buzzer. She stops singing, throws a look up the stairs, makes a few personal adjustments, and goes to the door. PAUL *enters, carrying a few books and two newspapers.)*

PAUL: Hello.
BILLIE: Hello.
PAUL: Morning papers.

*(*BILLIE *takes them.)*

BILLIE: You could of saved yourself the trouble. I don't read papers.
PAUL: Never?
BILLIE: Once in a while the back part.
PAUL: I think you should. The front part.
BILLIE: Why?

PAUL: It's interesting.

BILLIE: Not to me.

PAUL: How do you know if you never read it?

BILLIE: Look, if you're gonna turn out to be a pest, we could call the whole thing off right now.

PAUL: Sorry.

BILLIE: I look at the papers sometimes. I just never understand it. So what's the sense?

PAUL: Tell you what you do. You look through these. Anything you don't understand, make a mark. (*He hands her a red editing pencil.*) Then tomorrow, I'll explain whatever I can. All right?

BILLIE: All right.

PAUL (*handing her the books*): And I thought you might like these.

BILLIE: I'll try. (*She puts the books and papers on a near-by table.*)

PAUL: No, don't do that. Just start reading. If you don't like it, stop. Start something else.

BILLIE: There's only one thing. My eyesight isn't so hot.

PAUL: Well, why don't you wear glasses?

BILLIE: Glasses!

PAUL: Why not?

BILLIE: Because it's terrible.

(*They look at each other for a time. She notices his glasses, but can't think of anything to say that will soften her remark. She moves in closer to him. Then closer still. It looks as though they are about to dance. She leans toward him. Now they are touching.* PAUL *responds. He puts his arms about her and kisses her. A long, expert kiss. They come out of it.*)

BILLIE: Of course, they're not so bad on men.

PAUL (*softly*): Good night, Billie.

BILLIE: Good night.

(PAUL *leaves.* BILLIE *looks around for the light switch, finds it, and turns out the lights in the sitting room. The balcony, however, is still illuminated. She starts up the stairs, slowly, and begins singing again.*)

BILLIE: "Good authors, too, who once knew better words

Now only use four-letter words
Writing prose (tyah dah—"

(*She stops, turns, and looks back at the books and papers, her new key to something or other. She moves back into the room, picks them up, and, clutching them tightly, starts up again, continuing the song.*)

"Writing prose (tyah dah)—"

(*She turns out the balcony light, sings the "Tyah dah" at the door to* BROCK'S *room as two notes of derision, then goes into her room and slams the door as we hear her last triumphant.*)

"Anything goes—!"

CURTAIN

ACT TWO

SCENE: *Two months or so have passed. The room looks lived in. A new piece of furniture has been added—a desk, which stands to one side. It is loaded with books, papers, magazines, and clippings. On the walls are some lovely framed reproductions of French and American moderns, and one or two small originals. In another part of the room stands a large globe-map. There is also a library dictionary on a stand near the desk. At the other side of the room, a Capehart. On the floor beside the instrument are stacks of record albums. In every part of the room, more books, magazines, pictures, and books. It is early evening and* BILLIE, *wearing lounging pajamas and eyeglasses, is sitting on the sofa, her legs stretched out before her, reading a newspaper. She makes a mark on the paper, then lifts it high to continue her reading. The front page of the paper is covered with red marks. It looks like a newspaper with the measles. She puts the paper down with a sign of fatigue and moves to the Capehart, stretching. She selects a few records, puts them on the machine, starts it, and goes back to the sofa. The room is soon filled with the soothing sounds of the Sibelius "Concerto in D Minor for Violin and Orchestra, op. 47." The door buzzer sounds.* EDDIE *comes through, still wearing his hat, and opens the door to admit* PAUL. BILLIE *looks around and smiles. She takes off her glasses, quickly.*

PAUL: How are you, Eddie?

EDDIE: Great.

BILLIE: Hello.

(EDDIE *goes.*)

PAUL: Hello, smarty-pants. (*He moves to her.*) How you coming?

BILLIE: Not so bad?

PAUL: Hm?

BILLIE: -*ly,* bad*ly.* Would you like some tea?

PAUL (*sitting down*): No, thanks. (*He indicates the music.*) Nice, that.

BILLIE: Sibelius, opp forty-seven. (*They listen for a moment.*) Guess who I just had for tea? *To* tea?

PAUL: Who?

BILLIE: Mrs. Hedges.

PAUL: Really? How was it?

BILLIE: Don't ask! You know, she's pretty stupid, too, but in a refined sort of way. Of course, we didn't have very much to talk about—so then she happened to notice my book laying there—

PAUL: Lying.

BILLIE: —my book lying there, and she said, "Oh, I've been meaning to read that again for years!"

PAUL: What was it?

BILLIE: *David Copperfield.*

PAUL: Oh, yes.

BILLIE: So then we got to talking about it and you want to know something?

PAUL: What?

BILLIE: She's never read it at all.

PAUL: How do you know?

BILLIE: I could tell from the way we were talking.

PAUL: Does that surprise you?

BILLIE: What, that she'd never read it?

PAUL: Yes.

BILLIE: No.

PAUL: Then what?

BILLIE: Well, why should she make out like she did? It's no crime if she didn't.

PAUL: Everybody does that, more or less.

BILLIE: Do you?

PAUL: Sometimes.

BILLIE: I don't.

PAUL: I know, Billie. You have the supreme virtue of honesty.

BILLIE: Thanks.

(*A* WAITER *comes in from the service wing, crosses to the coffee table, and picks up the tray. A letter lies under it.*)

BILLIE: I'm glad I got something after two months of this.

(*The* WAITER *starts out.*)

PAUL: You didn't get that from me, I'm afraid.

BILLIE: I'm not so sure.

PAUL (*prompting*): Thank you.

BILLIE: You're welcome.

PAUL (*indicating the waiter*): No.

BILLIE: Oh . . . (*She calls out to the* WAITER.) Thank you! (*The* WAITER *nods and leaves. She picks up the letter.*) I got this letter today. From my father.

PAUL: New York?

BILLIE: Yes. I can't get over it.

PAUL: Why?

BILLIE: Well, it's the first time he ever wrote me in about eight years. We had a fight, sort of. He didn't want me to go with Harry.

PAUL: What does he do?

BILLIE: My father?

PAUL: Yes.

BILLIE: Gas Company. He used to read meters, but in this letter he says how he can't get around so good any more so they gave him a different job. Elevator man. (*A pause, as she remembers back. The music is still playing.*) Goofy old guy. He used to take a little frying pan to work every morning, and a can of Sterno, and cook his own lunch. He said everybody should have a hot lunch. (*Another pause.*) I swear I don't know how he did it. There were four of us. Me and my three brothers, and he had to do everything. My mother died. I never knew her. He used to feed us and give us a bath and buy our clothes. Everything. That's why all my life I used to think how some day I'd like to pay him back. Funny how it worked out. One night, I brought home a hundred dollars and I gave it to him. You know what he did? He threw it in the toilet and pulled the chain. I thought he was going to hit me, sure, but he didn't. In his whole life, he never hit me once.

PAUL (*carefully*): How'd he happen to write you? I mean, after all this time.

BILLIE: Because I wrote *him*.

PAUL (*smiling*): Oh.

BILLIE: He says he's thought about me every day. God. I haven't thought about him, I bet, once even, in five years. That's nothing against him. I haven't thought of anything.

PAUL: Be nice to see him, maybe.

BILLIE: I guess so—but he said I should write him again and I should have a hot lunch every day and I should let him know how I am but that he didn't want to see me if I was still living the life of a concubine. I looked it up. . . . He always used to say: "Don't ever do nothin' you wouldn't want printed on the front page of the New York *Times*." (*A pause.*) Hey—I just realized. I've practically told you the whole story of my life by now, practically.

PAUL: I've enjoyed it very much.

BILLIE: How about the story of *your* life?

PAUL: Oh, no. It's too long—and mostly untrue. (BILLIE *takes the letter over to the desk and puts it in a drawer.*) What'd you do this morning?

BILLIE (*brightening*): Oh, I went to the newsreel and then over to the National Gallery like you said.

PAUL: How was it?

BILLIE: Wonderful. Quiet and peaceful and so interesting and did you ever notice? It smells nice. (PAUL *smiles.*) It does.

PAUL: How long did you stay?

BILLIE: Oh—a couple hours. I'm going again.

PAUL: Good.

BILLIE: Only the next time I wish you could come along.

PAUL: All right.

BILLIE: Boy, there's sure some things *there* that could use some explaining. (*She moves toward* PAUL.) Oh, and you know what else I did today? I went down to Brentano's and I just walked around, like you said I should, and looked at all the different kinds of books, and then the ones I thought maybe I'd like to read I took.

PAUL: That's right.

BILLIE: Well, pretty soon I had a whole big pile, too big to carry even. So I stopped. And I thought, my God, it'll take me about a year to read this many. Then I looked around, and compared to all the books there, my little pile was like nothing. So then I realized that even if I read my eyes out till the day I die I couldn't even make a little dent in that one store. Next thing you know I bust out crying.

(*She sits down, dejected.*)

PAUL: Nobody reads everything.

BILLIE: They don't?

PAUL: Of course not.

BILLIE: I've sure been trying to.

PAUL (*rising and going to the desk*): I don't suppose you got a chance to read *my* piece? (*He holds up a copy of the* New Republic.)

BILLIE: What are you talking? Of course I read it. Twice. (*A pause.*)

PAUL: What'd you think?

BILLIE (*slowly*): Well, I think it's the best thing I ever read. I didn't understand one word.

PAUL: What didn't you understand?

BILLIE: None of it.

PAUL: Here. Show me what.

(BILLIE *puts on her eyeglasses and moves to join him at the desk.* PAUL *laughs.*)

BILLIE: What's so funny? That I'm blind, practically?

PAUL: Practically blind.

BILLIE: —practically blind?

PAUL: You're wonderful.

BILLIE: I'm sorry I look funny to you.

PAUL: You don't. They make you look lovelier than ever.

BILLIE: You sound like one of those ads for eyeglasses. (*She sits down at the desk and puts her attention on the article.* PAUL *points to it.*)

PAUL: What?

BILLIE: Well, like the name of it. "The Yellowing Democratic Manifesto."

PAUL: Simple.

BILLIE: To who? Whom.—Whom? Well, anyway, not to me.

PAUL: Well, look. You know what "yellowing" means?

BILLIE: Not this time.

PAUL: When a piece of paper gets old, what happens to it?

(BILLIE *thinks.*)

BILLIE: You throw it away.

PAUL: No, it turns yellow.

BILLIE: It does?

PAUL: Of course.

BILLIE: What do you know?

PAUL: Now, "democratic." You know what that means, don't you?

BILLIE (*nodding*): Not Republican.

PAUL: Well, not exactly. It just means pertaining to our form of government, which is a democracy.

(*There is a pause.*)

BILLIE (*understanding*): Oh. (*A sudden frown.*) What's "pertaining"?

PAUL (*with a gesture*): Has to do with.

BILLIE (*musing*): Pertaining. Nice word.

(*She makes a note of it.*)

PAUL: All right, now—"manifesto."

BILLIE: I don't know.

PAUL: Why didn't you look it up?

BILLIE: I did look it up. I still don't know.

PAUL: Well, look—when I say "manifesto," I mean the set of rules and ideals and—principles and hopes on which the United States is based.

BILLIE: And you think it's turning yellow.

PAUL: Well, yes. I think the original inspiration has been neglected, and forgotten.

BILLIE: And that's bad.

PAUL: And that's bad.

(*She thinks it over for a moment, hard. We seem to see it soaking in. She picks up the magazine.*)

BILLIE (*reading*): "Even a—(*She looks at* PAUL.)—cursory? (*He nods.*)—examination of contemporary society in terms of the Greek philosophy which defines the whole as a representation of its parts, sends one immediately to a consideration of the individual as a citizen and the citizen as an individual."

PAUL: Well—

BILLIE: I looked up every word!

PAUL: Well, listen—thousands of years ago, a Greek philosopher—(*He pauses to make sure she is following.*)—once said that the world could only be as good as the people who lived in it.

(*There is a pause as* BILLIE *thinks this over.*)

BILLIE: Makes sense.

PAUL: All right. So I said, you take one look at America today and right away you figure you better take a look at the people in it. One by one, sort of.

BILLIE: Yuh.

PAUL: That's all.

BILLIE (*pointing to the article*): That's this?

PAUL: Sure.

BILLIE: Well, why didn't you say so?

PAUL: Too fancy, huh? (*He moves to the other side of the room.*) You know, I think I'm going to do that piece again. Plainer.

BILLIE: Oh, and you know that little thing you gave me about Napoleon?

PAUL: No, what?

BILLIE: By Robert G. Ingersoll?

PAUL: Oh, yes.

BILLIE: Well, I'm not sure if I get that either.

PAUL: No deep meaning there.

BILLIE: There must be. He says about how he goes and looks in Napoleon's tomb.

PAUL: Yuh.

BILLIE: And he thinks of Napoleon's whole sad life.

PAUL: Yuh.

BILLIE: And then in the end he says he himself would have rather been a happy farmer.

PAUL (*quoting*): "—and I said I would rather have been a French peasant and worn wooden shoes. I would rather have lived in a hut with a vine growing over the door, and the grapes growing purple in the kisses of the autumn sun. I would rather have been that poor peasant, with my loving wife by my side, knitting as the day died out of the sky—with my children upon my knees and their arms about me—I would rather have been that man and gone down to the tongueless silence of the dreamless dust, than to have been that imperial impersonation of force and murder, known as 'Napoleon the Great.'"

BILLIE (*impressed*): How can you remember all that stuff?

(*The music, which has by now become part of the background, suddenly changes. A Debussy record comes to a close and a wild Benny Goodman side replaces it.* PAUL *is startled, so is* BILLIE. *Then* BILLIE *rushes over and turns it off.*)

BILLIE: Once in a while. Just for a change.

(PAUL *laughs.*)

PAUL: Don't try so hard, Billie. Please. You miss the whole point.

BILLIE: Well, I like to like what's better to like.

PAUL: There's room for all sorts of things in you. The idea of learning is to be bigger, not smaller.

BILLIE: You think I'm getting bigger?

PAUL: Yes.

BILLIE: Glad to hear it. (*She sits at the desk again.*) So he would rather be a happy peasant than be Napoleon. So who wouldn't?

PAUL: So Harry wouldn't, for one.

BILLIE: What makes you think not?

PAUL: Ask him.

BILLIE: He probably never heard of Napoleon.

PAUL: What's worse, he probably never heard of a peasant.

BILLIE: Do you hate him like poison?

PAUL: Who, Harry?

BILLIE: Yuh.

PAUL: No.

BILLIE: But you don't like him.

PAUL (moving away): No.

BILLIE: On account of me and him?

PAUL: One reason. There are lots more.

BILLIE: What?

PAUL: Well, if you think about it, you'll see that Harry is a menace.

BILLIE: He's not so bad. I've seen worse.

PAUL: Has he ever done anything for anyone, except himself?

BILLIE: Me.

PAUL: What?

BILLIE: Well, I got two mink coats.

PAUL: That was a trade. You gave him something, too.

(There is an awkward pause before BILLIE replies, very quietly.)

BILLIE: Don't get dirty. You're supposed to be so wonderful, so don't get dirty.

PAUL: Has he ever thought about anybody but himself?

BILLIE: Who does?

PAUL (with increasing fervor and volume): Millions of people, Billie. The whole damned history of the world is the story of a struggle between the selfish and the unselfish!

BILLIE: I can hear you.

PAUL (patiently): All the bad things in the world are bred by selfishness. Sometimes selfishness even gets to be a cause, an organized force, even a government. Then it's called Fascism. Can you understand that?

BILLIE: Sort of.

PAUL (loudly): Well, think about it, Billie.

BILLIE (*softly*): You're crazy about me, aren't you.

PAUL: Yes.

BILLIE: That's why you get so mad at Harry.

PAUL: Billie, listen, I hate his life, what he does, what he stands for. Not him. He just doesn't know any better.

BILLIE: I go for you, too.

PAUL: I'm glad, Billie.

BILLIE: That's why I started doing all this. I guess you know.

PAUL: No, I didn't.

BILLIE: A lot of good it did me. I never had this kind of trouble before, I can tell you.

PAUL: Trouble?

BILLIE: After that first night when I met you—I figured it was all going to work dandy. Then, when you wouldn't step across the line—I figured maybe the way to *you* was through your head.

PAUL (*very slowly*): Well—no.

BILLIE: Anyway, it doesn't matter now—but I like you anyway. Too late for the rest.

PAUL: Why?

BILLIE: Why? Look Paul, there's a certain time between a fellow and a girl when it either comes off or not and if it doesn't then, then it never does.

PAUL: Maybe we haven't got to our time yet.

BILLIE: I think we did. And you dropped the ball.

PAUL: Don't be so sure.

BILLIE: I know. I've had lots of fellas and I *haven't* had lots of fellas. If you know what I mean.

PAUL: Yes.

BILLIE (*moving away*): But I sure never thought I'd go through a thing like this for anybody.

PAUL: Like what?

BILLIE: Like getting all mixed up in my head. Wondering and worrying and *thinking*—and stuff like that. And, I don't know if it's good to find out so much so quick. (*She sits on the sofa.*)

PAUL: What the hell, Billie. Nobody's *born* smart. You know what's the stupidest thing on earth? An infant.

BILLIE: What've you got against babies all of a sudden?

PAUL: Nothing. I've got nothing against a brain three weeks old and empty. But when it hangs around for thirty years without absorbing anything, I begin to think something's the matter with it.

BILLIE (*rising in fury*): What makes you think I'm thirty?

PAUL: I didn't mean you, especially.

BILLIE: Yes, you did.

PAUL: I swear.

BILLIE: You certainly know how to get me sore.

PAUL: I'm sorry.

BILLIE: Thirty! Do I look thirty to you?

PAUL: No.

BILLIE: Then what'd you say it for?

PAUL: I don't know. (*A short pause.*) How old *are* you?

BILLIE: Twenty-nine.

(*They look at each other.* PAUL *smiles. She responds. He comes over and kisses her, softly.*)

PAUL: Don't stop. (*She kisses him.*) I meant don't stop studying.

BILLIE: Oh.

PAUL: Will you?

BILLIE: I don't know why it's so important to you.

PAUL: It's sort of a cause. I want everybody to be smart. As smart as they can be. A world full of ignorant people is too dangerous to live in.

BILLIE (*sitting again*): I know. That's why I wish I was doing better.

PAUL: You're doing wonderfully.

BILLIE: Yeah, but it's just no use. I bet most people would laugh at me if they knew what I was trying to do.

PAUL: I'm not laughing.

BILLIE: I am. I'm sort of laughing at myself. Who do I think I am anyway?

PAUL: What's the matter?

BILLIE: All them books!

PAUL (*coming to her*): It isn't only books, Billie. I've told you a hundred times.

BILLIE: It's mostly.

PAUL (*sitting beside her*): Not at all. Listen, who said this? "The proper study of Mankind is Man."

BILLIE: I don't know.

PAUL: You should.

BILLIE: Why?

PAUL: I've told you.

BILLIE: I forgot.

PAUL: Pope.

BILLIE: The Pope?

PAUL: No, not the Pope. Alexander Pope.

BILLIE: "The proper study of—

PAUL: —Mankind is Man."

BILLIE: —Mankind is Man." Of course, that means women, too.

PAUL: Yes.

BILLIE: Yes, I know.

PAUL: Don't worry about books so much.

BILLIE: I *been* studying different mankind lately. The ones you told me. Jane Addams last week, and this week Tom Paine. And then all by myself I got to thinking about Harry. He works so hard to get what he wants, for instance, but he doesn't know what he wants.

PAUL: More of what he's got, probably.

BILLIE: Money.

PAUL: Money, more people to push around, money.

BILLIE: He's not so bad as you think he is.

PAUL: I know. He's got a brain of gold.

(*There is the sound of a key in the door.* BROCK *comes in.*)

BROCK: Hello.

PAUL: Hello, Harry. We were just talking about you.

BROCK (*removing his hat and coat and putting them on a chair*): Yeah? Well, that ain't what I pay you for. She knows enough about me. Too much, in fact. Ed here?

BILLIE: No.

BROCK: God damn it! He's supposed to meet me. (*He sits down and removes his shoes.*)

PAUL (*to* BILLIE): What did you find out about Tom Paine?

BILLIE: Well, he was quite a fella.

PAUL: Where was he born? Do you remember?

BILLIE: London. Or England. Some place like that.

BROCK: What do you mean. London or England? It's the same thing.

BILLIE: It is?

BROCK: London is *in* England. It's a city, London. England is a whole country.

BILLIE: I forgot.

BROCK (*to* PAUL): Honest to God, boy. You got some patience.

PAUL: Take it easy.

BROCK: How can anybody get so dumb?

PAUL: We can't all know everything, Harry.

BILLIE (*to* HARRY): Who's Tom Paine, for instance?

BROCK: What?

BILLIE: You heard me. Tom Paine.

BROCK: What the hell do I care who he is?

BILLIE: *I* know.

BROCK: So what? If I wanted to know who he is I'd know who he is. I just don't care. (*To* PAUL.) Go ahead. Don't let me butt in.

PAUL (*to* BILLIE): Which of his books did you like best?

BILLIE: Well, I didn't read *by* him yet—only about him.

PAUL: Oh.

BILLIE: But I made a list of—

BROCK (*suddenly*): Who's Rabbit Maranville?

BILLIE: Who?

BROCK: Rabbit Maranville.

BILLIE: I don't know any rabbits.

BROCK: Think you're so smart.

PAUL: Used to play shortstop for the Braves, didn't he?

BROCK (*to* PAUL): What are you? Some kind of genius?

PAUL: No.

BROCK: I hire and fire geniuses every day.

PAUL: I'm sure you do. (*He turns to* BILLIE.) Where's that list?

BILLIE (*handing it over*): Here.

PAUL (*studying it*): Well, suppose you start with *The Age of Reason*.

BILLIE (*writing it down*): The—Age—of—Reason.

PAUL: Then, next, you might—

BROCK: Who's Willie Hop?

PAUL (*turning slightly*): National billiard champion. And I think it's pronounced—Hoppe.

BROCK: That's what I said. Anyway, I didn't ask you, I asked her.

PAUL: Sorry. (*He turns back to* BILLIE.) Where were we?

BILLIE: *Age of Reason.*

PAUL: All right, then try *The Rights of Man.*

BILLIE (*writing*): The—Rights—of—Man.

PAUL: I think that'll give you a rough idea of what—

BROCK (*coming over to them*): What's a peninsula?

BILLIE: Sshhh!!

BROCK: Don't give me that shush—! You think you know so much— what's a peninsula?

PAUL: It's a—

BROCK: Not you.

BILLIE (*with condescending superiority*): It's that new medicine!

BROCK: It is not.

BILLIE: What then?

BROCK: It's a body of land surrounded on three sides by water.

BILLIE: So what's that to know?

BROCK: So what's this Sam Paine to know?

BILLIE: Some difference! Tom Paine—not Sam Paine—*Tom* Paine practically started this whole country.

BROCK: You mean he's dead?

BILLIE: Of course.

BROCK (*to* PAUL): What the hell are you learnin' her about dead people? I just want her to know how to act with live people.

PAUL: Education is a difficult thing to control or to channel, Harry. One thing leads to another. It's a matter of awakening curiosity— stimulating imagination—developing a sense of independence.

BROCK (*cutting in*): Work on her, not me.

PAUL: No extra charge.

BROCK: I don't need nothin' you can tell me.

PAUL: Oh, I'm sure we could tell each other lots of interesting things, Harry.

BROCK (*a warning tone*): What the hell does that mean?

PAUL: Just trying to be friendly.

BROCK: Who asked you? You know, every time I see you I don't like you as much. For a chump who's got no place, you're pretty fresh. You better watch out—I got an eye on you.

PAUL: All right. Let's both watch out.

BROCK: You know, I could knock your block off, if I wanted.

PAUL: Yes, I know.

BROCK: All right, then—just go ahead and do what you're supposed to —and that's all.

PAUL: It's all right—we'll stop for now.

BROCK: No, go ahead. I want to see how you do it.

PAUL: Not just now, if you don't mind—I've got to go lie down. You don't realize how hard I work.

BILLIE: Ha ha. Some joke.

BROCK (*petulant*): Two hundred bucks a week and I can't even watch!

PAUL (*to* BILLIE): See you later.

BILLIE: Goodbye, Paul. Thanks.

PAUL: Not a bit.

(*He leaves.*)

BROCK: London or England. Honest to God.

(*He opens an envelope on the desk and studies its contents throughout the following, without once looking at* BILLIE.)

BILLIE: Harry.

BROCK: Yeah?

BILLIE: What's this business we're in down here? Could you tell me?

BROCK: What do you mean—*we?*

BILLIE: Well, I figure I'm sort of a partner, in a way.

BROCK: A silent partner.

BILLIE: So?

BROCK: So shut up.

BILLIE: I got a right to know.

BROCK: You got a right to get the hell out of my hair. Just put your nose in your book and keep it.

BILLIE: I don't want to do anything if it's against the law. That's one sure thing.

BROCK: You'll do what I tell you.

ARSENIC AND OLD LACE
Edgar Stehli, Boris Karloff, John Alexander, Josephine Hull, Jean Adair.

HARVEY
Frank Fay as Elwood P. Dowd.

BORN YESTERDAY—Paul Douglas, Judy Holliday.

BORN YESTERDAY—Paul Douglas in barber's chair as Judy Holliday looks on.

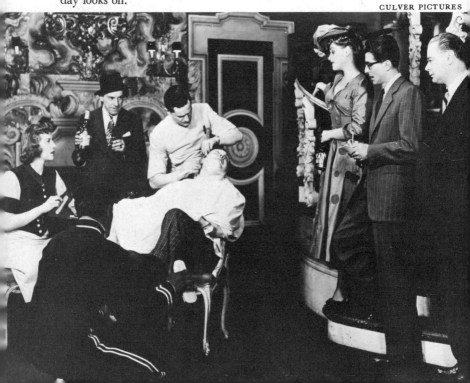

MARY, MARY   JOSEPH ABELES STUDIO
Barry Nelson, Barbara Bel Geddes.

CULVER PICTURES

MISTER ROBERTS
Murray Hamilton, Robert Keith, Henry Fonda.

THE ODD COUPLE—Walter Matthau, Art Carney.

JOSEPH ABELES STUDIO

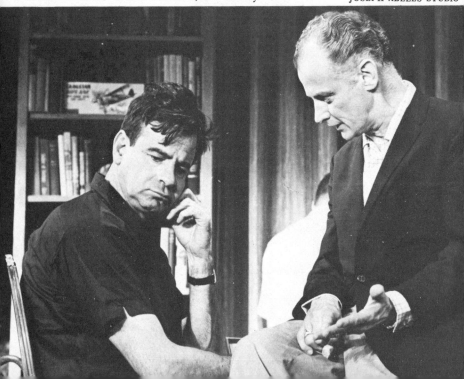

BILLIE: I think I know what it is—only I'm not sure.

BROCK: You should worry. You're doin' all right. Somethin' you want you ain't got maybe?

BILLIE: Yuh.

BROCK: What?

BILLIE: I want to be like the happy peasant.

BROCK: I'll buy it for you.

(HELEN *enters from the service wing, carrying a book.*)

BROCK: *Now* will you stop crabbing?

(HELEN *puts the book on one of the shelves.*)

HELEN: Well, I finished finally. Thanks loads for the loan of it.

BILLIE: How'd you like it?

HELEN: Pretty punk.

BILLIE: Really, Helen? I enjoyed it.

HELEN: Not me. I don't go for these stories where it shows how miserable it is to be rich.

BILLIE: Well, it can be.

BROCK: All—right—can the coffee klotch. (*To* HELEN.) Knock off.

HELEN: Sorry, Mr. Brock. (*She leaves, quickly, with a little see-you-later wave to* BILLIE.)

BROCK: Don't get so pally with everybody.

BILLIE: Paul says it's all right.

BROCK: Never mind Paul says. I don't like it.

BILLIE: You know what you are?

BROCK: What?

BILLIE: Uh—

(*She can't think of it, so she goes to the large dictionary and starts looking for the word. The door buzzer sounds.* EDDIE *comes in to open the front door.* BILLIE *finds what she has been looking for. She looks up from the dictionary.*)

BILLIE: Antisocial!

BROCK: You're God damn right I am!

(EDDIE *opens the door to admit* DEVERY *and* SENATOR HEDGES.)

DEVERY: Good evening.

BROCK: Where the hell have you guys been? You know what time it is?

DEVERY: Sorry.

BROCK: You're always sorry.

HEDGES: My fault. (*To* BILLIE.) Good evening.

BILLIE: Good evening. Won't you sit down?

HEDGES: Thank you.

DEVERY: How are you, Billie?

BILLIE: Superb. New word.

BROCK: All right—all right. What happened?

(*An awkward pause.* DEVERY *and* HEDGES *exchange a look and silently gird their loins.*)

HEDGES (*softly*): It's just this, Harry. I'm afraid it's going to take a little more time and—(*He pauses.*)

DEVERY (*picking it up*): —and a little more money.

BROCK (*angry*): Why?

DEVERY: Well, for one thing, the whole amendment has to be re-drafted.

BROCK: I don't want no re-drafted and I don't want to wait.

HEDGES: I'm afraid you'll have to.

BROCK: Don't tell me what I have to!

HEDGES: If you'd let me—

BROCK: Listen, I don't like you. You're makin' me feel like some sucker.

DEVERY: I'm sure Norval's doing his best.

BROCK: Well, his best ain't good enough.

DEVERY: Don't be unreasonable, Harry. There are ninety-six votes up there. Norval's just one guy.

BROCK: He's the wrong guy. What the hell? We've handled it before.

HEDGES: Things aren't the same.

BROCK: We'll make 'em the same. That's your job, ain't it?

DEVERY: Pretty tough assignment.

BROCK: What do I care? (*To* HEDGES.) And you. You better get movin' or I'll butcher you—you'll wind up a God-damn YMCA secretary again before you know it.

DEVERY: Harry—

BROCK: I'm gonna get it fixed so I can do business where I want and how I want and as big as I want. If you ain't with me, you're against me.

HEDGES: I'm with you.

BROCK (*starting up the stairs*): All right, then, you'll have to pull your weight in the God-damn boat or I'll get somebody who can. You understand me?

(*He slams out. There is an awkward pause.*)

HEDGES: He has quite a temper, hasn't he?

DEVERY: Don't mind him, he's always lived at the top of his voice. (*Pouring a drink.*) Anybody with me? Norval?

HEDGES: No, thank you.

BILLIE (*to* HEDGES): I don't think Harry should talk to you like that. After all, you're a Senator.

HEDGES: Oh, well.

BILLIE: I don't think anybody should talk to a Senator like that or be able too. A Senator is a wonderful thing.

HEDGES: Thank you.

BILLIE: The way it looks to me—if he pushes you around, it's like he's pushing a few million people around.

HEDGES: How do you mean?

BILLIE: The people who picked you.

HEDGES: Well, not quite that many.

BILLIE: How many then?

HEDGES: Eight hundred and six thousand, four hundred and thirty-four.

BILLIE: Well, *that's* quite a few to push around.

HEDGES: *You're* not one of my constituents by any chance, are you?

BILLIE (*after thinking a moment*): I don't think I know that one.

DEVERY: The Senator means are you one of the people who voted for him?

BILLIE: I never voted for anybody.

HEDGES (*smiling*): Why not?

BILLIE: I don't know. I guess I wouldn't know how.

DEVERY: Very simple. You just press a button.

BILLIE: Yuh, but which one? Like suppose it's between different people?

DEVERY (*smiling*): Well, you listen to the speeches—you read the papers—you make up your own mind. You take a look and see who's for who—that's *very* important. Once you take a stand on something—take a look and see who's on the other side and who's on your side.

HEDGES (*lightly*): That's all there is to it.

BILLIE (*to* HEDGES): Well, why do you take it from Harry? That's what I want to know. You're more important than him. You're a Senator.

HEDGES: Yes, and as such, you see—I have a great many duties and responsibilities—

BILLIE: Yuh?

HEDGES (*stalling*): The operation of government is very complex.

BILLIE: Why should it be? I understand it pretty good in the books and when Paul tells me—but then when I see a thing like this—it's like different.

HEDGES: How?

BILLIE: Well, when it comes down to what should be the laws and what shouldn't—is Harry more important than anybody else?

HEDGES (*meaning yes*): No.

BILLIE: Then how come he's got so much to say? After all, nobody ever voted for *him*.

HEDGES (*rising and starting out*): Well, we'll have a nice long talk about it sometime.

BILLIE: All right.

HEDGES: Goodbye.

BILLIE: Goodbye.

(DEVERY *takes* HEDGES *up to the door*.)

HEDGES: Quite a little girl.

DEVERY: Oh, yes.

HEDGES: Goodbye.

DEVERY: Goodbye.

(HEDGES *leaves*. DEVERY *goes quietly to his brief case and takes out a sheaf of papers*.

DEVERY (*to* BILLIE): Few things here for you.

(He spreads the papers out for signing. BILLIE *comes over. She picks up her glasses. He hands her his fountain pen, then goes over and pours another drink.* BILLIE *puts on her glasses and stands looking at the papers. She starts to read the top one. A moment later,* DEVERY *turns back into the room. He looks at* BILLIE *in amazement, then takes a step or two into the room.)*

BILLIE: What is this?

DEVERY: Same old stuff.

BILLIE: What?

DEVERY: Take too long to explain.

BILLIE: No it wouldn't. I like having things explained to me. I found that out.

DEVERY: Some other time.

BILLIE: Now.

DEVERY: You want me to tell Harry?

BILLIE: Tell him what?

DEVERY: That you won't sign this stuff?

BILLIE: Who said anything about that? I just want to know what it is.

DEVERY: A merger.

BILLIE: What's that?

DEVERY: Several companies being formed into one.

BILLIE: All Harry's?

DEVERY: No.

BILLIE: Whose then?

DEVERY: A few of Harry's and some others. French, Italian, and so on.

BILLIE (*with the shock of recognition*): A cartel!

DEVERY: What are you talking about?

BILLIE: About cartels. If that's what this is, then I'm against it. Paul explained me the whole thing.

(DEVERY *is dumbfounded.*)

DEVERY: It's perfectly all right. Don't worry.

BILLIE: You sure?

DEVERY: Ask Harry.

BILLIE: All right.

DEVERY: He won't like it.

BILLIE: Why not?

DEVERY: He just won't, that's all. He doesn't like people butting in.

BILLIE: I'm not people.

DEVERY: Listen to me, Billie. Be smart.

BILLIE: How can I be smart if nobody ever tells me anything?

DEVERY: I'm telling you something.

BILLIE: What?

DEVERY: Sign the stuff and don't start up with him.

BILLIE: Tomorrow.

DEVERY: Why tomorrow?

BILLIE: I want to look them over, so I'll know what I'm doing.

DEVERY (*losing his temper*): It's all right!

BILLIE: Must be something fishy. If not, you'd tell me.

DEVERY: Take my word for it.

BILLIE: No.

(DEVERY *tries hard to think of another approach.*)

BILLIE: I know what you feel bad about. You don't like to be doing all his dirty work—because you know you're better than him.

DEVERY (*white*): That's enough.

BILLIE: But I'm not so sure—maybe you're worse!

(DEVERY *looks at her for a moment, then rushes up the stairs in angry determination.* BILLIE *picks up the papers, also a small dictionary, brings them to the sofa, and sits down to read. Now* BROCK *appears on the balcony. He comes down into the room, slowly. Too slowly.* BILLIE *looks up, once, and continues what she is doing.* BROCK *crosses the room. She senses his silent fury as he passes behind her. He goes to where the liquor is, directly behind* BILLIE, *and takes a drink. Then he moves into the room and sits down, facing her. He watches her, quietly.* BILLIE *looks up at him for a moment, but says nothing. She is frightened.* BROCK *gives no sign of anger or violence. He just looks at her. Finally, he breaks the silence.*)

BROCK: Interesting?

BILLIE (*without looking up*): Not very.

BROCK: I suppose you're used to reading more high-toned stuff.

BILLIE: Yes, I am.

(*There is another long pause.*)

BROCK: What's the matter, kid?

BILLIE: Nothing.

BROCK: All of a sudden.

BILLIE: I don't like that Ed.

BROCK: Why, what'd he do to you?

BILLIE: He didn't do nothing, *anything,* to me. It's what he's done to himself.

BROCK: Done what?

BILLIE: He used to be Assistant Attorney General of the United States.

BROCK: Who?

BILLIE: Ed.

BROCK: So what's wrong with that?

BILLIE: Nothing's wrong. Just look at him now.

(BROCK *frowns, trying hard to follow.*)

BILLIE: Did you know he once wrote a book? *The Roots of Freedom.* That was the name of it. I read it. It was wonderful.

BROCK: Where'd you get all this?

BILLIE: I looked it up.

BROCK: Why?

BILLIE: No reason. I was just in the library. And look at him now. He hangs around and helps you promote and lets you walk all over him just because you pay for it.

BROCK: Oh, so we finally got around to me.

BILLIE: Yuh. I'm not so sure I like you either. You're selfish, that's your trouble.

BROCK: Since when is all this?

BILLIE: Since now.

BROCK: You don't say.

BILLIE: I used to think you were a big man, Harry. Now I'm beginning to see you're not. All through history there's been bigger men than you and better. Now, too.

BROCK: Who, for instance?

BILLIE: Thousands.

BROCK: Name one.

BILLIE: My father.

BROCK (*contemptuously*): Twenty-five a week.

BILLIE: "—a brain of gold."

BROCK (*confused*): What?

BILLIE: Never mind.

(BROCK *rises, moves across the room, and sits beside her.*)

BROCK: Listen, cutie, don't get nervous just because you read a book. You're as dumb as you ever were.

BILLIE: You think so?

BROCK: Sure, but I don't mind. You know why? (*He makes a rude pass.*) Because you've got the best little—

BILLIE (*rising and moving away swiftly*): Leave me alone, Harry.

BROCK: Come here.

BILLIE: No.

BROCK: I never seen you like this.

BILLIE: I never been like this. I feel like I want to go away someplace.

BROCK: Where?

BILLIE: I don't know.

BROCK: I may wind up here in a few weeks. We'll go to Florida maybe.

BILLIE: I mean alone.

BROCK: You know what I think? I think you've gone nuts.

BILLIE: Maybe.

BROCK: Calm down.

BILLIE: I can't.

BROCK: Why not?

BILLIE: I don't know. I just know I hate my life. There's a better kind, I know it. If you read some of these books, you'd know it, too. Maybe it's right what you say, I'm still dumb, but I know one thing I never knew before. There's a better kind of life than the one I got. Or you.

BROCK (*as he gets up and moves to her*): I suppose you figure you'da been better off with that lousy saxophone player.

BILLIE: At least he was honest.

BROCK: He was a dime-a-dozen chump.

BILLIE: He worked for a living, that's one thing—

BROCK: I work. I been workin' since I was twelve years old—nobody ever give me nothin'.

BILLIE: If a man goes and robs a house—that's work, too.

BROCK: In my whole life—

(HELEN, *carrying towels, enters from the service wing and goes upstairs.* BROCK *holds it until she is out of sight.*)

BROCK: —in my whole life I never robbed a house. What the hell are you talkin' about?

BILLIE: You can hardly understand anything, can you?

BROCK: Get off that high horse—you dumb little pot!

BILLIE: You—(*She tries hard to think of something worse.*)—menace!

BROCK: I picked you up out of the gutter and I can throw you back there, too. Why, you never had a decent meal before you met me.

BILLIE: Yeah, but I had to have 'em with you. You eat terrible. You got no manners. Takin' your shoes off all the time—that's another thing . . . and pickin' your teeth. You're just not couth!

(HELEN *comes down the stairs and goes out through the service entrance.*)

BROCK (*shouting*): I'm as couth as you are!

BILLIE (*with considerable disgust*): And that cheap perfume you put on yourself.

BROCK: Cheap? I don't own nothin' cheap. Except you.

BILLIE (*very quietly*): You don't own me. Nobody can own anybody. There's a law says.

BROCK: Don't tell me about the law. If I was scared of the law, I wouldn't be where I am.

BILLIE: Where are you?

BROCK: All right, you've talked enough. If you don't like it here, beat it. You'll be back.

(BILLIE *starts out of the room.*)

BROCK: Wait a minute. (*He gets the documents from the coffee table.*) First this.

BILLIE: Not now.

BROCK: Right now.

BILLIE: No. (*She starts up the stairs.*)

BROCK (*loudly*): Come here!

BILLIE: I'm not going to sign anything any more till I know what I'm signing. From now on.

BROCK: Do what I'm telling you!

(BILLIE *stands rigid and frightened.* BROCK *is suddenly in front of her. He raises his arm to strike her.*)

BILLIE (*cringing*): Harry, please! Don't!

(*Her last word is cut in two by a stinging slap. Then another. The seed of her rebellion is suddenly uprooted. She sags and sobs, defeated.* BROCK *propels her to the desk in a series of rough shoves. Still sobbing, she follows his directions and signs the documents, one by one. When she has finished,* BROCK *takes them up, folds them, and puts them into his pocket.* BILLIE'S *head goes to her folded arms on the desk.* BROCK *crosses to the liquor and gets a drink.*)

BROCK: All right, now get the hell out of here.

BILLIE: What?

BROCK: Don't be bawlin' around here, that's what. I don't like it. I been treatin' you too good, that's the trouble. You don't appreciate it. Nothin'. I ain't gonna have nobody around here who don't know their place. So get the hell out of here. Go sit on a park bench someplace till you're ready to behave yourself. (BILLIE *is rigid with fright.*) Go on! (*She starts for the stairs.* BROCK *points to the front door.*) This way out.

BILLIE (*in a small voice*): I've got to put something on.

BROCK: Well, hurry up—I don't want you around here like this. You bother me.

(BILLIE *starts up the stairs. Halfway up, she stops and turns to* BROCK.)

BILLIE: Big Fascist!

BROCK: What?

(*She goes into her room quickly.* BROCK *turns and sees a pile of books before him. Instantly, he identifies them as the reason for his present despair. He pushes them to the floor, violently—he kicks them out of his way—he finds a strange release in this, so he picks up one of the books, and begins tearing out the pages. There is mingled fury, excitement, and satisfaction in his heart as he completes the destruction of the book. He starts on a second as* DEVERY *comes down.* BROCK *stops, as though discovered in an indecent act.*)

DEVERY: All set?

BROCK: Certainly all set. What'd you think—I'm gonna let a broad talk back?

DEVERY: Where is she?

BROCK: I told her to take a walk. If there's one thing I can't stand it's a crier.

DEVERY: What's she crying about?

BROCK: What do I know?

DEVERY: She's becoming a strange girl.

BROCK: She's all right. All this book stuff's got her nervous, that's all.

DEVERY (*softly*): "A little learning is a dangerous thing."

BROCK: What?

DEVERY (*sitting*): Nothing, Harry. Looks like your passion for educating her was a mistake.

BROCK: I didn't know it would turn out like this, did I?—Remind me to fire that four-eyed Verrall skunk.

DEVERY: Why blame him?

BROCK: He must have told her *too* much. (*A pause.*) You know what she called me before? A Fach-ist.

DEVERY (*almost smiling*): She did?

BROCK: What the hell's that? Some kinda European, ain't it? It don't make sense. I was born in Plainfield, New Jersey. She knows that.

(*He stares at the door of* BILLIE'S *room moodily.*)

DEVERY: What's the matter, Harry?

BROCK: I love that broad. (*There is a pause.* BROCK *appears to be thinking. He looks up, in despair.*) Ed. You think we could maybe find somebody to make her dumb again?

(BILLIE *comes down, dressed for the street, and moves toward the front door.*)

BROCK (*without turning*): And don't be late if you don't want a bloody nose.

(BILLIE *stops and moves a step into the room.*)

BILLIE (*very, very gently*): Would you do me a favor, Harry?
BROCK (*mean*): What?
BILLIE: Drop dead?

(*She leaves quickly, before* BROCK *recovers.*)

CURTAIN

ACT THREE

SCENE: *Later that evening.* DEVERY, *coatless, is on the sofa working over a pile of documents. He is somewhat drunker than before.* BROCK, *in pajamas and dressing gown, is pacing the floor.*

BROCK: What time is it already?
DEVERY: One-thirty.
BROCK: I'll slug her senseless when she comes back.
DEVERY: *If.*
BROCK: Listen, I've had this with her before. She always winds up where I want her.
DEVERY: I hope so.

(*There is a pause.*)

BROCK: What time is it?

DEVERY: One-thirty.

BROCK: You said that before.

DEVERY: One-thirty-one.

BROCK: What time she go out?

DEVERY: I don't know. Five, six o'clock.

BROCK: Eight hours.

DEVERY: What?

BROCK: She's been gone eight hours.

DEVERY: Maybe she's seeing a double feature.

BROCK: Yeah. . . . *That* don't take eight hours! (*A pause.*) She coulda got into an accident.

DEVERY: You'd hear.

BROCK: She coulda got raped! (DEVERY *looks at him.*) It happens all the time.

DEVERY: Not to Billie. Maybe the other way around, but not to Billie.

BROCK: You'd think Eddie'd call up at least.

(*A pause.*)

DEVERY: Be damned inconvenient if he doesn't find her. I've got some more for her to sign. It can't wait.

(EDDIE *comes in.*)

EDDIE: She here?

BROCK: What do you mean, "she here"? *No!*

EDDIE: The guy downstairs said he seen her go out and then he seen her come in.

BROCK: He's blind. Go out and look some more.

EDDIE: I been all over town.

BROCK: Well, go over it again. (*There is the slightest possible hesitation from* EDDIE.) Do what I'm tellin' you!

EDDIE: Sure. (*He starts for his room.*) Just change my shoes. (*He goes out.*)

DEVERY: If I thought I could make those stairs I'd go lie down.

(*There is a tiny pause.*)

BROCK: I sure never thought she was gonna turn out like this.

DEVERY: Have you thought any more about that matter we discussed in connection with her?

BROCK: What connection?

DEVERY: Marrying her.

BROCK: Still harpin', huh?

DEVERY: Seems to have gone beyond the reasons of appearance, Harry. If she's going to be truculent, I'm thinking of your legal safety. On paper, she owns—

BROCK: I know what she owns.

DEVERY: You've got to do it, Harry.

(*A long pause.*)

BROCK (*softly*): They always hook you in the end, them broads. (*He pours a drink.*) It's crazy, you know it?

DEVERY: How?

BROCK: A whole trouble because a dame reads a book.

DEVERY: Just goes to show you.

BROCK: Yuh.

DEVERY: It's the new world, Harry—force and reason change places. Knowledge is power. You can lead a horse to water.

BROCK: What?

DEVERY: Honesty is the best policy. A stitch in time saves nine. (*He starts up the stairs and trips.*)

BROCK: I don't like the way things are going around here. You stewed all the time—the broad outa line—and that's some fine Senator you bought me.

DEVERY: I think he's cute.

BROCK: I could get me a better Senator out of Lindy's.

DEVERY: Best I could do.

BROCK: I'd like to trade him in, no kiddin'.

DEVERY: They're not all for sale, Harry. That's the trouble with this town—too many honest men in it.

(DEVERY *goes off into* BROCK'S *room.* BROCK *paces, lights a cigarette —then stops and stares at the books. He selects a particularly slender one and moves to the sofa. He reads.* EDDIE *comes through.*)

EDDIE: I'll take a look downstairs and see if she's—

(*He stops abruptly at the unbelievable sight before his eyes.* BROCK *turns to see him gaping.*)

BROCK: What's the matter?

EDDIE: Nuthin'.

BROCK: Didn't you ever see a person readin' a book, for Christ's sake?

EDDIE: Sure.

BROCK: All right then. Get the hell out of here!

EDDIE: Sure.

(*He goes quietly.* BROCK *reads. Behind him the door opens noiselessly and* BILLIE *looks in. She closes the door.* BROCK *reads a bit longer, then gives up. He tears the book in two and throws it away. He goes upstairs and into his room, turning off the main light on his way. A moment later* BILLIE *comes in and looks around.*

She goes up the stairs, stops at BROCK'S *door, and listens. Then she comes down to the door again and whispers to someone just outside.*

PAUL *joins her and closes the door.* BILLIE *moves to the desk and starts looking through the papers on it. She holds one out to* PAUL. *He examines it carefully, and nods. Quietly, systematically, they go through the desk.* PAUL *makes a pile of documents, letters, check-books, and papers.* BILLIE *crosses and picks up the material left by* DEVERY. PAUL *follows her and adds this to his.*)

BILLIE (*in a whisper*): Okay?

PAUL: This ought to do it fine.

BILLIE: I probably won't see you again, Paul—

PAUL: What!

BILLIE: Ssshh!

PAUL (*whispering*): What?!

BILLIE: So I want to say goodbye and thank you for everything.

PAUL: Where are you going?

BILLIE: Just away from here, that's all I know.

PAUL: Where? You can tell *me*.

BILLIE: I don't know. I thought I might go see my father for a while.

PAUL: And have a hot lunch every day?

BILLIE: Yeah.

PAUL: I've got a better idea.

BILLIE: What?

PAUL: Let's get married.

BILLIE: You must be daffy.

PAUL: I love you, Billie.

BILLIE: You don't love me. You just love my brain.

PAUL: That, too.

BILLIE: What would the boss of the *New Republic* say?

PAUL: I don't know. Probably—congratulations.

BILLIE: I'll think it over, but I can tell you now the answer is no. And I wish you'd hurry up out of here. (PAUL *kisses her.*) What are you doing?

PAUL: Well, if you don't know, I must be doing it wrong. (*He kisses her again.*)

BILLIE (*sitting on the sofa*): What's more important right now—crabbing Harry's act—or romancing?

PAUL (*sitting next to her*): They're one and the same thing to me.

BILLIE: Honest, Paul—I wish you'd—

(*The door opens and* EDDIE *comes in. He switches on the lights. He stops on the landing, surprised.* PAUL *and* BILLIE *rise.*)

EDDIE: What's this? Night school? (*To* BILLIE.) Where were you anyway? I looked all over town.

BILLIE: I walked over to the White House and back.

EDDIE: How's everybody over there? (*To* PAUL.) You better knock off, brother.

PAUL: Why?

EDDIE: I'm supposed to tell him she's back. I don't think he'll like you horsin' around with his girl in the middle of the night. He's funny that way.

PAUL: I'll take a chance.

BILLIE: You better go.

EDDIE: She's right. Take my advice.

PAUL: What's it to you?

EDDIE: Listen—noise I can stand, but blood makes me nervous. (*He goes upstairs and into* BROCK'S *room.*)

BILLIE: Please, Paul.

PAUL: Sure you'll be all right?

BILLIE: Don't worry.

PAUL: Goodbye, Billie.

BILLIE: Goodbye.

(PAUL *goes.* BILLIE *picks up the phone.*)

BILLIE: Porter, please. (*She sorts out a few things on the desk.*) Hello, porter? This is 67D. Could you send somebody up for my bags? . . . No, right now . . . thank you.

(EDDIE *appears on the balcony, rubbing his stomach, and gasping softly.*)

BILLIE: What's the matter?

EDDIE: Right in the stomach he hit me.

BILLIE: Why didn't you hit him back?

EDDIE: What?

BILLIE: Why didn't you hit him back?

EDDIE: He's been sayin' you've gone nuts. I could believe it, you know it?

BILLIE: Would you do me a favor?

EDDIE: What?

BILLIE: Pack my things up there?

EDDIE: You scrammin' again?

BILLIE: For good.

EDDIE: I'll tell you the truth, I'm sorry. I think he's gonna be sorry, too.

BILLIE: He's going to be worse than sorry.

EDDIE: Where you goin'?

BILLIE: Never mind.

EDDIE: You sore at me, too?

BILLIE: In a way.

EDDIE: What'd *I* do? What'd I *do?*

BILLIE: It's a new thing with me, Eddie. I'm going to be sore at anybody who just takes it. From now on.

EDDIE: Listen, don't get me thinkin'. I got enough trouble now.

(*He goes into* BILLIE'S *room.* BILLIE *begins to sort out her belongings, as* BROCK *appears.*)

BROCK: Fine time.

BILLIE (*gay*): Hello, Harry.

BROCK (*coming down*): Where you been?

BILLIE: I took a walk like you told me.

BROCK: That took you till now?

BILLIE: What's the matter, Harry? You miss me?

BROCK: I decided somethin' to tell you. Somethin' good. I don't like to wait when I get an idea.

BILLIE: Yuh, I know.

BROCK: Now I see you, I don't know if I should tell you it.

BILLIE: Why not?

BROCK: Runnin' out, talkin' fresh, slammin' doors. I knew you'd be back, though.

BILLIE: You did, huh?

BROCK: I told Ed, even. He was worried. Not me.

BILLIE: Not yet.

BROCK: What took you so long?

BILLIE: I had a lot to think.

BROCK: For instance?

BILLIE: Just where I stand around here.

BROCK: That's what I'm tryin' to tell you.

BILLIE: What?

BROCK: Where you stand.

BILLIE: Yuh.

BROCK: Well—first thing, that Verrall stuff is through. It gets in my way —and I don't like you upset so much. It's bad for you. And the next thing—we're gonna get married.

BILLIE: No.

BROCK: Only you got to behave yourself . . . No?! What do you mean, no?

BILLIE: I don't want to, that's what I mean. No. In fact, I've never been so insulted.

BROCK (*in a whisper*): Well, that's the God damndest thing I ever heard.

BILLIE: Why?

BROCK: Who the hell are you to say no, if I tell you?

BILLIE: Don't knock yourself out, you've got a lot of surprises coming.

BROCK: Just tell me first.

BILLIE: What?

BROCK: How can *you* not want to marry *me?*

BILLIE: Well, you're too dumb—for one thing. I've got a different kind of life in mind, Harry. Entirely. I'm sorry, but you just wouldn't fit in.

BROCK: Listen, Billie, I don't understand what the hell's happenin'!

BILLIE: I do.

BROCK: What'd I do? What did I? All right, I talked rough to you once in a while. Maybe I hit you a couple of times. Easy. Is that a reason to treat me like this? I done good for you, too. Couldn't we straighten it out?

BILLIE: No.

BROCK: Why not?

BILLIE (*very simply*): Well, all this stuff I've been reading—all that Paul's been telling me—it just mixed me up. But when you hit me before, it was like everything knocked itself together in my head—and made sense. All of a sudden I realized what it means. How some people are always giving it and some taking. And it's not fair. So I'm not going to let you any more. *Or anybody else.*

(*She goes back to the desk.*)

BROCK: Listen, kid. I got an idea. Come on upstairs and I'll calm you down. (BILLIE *continues her work.*) We used to have a pretty good time, remember? (BILLIE *slams a drawer.*) You want to come to Florida? I think you ought to marry me, don't you? (*He is suddenly off the handle.*) Listen, Billie. I want you to marry me. I don't want to argue about it. I've heard enough. Now you do what I'm tellin' you or you'll be damn good and sorry.

BILLIE: I'm not scared of you any more, Harry, that's another thing.

BROCK: You're not, huh?

(*He starts moving toward her, ominously, but stops as the door buzzer sounds. The door opens and two bellhops appear.*)

BILLIE: Come on in! Right up there.

BROCK: What the hell's this?

BILLIE: Oh, didn't I tell you? I'm leaving.

BROCK: What?

BILLIE: Yuh, for good.

BROCK (*to the bellhops*): Wait a second. (*They stop.*) Beat it. (*The bellhops hesitate.*) Hurry up! (*They hurry down and out.*)

BELLHOP (*at the door*): Thank you, sir.

BROCK (*to* BILLIE): Let's get organized around here! You can't just walk out, cutie. You're in too deep with me. I'm right in the middle of the biggest thing I ever done. Maybe I made a mistake hookin' you in with it—but you're in.

BILLIE: Well, I'm not going to be. I decided.

BROCK: All right, fine. You want to wash it up, we'll wash it up. I'm too important to monkey around with what you think. (*He shouts up.*) Ed! (*He looks through the papers on the desk.*) I'll fix it so you can be out of here in no time. You're spoiled. I spoiled you. You're no good to me no more. I was ready to make you a real partner. So you don't want it? So fine. See how you'll do without me. You don't look like you looked nine years ago. In fact, you look lousy, if you want the truth. I'm glad to get rid of you.

BILLIE: And as far as I'm concerned . . .

BROCK: Yeah?

BILLIE: *Vice versa!*

(DEVERY *comes down.*)

DEVERY (*to* BILLIE): You're back. (*To* BROCK.) All set?

BROCK: Shut up!

DEVERY: What's the matter?

BROCK (*rummaging through the desk*): She's off her nut. We're gonna settle everything up and get her the hell outa here.

DEVERY (*to* BILLIE): You sure you know what you're doing?

BILLIE: First time in my life I *do* know.

BROCK: What'd you do with that stuff you wanted her to . . . ?

DEVERY (*pointing to the sofa*): Right there.

BROCK: Where right there?

(DEVERY *moves to the desk. They begin looking, feverishly.*)

BILLIE (*nonchalantly*): With blue covers?

DEVERY: Yeah.

(*A pause.*)

BILLIE: Three copies?

BROCK: That's right.

(*Another pause.*)

BILLIE: I gave 'em to Paul.

(BROCK *and* DEVERY *freeze at the desk in odd positions.*)

BROCK: When?

BILLIE: Just now.

DEVERY: What for?

BILLIE: What do you think for? To put in the paper, I guess.

BROCK: There's some kinda jokes I don't like.

BILLIE: It's no joke. Paul says it's the worst swindle since—uh—the teapot. Something like that.

(DEVERY *and* BROCK *exchange a horrified look.*)

BILLIE: What are you getting so white about? You told me yourself it was perfectly all right.

BROCK: You double-crossing little—

BILLIE: I don't see it like that. If there's a fire and I call the engines— so who am I double-crossing—the fire?

DEVERY: I'd better get Norval.

BROCK: I know who to get. Eddie!!

DEVERY (*on the phone*): Decatur 9124.

(EDDIE *appears.*)

BROCK: You know where Verrall's room is?

EDDIE: Sure.

BROCK: Tell him to get in here right away.

EDDIE: Right. (*He starts out.*)

BROCK: Wait a minute—tell him Billie wants him.

(EDDIE *goes.*)

DEVERY (*on the phone*): Hello, Norval? Ed. Wake you? . . . Oh, good.

I'm over here at Harry's. Can you drop by? Important. . . . No, it can't. . . . All right.

(*He hangs up.*)

BILLIE: Paul's got nothing to do with this. It was my own idea.

BROCK: I'll show you ideas.

BILLIE: If you think you can strong-arm him—you're wasting your time. For a fellow with eyeglasses, he's very stubborn.

DEVERY (*pouring a drink*): Oh, dear.

BROCK (*to* DEVERY): If you don't stop bellyachin', get the hell out of here!

DEVERY: We're in trouble, Harry.

BROCK: Is that gonna help?

DEVERY: No. (*He downs his drink.*)

BROCK: I'll trim this guy. Watch me.

DEVERY: All right.

BROCK: You get in a spot, you fold up. Remind me to have a heart-to-heart talk with you.

DEVERY: Be that as it may—if this stuff breaks—nobody'll play with us.

BROCK: So what's to do?

DEVERY: Might be best—under the circumstances—to forget the whole deal. Let him publish. If nothing happens, he looks silly.

BROCK: What do you mean if nothin' happens? I've spent two months down here and I don't know how much dough. I'm supposed to let all that ride?

DEVERY: If you want to play it safe.

BROCK: Well, I don't. I want what I'm after.

DEVERY: Going to be tough to get.

BROCK: Why? Because some little weasel with eyeglasses wants to get noisy? I'll cut his tongue out!

DEVERY: Listen, Harry!

BROCK: You're chicken!

DEVERY: You think so?

BROCK: I think so.

DEVERY: You're off the handle because it looks like I've been right and you've been wrong.

BROCK: Talk.

DEVERY: I've told you again and again. Get too big and you become a target. It's easier to steal diamonds than elephants.

BROCK: Shut up! I'll handle this.

DEVERY: All right.

BROCK: You brought this guy around in the first place. Remember that. (DEVERY *sighs*.) You're about as much help to me as a boil on the—

(EDDIE *comes back with* PAUL, *who immediately senses the trap.* BROCK *crosses to him and speaks with quiet menace.*)

BROCK: I think you got somethin' by mistake that belongs to me.

PAUL: That so?

BROCK: How about it?

(*There is no answer.* BROCK *signals* EDDIE, *who grabs* PAUL'S *arms.* BROCK *frisks him.*)

BROCK: Sit down.

(PAUL *sits beside* BILLIE.)

PAUL: Hello.

BILLIE: How've you been?

PAUL: Fine, and you?

BILLIE: Fine.

BROCK (*to* DEVERY): Get the stuff out of his room.

(DEVERY *starts out.*)

PAUL: Not there, Ed.

(DEVERY *stops.*)

BROCK: Where, then? (PAUL *looks at him and smiles.*) All right, if you want to play it rough. I know how to do that.

(BROCK *walks to the service wing and bolts the door. Then* EDDIE *moves to the front door and does the same.* BROCK'S *determination and purpose strike a kind of terror in the room. He moves back to the sofa.*)

BROCK: Now you listen, you two heels. I mean business. I got too much at stake down here. You got somethin' that belongs to me. And if you wanna get out of here alive—you're gonna give it back. I'm no blowhard. (*To* BILLIE.) Tell him.

BILLIE: He's no blowhard. He's had people killed before. Like once, about six years ago, there was a strike at one of his—

BROCK: Shut up! You ain't gonna be tellin' nobody nothin' pretty soon.

BILLIE (*derisively*): Double negative. (*To* PAUL.) Right?

PAUL: Right.

BROCK: You don't seem to be gettin' the idea. You never been in trouble like you're gonna be if you don't do what I'm tellin' you.

DEVERY: Wait a minute, Harry. There's another way to handle this. (*To* PAUL.) I really think you've pulled a boner, Paul. My advice to you is to lay off.

PAUL: And my advice to you is to stop sticking your noses into my business.

BILLIE: Yuh!

BROCK: Look who's talkin' about stickin' noses. You're the Goddamndest buttinski I ever run into!

PAUL: I think I told you once before, Harry, that's my job.

BROCK: What? Gettin' in my way?

PAUL: Not exactly.

BROCK: What then? I'd like to know. No kiddin'.

PAUL: To find out what goes on and get it to the people.

BROCK: The people?

PAUL: The people.

BROCK: Never heard of them.

BILLIE: You will, Harry, some day. They're getting to be more well-known all the time. (EDDIE *brings* BROCK *a drink.*)

DEVERY: What if I told you this whole operation is strictly according to law?

PAUL: Then I'd say the law needs revision.

BROCK: Who are you? The government?

PAUL: Of course.

BROCK: Since when?

BILLIE: Since—uh—1779! (*To* PAUL.) Right?

BROCK: What?

PAUL: Of course I'm the government. What do you think the government is, Harry? A man, a monster, a machine? It's you and me and a few million more. We've got to learn to look after each other.

BROCK: Thanks, I can look after myself.

BILLIE (*to* PAUL): He doesn't get it. I think it's because you still talk too fancy. (*To* BROCK.) Look, Harry, the idea is that you can only get away with your kind of shenanigans if nobody cares about it.

BROCK: I know what I'm doin'. I got my rights the same as anybody else.

BILLIE: More! You keep buying more and more rights for yourself.

BROCK: You got nothin' to say to me.

(*The door buzzer.* EDDIE *goes to the door, unlocks and opens it, and* SENATOR HEDGES *comes in. Then he locks it again.*)

HEDGES: Good evening, Eddie! (*Gay.*) Well, this is a late little party, isn't it?

BROCK: Shut up!

HEDGES: What?

BROCK: Don't be so happy!

HEDGES: What's the trouble?

DEVERY: Well, Verrall here has—uh—stumbled on a whole pocketful of information. I don't know what he thinks it means.

PAUL: I'll tell you. Just that the connection between Harry's combine and the Senator's amendment is more than coincidence.

HEDGES: Now, just a moment, son. I've got nothing against you young radicals—used to be one myself—but you simply won't be practical. Now, what we're doing is common practice. Done every day. I don't know why you single us out to make a fuss about.

BROCK: Yeah, why?

PAUL: It's done every day, sir, right. I have no doubt that an undiscovered murder is committed every day. What does that prove? All this under-cover pressure—this bribery—and corruption—this government between friends—sure it goes on all the time and it's tough to crack. Ask me. I've tried for years. You need more than the knowing about it. You've got to have the facts and the figures and, most important—the names.

BILLIE: And he's got 'em.

HEDGES (*angry*): You be careful, young man, when you use the word bribery in my presence.

BILLIE: Eighty thousand dollars you got. What word would you like him to use?

(HEDGES *pales and looks helplessly over to* BROCK.)

HEDGES: Harry, I honestly feel—

BROCK: What the hell do I care what you feel? I feel, too.

HEDGES: I can't take any smearing now. It's a bad time.

BROCK: Knock off. (*To* PAUL.) All right, now we've all had our little beat around the bush, let's get down to it. What can we work out?

PAUL: You just heard your lawyer say it was all according to law.

BROCK: Yeah.

PAUL: If that's the case, what's bothering you?

BROCK: I don't like a lot of noise, that's all.

PAUL: I'll be very quiet.

DEVERY: It just starts a lot of snooping, you know that. Gets to be uncomfortable.

BILLIE: Maybe if it gets to be uncomfortable enough, you'll cut it out.

(HEDGES *sits down, miserable.*)

BROCK: What'll you take, Paul?

PAUL: I'll take a drink, please, if I may.

BROCK: Don't be fancy with me. I never met a guy yet who didn't have his price.

PAUL (*pouring drink*): I have.

BROCK (*to* PAUL): I'm talkin' about big numbers.

BILLIE: You and your big numbers. If you don't watch out you'll be wearing one across your chest.

BROCK: I'll get to you later. (*To* PAUL.) Make up your mind. There's just two ways we can do business. One—you play ball—make it worth your while. Two—you better start watchin' your step. There'll be no place you can walk—no place you can live, if you monkey-wrench me! What do you say?

PAUL: I'd like to think it over!

BROCK: All right. You got two minutes.

(PAUL *sits down and thinks. He looks at* BILLIE. *He smiles. She smiles. He looks at* DEVERY. *She looks at* HEDGES. *They both look at* BROCK. *Suddenly,* PAUL *rises.*)

PAUL: Come on, Billie.

(BILLIE *rises.* PAUL *is moving to the door.* EDDIE *seems about to intercept him.* BROCK *is moving toward him.*)

DEVERY: Wait a minute, Harry!

HEDGES: Now, let's not lose our tempers.

(BROCK, *in a sudden inhuman burst, swings* PAUL *around, grabs him by the throat, and begins to choke him.* PAUL *goes to his knees.* BROCK *hangs on.*)

DEVERY (*in a panic*): Stop it!

BILLIE: Harry!

HEDGES: Oh, my God!

(HEDGES, DEVERY, *and* EDDIE *are desperately attempting to prevent murder.* BILLIE *rushes to the phone and screams.*)

BILLIE: Operator! *Operator!!!*

(*A signal from* DEVERY, *and* EDDIE *goes to* BILLIE, *removes the phone from her hands, and seats her. The combined forces of* DEVERY *and* HEDGES *now tear* BROCK *loose. They throw him on the sofa, where he sits, spent, and subdued.* BILLIE *is helping* PAUL, *who sits on the stairs, groggy.*)

DEVERY (*to* BROCK): You God-damned fool! Where the hell do you think you are? Can't you see all this muscle stuff is a thing of the past? You cut it out, or you'll be a thing of the past, too.

BROCK: I got mad.

PAUL (*coming down to* BROCK): Who are *you* to get mad? You big baboon! You ought to be grateful you're allowed to walk around free.

BROCK (*in a warning tone*): You don't know me good enough for that kind of talk.

PAUL: I know you. I've seen your kind down here for years—with red hair and white hair and no hair—but you're always the same—you're usually right here in this room. What the hell do you guys want, anyway? You've *got* damn near all the oil and the lumber and the steel and coal and aluminum—what do you want now—all the people? All the laws?

BROCK (*rising*): Don't blow your top. I'm still ready to do business. How's a hundred grand?

PAUL: A hundred grand is beautiful—but I can't do it.

BROCK: Why not?

(*A pause.*)

PAUL: My wife wouldn't like it.

BILLIE (*softly*): She certainly wouldn't.

BROCK: All right, then, what's your idea?

PAUL: To try and stop you from buying and selling legislation as though it were junk.

BILLIE: "This country with its institutions belongs to the people who inhibit it."

PAUL: "Inhabit."

BILLIE: "Inhabit."

BROCK: What the hell are you two battin' about? I don't see what I'm doin' so wrong. This is America, ain't it? Where's all this free enterprise they're always talkin' about?

DEVERY (*toasting*): To free enterprise.

BROCK: You're just sore because I made good and you ain't. Everybody had the same chance as me—all them kids I used to know—so where are they now?

BILLIE: No place. Because you beat them out, like you said. You always want to hold everybody down so you can get it all for yourself. That's why there's people like my father—and like me. He couldn't give me what he wanted—so I wind up with an empty head and with you.

BROCK: I always did what I want and I'm always gonna.

BILLIE: Try it.

BROCK: Who's gonna stop me?

BILLIE: Us two.

BROCK: Youse two? Don't make me split a gut. Be some fine country where a hundred-and-a-quarter-a-week hick and a broad that ain't been off her end for ten years can stop *me*. (*He turns and crosses to* DEVERY, *in a fury*.) What the hell are you standin' around like a deaf-and-dumby? What do I pay you for? Go on, say somethin'!

DEVERY: All right. I'll say something.

BROCK: Well?

DEVERY: They're right.

BROCK: You think they can stop me? Stop a Senator? What the hell kind of a world is it if your money's no good? How can they lick me? *I* got all the money.

DEVERY: The Republicans had all the money, too. Remember?

(EDDIE *puts another drink into* BROCK'S *hand*.)

BROCK (*to* EDDIE): What the hell do *you* want?

EDDIE: Rye ginger ale.

BROCK: Who asked you? Knock off!

(EDDIE *retreats*.)

PAUL: Maybe another time, Harry, not now. And if you're going to try again—do it fast. It gets harder all the time—people get wiser—they hear more—they read more—they talk more. When enough of them know enough—that'll be the end of you.

BROCK: Don't worry about me.

PAUL: I do, though. I worry like hell. I stay up nights. When you live in Washington, it's enough to break your heart. You see a perfect piece of machinery—the democratic structure—and somebody's always tampering with it and trying to make it hit the jackpot.

DEVERY (*toasting*): To the jackpot.

BROCK: I'm no gambler. I'm a business man.

PAUL: You certainly are, but you're in the wrong business now.

BILLIE: When you steal from the government, you're stealing from yourself, you dumb ox.

PAUL: Sure, you nearsighted empire-builders have managed to *buy* little pieces of it once in a while—but you can't have it all—if you do, it won't be this country any more.

BROCK (*to* DEVERY, *softly*): Of all the guys in this town—why the hell did you have to pick *him* out? (*To* PAUL.) Do what you want. I'm goin' ahead.

BILLIE: Wait a minute! I'll tell you where you're going.

BROCK: You?!

BILLIE: Sure. In this whole thing—I guess you forgot about me—about how I'm a partner? Ed once told me—a hundred and twenty-six different yards I own.

DEVERY: Control.

BILLIE (*to* DEVERY): Same thing. (*To* BROCK.) So here's how it's going to be. I don't want them. I don't want anything of yours—or to do with you. So I'm going to sign them all back.

BROCK: All right!

BILLIE: Only not all at once—just one at a time—*one a year!* (BROCK *is stunned.*) Only you've got to behave yourself—because if you don't, I'm going to let go on everything. For what you've done— even since I've known you only—I bet you could be put in jail for about nine hundred years. You'd be a pretty old man when you got out.

BROCK (*to* DEVERY): What's goin' on around here?

DEVERY: A revolution.

BROCK: You got me into this—*get me out!*

DEVERY: Somehow, I don't feel as clever as I used to.

BILLIE: Come on, Paul. (*To* BROCK.) I'll send for my things.

BROCK: You little crumb—you'll be sorry for this day—wait and see. Go on—go with him—you ain't got a chance. If I ever seen anybody outsmart themselves, it's you.

BILLIE (*starts to go*): Goodbye, all.

BROCK (*to* PAUL): And you!

PAUL: Me?

BROCK: Yeah—you're fired!

PAUL: I'm sorry, Harry. I've enjoyed working for you very much indeed.

(BILLIE *is at the door.*)

BILLIE (*to* EDDIE): Open up!

EDDIE: All right, Harry?

BILLIE (*to* EDDIE, *in imitation of* BROCK): Do what I'm tellin' you!

(EDDIE *opens the door quickly.* BILLIE *and* PAUL *go out, smiling.* DEVERY *pours himself a drink.*)

BROCK (*trying hard to laugh off his disaster*): How do you like that? He coulda had a hundred grand—and she coulda had me. So they both wind up with nothin'. (*A pause.*) Dumb chump.

HEDGES: Yes.

BROCK: Crazy broad.

HEDGES: Quite right.

DEVERY (*toasting, his glass held high*): To all the dumb chumps and all the crazy broads, past, present, and future—who thirst for knowledge —and search for truth—who fight for justice—and civilize each other—and make it so tough for sons-of-bitches like you— (*To* HEDGES.) —and you— (*To* BROCK.) —and me. (*He drinks.*)

CURTAIN

Mister Roberts

THOMAS HEGGEN
and
JOSHUA LOGAN

Why our respondents liked

 MISTER ROBERTS

"A fine depiction of Navy life with hilarious humor."
GEORGE OPPENHEIMER

*"A special look at our attitudes about war,
laughter and motivation."*
DORE SCHARY

"A first rate play."
HOWARD TEICHMANN

Mister Roberts, originally a novel by Thomas Heggen, was brought to the stage through the joint efforts of the author, director Joshua Logan (who coauthored the play), and producer Leland Hayward—who steered it to Broadway success. Heggen, who had served as a lieutenant in the Navy and in active combat in the Pacific during World War II, drew from his own experiences to write the book *Mister Roberts,* which was published when he was twenty-six years old. Joshua Logan read Heggen's book while vacationing in Cuba and became very excited by the theatrical potential he saw in it. His own military service had been in Air Forces Combat Intelligence overseas, and together with Heggen they worked on the dialogue and structure for the play. Word of mouth based on tryouts of *Mister Roberts* was very enthusiastic, and the Broadway box office had a huge advance sale before opening night. Henry Fonda had canceled his plans to film a movie in order to appear on Broadway in the role of Lieutenant Roberts. The London company's lead was Tyrone Power, with Jackie Cooper as Pulver; the national company's lead was John Forsythe. *Mister Roberts* was the recipient of the 1948 Tony Award; the award was also given to Henry Fonda and producer Leland Hayward that year.

Mister Roberts was presented by Leland Hayward on February 18, 1948, at the Alvin Theatre, New York City. The cast was as follows:

Chief Johnson	Rusty Lane
Lieutenant (JG) Roberts	Henry Fonda
Doc	Robert Keith
Dowdy	Joe Marr
The Captain	William Harrigan
Insigna	Harvey Lembeck
Mannion	Ralph Meeker
Lindstrom	Karl Lukas
Stefanowski	Steven Hill
Wiley	Robert Baines
Schlemmer	Lee Krieger
Reber	John Campbell
Ensign Pulver	David Wayne
Dolan	Casey Walters
Gerhart	Fred Barton
Payne	James Sherwood
Lieutenant Ann Girard	Jocelyn Brando
Shore Patrolman	John Jordan
Military Policeman	Marshall Jamison
Shore Patrol Officer	Murray Hamilton
Seamen, Firemen and Others:	Tiger Andrews, Joe Bernard, Ellis Eringer, Mikel Kane, Bob Keith, Jr., Walter Mullen, John (Red) Kullers, Jack Pierce, Len Smith, Jr., Sanders (Sandy) Turner

Directed by Joshua Logan
Settings and Lighting by Jo Mielziner

SCENE

*Aboard the U.S. Navy Cargo Ship, AK 601, operating
in the back areas of the Pacific.*

TIME

*A few weeks before V-E Day until a few weeks
before V-J Day.*

NOTE: In the U. S. Navy, all officers below the rank
of Commander are addressed as "Mister."

ACT ONE

SCENE I

The curtain rises on the main set, which is the amidships section of a navy cargo ship. The section of the ship shown is the house, and the deck immediately forward of the house. Dominating center stage is a covered hatch. The house extends on an angle to the audience from downstage left to upstage right. At each side is a passageway leading to the after part of the ship. Over the passageways on each side are twenty-millimeter gun tubs; ladders lead up to each tub. In each passageway and hardly visible to the audience is a steep ladder leading up to a bridge. Downstage right is a double bitt. At the left end of the hatch cover is an opening. This is the entrance to the companionway which leads to the crew's compartment below. The lower parts of two kingposts are shown the house. A life raft is also visible. A solid metal rail runs from stage right and disappears behind the house. Upstage center is the door to the Captain's cabin. The pilothouse with its many portholes is indicated on the bridge above. On the flying bridge are the usual nautical furnishings: a searchlight and two ventilators. Over the door is a loudspeaker. There is a porthole to the left of the door and two portholes to the right. These last two look into the Captain's cabin.

The only object which differentiates this ship from any other navy cargo ship is a small scrawny palm tree, potted in a five-gallon can, standing to the right of the Captain's cabin door. On the container, painted in large white letters, is the legend: "PROP.T OF CAPTAIN, KEEP AWAY."

At rise, the lighting indicates that it is shortly after dawn. The stage is empty and there is no indication of life other than the sound of snoring from below.

CHIEF JOHNSON, *a bulging man about forty, enters through passageway upstage left. He wears dungaree shirt and pants and a chief petty officer's cap. He is obviously chewing tobacco, and he starts down the hatchway, notices the palm tree, crosses to the Captain's door cautiously, peering into the porthole to see that he is not being watched, then deliberately spits into the palm tree container. He wipes his mouth smugly and shuffles over to the hatch. There he stops, takes out his watch and looks at it, then disappears down the hatchway. A shrill whistle is heard.*

JOHNSON (*offstage—in a loud singsong voice which is obviously just carrying out a ritual*): Reveille . . . Hit the deck . . . Greet the new day . . . (*The whistle is heard again.*) Reveille . . .

INSIGNA (*offstage*): Okay, Chief, you done your duty—now get your big fat can out of here!

(JOHNSON *reappears at the head of hatchway calling back.*)

JOHNSON: Just thought you'd like to know about reveille. And you're going to miss chow again.

STEFANOWSKI (*offstage*): Thanks, Chief. Now go back to bed and stop bothering us.

(*His duty done,* JOHNSON, *still chewing, shuffles across the stage and disappears. There is a brief moment of silence, then the snoring is resumed below.*)

(*After a moment,* ROBERTS *enters from the passageway at right. He wears khaki shirt and trousers and an officer's cap. On each side of his collar he wears the silver bar indicating the rank of Lieutenant [junior grade]. He carries a rumpled piece of writing paper in his left hand, on which there is a great deal of writing and large black marks indicating that much has been scratched out. He walks slowly to the bitt, concentrating, then stands a moment looking out right. He suddenly gets an idea and goes to hatch cover, sitting and writing on the paper.* DOC *enters from the left passageway.* DOC *is between thirty-five and forty and he wears khakis and an officer's fore-and-aft cap; he wears medical insignia and the bars of Lieutenant [senior grade] on his collar. A stethoscope sticks out of his hip pocket. He is wiping the sweat off his neck with his handkerchief as he crosses above hatch cover. He stops as he sees* ROBERTS.)

DOC: That you, Doug?

ROBERTS (*wearily, looking up*): Hello, Doc. What are you doing up?

DOC: I heard you were working cargo today so I thought I'd get ready. On days when there's any work to be done I can always count on a big turnout at sick call.

ROBERTS (*smiles*): Oh, yeah.

DOC: I attract some very rare diseases on cargo days. That day they knew you were going to load five ships I was greeted by six more cases of beriberi—double beriberi this time. So help me, I'm going down to the ship's library and throw that old copy of *Moby Dick* overboard!

(*He sits on hatch cover.*)

ROBERTS: What are you giving them these days for double beriberi?

DOC: Aspirin—what else? (*He looks at* ROBERTS.) Is there something wrong, Doug?

ROBERTS: (*preoccupied*): No.

DOC (*lying back on the hatch*): We missed you when you went on watch last night. I gave young Ensign Pulver another drink of alcohol and orange juice and it inspired him to relate further sexual feats of his. Some of them bordered on the supernatural!

ROBERTS: I don't doubt it. Did he tell you how he conquered a forty-five-year-old virgin by the simple tactic of being the first man in her life to ask her a direct question?

DOC: No. Last night he was more concerned with quantity. It seems that on a certain cold and wintry night in November, 1939—a night when most of us mortal men would have settled for a cup of cocoa—he rendered pregnant three girls in Washington, D.C., caught the 11:45 train, and an hour later performed the same service for a young lady in Baltimore.

ROBERTS (*laughing*): Oh, my God!

DOC: I'm not sure what to do with young Pulver. I'm thinking of reporting his record to the American Medical Association.

ROBERTS: Why don't you just get him a job as a fountain in Radio City?

DOC: Don't be too hard on him, Doug. He thinks you are approximately God. . . . Say, there *is* something wrong, isn't there?

ROBERTS: I've been up all night, Doc.

DOC: What is it? What's the matter?

ROBERTS: I saw something last night when I was on watch that just about knocked me out.

DOC (*alarmed*): What happened?

ROBERTS (*with emotion*): I was up on the bridge. I was just standing there looking out to sea. I couldn't bear to look at that island any more. All of a sudden I noticed something. Little black specks crawling over the horizon. I looked through the glasses and it was a formation of our ships that stretched for miles! Carriers and battleships and cans—a whole task force, Doc!

DOC: Why didn't you break me out? I've never seen a battleship!

ROBERTS: They came on and they passed within half a mile of that reef! Carriers so big they blacked out half the sky! And battlewagons sliding along—dead quiet! I could see the men on the bridges. And this is what knocked me out, Doc. Somehow—I thought I was on those bridges—I thought I was riding west across the Pacific. I watched them until they were out of sight, Doc—and I was right there on those bridges all the time.

DOC: I know how that must have hurt, Doug.

ROBERTS: And then I looked down from our bridge and saw our Captain's palm tree! (*Points at palm tree, then bitterly.*) Our trophy for superior achievement! The Admiral John J. Finchley award for delivering more toothpaste and toilet paper than any other Navy cargo ship in the safe area of the Pacific. (*Taking letter from pocket and handing it to* DOC.) Read this, Doc—see how it sounds.

DOC: What is it?

ROBERTS: My application for transfer. I've been rewriting it ever since I got off watch last night.

DOC: O God, not another one!

ROBERTS: This one's different—I'm trying something new, Doc—a stronger wording. Read it carefully.

(DOC *looks for a moment skeptically, then noticing the intensity in his face decides to read the letter.*)

DOC (*reading*): "From: Lieutenant (jg) Douglas Roberts
To: Bureau of Naval Personnel

16 April 1945
Subject: Change of Duty, Request for . . ."

(*He looks up.*)

Boy, this is sheer poetry.

ROBERTS (*rises nervously*): Go on, Doc.

DOC (*reads on*): "For two years and four months I have served aboard
this vessel as Cargo Officer. I feel that my continued service aboard
can only reduce my own usefulness to the Navy and increase disharmony aboard this ship."

(*He looks at* ROBERTS *and rises.* ROBERTS *looks back defiantly.*)

ROBERTS: How about *that!*

DOC (*whistles softly, then continues*): "It is therefore urgently re-
quested that I be ordered to combat duty, preferably aboard a destroyer."

ROBERTS (*tensely, going to* DOC): What do you say, Doc? I've got a
chance, haven't I?

DOC: Listen, Doug, you've been sending in a letter every week for God
knows how long . . .

ROBERTS: Not like this . . .

DOC: . . . and every week the Captain has screamed like a stuck pig,
*dis*approved your letters and forwarded them that way. . . .

ROBERTS: That's just my point, Doc. He *does* forward them. They go
through the chain of command all the way up to the Bureau . . . Just
because the Captain doesn't . . .

DOC: Doug, the Captain of a Navy ship is the most absolute monarch
left in this world!

ROBERTS: I know that.

DOC: If he endorsed your letter "approved" you'd get your orders in a
minute . . .

ROBERTS: Naturally, but I . . .

(*Turns away from* DOC.)

DOC: . . . but "disapproved," you haven't got a prayer. You're stuck on
this old bucket, Doug. Face it!

ROBERTS (*turns quickly back*): Well, grant me this much, Doc. That one day I'll find the perfect wording and one human guy way up on top will read those words and say, "Here's a poor son-of-a-bitch screaming for help. Let's put him on a fighting ship!"

DOC (*quietly*): Sure . . .

ROBERTS (*after a moment*): I'm not kidding myself, am I, Doc? I've got a chance, haven't I?

DOC: Yes, Doug, you've got a chance. It's about the same chance as putting your letter in a bottle and dropping it in the ocean . . .

ROBERTS (*snatching letter from* DOC): But it's still a chance, goddammit! It's still a chance!

(ROBERTS *stands looking out to sea.* DOC *watches him for a moment, then speaks gently.*)

DOC: I wish you hadn't seen that task force, Doug. (*Pauses.*) Well, I've got to go down to my hypochondriacs.

(*He goes off slowly through passageway.*)

(ROBERTS *is still staring out as* DOWDY *enters from the hatchway. He is a hard-bitten man between thirty-five and forty and is wearing dungarees and no hat. He stands by hatchway with a cup of coffee in his hand.*)

DOWDY: Morning, Mister Roberts.

ROBERTS: Good morning, Dowdy.

DOWDY: Jeez, it's even hotter up here than down in that mess hall! (*He looks off.*) Look at that cruddy island . . . smell it! It's so hot it *already* smells like a hog pen. Think we'll get out of here today, sir?

(ROBERTS *takes* DOWDY'S *cup as he speaks and drinks from it, then hands it back.*)

ROBERTS: I don't know, Dowdy. There's one LCT coming alongside for supplies . . . (*Goes to hatchway, looks down.*) Are they getting up yet?

DOWDY (*also looking down hatch*): Yeah, they're starting to stumble around down there—the poor punch-drunk bastards. Mister Roberts, when are you going to the Captain again and ask him to give this crew a liberty? These guys ain't been off the ship for over a year except on duty.

ROBERTS: Dowdy, the last time I asked him was last night.

DOWDY: What'd he say?

ROBERTS: He said "No."

DOWDY: We gotta get these guys ashore! They're going Asiatic! (*Pause.*) Will you see him anyhow, Mister Roberts—just once more?

ROBERTS: You know I will, Dowdy. (*Hands* DOWDY *the letter.*) In the meantime, have Dolan type that up for me. (*He starts off right.*)

DOWDY (*descending hatchway*): Oh, your letter. Yes, sir!

ROBERTS (*calling over his shoulder*): Then will you bring a couple of men back aft? (*He exits through passageway.*)

DOWDY: Okay, Mister Roberts. (*He disappears down hatchway. He is heard below.*) All right, you guys in there. Finish your coffee and get up on deck. Stefanowski, Insigna, off your tails . . .

(*After a moment the center door opens and the* CAPTAIN *appears wearing pajamas and bathrobe and his officer's cap. He is carrying water in an engine-room oil can. He waters the palm tree carefully, looks at it for a moment tenderly and goes back into his cabin. After a moment,* DOWDY'S *voice is heard from the companionway and he appears followed by members of the crew.*)

DOWDY: All right, let's go! Bring me those glasses, Schlemmer. (SCHLEMMER *exits by ladder to the bridge. Other men appear from the hatchway. They are* INSIGNA, STEFANOWSKI, MANNION, WILEY, REBER *and* LINDSTROM—*all yawning, buttoning pants, tucking in shirts and, in general, being comatose. The men do not appear to like one another very much at this hour—least of all* INSIGNA *and* MANNION.) All right, I got a little recreation for you guys. Stefanowski, you take these guys and get this little rust patch here. (*He hands* STEFANOWSKI *an armful of scrapers and wire brushes, indicating a spot on the deck.* STEFANOWSKI *looks at instruments dully, then distributes them to the men standing near him.* SCHLEMMER *returns from the bridge, carrying four pairs of binoculars and a spy glass. He drops them next to* INSIGNA *who is sitting on the hatch.*) Insigna, I got a real special job for you. You stay right here and clean these glasses.

INSIGNA: Ah, let me work up forward, Dowdy. I don't want to be around this crud, Mannion.

MANNION: Yeah, Dowdy. Take Insigna with you!

DOWDY: Shut up, I'm tired of you two bellyaching! (*Nodding to others to follow him.*) All right, let's go, Reber . . . Schlemmer.

(DOWDY, REBER *and* SCHLEMMER *leave through passageway right. The others sit in sodden silence.* LINDSTROM *wanders slowly over to* INSIGNA. *He picks up spy glass and examines it. He holds the large end toward him and looks into it.*)

LINDSTROM: Hey, look! I can see myself!

STEFANOWSKI: Terrifying, ain't it?

(INSIGNA *takes the spy glass from him and starts polishing it.* LINDSTROM *removes his shoe and feels inside it, then puts it back on.*)

MANNION (*after a pause*): Hey, what time is it in San Francisco?

INSIGNA (*scornfully*): When?

MANNION: Anybody ask you? (*Turns to* WILEY.) What time would it be there?

WILEY: I don't know. I guess about midnight last night.

STEFANOWSKI (*studying scraper in his hand*): I wonder if you could get sent back to the States if you cut off a finger.

(*Nobody answers.*)

INSIGNA (*looking offstage*): Hey, they got a new building on that island. Fancy—two stories . . .

(*Nobody shows any curiosity.*)

MANNION: You know, I had a girl in San Francisco wore flowers in her hair—instead of hats. Never wore a hat . . .

(*Another sodden pause.*)

INSIGNA (*holding spy glass*): Hey, Stefanowski! Which end of this you look through?

STEFANOWSKI: It's optional, Sam. Depends on what size eyeball you've got.

(INSIGNA *idly looks through spy glass at something out right. Another pause.*)

INSIGNA: Hey, the Japs must've took over this island—there's a red and white flag on that new building.

MANNION: Japs! We never been within five thousand miles of a Jap! Japs! You hear that, Wiley?

WILEY: Yeah, smart, ain't he?

MANNION: Japs! That's a hospital flag!

INSIGNA: Anybody ask you guys? (*Nudging* LINDSTROM *and pointing to the other group.*) The goldbrick twins! (*Looks through spy glass.*) Hey, they got a fancy hospital . . . big windows and . . . (*Suddenly rises, gasping at what he sees.*)

STEFANOWSKI: What's the matter, Sam?

INSIGNA: Oh, my God! She's bare-assed!

STEFANOWSKI: *She!*

INSIGNA: Taking a shower . . . in that bathroom . . . that nurse . . . upstairs window!

(*Instantly the others rush to hatch cover, grab binoculars and stand looking out right.*)

WILEY: She's a blonde—see!

LINDSTROM: I never seen such a beautiful girl!

MANNION: She's sure taking a long time in that shower!

WILEY: Yeah, honey, come on over here by the window!

INSIGNA: Don't you do it, honey! You take your time!

STEFANOWSKI: There's another one over by the washbasin—taking a shampoo.

INSIGNA (*indignantly*): Yeah. But why the hell don't she take her bathrobe off! That's a stupid goddamn way to take a shampoo!

(*For a moment the men watch in silent vigilance.*)

STEFANOWSKI: Ah-hah!

WILEY: She's coming out of the shower!

MANNION: She's coming over to the window! (*A pause.*) Kee-ri-mi-ny!

(*For a moment the men stand transfixed, their faces radiant. They emit rapturous sighs. That is all.*)

LINDSTROM: Aw, she's turning around the other way!

MANNION: What's that red mark she's got . . . there?

INSIGNA (*authoritatively*): That's a birthmark!

MANNION (*scornfully*): Birthmark!

INSIGNA: What do you think it is, wise guy?

MANNION: Why, that's paint! She's sat in some red paint!

INSIGNA: Sat in some red paint! I'm tellin' you, that's a birthmark!

MANNION: Did you ever see a birthmark down there?

INSIGNA (*lowers his spy glass, turns to* MANNION): Why, you stupid jerk! I had an uncle once had a birthmark right down . . .

WILEY: Aww!

(INSIGNA *and* MANNION *return quickly to their glasses.*)

STEFANOWSKI (*groaning*): She's put her bathrobe on!

MANNION: Hey, she's got the same color bathrobe as that stupid bag taking the shampoo!

(*The four men notice something and exclaim in unison.*)

INSIGNA: Bag, hell! Look at her now with her head out of the water . . .

LINDSTROM: She's just as beautiful as the other one . . .

STEFANOWSKI: They look exactly alike with those bathrobes on. Maybe they're twins.

MANNION: That's my girl on the right—the one with the red birthmark.

INSIGNA: You stupid crud, the one with the birthmark's on the left!

MANNION: The hell she is . . .

(MANNION *and* INSIGNA *again lower their glasses.*)

INSIGNA: The hell she ain't . . .

WILEY: Awwww!

(MANNION *and* INSIGNA *quickly drop their argument and look.*)

STEFANOWSKI: They're both leaving the bathroom together. . . .

(*The men are dejected again.*)

LINDSTROM: Hey, there ain't no one in there now!

STEFANOWSKI (*lowering his glasses*): Did you figure that out all by yourself?

(*He looks through his glasses again.*)

MANNION (*after a pause*): Come on, girls, let's go!

WILEY: Yeah. Who's next to take a nice zippy shower?

INSIGNA (*after a pause*): They must think we got nothing better to do than stand here!

LINDSTROM: These glasses are getting heavy!

STEFANOWSKI: Yeah. We're wasting manpower. Let's take turns, okay? (*The others agree.*) All right, Mannion, you take it first.

(MANNION *nods, crosses and sits on bitt, keeping watch with his binoculars. The others pick up their scrapers and wire brushes.*)

INSIGNA (*watching* MANNION): I don't trust that crud.

LINDSTROM: Gee, I wish we was allowed to get over to that island. We could get a closer look.

STEFANOWSKI: No, Lindstrom. They'd see us and pull the shades down.

LINDSTROM: No, they wouldn't. We could cover ourselves with leaves and make out like we was bushes—and sneak up on them—like them Japs we seen in that movie . . . (*He starts to sneak around front of hatch, holding his wire brush before his face.* STEFANOWSKI *hears a noise from the* CAPTAIN'S *cabin and quickly warns the others.*)

STEFANOWSKI: Flash Red! (*The men immediately begin working in earnest as the* CAPTAIN, *now in khaki, enters. He stands for a moment, looking at them, and then wanders over to the group scraping the rust patch to inspect their work. Then, satisfied that they are actually working, he starts toward passageway. He sees* MANNION, *sitting on the bitt, looking through his glasses and smiling. The* CAPTAIN *goes over and stands beside him, looking off in the same direction.* STEFANOWSKI *tries frantically to signal a warning to* MANNION *by beating out code with his scraper.* MANNION *suddenly sees the* CAPTAIN *and quickly lowers his glasses and pretends to clean them, alternately wiping the lenses and holding them up to his eyes to see that they are clean. The* CAPTAIN *watches him suspiciously for a moment, then he exits by the ladder to the bridge.* STEFANOWSKI *rises and looks up ladder to make certain the* CAPTAIN *has gone.*) Flash White!

(*He turns and looks at* MANNION.) Hey, Mannion. Anyone in there yet?

MANNION (*watching something happily through glasses*): No, not yet!

INSIGNA (*picks up spy glass and looks, and rises quickly*): Why, you dirty, miserable cheat!

(*Instantly all the men are at the glasses.*)

LINDSTROM: There's one in there again!

STEFANOWSKI: The hell with her—she's already got her clothes on!

INSIGNA: And there she goes! (*Slowly lowers his glass, turning to* MANNION *threateningly.*) Why, you lousy, cheating crud!

MANNION (*idly swinging his glasses*): That ain't all. I seen three!

STEFANOWSKI: You lowdown Peeping Tom!

LINDSTROM (*hurt*): Mannion, that's a real dirty trick.

INSIGNA: What's the big idea?

MANNION: Who wants to know?

INSIGNA: *I* want to know! And you're damn well going to tell me!

MANNION: You loud-mouthed little bastard! Why don't you make me?

INSIGNA: You're damn right I will. Right now! (*He swings on* MANNION *as* LINDSTROM *steps clumsily between them.*)

LINDSTROM: Hey, fellows! Fellows!

INSIGNA: No wonder you ain't got a friend on this ship . . . except this crud, Wiley. (*He jerks his head in direction of* WILEY *who stands behind him on hatch cover.* WILEY *takes him by shoulder and whirls him around.*)

WILEY: What'd you say?

STEFANOWSKI (*shoving* WILEY): You heard him!

(MANNION *jumps on hatch cover to protect* WILEY *from* STEFANOWSKI. INSIGNA *rushes at* MANNION *and for a moment they are all in a clinch.* LINDSTROM *plows up on the hatch and breaks them apart. The men have suddenly formed into two camps—*MANNION *and* WILEY *on one side,* INSIGNA *and* STEFANOWSKI *facing them.* LINDSTROM *is just an accessory, but stands prepared to intervene if necessary.*)

MANNION (*to* WILEY): Look at them two! Everybody on the ship hates their guts! The two moochingest, no-good loud-mouths on the ship!

(STEFANOWSKI *starts for* MANNION *but* INSIGNA *pulls him back and steps menacingly toward* MANNION.)

INSIGNA: Why, you slimy, lying son-of-a-bitch!

(*Suddenly* MANNION *hits* INSIGNA, *knocking him down. He jumps on* INSIGNA *who catches* MANNION *in the chest with his feet and hurls him back.* WILEY *and* STEFANOWSKI *start fighting with* LINDSTROM, *attempting to break them apart.* MANNION *rushes back at* INSIGNA. INSIGNA *sidesteps* MANNION'S *lunge and knocks him to the deck.* INSIGNA *falls on him. They wrestle to their feet and stand slugging. At this point* ROBERTS *and* DOWDY *run on from passageway.* ROBERTS *flings* INSIGNA *and* MANNION *apart.* DOWDY *separates the others.*)

ROBERTS: Break it up! Break it up, I tell you!

(INSIGNA *and* MANNION *rush at each other.* ROBERTS *and* DOWDY *stop them.*)

DOWDY: Goddamn you guys, break it up!

ROBERTS: All right! What's going on?

INSIGNA (*pointing at* MANNION): This son-of-a-bitch here . . .

ROBERTS: Did you hear me?

MANNION (*to* INSIGNA): Shut your mouth!

DOWDY: Shut up, both of you!

INSIGNA: Slimy son-of-a-bitch! (*Picks up scraper and lunges at* MANNION *again.* ROBERTS *throws him back.*)

ROBERTS: I said to cut it out! Did you hear me? (*Wheels on* MANNION.) That goes for you too! (*Includes entire group.*) I'm going to give it to the first one who opens his mouth! (*The men stand subdued, breathing hard from the fight.*) Now get to work! All of you! (*They begin to move sullenly off right.*) Mannion, you and the rest get to work beside number two! And, Insigna, take those glasses way up to the bow and work on them! Stefanowski, keep those two apart.

STEFANOWSKI: Yes, sir.

(*The men exit.* ROBERTS *and* DOWDY *look after them.*)

DOWDY (*tightly*): You seen that, Mister Roberts. Well, last night down in the compartment I stopped three of them fights—worse than that. They've got to have a liberty, Mister Roberts.

ROBERTS: They sure do. Dowdy, call a boat for me, will you? I'm going ashore.

DOWDY: What are you going to do?

ROBERTS: I just got a new angle.

DOWDY: Are you going over the Captain's head?

ROBERTS: No, I'm going around his end—I hope. Get the lead out, Dowdy. (*He exits left as* DOWDY *goes off right and the lights*

Fade Out

(*During the darkness, voices can be heard over the squawk box saying:*)

Now hear this . . . now hear this. Sweepers, man your brooms. Clean sweep-down fore and aft. Sweep-down all ladders and all passageways. Do *not* throw trash over the fantail.

Now, all men on report will see the master-at-arms for assignment to extra duty.

Now hear this . . . now hear this. Because in violation of the Captain's orders, a man has appeared on deck without a shirt on, there will be no movies again tonight—by order of the Captain.

SCENE II

The lights dim up revealing the stateroom of PULVER *and* ROBERTS. *Two lockers are shown, one marked "Ensign F. T. Pulver," the other marked "Lt. (jg) D. A. Roberts." There is a double bunk along the bulkhead right. A desk with its end against the bulkhead left has a chair at either side. There is a porthole in the bulkhead above it. Up center, right of* PUL-VER'S *locker is a washbasin over which is a shelf and a medicine chest. The door is up center.*

An officer is discovered with his head inside ROBERTS' *locker, throwing skivvy shirts over his shoulder as he searches for something.* DOLAN, *a young, garrulous, brash yeoman, second class, enters. He is carrying a file folder.*

DOLAN: Here's your letter, Mister Roberts. (*He goes to the desk, taking fountain pen from his pocket.*) I typed it up. Just sign your old John

Henry here and I'll take it in to the Captain . . . then hold your ears. (*No answer.*) Mister Roberts! (PULVER's *head appears from the locker.*) Oh, it's only you, Mister Pulver. What are you doing in Mister Roberts' locker?

PULVER (*hoarsely*): Dolan, look in there, will you? I know there's a shoe box in there, but I can't find it.

(DOLAN *looks in the locker.*)

DOLAN: There ain't no shoe box in there, Mister Pulver.

PULVER: They've stolen it! There's nothing they'll stop at now. They've broken right into the sanctity of a man's own locker. (*He sits in chair at desk.*)

DOLAN (*disinterested*): Ain't Mister Roberts back from the island yet?

PULVER: No.

DOLAN: Well, as soon as he gets back, will you ask him to sign this baby?

PULVER: What is it?

DOLAN: What is it! It's the best damn letter Mister Roberts writ yet. It's going to blow the Old Man right through the overhead. And them big shots at the Bureau are going to drop their drawers too. This letter is liable to get him transferred.

PULVER: Yeah, lemme see it.

DOLAN (*handing letter to* PULVER): Get a load of that last paragraph. Right here.

PULVER (*reading with apprehension*): ". . . increase disharmony aboard this ship . . ."

DOLAN (*interrupting gleefully*): Won't that frost the Old Man's knockers? I can't wait to jab this baby in the Old Man's face. Mr. Pulver, you know how he gets sick to his stomach when he gets extra mad at Mister Roberts—well, when I deliver this letter I'm going to take along a wastebasket! Let me know when Mister Roberts gets back.

(DOLAN *exits.* PULVER *continues reading the letter with great dismay. He hears* ROBERTS *and* DOC *talking in the passageway, offstage, and quickly goes to his bunk and hides the letter under a blanket. He goes to the locker and is replacing skivvy shirts as* ROBERTS *and* DOC *enter.*)

ROBERTS: . . . so after the fight I figured I had to do something and do it quick!

DOC: What did you do over on the island, Doug?

ROBERTS (*sitting in chair and searching through desk drawer*): Hey, Frank, has Dolan been in here yet with my letter?

PULVER (*innocently*): I don't know, Doug boy. I just came in here myself.

DOC: You don't know anybody on the island, do you, Doug?

ROBERTS: Yes. The Port Director—the guy who decides where to send this ship next. He confided to me that he used to drink a quart of whiskey every day of his life. So this morning when I broke up that fight it came to me that he might just possibly sell his soul for a quart of Scotch.

PULVER (*rises*): Doug, you didn't give that shoe box to the Port Director!

ROBERTS: I did. "Compliments of the Captain."

DOC: You've had a quart of Scotch in a shoe box?

ROBERTS: Johnny Walker! I was going to break it out the day I got off this ship—Resurrection Day!

PULVER: Oh, my God! It's really gone! (*He sinks to the bunk.*)

DOC: Well, did the Port Director say he'd send us to a Liberty Port?

ROBERTS: Hell, no. He took the Scotch and said, "Don't bother me, Roberts. I'm busy." The rummy!

PULVER: How could you do it!

DOC: Well, where there's a rummy, there's hope. Maybe when he gets working on that Scotch he'll mellow a little.

PULVER: You gave that bottle to a goddamn *man!*

ROBERTS: Man! Will you name me another sex within a thousand miles . . . (PULVER, *dejected, goes up to porthole.*) What the hell's eating you anyway, Frank?

(DOC *crosses to bunk. He sees two fancy pillows on bottom bunk, picks up one and tosses it to* ROBERTS. *He picks up the other.*)

DOC: Well, look here. Somebody seems to be expecting company!

ROBERTS: Good Lord!

DOC (*reads lettering on pillowcase*): "Toujours l'amour . . . Souvenir of San Diego . . . Oh, you kid!"

ROBERTS (*reading from his pillowcase*): "Tonight or never . . . Compliments of Allis-Chalmers, Farm Equipment . . . We plow deep while others sleep." (*He looks at* DOC, *then rises.*) Doc—that new hospital over there hasn't got nurses, has it?

DOC: Nurses! It didn't have yesterday!

PULVER (*turning from porthole*): It has today!

DOC: But how did you find out they were there?

PULVER (*trying to recall*): Now let me think . . . it just came to me all of a sudden. This morning it was so hot I was just lying on my bunk —thinking . . . There wasn't a breath of air. And then, all of a sudden, a funny thing happened. A little breeze came up and I took a deep breath and said myself, "Pulver boy, there's women on that island."

ROBERTS: Doc, a thing like this could make a bird dog self-conscious as hell.

PULVER (*warming up*): They just flew in last night. There's eighteen of them—all brunettes except for two beautiful blondes—twin sisters! I'm working on one of those. I asked her out to the ship for lunch and she said she was kind of tired. So then I got kind of desperate and turned on the old personality—and I said, "Ain't there anything in the world that'll make you come out to the ship with me?" And she said, "Yes, there is, one thing and one thing only—" (*Crosses to* ROBERTS, *looks at him accusingly.*) "A good stiff drink of Scotch!" (*He sinks into the chair.*)

ROBERTS (*after a pause*): I'm sorry, Frank. I'm really sorry. Your first assignment in a year. (*He pats* PULVER *on the shoulder.*)

PULVER: I figured I'd bring her in here . . . I fixed it up real cozy . . . (*Fondling pillow on desk.*) . . . and then I was going to throw a couple of fast slugs of Scotch into her and . . . but, hell, without the Scotch, she wouldn't . . . she just wouldn't, that's all.

ROBERTS (*after a pause*): Doc, let's make some Scotch!

DOC: Huh?

ROBERTS: As naval officers we're supposed to be resourceful. Frank here's got a great opportunity and I've let him down. Let's fix him up!

DOC: Right! (*He goes to desk.* ROBERTS *begins removing bottles from medicine chest.*) Frank, where's the rest of that alcohol we were drinking last night?

PULVER (*pulling a large vinegar bottle half filled with colorless liquid from the wastebasket and handing it to* DOC): Hell, that ain't even the right color.

DOC (*taking the bottle*): Quiet! (*Thinks deeply.*) Color . . . (*With sudden decision.*) Coca-Cola! Have you got any?

ROBERTS: I haven't seen a Coke in four months—no, by God, it's five months!

PULVER: Oh, what the hell! (*He rises, crosses to bunk, reaches under mattress of top bunk and produces a bottle of Coca-Cola. The others watch him.* DOC *snatches the bottle.* PULVER *says apologetically.*) I forgot I had it.

(DOC *opens the bottle and is about to pour the Coca-Cola into the vinegar bottle when he suddenly stops.*)

DOC: Oh—what shade would you like? Cutty Sark . . . Haig and Haig . . . Vat 69 . . .

PULVER (*interested*): I told her Johnny Walker.

DOC: Johnny Walker it is! (*He pours some of the Coca-Cola into the bottle.*)

ROBERTS (*looking at color of the mixture*): Johnny Walker Red Label!

DOC: Red Label!

PULVER: It may look like it—but it won't taste like it!

ROBERTS: Doc, what does Scotch taste like?

DOC: Well, it's a little like . . . uh . . . it tastes like . . .

ROBERTS: Do you know what it's always tasted a little like to me? Iodine.

DOC (*shrugs as if to say "Of course" and rises. He takes dropper from small bottle of iodine and flicks a drop in the bottle*): One drop of iodine—for taste. (*Shakes the bottle and pours some in glass.*)

PULVER: Lemme taste her, Doc!

DOC (*stops him with a gesture*): No. This calls for a medical opinion. (*Takes a ceremonial taste while the others wait for his verdict.*)

PULVER: How about it?

DOC: We're on the right track! (*Sets glass down. Rubs hands professionally.*) Now we need a little something extra—for age! What've you got there, Doug?

ROBERTS (*reading labels of bottles on desk*): Bromo-Seltzer . . . Wildroot Wave Set . . . Eno Fruit Salts . . . Kreml Hair Tonic . . .

DOC: Kreml! It has a coal-tar base! And it'll age the hell out of it! (*Pours a bit of Kreml into mixture. Shakes bottle solemnly.*) One drop Kreml for age. (*Sets bottle on desk, looks at wrist watch for a fraction of a second.*) That's it! (*Pours drink into glass.* PULVER *reaches for it.* ROBERTS *pushes his arm aside and tastes it.*)

ROBERTS: By God, it does taste a little like Scotch!

(PULVER *again reaches for glass.* DOC *pushes his arm aside and takes a drink.*)

DOC: By God, it does!

(PULVER *finally gets glass and takes a quick sip.*)

PULVER: It's delicious. That dumb little blonde won't know the difference.

DOC (*hands the bottle to* PULVER): Here you are, Frank. Doug and I have made the Scotch. The *nurse* is your department.

(PULVER *takes the bottle and hides it under the mattress, then replaces the pillows.*)

PULVER (*singing softly*): Won't know the difference . . . won't know the difference. (DOC *starts to drink from Coca-Cola bottle as* PULVER *comes over and snatches it from his hand.*) Thanks, Doc. (*Puts cap on the bottle and hides it under the mattress. Turns and faces the others.*) Thanks, Doug. Jeez, you guys are wonderful to me.

ROBERTS (*putting bottles back in medicine chest*): Don't mention it, Frank. I think you almost deserve it.

PULVER: You do—really? Or are you just giving me the old needle again? What do you really think of me, Doug—honestly?

ROBERTS (*turning slowly to* PULVER): Frank, I like you. No one can get around the fact that you're a hell of a likable guy.

PULVER (*beaming*): Yeah—yeah . . .

ROBERTS: *But* . . .

PULVER: But what?

ROBERTS: But I also think you are the most hapless . . . lazy . . . disorganized . . . and, in general, the most lecherous person I've ever known in my life.

PULVER: I am not.

ROBERTS: Not what?

PULVER: I'm not disorganized—for one thing.

ROBERTS: Have you ever in your life finished anything you started out to do? You sleep sixteen hours a day. You pretend you want me to improve your mind and you've never even finished a book I've given you to read!

PULVER: I finished *God's Little Acre,* Doug boy!

ROBERTS: I didn't give you that! (*To* DOC.) He's been reading *God's Little Acre* for over a year! (*Takes dog-eared book from* PULVER'S *bunk.*) He's underlined every erotic passage, and added exclamation points—and after a certain pornographic climax, he's inserted the words "well written." (*To* PULVER.) You're the Laundry and Morale Officer and I doubt if you've ever seen the Laundry.

PULVER: I was down there only last week.

ROBERTS: And you're scared of the Captain.

PULVER: I'm not scared of the Captain.

ROBERTS: Then why do you hide in the passageway every time you see him coming? I doubt if he even knows you're on board. You're scared of him.

PULVER: I am not. I'm scared of myself—I'm scared of what I might do to him.

ROBERTS (*laughing*): What you might do to him! Doc, he lies in his sack all day long and bores me silly with great moronic plots against the Captain and he's never carried out one.

PULVER: I haven't, huh.

ROBERTS: No, Frank, you haven't. What happened to your idea of plugging up the line of the Captain's sanitary system? "I'll make it overflow," you said. "I'll make a backwash that'll lift him off the throne and knock him clean across the room."

PULVER: I'm workin' on that. I thought about it for half an hour—yesterday.

ROBERTS: Half an hour! There's only one thing you've thought about for half an hour in your life! And what about those marbles that you were going to put in the Captain's overhead—so they'd roll around at night and keep him awake?

PULVER: Now you've gone too far. Now you've asked for it. (*Goes to bunk and produces small tin box from under mattress. Crosses to* ROBERTS *and shakes it in his face. Opens it.*) What does that look like? Five marbles! I'm collecting marbles all the time. I've got one right here in my pocket! (*Takes marble from pocket, holds it close to*

ROBERTS' *nose, then drops it in box. Closes box.*) Six marbles! (*Puts box back under mattress, turns defiantly to* ROBERTS.) I'm looking for marbles all day long!

ROBERTS: Frank, you asked me what I thought of you. Well, I'll tell you! The day you finish one thing you've started out to do, the day you actually put those marbles in the Captain's overhead, and then have the guts to knock on his door and say, "Captain, I put those marbles there," that's the day I'll have some respect for you—that's the day I'll look up to you as a man. Okay?

PULVER (*belligerently*): Okay!

(ROBERTS *goes to the radio and turns it up. While he is listening,* DOC *and* PULVER *exchange worried looks.*)

RADIO VOICE: . . . intersecting thirty miles north of Hanover. At the same time, General George S. Patton's Third Army continues to roll unchecked into Southern Germany. The abrupt German collapse brought forth the remark from a high London official that the end of the war in Europe is only weeks away—maybe days . . .

(ROBERTS *turns off radio.*)

ROBERTS: Where the hell's Dolan with that letter! (*Starts toward the door.*) I'm going to find him.

PULVER: Hey, Doug, wait! Listen! (ROBERTS *pauses at the door.*) I wouldn't send in that letter if I were you!

ROBERTS: What do you mean—*that* letter!

PULVER (*hastily*): I mean any of those letters you been writin'. What are you so nervous about anyway?

ROBERTS: Nervous!

PULVER: I mean about getting off this ship. Hell, this ain't such a bad life. Look, Doug. We're a threesome, aren't we—you and Doc and me? Share and share alike! Now look, I'm not going to keep those nurses all to myself. Soon as I get my little nursie organized today, I'm going to start working on her twin sister—for you.

ROBERTS: All right, Frank.

PULVER: And then I'm going to scare up something for you too, Doc. And in the meantime you've got a lot of work to do, Doug boy— improvin' my mind and watching my grammar. And speaking of grammar, you better watch your grammar. You're going to get in trouble, saying things like "disharmony aboard this ship!" (ROBERTS *looks at* PULVER *quickly.* PULVER *catches himself.*) I mean just in

case you ever said anything like "disharmony aboard this ship" . . .
or . . . uh . . . "harmony aboard this ship" or . . .

ROBERTS: Where's that letter?

PULVER: I don't know, Doug boy . . . (*As* ROBERTS *steps toward him,
he quickly produces the letter from the blanket.*) Here it is, Doug.

ROBERTS (*snatching the letter*): What's the big idea!

(ROBERTS *goes to desk, reading and preparing to sign the letter.*
PULVER *follows him.*)

PULVER: I just wanted to talk to you before you signed it. You can't
send it in that way—it's too strong! Don't sign that letter, Doug,
please don't! They'll transfer you and you'll get your ass shot off.
You're just running a race with death, isn't he, Doc? It's stupid to
keep asking for it like that. The Doc says so too. Tell him what you
said to me last night, Doc—about how stupid he is.

ROBERTS (*coldly to* DOC): Yes, Doc, maybe you'd like to tell me to
my face.

DOC (*belligerently*): Yes, I would. Last night I asked you why you
wanted to fight this war. And you said: anyone who doesn't fight it is
only half-alive. Well, I thought that over and I've decided that's just a
crock, Doug—just a crock.

ROBERTS: I take it back, Doc. After seeing my task force last night I
don't even feel half-alive.

DOC: You are stupid! And I can prove it! You quit medical school to
get into this thing when you could be saving lives today. Why? Do
you even know yourself?

ROBERTS: Has it ever occurred to you that the guys who fight this war
might also be saving lives . . . yours and mine, for instance! Not just
putting men together again, but *keeping* them together! Right now I'd
rather practice that kind of medicine—Doctor!

DOC (*rising*): Well, right now, that's exactly what you're doing.

ROBERTS: What, for God's sake!

DOC: Whether you like it or not, this sorry old bucket does a necessary
job. And you're the guy who keeps her lumbering along. You keep
this crew working cargo, and more than that—you keep them *alive*.
It might just be that right here, on this bucket, you're deeper and
more truly in this war than you ever would be anywhere else.

ROBERTS: Oh, Jesus, Doc. In a minute, you'll start quoting Emerson.

DOC: *That* is a lousy thing to say!

ROBERTS: We've got nothing to do with the war. Maybe that's why we're on this ship—because we're not good enough to fight. (*Then quietly with emotion.*) Maybe there's some omniscient son-of-a-bitch who goes down the line of all the servicemen and picks out the ones to send into combat, the ones whose glands secrete enough adrenalin, or whose great-great-grandfathers weren't afraid of the dark or something. The rest of us are packed off to ships like this where we can't do any harm.

DOC: What is it you want to be—a hero or something?

ROBERTS (*shocked*): Hero! My God, Doc! You haven't heard a word I said! Look, Doc, the war's way out there! I'm here. I don't want to be here—I want to be out there. I'm sick and tired of being a lousy spectator. I just happen to believe in this thing. I've got to feel I'm *good* enough to be in it—to *participate!*

DOC: Good enough! Doug, you're good enough! You just don't have the opportunity. That's mostly what physical heroism is—opportunity. It's a reflex. I think seventy-five out of a hundred young males have that reflex. If you put any one of them—say, even Frank Thurlow Pulver, here—in a B-29 over Japan, do you know what you'd have?

ROBERTS: No, by God, I don't.

DOC: You'd have Pulver, the Congressional Medal of Honor winner! You'd have Pulver, who, singlehanded, shot down twenty-three attacking Zeroes, then with his bare hands held together the severed wing struts of his plane, and with his bare feet successfully landed the mortally wounded plane on his home field. (PULVER *thinks this over.*) Hell, it's a reflex. It's like the knee jerk. Strike the patella tendon of any human being and you produce the knee jerk. Look. (*He illustrates on* PULVER. *There is no knee jerk. He strikes again—still no reaction.*)

PULVER: What's the matter, Doc?

DOC: Nothing. But stay out of B-29's, will you, Frank?

ROBERTS: You've made your point very vividly, Doc. But I still want to get into this thing. I've got to get into it! And I'm going to keep on sending in these letters until I do.

DOC: I know you are, Doug.

ROBERTS (*signs the letter. Then to* DOC): I haven't got much time. I found that out over on the island. That task force I saw last night is on its way to start our last big push in the Pacific. And it went by me, Doc. I've got to catch it. (*He exits.*)

PULVER (*after a pause*): Doc, what are you going to give Doug on his birthday?

DOC: I hadn't thought of giving him anything.

PULVER: You know what? I'm gonna show him he's got old Pulver figured out all wrong. (*Pulls small cardboard roll from under mattress.*) Doc, what does that look like?

DOC: Just what it is—the cardboard center of a roll of toilet paper.

PULVER: I suppose it doesn't look like a firecracker.

DOC: Not a bit like a firecracker.

PULVER (*taking a piece of string from the bunk*): I suppose that doesn't look like a fuse.

DOC (*rising and starting off*): No, that looks like a piece of string. (*He walks slowly out of the room.* PULVER *goes on.*)

PULVER: Well, you just wait till old Pulver gets through with it! I'm going to get me some of that black powder from the gunner's mate. No, by God, this isn't going to be any peanut firecracker—I'm going to pack this old thing full of that stuff they use to blow up bridges, that fulminate of mercury stuff. And then on the night of Doug's birthday, I'm going to throw it under the Old Man's bunk. Bam—bam—bam! (*Knocks on* ROBERTS' *locker, opens it.*) Captain, it is I, Ensign Pulver. I just threw that firecracker under your goddamn bunk. (*He salutes as the lights*

Fade Out

(*In the darkness we hear the sound of a winch and shouted orders:*)

LCT OFFICER: On the AK—where do you want us?

AK VOICE: Starboard side, up for'd—alongside number two!

LCT OFFICER: Shall we use our fenders or yours?

AK VOICE: No, we'll use ours! Stand off till we finish with the barge!

SCENE III

The curtain rises and the lights dim up on the deck. ROBERTS *stands on the hatch cover.* SCHLEMMER, GERHART *and another*

*seaman are sitting on the hatch cover. They are tired and hot.
A cargo net, filled with crates, is disappearing off right.
Offstage we hear the shouts of men working cargo. Two officers
walk across the stage. Everyone's shirt is wet with perspiration.*

ROBERTS (*calling through megaphone*): Okay—take it away—that's
all for the barge. On the LCT—I'll give you a bow line.

LCT OFFICER (*offstage*): Okay, Lieutenant.

ROBERTS (*to crew*): Get a line over!

DOWDY (*offstage*): Yes, sir!

REBER (*off right*): Heads up on the LCT!

ROBERTS: That's good. Make it fast.

(PAYNE, *wearing the belt of a messenger, enters from companionway as* DOWDY *enters from right*.)

PAYNE: Mister Roberts, the Captain says not to give this LCT any fresh
fruit. He says he's going to keep what's left for his own mess.

ROBERTS: Okay, okay . . .

PAYNE: Hold your hat, Mister Roberts. I just saw Dolan go in there
with your letter. (*He grins and exits as* ROBERTS *smiles at* DOWDY.)

DOWDY: Here's the list of what the LCT guy wants.

ROBERTS (*reading rapidly*): One ton dry stores . . . quarter-ton frozen
food . . . one gross dungarees . . . twenty cartons toothpaste . . . two
gross skivvy shirts . . . Okay, we can give him all that.

DOWDY: Can these guys take their shirts off while we're working?

ROBERTS: Dowdy, you know the Captain has a standing order . . .

DOWDY: Mister Roberts, Corcoran just passed out from the heat.

ROBERTS (*looks at men who wait for his decision*): Hell, yes, take 'em
off. (DOWDY *exits.* SCHLEMMER, REBER *and seaman remove shirts
saying "Thanks,* MISTER ROBERTS" *and exit right.* ROBERTS *calls
through megaphone.*) LCT, want to swap movies? We've got a new
one.

LCT (*offstage*): What's that?

ROBERTS: *Charlie Chan at the Opera.*

LCT (*offstage*): No, thanks, we've seen that three times!

ROBERTS: What you got?

LCT (*offstage*): Hoot Gibson in *Riders of the Range.*

ROBERTS: Sorry I brought the subject up.

DOWDY (*entering from right*): All set, Mister Roberts.

LCT (*offstage*): Lieutenant, one thing I didn't put on my list because I wanted to ask you—you couldn't spare us any fresh fruit, could you?

ROBERTS: You all out?

LCT (*offstage*): We haven't seen any for two months.

ROBERTS (*to* DOWDY): Dowdy, give 'em a couple of crates of oranges.

DOWDY: Yes, sir.

ROBERTS: Compliments of the Captain.

DOWDY: Aye-aye, sir. (*He exits.*)

ROBERTS (*to* LCT): Here comes your first sling-load! (*There is the grinding sound of a winch. With hand-signals* ROBERTS *directs placing of the sling-load. Then he shouts:*) Watch that line!

(DOWDY'S *voice is heard offstage:*)

DOWDY: Slack off, you dumb bastards! Slack off!

(PAYNE *enters.* ROBERTS *turns to him sharply.*)

ROBERTS: What!

PAYNE: The Captain wants to see you, Mister Roberts.

DOWDY (*offstage*): Goddammit, there it goes! You've parted the line!

ROBERTS: Get a fender over! Quick! (*To* PAYNE.) You go tell the Captain I'm busy! (PAYNE *exits.* ROBERTS *calls offstage.*) Get a line over —his bow's coming in!

REBER (*offstage*): Heads up!

GERHART (*offstage*): Where shall we secure?

DOWDY (*offstage*): Secure here!

ROBERTS: No. Take it around the bitt!

DOWDY (*offstage*): Around the bitt!

ROBERTS: That's too much! Give him some slack this time! (*Watches intently.*) That's good. Okay, let's give him the rest of his cargo.

GERHART (*entering quickly and pointing toward companionway*): Flash Red! (*He exits. The* CAPTAIN *enters, followed by* PAYNE *and* DOLAN.)

CAPTAIN: All right, Mister! Let's have this out right here and now! What do you mean—telling me you're busy!

ROBERTS: We parted a line, Captain. You didn't want me to leave the deck with this ship coming in on us?

CAPTAIN: You're damn right I want you to leave the deck. When I tell you I want to see you, I mean *now,* Mister! I mean jump! Do you understand?

(*At this point a group of men, attracted by the noise, crowd in. They are naked to the waist. They pretend they are working, but actually they are listening to the* CAPTAIN'S *fight with* ROBERTS.)

ROBERTS: Yes, Captain. I'll remember that next time.

CAPTAIN: You're damn right you'll remember it! Don't *ever* tell me you're too busy to see me! Ever! (ROBERTS *doesn't answer. The* CAPTAIN *points to the letter he is carrying.*) By God, you think you're pretty cute with this letter, don't you? You're trying to get me in bad with the Admiral, ain't you? Ain't you?

ROBERTS: No, I'm not, Captain.

CAPTAIN: Then what do you mean by writing "disharmony aboard this ship"?

ROBERTS: Because it's true, Captain.

(*The men grin at each other.*)

CAPTAIN: Any disharmony on this ship is my own doing!

ROBERTS: That's true too, Captain.

CAPTAIN: Damn right it's true. And it ain't gonna be in any letter that leaves this ship. Any criticism of this ship stays on this ship. I got a reputation with the Admiral and I ain't gonna lose it on account of a letter written by some smart-alec college officer. Now you retype that letter and leave out that disharmony crap and I'll send it in. But this is the last one, understand?

ROBERTS: Captain, every man in the Navy has the right to send in a request for transfer . . . and no one can change the wording. That's in Navy regs.

CAPTAIN (*after a pause*): How about that, Dolan?

DOLAN: That's what it says, sir.

CAPTAIN: This goddamn Navy! I never put up with crap like that in the merchant service. All right, I'll send this one in as it is—*dis*approved, like I always do. But there's one thing I don't have to do and that's send in a letter that ain't been written. And, Mister, I'm tellin' you here and now—you ain't gonna write any more. You bring one next week and you'll regret it the rest of your life. You got a job right here and, Mister, you ain't *never* going to leave this ship. Now get on with your work. (*He looks around and notices the men. He shouts.*) Where are your shirts?

ROBERTS: Captain, I . . .

CAPTAIN: Shut up! *Answer me, where are your shirts?* (*They stare at him.*) Get those shirts on in a goddamn quick hurry.

(*The men pick up their shirts, then pause, looking at* ROBERTS.)

ROBERTS: Captain, it was so hot working cargo, I . . .

CAPTAIN (*shouting louder*): I told you to shut up! (*To the men.*) I'm giving you an order: get those shirts on!

(*The men do not move.*)

ROBERTS (*quietly*): I'm sorry. Put your shirts on.

(*The men put on their shirts. There is a pause while the* CAPTAIN *stares at the men. Then he speaks quietly:*)

CAPTAIN: Who's the Captain of this ship? By God, that's the rankest piece of insubordination I've seen. You've been getting pretty smart playing grab-ass with Roberts here . . . but now you've gone too far. I'm givin' you a little promise—I ain't never gonna forget this. And in the meantime, every one of you men who disobeyed my standing order and appeared on deck without a shirt—every one—is on report, do you hear? On report!

ROBERTS: Captain, you're not putting these men on report.

CAPTAIN: What do you mean—I'm not!

ROBERTS: I'm responsible. I gave them permission.

CAPTAIN: You disobeyed my order?

ROBERTS: Yes, sir. It was too hot working cargo in the sun. One man passed out.

CAPTAIN: I don't give a damn if fifty men passed out. I gave an order and you disobeyed it.

LCT (*offstage*): Thanks a million for the oranges, Lieutenant.

CAPTAIN (*to* ROBERTS): Did you give that LCT fresh fruit?

ROBERTS: Yes, sir. We've got plenty, Captain. They've been out for two months.

CAPTAIN: I've taken all the crap from you that I'm going to. You've just got yourself ten days in your room. Ten days, Mister! Ten days!

ROBERTS: Very well, Captain. Do you relieve me here?

CAPTAIN: You're damn right, I relieve you. You can go to your room for ten days! See how you like that!

LCT (*offstage*): We're waiting on you, Lieutenant. We gotta shove off.

(ROBERTS *gives the megaphone to the* CAPTAIN *and starts off. The* CAPTAIN *looks in direction of the* LCT *then calls to* ROBERTS.)

CAPTAIN: Where do you think you're going?

ROBERTS (*pretending surprise*): To my room, Captain!

CAPTAIN: Get back to that cargo! I'll let you know when you have ten days in your room and you'll damn well know it! You're going to stay right here and do your job! (ROBERTS *crosses to the crew. The* CAPTAIN *slams the megaphone into* ROBERTS' *stomach.* PULVER *enters around the corner of the house, sees the* CAPTAIN *and starts to go back. The* CAPTAIN *sees* PULVER *and shouts:*) Who's that? Who's that officer there?

PULVER (*Turning*): Me, sir?

CAPTAIN: Yes, you. Come here, boy. (PULVER *approaches in great confusion and can think of nothing better to do than salute. This visibly startles the* CAPTAIN.) Why, you're one of my officers!

PULVER (*turning*): Me, sir?

CAPTAIN: What's your name again?

PULVER: Ensign Pulver, sir. (*He salutes again. The* CAPTAIN, *amazed, returns the salute, then says for the benefit of* ROBERTS *and the crew:*)

CAPTAIN: By God, I'm glad to see one on this ship knows how to salute. (*Then to* PULVER.) Pulver . . . oh, yes . . . Pulver. How is it I never see you around?

PULVER (*terrified*): I've wondered about that myself, sir.

CAPTAIN: What's your job?

PULVER (*trembling*): Officer in charge of laundry and morale, sir.

CAPTAIN: How long you been aboard?

PULVER: Fourteen months, sir.

CAPTAIN: Fourteen months! You spend most of your time down in the laundry, eh?

PULVER: Most of the time, sir. Yes, sir.

(ROBERTS *turns his face to hide his laughter.*)

CAPTAIN: Well, you do a good job, Pulver, and . . . you know I'd like to see more of you. Why don't you have lunch with me in my cabin today?

PULVER: Oh, I can't today.

CAPTAIN: Can't? Why not?

PULVER: I'm on my way over to the hospital on the island. I've got to go pick up a piece . . . of medical equipment.

ROBERTS (*calling over*): Why, I'll take care of that, Frank.

CAPTAIN: That's right, Roberts. You finish here and you go over and fetch it.

ROBERTS: Yes, sir. (*He nods and turns away grinning.*)

CAPTAIN (*to* PULVER): Well, how about it?

PULVER: This is something I've got to take care of myself, sir. If you don't mind, sir.

CAPTAIN: Well, some other time then.

PULVER: Yes, sir. Thank you, sir.

CAPTAIN: Okay, Pulver.

(*The* CAPTAIN *baits another salute from* PULVER, *then exits.* PULVER *watches him go, then starts to sneak off.*)

ROBERTS (*grinning and mimicking the* CAPTAIN): Oh, boy! (PULVER *stops uneasily.* ROBERTS *salutes him.*) I want to see more of you, Pulver!

PULVER (*furiously*): That son-of-a-bitch! Pretending he doesn't know me! (*He looks at watch and exits.* ROBERTS *turns laughing to the crew who are standing rather solemnly.*)

DOWDY (*quietly*): Nice going, Mister Roberts.

SCHLEMMER: It was really beautiful the way you read the Old Man off!

GERHART: Are you going to send in that letter next week, Mister Roberts?

ROBERTS: Are we, Dolan?

DOLAN: You're damn right we are! And I'm the baby who's going to deliver it!

SCHLEMMER: He said he'd fix you good. What do you think he'll do?

REBER: You got a promotion coming up, haven't you?

SCHLEMMER: Yeah. Could he stop that or something?

DOLAN: Promotion! This is Mister Roberts. You think he gives a good hoot-in-hell about another lousy stripe?

ALL: Yeah.

GERHART: Hey, Mister Roberts, can I take the letter in next week?

DOLAN (*indignantly*): You can like hell! That's my job—isn't it, Mister Roberts?

GERHART: Can I, Mister Roberts?

ROBERTS: I'm afraid I've promised that job to Dolan.

DOLAN (*pushing* GERHART *away*): You heard him (*To* ROBERTS.) We gotta write a really hot one next week.

ROBERTS: Got any asbestos paper? (*He starts off, the men follow happily as the lights*

Fade Out

SCENE IV

The lights come up immediately on the main set. REBER *and* GERHART *enter from right passageway. As they get around the corner of the house, they break into a run.* REBER *dashes off through left passageway.*

GERHART (*excitedly, descending hatchway*): Hey, Schlemmer! Schlemmer!

(MISS GIRARD, *a young, attractive, blonde Army nurse, and* PULVER *enter from right passageway.*)

PULVER: Well, here it is.

MISS GIRARD: This is a ship?

PULVER: Unh-hunh.

MISS GIRARD: My sister and I flew over some warships on our way out from the States and they looked so busy—men running around like mad.

PULVER: It's kinda busy sometimes up on deck.

MISS GIRARD: Oh, you mean you've seen a lot of action?

PULVER: Well, I sure as hell haven't had much in the last year . . . Oh, battle action! Yeah . . . Yeah . . .

MISS GIRARD: Then you must have a lot of B.F. on here.

PULVER: Hunh?

MISS GIRARD: You know—battle fatigue?

PULVER: Yeah, we have a lot of that.

MISS GIRARD: Isn't that too bad! But they briefed us to expect a lot of that out here. (*Pause.*) Say, you haven't felt any yourself, have you?

PULVER: I guess I had a little touch of it . . . just a scratch.

MISS GIRARD: You know what you should do then? You should sleep more.

PULVER: Yeah.

MISS GIRARD: What's your job on the ship?

PULVER: Me? I'm . . . Executive Officer . . .

MISS GIRARD: But I thought that Executive Officers had to be at least a . . .

PULVER: Say, you know what I was thinking? That we should have that little old drink of Scotcharoo right now—

MISS GIRARD: I think so too. You know, I just love Scotch. I've just learned to drink it since I've joined the Army. But I'm already an absolute connoisseur.

PULVER (*dismayed*): Oh, you are?

MISS GIRARD: My twin sister has a nickname for me that's partly because I like a particular brand of Scotch . . . (*Giggles.*) and partly because of a little personal thing about me that you wouldn't understand. Do you know what she calls me? "Red Label!" (*They both laugh.*) What are you laughing at? You don't know what I'm talking about—and what's more you never will.

PULVER: What I was laughing about is—that's the kind I've got.

MISS GIRARD: Red Label! Oh, you're God's gift to a thirsty nurstie! But where can we drink it? This is a Navy ship . . . isn't it?

PULVER: Oh, yeah, yeah, we'll have to be careful . . . We mustn't be seen . . . Lemme see, where shall we go . . . (*Considers.*) I have it! We'll go back to my cabin. Nobody'd bother us there.

MISS GIRARD: Oh, you're what our outfit calls an operator. But you look harmless to me.

PULVER: Oh, I don't know about that.

MISS GIRARD: What's your first name—Harmless?

PULVER: Frank.

MISS GIRARD: Hello, Frank. Mine's Ann.

PULVER: Hello, Ann.

MISS GIRARD: All right. We'll have one nice little sip in your room.

PULVER: Right this way. (*They start off toward left passageway.* INSIGNA, MANNION, STEFANOWSKI, WILEY *and* LINDSTROM *enter from right, carrying the spy glass and binoculars.* STEFANOWSKI *trips on hatch cover.* MISS GIRARD *and* PULVER *turn.*) Hello, Mannion . . . Insigna . . . Stefanowski . . .

MANNION (*hoarsely*): Hello, Mister Pulver . . .

PULVER: This is—Lieutenant Girard.

(*The men murmur a greeting.*)

MISS GIRARD: What're you all doing with those glasses?

INSIGNA: We're . . . cleaning them. (*Suddenly pulls out shirt tail and begins lamely polishing spy glass. The others follow his example. More men crowd onto the stage.*)

PULVER: Well, don't work too hard . . . (*They turn to leave, but find themselves hemmed in by the men.*) It's getting a little stuffy up here, I guess we better . . .

(ROBERTS *enters, very excited, carrying a piece of paper and a small book.*)

ROBERTS (*entering*): Hey, Insigna . . . Mannion . . . get a load of this . . . Hey, Frank . . . (*He stops short seeing* MISS GIRARD.)

PULVER: Hiya, Doug boy! This is Ann Girard—Doug Roberts.

ROBERTS: How do you do?

MISS GIRARD (*beaming*): How do you do? You're Frank's roommate. He's told me all about you.

ROBERTS: Really?

MISS GIRARD: What are you doing on this ship?

ROBERTS: Now there you've got me.

MISS GIRARD: No, I mean what's your job? Like Frank here is Executive Officer.

ROBERTS: Oh, I'm just the Laundry and Morale Officer.

MISS GIRARD: Why, that's wonderful—I've just been made Laundry and Morale Officer in our outfit!

PULVER: Oh, for Christ's sake!

(MANNION *and* INSIGNA *begin an argument in whispers.*)

MISS GIRARD: Maybe we can get together and compare notes.

ROBERTS: I'd enjoy that very much.

PULVER (*attempting to usher* MISS GIRARD *off*): Look, Doug. Will you excuse us? We're going down to have a little drink.

MISS GIRARD: Frank, I don't think that's very nice. Aren't you going to ask Doug to join us?

PULVER: Hell, no—I mean—he doesn't like Scotch.

ROBERTS: That's right, Miss Girard. I stay true to alcohol and orange juice.

PULVER: Come on, Ann . . .

MISS GIRARD: Wait a minute! A lot of the girls at the hospital swear by alcohol and orange juice. We ought to all get together and have a party in our new dayroom.

INSIGNA (*to* MANNION): I bet you fifty bucks . . .

(STEFANOWSKI *moves* INSIGNA *and* MANNION *away from* MISS GIRARD.)

MISS GIRARD: Seems to be an argument.

PULVER: Yeah.

MISS GIRARD: Well, anyhow, we're fixing up a new dayroom. (*She looks offstage.*) Look, you can see it! The hospital! And there's our new dormitory! That first window . . .

(PULVER *takes glasses from* WILEY *to look at island.*)

INSIGNA (*to* MANNION, *his voice rising*): All right, I got a *hundred* bucks says that's the one with the birthmark on her ass.

(*There is a terrible silence.* MISS GIRARD, *after a moment, takes the glasses from* PULVER *and looks at the island. After a moment she lowers the glass and speaks to* PULVER.)

MISS GIRARD: Frank, I won't be able to have lunch with you after all. Would you call the boat, please? (*To* ROBERTS.) Good-bye, Doug. It was nice knowing you. You see, I promised the girls I'd help them hang some curtains and I think we'd better get started right away. Good-bye, everybody. (*To* MANNION.) Oh, what's your name again?

INSIGNA: Mine?

MISS GIRARD: No. Yours.

MANNION: Mine? (MISS GIRARD *nods.*) Mannion.

MISS GIRARD: Well, Mannion. I wouldn't take that bet if I were you because you'd lose a hundred bucks. (*To* PULVER.) Come on, Harmless. (*She exits, followed by a bewildered* PULVER. *The men watch her off.* STEFANOWSKI *throws his cap on the ground in anger.*)

MANNION (*to* INSIGNA): You loud-mouthed little bastard! Now you've gone and done it!

ROBERTS: Shut up! Insigna, how did you . . .

INSIGNA: We seen her taking a bath.

LINDSTROM: Through these glasses, Mister Roberts! We could see everything!

STEFANOWSKI (*furious*): You heard what she said—she's going to hang some curtains.

MANNION: Yeah . . .

LINDSTROM: Gee, them nurses was pretty to look at. (*He sighs. There is a little tragic moment.*)

ROBERTS: She's got a ten-minute boat ride. You've still got ten minutes.

WILEY: It wouldn't be any fun when you know you're going to be rushed.

LINDSTROM: This was the first real good day this ship has ever had. But it's all over now.

ROBERTS: Well, maybe you've got time then to listen to a little piece of news . . . (*He reads from the paper in his hands.*) "When in all respects ready for sea, on or about 1600 today, the *AK 601* will proceed at ten knots via points X-Ray, Yolk and Zebra to Elysium Island, arriving there in seven days and reporting to the Port Director for cargo assignment." (*Emphatically.*) "During its stay in Elysium, the ship will make maximum use of the recreational facilities of this port."

(*The men look up in slow surprise and disbelief.*)

STEFANOWSKI: But that means liberty!

LINDSTROM: That don't mean liberty, Mister Roberts?

ROBERTS: That's exactly what it means!

INSIGNA (*dazed*): Somebody must've been drunk to send us to a Liberty Port!

(ROBERTS *nods.*)

LINDSTROM: Has the Old Man seen them orders?

ROBERTS: He saw them before I did. (*Now the men are excited.*)

WILEY: Elysium! Where's that?

MANNION: Yeah! Where's that, Mister Roberts?

(*The men crowd around* ROBERTS *as he sits on the hatch.*)

ROBERTS (*reading from guide-book*): "Elysium is the largest of the Limbo Islands. It is often referred to as the 'Polynesian Paradise.' Vanilla, sugar, cocoa, coffee, copra, mother-of-pearl, phosphates and rum are the chief exports."

INSIGNA: Rum! Did you hear that? (*He gooses* LINDSTROM.)

LINDSTROM: Cut that out!

(DOLAN *gooses* INSIGNA.)

INSIGNA: Cut that out!

MANNION: Shut up!

ROBERTS: "Elysium City, its capital, is a beautiful metropolis of palm-lined boulevards, handsome public buildings and colorful stucco homes. Since 1900, its population has remained remarkably constant at approximately 30,000.

INSIGNA: I'll fix that!

(*The men shout him down.*)

ROBERTS: That's all there is here. If you want the real dope on Elysium, there's one man on this ship who's been there.

STEFANOWSKI: Who's that?

MANNION: Who?

ROBERTS: Dowdy!

(*The men run off wildly in every direction, shouting for* DOWDY. *The call is taken up all over the ship.* ROBERTS *listens to them hap-*

*pily, then notices a pair of binoculars. He looks toward the island for
a moment, shrugs and is lifting the binoculars to his eyes as the lights*

Fade Out

SCENE V

*During the darkness we can hear the exciting strains of Polyne-
sian music.*

*The lights come up slowly through a porthole, casting a
strong late-afternoon shaft of light onto motionless white
figures. It is the enlisted men's compartment below decks. Except for a few not yet fully dressed, the men are all in white
uniforms. The compartment is a crowded place with three-
tiered bunks against the bulkheads. Most of the men are
crowded around the porthole, downstage left. The men who
cannot see are listening to the reports of* INSIGNA, *who is standing on a bench, looking out the porthole. The only man who is
not galvanized with excitement is* DOWDY, *who sits calmly on a
bench, downstage center, reading a magazine*—True Detective.

GERHART (*to* INSIGNA): What do you see now, Sam?

INSIGNA: There's a lot of little boats up forward—up around the bow.

PAYNE: What kind of boats?

INSIGNA: They're little sort of canoes and they're all filled up with
flowers and stuff. And there's women in them boats, paddling
them . . .

PAYNE: Are they coming down this way?

INSIGNA: Naw. They're sticking around the bow.

STEFANOWSKI: Sam, where's that music coming from?

INSIGNA: There's a great big canoe up there and it's all filled with fat
bastards with flowers in their ears playing little old gittars . . .

SCHLEMMER: Why the hell can't we go up on deck? That's what I'd like
to know!

LINDSTROM: When are we going ashore! That's what I'd like to know!

(INSIGNA *suddenly laughs.*)

PAYNE: What is it, Sam?

INSIGNA: I wish you could see this . . .

(CHIEF JOHNSON *enters, looking knowingly at the men, shakes his head and addresses* DOWDY.)

JOHNSON: Same story in here, eh? Every porthole this side of the ship!

DOWDY: They're going to wear themselves down to a nub before they ever get over there . . .

LINDSTROM (*takes coin from pocket and thrusts it at* INSIGNA): Hey, Sam, here's another penny. Make them kids down below dive for it.

INSIGNA (*impatiently*): All right! (*Throws coin out the port.*) Heads up, you little bastards!

(*The men watch tensely.*)

LINDSTROM: Did he get that one too?

INSIGNA: Yeah . . .

(*The men relax somewhat.*)

LINDSTROM: Them kids don't ever miss!

INSIGNA: Hey, Dowdy—where's that little park again? Where you said all the good-looking women hang out?

DOWDY: For the last time—you see that big hill over there to the right . . .

INSIGNA: Yeah.

DOWDY: You see a big church . . . with a street running off to the left of it.

INSIGNA: Yeah.

DOWDY: Well, you go up that street three blocks . . .

INSIGNA: Yeah, I'm there.

DOWDY: That's the park.

INSIGNA: Well, I'll be damned . . .

LINDSTROM: Hey, show me that park, Sam?

(*The other men gather around* INSIGNA, *asking to see the park.*)

INSIGNA (*the authority now*): All right, you bastards, line up. I'll show you where the women hang out.

(*The men form a line and each steps up to the porthole where* INSIGNA *points out the park.*)

JOHNSON (*to* DOWDY): Smell that shoe polish? These guys have gone nuts!

DOWDY: I went down the ship's store the other day to buy a bar of soap and, do you know, they been sold out for a week! No soap, no Listerine, no lilac shaving lotion—hell, they even sold eighteen jars of Mum! Now these bastards are bootlegging it! They're gettin' ten bucks for a used jar of Mum!

(REBER, *wearing the messenger's belt, enters. The men greet him excitedly.*)

STEFANOWSKI: What's the word on liberty, Reber? Is the Old Man still asleep?

MANNION: Yeah, what's the word?

REBER: I just peeked in on him. He's snoring like a baby.

GERHART: Jeez, how any guy can sleep at a time like this!

INSIGNA: I'll get him up! I'm going up there and tap on his door! (*Picks up a heavy lead pipe.*)

DOWDY (*grabbing* INSIGNA): Like hell you are! You're going to stay right here and pray. You're going to pray that he wakes up feeling good and decides he's kept you guys sweating long enough!

MANNION: That's telling the little crud!

(INSIGNA *and* MANNION *threaten each other.*)

REBER: Hey, Lindstrom. I got good news for you. You can take them whites off.

LINDSTROM: I ain't got the duty *tonight?*

REBER: That's right. You and Mister Roberts got the duty tonight—the twelve to four watch. The Exec just posted the list . . . (*He is interrupted by the sound of static on the squawk box. Instantly all men turn toward it eagerly.*)

DOLAN (*on squawk box*): Now hear this! Now hear this!

WILEY: Here we go! Here we go!

STEFANOWSKI (*imitating the squawk box*): Liberty . . . will commence . . . immediately!

GERHART: Quiet!

DOLAN (*on squawk box*): Now hear this! The Captain's messenger will report to the Captain's cabin on the double!

REBER: My God! He's awake! (*He runs out.*)

PAYNE: Won't be long now!

WILEY: Get going, Mannion! Get into those whites! We're going to be the first ones over the side!

MANNION: Hell, yes! Give me a hand!

(*Now there is a general frenzy of preparation—the men put the last-minute touches to shoes, hair, uniforms.*)

GERHART (*singing to the tune of "California, Here I Come"*): Ee-liss-*ee*-um, here I come! . . . Ta-ta-ta-ta-*ta*-da-tah . . .

SCHLEMMER (*to* GERHART): Watch where you're going! You stepped on my shine!

INSIGNA: Schlemmer . . . Stef . . . Gerhart . . . come here! (*These men gather around him.* LINDSTROM *remains unhappily alone.*) Now listen! Stefanowski and me are going to work alone for the first hour and a half! But if you pick up something first . . . (*Produces small map from his pocket.*) We'll be working up and down this street here . . .

(*They study the map. Now the squawk box is clicked on again. All the men stand rigid, listening.*)

DOLAN (*on squawk box*): Now hear this! Now hear this! The Captain is now going to make a personal announcement.

(*Sound of squawk-box switch.*)

CAPTAIN (*on squawk box*): Goddammit, how does this thing work? (*Sound of squawk-box switch again.*) This is the Captain speaking. I just woke up from a little nap and I got a surprise. I found out there were men on this ship who were expecting liberty. (*At this point, the lights start dimming until the entire scene is blacked out. The speech continues throughout the darkness. Under the* CAPTAIN'S *speech the strains of Polynesian music can be heard.*) Now I don't know how such a rumor got around, but I'd like to clear it up right now. You see, it's like this. Because of cargo requirements and security conditions which has just come to my personal attention there will be no liberty as long as we're in this here port. And one other thing—as long as we're here, no man will wear white uniforms. Now I would

like to repeat for the benefit of complete understanding and clearness,
NO LIBERTY. That is all.

SCENE VI

The lights come up on the CAPTAIN's *cabin. Against the left
bulkhead is a settee. A chair is placed center. Up center is the
only door. The* CAPTAIN *is seated behind his desk, holding a
watch in one hand and the microphone in the other, in an attitude of waiting. Just over the desk and against the right
bulkhead is a ship's intercommunication board. There is a wall-
safe in the right bulkhead. After a moment there is a knock on
the door.*

CAPTAIN: Come in, Mister Roberts. (*As* ROBERTS *enters, the* CAPTAIN
puts the microphone on the desk.) Thirty-eight seconds. Pretty good
time! You see, I been expectin' you ever since I made my little announcement.

ROBERTS: Well, as long as you're expecting me, what about it—when
does this crew get liberty?

CAPTAIN: Well, in the first place, just kinda hold your tongue. And in
the second place, sit down.

ROBERTS: There's no time to sit down. When are you going to let this
crew go ashore?

CAPTAIN: I'm not. This wasn't my idea—coming to a Liberty Port. One
of my officers arranged it with a certain Port Director—gave him a
bottle of Scotch whiskey—compliments of the Captain. And the Port
Director was kind enough to send me a little thank-you note along
with our orders. Sit down, Mister Roberts. (ROBERTS *sits.*) Don't
worry about it. I'm not going to make trouble about that wasted bottle of Scotch. I'll admit I was a little pre-voked about not being con-
sulted. Then I got to thinking maybe we oughta come to this port
anyway so's you and me could have a little talk.

ROBERTS: You can make all the trouble you want, Captain, but let's
quit wasting time. Don't you hear that music? Don't you know it's
tearing those guys apart? They're breakable, Captain! I promise you!

CAPTAIN: That's enough! I've had enough of your fancy educated talk.
(*Rises, goes to* ROBERTS.) Now you listen to me. I got two things I
want to show you. (*He unlocks the wall-safe, opens it and takes out*

a commander's cap with gold braid "scrambled eggs" on the visor.)
You see that? That's the cap of a full commander. I'm gonna wear
that cap some day and you're going to help me. (*Replaces cap in
safe, goes back to* ROBERTS.) I guess there's no harm in telling you
that you helped me get that palm tree by working cargo. Now don't
let this go to your head, but when Admiral Finchley gave me that
award, he said, "You got a good Cargo Officer, Morton; keep him at
it, you're going places." So I went out and bought that hat. There's
nothing gonna stand between me and that hat—certainly not you.
Now last week you wrote a letter that said "disharmony aboard this
ship." I told you there wasn't going to be any more letters. But what
do I find on my desk this morning . . . (*Taking letter from desk.*)
Another one. It says "friction between myself and the Commanding
Officer." That ain't gonna go in, Mister.

ROBERTS: How are you going to stop it, Captain?

CAPTAIN: I ain't, you are. (*Goes to his chair and sits.*) Just how much
do you want this crew to have a liberty anyhow? Enough to stop this
"disharmony"? To stop this "friction"? (*Leans forward.*) Enough
to get out of the habit of writing letters ever? Because that's the only
way this crew is ever gonna get ashore. (*Leans back.*) Well, we've
had our little talk. What do you say?

ROBERTS (*after a moment*): How did you get in the Navy? How did
you get on our side? You're what I joined to fight *against*. You ignorant, arrogant, ambitious . . . (*Rises.*) jackass! Keeping a hundred
and sixty-seven men in prison because you got a palm tree for the
work *they* did. I don't know which I hate worse—you or that other
malignant growth that stands outside your door!

CAPTAIN: Why, you goddamn . . .

ROBERTS: How did you ever get command of a ship? I realize that in
wartime they have to scrape the bottom of the barrel, but where the
hell did they ever scrape you up?

CAPTAIN (*shouting*): There's just one thing left for you, by God—a
general court-martial.

ROBERTS: That suits me fine. Court-martial me!

CAPTAIN: By God, you've got it!

ROBERTS: I'm asking for it!

CAPTAIN: You don't have to ask for it, you've got it now!

ROBERTS: If I can't get transferred off here, I'll get court-martialed off!
I'm fed up! But you'll need a witness. Send for your messenger. He's
down below. I'll say it all again in front of him. (*Pauses.*) Go on, call

in Reber! (*The* CAPTAIN *doesn't move.*) Go on, call him. (*Still the* CAPTAIN *doesn't move.*) Do you want me to call him?

CAPTAIN: No. (*He walks upstage, then turns to* ROBERTS.) I think you're a pretty smart boy. I may not talk very good, Mister, but I know how to take care of smart boys. Let me tell you something. Let me tell you a little secret. I hate your guts, you college son-of-a-bitch! You think you're better than I am! You think you're better because you've had everything handed to you! Let me tell you something, Mister—I've worked since I was ten years old, and all my life I've known you superior bastards. I knew you people when I was a kid in Boston and I worked in eating-places and you ordered me around. . . . "Oh, bus-boy! My friend here seems to have thrown up on the table. Clean it up, please." I started going to sea as a steward and I worked for you then . . . "Steward, take my magazine out to the deck chair!" . . . "Steward, I don't like your looks. Please keep out of my way as much as possible!" Well, I took that crap! I took that for years from pimple-faced bastards who weren't good enough to wipe my nose! And now I don't have to take it any more! There's a war on, by God, and I'm the Captain and you can wipe my nose! The worst thing I can do to you is to keep you on this ship! And that's where you're going to stay! Now get out of here! (*He goes to his chair and sits.* ROBERTS *moves slowly toward the door. He hears the music, goes to the porthole and listens. Then he turns to the* CAPTAIN.)

ROBERTS: Can't you hear that music, Captain?

CAPTAIN: Yeah, I hear it. (*Busies himself at desk, ignoring* ROBERTS.)

ROBERTS: Don't you know those guys below can hear it too? Oh, my God.

CAPTAIN: Get out of here.

(*After a moment,* ROBERTS *turns from the porthole and slumps against the* CAPTAIN'S *locker. His face is strained.*)

ROBERTS: What do you want for liberty, Captain?

CAPTAIN: I want plenty. You're through writin' letters—ever.

ROBERTS: Okay.

CAPTAIN: That's not all. You're through givin' me trouble. You're through talkin' back to me in front of the crew. You ain't even gonna open your mouth—except in civil answer. (ROBERTS *doesn't answer.*) Mister Roberts, you know that if you don't take my terms I'll let you out that door and that's the end of any hope for liberty.

ROBERTS: Is that all, Captain?

CAPTAIN: No. Anyone know you're in here?

ROBERTS: No one.

CAPTAIN: Then you won't go blabbin' about this to anyone ever. It might not sound so good. And besides I don't want you to take credit for gettin' this crew ashore.

ROBERTS: Do you think I'm doing this for credit? Do you think I'd *let* anyone know about this?

CAPTAIN: I gotta be sure.

ROBERTS: You've got my word, that's all.

CAPTAIN (*after a pause*): Your word. Yes, you college fellas make a big show about keeping your word.

ROBERTS: How about it, Captain. Is it a deal?

CAPTAIN: Yeah. (ROBERTS *picks up the microphone, turns on a switch and thrusts the microphone at the* CAPTAIN.) Now hear this. This is the Captain speaking. I've got some further word on security conditions in this port and so it gives me great pleasure to tell you that liberty, for the starboard section . . .

ROBERTS (*covering the microphone with his hand*): For the entire crew, goddammit.

CAPTAIN: Correction: Liberty for the entire crew will commence immediately.

(ROBERTS *turns off the microphone. After a moment we hear the shouts of the crew.* ROBERTS *goes up to porthole. The* CAPTAIN *leans back on his chair. A song, "Roll Me Over," is started by someone and is soon taken up by the whole crew.*)

ROBERTS (*looking out of the porthole. He is excited and happy*): Listen to those crazy bastards. Listen to them.

(*The crew continues to sing with increasing volume. Now the words can be distinguished:*

> *Roll me over in the clover,*
> *Roll me over, lay me down*
> *And do it again.*)

THE CURTAIN FALLS

ACT TWO

SCENE I

The curtain rises on the main set. It is now 3:45 A.M. The night is pitch-black, but we can see because of a light over the head of the gangway, where a temporary desk has been rigged; a large ship's logbook lies open on this desk. A small table on which are hospital supplies is at left of the door.

At rise, ROBERTS, DOC, LINDSTROM, JOHNSON *and four* SEAMEN *are discovered onstage.* LINDSTROM, *in web belt, is writing in the log.* ROBERTS *is standing with a pile of yellow slips in his hand; he wears the side-arms of the Officer of the Deck.* JOHNSON *and a* SEAMAN *are standing near the hatchway, holding the inert body of another* SEAMAN, *who has court plaster on his face. Two more* SEAMEN *lie on the hatch cover where* DOC *is kneeling, bandaging one of them. As the curtain rises we hear the sound of a siren off right. Everyone turns and looks—that is, everyone who is conscious.*

LINDSTROM: Here's another batch, Mister Roberts—a whole paddy wagon full. And this one's an Army paddy wagon.

ROBERTS: We haven't filed away this batch yet. (*To* DOC.) Hurry up, Doc.

JOHNSON (*to* DOC, *indicating body he is carrying*): Where do we put number twenty-three here, Doc? Sick bay or what?

DOC: Just put him to bed. His condition's only critical.

JOHNSON (*carrying* SEAMAN *off*): They just roll out of their bunks, Doc. Now I'm stacking 'em on the deck down there—I'm on the third layer already.

VOICE (*offstage*): Okay, Lieutenant! All set down here! You ready?

ROBERTS (*calling offstage—and giving hand signal*): Okay! (*To* DOC.) Here they come, Doc! Head's up!

SHORE PATROLMAN'S VOICE (*offstage*): Lieutenant!

ROBERTS: Oh, not you again!

SHORE PATROLMAN'S VOICE (*offstage*): I got a bunch of real beauties for you this time.

ROBERTS (*calling offstage*): Can they walk?

SHORE PATROLMAN'S VOICE (*offstage*): Just barely!

ROBERTS (*calling*): Then send 'em up.

LINDSTROM: Man, oh, man, what a liberty! We got the record now, Mister Roberts! This makes the seventh batch since we went on watch!

(*The sound of a cargo winch and a voice offstage singing the Army Air Corps song are heard.* ROBERTS *is looking offstage.*)

ROBERTS (*signaling*): Looks like a real haul this time. Schlemmer, look out!

LINDSTROM: Schlemmer, look out!

ROBERTS: Okay, Doc. (DOC *and* ROBERTS *lift the two bodies from the hatch cover and deposit them farther upstage. At this moment, the cargo net appears, loaded with bodies in once-white uniforms and leis. Riding on top of the net is* SCHLEMMER, *wearing a lei and singing "Off We Go into the Wild Blue Yonder."*) Let her in easy . . .

LINDSTROM: Let her in easy . . .

(*The net is lowered onto the hatch cover and* LINDSTROM *detaches it from the hook. All start untangling bodies.*)

ROBERTS: Well, they're peaceful anyhow.

(*At this point a* SHORE PATROLMAN *enters from the gangway.*)

SHORE PATROLMAN (*handing* ROBERTS *a sheaf of yellow slips*): For your collection. (*Points down gangway.*) Take a look at them.

ROBERTS (*looks upstage*): My God, what did they do?

SHORE PATROLMAN: They done all right, Lieutenant. Six of them busted into a formal dance and took on a hundred and twenty-eight Army bastards. (*Calls off.*) All right, let's go!

(STEFANOWSKI, REBER, WILEY, PAYNE *and* MANNION, *with his arm around* INSIGNA, *straggle on—a frightening sight—followed by a* MILITARY POLICEMAN: INSIGNA'S *uniform is torn to shreds.* MANNION *is clad in a little diaper of crepe paper. All have bloody faces and uniforms. A few bear souvenirs—a Japanese lantern, leis, Army caps, a*

Shore Patrol band, etc. They throw perfunctory salutes to the colors, then murmur a greeting to ROBERTS.)

MILITARY POLICEMAN: Duty Officer?

ROBERTS: That's right.

MILITARY POLICEMAN (*salutes*): Colonel Middleton presents his compliments to the Captain and wishes him to know that these men made a shambles out of the Colonel's testimonial dinner-dance.

ROBERTS: Is this true, Insigna?

INSIGNA: That's right, Mister Roberts. A shambles. (*To* MANNION.) Ain't that right, Killer?

MANNION: That's right, Mister Roberts.

ROBERTS: You men crashed a dance for Army personnel?

MANNION: Yes, sir! And they made us feel unwelcome! (*To* INSIGNA.) Didn't they, Slugger?

ROBERTS: Oh, they started a fight, eh?

WILEY: No, sir! *We* started it!

STEFANOWSKI: We finished it too! (*To* MILITARY POLICEMAN.) Tell Mister Roberts how many of you Army bastards are in the hospital.

MANNION: Go on.

MILITARY POLICEMAN: Thirty-eight soldiers of the United States Army have been hospitalized. And the Colonel himself has a very bad bruise on his left shin!

PAYNE: *I* did that, Mister Roberts.

MILITARY POLICEMAN: And that isn't all, Lieutenant. There were young ladies present—fifty of them. Colonel Middleton had been lining them up for a month, from the best families of Elysium. And he had personally guaranteed their safety this evening. Well, sir . . .

ROBERTS: Well?

MILITARY POLICEMAN: Two of those young ladies got somewhat mauled, one actually got a black eye, six of them got their clothes torn off and then went screaming off into the night and they haven't been heard from since. What are you going to do about it, Lieutenant?

ROBERTS: Well, I'm due to get relieved here in fifteen minutes—I'll be glad to lead a search party.

MILITARY POLICEMAN: No, sir. The Army's taking care of that end. The Colonel will want to know what punishment you're going to give these men.

ROBERTS: Tell the Colonel that I'm sure our Captain will think of something.

MILITARY POLICEMAN: But . . .

ROBERTS: That's all, Sergeant.

MILITARY POLICEMAN (*salutes*): Thank you, sir. (*He goes off.*)

SHORE PATROLMAN: Lieutenant, I been pretty sore at your guys up till now—we had to put on ten extra Shore Patrolmen on account of this ship. But if you knew Colonel "Chicken" Middleton—well, I'd be willing to do this every night. (*To the men.*) So long, fellows!

(*The men call "So long."* SHORE PATROLMAN *exits, saluting* ROBERTS *and quarter-deck.*)

ROBERTS: Well, what've you got to say for yourselves?

STEFANOWSKI (*after a moment*): Okay if we go ashore again, Mister Roberts?

ROBERTS (*to* LINDSTROM): Is this the first time for these guys?

LINDSTROM (*showing log*): Yes, sir, they got a clean record—they only been brought back once.

ROBERTS: What do you say, Doc?

(*The men turn eagerly to* DOC.)

DOC: Anybody got a fractured skull?

MEN: No.

DOC: Okay, you pass the physical.

ROBERTS: Go down and take a shower first and get into some clothes.

(*The men rush to the hatchway.*)

STEFANOWSKI: We still got time to get back to that dance!

(*As they descend hatchway,* INSIGNA *pulls crepe paper from around* MANNION *as he is halfway down the hatchway.*)

ROBERTS: How you feeling, Doc?

DOC: These alcohol fumes are giving me a cheap drunk—otherwise pretty routine. When do you get relieved, Doug? (*Takes box from table and gestures for men to remove table. They carry it off.*)

ROBERTS: Soon as Carney gets back from the island. Any minute now.

DOC: What are you grinning like a skunk for?

ROBERTS: Nothing. I always grin like a skunk. What have you got in the box?

DOC (*descending hatchway—holding up small packet he has taken from the box*): Little favors from the Doc. I'm going to put one in each man's hand and when he wakes up he'll find pinned to his shirt full instructions for its use. I think it'll save me a lot of work later on. (*His head disappears.*)

LINDSTROM: I wish Gerhart would get back here and relieve me. I've got to get over to that island before it runs out of women.

(DOLAN *enters from gangway.*)

DOLAN: Howdy, Mister Roberts! I'm drunk as a goat! (*Pulls a goat aboard.*) Show him how drunk I am. Mister Roberts, when I first saw her she was eatin', and you know, she just eat her way into my heart. She was eatin' a little old palm tree and I thought to myself, our ship needs a mascot. (*He points out palm tree to goat.*) There you are, kid. Chow!

(ROBERTS *blocks his way.*)

ROBERTS: Wait a minute . . . wait a minute. What's her name?

DOLAN: I don't know, sir.

ROBERTS: She's got a name plate.

DOLAN: Oh, so she has . . . her name is . . . (*Reads from tag on goat's collar.*) . . . Property Of.

ROBERTS: What's her last name?

DOLAN: Her last name . . . (*Reads again.*) Rear Admiral Wentworth.

(*Approaching siren is heard offstage.*)

ROBERTS: Okay, Dolan, hit the sack. I'll take care of her.

DOLAN: Okay, Mister Roberts. (*Descends hatchway.*) See that she gets a good square meal. (*He points to the* CAPTAIN'S *palm tree and winks, then disappears.* GERHART *enters from gangway.*)

LINDSTROM: Gerhart! (LINDSTROM *frantically removes his web belt and shoves it at* GERHART.)

GERHART: Okay, okay—you're relieved.

LINDSTROM (*tosses a fast salute to* ROBERTS *and says in one breath*): Requestpermissiontogoashore! (*He hurries down gangway.*)

(SHORE PATROLMAN *enters from gangway.*)

SHORE PATROLMAN: Lieutenant, has one of your men turned up with a . . . (*Sees goat and takes leash.*) Oh, Thanks. (*To goat.*) Come on, come on, your papa over there is worried about you. (*Pulls goat down gangway.*)

GERHART: Where's your relief, Mister Roberts?

ROBERTS (*sitting on hatch*): He'll be along any minute. How was your liberty, Gerhart?

(GERHART *grins. So does* ROBERTS. DOC *enters from hatchway.*)

DOC: What are you looking so cocky about anyway?

ROBERTS: Am I looking cocky? Maybe it's because for the first time since I've been on this ship, I'm seeing a crew.

DOC: What do you think you've been living with all this time?

ROBERTS: Just a hundred and sixty-seven separate guys. There's a big difference, Doc. Now these guys are bound together. You saw Insigna and Mannion. Doc, I think these guys are strong enough now to take all the miserable, endless days ahead of us. I only hope I'm strong enough.

DOC: Doug, tomorrow you and I are going over there and take advantage of the groundwork that's been laid tonight. You and I are going to have ourselves a liberty.

(PULVER *enters slowly from the gangway and walks across the stage.* DOC *calls* ROBERTS' *attention to him.*)

ROBERTS: Hello, Frank. How was your liberty?

(PULVER *half turns, shrugs and holds up seven fingers, then exits. A* SHORE PATROL OFFICER *enters from the gangway and calls offstage. He speaks with a Southern accent.*)

SHORE PATROL OFFICER: That's your post and that's your post. You know what to do. (*He salutes the quarter-deck, then* ROBERTS.) Officer of the Deck? (ROBERTS *nods. The* SHORE PATROL OFFICER *hesitates a moment.*) I hope you don't mind but I've stationed two of my men at the foot of the gangway. I'm sorry but this ship is restricted for the rest of its stay in Elysium. Your Captain is to report to the Island Commander at seven o'clock this morning. I'd recommend that he's there on time. The Admiral's a pretty tough cookie when he's mad, and he's madder now than I've ever seen him.

ROBERTS: What in particular did this?

SHORE PATROL LIEUTENANT: A little while ago six men from your ship broke into the home of the French Consul and started throwing things through the plate-glass living-room window. We found some of the things on the lawn: a large world globe, a small love seat, a lot of books and a bust of Balzac—the French writer. We also found an Army private first class who was unconscious at the time. He claims they threw him too.

ROBERTS: Through the window?

SHORE PATROL LIEUTENANT: That's right! It seems he took them there for a little joke. He didn't tell them it was the Consul's house; he said it was a—what we call in Alabama—a cat-house. (ROBERTS and DOC *nod*.) Be sure that your Captain is there at seven o'clock sharp. If it makes you feel any better, Admiral Wentworth says this is the worst ship he's ever seen in his entire naval career. (*Laughs, then salutes.*) Good night, Lieutenant.

ROBERTS (*returning salute*): Good night.

(*The* SHORE PATROL LIEUTENANT *exits down gangway—saluting the quarter-deck.*)

GERHART: Well, there goes the liberty. That was sure a wham-bam-thank you, ma'am!

DOC: Good night. (*He exits through left passageway.*)

GERHART: But, by God, it was worth it. That liberty was worth anything!

ROBERTS: I think you're right, Gerhart.

GERHART: Hunh?

ROBERTS: I think you're right.

GERHART: Yeah. (*He smiles.* ROBERTS *looks over the log.* GERHART *whistles softly to himself "Roll Me Over" as the lights slowly*

Fade Out

During the darkness we hear JOHNSON *shouting:*

JOHNSON: All right, fall in for muster. Form two ranks. And pipe down.

SCENE II

The lights come up, revealing the deck. Morning sunlight. A group of men, right and left, in orderly formation. They are talking.

JOHNSON: 'Ten-shun!

(*The command is relayed through the ship. The* CAPTAIN *enters from his cabin, followed by* ROBERTS. *The* CAPTAIN *steps up on the hatch cover.* ROBERTS *starts to fall in with the men.*)

CAPTAIN (*calling to* ROBERTS *and pointing to a place beside himself on hatch cover*): Over here, Roberts. (ROBERTS *takes his place left of* CAPTAIN.) We're being kicked out of this port. I had a feeling this liberty was a bad idea. That's why we'll never have one again. We're going to erase this blot from my record if we have to work twenty-four hours a day. We're going to move even more cargo than we've ever moved before. And if there ain't enough cargo work, Mister Roberts here is gonna find some. Isn't that right, Mister Roberts? (ROBERTS *doesn't answer.*) Isn't that right, Mister Roberts?

ROBERTS: Yes, sir.

CAPTAIN: I'm appointing Mister Roberts here and now to see that you men toe the line. And I can't think of a more honorable man for the job. He's a man who keeps his word no matter what. (*Turns to* ROBERTS.) Now, Roberts, if you do a good job—and if the Admiral begins to smile on us again—there might be something in it for you. What would you say if that little silver bar on your collar got a twin brother some day? (ROBERTS *is startled. The* CAPTAIN *calls offstage.*) Officer of the Deck!

OFFSTAGE VOICE: Yes, sir!

CAPTAIN (*to* ROBERTS): You wasn't expectin' that, was you? (*Calling offstage.*) Get ready to sail!

OFFSTAGE VOICE: Aye-aye, sir!

CAPTAIN: You men are dismissed!

JOHNSON: Fall out!

(*The men fall out. Some exit. A little group forms downstage.*)

CAPTAIN: Wait a minute! Wait a minute! Roberts, take these men here back aft to handle lines. And see that they work up a sweat. (ROBERTS *and men look at him.*) Did you hear me, Roberts? I gave you an order!

ROBERTS (*carefully*): Yes, Captain. I heard you.

CAPTAIN: How do you answer when I give an order?

ROBERTS (*after a pause*): Aye-aye, sir.

CAPTAIN: That's more like it . . . that's more like it! (*He exits into his cabin.*)

STEFANOWSKI: What'd he mean, Mister Roberts?

ROBERTS: I don't know. Just what he said, I guess.

GERHART: What'd you let him give you all that guff for?

DOLAN (*stepping up on hatch, carrying a file folder*): Because he's tired, that's why. He had the mid-watch last night. Your tail'd be dragging too if you had to handle all them customers.

ROBERTS: Come on. Let's get going . . .

DOLAN: Wait a minute, Mister Roberts. Something come for you in the mail this morning—a little love letter from the Bureau. (*Pulls out paper from file folder.*) Get a load of this! (*Reads.*) "To All Ships and Stations: Heightened war offensive has created urgent need aboard combat ships for experienced officers. (*He clicks his teeth and winks at* ROBERTS.) All commanding officers are hereby directed to forward with their endorsements all applications for transfer from officers with twenty-four months' sea duty." (ROBERTS *grabs the directive and reads it.* DOLAN *looks at* ROBERTS *and smiles.*) You got twenty-nine months—you're the only officer aboard that has. Mister Roberts, the Old Man is hanging on the ropes from the working-over the Admiral give him. All he needs to flatten him is one more little jab. And here it is. Your letter. I typed it up. (*He pulls out triplicate letter from file cover—then a fountain pen which he offers to* ROBERTS.) Sign it and I'll take it in—

MANNION: Go on, sign it, Mister Roberts. He'll take off like a bird.

DOLAN: What're you waitin' for, Mister Roberts?

ROBERTS (*handing directive back to* DOLAN): I'll want to look it over first, Dolan. Come on, let's get going.

DOLAN: There's nothing to look over. This is the same letter we wrote yesterday—only quoting this new directive.

ROBERTS: Look, Dolan, I'm tired. And I told you I wanted—

DOLAN: You ain't too tired to sign your name!

ROBERTS (*sharply*): Take it easy, Dolan. I'm not going to sign it. So take it easy! (*Turns to exit right, finds himself blocked by crew.*) Did you hear me? Let's get going! (*Exits.*)

STEFANOWSKI: What the hell's come over him?

(*They look at one another.*)

INSIGNA: Aye-aye, sir—for Christ's sake!

MANNION (*after a moment*): Come on. Let's get going.

DOLAN (*bitterly*): "Take it easy . . . take it easy!"

(*The men start to move off slowly as the lights*

Fade Out

During the darkness we hear a radio. There is considerable static.

AMERICAN BROADCASTER: Still, of course, we have no official word from the Headquarters of the Supreme Allied Command in Europe. I repeat, there is no official announcement yet. The report that the war in Europe has ended has come from only one correspondent. It has not been confirmed by other correspondents or by SHAEF headquarters. But here is one highly intriguing fact—that report has not been denied either in Washington or in SHAEF headquarters in Europe. IT HAS NOT BEEN DENIED. Right now in those places the newsmen are crowded, waiting to flash to the world the announcement of V-E Day.

SCENE III

The lights come up on ROBERTS' *and* PULVER'S *cabin.* DOC, *at the desk, and* PULVER, *up in his bunk, are listening to the radio.*

PULVER: Turn that damn thing off, Doc. Has Doug ever said anything to you about wanting a promotion?

DOC: Of course not. I doubt if he's even conscious of what rank he is.

PULVER: You can say that again!

DOC: I doubt if he's even conscious of what rank he is.

PULVER: That's what I said. He doesn't even think about a promotion. The only thing he thinks about is the war news—up in the radio shack two weeks now—all day long—listening with a headset, reading all the bulletins . . . Anyone who says he's bucking for another stripe is a dirty liar.

DOC: Who says he is, Frank?

PULVER: Insigna, Mannion and some of the other guys. I heard them talking outside the porthole. They were talking loud on purpose so I could hear them—they must've guessed I was lying here on my bunk. What's happened to Doug anyway, Doc?

DOC: How would I know! He's spoken about ten words to me in as many days. But I'm damn well going to find out.

PULVER: He won't talk, Doc. This morning I followed him all around the room while he was shaving. I begged him to talk to me. I says, "You're a fellow who needs a friend and here I am." And I says, "What's all this trouble you're having with the crew? You tell me and I'll fix it up like that." And then I give him some real good advice—I says, "Keep your chin up," and things like that. And then do you know what he did? He walked out of the room just as though I wasn't here.

(*There is a knock on the door.*)

DOC: Come in.

(DOWDY *enters.*)

DOWDY: Doc, Mister Pulver—could we see you officers a minute?

DOC: Sure. (GERHART *and* LINDSTROM *enter, closing the door.*) What is it?

DOWDY: Tell them what happened, Gerhart.

GERHART: Well, sir, I sure don't like to say this but . . . Mister Roberts just put Dolan on report.

LINDSTROM: Me and Gerhart seen him.

PULVER: On report!

GERHART: Yes, sir. Tomorrow morning Dolan has to go up before the Captain—on account of Mister Roberts.

LINDSTROM: On account of Mister Roberts.

GERHART: And we was wondering if you officers could get him to take Dolan off report before . . . well, before—

DOC: Before what, Gerhart?

GERHART: Well, you see, the guys are all down in the compartment, talking about it. And they're saying some pretty rough things about Mister Roberts. Nobody just ever expected to see him put a man on report and . . .

LINDSTROM: He ain't gonna turn out to be like an officer, is he, Doc?

DOWDY: Lindstrom . . .

LINDSTROM: Oh, I didn't mean you, Doc . . . or even you, Mister Pulver!

DOC: That's all right, Lindstrom. What was this trouble with Dolan?

DOWDY: This letter business again!

GERHART: Yes, sir. Dolan was just kiddin' him about not sending in any more letters. And all of a sudden Mister Roberts turned just white and yelled, "Shut up, Dolan. Shut your goddamn mouth. I've had enough." And Dolan naturally got snotty back at him and Mister Roberts put him right on report.

LINDSTROM: Right on report.

(ROBERTS *enters.*)

PULVER: Hello, Doug boy. Aren't you listening to the war news?

DOWDY: All right, Doctor. We'll get that medical store room cleaned out tomorrow.

(DOWDY, GERHART *and* LINDSTROM *leave.*)

PULVER: We thought you were up in the radio shack.

ROBERTS (*to* PULVER): Don't you want to go down to the wardroom and have a cup of coffee?

PULVER (*jumping down from bunk*): Sure. I'll go with you.

ROBERTS: I don't want any. Why don't you go ahead?

PULVER: Nah. (*He sits back on bunk. There is another little pause.*)

ROBERTS: Will you go on out anyway? I want to talk to Doc.

PULVER (*rising and crossing to door*): All right, I will. I'm going for a cup of coffee. (*Stops, turns and gets cap from top of locker.*) No! I'm going up to the radio shack. You aren't the only one interested in the war news. (*He exits.*)

ROBERTS (*with emotion*): Doc, transfer me, will you? (DOC *looks at him.*) Transfer me to the hospital on this next island! You can do it. You don't need the Captain's approval! Just put me ashore for examination—say there's something wrong with my eyes or my feet or my head, for Christ's sake! You can trump up something!

DOC: What good would that do?

ROBERTS: Plenty! I could lie around that hospital for a couple of weeks. The ship would have sailed—I'd have missed it! I'd be off this ship. Will you do it, Doc?

DOC: Doug, why did you put Dolan on report just now?

ROBERTS (*angrily*): I gave him an order and he didn't carry it out fast enough to suit me. (*Glares at* DOC, *who just studies him.* ROBERTS *rises and paces right.*) No, that's not true. It was the war. I just heard the news. The war is ending and I couldn't get to it and there was Dolan giving me guff about something—and all of a sudden I hated him. I hated all of them. I was sick of the sullen bastards staring at me as though I'd sold them down the river or something. If they think I'm bucking for a promotion—if they're stupid enough to think I'd walk ten feet across the room to get anything from that Captain, then I'm through with the whole damn ungrateful mob!

DOC: Does this crew owe you something?

ROBERTS: What the hell do you mean by that?

DOC: You talk as if they did. (ROBERTS *rises and crosses to bunk.*)

ROBERTS (*quietly*): That's exactly how I'm talking. I didn't realize it but that's exactly the way I've been feeling. Oh, Jesus, that shows you how far gone I am, Doc. I've been taking something out on them. I've been blaming them for something that . . .

DOC: What, Doug? Something what? You've made some sort of an agreement with the Captain, haven't you, Doug!

ROBERTS (*turns*): Agreement? I don't know what you mean. Will you transfer me, Doc?

DOC: Not a chance, Doug. I could never get away with it—you know that.

ROBERTS: Oh, my God!

PULVER (*offstage*): Doug! Doc! (*Entering.*) Listen to the radio, you uninformed bastards! Turn it up!

(ROBERTS *reaches over and turns up the radio. The excited voice of an announcer can be heard.*)

ANNOUNCER: . . . this broadcast to bring you a special news flash! The war is over in Europe! THE WAR IS OVER IN EUROPE! (ROBERTS *grasps* DOC's *arm in excitement.*) Germany has surrendered unconditionally to the Allied Armies. The surrender was signed in a schoolhouse in the city of Rheims . . .

(ROBERTS *stands staring.* DOC *turns off the radio. For a moment there is silence, then:*)

DOC: I would remind you that there's still a minor skirmish here in the Pacific.

ROBERTS: I'll miss that one too. But to hell with me. This is the greatest day in the world. We're going to celebrate. How about it, Frank?

PULVER: Yeah, Doug. We've got to celebrate!

DOC (*starting to pull alcohol from waste basket*): What'll it be— alcohol and orange juice or orange juice and alcohol?

ROBERTS: No, that's not good enough.

PULVER: Hell, no, Doc! (*He looks expectantly at* ROBERTS.)

ROBERTS: We've got to think of something that'll lift this ship right out of the water and turn it around the other way.

(PULVER *suddenly rises to his feet.*)

PULVER (*shouting*): Doug! Oh, my God, why didn't I think of this before. Doug! Doc! You're going to blow your tops when you hear the idea I got! Oh, Jesus, what a wonderful idea! It's the only thing to do. It's the only thing in the whole world to do! That's all! Doug, you said I never had any ideas. You said I never finished anything I started. Well, you're wrong—tonight you're wrong! I thought of something and I finished it. I was going to save it for your birthday, but I'm going to give it to you tonight, because we gotta celebrate . . .

ROBERTS (*waves his hands in* PULVER'S *face for attention*): Wait a minute, Frank! What is it?

PULVER: A firecracker, by God. (*He reaches under his mattress and pulls out a large, wobbly firecracker which has been painted red.*) We're gonna throw a firecracker under the Old Man's bunk. Bam-bam-bam! Wake up, you old son-of-a-bitch, IT'S V-E DAY!

ROBERTS (*rising*): Frank!

PULVER: Look at her, Doc. Ain't it a beauty? Ain't that the greatest hand-made, hand-painted, hand-packed firecracker you ever saw?

ROBERTS (*Smiling and taking firecracker*): Yes, Frank. That's the most beautiful firecracker I ever saw in my life. But will it work?

PULVER: Sure it'll work. At least, I think so.

ROBERTS: Haven't you tested it? It's got to work, Frank, it's just got to work!

PULVER: I'll tell you what I'll do. I'll take it down to the laundry and test it—that's my laboratory, the laundry. I got all the fixings down there—powder, fuses, everything, all hid behind the soapflakes. And if this one works, I can make another one in two minutes.

ROBERTS: Okay, Frank. Take off. We'll wait for you here. (PULVER *starts off*.) Be sure you got enough to make it loud. What'd you use for powder?

PULVER: Loud! This ain't a popgun. This is a firecracker. I used fulminate of mercury. I'll be right back. (*He runs out*.)

ROBERTS: Fulminate of mercury! That stuff's murder! Do you think he means it?

DOC (*taking alcohol bottle from waste basket*): Of course not. Where could he get fulminate of mercury?

ROBERTS: I don't know. He's pretty resourceful. Where did he get the clap last year?

DOC: How about a drink, Doug? (*He pours alcohol and orange juice into two glasses*.)

ROBERTS: Right! Doc, I been living with a genius. This makes it all worth while—the whole year and a half he spent in his bunk. How else could you celebrate V-E Day? A firecracker under the Old Man's bunk! The silly little son-of-a-bitch!

DOC (*handing* ROBERTS *a drink*): Here you are, Doug. (DOC *holds the drink up in a toast*.) To better days!

ROBERTS: Okay. And to a great American, Frank Thurlowe Pulver . . . Soldier . . . Statesman . . . Scientist . . .

DOC: Friend of the Working Girl . . .

(*Suddenly there is a tremendous explosion*. DOC *and* ROBERTS *clutch at the desk*.)

ROBERTS: Oh, my God!

DOC: He wasn't kidding! That's fulminate of mercury!

CAPTAIN (*offstage*): What was that?

(ROBERTS *and* DOC *rush to porthole, listening.*)

JOHNSON (*offstage*): I don't know, Captain. I'll find out!

(*We hear the sounds of running feet.*)

ROBERTS: Doc, we've got to go down and get him.
DOC: This may be pretty bad, Doug.

(*They turn to start for the door when suddenly a figure hurtles into the room and stops. For a moment it looks like a combination scarecrow and snowman but it is* PULVER—*his uniform tattered; his knees, arms and face blackened; he is covered with soapsuds and his eyes are shining with excitement.* ROBERTS *stares in amazement.*)

PULVER: Jeez, that stuff's terrific!
DOC: Are you all right?
PULVER: I'm great! Gee, you should've been there!
ROBERTS: You aren't burned—or anything?
PULVER: Hell, no. But the laundry's kinda beat up. The mangle's on the other side of the room now. And there's a new porthole on the starboard side where the electric iron went through. And I guess a steam-line must've busted or something—I was up to my ass in lather. And soapflakes flyin' around—it was absolutely beautiful!

(*During these last lines,* DOC *has been making a brisk, professional examination.*)

DOC: It's a miracle. He isn't even scratched!
PULVER: Come on down and see it, Doug. It's a Winter Wonderland!
CAPTAIN (*offstage*): Johnson!
ROBERTS: Quiet!
JOHNSON (*offstage*): Yes, sir.
CAPTAIN (*offstage*): What was it?
JOHNSON (*offstage*): The laundry, Captain. A steam-line must've blew up.
PULVER (*explaining*): Steam-line came right out of the bulkhead. (*He demonstrates.*) Whish!

CAPTAIN (*offstage*): How much damage?

JOHNSON (*offstage*): We can't tell yet, Captain. We can't get in there —the passageway is solid soapsuds.

PULVER: Solid soapsuds. (*He pantomimes walking blindly through soapsuds.*)

CAPTAIN (*offstage*): Tell those men to be more careful.

ROBERTS (*excitedly*): Frank, our celebration is just getting started. The night is young and our duty's clear.

PULVER: Yeah? What're we gonna do now, Doug?

ROBERTS: Get cleaned up and come with me.

PULVER: Where we goin' now, Doug?

ROBERTS: We're going down and get the rest of your stuff. You proved it'd work—you just hit the wrong target, that's all. We're going to make another firecracker, and put it where it really belongs.

PULVER (*who has slowly wilted during* ROBERTS' *speech*): The rest of my stuff was—in the laundry, Doug. It all went up. There isn't any more. I'm sorry, Doug. I'm awful sorry.

ROBERTS (*sinks into chair*): That's all right, Frank.

PULVER: Maybe I can scrounge some more tomorrow.

ROBERTS: Sure.

PULVER: You aren't sore at me, are you, Doug?

ROBERTS: What for?

PULVER: For spoilin' our celebration?

ROBERTS: Of course not.

PULVER: It was a good idea though, wasn't it, Doug?

ROBERTS: Frank, it was a great idea. I'm proud of you. It just didn't work, that's all. (*He starts for the door.*)

DOC: Where are you going, Doug?

ROBERTS: Out on deck.

PULVER: Wait'll I get cleaned up and I'll come with you.

ROBERTS: No, I'm going to turn in after that. (*To* PULVER.) It's okay, Frank. (*He exits.*)

(PULVER *turns pleadingly to* DOC.)

PULVER: He was happy there for a minute though, wasn't he, Doc? Did you see him laughing? He was happy as hell. (*Pause.*) We gotta do something for that guy, Doc. He's in bad shape. What's the matter with him anyhow, Doc. Did you find out?

DOC: No, he wouldn't tell me. But I know one thing he's feeling tonight and that's panic. Tonight he feels his war is dying before he can get to it. (DOC *goes to radio and turns up volume.*)

PULVER: I let him down. He wanted to celebrate and I let him down. (*He drops his head.*)

ANNOUNCER'S VOICE *on radio comes up as the lights*

Fade Out

(*During the darkness and under the first part of Scene IV we hear the voice of a British broadcaster:*)

BRITISH BROADCASTER: . . . we hope that the King and Queen will come out. The crowds are cheering—listen to them—and at any second now we hope to see Their Majesties. The color here is tremendous—everywhere rosettes, everywhere gay, red-white-and-blue hats. All the girls in their summer frocks on this lovely, mild, historic May evening. And although we celebrate with joyous heart the great victory, perhaps the greatest victory in the history of mankind, the underlying mood is a mood of thanksgiving. And now, I believe, they're coming. They haven't appeared but the crowd in the center are cheering madly. Handkerchiefs, flags, hands waving—HERE THEY COME! First, Her Majesty, the Queen, has come into view. Then the King in the uniform of an Admiral of the Fleet. The two Princesses standing on the balcony—listen to the crowd—

(*Sound of wild cheering.*)

(*This broadcast continues throughout the blackout and the next scene. Several times the station is changed, from a broadcast of the celebration in San Francisco to the speaker in New York and the band playing "The Stars and Stripes Forever" in Times Square.*)

SCENE IV

The lights dim up on the main set. It is a few minutes later, and bright moonlight. The ship is under way—this is indicated by the apparent movement of the stars, slowly up and down. A group of men are sitting on the hatch cover in a late bull session. They are INSIGNA, MANNION, DOLAN and STEFANOWSKI.

GERHART *stands over them; he has obviously just returned from some mission for the group.*

GERHART: I'm telling you, that's all it was. A steam pipe busted in the laundry—they're cleaning it up now. It ain't worth going to see.

(*The others make way for him and he sits down beside them.* INSIGNA *cocks his head toward the sound of the radio.*)

INSIGNA: What the hell's all the jabbering on the radio now?

MANNION: I don't know. Something about the King and Queen . . .

(*The men listen for a moment without curiosity; then, as the radio fades, they settle back in indolent positions.*)

INSIGNA: Well, anyhow, like I was telling you, this big sergeant in Elysium was scared to fight me! Tell 'em how big he was, Killer.

MANNION: Six foot seven or eight . . .

STEFANOWSKI: That sergeant's grown eight inches since we left Elysium . . . Did you see me when I swiped that Shore Patrol band and went around arresting guys? That Shore Patrol Lieutenant said I was the best man he had. I arrested forty-three guys . . .

MANNION (*smiles at* DOLAN *who is looking depressed*): Come on, Dolan, don't let him get you down.

INSIGNA: Yeah, come on, Dolan.

(ROBERTS *enters. He looks at the men, who have their backs turned, hesitates, then goes slowly over to them.*)

GERHART (*idly*): What was them croquette things we had for chow to-night?

(STEFANOWSKI *looks up and notices* ROBERTS. *Instantly he sits upright.*)

STEFANOWSKI: Flash Red!

(*The men sit up. There is an embarrassed silence.*)

ROBERTS: Good evening. (*The men smile politely.* ROBERTS *is very embarrassed.*) Did you hear the news? The war's over in Europe.

MANNION (*smiling*): Yes, sir. We heard.

STEFANOWSKI (*helping out the conversation*): Sure. Maybe somebody'll get on the ball out here now . . .

(DOLAN *rises, starts down hatchway.*)

ROBERTS: Dolan, I guess I kind of blew my top tonight. I'm sorry. I'm taking you off report.

DOLAN: Whatever you want, sir . . . (*He looks ostentatiously at his watch and yawns.*) Well, I guess I'll hit the old sack . . . (*He goes down hatchway.*)

MANNION: Yeah, me too . . .

INSIGNA: Yeah . . .

GERHART: It's late as hell.

STEFANOWSKI: I didn't realize how late it was . . .

(*All the men get up, then go down the hatchway.* ROBERTS *stands looking after them. Now the radio is heard again.* ROBERTS *goes to hatchway and sits listening.*)

SPEAKER: . . . Our boys have won this victory today. But the rest is up to you. You and you alone must recognize our enemies: the forces of ambition, cruelty, arrogance and stupidity. You must recognize them, you must destroy them, you must tear them out as you would a malignant growth! And cast them from the surface of the earth!

(*The end of the speech is followed by a band playing "The Stars and Stripes Forever."* ROBERTS' *face lights up and a new determination is in it. He repeats the words "malignant growth." The band music swells. He marches to the palm tree, salutes it, rubs his hands together and, as the music reaches a climax, he jerks the palm tree, earth and all, from the container and throws it over the side. Then, as the music continues, loud and climactic, he brushes his hands together, shrugs, and walks casually off left singing the tune to himself.*)

(*For a moment the stage is empty. Then the lights go up in the* CAPTAIN'S *cabin. The door to the* CAPTAIN'S *cabin opens and the* CAPTAIN *appears. He is in pajamas and bathrobe, and in one hand he carries his watering can. He discovers the empty container. He looks at it, then plunges into his cabin. After a moment, the General Alarm is heard. It is a terrible clanging noise designated to rouse the dead. When the alarm stops, the* CAPTAIN'S *voice is heard, almost hysterical, over the squawk box.*)

CAPTAIN: General Quarters! General Quarters! Every man to his battle station on the double!

(JOHNSON, *in helmet and life jacket, scurries from hatchway into the* CAPTAIN'S CABIN. WILEY *enters from right passageway and climbs into the right gun tub. Now men appear from all directions in various degrees of dress. The stage is filled with men frantically running everywhere, all wearing helmets and life preservers.*)

INSIGNA (*appearing from hatchway*): What happened? (*He runs up the ladder and into the left gun tub.* PAYNE *enters from left and starts to climb up to left gun tub.*) Get the hell out of here, Payne. This ain't your gun—your gun's over there!

DOLAN (*also trying to climb the ladder with* PAYNE): Over there . . . over there . . .

(PAYNE *crosses to right gun tub.*)

REBER (*entering from hatchway*): What the hell happened?

SCHLEMMER: Are *we* in an air raid?

PAYNE: Submarine . . . must be a submarine!

GERHART: Hey, Wiley, what happened?

DOWDY (*calling to someone on life raft*): Hey, get away from that life raft. He didn't say abandon ship!

(*During the confusion,* STEFANOWSKI, *bewildered, emerges from the hatchway and wanders over to right gun tub.*)

STEFANOWSKI: Hey, Wiley, Wiley—you sure you're supposed to be up there?

WILEY: Yeah.

STEFANOWSKI (*crossing to left gun tub*): Hey, Sam. Are you supposed to be up there?

INSIGNA: Yeah, we was here last year!

STEFANOWSKI: Hey, Dowdy. Where the hell's my battle station?

DOWDY: I don't know where your battle station is! Look around!

(STEFANOWSKI *wanders aimlessly about.* WILEY, *in the gun tub right, is receiving reports of battle readiness from various parts of the ship:*)

WILEY: Twenty millimeters manned and ready. (*Pause.*) Engine room manned and ready. (*Pause.*) All battle stations manned and ready.

STEFANOWSKI (*sitting on corner of hatch*): Yeah, all but mine . . .

JOHNSON'S VOICE (*in* CAPTAIN'S *cabin*): All battle stations manned and ready, Captain.

CAPTAIN'S VOICE: Give me that thing.

JOHNSON'S VOICE (*"on mike"—that is, speaking directly into squawk-box microphone. "Off mike" means speaking unintentionally into this live microphone*): Attention . . . Attention . . . The Captain wishes to . . .

CAPTAIN'S VOICE (*off mike*): Give me that thing! (*On mike.*) All right, who did it? Who did it? You're going to stay here all night until someone confesses. You're going to stay at those battle stations until hell freezes over until I find out who did it. It's an insult to the honor of this ship, by God! The symbol of our cargo record has been destroyed and I'm going to find out who did it if it takes all night! (*Off mike.*) Johnson, read me that muster list!

JOHNSON'S VOICE (*reading muster list off mike*): Abernathy . . .

MANNION
Symbol of our cargo record? What the hell's that?

(STEFANOWSKI *rises, sees empty container, kneels and ceremoniously bows to it.*)

DOWDY
For God's sake, Stefanowski, find some battle station!

CAPTAIN'S VOICE
No, not Abernathy . . .

JOHNSON'S VOICE
Baker . . .

CAPTAIN'S VOICE
No . . .

JOHNSON'S VOICE
Bartholomew . . . Becker . . . Billings . . . Carney . . . Daniels . . . Dexter . . . Ellison . . . Everman . . . Jenkins . . . Kelly . . . Kevin . . . Martin . . .

(STEFANOWSKI *points to empty container*. DOWDY *sees it and spreads the news to the men on left*. SCHLEMMER *sees it and tells the other men. Now from all parts of the ship men enter and jubilantly look at the empty container. Bits of soil fly into the air as the men group around the empty can*.).

Olsen . . .

O'Neill . . .

CAPTAIN'S VOICE

No, not O'Neill . . .

Pulver . . .

CAPTAIN'S VOICE

No, not Pulver. He hasn't the guts . . .

JOHNSON'S VOICE

Roberts . . .

CAPTAIN'S VOICE (*roaring, off mike*): Roberts! He's the one! Get him up here!

JOHNSON'S VOICE (*on mike*): Mister Roberts will report to the Captain's cabin on the double!

(*The men rush back to their battle stations.*)

CAPTAIN'S VOICE: Get him up here, I tell you! Get him up here . . .

JOHNSON'S VOICE (*on mike*): Mister Roberts will report to the Captain's cabin on the . . .

CAPTAIN (*off mike*): Give me that thing. (*On mike.*) Roberts, you get up here in a goddamn quick hurry. Get up here! Roberts, I'm giving you an order—get the lead out of your pants.

(ROBERTS *appears from left passageway and, walking slowly, enters the* CAPTAIN'S *cabin.*)

(*The men move onstage and* LINDSTROM *gets to a position on the ladder where he can look through the porthole of the* CAPTAIN'S *cabin.*)

ROBERTS' VOICE: Did you want to see me, Captain?

CAPTAIN'S VOICE: You did it. You did it. Don't lie to me. Don't stand there and lie to me. Confess it!

ROBERTS' VOICE: Confess what, Captain? I don't know what you're talking about.

CAPTAIN'S VOICE: You know damn well what I'm talkin' about because you did it. You've doublecrossed me—you've gone back on your word!

ROBERTS' VOICE: No, I haven't, Captain.

CAPTAIN: Yes, by God, you have. I kept my part of the bargain! I gave this crew liberty—I gave this crew liberty, by God, but you've gone back on *your* word.

(DOWDY *takes off his helmet and looks at the men.*)

ROBERTS' VOICE: I don't see how you can say that, Captain. I haven't sent in any more letters.

(DOLAN, *on gun tub ladder, catches* INSIGNA'S *eye.*)

CAPTAIN'S VOICE: I'm not talkin' about your goddamn sons-a-bitchin' letters. I'm talkin' about what you did tonight.

ROBERTS' VOICE: Tonight? I don't understand you, Captain. What do you think I did?

CAPTAIN: Quit saying that, goddammit, quit saying that. You know damn well what you did. You stabbed me in the back. You stabbed me in the back . . . aaa . . . aa . . .

JOHNSON'S VOICE: Captain! Get over to the washbasin, Captain!

CAPTAIN'S VOICE: Aaaaaaa . . .

INSIGNA: What the hell happened?

DOLAN: Quiet!

JOHNSON (*on mike*): Will the Doctor please report to the Captain's cabin on the double?

(DOC *appears from left, pushing his way through the crowd, followed by two* MEDICAL CORPSMEN *wearing Red Cross brassards and carrying first-aid kits and a stretcher.* DOC *walks slowly; he is idly attaching a brassard and smoking a cigarette. He wears his helmet sloppily.*)

DOC: Gangway . . . gangway . . .

DOWDY: Hey, Doc, tell us what's going on.

DOC: Okay. Okay. (*He enters the* CAPTAIN'S *cabin followed by the* CORPSMEN *who leave stretcher leaning against the bulkhead. The door closes. There is a tense pause. The men gather around the cabin again.* LINDSTROM *is at the porthole.*)

REBER: Hey, Lindstrom, where's the Old Man?

LINDSTROM: He's sittin' in the chair—leaning way forward.

PAYNE: What's the Doc doin'?

LINDSTROM: He's holdin' the waste basket.

REBER: What waste basket?

LINDSTROM: The one the Old Man's got his head in. And he needs it too. (*Pause.*) They're helpin' him over to the couch. (*Pause.*) He's lying down there and they're takin' off his shoes. (*Pause.*) Look out, here they come.

(*The men break quickly and rush back to their battle stations. The door opens and* ROBERTS, DOC *and the* CORPSMEN *come out.*)

DOC (*to* CORPSMEN): We won't need that stretcher. Sorry. (*Calls.*) Dowdy! Come here.

(DOWDY *comes down to* DOC. *He avoids* ROBERTS' *eyes.*)

ROBERTS: Dowdy, pass the word to the crew to secure from General Quarters.

DOC: And tell the men not to make any noise while they go to their bunks. The Captain's resting quietly now, and I think that's desirable.

ROBERTS: Pass the word, will you, Dowdy?

DOWDY: Yes, Mister Roberts. (*He passes the word to the crew who slowly start to leave their battle stations. They are obviously stalling.*)

DOC (*to* ROBERTS): Got a cigarette? (ROBERTS *reaches in his pocket and offers* DOC *a cigarette. Then he lights* DOC'S *cigarette.* DOC *notices the men stalling.*) Well, guess I'd better get back inside. I'll be down to see you after I get through. (*He enters cabin and stands there watching. The men move offstage, very slowly, saying "Good night, Mister Roberts," "Good night, sir." Suddenly* ROBERTS *notices that all the men are saying good night to him.*)

DOLAN (*quietly*): Good night, Mister Roberts. (ROBERTS *does not hear him.*) Good night, Mister Roberts.

ROBERTS: Good night, Dolan.

(DOLAN *smiles and exits down hatch.* ROBERTS *steps toward hatch, removes helmet, looks puzzled as the lights*

Fade Out

(*During the darkness, over the squawk box the following announcements are heard:*)

FIRST VOICE: Now hear this . . . Now hear this . . . C, E and S Divisions and all Pharmacist's Mates will air bedding today—positively!

SECOND VOICE: There is now available at the ship's store a small supply of peanut brittle. Ship's store will be open from 1300 to 1315.

THIRD VOICE: Now, Dolan, Yeoman Second Class, report to the radio shack immediately.

SCENE V

The lights come up on the stateroom of ROBERTS *and* PULVER. PULVER *is lying in the lower bunk.* DOC *is sitting at the desk with a glass and a bottle of grain alcohol in front of him.* ROBERTS *is tying up a sea bag. A small suitcase stands beside it. His locker is open and empty.* WILEY *picks up the sea bag.*

WILEY: Okay, Mister Roberts. I'll take these down to the gangway. The boat from the island should be out here any minute for you. I'll let you know.

ROBERTS: Thanks, Wiley.

WILEY (*grinning*): That's okay, Mister Roberts. Never thought you'd be taking this ride, did you? (*He exits with the bags.*)

ROBERTS: I'm going to be off this bucket before I even wake up.

DOC: They flying you all the way to the *Livingston?*

ROBERTS: I don't know. The radio dispatch just said I was transferred and travel by air if possible. I imagine it's all the way though. They're landing planes at Okinawa now and that's where my can is probably running around. (*Laughs a little.*) Listen to me, Doc—my can!

PULVER (*studying map by* ROBERTS' *bunk*): Okinawa! Jeez, you be might-y careful, Doug.

ROBERTS: Okay, Frank. This is *too* much to take, Doc. I even got a destroyer! The *Livingston!* That's one of the greatest cans out there.

PULVER: I know a guy on the *Livingston.* He don't think it's so hot.

DOLAN (*entering. He has a file folder under his arm*): Here you are, Mister Roberts. I typed up three copies of the radio dispatch. I've got to keep a copy and here's two for you. You're now officially detached from this here bucket. Let me be the first.

ROBERTS: Thanks, Dolan. (*They shake hands.* ROBERTS *takes papers, and looks at them.*) Dolan, how about these orders? I haven't sent in a letter for a month!

DOLAN (*carefully*): You know how the Navy works, Mister Roberts.

ROBERTS: Yeah, I know, but it doesn't seem . . .

DOLAN: Listen, Mister Roberts, I can tell you exactly what happened. Those guys at the Bureau need men for combat duty awful bad and they started looking through all the old letters and they just come across one of yours.

ROBERTS: Maybe—but still you'd think . . .

DOLAN: Listen, Mister Roberts. We can't stand here beating our gums! You better get cracking! You seen what it said there, "Proceed immediately." And the Old Man says if you ain't off of here in an hour, by God, he's going to throw you off!

ROBERTS: Is that all he said?

DOLAN: That's all he said.

ROBERTS (*grinning at* DOC): After fighting this for two years you'd think he'd say more than that . . .

CAPTAIN'S VOICE (*offstage*): Be careful of that one. Put it down easy.

DOC: What's that?

DOLAN: A new enlarged botanical garden. That's why he can't even be bothered about you today, Mister Roberts. Soon as we anchored this morning he sent Olsen over with a special detail—they dug up two palm trees . . . He's busy as a mother skunk now and you know what he's done—he's already set a twenty-four-hour watch on these new babies with orders to shoot to kill. (*To* PULVER.) That reminds me, Mister Pulver. The Captain wants to see you right away.

PULVER: Yeah? What about?

DOLAN: I don't know, sir. (*To* ROBERTS.) I'll be back to say good-bye, Mister Roberts. Come on, Mister Pulver. (*He exits.*)

PULVER (*following* DOLAN *out*): What the hell did I do with his laundry this week?

(ROBERTS *smiles as he starts putting on his black tie.*)

DOC: You're a happy son-of-a-bitch, aren't you?

ROBERTS: Yep. You're happy about it too, aren't you, Doc?

DOC: I think it's the only thing for you. (*Casually.*) What do you think of the crew now, Doug?

ROBERTS: We're all right now. I think they're nice guys—all of them.

DOC: Unh-hunh. And how do you think they feel about you?

ROBERTS: I think they like me all right . . . till the next guy comes along.

DOC: You don't think you're necessary to them?

ROBERTS (*sitting on bunk*): Hell, no. No officer's necessary to the crew, Doc.

DOC: Are you going to leave this ship believing that?

ROBERTS: That's nothing against them. A crew's too busy looking after themselves to care about anyone else.

DOC: Well, take a good, deep breath, Buster. (*He drinks some alcohol.*) What do you think got you your orders? Prayer and fasting? Sending in enough Wheatie box tops?

ROBERTS: My orders? Why, what Dolan said—one of my old letters turned up . . .

DOC: Bat crap! This crew got you transferred. They were so busy looking out for themselves that they took a chance of landing in prison for five years—any one of them. Since you couldn't send in a letter for transfer, they sent one in for you. Since they knew the Captain wouldn't sign it approved, they didn't bother him—they signed it for him.

ROBERTS: What do you mean? They forged the Captain's name?

DOC: That's right.

ROBERTS (*rising*): Doc! Who did? Which one of them?

DOC: That would be hard to say. You see, they had a mass meeting down in the compartment. They put guards at every door. They called it the Captain's-Name-Signing contest. And every man in this crew—a hundred and sixty-seven of them—signed the Captain's name on a blank sheet of paper. And then there were judges who compared these signatures with the Captain's and selected the one to go in. At the time there was some criticism of the decision on the grounds that the judges were drunk, but apparently, from the results, they chose well.

ROBERTS: How'd you find out about this, Doc?

DOC: Well it was a great honor. I am the only officer aboard who does know. I was a contestant. I was also a judge. This double honor was accorded me because of my character, charm, good looks and because the medical department contributed four gallons of grain alcohol to the contest. (*Pauses.*) It was quite a thing to see, Doug. A hundred and sixty-seven guys with only one idea in their heads—to do something for Mister Roberts.

ROBERTS (*after a moment*): I wish you hadn't told me, Doc. It makes me look pretty silly after what I just said. But I didn't mean it, Doc. I was afraid to say what I really feel. I love those bastards, Doc. I think they're the greatest guys on this earth. All of a sudden I feel that there's something wrong—something terribly wrong—about leaving them. God, what can I say to them?

DOC: You won't say anything—you don't even know. When you're safely aboard your new ship I'm supposed to write and tell you about it. And at the bottom of the letter, I'm supposed to say, "Thanks for the liberty, Mister Roberts. Thanks for everything."

ROBERTS: Jesus!

(PULVER *enters, downcast.*)

PULVER: I'm the new Cargo Officer. And that's not all—I got to have dinner with him tonight. He *likes* me!

(*There is a polite rap on the door.*)

DOC: Come in. (*Enter* PAYNE, REBER, GERHART, SCHLEMMER, DOLAN *and* INSIGNA, *all carrying canteen cups except* INSIGNA *whose cup is in his belt. He carries a large, red fire extinguisher.*) What's this?

INSIGNA: Fire and rescue party. Heard you had a fire in here.

(*All are looking at* ROBERTS.)

ROBERTS: No, but—since you're here—I—

INSIGNA: Hell, we got a false alarm then. Happens all the time. (*Sets extinguisher on desk.*) In that case, we might as well drink this stuff. Give me your glass, Mister Roberts, and I'll put a head on it—yours too, Doc. I got one for you, Mister Pulver. (*He fills their glasses from the fire extinguisher.*)

ROBERTS: What's in that, a new batch of jungle juice?

INSIGNA: Yeah, in the handy, new, portable container. Everybody loaded?

(*All nod.*)

DOLAN: Go ahead, Sam.

INSIGNA (*to* ROBERTS): There's a story going around that you're leaving us. That right?

ROBERTS (*carefully*): That's right, Sam. And I . . .

INSIGNA: Well, we didn't want you to get away without having a little drink with us and we thought we ought to give you a little sort of going-away present. The fellows made it down in the machine shop. It ain't much but we hope you like it. (REBER *prompts him.*) We all sincerely hope you like it. (*Calls offstage.*) All right, you bastards, you can come in now.

(*Enter* LINDSTROM, MANNION, DOWDY *and* STEFANOWSKI. MANNION *is carrying a candy box. He walks over to* ROBERTS *shyly and hands him the box.*)

ROBERTS: What is it?

SCHLEMMER: Open it.

(ROBERTS *opens the box. There is a deep silence.*)

PULVER: What is it, Doug?

(ROBERTS *holds up the box. In it is a brass medal shaped like a palm tree attached to a piece of gaudy ribbon.*)

LINDSTROM: It's a palm tree, see.

DOLAN: It was Dowdy's idea.

DOWDY: Mannion here made it. He cut it out of sheet brass down in the machine shop.

INSIGNA: Mannion drilled the words on it too.

MANNION: Stefanowski thought up the words.

STEFANOWSKI (*shoving* LINDSTROM *forward*): Lindstrom gets credit for the ribbon from a box of candy that his sister-in-law sent him. Read the words, Mister Roberts.

ROBERTS (*with difficulty*): "Order . . . order of . . ." (*He hands the medal to* DOC.)

DOC (*rises and reads solemnly*): "Order of the palm. To Lieutenant (jg) Douglas Roberts for action against the enemy, above and beyond the call of duty on the night of eight May 1945." (*He passes the medal back to* ROBERTS.)

ROBERTS (*after a moment—smiling*): It's very nice but I'm afraid you've got the wrong guy.

(*The men turn to* DOWDY, *grinning.*)

DOWDY: We know that, but we'd kinda like for you to have it anyway.

ROBERTS: All right, I'll keep it.

(*The men beam. There is an awkward pause.*)

GERHART: Stefanowski thought up the words.

ROBERTS: They're fine words.

(WILEY *enters.*)

WILEY: The boat's here, Mister Roberts. I put your gear in. They want to shove off right away.

ROBERTS (*rising*): Thanks. We haven't had our drink yet.

REBER: No, we ain't.

(*All get to their feet.* ROBERTS *picks up his glass, looks at the crew, and everyone drinks.*)

ROBERTS: Good-bye, Doc.

DOC: Good-bye, Doug.

ROBERTS: And thanks, Doc.

DOC: Okay.

ROBERTS: Good-bye, Frank.

PULVER: Good-bye, Doug.

ROBERTS: Remember, I'm counting on you.

(PULVER *nods.* ROBERTS *turns to the crew and looks at them for a moment. Then he takes the medal from the box, pins it on his shirt, shows it to them, then gives a little gestured salute and exits as the lights*

Fade Out

During the darkness we hear voices making announcements over the squawk box:

FIRST VOICE: Now hear this . . . now hear this . . . Sweepers, man your brooms. Clean sweep-down fore and aft!

SECOND VOICE: Now hear this! All men put on report today will fall in on the quarter-deck—and form three ranks!

THIRD VOICE: Now hear this! All divisions will draw their mail at
1700—in the mess hall.

SCENE VI

The lights come up showing the main set at sunset. DOC *is sitting on the hatch, reading a letter.* MANNION, *wearing sidearms,
is pacing up and down in front of the* CAPTAIN'S *cabin. On
each side of the door is a small palm tree in a five-gallon
can—on one can is painted in large white letters, "Keep
Away"; on the other, "This Means You." After a moment,*
PULVER *enters from the left passageway, carrying a small
packet of letters.*

PULVER: Hello, Mannion. Got your mail yet?

MANNION: No. I've got the palm tree watch.

PULVER: Oh. (*To* DOC.) What's your news, Doc?

DOC: My wife got some new wallpaper for the living room.

(PULVER *sits on hatch cover.* DOWDY *enters wearing work gloves.*)

DOWDY: Mister Pulver, we'll be finished with the cargo in a few minutes.

PULVER: How'd it go?

DOWDY: Not bad. I've got to admit you were right about Number Three
hold. It worked easier out of there. Mister Pulver, I just found out
what the Captain decided—he ain't going to show a movie again tonight.

PULVER: Why not?

DOWDY: He's still punishing us because he caught Reber without a shirt
on two days ago. You've got to go in and see him.

PULVER: I did. I asked him to show a movie yesterday.

DOWDY: Mister Pulver, what the hell good does that do us today?
You've got to keep needlin' that guy—I'm tellin' you.

PULVER: Don't worry. I'll take care of it in my own way.

DOWDY (*going off, but speaking loud enough to be heard*): Oh, God,
no movie again tonight. (*He exits.* PULVER *starts looking at his
packet of mail.*)

PULVER (*looking at first letter*): This is from my mother. All she ever says is stay away from Japan. (*He drops it on the hatch cover.*) This is from Alabama. (*Puts it in his pocket and pats it. Looks at third letter.*) Doc! This is from Doug!

DOC: Yeah? (PULVER *rips open the envelope.*) What does he say?

PULVER (*reading*): "This will be short and sweet, as we're shoving off in about two minutes . . ." (*Pauses and remarks.*) This is dated three weeks ago.

DOC: Does he say where he is?

PULVER: Yeah. He says: "My guess about the location of this ship was just exactly right." (*Looks up.*) That means he's around Okinawa all right! (*Reads on and chuckles.*) He's met Fornell. That's that friend of mine . . . a guy named Fornell I went to college with. Listen to this: "Fornell says that you and he used to load up your car with liquor in Omaha and then sell it at an indecent profit to the fraternity boys at Iowa City. How about that?" We did too. (*Smiles happily.*) "This part is for Doc." (DOC *gestures for him to read it.*) "I've been aboard this destroyer for two weeks now and we've already been through four air attacks. I'm in the war at last, Doc. I've caught up with that task force that passed me by. I'm glad to be here. I had to be here, I guess. But I'm thinking now of you, Doc, and you, Frank, and Dolan and Dowdy and Insigna and everyone else on that bucket —all the guys everywhere who sail from Tedium to Apathy and back again—with an occasional side trip to Monotony. This is a tough crew on here, and they have a wonderful battle record. But I've discovered, Doc, that the most terrible enemy of this war is the boredom that eventually becomes a faith and, therefore, a sort of suicide—and I know now that the ones who refuse to surrender to it are the strongest of all.

"Right now, I'm looking at something that's hanging over my desk: a preposterous hunk of brass attached to the most bilious piece of ribbon I've ever seen. I'd rather have it than the Congressional Medal of Honor. It tells me what I'll always be proudest of—that at a time in the world when courage counted most, I lived among a hundred and sixty-seven brave men.

"So, Doc, and especially you, Frank, don't let those guys down. Of course, I know that by this time they must be very happy because the Captain's overhead is filled with marbles and . . ." (*He avoids* DOC's *eyes.*) "Oh, hell, here comes the mail orderly. This has to go now. I'll finish it later. Meanwhile you bastards can write too, can't you?

                                              "Doug."

DOC: Can I see that, Frank?

(PULVER *hands him the letter, looks at the front of his next letter and says quietly:*)

PULVER: Well, for God's sake, this is from Fornell!

DOC (*reading* ROBERTS' *letter to himself*): ". . . I'd rather have it than the Congressional Medal of Honor." I'm glad he found that out. (*He looks at* PULVER, *sensing something wrong.*) What's the matter? (PULVER *does not answer.*) What's the matter, Frank? (PULVER *looks at him slowly as* DOWDY *enters.*)

DOWDY: All done, Mister Pulver. We've secured the hatch cover. No word on the movie, I suppose.

DOC (*louder, with terror*): Frank, what is it?

PULVER: Mister Roberts is dead. (*Looks at letter.*) This is from Fornell . . . They took a Jap suicide plane. It killed everyone in a twin-forty battery and then it went on through and killed Doug and another officer in the wardroom. (*Pause.*) They were drinking coffee when it hit.

DOWDY (*quietly*): Mister Pulver, can I please give that letter to the crew?

DOC: No. (*Holding out* ROBERTS' *letter.*) Give this one. It's theirs. (DOWDY *removes gloves and takes the letter from* DOC *and goes off.*) Coffee . . .

(PULVER *gets up restlessly.* DOC *stares straight ahead.* PULVER *straightens. He seems to grow. He walks casually over to* MANNION.)

PULVER (*in a friendly voice*): Go on down and get your mail. I'll stand by for you.

MANNION (*surprised*): You will? Okay, thanks, Mister Pulver.

(MANNION *disappears down hatch. As soon as he exits* PULVER *very calmly jerks the rooted palms, one by one, from their containers and throws them over the side.* DOC *looks up to see* PULVER *pull second tree.* DOC *ducks as tree goes past him. Then* PULVER *knocks loudly on the* CAPTAIN'S *door.*)

CAPTAIN (*offstage. His voice is very truculent*): Yeah. Who is it?

PULVER: Captain, this is Ensign Pulver. I just threw your palm trees overboard. Now what's all this crap about no movie tonight? (*He throws the door open, banging it against the bulkhead, and is entering the* CAPTAIN'S *cabin as*

THE CURTAIN FALLS

Mary, Mary

JEAN KERR

Why our respondents liked

 MARY, MARY

"Jean Kerr's Mary, Mary *is still one of the cleverest American comedies ever written. Still holds up in the re-reading. A great comedy by a great lady."*

EARL WILSON

"A very durable example of domestic comedy, it is playable by anyone loud enough to be heard."

HEYWOOD HALE BROUN

"It's still as charming as originally."

HELEN HAYES

Mary, Mary—the smash hit comedy with its irrepressible heroine Mary McKellaway—after concluding its 1,572nd performance at the Helen Hayes Theatre in December 1964, earned the distinction of being Broadway's ninth longest running production and fifth longest-run play. Its road companies went on to successfully tour every part of the country. Theatregoers delighted in Miss Kerr's sharp wit and keen understanding of domestic problems in this funny and touching play. Jean Kerr had previously gained prominence as an author with her best-selling books *Please Don't Eat the Daisies* and *The Snake Has All the Lines*. She wrote sketches for a musical revue and the book for the musical *Goldilocks* with her husband Walter Kerr, New York *Times* Drama Critic. Other works which show off her witty and winning style are *King of Hearts* (co-authored with Eleanor Brooke), *Penny Candy,* and her plays, including *Finishing Touches* and *Poor Richard*.

Mary, Mary was presented by Roger L. Stevens, in association with Lyn Austin, on March 8, 1961, at the Helen Hayes Theatre, New York City. The cast was as follows:

Bob McKellaway	Barry Nelson
Tiffany Richards	Betsy von Furstenberg
Oscar Nelson	John Cromwell
Dirk Winston	Michael Rennie
Mary McKellaway	Barbara Bel Geddes

Staged by Joseph Anthony
Setting by Oliver Smith
Costumes by Theoni V. Aldredge
Lighting by Peggy Clark
Production Stage Manager, Bill Ross
Stage Manager, John Drew Devereaux
Press Representative, Seymour Krawitz

The action of the play takes place in Bob McKellaway's living room in a New York apartment building. The time is the present.

ACT ONE

A Saturday morning in winter

ACT TWO

Saturday night; late

ACT THREE

Sunday morning

ACT ONE

AT RISE: BOB *is on the telephone. Several morning newspapers, open to the book page, are spread out in front of him. He dials a number.*

BOB: I want to speak to Mr. Howard Nieman. (*The doorbell rings once, perfunctorily*) Okay, I'll hold on.

TIFFANY (*letting herself in at the front door; she carries a jar of wheat germ*): Bob!

BOB: Hi, honey.

TIFFANY (*leaving the door ajar and coming into the room apprehensively*): I've read the reviews. How are you feeling?

BOB: I'm not exactly dancing with glee.

TIFFANY: Well, it's not fair!

BOB (*rising, phone in hand*): Shhhh! This is Nieman. I'm waiting for him to get off the other line.

TIFFANY (*coming to* BOB *at the desk*): But it isn't fair. You publish books of quality and distinction and you should get the credit.

BOB: You're one hundred percent correct and beautiful besides. (*They kiss.*) (*Into the phone.*) Hello, Howard! How are you? (*He sits, pulling newspapers toward him.*) Yes, sure I read the notices. Well, Howard, we were both hoping for a better break, but on the other hand there are a lot of good quotes here. (*Running his finger down a page and having some difficulty finding a decent quote.*) "A magician with words" and so forth. (TIFFANY *hangs her coat on the railing, and quietly feeds wheat germ to the fish.*) And with a book like yours we can hope for something more in the weeklies. I'm confident we'll go into another printing. What did you think about the notices? Sure, we all wish Orville Prescott would write a novel. Look, Howard, please calm down. I hope you're not going around talking this way.

Well, for one thing, people don't read reviews that carefully. All you do is spread the bad word. (*Rises, fidgeting.*) Let me give you some advice from Jake Cooper, in publicity. In his coarse but memorable phrase, nobody knows you've got a boil on your behind if you don't tell them. (BOB *listens a second longer, then shrugs and hangs up.*)

TIFFANY: What did he say?

BOB: He said the boil was not on his behind. (*Picks up a newspaper.*) It was on page 34 of the New York *Times.*

TIFFANY: Why shouldn't he be mad? It's a wonderful book!

BOB: That's what I like. Loyalty. (*Suddenly remembering, picking up a box of candy.*) I have a present for you and I forgot about it.

TIFFANY: A present?

BOB: It's Valentine's Day. (*Bringing her the box.*) Did you forget? To the sweet. Will you be my valentine? (*Kiss.*)

TIFFANY: Sure I'll be your valentine. (*Pulls* BOB *down onto the sofa. He is kissing her as* OSCAR *appears from the corridor with a brief case.*)

OSCAR (*pushing the door wider*): The door is open. Shall I come in?

BOB: Oh, Oscar—by all means. Tiffany, I want you to meet Oscar Nelson. My old friend and my new tax lawyer.

TIFFANY: Hello.

BOB: And this is Tiffany Richards. We're getting married next month.

OSCAR: And she'll be deductible. (*Comes down to shake hands with* TIFFANY.) Congratulations. (BOB *closes the door.*)

TIFFANY: Well, I'm very happy he's got you as a tax lawyer. Don't you think it's just outrageous—the government investigating his back taxes just like he was Frank Sinatra?

OSCAR: Under the law we're all equals.

BOB: Oscar—think of that clunk from the FBI who came charging in here and accused me of fleecing the government of six thousand dollars!

OSCAR: Wait, wait, wait. In the first place, this clunk is not from the FBI. He's from the Internal Revenue Service, a small but real distinction. In the second place, he is not accusing you of anything. He is merely asking you to produce proof that this six thousand dollars was legitimate professional expenses.

BOB: All I can tell you is that I am not coughing up any six thousand dollars. I'll move to Alaska.

OSCAR: You're too late. It's come into the Union.

TIFFANY: Darling, there's nothing to be upset about. Mr. Nelson will handle this man. (*Rises.*) Now *I'm* going to get you your midafternoon cocktail. (*To* OSCAR.) Would you like one?

OSCAR: Not this early, thank you.

TIFFANY: It's not alcohol. It's raw milk, brewer's yeast, and wheat germ.

OSCAR: Not this early, thank you.

BOB (*aware of* OSCAR'S *expression*): It does sound awful, but it's incredible the energy it gives you.

OSCAR: I'll have to try it sometime.

TIFFANY: You have no intention of trying it. And you know what? You should, because you're definitely undernourished. Look at your ears.

OSCAR: What about them? I know they stick out.

TIFFANY: They're whitish. Here, let me look at your fingernails. (*She picks up his hand.*) See how pale they are? A really healthy person will have pink ears and pink fingernails. Another thing—a healthy person will have a tongue the color of beefsteak.

OSCAR (*backing away, hand to mouth*): No, no—I will spare you that.

TIFFANY: I'm going to bring you a cocktail, and you try it. (*She goes off to the kitchen and closes the door.*)

BOB: You think that's a lot of damn nonsense.

OSCAR: How did you know?

BOB: Because that's what I thought, in the beginning. But I have seen the results and I am completely sold. And if you want to know—I *love* being clucked over.

OSCAR: I'm delighted to hear it. And your ears were never lovelier. Now, shall we get down to business? (*Goes to the desk with his brief case.*)

BOB: Please, let's. I'm in a real mess, Oscar. Actually, it's been a muddle ever since I started to pay alimony. And now this tax thing. What am I going to do? You probably read those notices today. I won't make anything on the Nieman book. Somewhere, something's got to give. And it's got to be straightened out before Tiffany and I get married.

OSCAR (*spreading out various papers on the desk*): We'll see what we can do.

BOB: What I want is a bird's-eye view of my whole financial picture. What I'm spending. What I should be spending. Where I should be cutting corners.

OSCAR: All right. I've already come to a few conclusions, but I'll want to look at your files—(*Makes a gesture toward the inner office*).

BOB: Thanks, Oscar. And I appreciate your coming over here on a Saturday. In fact, I appreciate your taking on this whole dumb job. I didn't think you would.

OSCAR: Why not?

BOB: Well, (*Glancing toward the kitchen door*) you wouldn't handle the divorce.

OSCAR: Bob, how could I have handled the divorce? Mary was just as much my friend as you were. Besides, I never thought you'd go through with it. I thought of you as the golden couple—smiling over steaming bowls of Campbell's chicken soup—

BOB: Oh, brother.

OSCAR: What happened?

BOB (*with a shrug*): What happens to any marriage. You're in love, and then you're not in love. I married Mary because she was so direct and straightforward and said just exactly what she meant.

OSCAR: And why did you divorce her?

BOB: Because she was so direct and straightforward and said just exactly what she meant.

OSCAR: When did you see her last?

BOB: Eight, nine months ago.

OSCAR: Well, you're going to see her this afternoon.

BOB: Like hell!

OSCAR: Bob, I called Mary in Philadelphia and asked her—as a special favor—to come up here this afternoon.

BOB: But why would you do that? Why in God's name would you—?

OSCAR: Why? Because you have five thousand dollars' worth of canceled checks that you can neither identify nor explain. Some of them Mary signed. I'm hoping that her memory will be a little better than yours.

BOB (*searching for an out*): But I've got an appointment here in ten minutes. Do you remember Dirk Winston?

OSCAR: The movie actor? Sure.

BOB: We were in the Navy together. Now he's moved into this building.

OSCAR: Well, it's nice you two old sailors can get together. There ought to be many a salty story, many a hearty laugh.

BOB: You don't get the picture. He's written a book.

OSCAR: A book?

BOB: That's right. The story of his life in three hundred and eighteen ungrammatical pages. (*Hands him a manuscript from the low book-case.*)

OSCAR (*glancing at it*): *Life Among the Oranges.* Not a bad title.

BOB: It's all right, I suppose. (*Picks up a small bowl of dried apricots and begins to eat one, nervously*) I can't imagine it on our lists.

OSCAR: I gather you're not going to do it.

BOB: Of course I'm not going to do it. But I dread talking to him. There is no right way to tell an author you don't want to publish his book.

OSCAR: If it's not going to be sweet, make it short. I can take Mary into the office—

BOB: Oh—Mary. (*Suddenly turning on* OSCAR.) Don't you leave me alone with her for one minute, do you hear?

OSCAR: She's only five feet three.

BOB: Never mind that. (*Going to the file cabinet, upset, and picking up a set of galleys.*) And when will I get to these galleys? They have to be back to the printer on Monday.

OSCAR: What are you eating?

BOB: Dried apricots. (OSCAR *remains silent.*) They're full of vitamin C.

OSCAR: The things I'm learning today! (*Indicating the galleys* BOB *is fretting over.*) What's that one like?

BOB: It's absolutely fascinating. I want you to read it. (*Enthusing, partly to distract himself.*) It's told in the first person, and when the story opens we're coming back from a funeral. But only gradually do we come to realize that the narrator of the story is the dead man.

OSCAR: It sounds sensitive, very sensitive.

BOB (*an extravagant little flare-up*): Oscar, I can think of only one sure way to clean up in this business! A new series. I could take the great sex novels—*Lady Chatterley, Peyton Place*—and have them rewritten for the ten-to-twelve age group.

(TIFFANY *enters with drinks, bringing one to* BOB.)

TIFFANY: It took me longer because the Waring Blendor was broken
. . .

BOB: Thank you, darling.

TIFFANY: And I had to use an egg beater. (*Handing a glass to* OSCAR, *who rises.*) You've *got* to *taste* it, anyway. (*He doesn't.*)

BOB (*taking over*): Honey, I want you to put on your new gray bonnet and get out of here.

TIFFANY (*surprised*): Bob! Aren't we driving up to Goshen? Dad's expecting us!

BOB: Certainly. I'll pick you up at five-thirty. No, make it six.

TIFFANY (*really puzzled*): But why do I have to *go*?

BOB: Because in my winning, boyish way, I'm asking you to.

TIFFANY: I know why! Because that sexy movie actor is coming. You think in ten minutes I'll be sitting on his lap giving little growls of rapture.

BOB: Nonsense. Why should you care about vulgar good looks when you have me? No—(*With a sigh and moving away from her*)—the truth is my ex-wife is descending upon me this afternoon.

OSCAR: It was my suggestion. I thought she might be able to shed some light on this tax matter.

TIFFANY (*abruptly*): I'm delighted. I want to meet her. I've always wanted to meet her.

BOB: Well, you're not *going* to meet her—

TIFFANY (*sitting down, firmly, in a chair*): Yes, I am.

(OSCAR, *sensing that he'd better, slips away into the inner offie with his papers and closes the door.*)

BOB: Darling, you are a sweet, reasonable girl, and I insist that you stay in character. Besides, I have those galleys to finish. (*As though to conclude the matter.*) Kiss me, and stop all this nonsense.

TIFFANY (*deliberately refusing to move*): I won't. I am not going to turn into Joan Fontaine.

BOB: What the hell are you talking about?

TIFFANY: Don't you remember Joan Fontaine in *Rebecca*? She was always thinking about the first Mrs. de Winter. She used to imagine that she could see her ghost on the staircase with that straight black Indian hair floating out behind her. Don't you remember? And she'd shudder when she saw the monogram on the silver brushes.

BOB (*with a snort*): Silver brushes! Mary used to use plastic combs with little tails, and she'd crack off the tails so they'd fit in her purse. And her hair was tied back in a bun. Tiffany—this is so silly!

TIFFANY: I'll tell you another reason why I ought to meet Mary. We'd

probably have a lot in common. Daddy says that a man goes on making the same mistake indefinitely.

BOB: Is that supposed to be an epigram? Because I don't get it.

TIFFANY: Practically everybody Daddy knows is divorced. It's not that
they're worse than other people, they're just richer. And you do begin
to see the pattern. You know Howard Pepper. When he divorced his
first wife, everybody said "Oh, what he endured with Maggie! It was
hell on earth!" Then when he married the new girl, everybody said
"She's so *good* for him." Except when you met her she looked like
Maggie, she talked like Maggie, it was Maggie all over again. And
now his *third* wife—

BOB: Okay, okay. I get the whole ghastly picture. But I promise you on
my sacred oath as a Yale man that you don't resemble my ex-wife in
any way, shape, or form.

TIFFANY: Is that good?

BOB (*relaxing for a moment with* TIFFANY *on the sofa*): Good? It's a
benediction from heaven. You—sweet, idiot child—soothe my
feathers. Mary always, always ruffled them. Life with Mary was like
being in a phone booth with an open umbrella—no matter which way
you turned, you got it in the eye.

TIFFANY: Well, at last—a plain statement! Now that you've opened up
a little, tell me, where did you meet her? Who introduced you?

BOB: I don't think we *were* introduced.

TIFFANY: You picked her up.

BOB: In a way. Do you remember that novel we published—*Our Kingdom Come*? It was sort of an allegory—the pilot of the plane turned
out to be God?

TIFFANY: I don't think so.

BOB: Well, they made a play out of it. So of course I had to go to the
opening night. And it was awful. Really grisly. After the second act,
we were all standing out on the sidewalk. We were too stunned to
talk. In fact, there didn't seem to be anything to say. Finally this girl
spoke. She was standing there by herself in a polo coat, smoking—
and she said, "Well, it's *not* uneven." So I laughed, and we started to
talk—

TIFFANY: And you said, "We don't have to go back in there, let's have
a drink—"

BOB: See? I don't have to tell you. You know. (*Rises and gets her
coat.*)

TIFFANY (*rising, too, pursuing the subject*): Did you kiss her that night?

BOB: Come on. Put on your coat. You're just stalling for time.

TIFFANY: I'll bet you did.

BOB: What?

TIFFANY: Kiss her that night.

BOB: I didn't kiss her for weeks.

TIFFANY: I don't believe it. You kissed me on the second night—in the elevator—do you remember?

BOB (*thinking of* MARY): Oh, I made certain fumbling attempts—but she'd make some little joke, like "Let's not start something we can't finish in a cab on Forty-fourth Street"—

TIFFANY: Well, for goodness sake, where was she when you finally did kiss her? On an operating table, under ether?

BOB: No, as it happens she was in a cab on Forty-fourth Street. Somehow or other she got her fingers slammed in the door. She pretended it was nothing, and we were chatting along. Then suddenly—this was blocks later—she started to cry. I looked at her fingers. (*Taking* TIFFANY'S *hand.*) Two of the nails were really smashed. And it started out I was just trying to comfort her, and—

TIFFANY: That is the most *un*romantic story I ever heard!

BOB: They certainly won't get a movie out of it. (*Urging her toward door.*) I told you it wasn't worth discussing.

TIFFANY (*picks up her handbag*): I know, I kept fishing. Did she cry a lot in taxicabs?

BOB: She never cried again. Not anyplace—ever—not once.

(OSCAR *appears from inner office, frowning over a sheaf of papers.*)

OSCAR: These figures for the year—can they represent the *total* profit?

BOB: I'm afraid so. (*Doorbell.* BOB *thinks quickly.*) Oscar, will you get that?

TIFFANY: Just let me *meet* her. Two minutes and I promise I'll go!

BOB (*pulling her toward the kitchen*): We'll go out the back door and I'll get you a cab.

TIFFANY: I feel like I was caught in a raid!

(OSCAR *has been looking on as* BOB *gets* TIFFANY *into the kitchen.*)

BOB: I'm *not* adult and Noël Coward would wash his hands of me.

(*He slips into the kitchen, too, and closes the door as* OSCAR *crosses to the main door and opens it not to* MARY *but to* DIRK WINSTON, *who has a large, partially wrapped piece of wood carving in his arms.*)

OSCAR: Hello. Come in.

DIRK: I'm—

OSCAR: Yes, I know. You're Dirk Winston. Bob will be right back. My name is Oscar Nelson. (*We hear* TIFFANY *giggling and protesting "Please, Bob—please!" off in the kitchen area.* OSCAR *and* DIRK *hear it, too.*) Her name is Tiffany Richards. (*Squeals from* TIFFANY, *off.*)

DIRK: It kind of makes me homesick for the back lot at Paramount. I thought I was late, but . . . (OSCAR, *puzzled, is looking at the package in* DIRK's *arms*). Suppose I take this thing downstairs and I'll be back in ten minutes.

OSCAR: I think recess should be over by that time.

DIRK (*feeling he should explain the package*): I saw this in an antique shop. (*Undoing the wrapping a bit.*) It's supposed to be Geronimo, but it looks so much like Jack Warner I couldn't resist. (*He goes, closing the door.* OSCAR *notices the drink* TIFFANY *has left for him. He tastes it, then crosses to the liquor table and pours a generous slug into the drink. He takes a sip. It's better. He looks at his fingernails, then goes to the mantel, puts down his drink, picks up a mirror, and examines his tongue. While he is doing so,* MARY *enters by the main door. She puts down her overnight bag and then sees* OSCAR.)

MARY: Oscar!

OSCAR: Mary, darling.

MARY: Are you sick?

OSCAR: Of course not. I'm out of my mind. (*Going to her and embracing her.*) Hey! I want you to concentrate and give me a better hug than that! (*We are aware that* MARY *is somewhat abstracted and apprehensive. Also that she is getting her feel of the room again, after all this time.*)

MARY: Oscar—dear Oscar—it's lovely to see you. (*Hesitantly.*) Where's—?

OSCAR: He'll be right back. He just—(*Interrupting himself, staring at her*). Wait a minute! What's happened to you? You look absolutely marvelous.

MARY: Did you say that right?

OSCAR: Apparently not, because I didn't get an answer.

MARY (*adopting a television commercial tone, mechanically*): Well, you see, I *had* been using an ordinary shampoo, which left a dull, unattractive film on my hair . . .

OSCAR: Come on, I'm interested. The hair is different—the clothes—the makeup. Clearly loving hands have been at work.

MARY (*putting her coat and handbag aside and sitting down, tentatively*): Yes, but you're not supposed to notice. I mean you're supposed to have an appreciative gleam in your eye, but you don't have to remind me of the dreary hours at Elizabeth Arden's—

OSCAR: Appreciative gleam? I've been casting you lustful glances. You're just too pure to notice. What caused the transformation?

MARY (*still not located in space*): Well, being divorced is like being hit by a Mack truck. If you live through it, you start looking very carefully to the right and to the left. While I was looking I noticed that I was the only twenty-eight-year-old girl wearing a polo coat and no lipstick.

OSCAR: You were? I never noticed. (*Starting toward kitchen.*) But let me see if I can locate our—

MARY (*quickly taking a cigarette from a box on the table*): No, no—please—wait. Let me have a cigarette first.

OSCAR (*lighting it for her*): You nervous?

MARY: Certainly not. But I haven't seen Bob in nine months. I guess I can last another five minutes. Besides, you and I have a lot to talk about. How's Jennifer?

OSCAR (*quiet and offhand tone*): Well, she had this illegitimate baby after she met that man from Gristede's, but it's all right now. . . .

MARY (*nodding, looking about the room*): Oh? Good! And how's everything at the office?

OSCAR: You haven't heard one word I said.

MARY (*caught*): You're right. I'm not listening. And I *am* nervous. I shouldn't have come.

OSCAR (*puts his hands on the arm of her chair. Sympathetically*): Mary, do you still—

MARY (*quickly*): I don't still—anything.

OSCAR: I'm sorry. I should have realized that—

MARY: Stop it. Don't give me that sad spaniel exrpession, as though you'd just looked at the X rays. I'm all right, Doctor. Just fine.

(BOB *appears from kitchen, stops short. His words are awkwardly spaced.*)

BOB: Well. Hello. You did get here.

OSCAR: Of course, she knew the address. (OSCAR *starts toward the office.*)

BOB (*not wanting to be left alone*): Oscar! (MARY *gets to her feet, ill at ease.*)

OSCAR: Be right back. (OSCAR *goes into office, leaving the door open. MARY turns toward BOB and her nerves now vanish. But BOB'S are quickly in bad shape.*)

MARY: Hello.

BOB (*a step to her*): You look very different. You've changed. I was going to ask you how you've been. But I can see. You've been fine.

MARY: How about you? Did you ever clear up that case of athlete's foot?

BOB (*almost under his breath*): No—you haven't changed.

MARY (*this flusters her briefly. She crosses to the desk, dips a hand into the bowl of dried apricots*): Well, you know what they say—the more we change, the more we stay the same. Good Lord! These are dried apricots.

BOB: What did you think they were?

MARY: Ears.

BOB (*ignoring it*): I want to say that I appreciate your coming. I'm sure you didn't *want* to.

MARY (*circling below the desk toward a plant on a low bookcase*): Nonsense. It put my mind at ease. You can't think how often I've worried about the philodendron.

BOB (*picking up tax papers*): I'm sure. Now, Oscar has explained to you that my—our—1962 income tax returns are being—

MARY: I advise you to make a clean breast of it. Admit everything.

BOB: This does not happen to be a subject for comedy. I've got to get this straightened out. I'm getting married in two weeks.

MARY (*really stunned*): Oh?

BOB: I thought you knew. Surely Oscar must have—

MARY: Of course! And it went right out of my head. (*Sitting near the desk.*) But how nice! Do I know her?

BOB: No, you don't.

MARY: Do you?

BOB (*chooses to ignore this*): Her name is Tiffany Richards.

MARY: Tiffany. I'll bet she uses brown ink. And when she writes she draws little circles over the *i*'s.

BOB: She is a beautiful, lovely girl with a head on her shoulders.

MARY: How useful!

BOB (*spluttering with irritation*): You really do have a talent for— you've been here five minutes, and already I'm—

MARY (*with maddening calm*): Have a dried apricot.

BOB (*striding to office door*): Oscar, have you fallen asleep in there?

OSCAR (*off*): Coming!

BOB (*moving away from* MARY *as* OSCAR *appears from office*): Shall we get on with this? (*To* MARY) I know you have to get back to Philadelphia—

MARY: I'm staying in town tonight, so you may consider that my time is your time.

OSCAR (*sits at the desk, handing* MARY *a batch of canceled checks*): Okay, Mary, will you look through these checks? Most of them you've signed.

MARY: Oh, dear—I'm not going to remember *any* of these, Oscar—

OSCAR: It'll come. Just give yourself time. You understand that we're particularly looking for items that might be deductible. Business entertaining, professional gifts, and so forth.

MARY (*working her way through the checks*): L. Bernstein—seventy-eight dollars. That's impossible. The only L. Bernstein I know is Leonard Bernstein and I don't know Leonard Bernstein.

OSCAR (*pointing it out*): This is L. Bernstein, D.D.S. A dentist.

BOB (*shaking his head*): I told you—Sidney Bauer is my dentist.

MARY: Dentist, dentist, dentist. (*Snapping her fingers.*) Listen—it's that man in Boston!

BOB: What man in Boston?

MARY: Don't you remember that crazy restaurant where you go down all the stairs? And you thought you got a stone in the curry—but it was your inlay?

BOB: Oh.

MARY: And we drove all the way out to Framingham because he was the only dentist who'd take you on Sunday?

BOB: Yeah, yeah, yeah.

MARY: By the way, how is that inlay?

BOB: Just grand. How are your crowns? (*They turn from each other.*)

OSCAR (*stopping this*): *And* we have Mrs. Robert Connors—three hundred dollars.

BOB: Mrs. Connors?

MARY: I thought so long as you walked this earth you'd remember Mrs. Connors. Bootsie Connors and her fish?

BOB: Oh, God. That ghastly weekend in Greenwich.

OSCAR: Okay, tell Daddy.

BOB: Do you remember that young English critic, Irving Mannix?

OSCAR: The angry young man?

BOB: This was two years ago, when he was just a cross young man. At that time he was writing long scholarly articles proving that Shakespeare was a homosexual.

MARY: Sort of the intellectual's answer to *Photoplay*.

BOB: Anyway, he was staying here. And we'd been invited to a party at the Connors'.

MARY: So we brought along dear old Irving.

BOB: Do you know the Connors' place in Greenwich?

OSCAR: No.

BOB: Well, the living room is about the size of the ball room at the St. Regis. You feel it would be just the place to sign a treaty. (*As they become interested in the details of the story* BOB *and* MARY *gradually forget their present situation and relax.*) Anyway, it was all too rich for Irving and he started to lap up martinis. In fifteen minutes he was asking our hostess if it was true that the Venetian paneling had been brought over piece by piece from Third Avenue.

OSCAR: Why didn't you take this charmer home?

BOB: Because he passed out. In the library.

MARY (*it comes back*): On that damn velvet sofa.

BOB: But he came to just long enough to light a cigarette. Presently the sofa was on fire—really on fire. Our hero jumped up and, with stunning presence of mind, put out the blaze with a tank of tropical fish.

MARY: And these were no run-of-the-bowl goldfish. They came from Haiti and were friends of the family. I mean, they had *names*.

OSCAR: Well, he was a writer. I think we can call that professional entertainment. Okay—we have twenty-five dollars to the Beach Haven Inn.

MARY: That must be yours.

BOB: Nonsense! I was never in . . . (*And then he remembers.*) The Booksellers—

MARY and BOB (*together*): Convention.

BOB: That awful hotel with the iron deer in front.

MARY (*nodding, her eyes lighting up*): With the night clerk who looked like Norman Vincent Peale and was so suspicious.

BOB: No wonder he was suspicious! (*To* OSCAR, *indicating* MARY.) He turns around to get the key and this one says just loud enough for him to hear, "Darling, are we doing the right thing? Maybe we ought to *wait.*"

MARY: He was *delighted* to come face to face with sin.

BOB: That's probably why he charged us four bucks to bring up three bottles of beer.

MARY (*to* OSCAR): He forgot the bottle opener, and we had to pry them open on the handle of the radiator.

BOB: And one of them was warm or something, so it shot up to the ceiling and all over one of the beds. So we both had to sleep in the other twin bed. . . . (*His voice has slowed down on this last thought. The remembering is suddenly a bit painful. There is a short, awkward silence before* MARY *gets to her feet, deliberately breaking the mood.*)

MARY: Oscar, we're being inefficient. We don't need total recall—just the facts. I'll take these checks into the office and make notes on the ones I can remember.

(*Almost before they realize it, she has left them.* OSCAR *and* BOB *look at one another, then* BOB *looks away.*)

OSCAR: Mary looks wonderful, don't you think?

BOB: Great.

OSCAR: Like a million bucks.

BOB (*nettled*): I'm afraid the figure that comes into my mind is five thousand bucks in alimony.

OSCAR (*notices* DIRK, *who has just stuck his head in at the main door*): Your friend from California.

BOB (*relieved at the interruption; his exuberance is a bit excessive after the strain with* MARY): Dirk! It's good to see you! How long has it been?

DIRK: I don't know. We were still in sailor suits.

BOB (*indicating* OSCAR): By the way, do you know—

OSCAR: We've met.

BOB: You know, Dirk is the expert we *should* consult! (*To* DIRK.) You've been married four or five times. How the hell did you manage it?

DIRK (*relaxing into a chair*): I feel like a failure to admit that I was only married three times. Actually, I married my first wife twice—so while there were three marriages, there were just two wives involved.

BOB: Now what? Do you pay both of them alimony?

DIRK: No, my second wife just married a very nice plastic surgeon. He fell in love with her while removing a wart from her shoulder blade. I always thought there was a popular song in that.

BOB: What about your first wife?

DIRK: She died.

BOB: See? Them that has, gets!

OSCAR (*rises, picks up manuscript from desk, and gives it to* BOB): I know you two have business to talk about—(BOB *glances at* DIRK'S *manuscript, and his face shows his dismay at having to deal with it.*) —so I'll get back to my arithmetic. (*He joins* MARY *in the small office, closing the door.*)

DIRK: Yes! Down to business.

BOB (*avoiding the subject and trying to hold onto his own momentary better spirits.*): Dirk, you look great. Younger than ever. How do you do it?

DIRK: I'll tell you this—it gets harder and harder. If I don't get ten full hours' sleep, they can't do a close-up. If I eat a ham sandwich after four o'clock, it shows on the scales. Ham sandwich, hell. I can gain weight from two Bayer aspirins.

BOB: You sound like the curator of your own museum. Come on, now. It's been worth it, hasn't it?

DIRK: Sure. Except that you develop such nutty habits. Do you know what all middle-aged actors do when they're alone in taxicabs?

BOB: What do they do? (DIRK *now demonstrates the business of biting, open-mouthed, from left to right, to strengthen the jaw muscles.*) What's that for?

DIRK: It firms up the jawline, old boy. I'll tell you what I dream of doing. My dearest ambition in life is to let my damn jawline go. In fact, that's why I wrote this book.

BOB (*brought back to the subject, embarrassed*): I see. But—uh—

DIRK: Have you read it?

BOB: Certainly I've read it. Now—the question is, shall I be perfectly frank? (DIRK *immediately rises and picks up the manuscript as if to go.*) You bruise easily. Have you shown this to anybody else?

DIRK: My agent, who thought it was brave, haunting, and hilarious. I brought it to you first because I knew you.

BOB: I'm sorry, Dirk—but the truth is it's not a book at all. For the moment we'll rule out the quality of the writing.

DIRK: Let's not rule out anything. What about the quality of the writing?

BOB: Well, it's—it's—

DIRK: Is "lousy" the word you're groping for?

BOB: Well, let's say it's not prose. Actually, it's not even punctuated. I get the feeling that you waited until you were out of breath and then threw in a semicolon.

DIRK: Hm.

BOB: However, that could be fixed. What can't be fixed is the content. It's nothing but anecdotes, really. It's as though you were just taking up where Louella left off.

DIRK: I gather you do not wish to publish this book. Do you think someone else would take it?

BOB: There are a couple of fringe outfits that I imagine would—

DIRK: I don't want a fringe outfit. Tell me this. How much does it cost to publish a book? Any book?

BOB: It depends on the size of the first printing, the length of the book, the kind of promotion—

DIRK: Let's get down to cases. How much would it cost to bring out my book with a first printing of, say, twelve thousand copies?

BOB: Oh—eight, nine thousand dollars.

DIRK: Let's say I made a check out to you for eighteen thousand dollars. Would you do the book?

BOB: If you proposition women with this same kind of finesse you must get your face slapped a lot.

DIRK: I thought it was worth a try, but don't get mad.

BOB: I'm not mad. I'm surprised. Why does that book mean so much to you? Obviously it isn't the money.

DIRK: It may sound naïve to say it—but being a star has never killed my urge to become an actor. Ten years ago I started to campaign for real parts. But the formula was still making money. So I went right on—passionate kisses and then I'd build the Suez Canal—passionate kisses and then I'd open the golden West—

BOB: What do you figure—you're all through in Hollywood?

DIRK: Technically, no. I have two more pictures to go on my present contract. But when I left, they knew and I knew that I was the sinking ship leaving the rats.

BOB: But why this jump into literature?

DIRK: Well, my press agent thought . . . what the hell, why blame him? *I* thought it might stir up a little interest in me as a man instead of a windup toy. In my fantasies I imagined it would be serialized in *The Saturday Evening Post* with pictures of me looking very seedy. And all of a sudden producers would be saying, "Don't laugh, but do you know who'd be perfect for the degenerate father—Dirk Winston!"

(MARY *enters from the office, leaving the door open.*)

MARY: Bob, I've done my half. Oscar would like to see you. (*Seeing* DIRK.) Oh, excuse me.

DIRK (*rising, pleasantly*): Hello, there.

BOB: This is my—former wife, Mary McKellaway.

MARY: You're Dirk Winston. And your real name is Winston Krib. Dirk is Krib spelled backwards.

DIRK: Good Lord, how did you remember that?

MARY: Oh, I have a head full of the most useless information. I still remember the names of each of the Dionne quintuplets, and the width of the Amazon River.

DIRK: Oh?

MARY: You have no idea how few people care about the width of the Amazon River. I understand you've written a book.

DIRK: That's what I understood, until I talked to Bob here.

MARY: Bob's a special case. He was frightened at an early age by a best seller. (*She is picking up her coat and handbag.*)

DIRK: He was?

BOB: I was not. Why do you say that? It's simply not true. I happen to believe that there's great wisdom in Emerson's remark that you should never read any book until it's a year old. And I'd like to think I'm publishing the kind of books that will be around next year. I'm fed up with novels about tangled lives in Scarsdale—or Old Salem for that matter: (*Quoting, in a mock literary rhythm.*) "All he knew was that he was a man and she was a woman or had he made some dreadful mistake."

OSCAR (*off*): Bob! Are you coming?

BOB (*on his way to office*): Be right back, Dirk.

DIRK: Don't think about me. We're all through. I wouldn't want you to be any clearer.

MARY: Bob, I suppose I might as well go too.

BOB (*turns back to* MARY, *something new on his mind*): Right now?

MARY: Well, don't you have a date?

BOB: I am meeting Tiffany—but couldn't you spare just five minutes? There's something I'd like to ask you.

(*Assuming her consent,* BOB *goes into the office.* MARY *stares after him a moment, absently reaching for a cigarette. Then she becomes aware of* DIRK *again, who has started for the main door but is now hesitating, watching her.*)

MARY: I used to love your movies. Of course, I didn't see all of them. My mother wouldn't let me.

DIRK: That's all right. I didn't see all of them, either. My agent wouldn't let me. Are you a writer?

MARY: No, I work for the *Ladies' Home Journal.* I edit the letters to the editor.

DIRK: You mean they have to be edited?

MARY (*nodding*): It does seem a little like incest, doesn't it?

DIRK: Bob did say you were his *former* wife, didn't he?

MARY: That's right.

DIRK: I'm so glad.

MARY: Why?

DIRK: Because I can ask you to dinner. Will you have dinner with me?

MARY: Tonight?

DIRK: You have a date?

MARY: No—no.

DIRK: Then what's wrong with tonight?

MARY: I guess I think we should have known each other longer—like, say, another five minutes.

DIRK: You think you're letting yourself in for an orgy. You think I will ply you with liquor, lure you to my sinful bachelor lodgings, and chase you around the king-sized bed.

MARY (*with a look toward the office*): Well, I've never been plied with liquor. Maybe I'd like it, but—

DIRK: Come on, we'll have dinner. And *Duck Soup* is playing at the Museum of Modern Art. I promise you I'll be so respectable you'll find me quite tiresome.

MARY (*on an impulse*): I have a new dress that would look pretty silly all by itself in Schrafft's. Why not? I'd love to. Do you want to pick me up here? What time?

DIRK: Half an hour? (*It occurs to him he'd better check.*) By the way, you don't—live here, do you?

MARY: Oh, no. We're not as civilized as all that. This is business.

DIRK: Fine. (*Passing office door.*) See you, Bob. I've got a call in to the Coast. (*On his way to the main door, turning back to* MARY.) Half an hour?

(MARY *nods, smiling.* DIRK *goes, closing the door.* MARY *turns, a little unsure of herself, sees the galleys on the sofa table, abstractedly picks them up, and puts her cigarette on an ash tray on the table. At almost the same time,* BOB *appears from the office, as though in response to* DIRK'S *farewell, then realizes he is alone with* MARY.)

BOB: Oh. Mary—thanks for waiting—I—

MARY (*she has been aware of his return, but has not looked at him. Now she deliberately reads from the galleys, in a somewhat questioning voice*): "He was alone in the middle of the field. He was grateful once again to be in possession of his own body. The Queen Anne's lace waved in the breeze like a thousand tiny handkerchiefs . . ." (*Looks up.*) This sounds suspiciously like our friend O'Brynner. (*Glancing at the first page of the galleys.*) And no wonder! I thought you weren't going to do this one.

BOB: Why?

MARY: Because this man writes like a sick elf.

BOB (*wanting to brush the matter aside before he is irritated again*): Let's skip that. (*In a hesitant, slightly strained voice.*) Mary—

MARY (*adopting his tone*): Bob—

BOB: I've been thinking. (*Starts to sit on the ottoman.*)

MARY: I thought you had an odd expression.

BOB (*jumping up again, a sudden, desperate explosion*): Could you—

would it be absolutely impossible for you to listen to me for three minutes without making one single wisecrack?

MARY (*stung—but concealing it*): I could try.

BOB (*earnestly*): I wish you would. I really wish you would. There is something I want to ask you and I can't do it through a barrage of flippantries.

MARY: You'd be surprised. I don't feel flippant at all. What is it you want to ask me?

BOB (*sitting*): You—know I'm getting married again.

MARY: Yes, I know that.

BOB: Well, I find myself stewing over a very curious thing Tiffany said today.

MARY: Oh?

BOB: Her idea was that people go right on making the same mistakes. I had an eerie feeling that there was something true about that. (*Realizing that he is groping.*) What I'm trying to say is that I have by God got to make a better job of it this time. (MARY *turns her head away.* BOB *leans toward her.*) Yes?

MARY: I didn't say anything.

BOB: But you were thinking—

MARY (*turns back to him sharply*): Look, you say your lines, I'll say my lines. You're hoping for better luck this time. I hope you'll have better luck this time. Beyond that, I don't see—

BOB: You could tell me what *I* did wrong. When we broke up, I spent many drunken hours thinking how it was all your fault. (MARY *starts to speak.*) Yes, I know I'm painting a charming portrait of myself— Bob McKellaway as a slob and sorehead. But that's how I felt.

MARY: And that's how you still feel.

BOB: No, by the time I calmed down and cleared the last of your bobby pins out of the bathroom, I realized that half the trouble had to be me.

MARY: You think it can be divided into two equal parts—like a sandwich?

BOB: I think success has no rules, but you can learn a great deal from failure.

MARY: I see. And what you're really looking for is the formula for instant marriage.

BOB: No, I'm not as sappy as that. I'm prepared to make a number of different mistakes this time. I would like not to make the same ones. And I would like some advice.

MARY: Had you thought of writing to Dear Abby? (*He rises and moves away. She is immediately penitent.*) Bob, I'm sorry for that. That's the kind of thing I promised not to say. (BOB *returns to her, hopefully.*) But what you're asking is impossible. I can't give you a report card. Is he punctual? Does he complete the task assigned? But you know what? This is so like you. This determination to be sensible in a situation where it isn't sensible to be sensible. You want to analyze, analyze. Like those people who take an overdose of sleeping pills, and sit there making notes while they're dying. "Four A.M. Vision beginning to blur." You'd do that. You would.

BOB: Maybe.

MARY: What shall I say? That you used to leave your ties on the coffee table? And you always grabbed *The New Yorker* first and took it to the bathroom? And you never talked to me in cars?

BOB: Of course I talked in cars.

MARY: Yes, to the traffic signals. "Come on, dammit, turn green."

BOB: I concentrate when I drive.

MARY: And you were always asking solemn, editorial-type questions beginning Don't You Ever. Don't You Ever order lunch meat? Don't You Ever put the lid back on the mayonnaise? Don't You Ever put your cigarettes out?

BOB (*brandishing* MARY'S *still-smoking cigarette and putting it out with great vigor*): Because you never in your life put a cigarette out!

MARY: And you always, always put the ice-cube trays back without filling them.

BOB (*gesturing toward the kitchen*): Ice-cube trays? Is that all you remember?

MARY: Aren't you forgetting one small detail? You're the one who walked out.

BOB: Technically, I suppose that's true.

MARY: Technically? There was nothing technical about it. You got up in the middle of the night and slammed out of here. And you know what? I never knew why.

BOB: Like hell you didn't.

MARY: All I knew was, one moment you were in bed, and the next minute you were banging drawers and dumping shirts into a suitcase.

BOB: And that's *all* you remember? (*Coming nearer.*) Let me reconstruct the scene for you. You were in bed reading *McCall's*. I was in the bathroom brushing my teeth. Then I put the lights out, came to bed, put my arms around you, and you said, "Okay, let's get those colored lights going."

MARY: I said that?

BOB: I wouldn't be capable of inventing it.

MARY: And was that so terrible?

BOB: Maybe not. But let us say that it had the effect of a cold shower when I wasn't in the mood for a cold shower.

MARY: I see.

BOB: I grant you it was a very small straw to be the last straw. Another time it would have bounced off me. But it had been such a stinker of a day. We got bad notices on the Caine book. The deal for the serial rights fell through. Oh, the usual. Except that I felt a peculiar need for some warmth. I guess I felt I needed a wife.

MARY (*hotly*): I think I was wifely—a lot.

BOB: Sure. On and off. Between jokes. (MARY *grabs a sofa pillow as though she were going to hit him with it, but is deflected by* OSCAR'S *return from the office. He sees what she is doing.*)

OSCAR: Please don't be embarrassed on my account. I'm delighted. I hate a friendly divorce. A lawyer is never entirely comfortable with a friendly divorce, any more than a good mortician wants to finish his job and then have the patient sit up on the table. (MARY, *without saying a word, picks up her coat, her suitcase, gloves, and handbag and leaves by the main door.* OSCAR *looks at* BOB.) Did you read Walter Lippmann today? I thought it was an awfully good piece.

BOB: Oscar, don't be urbane all the time. I can't stand it. (*Fuming.*) You see why I didn't want to see her again? When you said she was coming, I should have walked out that front door! I don't understand it. I thought she had lost the power to enrage me. Maybe I took the bandages off too soon. Maybe I—(*Stops as he sees* MARY *returning with her suitcase.*) Did you forget something?

MARY: No, dammit, I *remembered* something. Having made my dramatic exit, I realized that this is where I'm being picked up. I *have* to stay here for another ten minutes.

BOB: I see.

MARY: And furthermore, I will have to use your room to change in. (*To* OSCAR.) Oscar, if the phone rings, it may be for me. Will *you* take it? The Algonquin is supposed to call and confirm my room for tonight.

BOB: There's a new telephone in the . . .

(MARY *goes off to the bedroom, not exactly slamming the door but letting it close pretty arrogantly behind her.* BOB *starts to follow but is stopped by* OSCAR.)

OSCAR: Never mind her. We have something more important to talk about. (*Sitting at the desk.*) I have been over all the figures and am now ready to give my state of the Union address.

BOB (*trying to tear his mind away from* MARY, *but still edgy and upset*): First, tell me about that tax thing.

OSCAR: Oh, my guess is that we'll get it down somewhere in the neighborhood of eighteen hundred, two thousand dollars.

BOB: That would be more like it.

OSCAR: You said you wanted my advice on the over-all picture. Let me ask you a couple of questions. Tiffany comes from a wealthy family, doesn't she?

BOB: What has that got to do with anything?

OSCAR: A lot. She has to be supported. You can't support her. I have now been through what we shall laughingly call your books, and you're not supporting yourself.

BOB: You're joking.

OSCAR: Then why aren't you laughing?

BOB: Look. If you're trying in some left-handed way to tell me I can't get married, you're wasting your breath. I'm thirty-six years old, and this is a—

OSCAR: Free country? Don't you believe it. People pick up the most erroneous ideas from popular songs. Let me tell you something. If all you've got is the sun in the morning and the moon at night, you're in trouble.

BOB: What are you talking about? I take eighteen thousand a year out of the company—plus bonuses.

OSCAR: That's right.

BOB: That may be cigarette money to the Rockefellers, but it still feels like a lot to me. Hell, my father never made more than five thousand a year in his life and he put four boys through college.

OSCAR: Let's not dwell on the glories of the past. *I* have the figures for *this* year. Do you want to hear them?

BOB: No. (*Starts for bedroom and stops.*) Oh, yes, I suppose so.

OSCAR (*referring to a work sheet*): We start with your base salary—eighteen thousand—plus one thousand dollars sales bonus. By the way, that was down from preceding years.

BOB: Sales were down.

OSCAR: So that's nineteen thousand dollars. Against that, we have thirty-two hundred, rent; two thousand, eighty, maid service; four thousand, nine hundred, food and liquor; five thousand, alimony to Mary—

BOB: And that's ridiculous. (*Shouting at the bedroom door.*) She's working.

OSCAR: That was the decision of the court. You can't do anything about it. (*Picking up where he left off.*) Five thousand to Mary. Six hundred and eighty, club dues and entertainment. Six hundred, clothes. Nine hundred, books, furnishings, dry cleaning. Eleven hundred, insurance and medical. Twenty-seven hundred, taxes. We now have a total of twenty-one thousand, one hundred and sixty dollars. You do have three thousand in available savings, but most of that will go for that old tax bill.

BOB: Here, let me see that thing. (*Takes work sheet from* OSCAR.)

OSCAR: You can juggle those figures any way you want to. But you're not going to change the fact that you are already spending twenty-one thousand on an income of nineteen. It's not just that you can't support another wife. You'd be ill-advised to buy a canary.

BOB: It can't be as complicated as you're pretending—

OSCAR: Actually, it's even more complicated. You must keep in mind that if you ever wanted to divorce Tiffany, you'd be in a hopeless position, financially.

BOB (*outburst*): I'm not going to divorce Tiffany! Why would I divorce Tiffany?

OSCAR: Your attitude does you credit.

BOB: Here. Some of these expenses I can cut.

OSCAR: Yes, you could move to a cheaper apartment. You don't have to belong to the New York Athletic Club. You might save seven or eight hundred dollars. However, I have met Tiffany. I doubt that you could keep her in cashmere sweaters for that. She doesn't work, does she?

BOB: Oh, she does volunteer things.

OSCAR: Maybe her father would give her an allowance.

BOB: Maybe we could take in boarders. Any more bright ideas? What the hell am I supposed to do? Stay single for the rest of my life and sleep around? Or do I remain celibate and take cold showers and get plenty of exercise?

OSCAR: Fortunately, you belong to the Athletic Club. (*Telephone rings.* OSCAR *answers it.*) Hello. That's right. Can I take the message? (MARY, *in dressing gown, pokes her head out of the bedroom door.*) I see. Will you wait one minute? (*To* MARY) They haven't got a single but they can give you a suite!

MARY: Tell them never mind. I'm not paying twenty-four dollars for one night. I'll go to the Biltmore.

BOB (*not graciously, just realistically*): If you want to, you can stay here. I'm going to be in Goshen for the weekend.

MARY: Stay here?

BOB: I won't be here. You'll be perfectly safe.

MARY: I'm not worried. I was perfectly safe when you *were* here. (MARY *disappears, shutting the door again.*)

BOB: I shouldn't have divorced her. I should have shot her.

OSCAR (*into phone*): Thank you, she'll make other arrangements. (*Doorbell, as* OSCAR *hangs up.*)

BOB (*going to the front door*): With my luck, this'll be a telegram saying that my rich old uncle died and left his money to a kindly waitress. (BOB *opens the door to* DIRK, *and is surprised to see him.*) Oh. Hello again.

DIRK: Hello. Is she ready?

BOB: Who?

DIRK: Do I get a choice? I'm calling for Mary.

BOB: For Mary? For what?

DIRK: For dinner. Isn't that all right? Should my mother have called your mother?

BOB: Don't be ridiculous. I just didn't know, that's all.

OSCAR: You see, Bob thinks when he brings a book back to the library, it'll never go out again.

BOB: Bob doesn't think anything. I had always supposed that Mr. Winston only went out with women whose names ended in *a*. Like Lana. Or Ava. And I'm a little puzzled as to why he wants to take my ex-wife to dinner.

DIRK: Because she looked hungry. You damn fool! Because she strikes me as an exceptionally attractive girl.

BOB: And you would know.

DIRK: That's right. I don't want to pull rank or anything—but I think it might be fair to assume I know at least as much about women as you do about books. Perhaps more.

BOB: Look, you misunderstand me. I am delighted that you find my former wife attractive. I'm charmed that you are taking her out. If you decide to marry her, I'll send up rockets. In fact, you can count on me as your best man.

OSCAR: Marry her and you count on him as your publisher.

BOB (*overheated*): Absolutely! Now, there's a brilliant idea! Why didn't I think of it? Oscar's got a head on both his shoulders. I could solve your problems, you could solve my problems.

DIRK: You've got to be joking.

BOB (*lying back on the sofa and kicking off his loafers*): Why? This is the age of the deal! You scratch me and I'll scratch you! Don't you read the papers? Why should I be out of touch?

OSCAR: Bob—

DIRK: No, let's listen to him. I couldn't be more impressed. It stirs memories of the past—I keep thinking, "Louis B. Mayer, thou shouldst be living at this hour!"

BOB (*To* OSCAR): See? You're shocked. But he's been around!

DIRK: And back. It couldn't be more reasonable. He has an unmarketable wife and I have an unmarketable book. He thinks we should pool our lack of resources. I haven't had such a fascinating offer in years.

(*The bedroom door opens and* MARY *appears, beautiful in a low-cut dress.*)

MARY: Hello! I think I'm all collected. (*All rise.*) (*She senses the tension in the air.*) What are you all staring at? Is something showing?

DIRK: Yes, and it looks delicious. Are we ready?

(*He gets* MARY'S *coat as* MARY *goes to* OSCAR *and kisses him.*)

MARY (*to* BOB): I suppose it's all right if I pick up that bag later tonight?

BOB: Certainly. But how will you get in?

MARY (*waving a bunch of keys from out of her hand bag*): I still have my keys. Have you been missing things?

DIRK: Shall we run along? I double-parked down there.

MARY (*breezing through doorway, calling back to* OSCAR *and* BOB): Good night!

BOB and OSCAR (*she's already gone*): Good night.

DIRK (*ready to go, turning back to* BOB *from the doorway, grinning*): I think you've got yourself a deal.

(DIRK *goes, closing door behind him.* BOB *heaves a great sigh of exasperation and snatches up the galleys.*)

OSCAR (*after watching* BOB *for a moment*): I've known you for twenty years and I never realized you had this flair for comedy. (*No answer from* BOB, *trying to concentrate on galleys.*) You *were* joking?

BOB (*crossly*): Of course I was joking. (*Looking up as the thought crosses his mind.*) But wouldn't I like to see him try! It'd be an education for him. (OSCAR *pokes the work sheet under his nose.*) Don't, don't, don't. I don't want to hear another word about my untidy affairs. (*Turns his attention to galleys again.*)

OSCAR (*following* BOB *to the desk*): What's the matter with you?

BOB (*sharply, not lyrically, and without looking up*): Say I'm weary, say I'm sad, say that health and wealth have missed me, and you've said it.

(BOB *is now rapidly crossing out great sections of the galleys.*)

OSCAR: Why are you *slashing* at those galleys?

BOB: Because this man writes like a sick elf!

(*And* BOB *is going at it with renewed vigor as the* CURTAIN FALLS.)

END OF ACT ONE

ACT TWO

The moment the curtain is up, DIRK *and* MARY *enter by the main door, stomping their feet and brushing snow from their clothes. It is shortly after midnight and the room is dark except for the glow from the window.* MARY *turns on the hall light just inside the front door.*

DIRK: Did you get wet?

MARY: No, except for my hair.

DIRK: It doesn't look wet.

MARY: No, but you watch. In five minutes it'll be so fuzzy I'll be able to cut a piece off and clean my suede shoes.

DIRK: Would you feel safer if I left the door open?

MARY: Oh dear! I felt perfectly safe until you asked that question.

DIRK: The question is withdrawn.

MARY: Isn't this the silliest snowstorm? (*Going to the window, looking out.*)

DIRK (*closing the door and following her*): I come from California. I think it's a lovely snowstorm.

MARY: But those great big flakes swirling around! It looks so phoney. Like—do you remember those big glass paperweights and you turned them upside down and it snowed? That's how it looks. (*Turns and is surprised to find him right behind her. Unsettled, she points to her bag near the bedroom door.*) Here's that damn bag. Remember— you're not coming back out with me. I'll get a cab.

DIRK: In *this?* You'd never. And here I am—ready—willing—cheaper.

MARY: If I had a brain in my head, I'd have taken it with me and we could have dropped it off at the Biltmore.

(MARY *is holding the suitcase in her hand. As* DIRK *goes to take it from her, his hand rests on hers a moment.*)

DIRK: Does everybody tell you how pretty you are?

MARY (*takes her hand away—flustered*): Oh, you *are* a good actor! You could play anything. (*Changing the subject.*) You know what? It's really idiotic, our going back out in that blizzard. We're not delivering the serum. (*She comes into the room and turns on a lamp.*) Why don't I just *stay* here? (DIRK *puts the bag down and looks toward the bedroom. In answer to his unspoken question*) Oh, he's safely in Goshen with a beautiful, lovely girl with a head on her shoulders.

(*She has remembered* BOB'S *description word for word.* DIRK *stares at her a second, then heads for the bar table.*)

DIRK: Do you suppose we can have a drink, or did Bob get the custody of the liquor?

MARY (*she is already a couple of cocktails in, and is beginning to like it*): Sure, let's have a drink. But make mine light. I'm beginning to feel that champagne. (*She turns on another lamp.*) Do you realize we were three hours in that restaurant? That's the nice thing about having dinner with somebody you're not married to. (*She starts to sit on the sofa, then after a glance at* DIRK, *who is making the drinks, discreetly chooses a chair.*) You have so much more to talk about.

DIRK: All I found out about you is that you're allergic to penicillin and you love *The Catcher in the Rye.*

MARY: That's all? That's a lot. I want to hear about you. Are you going to get your book published?

DIRK: I am going to make every possible effort. (*Hands her a drink.*) That's mostly water. (*He moves a chair close to her and sits.*) You and Bob must have spent a lot of time with authors. What do *they* talk about?

MARY: You don't think they talk about *books*? They talk about first serial rights, second serial rights, movie rights, and how they're going to form a corporation to publish their next one so they can call it a capital gain and move to Jamaica.

DIRK: They sound just like actors.

MARY: It's terrible when you feel a writer is trying out his material on you. You never know exactly what reaction they expect, but you have to keep looking so *interested* your eyebrows get tired. (*She has made a concentrated face to show what she means.* DIRK *grins.*)

DIRK: I know a guy who used to work with Disney. He'd actually tell you the whole plot of an animated cartoon—frame by frame. But he was a classic case. He could bore the birds back onto the trees. He never stepped talking—never. If he took a drink, he'd hold his hand up—(*He demonstrates this*)—so you couldn't put a word in until he was back with you. (MARY *laughs at the demonstration, then calms down into a small silence, which* DIRK *fills.*) Your eyes are so blue—and so liquid. I feel they might spill right down your cheeks.

MARY (*quick with the answer, moving away to get a cigarette, leaving her drink behind*): That's because I need glasses and won't wear them.

DIRK (*curious and interested*): Why do you do that?

MARY: Do what?

DIRK: You jump when you get a compliment.

MARY (*too quickly*): No, I don't.

DIRK: You're actually embarrassed.

MARY (*a shade defensively, lighting her cigarette*): Why should I be embarrassed?

DIRK: I don't know. But you are. You come bustling in to change the subject, like a nervous hostess who's discovered that two of the guests are quarreling. (*Imitating the hostess.*) "Now, come along, Harry—there's somebody very nice I want you to meet."

MARY (*sits at one end of sofa*): All right. Pay me pretty compliments and I won't change the subject.

DIRK: And you won't make jokes? (MARY *is stunned by the echo of* BOB'S *remark.*)

MARY: What? What?

DIRK: Shouldn't I have said that?

MARY: No, that's all right. It's been said before. Just recently, in fact. I suppose I should take a course and find out what a girl should answer when a gentleman says "Tell me, pretty maiden, are there any more at home like you?" Though it would hardly pay. It doesn't come up that often.

DIRK: I thought little girls learned things like that when they were three years old. (*He moves nearer to her, bringing her drink.*)

MARY: Oh, but I'm a very retarded case. It's only just this year I learned how to put my hair up in rollers.

DIRK: What did you do before that?

MARY: I wore it pinned back in a bun. And when it had to be cut, *I* cut it, or I went somewhere and *they* cut it. Lately I've been going to Elizabeth Arden, and I want you to know that it's a whole new way of life.

DIRK: So I'm told.

MARY: At Arden's they don't just cut your hair—never. They *shape* it. And they honestly think a good shaping is as important as a cure for cancer. The hairdresser really blanched when he saw my bun. I could hear him thinking, "Thank God she came to me—another month and it might have been too late."

DIRK: Well, I think your hair looks lovely. Now say thank you.

MARY: Thank you.

DIRK: See how easy it is?

MARY (*jumping up, self-conscious*): I—Oh—Tell me about your book. (*Picks up the manuscript.*)

DIRK (*taking the manuscript from* MARY): What can I tell you? It weighs three quarters of a pound. It takes eighty-four cents in stamps to mail it. (*Tosses it on sofa table and goes to the bar for another drink.*)

MARY: Don't talk like that. You mustn't lose faith in it just because Bob didn't like it. Bob's a good publisher but he makes mistakes. Did you have any help with this book?

DIRK: You mean, did I *tell* it to somebody? No.

MARY: I'm glad. All these "as told to" books have such a spooky flavor about them. First the personality is all drained off. Then, to compensate, something else is pumped in—sex or religion or Scott Fitzgerald. I fully expect that any day now we're going to have The Confessions of Saint Augustine—as told to Gerold Frank.

DIRK (*returning to her*): Mary—

MARY: What?

DIRK: You just said Bob makes mistakes. But how did he ever let you slip through his fingers?

MARY: Just lucky, I guess.

DIRK: I think I am beginning to see the clue to this little puzzle.

MARY: What puzzle?

DIRK: You.

MARY: I'd love to think I was a puzzle. A woman of mystery. Smiling and enigmatic on the surface—but underneath, a tigress. (*Change of mood, straightforward.*) I hate to admit it, but what you see is all there is. Underneath this plain, girlish exterior, there's a very plain girl.

DIRK: Ah, but what happened to make you *decide* it was such a plain exterior? It was the divorce, wasn't it? It was Bob.

MARY: Bob? I decided *that* when I was thirteen years old. We can't blame Bob for everything.

DIRK: At thirteen, all by yourself, you decided that?

MARY (*sitting on the ottoman*): Oh, there were people around, but I can't say they gave me any argument. Do you ever look at little girls?

DIRK: How little?

MARY (*rather intensely, as she remembers and thinks about it. The intensity is perhaps increased by the amount she's had to drink*): You take two little girls. One of them is pink and round, with curly hair and yards of eyelashes. The other one is pale and bony, with thin, wispy hair and two little ears poking through—like the handles on a sugar bowl. Okay, which one of these little girls is going to have to wear braces on her teeth?

DIRK: The wispy one.

MARY (*as though awarding him a prize*): You've got it. (*Seeing herself again, taking a sip of her drink.*) That was me. Braces on my teeth, Band-Aids on my knees, freckles on my nose. All elbows and shoulder blades. For two years running I got picked to play the consumptive orphan in *Michael O'Halloran*.

DIRK: That was talent.

MARY: That was typecasting.

DIRK: All adolescents go through something. I had the worst case of acne in the history of the world. For three years I was a Technicolor marvel. You wouldn't remember when Fleischmann's Yeast was the big thing. I used to eat Fleischmann's Yeast and drink water until I couldn't move without gurgling. I imagine I was actually fermenting.

MARY: I never ate yeast, but once I sent away secretly for Stillman's freckle cream. I guess I used too much, because I just peeled and peeled. I had to pretend it was a sunburn.

DIRK: I used to pretend I hated everybody. Especially girls, because I was too self-conscious to talk to them.

MARY: You made a spectacular recovery.

DIRK: I may even have overdone it. But why didn't you—

MARY: Make a recovery? Well, it was sort of different with me. When I was a kid, I mean really a kid, I never worried about the way I looked, because I thought—I *knew*—I'd grow up to be beautiful just like my sister Clara.

DIRK: Was she so beautiful?

MARY: Clara? She had bright red hair and brown eyes and she always had a faintly startled look, as if she'd just come out of a dark theater into the sunlight. People who met her would be so busy staring they'd forget to finish their sentences.

DIRK: I can see that would have been something of a cross for you.

MARY: No, I thought it was insurance. Clara was six years older than I was, and I thought "I'll grow up to look just like that." One day I was measuring myself—I was about fourteen—and I realized I hadn't grown at all, not an inch, in a whole year. And then it came to me. I wasn't going to grow any more. I was *up*. And I didn't look anything at all like Clara.

DIRK: And you weren't satisfied to look like Mary?

MARY: I certainly was not. I went rushing to my father, and I asked him when I was going to look like Clara. Poor man. He didn't know what to say.

DIRK: What did he say?

MARY: He said "Darling, we wouldn't want two Claras. You're the bright one." That did it. I could have faced being plain, but to be plain *and* bright! In the high school I went to, that was a beatable combination.

DIRK: So you decided to get on the debating team.

MARY: How did you know?

DIRK: Girls who feel they are not going to be invited to dances always get on the debating team.

MARY: And I worked on the school newspaper. And I imagined all the time that I was really Catherine Earnshaw.

DIRK: Catherine who?

MARY: The girl in *Wuthering Heights*. Cathy.

DIRK: Oh, Merle Oberon.

MARY: That's right. I used to dream that somewhere there was a strange, dark man whose heart was quietly breaking for me. On rainy nights I'd open the window and imagine I could hear him calling—"Oh, my wild, sweet Cathy!" The colds I got! And of course the only dark man I ever saw was the middle-aged dentist who used to adjust the braces on my teeth.

DIRK: And you're still cross about it.

MARY: Is that how I sound? I don't feel that way. I feel wistful. I think of that sappy little girl and I wonder what happened to her.

DIRK: Nothing happened. She hasn't changed at all.

MARY: You mean I haven't changed at all? That's a hell of a thing to say.

DIRK: Oh, I'm certain you've changed in appearance. That's clear enough. But you yourself haven't changed. Somewhere inside you, you're *still* wearing braces on your teeth.

MARY: Oh, come, come. I came to the big city. I learned to tip waiters. I read *The New Yorker*. I got married.

DIRK: And nothing took. Do you know what's strange?

MARY: What?

DIRK: Here you are—so lovely. And nobody falls in love with you.

MARY: Oh, is that so? And where did you get that idea?

DIRK: From you.

MARY: You're crazy. I never said—listen, lots of people—well, Bob certainly was in love with me—

DIRK: You really thought so?

MARY: Of course! Why else would he marry me? There was no dowry, or anything.

DIRK: I don't know. Why did he?

MARY (*seriously unsettled beneath her insistent assurance*): Because he felt that—because we both—listen, what is this? (*Rises.*) I haven't answered so many idiotic questions since I tried to open a charge account at Saks! (*Moves away to the fireplace.*) There must be a genteel, ladylike way of telling you that it's none of your damn business!

DIRK: I knew I'd get a rise out of you when I said that about Bob.

MARY: Then why did you say it?

DIRK: Of course Bob was in love with you. But you don't believe it. You never believed it.

MARY (*turns to him, alert*): What did he tell you?

DIRK: Nothing. You're the evidence. Women who believe they're attractive have a certain air about them. You don't. Your reflexes are off.

MARY (*now furious*): I will match my reflexes with your manners any old day! And now, unless you have some other little speech all rehearsed, I suggest you go upstairs or downstairs or wherever it is you call home!

DIRK: Now you're mad.

MARY: Oh, you *are* the quick one! Nothing is wasted on you. Of course I'm mad! What did you expect I'd be?

DIRK: I didn't know. I never met anybody quite like you before.

MARY: We're even. I never met anybody like you, either. (*Sitting at one end of the sofa.*) Which doesn't explain why I let myself be taken in by that richer, milder, longer-lasting M-G-M charm.

DIRK: Oh, *were* you—taken in?

MARY: I must have been. Why else would I sit here—babbling like an idiot, pouring out my little girlish secrets! That's not part of my regular act. I don't learn. (DIRK *sits near* MARY *on sofa.*) I guess I never will learn.

DIRK (*putting his hands on her shoulders and speaking earnestly and directly*): Mary, do you know what I feel? I feel—

MARY (*coolly, sarcastically*): You feel as though you were seeing me—for the first time.

DIRK: I'll tell you something you ought to learn. You really ought to learn when to shut up. (*With real dispatch, he takes her into his arms and kisses her firmly.* MARY *is too startled at first to protest, and later she is maybe too interested. When they break off,* DIRK *puts one finger gently to her lips.*) Shh! Now once more—quickly, before you lose your nerve. (*He kisses her again.*)

MARY (*finally*): I feel dizzy.

DIRK: That's suitable.

MARY: It's just that I haven't kissed anybody, lately. But it's like riding a bicycle. It does come back to you.

DIRK: And you don't even have to worry about the calories.

MARY: You know—you're very nice. And about ninety-five per cent correct.

DIRK: About what?

MARY: About a lot of things. But why are you bothering with me?

DIRK: I'm being bribed.

MARY (*taking it as a joke, of course*): I *knew* that. But there must be other reasons. I like *you* because you hurt my feelings and made me lose my temper.

DIRK: And that's a reason?

MARY: To me it is. I've gone so long not reacting to anything, it seems somehow reassuring. It's like—well—if you were absolutely convinced that you had no feeling in your hand, you'd be relieved to burn your fingers.

DIRK (*picking up her hand and kissing it*): What can we do for those fingers? I like you because I think that, with any encouragement, I might fall in love with you. (*She is silent.*) If you're going to say anything, say what you're thinking. Don't invent something.

MARY (*facing up to this*): I'm thinking I'd really like to believe that. So I will.

DIRK: That's my girl.

(*And he is kissing her again as* BOB *enters.* BOB, *too, is snowy as he comes in the main door. He stops dead at what he sees.*)

BOB: Mary. What are *you* doing here?

DIRK: Don't ask rhetorical questions. Surely you can see what she's doing.

BOB (*embarrassed, bothered by some instinctive reaction he doesn't understand, and trying to be cordial. After all, it's what he hoped for. His reactions are actually disturbingly mixed*): All I meant, really, was to indicate my surprise that Mary was *here*. I thought we left it that she was going to the Biltmore. I mean—what *is* the situation now? (*To* MARY, *and still floundering.*) I mean, are you just coming or going?

MARY (*sweetly. She's a little bit high*): I'm staying. What about you?

DIRK: We thought you were on your way to Goshen.

BOB (*taking off his coat*): I *was* on my way to Goshen, but there's a blizzard out there. We couldn't even get on the thruway.

MARY: And I wasn't privy to your change of plans. (*Turns to* DIRK.) Do you know I never in my whole life used the word privy before?

DIRK: Not even for—?

MARY (*shaking her head rapidly*): Nope, never. Don't you hate places where they have cute names for the men's room?

DIRK: I hate places where they have cute names for the places. Did you ever hear of a nightclub called the Chez When?

(BOB *moves toward the desk aimlessly. They are continuing their conversation as though he hadn't come in.*)

MARY (*eyes widening*): No.

DIRK: What do you call it when the words are accidentally twisted? Where the minister says the Lord is a shoving leopard—?

MARY: I think that's a spoonerism. I'm always getting words twisted like that. I was buying a hammock for the porch at home. And in a crowded elevator I said, "Miss, where do you have perch forniture?"

DIRK: Perch forniture?

MARY: Don't you just know the unsuitable things that would go on in perch forniture?

(*As they laugh, they become more aware of* BOB, *who is feeling very much like a fifth wheel and not liking it.*)

DIRK: Bob, why don't you get yourself a drink?

BOB: Thank you. You're the soul of hospitality. (*He does go to get himself a drink.*)

DIRK: Well . . .

MARY: Pay no attention to Bob. It's just that he's systematic. He has his day all planned out. He makes a list. And the snow wasn't on his list and you weren't on his list.

DIRK (*a sly look at* BOB): But we had such an interesting chat at six o'clock. I thought I was definitely in his plans—on his list.

BOB: I'm sorry if I sounded rude. But it happens to be one-thirty, and any hour now I'd like to know where I'm going to lay my head. (*To* MARY.) Did I understand you to say you were staying here?

MARY (*giddily*): Yes. I'm sleepy. I do not wish to go out into the night that covers me black as the pit from pole to pole. Remember, women and children first. That's the law of the sea. And I'm sure it goes for snowstorms.

BOB: Naturally I don't expect you to go out in this. (*Unable to restrain a note of irony.*) Would it be all right if I slept here on the couch?

MARY: Certainly. Be your guest.

DIRK (*to* MARY): Our host is beginning to look glassy-eyed. And since we seem to be sitting on his final resting place, I'd better leave. (*Rising.*) But it was a lovely evening. (*Takes* MARY's *hand.*)

MARY (*rising with* DIRK): I thought so. I really thought so.

(*They go hand in hand toward the door.* DIRK *gets his coat.*)

DIRK: I'll call you first thing in the morning. Is ten o'clock too early?

MARY: Ten o'clock is fine. (DIRK *kisses her lightly but definitely.*)

DIRK (*to* MARY): Good night—(*To* BOB, *cheerily.*) Good night!

BOB: Night. (DIRK *goes, closing the main door behind him.*) (*There is a slight moment of awkwardness, then* BOB *goes toward the closet.*) Well, I'll get myself a blanket and some sheets. I imagine that extra blanket is still in the storage closet.

MARY (*hasn't stirred*): I imagine.

BOB (*having got out a sheet and blanket*): Too bad we can't open the window. This place is full of smoke. (*Waving his arms about to dispel imaginary smoke.*)

MARY: Uh-hm.

BOB (*picks up a large ash tray from the coffee table and dumps the contents of the sofa table ash tray and the mantel ash tray into it. Then empties the large one into the fireplace. Finally, he speaks his mind*): I must say that I'm rather surprised at you.

MARY (*bright, cheery*): Yes. I'm a little surprised at me, too.

BOB: You've been drinking.

MARY (*airily*): Yep, that's exactly what I've been doing. It's taught me a valuable lesson. You know what's the matter with this country? Too much sobriety. Too many sober persons.

BOB: May I suggest that you get yourself to bed before you pass right out?

MARY: No, you may not suggest one thing. I do not require your solasitude.

BOB: Solasitude? Solicitude!

MARY (*pleasantly stretching out on the sofa*): All right, that's what I do not require. I feel fine, splendid, top of the morning.

BOB (*cleaning desk ash tray*): I don't get it. I thought you were the conservative, slow-to-warm-up type. Miss Birds Eye Frozen.

MARY: There *was* a rumor like that going round. Isn't it nice to know there's nothing in it.

   (BOB *empties the contents of the bookcase and desk ash trays into a wastebasket.*)

BOB: Mary, look. What you do is none of my business. I know that.

MARY: I'm glad you know that.

BOB (*edging toward her, worried*): I never wanted to see you retire to a convent. You *ought* to go out with men. You should get married again. To some man who's in love with you.

MARY (*listening*): What other kind of man would marry me?

BOB: There are men and men. And—well, you don't know what you're getting into here. The idea of you sitting around necking with that bum! What the hell do you know about him?

MARY: Well, let's see. He had a very bad case of acne when he was fourteen years old.

BOB: That clarifies everything. I'm telling you this league is too fast for you, dearie. These glamour boys collect women like stamps—if you want to be added to the collection.

MARY (*sits up on sofa, finally speaking up for herself*): All right. I'll tell you something. He thinks he's falling in love with me.

BOB (*alarmed; feeling responsible*): He said that? Oh, that bastard! But you *couldn't* have believed him?

MARY: Why not?

BOB: Now, honestly. Does it seem very likely that that big, caramel-covered movie idol would come along and just one, two, three, bang, fall in love with a girl like you?

MARY (*sharply hurt, and now fighting tears*): I guess I thought it was possible—even with a girl like me. Isn't that the height of something or other?

BOB (*distressed at what he has said*): Wait, I didn't mean a girl like *you*—I meant any ordinary—

MARY: I *know* what you meant. How could you be clearer? I'm the drab, colorless type and I should know better than to believe it when somebody tells me I'm—pretty. . . . (*She can't help the catch in her voice, try as she may.*)

BOB (*completely unsettled*): Are you going to cry about it?

MARY: Maybe. Maybe. Why not?

BOB: Because you never cry.

MARY: How do you know I never? How do you know? I'll cry if I please! And I please! (*And she lets herself go, having a real, satisfactory cry.*)

BOB: Mary—

MARY (*flinging herself face down on sofa*): Don't you Mary me!

BOB (*out of his depth and railing against it*): It must have something to do with the position of the moon—I don't get it. Some joker tells you you're beautiful and you go all to pieces. I used to tell you you were beautiful and your detachment was marvelous to behold! (*Leans over her.*)

MARY (*sits up—flaring*): You never, never, never told me I was beautiful!

BOB: Of course I did!

MARY: No, you didn't. You said you liked the way I looked.

BOB: That's the same thing.

MARY: It most certainly is not the same thing! The world is full of people that you like the way they look, but you wouldn't say they were beautiful!

BOB: Like who, for instance?

MARY: Like Mrs. Roosevelt!

BOB (*incredulous, entirely serious, and wonderfully maddening*): You didn't think Mrs. Roosevelt was beautiful? My God—the character in that face . . . !

MARY: See? Now I'm a Communist. I'm picking on Mrs. Roosevelt! I *loved* Mrs. Roosevelt. And I'm not talking about character. If there is one thing I'm not interested in having any more of—if there's one thing I'm lousy with—it's character! Oh, why did you come back here tonight? I felt so good. Now I'm cold sober and everything is spoiled!

BOB (*backtracking*): I see that you're upset. I'm sorry if I—

MARY: You're not sorry. You're merely embarrassed.

BOB: What I *am* is surprised. I never thought I'd find you sobbing on the sofa. For all the world like any other woman. Actually, it's quite becoming. (*Sits near* MARY *and offers his handkerchief.*)

MARY (*taking it and wiping her eyes*): Thank you. I'm so relieved to know that.

BOB: Funny you never cried in the whole five years we were married.

MARY: I figured you were sensitive enough for both of us. You decided right at the beginning that I was the airy type—impervious to wind and weather and small disappointments.

BOB: You make it sound as though I invented your character. For that matter, what's wrong with being the airy type?

MARY (*getting up*): It got to be a bit of a strain. I felt like I was on some damn panel show, twenty-four hours a day. Smiling, affable, humming little snatches of song. Laughing when I didn't know the answers. But affable, affable, affable! You don't know how I longed to get up some morning and feel free for once to be depressed, to be constipated, to be boring. (*Pause.*) All right. I was boring.

BOB: No, you were not boring. It's strange we talked so much without communicating. (*The fact has hit him, and he's considering it.*)

MARY: It was hard to communicate with you. You were always communicating with yourself. The line was busy.

BOB (*surprised*): Is that the way it seemed to you?

MARY: It seemed to me that you were taking your emotional temperature six times a day. I could almost hear you asking yourself: "Am I nervous? Am I tense? Did that upset me?" How are you feeling right now?

(BOB *almost doesn't hear this last thrust. He is seriously and soberly thinking back.* MARY *picks up the sheet and blanket.*)

BOB: You're right, of course. I do have a bad habit of asking myself questions—silly questions. But—am I nervous, am I tense? That's more or less reasonable. (*Looking at her.*) It was really more foolish than that. I used to ask myself—why doesn't she love me?

MARY (*shocked, unbelieving*): You asked yourself—that?

BOB: All the time.

MARY (*throws bedclothes on sofa, exploding*): That's why I hate intellectuals! They're all so dumb!

BOB: What kind of a statement is that?

MARY: An idiotic statement. I should save my breath and remember that I'm talking to the most sensible man in the western hemisphere.

BOB: Why do you harp on that? I'm not all that sensible.

MARY: But you are! You lead a sensible life. You eat a sensible breakfast. You limit yourself to one pack of cigarettes a day—no more than two cocktails before dinner. You're even sensible about sex.

BOB: Would you like to explain that crack?

MARY: Any man that would tap his wife on the shoulder at eleven o'clock and say "Are you in the mood tonight—because if you're not, I'm going to take a sleeping pill" is just about as sensible as you can get!

BOB (*blanching*): Of course, I don't have Mr. Dirk Winston's technique in these matters.

MARY: No, you don't, more's the pity.

BOB: Look, I didn't mean to bring out your heavy artillery. I merely wanted to save you—

MARY: From what? From Dirk? But I don't want to be saved.

BOB: Just a minute. Surely you—

MARY: If he's just toying with my affections, okay. Maybe I'm in the mood to have my affections toyed with.

BOB: Mary, I promise you—you don't have the whole picture—

MARY: But I've seen the previews. And there's not one thing in this whole world you can do about it. (*Going toward the bedroom.*)

BOB (*starts to follow her, but stops to steel himself*): Mary, I'm ashamed to tell you this, but I think I just *have* to—

MARY (*fiercely*): No, you don't have to, and you're not going to! I won't listen. I had a lovely time—a lovely time, do you hear? And you're not going to spoil it for me! Good night! (*She stomps off into the bedroom, letting the door bang behind her firmly.*)

(BOB *sees* DIRK'S *manuscript on sofa table, seizes it, and starts to throw it into the fireplace, then thinks better of it. He goes to his desk and picks up the telephone.*)

BOB: Mr. Winston's apartment, please. (*He fidgets, but the wait is not long.*) (*Into phone.*) Dirk? You asleep? No, I didn't call to ask if you were asleep. I'm coming down there. I've got to talk to you. (*Pause to listen.*) Who's there with you—your agent? Is she pretty? Oh, all right, all right. I believe you. Then you've got to come up here. . . . You make it sound like I was asking you to drive to New

Rochelle. It's only one flight up. No, it won't keep until Monday. Listen, it'll only take five minutes—okay, okay. (*Hangs up.*)

(MARY *appears from the bedroom with an alarm clock.* BOB *crosses quickly away from the phone.*)

MARY (*coolly*): Do you want the alarm or shall I keep it?

BOB: You can keep it. I'm hardly likely to *over*sleep on that damn sofa. I'm lucky if I get to sleep. (*Turning off one of the lights.*)

MARY: All right. I'll take the sofa. It doesn't bother me.

BOB (*quickly, alarmed that she'll still be on hand when* DIRK *arrives*): No, no, absolutely not. That's out of the question. Now if you're going to bed, would you *go* to bed? (*He starts pacing to the window and back to the bar table.*)

MARY (*crossing casually to the alcove bookcase*): What's the matter with you? What are you pacing up and down like that for?

BOB (*stops pacing*): I'm waiting for you to go, instead of which—what are you doing?

MARY: Looking for something to read.

BOB: The place is full of books. What do you want?

MARY: I want something guaranteed not to improve my mind. (*Glancing at books.*) *The Gathering Storm* . . . *The Riddle of Rilke* . . . (*Spies* DIRK'S *manuscript on the desk.*) Oh. Dirk's book. The very thing. (*She starts for the bedroom, slowing down as her interest is caught by something in the manuscript.*)

BOB: Okay, now. Will you go to bed?

MARY (*slightly puzzled by his urgency*): I'm going. I'm going. (*Taking her suitcase with her, she goes into the bedroom and closes the door.*)

(BOB *breathes a sigh of relief, goes to the main door, opens it slightly so that* DIRK *will not have to ring, then returns to finish making himself a drink. At just this moment* DIRK *can be seen arriving in the corridor. As he is about to put his finger to the bell,* BOB *notices and dives for the door.*)

BOB: *Don't* push that damn buzzer!

DIRK: What's the problem?

BOB: I simply don't want Mary to hear that bell.

DIRK: Shall I come in?

BOB: Yes, of course. (*Drawing him into the room, slightly away from bedroom door. Suddenly he is awkward and nervous in this new situation.*) Listen, can I make you a drink?

DIRK: No, I don't want a drink. I merely want to know why you hauled me up here in the middle of the night.

BOB: Actually, it's only two o'clock. The thing is, I thought that we should—really, what I mean is that I should—(*Doesn't know how to begin.*) You're sure you don't want a drink?

DIRK: Positive.

BOB (*after staring at him helplessly for a second*): Well, I want a drink. (*Goes and gets the one he was making.*)

DIRK: All right. Let's have it.

BOB (*gulping a shot, and taking the plunge*): Look here, Winston . . . you know damn well that all this talk about you and Mary—and my publishing your book—was supposed to be a joke.

DIRK: I thought it was funny.

BOB: Okay, you knew I wasn't serious. Then why—why—?

DIRK: Ah, but you *were* serious! You had the wild-eyed look of a man who knows he has just spoken a true word in jest.

BOB: Look, I shot off my face. A bad habit I must nip in the full bloom. However, I wish to make it absolutely clear that I never intended at any time to make a deal with you involving Mary.

DIRK: And I thought it was an admirable plan! You wouldn't have been losing a wife, you'd have been gaining an author.

BOB: But you've got the whole thing straight now?

DIRK: Certainly.

BOB (*relieved*): I never dreamt that you were *this* anxious to get into print. And I certainly never thought that Mary—of all people— would sink into girlish incoherence at her first exposure to an actor.

DIRK: Why do you say "of all people—Mary?"

BOB: Because she's got some sense. That she could swallow that corny line!

DIRK: Do you describe everything you don't understand as corny?

BOB: What do you mean?

DIRK: Nothing. I suppose it's all right for me to go now—or did you have some other little confidence to tell me?

BOB: No, that's all. And thank you for coming. You can see I had to clear this up. I'll make your excuses to Mary in the morning.

DIRK: You will what?

BOB: I'll tell her you had to go back to Hollywood—for retakes, or whatever people go back to Hollywood for.

DIRK: And why will you tell her that?

BOB: Well, you don't think you'd be doing her a kindness to continue this little farce?

DIRK: I'm not interested in doing her a kindness. And I *am* going to see her.

BOB (*not understanding at all*): But why? I thought we understood each other. I thought we talked things out!

DIRK: Yes, and you listened very carefully to every word you had to say.

BOB: What do you mean by that?

DIRK: I mean you should take that paper bag off your head. You notice everything but the obvious. What kind of a jerk are you? How dare you suppose that Mary is some kind of a charity case? Where do you get off to suggest that any man who's interested in her has to have three ulterior motives?

BOB (*at a real loss now*): I don't think *that*. I never thought—

DIRK: Well, you gave a very good imitation of somebody who thought that. What I told Mary may well have sounded corny. It seems that I lack literary qualities everywhere. (*Levelly.*) But it wasn't a line. (BOB *sinks into the chair at his desk, confused.*) You know, talking to you, I begin to see why Mary is so shy.

BOB (*aghast*): Mary? Shy?

DIRK: That's right. Shy *and* insecure. You probably don't believe that, either, even though you're at least two-thirds responsible.

BOB (*he can't be hearing anything right*): How could I be responsible?

DIRK: I don't know. My guess is that you treated her as though she were intelligent.

BOB: She *is* intelligent.

DIRK (*waving it aside*): Shhh! She'll hear you! (*Going toward door, pausing to size him up.*) Where did you get the habit of making assumptions based only on assumptions? Was your father a lawyer?

BOB (*staring at him*): I'll put it all in a letter.

DIRK: All right. Before I go, I want to say only one thing. Leave her alone. Just leave her alone. Okay? (BOB *isn't grasping.*) I mean—tonight. (*With a gesture to the sofa.*)

BOB (*rising as this penetrates, dumfounded*): Are you nuts? I'm getting married in two weeks!

DIRK: Dandy. I'll send you a pair of book ends.

(*He leaves.* BOB *follows him to the door and angrily shoots the bolt. He turns out the hall light, takes off his jacket, picks up the sheet, then throws it down and starts for the bedroom door. He starts to knock on it, but doesn't. Biting his lip, he looks around the room, sees the telephone. With an inspiration, he hurries to it.*)

BOB: Operator? Would you ring this number for me? *My* number. Thank you. (*He hangs up until the phone rings. Then he waits until it stops ringing after three rings. Picks it up.*) Mary? This is Bob. I'm in the living room.

(*Pause, while he listens for her to speak. Then the bedroom door whips open and* MARY *appears in the doorway, in pajamas, with the bedroom receiver in her hand.*)

MARY: My God, you *are* in the living room! (*Stares at receiver in her hand, then at him.*) What do you want? (*Holds up one finger, getting into the spirit of the thing, and is repeating her question into receiver as she returns to the bedroom.*) What do you want?

BOB (*exasperated now, into phone*): Oh, stop it! Hang up! You're just trying to make me feel foolish!

MARY (*appearing in bedroom doorway again, with receiver*): *I'm* trying to make *you* look foolish! Who called who from the living room?

BOB: Well, I wasn't going to go barging into your bedroom! (*He hangs up his phone.*) I had something to say to you and there seemed to be no reason why I couldn't say it on the telephone.

MARY (*turning to go*): I'll go back in. You call me again.

BOB: Stay right there! (MARY *merely reaches into the bedroom to hang up her receiver.*) This won't take one minute. I just feel—in all fairness—that I have an obligation to tell you—(*It's a struggle for him, but he's game.*)—that I was wrong, apparently, about Mr. Winston.

MARY: And by what curious process did you arrive at this conclusion?

BOB: I talked to him. He was just up here.

MARY (*her eyes popping*): He *wasn't*—you *didn't*—!

BOB: It was all right. Don't worry. (*Facing her.*) He merely told me that I was an insensitive clunk who never appreciated you.

MARY: And what did you say?

BOB: Oh, a number of stupid things. It was not my finest hour. Of course, when he says I didn't appreciate you, that's hogwash. I appreciated you, all right. (*Sits on the sofa.*) I just wasn't able to handle you.

MARY (*softened by* BOB'S *direct attitude and drifting into the room*): Don't reproach yourself. I didn't win any prizes for the way I handled you. It takes at least one to make a marriage.

BOB: Do you know how helpless you feel if you have a full cup of coffee in your hand and you start to sneeze? There's nothing to do but just let it splash. That's how I feel in all my relationships any more. Helpless—unable to co-ordinate—splashing everybody.

MARY: You're just tired. (*Without thinking about it, they seem to have drifted into a perfectly familiar domestic situation.*)

BOB: Listen, you should have heard my various exchanges with Winston today! And thank God you didn't! Talk about a comedy of errors! I try to grasp all sides of the picture. Nobody believes that—but I try.

MARY: Bob, honey—I mean, Bob—I believe it. I certainly believe it. I honestly think you're so busy grasping all sides of the picture that you never stand back and see it.

BOB (*willing to consider this*): Okay. Give me an example.

MARY: All right. I've been reading Dirk's book. I haven't got very far, but I think it's good.

BOB: Come on now—

MARY: No, you're going to let me finish. It may not win a Pulitzer prize, but it's readable. It's so nice and gossipy. I think it would sell.

BOB: I never said it wouldn't sell. I said I didn't want to do it.

MARY: But why not?

BOB: Oh, we've had this out a hundred times.

MARY: Bob, you won't believe this but I'm glad you have standards. I wouldn't want you to settle for trash. But it's no crime to stay in business. You've got to keep the shop open or you won't be there when a masterpiece comes along. (*Quickly.*) Let me get it. (*She dodges briefly into the bedroom for the manuscript, talking as she does, while* BOB *sits and stares at her.*) I'm willing to make you a small bet that you can open it at any page at all and find something that's— nice, interesting. (*Coming back and sitting at one end of the sofa.*

The atmosphere is casual and they are, for all intents and purposes, man and wife at home alone.) Maybe it goes to pieces at the end, but I wouldn't know about that. Okay, we'll just open it anywhere. (*Reading from manuscript.*) ". . . Starlets have a reputation for being dumb only because they have such blank expressions. And the smarter they are, the blanker they look, because they've learned that it's impossible to register any emotion without using some muscle which in time, will produce a wrinkle. Even to look a tiny bit puzzled causes twin lines over the bridge of the nose. (*Glancing at* BOB *to do the expression for him; it strikes her as amusing:* BOB *is simply looking at her. She goes on.*) By the time she is thirty, a starlet has been carefully taught to smile like a dead halibut. The eyes widen, the mouth drops open, but the muscles are never involved." (*Turning to* BOB *to explain.*) They don't smile like this—(*She smiles as most people do.*) See? You get all these wrinkles. (*Touching her forehead with her fingers to show him.*) They go like this. (*She lets her mouth drop open in a mechanized, slack smile that doesn't involve the eyes.* BOB *is not really hearing her as he looks at her. She becomes aware he isn't responding.*) You don't think that's funny.

BOB (*forced to say something, unable to identify what he's really feeling, the wrong thing pops out*): Haven't you got a robe? (*He rises and crosses away.*)

MARY (*blank*): What do you mean, haven't I got a robe?

BOB (*awkward*): Well—do *you* think it's right for you to be sitting here in your night clothes?

MARY (*blowing*): My night clothes! Good Lord, you'd think it was a black lace bikini! Eight million times you've seen me in pajamas!

BOB: We were married then.

MARY (*staring after him*): Well, look at it this way. The divorce won't be final for two weeks.

BOB (*turns on a lamp*): That may be precisely the point.

MARY: Oh, my, we are so proper! Do you feel yourself in danger of being compromised? Don't worry so much. If I should suddenly throw myself upon you, you could always scream.

BOB: Oh, shut up.

MARY (*continuing blithely*): However, as it happens, I don't have a robe but there must be something around here. (*Sees his overcoat on the window seat.*) Yes, here we are. (*Puts it on; it is, of course, too big for her.*) I trust this will show my good faith and restore your sense of fitness.

BOB: And how do you think you look in that?

MARY (*sweetly*): I don't know. Kind of cute, maybe?

BOB: Boy! All of a sudden you're cocky as hell, aren't you?

MARY: All of a sudden? It took months. It was work, work, work every minute!

BOB: But it's been worth it. Think of having Dirk Winston making passes at you! It must be like getting the Good Housekeeping Seal of Approval.

MARY: Um—sort of.

BOB: When you kissed him, I just hope you didn't damage his porcelain crowns.

MARY (*giggling*): Well, we can't worry about everything. But never mind his crowns, let's talk about his book. (*Reaching for the manuscript on the sofa, secretly pleased at BOB's attitude.*)

BOB: I refuse to talk about anything with you in that damn coat. You look like Jackie Coogan in *The Kid*. Here—take it off! (*Reaches for the coat.*)

MARY (*pretending to be shocked, as though fighting for her virtue*): Oh, no—no—please!

BOB (*starting to unbutton it*): Take it off. You only put it on to make me feel like an idiot.

MARY (*struggling*): You're going to break the buttons.

BOB: To hell with the buttons. (*He finally gets the coat off—and they stand facing each other in a moment of nervous intimacy. Instinctively, MARY puts her hand to the top of her pajamas. BOB backs away slightly*) No, that's as far as I mean to go. (*Angrily.*) Now would you do me a favor, please? Will you please go to bed?

MARY (*below sofa, unsettled herself, now*): Certainly. But what are you so intense about?

BOB: I'm the intense type. Surely you've remarked on that before. I'm asking myself how I feel. And I feel wretched.

MARY: What's the matter?

BOB: You know damn well what's the matter! I feel all involved again. And I won't have it! I will not have it! I was getting over you so nicely. I was cured. My God, I feel like somebody who was getting out of the hospital after nine long months and fell down in the lobby and broke a leg. (*Because he is furious with himself.*) And you did it deliberately!

MARY: Did it—did what?

BOB: If you want to pretend that your only purpose in the last half hour was to change my opinion of that book—all right!

MARY (*turns away, more quietly*): But I gather I'm not fooling you— great student of character that you are.

BOB: Okay, what *did* you have in mind—curling up on the sofa, cute as all get-out in your little blue pajamas? No, I'll tell you. You were conducting a little experiment.

MARY: I was?

BOB: You wanted to see—just for the record—if Old Bob wouldn't leap to the bait like our friend Mr. Winston. You just wanted to check and see if I had any little twinges left. (*She says nothing.*) Well?

MARY (*very quietly*): I'm just wondering if that could possibly be true.

BOB: There's no reason for you to be kept in suspense. Yes, if you want to know, I do still feel twinges. God help me. Every now and then a sharp one. Now what do you say?

MARY (*thoughtful for a split second, then, in her perplexity, reverting to type*): Well, I don't know—it *sounds* like a gall bladder attack. (BOB *stares a second, then turns on his heel and grabs his jacket.*) (MARY *impulsively, and now all regret.*) Bob, where are you going?

BOB (*putting on his jacket wildly*): Where am I going? Out! What am I going to do? Nothing! (*He struggles to get quickly into his overcoat, making a mess of the procedure.*)

MARY: Bob, don't be silly! It's still snowing! You'll get pneumonia.

BOB (*hurls his overcoat to the floor and storms out*): Don't you worry your little head. (*Leaving the door open.*)

MARY (*shouting after him*): But where can you possibly go at this hour in the morning? They'll think you're crazy—! (MARY *stands there a moment, her back to us. Then she slowly turns and picks up* BOB'S *coat. She comes down to a chair, the coat clutched in her arms. After a second or so, she begins to recite mechanically, like a child writing* "lines" *as a punishment.*) I must keep my big mouth shut. . . . I must keep my big mouth shut. . . . I must keep my big mouth shut. . . .

(*As the* CURTAIN FALLS)

END OF ACT TWO

ACT THREE

Next morning, rather early.

AT RISE: The stage is empty but the doorbell is ringing. The sofa is made up with sheet and blanket, but these are obviously unrumpled. In a moment MARY *comes from the bedroom, still half-asleep. She is in her pajamas.*

MARY: Bob . . . (*Staring at the sofa.*) Oh. He didn't come back at all. (*She stumbles to the phone.*) Hello. (*Doorbell.*) Hello. For heaven's sakes, hello. (*Doorbell again.* MARY *now realizes it isn't the phone.*) Oh. Excuse me. (*Hangs up.*) I'm coming. (*Before she can get to the door, it opens. It is* TIFFANY.) Oh, hello. Good morning. Oh—you're —I mean, you must be—

TIFFANY (*after a moment of staring at* MARY, *without showing her surprise, she closes the door and speaks cheerily*): I'm Tiffany Richards. And you're Mary, aren't you? Well, I'm delighted to meet you. May I come in?

MARY: Certainly. By all means. I don't know *where* Bob is . . .

TIFFANY (*taking off her coat*): He's probably taking a walk. Lately I've been getting him to take a walk before breakfast. It's the very best thing for a sluggish colon.

MARY (*vaguely, still sleepy and not knowing where to settle or what to do next*): Yes, I can imagine it would be.

TIFFANY (*opening the curtains*): I never dreamt I'd find you here. But I'm so pleased it worked out this way. I've been dying to meet you. And it's a good thing Bob isn't here.

MARY: Why?

TIFFANY: Oh, he'd be bustling me right out the front door. For some reason, he was determined I wasn't going to meet you. You know, you're much shorter than I expected.

MARY (*not bitchy*): Of course I don't have any shoes on.

TIFFANY: It's just that Bob always makes you sound so overpowering. I expected somebody with a husky voice who said "darling" a lot. Harlequin glasses, big jangling bracelets, black velvet toreador pants.

MARY: But I do have a bracelet that jangles. I just don't wear it to bed.

TIFFANY: No, I can tell what you're like just by looking at you. I think you're nice.

MARY: Oh, dear.

TIFFANY: What's the matter?

MARY: It's so early. And you want to be frank and disarming.

TIFFANY: But what's wrong with that?

MARY (*going toward the bedroom, quickly and apologetically*): Oh, nothing, nothing at all. It's just my low metabolism. I don't grasp things this early in the day. I mean, I hear voices, all right, but I can't pick out the verbs. (*Goes into the bedroom.*)

TIFFANY (*taking a dried apricot from the bowl*): You probably don't eat right. My grandmother is like that.

MARY (*returning, rummaging through her purse*): Oh, no. It's not possible! The way I feel and I don't even have a cigarette.

TIFFANY: Look, I wouldn't bother you, but Bob will be back and then I'll *never* get a chance to ask you.

MARY (*looks in the cigarette box on the sofa table*): Ask me? Ask me what?

(*From now on* MARY *is making an abstracted effort to listen to* TIFFANY *but what she is really doing is making a methodical and increasingly desperate effort to find a cigarette somewhere around the apartment.*)

TIFFANY: I guess I should warn you that I'm a very practical kind of person. People tease me about it all the time. Last Christmas, when I went to Palm Beach, everybody thought I was crazy because I took along my sun lamp, except it rained every day and I was the only one who came back with a tan.

MARY: Yes, but what did you want to ask me?

TIFFANY: I'm getting to that. Daddy always said that before you move into a house, you should consult the former tenant.

MARY: Oh. (*Checking the bookshelves and* BOB'S *desk for a cigarette.*)

TIFFANY: The person who's been living there will know where the storm windows are and whether there's a leak in the basement. Why should you spend six months finding out for yourself?

MARY (*at the desk, too foggy to understand*): They don't have storm windows in this building.

TIFFANY: I'm not talking about the apartment. I'm talking about Bob.

MARY: You want to know if Bob has a leak in the basement? (*Her last resort.*) Excuse me—you don't have a cigarette on you, do you?

TIFFANY: I'm sorry. I don't smoke. It's not that I worry about lung cancer, but it does stain your teeth.

MARY: Well, I worry terribly about lung cancer. I also worry about shortness of breath and heart disease. But what really worries me right this minute is that I'm not going to find a cigarette. (*Begins looking through the desk drawers.*)

TIFFANY: Oh, I guess you never do find out. My cousin Harriet knew this boy for seven years. I mean she *thought* she knew him. But on the day they were married they took an overnight train to Chicago. And when they shut the door of their roomette, do you know the first thing he did?

MARY: No, and don't tell me.

TIFFANY: Well, he picked up a book of matches, opened the cover, and started picking his teeth. Like this. (*Demonstrates "picking his teeth" with a lid of book matches.*) (*The key turns in the front door and* BOB *enters, the Sunday papers under his arm. He stops, startled and then embarrassed to find the two girls together.*) Hi.

BOB (*pulling himself together with an effort*): Well. This is cozy. (*Then rattled again, quick to overexplain.*) Tiffany, I should have explained to you last night that you'd find Mary here. (*Stopping to listen to himself.*) Of course, I didn't know last night. (*Now really confused, looking at* MARY.) I suppose you've introduced yourselves.

TIFFANY (*rising and kissing* BOB *on the cheek*): Oh yes, of course! (*She goes into the kitchen.*)

BOB: Good morning, Mary.

MARY: Good morning, Bob. Did you have to go without your overcoat?

BOB: At the time I thought so.

MARY: I made up your bed because I expected—(BOB *takes off his jacket.*) What did you do?

BOB: Walked, mostly. (*Looking for a cigarette on the low bookcase.*)

MARY: Don't tell me you're out of cigarettes, too?

BOB (*patting his pockets. But they're empty*): Yes, but you'll find some in the desk drawer.

MARY: No, I looked.

BOB: Well, did you try behind the—

MARY: Yes, and I tried the liquor cabinet and the stamp drawer. (TIFFANY *returns with wheat germ for the fish.*) And the last refuge of all—the Chinese vase—

BOB (*starting his own search*): Don't tell me I'm going to have to go trudging back out in that snow!

TIFFANY: Just for a cigarette? Would you like some breakfast? There's some orange-flavored yogurt.

BOB: Oh, no, no. Lord, no! Tiffany, be a lamb and fold up these sheets. There may be some under the—

MARY: See! If you hadn't dumped every single ash tray last night I could have found some medium-sized butts.

(TIFFANY *folds up the blanket, watching* MARY *and* BOB *feverishly search every conceivable nook.*)

BOB: We must remain calm. It is statistically impossible that in this whole big apartment there isn't one single—just ask yourself: Where would you go if you were a cigarette? (*From beneath the cushion of a chair he brings up a battered half package.*) Look! Success! (MARY *runs to him.*)

MARY (*as though cooing over a new baby*): There! Did you ever see anything so pretty in your life?

(BOB *is digging for matches to light* MARY'S *cigarette.*)

TIFFANY: But they're all squashed!

(MARY *and* BOB *simply turn to stare at* TIFFANY, *simultaneously and incredulously. Then they turn their attention to the serious business of getting the cigarettes lighted, after which they exhale. Forgetting themselves, they speak in unison.*)

MARY and BOB: Mmmm—that's *real* coffee! (*Becoming aware of what they have just done, they are a little embarrassed and pause awkwardly.*)

TIFFANY (*looking up as she puts blanket away*): Coffee? What's that about coffee?

BOB (*firmer*): Nothing. Absolutely nothing.

TIFFANY: It must be something.

BOB (TIFFANY *is obviously waiting for an explanation.* BOB *launches into it lamely*): We once heard this announcer on television. It was late at night and I suppose the poor joker was confused from having to talk about so many products all day. Anyway, he started to do a cigarette commercial. He sucked in and smiled and said "Mmmm— that's *real* coffee." (TIFFANY *does not react.*) You see, it *wasn't* worth going into. (*Determined to be brisk and cheerful.*) All of which reminds me that I haven't had any coffee. I think I'd better start some up.

(BOB *goes into the kitchen almost too quickly, closing the door. There is a slight pause as* TIFFANY *looks at* MARY.)

TIFFANY: How long does it take to have little private jokes?

MARY: What?

TIFFANY: Never mind. (*She begins to fold the sheet on the sofa.*) I must stop asking questions for which there are no answers. (*Stops folding and looks reflectively at the sheet.*) This sheet isn't even mussed. (*Looks at sofa.*) Nobody slept on this sofa last night.

MARY: No. Bob was going to, but—

TIFFANY: He changed his mind.

MARY (*not wanting to go into what really happened*): That couch is a little short for him. Anyway, he decided that—

TIFFANY:—he'd rather sleep with you. (*She finishes folding the sheet, matter-of-factly.* MARY'S *mouth drops open, but not for long.*)

MARY: You mean—for old times' sake? No, indeed. Bob went—well, as a matter of fact, I don't *know* where he went. But he certainly wasn't here. As you will discover when you ask him.

TIFFANY: I won't ask him.

MARY (*looking at her*): Because you don't believe me.

TIFFANY: No, I don't.

MARY: Tiffany, when you get a little older, you'll learn not to *invent* problems. All you have to do is wait, and real ones turn up.

TIFFANY: In a way—I think I'm just as glad it happened.

MARY: You are.

TIFFANY: Bob's attitude toward you has always been a little mysterious. I'm hoping this may clear the air.

MARY: Your theory is that he's a little bit homesick and a trip back to the old place may cure him?

TIFFANY: All right, yes. That's what I think.

(BOB *returns briskly from the kitchen, carrying a tray with coffee cups and an electric coffee maker on it.*)

MARY: Bob. I'm afraid our little secret is out.

BOB (*casually, unraveling electric cord*): What little secret?

MARY: No, Bob, please. Tiffany *knows*. And she's being very understanding.

BOB (*glancing at* MARY *but kneeling to put the cord into the light socket*): Would you care to be plainer? I'm simply not up to riddles this morning.

MARY: Certainly. I'm trying to tell you that Tiffany is glad we slept together last night. She thinks it will clear the air.

BOB (*hearing it, and instantly up*): What did you say? What?

MARY (*blithely*): I really must get dressed. (MARY *goes off to the bedroom, closing the door behind her.*)

BOB (*turning to* TIFFANY): Did I hear her correctly?

TIFFANY (*offering him the bowl of apricots*): Bob, whatever you do—please don't apologize.

BOB (*waving the bowl away and circling her*): You're damn right I won't apologize!

TIFFANY: All right, but are you going to snap at *me*?

BOB: Wait a minute. You accept this as a *fact*—and you're not even disturbed?

TIFFANY: Should I be?

BOB: Well, I can think of six reasons why you ought to be. And you can't even think of one?

TIFFANY: It isn't like it was somebody new. It isn't even like you planned it. You're put back into an old situation, and you fall into an old pattern.

BOB: I see.

TIFFANY: Anybody will tell you that the force of habit is stronger than —than love, even.

BOB: And in spite of the fact that I shack up with my ex-wife, you're willing to marry me?

TIFFANY: Certainly.

BOB: My God, haven't you got any principles, any ethics?

TIFFANY (*aroused, finally*): How did my principles ever get into this? What have *I* done?

BOB (*turning away and rubbing his forehead violently. Then he collapses into the chair behind the desk and begins rummaging through the desk drawers*): I've got to take some aspirin. I've got to clear my head.

TIFFANY: What's the matter?

BOB: You've heard of a lost weekend. Well, this has been a found weekend and it's worse.

TIFFANY: I'll get some water. (*She goes into the kitchen, leaving the door ajar.*)

(BOB *now brings out, one by one, about a dozen bottles of pills of varying sizes, including aspirin.*)

BOB: I feel in my bones that this is going to be one little peach of a day. I've got to take something to clear my head or I'm going to goof. I'm going to make some crucial mistake. (TIFFANY *returns with a glass of water.*) And where the hell is Oscar?

TIFFANY: On Sunday, what do you want with Oscar?

BOB (*taking the glass and two aspirins*): There!

TIFFANY: Also take two of those large vitamins. (*With a glance at the bedroom door;* MARY *is on her mind.*)

BOB: Why? (*He opens a bottle and takes out three capsules.*)

TIFFANY: Alcohol works directly on the blood stream. (*He swallows one.*) If you drink too much it lowers the white count, which is one reason why—

BOB (*with another one in his mouth*): No, no—don't give me the details. (*Downs a third.*) Now I've taken three. There. I can feel my white blood count going up already.

TIFFANY (*suddenly noticing the bottle and picking it up*): Bob. You didn't take these?

BOB: You told me to.

TIFFANY: You idiot! These aren't vitamins.

BOB: What are they?

TIFFANY: Sleeping pills. (BOB *snatches the bottle from her and looks at it.*)

BOB (*to heaven in despair*): Oh, great. Great!

TIFFANY: Do you feel peculiar?

BOB: Not yet.

TIFFANY: Well, you will. We'd better get something.

BOB: It's not going to kill me. You have to take a whole bottle—a hundred and twenty, or something. (*Doorbell.* TIFFANY *starts to answer it.*) That'll be Oscar.

TIFFANY (*on her way to door*): Don't sit down. (BOB *jumps up.*) I think you're supposed to keep walking around.

BOB: You're thinking of concussion. (*He drops into a chair again.*)

TIFFANY (*opening the door.* DIRK *appears*): Oh—come in! You're Dirk Winston, aren't you?

DIRK: Yes. And you're—?

TIFFANY: I'm Tiffany Richards. (*Pulling* DIRK *into the room.*) And we've got a problem. Bob has taken some sleeping pills.

DIRK: Bob has!

BOB: Tiffany, Please! Don't turn this into a melodrama. (*To* DIRK.) I just—

TIFFANY (*to* DIRK, *pointing to the coffee maker*): Do you think you could get him some coffee? I'll go to the drugstore and see if I can get some benzedrine or Dexamil—

BOB: They won't give that without a prescription.

TIFFANY (*slipping on her coat*): They'll give me something, don't you worry. I'd call a doctor, but they want to ask you a lot of crazy questions, like are you depressed. (*To* DIRK.) You'll watch out for him, won't you?

DIRK: Like a mother. Now, don't worry. (TIFFANY *rushes out the front door.* DIRK *wanders casually down to* BOB.) Why did you do it?

BOB: Because my life has suddenly become ashes. I didn't know which way to turn.

DIRK: Come off it. How many did you take?

BOB: Three. Look, I got the bottles mixed up. I thought I was taking vitamins. Any more questions?

DIRK: Yeah. Where's Mary?

BOB (*crossly*): Well, the last time I saw her, she was in pajamas, so I think we may safely suppose she's dressing.

DIRK: What the hell are you so irritable about?

BOB: Because I had a rotten night! I drank too much, slept too little—

DIRK: You're not fooling anybody. You're mad as a hornet because I'm here to get Mary.

BOB: Why should I be mad? I'm delighted!

DIRK: You *sound* delighted.

BOB: Never mind my inflections. I just haven't had your training.

DIRK: You know, there's something very mysterious about your feeling for Mary. It's like gas. You can't get it up and you can't get it down.

BOB (*the thought registers with* BOB *but he doesn't blanch*): There's a touch of the poet in you.

(MARY *enters from the bedroom, dressed, and looking just splendid.*)

MARY (*very cheery, seeing* DIRK): Good morning!

DIRK: Good morning. You just getting up?

MARY: Oh, I've been up for an hour. In fact, I've already had a heart-to-heart talk with Miss Richards.

BOB (*going to the bar table*): I've got to have some coffee.

MARY (*sweetly*): And would you bring me some, please? And a Danish that's—

BOB (*mechanically, swerving from the coffee maker toward the kitchen*):—cut down the middle, and no butter. I'll get it. (*Goes into the kitchen, closing the door.*)

DIRK: I woke up this morning thinking: What nice thing just happened to me? And it was you.

MARY: You're very sweet. And not like a movie actor at all.

DIRK (*pouring her a cup of coffee*): Sure I am. Movie actors are just ordinary, mixed-up people—with agents.

MARY: I should think it would be fun to be Dirk Winston.

DIRK: It is. There are all kinds of advantages. I can go into any restaurant at all and the headwaiter will automatically bring me a large pepper mill. Doctors don't get pepper mills—or lawyers. Not only that, but the headwaiter stands right there until I use it. I don't want him to feel a failure, so I grind away. With the result that I've had too much pepper on everything for twenty years. I love the way you smile.

MARY (*nervous, but meaning every word of it*): Dirk, I want you to know that I will never forget last evening. You couldn't possibly know what you did for me.

DIRK: Yes, but what have I done for you lately?

MARY: I'm not joking. I'm terribly pleased—and gratified.

DIRK (*urgently*): Gratified, hell! I don't want you to be gratified. I want you to be interested. I want you to say it would cause you a real pang if you thought you weren't going to see me again.

MARY: Oh, Dirk, it would—it does.

DIRK: I got a call from the studio at eight o'clock. They insist that I fly to New Orleans this morning for some personal appearance stuff. That picture of mine is opening there Thursday.

MARY: In New Orleans?

DIRK (*nodding*): The picture is called *King of the Mardi Gras*. That's how the great minds in publicity operate—the mayor meets me at the airport and hands me a praline or some damn thing. There's nothing I can do about it. It's in my contract. Anyway, here's the point. Why don't you come along?

MARY: But Dirk! I'm a working girl.

DIRK: Surely they could carry on without you for one week. Never underestimate the power of the *Ladies' Home Journal*.

MARY: But you just don't *do* that . . . !

DIRK: Sure you do. You call up and say that you've just had a recurrence of an old football injury. We could have a lot of fun. We could get to know each other.

MARY: But Dirk, I don't go off on trips with movie stars—I read about people like that in the *Journal-American* and I'm scandalized!

DIRK: Come on. Be rash. Fly now, pay later.

(BOB *returns with an empty paper carton.*)

BOB: Dirk, we seem to be all out of everything. Could I ask you to go down to the bakery and get a half-dozen Danish? It's for Mary.

MARY: Oh, let's have toast—anything.

BOB: No, there's nothing out there. I'd go myself, but I'm feeling so groggy.

DIRK (*rising and looking at his watch*): I don't *have* all that time . . . (*And looking at* MARY.)

BOB: It's right in the building. Go left after you get out of the elevator.

DIRK: Well, I started life as a messenger boy.

MARY: Oh, don't bother.

DIRK: That's all right. I have to see if they've got my luggage in the lobby anyway. (*With a curious glance at* BOB, *then at* MARY.) Mary —think about it. . . . (*He goes.*)

MARY: I don't know who ate them, but there was a whole bagful last night.

BOB: I stuffed them in the wastebasket.

MARY: You what?

BOB: I wanted to get him out of here so I could talk to you.

MARY (*starting for door as though to stop* DIRK): If that isn't the dumbest thing! Why should he have to—?

BOB (*grabbing her and spinning her around*): It won't hurt him a bit. You know—I'd like to shake you until your teeth rattled.

MARY: Oh, come on! In your whole life you never even shook a bottle of magnesia.

BOB: Why, why, *why* would you tell Tiffany that we slept together last night?

MARY (*honestly*): Look, Bob, whether you believe it or not, I said nothing to give Tiffany that impression.

BOB (*this rocks him a little*): Then why did she—?

MARY: I don't know. Some people have such a talent for making the best of a bad situation that they go around creating bad situations so they can make the best of them.

BOB (*trying to think*): She didn't seem upset at all.

MARY: Upset? I got the impression she was delighted.

BOB: I know. I don't understand it. I don't understand anything. (*He sinks into a chair.*) Mary, I'm so miserable.

MARY: Why?

BOB: You should know why. Look. In all the months we've been separated, have you been happier?

MARY (*reflectively*): No.

BOB: Have you—ever thought we might get back together again?

MARY (*trying to hide the emotion she feels*): It crossed my mind. (*She sits near him, tentatively.*)

BOB (*after a breath*): *Would* you consider it?

MARY (*struggling to control the relief and joy that want to come into her voice*): Bob, do you know what you're saying? Do you *mean* it?

BOB (*surprisingly making no move toward her*): I do mean it. (*Thinking, and even turning away.*) I've been behaving like a damn adolescent—refusing to face the simple facts.

MARY (*a little taken aback*): What simple facts?

BOB: Look at the whole thing in sequence. (*Counting the items on his fingers, logically.*) *A*—I wanted a divorce from you because—well, it boils down to something as simple as I didn't think you understood me. Okay. (*Next finger.*) *B*—the minute we got divorced, I discovered what I should have known in the first place—that I'm the kind of man who has to be married.

MARY (*hurt now, but keeping a level tone*): Is that what you discovered?

BOB (*going on with his explanation as though he were addressing a committee, completely unaware of the effect on* MARY): Absolutely. This business of going from flower to flower never did appeal to me. I hate to live alone. I hate to sleep alone. I keep finding myself, at four o'clock in the morning, sitting in the bathroom reading old magazines. So—I decided to get married again. That's *C*. In the circumstances, it seemed the logical thing to do.

MARY (*taking his tone*): I'd say so—yes.

BOB: But wait a minute. Now I discover that Tiffany really believes that I would actually sleep with one woman on the very eve of marrying another. By this time she should know me better than that. It isn't in my character. I'm really too square. But the point remains. *She* doesn't understand me, either.

MARY (BOB *doesn't notice the acid that begins to creep into her voice*): Okay, we've had *A, B,* and *C*. What about *D*?

BOB (*innocent, and eager to go on explaining*): Well, I ask myself—am I walking with my eyes wide open into another case of incompatibility? In five years will there be another divorce? I don't think I could face it. (*He sinks onto the sofa, yawning.*)

MARY (*casually, still playing along, though we can hear what's going on inside her*): No, and there would be more alimony, too.

BOB: Oh! More alimony, more scenes, more confusion! The thing is, you and I may be incompatible, but we know all about it now. I think we should get married again. It would be the sensible, reasonable thing to do. Don't you? (*He doesn't have to wait too long for his answer.* MARY *rises.*)

MARY: You clunk. You block of wood. You're dumb—you're obtuse—you're—do you know something? I was so much in love with you that when you left I thought I'd die. That's right—big, healthy, well-adjusted Mary—I thought I might just possibly die! I used to sleep with the light on because in the beginning I'd wake up in the dark and forget where I was—and I'd reach out for you. Do you know if I saw a man ahead of me in the subway who walked like you or had shoulders like you, I used to feel faint, really faint. And you have the gall to stand there and talk to me about the sensible reasons why I should come back to you. You and your damn, stinking ABC's! (*She starts for the bedroom.*)

BOB (*with his head blown off*): Wait a minute—just because I try to be rational doesn't mean I don't *feel* anything—

MARY: Well, we won't really know until after the autopsy. Let me give you a little piece of advice. I think you should go right ahead and marry Tiffany. It would be more than a marriage. It would be a merger. You should be as happy as two IBM machines clicking away together!

BOB (*trying to salvage his dignity*): So you're not coming back.

MARY: That's right. *A*—I don't want to, *B*—I don't want to, *C*—I don't want to! (*She starts into the bedroom.*)

(OSCAR *has let himself in,* DIRK *having left the door part-way open.*)

OSCAR: What don't you want to do?

MARY: Oh, hello, Oscar—(*She stops in the bedroom doorway, all passion spent.*)

OSCAR (*closing the door—to* BOB): I got your message. I'm shocked to see you looking so well.

BOB: What do you mean?

OSCAR (*getting out of his coat*): The answering service said it was absolutely urgent that I get over here this morning. *Urgent* was underlined three times.

BOB: Oh. (*An embarrassed glance in* MARY'S *direction.*)

OSCAR: I presumed that you were at death's door—waiting for me to draw up your will.

BOB: Of course not. It was really nothing that important. Actually it was really something minor. I mean, it could have—

MARY (*whirling on* BOB, *exasperated*): Oh, stop it! Why don't you tell him why you called him up this morning and asked him to come over? (*To* OSCAR.) He thought he'd come back and find nobody here but *me*—and he'd be left alone with me. But think of it—you're too late! The damage has been done.

BOB (*outraged, blowing*): That's right! Listen to *her!* She knows my mind so much better than I do.

MARY: Oscar, when you go back over his accounts, you may deduct the amount he pays me in alimony. I don't want it. I never wanted it. I'm working now, and I don't need it.

BOB (*angrily*): Oh, don't be noble, there's no necessity!

MARY: Oh, but there is! (*To* OSCAR.) Do you realize that if this poor soul had to go on paying alimony to me, he could never divorce Tiffany? Oscar, I sat at home and waited nine long months for him to call. Well, I'm not sitting home any longer. (*Heading for the bedroom.*) Now I'm going to pack. (MARY *goes, slamming door behind her.*)

OSCAR: Congratulations. You seem to have solved everything.

BOB: Oh, Oscar, you don't know what you're talking about! Even my problems have problems! (*Uncontrollably, he yawns right in* OSCAR'S *face, then plunges on without pausing, in the same overwrought way.*) What am I going to do? I can't marry Tiffany. She pushes in the bottoms of chocolates!

OSCAR: I never thought you would marry Tiffany.

BOB: Stop sounding like an owl and tell me what to do!

OSCAR: Get Mary back.

BOB: That's the conclusion I came to. But how?

OSCAR: Ask her.

BOB: Ask her? Last night I pleaded with her. Today I tried to be reasonable!

OSCAR (*quietly*): So that's what she's so mad about?

BOB: Yeah! And can you explain to me why *that* should make a woman mad?

OSCAR: Not in the time we have at our disposal. But I can tell you you'd be better off giving her one idiotic reason.

BOB: What do you mean?

OSCAR: Tell her you want her back so you can bite her shoulders.

BOB: You try and tell her something! Do you know that she's actually convinced I never noticed she was pretty? What does she think—I just arrived in from Mars? (*Yawn.*) I've got two eyes. Hell, she always was pretty. When I first saw her with that pale hair and that pale face I thought she looked like a lovely piece of white porcelain.

OSCAR: Did you tell her?

BOB: Are you crazy? She would have said "White porcelain—you mean like the kitchen sink?"

OSCAR: Come on, now, you exaggerate.

BOB: Exaggerate? You don't know the half of it. She thinks I'm made of cast iron. She thinks I've never felt even a pang. Like I was some sort of vegetable. Do you know why I put that stinking phone in the bedroom? Because after we broke up I thought she might call me in the middle of the night some night and I wanted to be sure that I'd hear it. And before she gets out of here this afternoon I'm going to tell her about that phone. She's going to hear a few plain truths. She's not going to call me a block of wood. (*He starts toward the bedroom.*) She's not going to—

(*He is stopped by the return of* TIFFANY, *who hurries in by the main door with a small package.*)

TIFFANY: Darling, how do you feel now? Are you all right? Hello, Mr. Nelson. I don't know what this is but he said it would help. (*Gives him a small box wrapped in blue paper.*)

BOB: Thank you, darling. It was sweet of you to dash out and get things. (*But he is plainly befuddled by his own mixed emotions.*)

TIFFANY (*sensing the problem*): Bob—you have something to tell me. You've had something to tell me ever since you came in this morning.

BOB (*evasive*): What? No, I didn't—I don't.

(OSCAR *is trying to make himself invisible by examining the fish tank.*)

TIFFANY: You think you're inscrutable. You're the most scrutable man I ever met. Now, *tell* me—sleepy or no. You know, if you repress things, eventually you become devious—tell me!

BOB: Tiffany! Oscar is going to think *you've* taken an overdose of something.

TIFFANY: Don't worry about Oscar. He hasn't been surprised by anything since Truman was elected president. Tell me!

BOB (*trying to avoid a showdown, scarcely knowing his own mind and not up to a decision anyway*): Tiffany—honey—please—

TIFFANY (*crisply*): All right, I'll tell you. You've discovered that you're still in love with Mary. (OSCAR *perks up an ear.*)

BOB (*shocked*): Did I say anything whatsoever to lead you to think that?

TIFFANY: Of course not. And you never would. You'd be much too embarrassed. You'd think it was adolescent and in rather bad taste. Instead, you were going to tell me all the reasons why it would be a mistake for me to marry you. (BOB *is trying to shake his head "no," but she goes confidently on.*) (*To* OSCAR) I figured it all out while I was going to the drugstore.

BOB (*groaning and blinking his eyes*): No, no—not today!

OSCAR: What *are* the reasons? I'm interested even if Bob isn't.

TIFFANY (*systematically and incontrovertibly*): Well, one, he's thirteen years older than I am. That may not seem important now, but in ten years the gap will seem even wider. Then, two—(*She is just as thorough and efficient in her reasoning as* BOB *was with* MARY.)—he's a divorced man, which makes him a bad risk to start with. A girl of my age really deserves better than that. Finally, he's not a rich man, never will be a rich man, and he could never provide the Dior originals and the sable stoles that a girl of my upbringing would naturally expect. (*She has given a good imitation of* BOB, *without sounding unlike herself.*)

BOB: Nonsense! I never would have brought up that part about the money. It never occurred to me.

TIFFANY (*slowly, pointedly, only a shade regretfully*): But all the rest of it—*did* occur to you?

BOB (*terribly embarrassed, and really fighting off sleep now*): Oh, Lord, I don't mind that I'm a bastard. What hurts is that I seem to be such an *inept* bastard. (*Yawning in spite of himself.*) Tiffany, what can I say that—(*At this moment* DIRK *returns by the main door, a bag of buns in his hand.*)

DIRK: I've got the buns.

OSCAR: Congratulations!

DIRK (*Noticing that although* BOB *is standing up, supporting himself with the back of a chair, his eyes are closed*): I thought only horses could sleep standing up.

OSCAR: Bob is exceptional. We shall not see his like again.

(MARY *enters from the bedroom with her suitcase and coat.*)

OSCAR (*To* BOB): What is the matter with you?

(BOB *shakes his head to wake himself.*)

BOB: I should have cards printed; I took three sleeping pills by accident. (*He lets himself into a chair, puts his feet on another, and instantly drowses off.*)

TIFFANY: Freud says there are no accidents. I think he wanted to pass out.

MARY: He was anticipating the popular demand. Dirk, I'll bet if I said I was coming to New Orleans with you—you'd go right into shock.

DIRK: What do you want to bet? Mary, are you . . . coming?

MARY (*struggling toward a decision*): I have half a mind to. I used to be superior to this kind of thing. But any minute now I'll be too old.

DIRK: That's right, you'll be seventy and you'll have nothing to repent.

OSCAR: May I come too? She might need a lawyer.

TIFFANY: But you wouldn't go and leave Bob like that!

MARY: We could cover him with a sheet. (*She starts to eat a bun, reflectively.*)

TIFFANY: How can you be so unfeeling?

MARY: My dear he has you. And when he wakes up he has all those dried apricots.

TIFFANY: But he doesn't have me. Not any more. We had an intelligent talk and I'm leaving.

MARY: That's my boy.

OSCAR: I wish he could hear this. I suggest you toss a coin. The loser takes Bob. (*He gives* BOB *an urgent, if surreptitious, poke in the ribs.*)

BOB: What, what? (*Jumping up, grabbing more coffee.*) There's something important going on. I've got to stay awake.

DIRK (*quickly, to* MARY): Honey, you know this plane is being met by a gaggle of city officials. That means you have to decide right now. We have to leave in ten minutes.

MARY: Yes, I realize that . . . !

OSCAR (*crossing to* MARY): You understand that once you get on that plane you can't change your mind and get off at 125th Street. Now I think we should thrash this out.

TIFFANY (*composing herself formally on the ottoman*): Yes, that's what I think.

MARY: Sure, why don't we call in David Susskind and have a panel discussion. (BOB *falls asleep again.*) Oh, Oscar, I don't mean to be short with you but if I want to go with Dirk why shouldn't I?

TIFFANY: Well, for one thing, when a conservative person like you decides to embark on an indiscretion, you should practice up on little things before you fly off with a movie actor. You don't start at the top.

OSCAR: You see what she means. There's a hierarchy of skills.

DIRK: Just a minute. What makes you all so certain that I'm just a movie star on the make and that Mary is another pickup?

TIFFANY: Well, you use a cigarette holder . . . and her very own husband wants her back.

MARY: He is no longer my very own husband.

TIFFANY: But he was and . . .

OSCAR: May I take this one? Remember you and Bob chose each other. Now you'd tell me that you chose Bob in spite of his faults. I'd tell you that you chose him because of his faults. What is missing in him is probably necessary for what is missing in you. Let us not to the marriage of true impediments admit minds.

DIRK: Am I hearing right? Are you suggesting that these two people stay together for mutual therapy? I haven't heard anything so dumb since my press agent told me he was getting married because it made it easier to register at the Plaza.

TIFFANY: Under what circumstances are you in favor of marriage?

DIRK: What do you mean, in favor? Marriage isn't something that has to be supported like low-cost housing or the bill of rights. It's something that happens like a sneeze . . . like lightning. Mary, I'll ask you once more. Will you take a chance? Will you come?

OSCAR: Why should she take a chance? (*To* MARY, *forcibly.*) You still yearn after *Bob*. I know you do.

(OSCAR'S *stress on the word "Bob" has penetrated the fog, like an alarm bell.* BOB *comes to slightly and looks around.*)

MARY: Are we going to be naïve about this? Asking me whether I yearn after Bob is about as sensible as asking a reformed alcoholic whether he ever thinks about bourbon! What difference does it make? I'm on the wagon for good and sufficient reasons. And I feel a lot better. Dirk, I *am* going with you.

BOB: Where are you going? (*To* OSCAR) Where is she going?

DIRK: She is going to New Orleans with me.

BOB (*coming between* MARY *and* DIRK): Nonsense. I wouldn't let her go as far as the mailbox with you.

DIRK: Look, van Winkle, you have nothing whatever to say about it.

BOB: That's what you think. (*Fighting hard for consciousness.*) I have something very important to say—and—I've been trying to say it since six o'clock this morning. (*He teeters a bit, tries to get a grip on himself.*) Now *everybody* listen—

(*With them all attentive, his mind starts to go blank again. He leans against the frame of the closet door and slowly slides to the floor. He is asleep again.*)

MARY (*worried now*): Maybe we should call a doctor. I don't like his color.

DIRK: I don't like his color. I didn't like it yesterday. Come on Mary, let's leave Wynken, Blynken and Nod. (*He picks up* MARY'S *suitcase and his coat.*)

MARY: But what if he's really—?

BOB (*with a supreme effort he rises*): Wait a minute, now. It's coming to me. (*Crossing blindly to* TIFFANY.) Mary . . . (*Sees his mistake and turns blinking to find* MARY.)

MARY (*going to* BOB *and extending her hand*): I don't know whether you can hear me, but—good-by, Bob.

BOB (*focusing on* DIRK): You are one of the chief causes of why I am so confused. (*Puts his arm around* MARY.) Don't you ever kiss my wife again.

MARY: Bob—you're making a fool of yourself—

BOB (*turning on* MARY *and pushing her toward the window seat*): You shut up. (*Back to* DIRK.) You leave her alone. She can't cope with a lounge lizard like you. She's got more goodness in her whole body than you've got in your little finger! (*He looks dazedly at* OSCAR.)

(OSCAR *shakes his head as if to say* "No, you didn't get that right.")

MARY (*moving toward the door*): All right, Dirk—the poor soul doesn't know what he's talking about—

(DIRK *exits with her suitcase and* MARY *is following him when* BOB *summons a last burst of energy and lunges after her.*)

BOB: Oh, don't I? I'm talking about you—you dumb little idiot—and you're not going anywhere with anybody! (*He grabs* MARY *around the waist and propels her into the storage closet. The others exclaim almost simultaneously.*)

MARY: Bob!

DIRK (*re-entering. He has dropped the suitcase in the hall*): Are you out of your . . . ? (*But* BOB *has quickly shut the door, and locked it with a key. He turns to the others fiercely.*)

BOB: I haven't slept in nine months and I'm sick of it!

DIRK: Hand me that key. If you were in *good* condition, I could take it from you.

BOB: That is an absolutely true statement. (*He walks to the window and calmly tosses the key through it.*)

DIRK: What did you do that for?

BOB: I was going to swallow it, but it was too big. (*He collapses on the window seat, leans out for some air, and almost overbalances.* OSCAR *grabs his feet to keep* BOB *from falling out.* TIFFANY *screams.*)

MARY (*off*): Let me out of here this minute!

DIRK (*going to the closet door, calling through*): Mary, can you hear? That lunatic has thrown the key out into the snow! (*A big groan from* MARY, *off.*) What are we going to do?

OSCAR: Oh, the snow will melt in a day or two.

TIFFANY: In the movies, they just break the door down.

DIRK: In the movies the door is pieced together by the prop men so all you have to do is blow on it!

MARY (*off*): Dirk! Dirk! Are you still there?

DIRK (*exasperated*): Sure, I'm still here!

MARY (*off*): Well, you shouldn't be! Go this minute!

DIRK: No!

MARY (*off*): Please, Dirk! Those people will be waiting. The studio will be furious!

DIRK: Let them be furious! (*Starting for the desk.*) I'll call them up. (*Remembers.*) Oh, Lord, I can't even *get* them now! And if I don't show up all the columns will say I was drunk or being held somewhere on a morals charge. (*Turning on* BOB *as if he'd like to wring his neck.*)

MARY (*off, urgently*): Dirk!

DIRK (*going to the closet door*): I *am* going, honey. I don't see what else to do. I'll call you tonight and we'll set up something. (*To* OSCAR.) I depend on you as the only sane member of the group to get her out of there.

BOB: Well, it's been grand seeing you. Do come again.

DIRK (*to* TIFFANY *and* OSCAR, *ignoring* BOB): Good-by. Where's my damn book? (*He sees it and starts for it.*)

BOB (*snatching up the manuscript*): What are you talking about? You offered this book to me. You can't take it back.

DIRK: You said it stank.

BOB: I did not. I said it wasn't punctuated. I'll punctuate it. (*Weaving toward the window seat.*)

OSCAR (*to* DIRK): You'd better let him keep it or he'll throw it out in the snow.

DIRK: And I left Hollywood and came to New York because I wanted to be among intelligent people! (*Getting into his coat with a sigh.*) You know I made three pictures for Cecil B. De Mille and he once said to me: "If you want to get hold of a woman, don't talk to her— get hold of her—pick her up and carry her away." I thought to myself: "This man is a jerk." (*With a glance toward heaven.*) Cecil, forgive me. (DIRK *exits.* OSCAR *picks up a telephone book.*)

BOB (*forcing himself to snap to, and going to the closet door*): Mary! Mary! (*Knocks.*)

TIFFANY: You don't suppose *she's* fallen asleep?

BOB: No, I suppose she's too mad to talk.

OSCAR (*at the desk, opening the classified section of the phone book*): Why don't you try calling a locksmith? Just start with the A's. . . .

(TIFFANY *is picking up her coat.*)

BOB (*blinking*): Oh—Tiffany.

TIFFANY (*holds out her hand*): Good-by.

BOB: Good-by. (*They shake hands. He helps her on with her coat.*) Tiffany, you really are a very sweet girl.

TIFFANY: Yes, I am. (*Turning to* OSCAR.) Good-by, Mr. Nelson.

OSCAR: Good-by, my dear. If you're ever looking for a job, I have a large law office and could always use a girl like you.

TIFFANY: Thank you.

(BOB *is now dialing a number from the phone book.*)

OSCAR (*following* TIFFANY *toward the door*): You're not too upset, are you?

TIFFANY: Oh, I'll be upset tomorrow, when the novocain wears off. But even tomorrow I think I'm going to feel it's just as well.

OSCAR: Why?

TIFFANY: I was attracted to Bob in the first place because he wasn't attracted to me. That intrigued me. I don't want to sound conceited but when you're twenty-one and you're sort of pretty and very rich, you get used to men falling in love with you. But now I ask myself—is it enough that a man is *not* attracted to you? Good-by. (*She goes.*)

BOB (*on the telephone*): Is this the locksmith? I've got a woman locked in here. Certainly I know the woman. Could you come right over? I know it's Sunday. Okay, so it's extra. Ninety-one East Seventy-first Street. (*To* OSCAR, *who is getting into his coat.*) He'll be right over.

OSCAR: Good. Then I may safely take my departure.

BOB (*rising, in terror*): Oscar—you wouldn't leave me alone with her?

OSCAR: You'll have the locksmith.

BOB: What will I say?

OSCAR: As little as possible. (*He starts out.*)

BOB (*clutching* OSCAR *by the arms*): Please stay.

OSCAR: No, my dear boy. This dismal scene you needs must act alone.

BOB: Do you think she'll take the next plane after him?

OSCAR: Well, there are other rooms, other keys.

BOB (*reeling a little, but steadying himself*): You're a big help.

OSCAR: All my clients tell me that. I'll call you tomorrow. (OSCAR *goes.*)

(BOB, *left alone, goes nervously to the closet door.*)

BOB: Mary? Mary, please answer me. (*He kneels down and calls through the keyhole.*) The locksmith is coming—(*The closet door opens unexpectedly and* MARY *appears. She walks past him into the room. He blinks.*) How did you get the door open?

MARY: My keys. (*Shows them.*)

BOB (*rising*): You mean you could have . . . ?

MARY: Yes. I could have.

BOB (*shaking himself, then nodding vaguely*): I know I behaved like a slob . . . doing this.

MARY: Like a slob.

BOB: I made a spectacle of myself.

MARY: You certainly did. It was the silliest thing I ever saw. And do you know what? I was so proud.

BOB (*it's all getting through to him*): Mary! My sweet, beautiful darling. I always thought you were beautiful. I thought you were as beautiful as—a piece of white porcelain.

MARY: White porcelain? You mean like—(*She catches herself.*) Oh, that's very sweet. (*He goes to her and takes her in his arms, her head on his shoulder.*) I missed your shoulder more than anything.

BOB: A hundred times I would have crawled on my hands and knees to Philadelphia, but I was afraid—Mary, come home.

MARY: I'm home.

(*They kiss. As they do,* BOB *begins to go slack again, sinking slowly onto the sofa.*)

BOB: Oh, Mary, what am I going to do?

MARY (*sitting next to him as he stretches out helplessly*): Why, what's the matter, darling?

BOB: I'm falling asleep again.

MARY (*she lifts his legs onto her lap*): That's all right.

BOB: Yeah. But how will we get those colored lights going?

MARY: We'll manage.

(*She starts to take off his shoes and, smiling,* BOB *falls asleep as the* CURTAIN FALLS.)

END OF PLAY

The Odd Couple

NEIL SIMON

Why our respondents liked

 THE ODD COUPLE

"Neil Simon at his very best. That's the best reason."
DORE SCHARY

"Neil Simon's best—it will live forever."
JOSHUA LOGAN

"Simon's best . . . human & humane."
GEORGE OPPENHEIMER

The Odd Couple is one of the numerous comedy hits, coming in brilliantly close succession, that Neil Simon has authored. Ever since his first Broadway play in 1961, *Come Blow Your Horn,* Mr. Simon has been providing countless hours of enjoyment for theatregoers—the book for the musical *Little Me, Barefoot in the Park, Sweet Charity, The Star-Spangled Girl, Plaza Suite, Promises, Promises, Last of the Red Hot Lovers, The Gingerbread Lady, The Prisoner of Second Avenue, The Sunshine Boys, The Good Doctor, God's Favorite,* and *California Suite. The Odd Couple* became the smash hit comedy of the season when it opened on March 10, 1965, with impressive performances by Walter Matthau as Oscar Madison—who won a Tony Award as Dramatic Actor—and Art Carney as Felix Ungar. Neil Simon was awarded the Tony for best playwright of the season. Mr. Simon's writing career was launched with his working on scripts for the TV shows in the 1950s of Phil Silvers, Sid Caesar, Imogene Coca, Garry Moore, and Tallulah Bankhead. He was also responsible for the successful adaptation of *The Odd Couple* into a movie, which he did with several of his other plays as well—including *Barefoot in the Park* and *The Prisoner of Second Avenue.* In receiving the Sam S. Shubert Award in 1968, Neil Simon was honored for his great contributions to the American theatre.

The Odd Couple was presented by Saint Subber on March 10, 1965, at the Plymouth Theatre, New York City. The cast was as follows:

Speed	Paul Dooley
Murray	Nathaniel Frey
Roy	Sidney Armus
Vinnie	John Fiedler
Oscar Madison	Walter Matthau
Felix Ungar	Art Carney
Gwendolyn Pigeon	Carole Shelley
Cecily Pigeon	Monica Evans

Directed by Mike Nichols
Setting by Oliver Smith
Lighting by Jean Rosenthal
Costumes by Ann Roth

The action takes place in an apartment on
Riverside Drive in New York City.

ACT ONE

A hot summer night.

ACT TWO

SCENE 1: *Two weeks later, about eleven at night.*
SCENE 2: *A few days later, about eight P.M.*

ACT THREE

The next evening, about seven-thirty.

ACT ONE

It is a warm summer night in OSCAR MADISON'S *apartment. This is one of those large eight-room affairs on Riverside Drive in the upper eighties. The building is about thirty-five years old and still has vestiges of its glorious past—high ceilings, walk-in closets and thick walls. We are in the living room with doors leading off to the kitchen, a bedroom and a bathroom, and a hallway to the other bedrooms.*

Although the furnishings have been chosen with extreme good taste, the room itself, without the touch and care of a woman these past few months, is now a study in slovenliness. Dirty dishes, discarded clothes, old newspapers, empty bottles, glasses filled and unfilled, opened and unopened laundry packages, mail and disarrayed furniture abound. The only cheerful note left in this room is the lovely view of the New Jersey Palisades through its twelfth-floor window. Three months ago this was a lovely apartment.

As the curtain rises, the room is filled with smoke. A poker game is in progress. There are six chairs around the table but only four men are sitting. They are MURRAY, ROY, SPEED *and* VINNIE. VINNIE, *with the largest stack of chips in front of him, is nervously tapping his foot; he keeps checking his watch.* ROY *is watching* SPEED *and* SPEED *is glaring at* MURRAY *with incredulity and utter fascination.* MURRAY *is the dealer. He slowly and methodically tries to shuffle. It is a ponderous and painful business.* SPEED *shakes his head in disbelief. This is all done wordlessly.*

SPEED (*cups his chin in his hand and looks at* MURRAY): Tell me, Mr. Maverick, is this your first time on the riverboat?

MURRAY (*with utter disregard*): You don't like it, get a machine.

(*He continues to deal slowly.*)

ROY: Geez, it stinks in here.

VINNIE (*looks at his watch*): What time is it?

SPEED: Again what time is it?

VINNIE (*whining*): My watch is slow. I'd like to know what time it is.

SPEED (*glares at him*): You're winning ninety-five dollars, that's what time it is. Where the hell are you running?

VINNIE: I'm not running anywhere. I just asked what time it was. Who said anything about running?

ROY (*looks at his watch*): It's ten-thirty.

(*There is a pause.* MURRAY *continues to shuffle.*)

VINNIE (*after the pause*): I got to leave by twelve.

SPEED (*looks up in despair*): Oh, Christ!

VINNIE: I told you that when I sat down. I got to leave by twelve. Murray, didn't I say that when I sat down? I said I got to leave by twelve.

SPEED: All right, don't talk to him. He's dealing. (*To* MURRAY.) Murray, you wanna rest for a while? Go lie down, sweetheart.

MURRAY: You want speed or accuracy, make up your mind.

(*He begins to deal slowly.* SPEED *puffs on his cigar angrily.*)

ROY: Hey, you want to do me a really big favor? Smoke toward New Jersey.

(SPEED *blows smoke at* ROY.)

MURRAY: No kidding, I'm really worried about Felix. (*Points to an empty chair.*) He's never been this late before. Maybe somebody should call. (*Yells off.*) Hey, Oscar, why don't you call Felix?

ROY (*waves his hand through the smoke*): Listen, why don't we chip in three dollars apiece and buy another window. How the hell can you breathe in here?

MURRAY: How many cards you got, four?

SPEED: Yes, Murray, we all have four cards. When you give us one more, we'll all have five. If you were to give us two more, we'd have six. Understand how it works now?

ROY (*yells off*): Hey, Oscar, what do you say? In or out?

(*From offstage we hear* OSCAR'*s voice.*)

OSCAR (*offstage*): Out, pussycat, out!

(SPEED *opens and the others bet.*)

VINNIE: I told my wife I'd be home by one the latest. We're making an eight o'clock plane to Florida. I told you that when I sat down.

SEED: Don't cry, Vinnie. You're forty-two years old. It's embarrassing. Give me two . . .

(*He discards.*)

ROY: Why doesn't he fix the air conditioner? It's ninety-eight degrees, and it sits there sweating like everyone else. I'm out.

(*He goes to the window and looks out.*)

MURRAY: Who goes to Florida in July?

VINNIE: It's off-season. There's no crowds and you get the best room for one-tenth the price. No cards . . .

SPEED: Some vacation. Six cheap people in an empty hotel.

MURRAY: Dealer takes four . . . Hey, you think maybe Felix is sick? (*He points to the empty chair.*) I mean he's never been this late before.

ROY (*takes a laundry bag from an armchair and sits*): You know, it's the same garbage from last week's game. I'm beginning to recognize things.

MURRAY (*throwing his cards down*): I'm out . . .

SPEED (*showing his hand*): Two kings . . .

VINNIE: Straight . . .

(*He shows his hand and takes in the pot.*)

MURRAY: Hey, maybe he's in his office locked in the john again. Did you know Felix was once locked in the john overnight? He wrote out his entire will on a half a roll of toilet paper! Heee, what a nut!

(VINNIE *is playing with his chips.*)

SPEED (*glares at him as he shuffles the cards*): Don't play with your chips. I'm asking you nice; don't play with your chips.

VINNIE (*to* SPEED): I'm not playing. I'm counting. Leave me alone. What are you picking on me for? How much do you think I'm winning? Fifteen dollars!

SPEED: Fifteen dollars? You dropped more than that in your cuffs!

(SPEED *deals a game of draw poker.*)

MURRAY (*yells off*): Hey, Oscar, what do you say?

OSCAR (*enters carrying a tray with beer, sandwiches, a can of peanuts, and opened bags of pretzels and Fritos*): I'm in! I'm in! Go ahead. Deal!

(OSCAR MADISON *is forty-three. He is a pleasant, appealing man who seems to enjoy life to the fullest. He enjoys his weekly poker game, his friends, his excessive drinking and his cigars. He is also one of those lucky creatures in life who even enjoys his work—he's a sportswriter for the New York* Post. *His carefree attitude is evident in the sloppiness of his household, but it seems to bother others more than it does* OSCAR. *This is not to say that* OSCAR *is without cares or worries. He just doesn't seem to have any.*)

VINNIE: Aren't you going to look at your cards?

OSCAR (*sets the tray on a side chair*): What for? I'm gonna bluff anyway. (*Opens a bottle of Coke.*) Who gets the Coke?

MURRAY: I get a Coke.

OSCAR: My friend Murray the policeman gets a warm Coke.

(*He gives him the bottle.*)

ROY (*opens the betting*): You still didn't fix the refrigerator? It's been two weeks now. No wonder it stinks in here.

OSCAR (*picks up his cards*): Temper, temper. If I wanted nagging I'd go back with my wife. (*Throws them down.*) I'm out. Who wants food?

OSCAR (*looks under the bread*): I got brown sandwiches and green sandwiches. Well, what do you say?

MURRAY: What's the green?

OSCAR: It's either very new cheese or very old meat.

MURRAY: I'll take the brown.

(OSCAR *gives* MURRAY *a sandwich.*)

ROY (*glares at* MURRAY): Are you crazy? You're not going to eat that, are you?

MURRAY: I'm hungry.

ROY: His refrigerator's been broken for two weeks. I saw milk standing in there that wasn't even in the bottle.

OSCAR (*to* ROY): What are you, some kind of a health nut? Eat, Murray, eat!

ROY: I've got six cards . . .

SPEED: That figures—I've got three aces. Misdeal.

(*They all throw their cards in.* SPEED *begins to shuffle.*)

VINNIE: You know who makes very good sandwiches? Felix. Did you ever taste his cream cheese and pimento on date-nut bread?

SPEED (*to* VINNIE): All right, make up your mind: poker or menus. (OSCAR *opens a can of beer, which sprays in a geyser over the players and the table. There is a hubbub as they all yell at* OSCAR. *He hands* ROY *the overflowing can and pushes the puddle of beer under the chair. The players start to go back to the game only to be sprayed again as* OSCAR *opens another beer can. There is another outraged cry as they try to stop* OSCAR *and mop up the beer on the table with a towel which was hanging on the standing lamp.* OSCAR, *undisturbed, gives them the beer and the bags of refreshments, and they finally sit back in their chairs.* OSCAR *wipes his hands on the sleeve of* ROY's *jacket which is hanging on the back of the chair.*) Hey, Vinnie, tell Oscar what time you're leaving.

VINNIE (*like a trained dog*): Twelve o'clock.

SPEED (*to the others*): You hear? We got ten minutes before the next announcement. All right, this game is five card stud. (*He deals and ad libs calling the cards, ending with* MURRAY's *card.*) . . . And a bullet for the policeman. All right, Murray, it's your bet. (*No answer.*) Do something, huh.

OSCAR (*getting a drink at the bar*): Don't yell at my friend Murray.

MURRAY (*throwing in a coin*): I'm in for a quarter.

OSCAR (*proudly looks in* MURRAY's *eyes*): Beautiful, baby, beautiful.

(*He sits down and begins to open the can of peanuts.*)

ROY: Hey, Oscar, let's make a rule. Every six months you have to buy fresh potato chips. How can you live like this? Don't you have a maid?

OSCAR (*shakes his head*): She quit after my wife and kids left. The work got to be too much for her. (*He looks on the table.*) The pot's shy. Who didn't put in a quarter?

MURRAY (*to* OSCAR): You didn't.

OSCAR (*puts in money*): You got a big mouth, Murray. Just for that, lend me twenty dollars.

(SPEED *deals another round.*)

MURRAY: I just loaned you twenty dollars ten minutes ago.

(*They all join in a round of betting.*)

OSCAR: You loaned me *ten* dollars *twenty* minutes ago. Learn to count, pussycat.

MURRAY: Learn to play poker, chicken licken! Borrow from somebody else. I keep winning my own money back.

ROY (*to* OSCAR): You owe everybody in the game. If you don't have it, you shouldn't play.

OSCAR: All right, I'm through being the nice one. You owe me six dollars apiece for the buffet.

SPEED (*dealing another round of cards*): Buffet? Hot beer and two sandwiches left over from when you went to high school?

OSCAR: What do you want at a poker game, a tomato surprise? Murray, lend me twenty dollars or I'll call your wife and tell her you're in Central Park wearing a dress.

MURRAY: You want money, ask Felix.

OSCAR: He's not here.

MURRAY: Neither am I.

ROY (*gives him money*): All right, here. You're on the books for another twenty.

OSCAR: How many times are you gonna keep saying it?

(*He takes the money.*)

MURRAY: When are you gonna call Felix?

OSCAR: When are we gonna play poker?

MURRAY: Aren't you even worried? It's the first game he's missed in over two years.

OSCAR: The record is fifteen years set by Lou Gehrig in 1939! I'll call! I'll call!

ROY: How can you be so lazy?

(*The phone rings.*)

OSCAR (*throwing his cards in*): Call me irresponsible, I'm funny that way.

(*He goes to the phone.*)

SPEED: Pair of sixes . . .

VINNIE: Three deuces . . .

SPEED (*throws up his hands in despair*): This is my last week. I get all the aggravation I need at home.

(OSCAR *picks up the phone.*)

OSCAR: Hello! Oscar the Poker Player!

VINNIE (*to* OSCAR): If it's my wife tell her I'm leaving at twelve.

SPEED (*to* VINNIE): You look at your watch once more and you get the peanuts in your face. (*To* ROY.) Deal the cards!

(*The game continues during* OSCAR's *phone conversation, with* ROY *dealing a game of stud.*)

OSCAR (*into the phone*): Who? Who did you want, please? *Dabby?* Dabby who? No, there's no Dabby here. Oh, *Daddy!* (*To the others.*) For crise sakes, it's my kid. (*Back into the phone, he speaks with great love and affection.*) Brucey, hello, baby. Yes, it's Daddy! (*There is a general outburst of ad libbing from the poker players. To the others.*) Hey, come on, give me a break, willya? My five-year-old kid is calling from California. It must be costing him a fortune.

(*Back into the phone.*) How've you been, sweetheart? Yes, I finally got your letter. It took three weeks. Yes, but next time you tell Mommy to give you a stamp. I know, but you're not supposed to draw it on. (*He laughs. To the others.*) You hear?

SPEED: We hear. We hear. We're all thrilled.

OSCAR (*into the phone*): What's that, darling? What goldfish? Oh, in your room! Oh, sure. Sure, I'm taking care of them. (*He holds the phone over his chest.*) Oh, God, I killed my kid's goldfish! (*Back into the phone.*) Yes, I feed them every day.

ROY: Murderer!

OSCAR: Mommy wants to speak to me? Right. Take care of yourself, soldier. I love you.

VINNIE (*beginning to deal a game of stud*): Ante a dollar . . .

SPEED (*to* OSCAR): Cost you a dollar to play. You got a dollar?

OSCAR: Not after I get through talking to this lady. (*Into the phone with false cheerfulness.*) Hello, Blanche. How are you? Err, yes, I have a pretty good idea why you're calling. I'm a week behind with the check, right? *Four* weeks? That's not possible. Because it's not possible. Blanche, I keep a record of every check and I *know* I'm only *three* weeks behind! Blanche, I'm trying the best I can. Blanche, don't threaten me with jail because it's not a threat. With my expenses and my alimony, a prisoner takes home more pay than I do! Very nice, in front of the kids. Blanche, don't tell me you're going to have my salary attached, just say good-bye! Good-bye! (*He hangs up. To the players.*) I'm eight hundred dollars behind in alimony so let's up the stakes.

(*He gets his drink from the poker table.*)

ROY: She can do it, you know.

OSCAR: What?

ROY: Throw you in jail. For nonsupport of the kids.

OSCAR: Never. If she can't call me once a week to aggravate me, she's not happy.

(*He crosses to the bar.*)

MURRAY: It doesn't bother you? That you can go to jail? Or that maybe your kids don't have enough clothes or enough to eat?

OSCAR: Murray, *Poland* could live for a year on what my kids leave over from lunch! Can we play cards?

(*He refills his drink.*)

ROY: But that's the point. You shouldn't *be* in this kind of trouble. It's because you don't know how to manage anything. I should know; I'm your accountant.

OSCAR (*crossing to the table*): If you're my accountant, how come I need money?

ROY: If you need money, how come you play poker?

OSCAR: Because I need money.

ROY: But you always lose.

OSCAR: That's why I need the money! Listen, *I'm* not complaining. *You're* complaining. I get along all right. I'm living.

ROY: Alone? In eight dirty rooms?

OSCAR: If I win tonight, I'll buy a broom.

(MURRAY *and* SPEED *buy chips from* VINNIE, *and* MURRAY *begins to shuffle the deck for a game of draw.*)

ROY: That's not what you need. What you need is a wife.

OSCAR: How can I afford a wife when I can't afford a broom?

ROY: Then don't play poker.

OSCAR (*puts down his drink, rushes to* ROY *and they struggle over the bag of potato chips, which rips, showering everyone. They all begin to yell at one another*): Then don't come to my house and eat my potato chips!

MURRAY: What are you yelling about? We're playing a friendly game.

SPEED: Who's *playing?* We've been sitting here talking since eight o'clock.

VINNIE: Since *seven.* That's why I said I was going to quit at *twelve.*

SPEED: How'd you like a stale banana right in the mouth?

MURRAY (*the peacemaker*): All right, all right, let's calm down. Take it easy. I'm a cop, you know. I could arrest the whole lousy game. (*He finishes dealing the cards.*) Four . . .

OSCAR (*sitting at the table*): My friend Murray the Cop is right. Let's just play cards. And please hold them up; I can't see where I marked them.

MURRAY: You're worse than the kids from the PAL.

OSCAR: But you still love me, Roy, sweety, right?

ROY (*petulant*): Yeah, yeah.

OSCAR: That's not good enough. Come on, say it. In front of the whole poker game. "I love you, Oscar Madison."

ROY: You don't take any of this seriously, do you? You owe money to your wife, your government, your friends . . .

OSCAR (*throws his cards down*): What do you want me to do, Roy, jump in the garbage disposal and grind myself to death? (*The phone rings. He goes to answer it.*) Life goes on even for those of us who are divorced, broke and sloppy. (*Into the phone.*) Hello? Divorced, Broke and Sloppy. Oh, hello, sweetheart. (*He becomes very seductive, pulls the phone to the side and talks low, but he is still audible to the others, who turn and listen.*) I told you not to call me during the game. I can't talk to you now. You *know* I do, darling. All right, just a minute. (*He turns.*) Murray, it's your wife.

(*He puts the phone on the table and sits on the sofa.*)

MURRAY (*nods disgustedly as he crosses to the phone*): I wish you *were* having an affair with her. Then she wouldn't bother *me* all the time. (*He picks up the phone.*) Hello, Mimi, what's wrong?

(SPEED *gets up, stretches and goes into the bathroom.*)

OSCAR (*in a woman's voice, imitating* MIMI): What time are you coming home? (*Then imitating* MURRAY.) I don't know, about twelve, twelve-thirty.

MURRAY (*into the phone*): I don't know, about twelve, twelve-thirty! (ROY *gets up and stretches.*) Why, what did you want, Mimi? "A corned beef sandwich and a strawberry malted!"

OSCAR: Is she pregnant again?

MURRAY (*holds the phone over his chest*): No, just fat! (*There is the sound of a toilet flushing, and after* SPEED *comes out of the bathroom,* VINNIE *goes in. Into the phone again.*) What? How could you hear that, I had the phone over my chest? Who? Felix? No, he didn't show up tonight. What's wrong? You're kidding! How should I know? All right, all right, good-bye. (*The toilet flushes again, and after* VINNIE *comes out of the bathroom,* ROY *goes in.*) Good-bye Mimi. Good-bye. (*He hangs up. To the others.*) Well, what did I tell you? I knew it!

ROY: What's the matter?

MURRAY (*pacing by the couch*): Felix is missing!

OSCAR: Who?

MURRAY: Felix! Felix Ungar! The man who sits in that chair every week and cleans ashtrays. I told you something was up.

SPEED (*at the table*): What do you mean, missing?

MURRAY: He didn't show up for work today. He didn't come home tonight. No one knows where he is. Mimi just spoke to his wife.

VINNIE (*in his chair at the poker table*): Felix?

MURRAY: They looked everywhere. I'm telling you he's missing.

OSCAR: Wait a minute. No one is missing for one day.

VINNIE: That's right. You've got to be missing for forty-eight hours before you're missing. The worst he could be is lost.

MURRAY: How could he be lost? He's forty-four years old and lives on West End Avenue. What's the matter with you?

ROY (*sitting in an armchair*): Maybe he had an accident.

OSCAR: They would have heard.

ROY: If he's laying in a gutter somewhere? Who would know who he is?

OSCAR: He's got ninety-two credit cards in his wallet. The minute something happens to him, America lights up.

VINNIE: Maybe he went to a movie. You know how long those pictures are today.

SPEED (*looks at* VINNIE *contemptuously*): No wonder you're going to Florida in July! Dumb, dumb, dumb!

ROY: Maybe he was mugged?

OSCAR: For thirty-six hours? How much money could he have on him?

ROY: Maybe they took his clothes. I knew a guy who was mugged in a doctor's office. He had to go home in a nurse's uniform.

(OSCAR *throws a pillow from the couch at* ROY.)

SPEED: Murray, you're a cop. What do you think?

MURRAY: I think it's something real bad.

SPEED: How do you know?

MURRAY: I can feel it in my bones.

SPEED (*to the others*): You hear? Bulldog Drummond.

ROY: Maybe he's drunk. Does he drink?

OSCAR: Felix? On New Year's Eve he has Pepto-Bismal. What are we guessing? I'll call his wife.

(*He picks up the phone.*)

SPEED: Wait a minute! Don't start anything yet. Just 'cause we don't know where he is doesn't mean somebody else doesn't. Does he have a girl?

VINNIE: A what?

SPEED: A girl? You know. Like when you're through work early.

MURRAY: Felix? Playing around? Are you crazy? He wears a vest and galoshes.

SPEED (*gets up and moves toward* MURRAY): You mean you automatically know who has and who hasn't got a girl on the side?

MURRAY (*moves to* SPEED): Yes, I automatically know.

SPEED: All right, you're so smart. Have I got a girl?

MURRAY: No, you haven't got a girl. What you've got is what *I've* got. What you *wish* you got and what you *got* is a whole different civilization! *Oscar* maybe has a girl on the side.

SPEED: That's different. He's divorced. That's not on the side. That's in the middle.

(*He moves to the table.*)

OSCAR (*to them both as he starts to dial*): You through? 'Cause one of our poker players is missing. I'd like to find out about him.

VINNIE: I thought he looked edgy the last couple of weeks. (*To* SPEED.) Didn't you think he looked edgy?

SPEED: No. As a matter of fact, I thought *you* looked edgy.

(*He moves down to the right.*)

OSCAR (*into the phone*): Hello? Frances? Oscar. I just heard.

ROY: Tell her not to worry. She's probably hysterical.

MURRAY: Yeah, you know women.

(*He sits down on the couch.*)

OSCAR (*into the phone*): Listen, Frances, the most important thing is not to worry. Oh! (*To the others.*) She's not worried.

MURRAY: Sure.

OSCAR (*into the phone*): Frances, do you have *any* idea where he could be? He what? You're kidding? Why? No, I didn't know. Gee, that's too bad. All right, listen, Frances, you just sit tight and the minute I hear anything I'll let you know. Right. G'bye.

(*He hangs up. They all look at him expectantly. He gets up wordlessly and crosses to the table, thinking. They all watch him a second, not being able to stand it any longer.*)

MURRAY: Ya gonna tell us or do we hire a private detective?

OSCAR: They broke up!

ROY: Who?

OSCAR: Felix and Frances! They broke up! The entire marriage is through.

VINNIE: You're kidding!

ROY: I don't believe it.

SPEED: After twelve years?

(OSCAR *sits down at the table.*)

VINNIE: They were such a happy couple.

MURRAY: Twelve years doesn't mean you're a *happy* couple. It just means you're a *long* couple.

SPEED: Go figure it. Felix and Frances.

ROY: What are you surprised at? He used to sit there every Friday night and tell us how they were fighting.

SPEED: I know. But who believes Felix?

VINNIE: What happened?

OSCAR: She wants out, that's all.

MURRAY: He'll go to pieces. I know Felix. He's going to try something crazy.

SPEED: That's all he ever used to talk about. "My beautiful wife. My wonderful wife." What happened?

OSCAR: His beautiful, wonderful wife can't stand him, that's what happened.

MURRAY: He'll kill himself. You hear what I'm saying? He's going to go out and try to kill himself.

SPEED (*to* MURRAY): Will you shut up, Murray? Stop being a cop for two minutes. (*To* OSCAR.) Where'd he go, Oscar?

OSCAR: He went out to kill himself.

MURRAY: What did I tell you?

ROY (*to* OSCAR): Are you serious?

OSCAR: That's what she said. He was going out to kill himself. He didn't want to do it at home 'cause the kids were sleeping.

VINNIE: Why?

OSCAR: Why? Because that's Felix, that's why. (*He goes to the bar and refills his drink.*) You know what he's like. He sleeps on the window sill. "Love me or I'll jump." 'Cause he's a nut, that's why.

MURRAY: That's right. Remember he tried something like that in the army? She wanted to break off the engagement so he started cleaning guns in his mouth.

SPEED: I don't believe it. Talk! That's all Felix is, talk.

VINNIE (*worried*): But is that what he said? In those words? "I'm going to kill myself?"

OSCAR (*pacing about the table*): I don't know in what words. She didn't read it to me.

ROY: You mean he left her a note?

OSCAR: No, he sent a telegram.

MURRAY: A *suicide telegram?* Who sends a suicide telegram?

OSCAR: Felix, the nut, that's who! Can you imagine getting a thing like that? She even has to tip the kid a quarter.

ROY: I don't get it. If he wants to kill himself, why does he send a telegram?

OSCAR: Don't you see how his mind works? If he sends a note, she might not get it till Monday and he'd have no excuse for not being dead. This way, for a dollar ten, he's got a chance to be saved.

VINNIE: You mean he really doesn't want to kill himself? He just wants sympathy.

OSCAR: What he'd really like is to go to the funeral and sit in the back. He'd be the biggest crier there.

MURRAY: He's right.

OSCAR: Sure I'm right.

MURRAY: We get these cases every day. All they want is attention. We got a guy who calls us every Saturday afternoon from the George Washington Bridge.

ROY: I don't know. You never can tell what a guy'll do when he's hysterical.

MURRAY: Nahhh. Nine out of ten times they don't jump.

ROY: What about the tenth time?

MURRAY: They jump. He's right. There's a possibility.

OSCAR: Not with Felix. I know him. He's too nervous to kill himself. He wears his seatbelt in a drive-in movie.

VINNIE: Isn't there someplace we could look for him?

SPEED: Where? Where would you look? Who knows where he is?

(*The doorbell rings. They all look at* OSCAR.)

OSCAR: Of course! If you're going to kill yourself, where's the safest place to do it? With your friends!

(VINNIE *starts for the door.*)

MURRAY (*stopping him*): Wait a minute! The guy may be hysterical. Let's play it nice and easy. If *we're* calm, maybe *he'll* be calm.

ROY (*getting up and joining them*): That's right. That's how they do it with those guys out on the ledge. You talk nice and soft.

(SPEED *rushes over to them, and joins in the frenzied discussion.*)

VINNIE: What'll we say to him?

MURRAY: We don't say nothin'. Like we never heard a thing.

OSCAR (*trying to get their attention*): You through with this discussion? Because he already could have hung himself out in the hall. (*To* VINNIE.) Vinnie, open the door!

MURRAY: Remember! Like we don't know nothin'.

(*They all rush back to their seats and grab up cards, which they concentrate on with the greatest intensity.* VINNIE *opens the door.* FELIX UNGAR *is there. He's about forty-four. His clothes are rumpled as if he had slept in them, and he needs a shave. Although he tries to act matter-of-fact, there is an air of great tension and nervousness about him.*)

FELIX (*softly*): Hi, Vin! (VINNIE *quickly goes back to his seat and studies his cards.* FELIX *has his hands in his pockets, trying to be very nonchalant. With controlled calm.*) Hi, fellas. (*They all mumble hello, but do not look at him. He puts his coat over the railing and crosses to the table.*) How's the game going? (*They all mumble appropriate remarks, and continue staring at their cards.*) Good! Good! Sorry I'm late. (FELIX *looks a little disappointed that no one asks "What?" He starts to pick up a sandwich, changes his mind and makes a gesture of distaste. He vaguely looks around.*) Any Coke left?

OSCAR (*looking up from his cards*): Coke? Gee, I don't think so. I got a Seven-Up!

FELIX (*bravely*): No, I felt like a Coke. I just don't feel like Seven-Up tonight!

(*He stands watching the game.*)

OSCAR: What's the bet?

SPEED: You bet a quarter. It's up to Murray. Murray, what do you say? (MURRAY *is staring at* FELIX.) Murray! Murray!

ROY (*to* VINNIE): Tap his shoulder.

VINNIE (*taps* MURRAY'*s shoulder*): Murray!

MURRAY (*startled*): What? What?

SPEED: It's up to you.

MURRAY: Why is it always up to me?

SPEED: It's not always up to you. It's up to you now. What do you do?

MURRAY: I'm in. I'm in.

(*He throws in a quarter.*)

FELIX (*moves to the bookcase*): Anyone call about me?

OSCAR: Er, not that I can remember. (*To the others.*) Did anyone call for Felix? (*They all shrug and ad lib "No."*) Why? Were you expecting a call?

FELIX (*looking at the books on the shelf*): No! No! Just asking.

(*He opens a book and examines it.*)

ROY: Er, I'll see his bet and raise it a dollar.

FELIX (*without looking up from the book*): I just thought someone might have called.

SPEED: It costs me a dollar and a quarter to play, right?

OSCAR: Right!

FELIX (*still looking at the book, in a sing song*): But, if no one called, no one called.

(*He slams the book shut and puts it back. They all jump at the noise.*)

SPEED (*getting nervous*): What does it cost me to play again?

MURRAY (*angry*): A dollar and a quarter! A *dollar and a quarter!* Pay attention, for crise sakes!

ROY: All right, take it easy. Take it easy.

OSCAR: Let's calm down, everyone, heh?

MURRAY: I'm sorry. I can't help it. (*Points to* SPEED.) He makes me nervous.

SPEED: I make *you* nervous. You make *me* nervous. You make *every-one* nervous.

MURRAY (*sarcastic*): I'm sorry. Forgive me. I'll kill myself.

OSCAR: Murray!

(*He motions with his head to* FELIX.)

MURRAY (*realizes his error*): Oh! Sorry.

(SPEED *glares at him. They all sit in silence a moment, until* VINNIE *catches sight of* FELIX, *who is now staring out an upstage window. He quickly calls the others' attention to* FELIX.)

FELIX (*looking back at them from the window*): Gee, it's a pretty view from here. What is it, twelve floors?

OSCAR (*quickly crossing to the window and closing it*): No. It's only eleven. That's all. Eleven. It says twelve but it's really only eleven. (*He then turns and closes the other window as* FELIX *watches him.* OSCAR *shivers slightly.*) Chilly in here. (*To the others.*) Isn't it chilly in here?

(*He crosses back to the table.*)

ROY: Yeah, that's much better.

OSCAR (*to* FELIX): Want to sit down and play? It's still early.

VINNIE: Sure. We're in no rush. We'll be here till three, four in the morning.

FELIX (*shrugs*): I don't know; I just don't feel much like playing now.

OSCAR (*sitting at the table*): Oh! Well, what *do* you feel like doing?

FELIX (*shrugs*): I'll find *some*thing. (*He starts to walk toward the other room.*) Don't worry about me.

OSCAR: Where are you going?

FELIX (*stops in the doorway. He looks at the others who are all staring at him*): To the john.

OSCAR (*looks at the others, worried, then at* FELIX): Alone?

FELIX (*nods*): I always go alone! Why?

OSCAR (*shrugs*): No reason. You gonna be in there long?

FELIX (*shrugs, then says meaningfully, like a martyr*): As long as it takes.

   (*Then he goes into the bathroom and slams the door shut behind him. Immediately they all jump up and crowd about the bathroom door, whispering in frenzied anxiety.*)

MURRAY: Are you crazy? Letting him go to the john alone?

OSCAR: What did you want me to do?

ROY: Stop him! Go in with him!

OSCAR: Suppose he just has to go to the john?

MURRAY: Supposing he does? He's better off being embarrassed than dead!

OSCAR: How's he going to kill himself in the john?

SPEED: What do you mean, how? Razor blades, pills. Anything that's in there.

OSCAR: That's the kids' bathroom. The worst he could do is brush his teeth to death.

ROY: He could jump.

VINNIE: That's right. Isn't there a window in there?

OSCAR: It's only six inches wide.

MURRAY: He could break the glass. He could cut his wrists.

OSCAR: He could also flush himself into the East River. I'm telling you he's not going to try anything!

   (*He moves to the table.*)

ROY (*goes to the doorway*): Shhh! Listen! He's crying. (*There is a pause as all listen as* FELIX *sobs.*) You hear that. He's crying.

MURRAY: Isn't that terrible? For God's sakes, Oscar, do something! Say something!

OSCAR: What? What do you say to a man who's crying in your bathroom?

(*There is the sound of the toilet flushing and* ROY *makes a mad dash back to his chair.*)

ROY: He's coming!

(*They all scramble back to their places.* MURRAY *gets mixed up with* VINNIE *and they quickly straighten it out.* FELIX *comes back into the room. But he seems calm and collected, with no evident sign of having cried.*)

FELIX: I guess I'll be running along.

(*He starts for the door.* OSCAR *jumps up. So do the others.*)

OSCAR: Felix, wait a second.

FELIX: No! No! I can't talk to you. I can't talk to anyone.

(*They all try to grab him, stopping him near the stairs.*)

MURRAY: Felix, please. We're your friends. Don't run out like this.

(FELIX *struggles to pull away.*)

OSCAR: Felix, sit down. Just for a minute. Talk to us.

FELIX: There's nothing to talk about. There's nothing to say. It's over. Over. Everything is over. Let me go!

(*He breaks away from them and dashes into the stage-right bedroom. They start to chase him and he dodges from the bedroom through the adjoining door into the bathroom.*)

ROY: Stop him! Grab him!

FELIX (*looking for an exit*): Let me out! I've got to get out of here!

OSCAR: Felix, you're hysterical.

FELIX: Please let me out of here!

MURRAY: The john! Don't let him get in the john!

FELIX (*comes out of the bathroom with* ROY *hanging onto him, and the others trailing behind*): Leave me alone. Why doesn't everyone leave me alone?

OSCAR: All right, Felix, I'm warning you. Now cut it out!

(*He throws a half-filled glass of water, which he has picked up from the bookcase, into* FELIX'S *face.*)

FELIX: It's *my* problem. I'll work it out. Leave me alone. Oh, my stomach.

(*He collapses in* ROY'S *arms.*)

MURRAY: What's the matter with your stomach?

VINNIE: He looks sick. Look at his face.

(*They all try to hold him as they lead him over to the couch.*)

FELIX: I'm not sick. I'm all right. I didn't take anything, I swear. Ohh, my stomach.

OSCAR: What do you mean you didn't take anything? What did you take?

FELIX (*sitting on the couch*): Nothing! Nothing! I didn't take anything. Don't tell Frances what I did, please! Oohh, my stomach.

MURRAY: He took something! I'm telling you he took something.

OSCAR: What, Felix? *What?*

FELIX: Nothing! I didn't take anything.

OSCAR: Pills? Did you take pills?

FELIX: No! No!

OSCAR (*grabbing* FELIX): Don't lie to me, Felix. Did you take pills?

FELIX: No, I didn't. I didn't take anything.

MURRAY: Thank God he didn't take pills.

(*They all relax and take a breath of relief.*)

FELIX: Just a few, that's all.

(*They all react in alarm and concern over the pills.*)

OSCAR: He took pills.

MURRAY: How many pills?

OSCAR: What kind of pills?

FELIX: I don't know what kind. Little green ones. I just grabbed anything out of her medicine cabinet. I must have been crazy.

OSCAR: Didn't you look? Didn't you see what kind?

FELIX: I couldn't see. The light's broken. Don't call Frances. Don't tell her. I'm so ashamed. So ashamed.

OSCAR: Felix, how many pills did you take?

FELIX: I don't know. I can't remember.

OSCAR: I'm calling Frances.

FELIX (*grabs him*): No! Don't call her. Don't call her. If she hears I took a whole bottle of pills . . .

MURRAY: A whole bottle? *A whole bottle of pills?* (*He turns to* VINNIE.) My God, call an ambulance!

(VINNIE *runs to the front door.*)

OSCAR (*to* MURRAY): You don't even know what *kind!*

MURRAY: What's the difference! He took a whole bottle!

OSCAR: Maybe they were vitamins. He could be the healthiest one in the room! Take it easy, will you?

FELIX: Don't call Frances. Promise me you won't call Frances.

MURRAY: Open his collar. Open the window. Give him some air.

SPEED: Walk him around. Don't let him go to sleep.

(SPEED *and* MURRAY *pick* FELIX *up and talk him around, while* ROY *rubs his wrists.*)

ROY: Rub his wrists. Keep his circulation going.

VINNIE (*running to the bathroom to get a compress*): A cold compress. Put a cold compress on his neck.

(*They sit* FELIX *in the armchair, still chattering in alarm.*)

OSCAR: One doctor at a time, heh? All the interns shut the hell up!

FELIX: I'm all right. I'll be all right. (*To* OSCAR *urgently.*) You didn't call Frances, did you?

MURRAY (*to the others*): You just gonna stand here? No one's gonna do anything? I'm calling a doctor.

(*He crosses to the phone.*)

FELIX: No! No doctor.

MURRAY: You *gotta* have a doctor.

FELIX: I don't need a doctor.

MURRAY: You gotta get the pills out.

FELIX: I got them out. I threw up before! (*He sits back weakly.* MURRAY *hangs up the phone.*) Don't you have a root beer or a ginger ale?

(VINNIE *gives the compress to* SPEED.)

ROY (*to* VINNIE): Get him a drink.

OSCAR (*glares angrily at* FELIX): He threw them up!

VINNIE: Which would you rather have, Felix, the root beer or the ginger ale?

SPEED (*to* VINNIE): Get him the drink! Just get him the drink.

(VINNIE *runs into the kitchen as* SPEED *puts the compress on* FELIX's *head.*)

FELIX: Twelve years. Twelve years we were married. Did you know we were married twelve years, Roy?

ROY (*comforting him*): Yes, Felix. I knew.

FELIX (*with great emotion in his voice*): And now it's over. Like that, it's over. That's hysterical, isn't it?

SPEED: Maybe it was just a fight. You've had fights before, Felix.

FELIX: No, it's over. She's getting a lawyer tomorrow. *My* cousin. She's using *my* cousin! (*He sobs.*) Who am *I* going to get?

(VINNIE *comes out of the kitchen with a glass of root beer.*)

MURRAY (*patting his shoulder*): It's okay, Felix. Come on. Take it easy.

VINNIE (*gives the glass to* FELIX): Here's the root beer.

FELIX: I'm all right, honestly. I'm just crying.

(*He puts his head down. They all look at him helplessly.*)

MURRAY: All right, let's not stand around looking at him. (*Pushes* SPEED *and* VINNIE *away.*) Let's break it up, heh?

FELIX: Yes, don't stand there looking at me. Please.

OSCAR (*to the others*): Come on, he's all right. Let's call it a night.

(MURRAY, SPEED *and* ROY *turn in their chips at the poker table, get their coats and get ready to go.*)

FELIX: I'm so ashamed. Please, fellas, forgive me.

VINNIE (*bending to* FELIX): Oh, Felix, we—we understand.

FELIX: Don't say anything about this to anyone, Vinnie. Will you promise me?

VINNIE: I'm going to Florida tomorrow.

FELIX: Oh, that's nice. Have a good time.

VINNIE: Thanks.

FELIX (*turns away and sighs in despair*): We were going to go to Florida next winter. (*He laughs, but it's a sob.*) Without the kids! Now they'll go without me.

(VINNIE *gets his coat and* OSCAR *ushers them all to the door.*)

MURRAY (*stopping at the door*): Maybe one of us should stay?

OSCAR: It's all right, Murray.

MURRAY: Suppose he tries something again?

OSCAR: He won't try anything again.

MURRAY: How do you *know* he won't try anything again?

FELIX (*turns to* MURRAY): I won't try anything again. I'm very tired.

OSCAR (*to* MURRAY): You hear? He's very tired. He had a busy night. Good night, fellows.

(*They all ad lib good-byes and leave. The door closes but opens immediately and* ROY *comes back in.*)

ROY: If anything happens, Oscar, just call me.

(*He exits, and as the door starts to close, it reopens and* SPEED *comes in.*)

SPEED: I'm three blocks away. I could be here in five minutes.

(*He exits, and as the door starts to close, it reopens and* VINNIE *comes back in.*)

VINNIE: If you need me I'll be at the Meridian Motel in Miami Beach.

OSCAR: You'll be the first one I'll call, Vinnie.

(VINNIE *exits. The door closes and then reopens as* MURRAY *comes back.*)

MURRAY (*to* OSCAR): You're sure?

OSCAR: I'm sure.

MURRAY (*loudly to* FELIX, *as he gestures to* OSCAR *to come to the door*): Good night, Felix. Try to get a good night's sleep. I guarantee you things are going to look a lot brighter in the morning. (*To* OSCAR, *sotto voce.*) Take away his belt and his shoe laces.

(*He nods and exits.* OSCAR *turns and looks at* FELIX *sitting in the armchair and slowly moves across the room. There is a moment's silence.*)

OSCAR (*he looks at* FELIX *and sighs*): Ohh, Felix, Felix, Felix, Felix!

FELIX (*sits with his head buried in his hands. He doesn't look up*): I know, I know, I know, I know! What am I going to do, Oscar?

OSCAR: You're gonna wash down the pills with some hot, black coffee. (*He starts for the kitchen, then stops.*) Do you think I could leave you alone for two minutes?

FELIX: No, I don't think so! Stay with me, Oscar. Talk to me.

OSCAR: A cup of black coffee. It'll be good for you. Come on in the kitchen. I'll sit on you.

FELIX: Oscar, the terrible thing is, I think I still love her. It's a lousy marriage but I still love her. I didn't want this divorce.

OSCAR (*sitting on the arm of the couch*): How about some Ovaltine? You like Ovaltine? With a couple of fig newtons or chocolate mallomars?

FELIX: All right, so we didn't get along. But we had two wonderful kids, and a beautiful home. Didn't we, Oscar?

OSCAR: How about vanilla wafers? Or Vienna fingers? I got everything.

FELIX: What more does she want? What does *any* woman want?

OSCAR: I want to know what *you* want. Ovaltine, coffee or tea. Then we'll get to the divorce.

FELIX: It's not fair, damn it! It's just not fair! (*He bangs his fist on the arm of the chair angrily, then suddenly winces in great pain and grabs his neck.*) Oh! Ohh, my neck. My neck!

OSCAR: What? What?

FELIX (*he gets up and paces in pain. He is holding his twisted neck*): It's a nerve spasm. I get it in the neck. Oh! Ohh, that hurts.

OSCAR (*rushing to help*): Where? Where does it hurt?

FELIX (*stretches out an arm like a halfback*): Don't touch me! Don't touch me!

OSCAR: I just want to see where it hurts.

FELIX: It'll go away. Just let me alone a few minutes. Ohh! Ohh!

OSCAR (*moving to the couch*): Lie down; I'll rub it. It'll ease the pain.

FELIX (*in wild contortions*): You don't know how. It's a special way. Only Frances knows how to rub me.

OSCAR: You want me to ask her to come over and rub you?

FELIX (*yells*): No! No! We're getting divorced. She wouldn't want to rub me any more. It's tension. I get it from tension. I must be tense.

OSCAR: I wouldn't be surprised. How long does it last?

FELIX: Sometimes a minute, sometimes hours. I once got it while I was driving. I crashed into a liquor store. Ohhh! Ohhh!

(*He sits down, painfully, on the couch.*)

OSCAR (*getting behind him*): You want to suffer or do you want me to rub your stupid neck?

(*He starts to massage it.*)

FELIX: Easy! Easy!

OSCAR (*yells*): Relax, damn it: relax!

FELIX (*yells back*): Don't yell at me! (*Then quietly.*) What should I do? Tell me nicely.

OSCAR (*rubbing the neck*): Think of warm jello!

FELIX: Isn't that terrible? I can't do it. I can't relax. I sleep in one position all night. Frances says when I die on my tombstone it's going to say, "Here Stands Felix Ungar." (*He winces.*) Oh! Ohh!

OSCAR (*stops rubbing*): Does that hurt?

FELIX: No, it feels good.

OSCAR: Then say so. You make the same sound for pain or happiness.

(*Starts to massage his neck again.*)

FELIX: I know. I know. Oscar—I think I'm crazy.

OSCAR: Well, if it'll make you feel any better, I think so too.

FELIX: I mean it. Why else do I go to pieces like this? Coming up here, scaring you to death. Trying to kill myself. What is that?

OSCAR: That's panic. You're a panicky person. You have a low threshold for composure.

(He stops rubbing.)

FELIX: Don't stop. It feels good.

OSCAR: If you don't relax I'll break my fingers. *(Touches his hair.)* Look at this. The only man in the world with clenched hair.

FELIX: I do terrible things, Oscar. You know I'm a cry baby.

OSCAR: Bend over.

(FELIX bends over and OSCAR begins to massage his back.)

FELIX *(head down)*: I tell the whole world my problems.

OSCAR *(massaging hard)*: Listen, if this hurts just tell me, because I don't know what the hell I'm doing.

FELIX: It just isn't nice, Oscar, running up here like this, carrying on like a nut.

OSCAR *(finishes massaging)*: How does your neck feel?

FELIX *(twists his neck)*: Better. Only my back hurts.

(He gets up and paces, rubbing his back.)

OSCAR: What you need is a drink.

(He starts for the bar.)

FELIX: I can't drink. It makes me sick. I tried drinking last night.

OSCAR *(at the bar)*: Where *were* you last night?

FELIX: Nowhere. I just walked.

OSCAR: All night?

FELIX: All night.

OSCAR: In the rain?

FELIX: No. In a hotel. I couldn't sleep. I walked around the room all night. It was over near Times Square. A dirty, depressing room. Then

I found myself looking out the window. And suddenly, I began to think about jumping.

OSCAR (*he has two glasses filled and crosses to* FELIX): What changed your mind?

FELIX: Nothing. I'm still thinking about it.

OSCAR: Drink this.

(*He hands him a glass, crosses to the couch and sits.*)

FELIX: I don't want to get divorced, Oscar. I don't want to suddenly change my whole life. (*He moves to the couch and sits next to* OSCAR.) Talk to me, Oscar. What am I going to do? What am I going to do?

OSCAR: You're going to pull yourself together. And then you're going to drink that Scotch, and then you and I are going to figure out a whole new life for you.

FELIX: Without Frances? Without the kids?

OSCAR: It's been done before.

FELIX (*paces around*): You don't understand, Oscar. I'm nothing without them. I'm—*nothing!*

OSCAR: What do you mean, nothing? You're something! (FELIX *sits in the armchair.*) A person! You're flesh and blood and bones and hair and nails and ears. You're not a fish. You're not a buffalo. You're *you!* You walk and talk and cry and complain and eat little green pills and send suicide telegrams. No one else does that, Felix. I'm telling you, *you're the only one of its kind in the world!* (*He goes to the bar.*) Now drink that.

FELIX: Oscar, you've been through it yourself. What did you do? How did you get through those first few nights?

OSCAR (*pours a drink*): I did exactly what you're doing.

FELIX: Getting hysterical!

OSCAR: No, drinking! *Drinking!* (*He comes back to the couch with the bottle and sits.*) I drank for four days and four nights. And then I fell through a window. I was bleeding but I was forgetting.

(*He drinks again.*)

FELIX: How can you forget your kids? How can you wipe out twelve years of marriage?

OSCAR: You can't. When you walk into eight empty rooms every night it hits you in the face like a wet glove. But those are the facts, Felix. You've got to face it. You can't spend the rest of your life crying. It annoys people in the movies! Be a good boy and drink your Scotch.

(*He stretches out on the couch with his head near* FELIX.)

FELIX: I can imagine what Frances must be going through.

OSCAR: What do you mean, what *she's* going through?

FELIX: It's much harder on the woman, Oscar. She's all alone with the kids. Stuck there in the house. She can't get out like me. I mean where is she going to find someone now at her age? With two kids. Where?

OSCAR: I don't know. Maybe someone'll come to the door! Felix, there's a hundred thousand divorces a year. There must be *something* nice about it. (FELIX *suddenly puts both his hands over his ears and hums quietly.*) What's the matter now?

(*He sits up.*)

FELIX: My ears are closing up. I get it from the sinus. It must be the dust in here. I'm allergic to dust.

(*He hums. Then he gets up and tries to clear his ears by hopping first on one leg then the other as he goes to the window and opens it.*)

OSCAR (*jumping up*): What are you doing?

FELIX: I'm not going to jump. I'm just going to breathe. (*He takes deep breaths.*) I used to drive Frances crazy with my allergies. I'm allergic to perfume. For a while the only thing she could wear was my after-shave lotion. I was impossible to live with. It's a wonder she took it this long.

(*He suddenly bellows like a moose. He makes this strange sound another time.* OSCAR *looks at him dumbfounded.*)

OSCAR: What are you doing?

FELIX: I'm trying to clear my ears. You create a pressure inside and then it opens it up.

(*He bellows again.*)

OSCAR: Did it open up?

FELIX: A little bit. (*He rubs his neck.*) I think I strained my throat.

(*He paces about the room.*)

OSCAR: Felix, why don't you leave yourself alone? Don't tinker.

FELIX: I can't help myself. I drive everyone crazy. A marriage counselor once kicked me out of his office. He wrote on my chart, "Lunatic!" I don't blame her. It's impossible to be married to me.

OSCAR: It takes two to make a rotten marriage.

(*He lies back down on the couch.*)

FELIX: You don't know what I was like at home. I bought her a book and made her write down every penny we spent. Thirty-eight cents for cigarettes; ten cents for a paper. Everything had to go in the book. And then we had a big fight because I said she forgot to write down how much the book was. Who could live with anyone like that?

OSCAR: An accountant! What do I know? We're not perfect. We all have faults.

FELIX: Faults? Heh! Faults. We have a maid who comes in to clean three times a week. And on the other days, Frances does the cleaning. And at night, after they've both cleaned up, I go in and clean the whole place again. I can't help it. I like things clean. Blame it on my mother. I was toilet-trained at five months old.

OSCAR: How do you remember things like that?

FELIX: I loused up the marriage. Nothing was ever right. I used to recook everything. The minute she walked out of the kitchen I would add salt or pepper. It's not that I didn't trust her, it's just that I was a better cook. Well, I cooked myself out of a marriage. (*He bangs his head with the palm of his hand three times.*) *God damned idiot!*

(*He sinks down in the armchair.*)

OSCAR: Don't do that; you'll get a headache.

FELIX: I can't stand it, Oscar. I hate me. Oh, boy, do I hate me.

OSCAR: You don't hate you. You love you. You think no one has problems like you.

FELIX: Don't give me that analyst jazz. I happen to know I hate my guts.

OSCAR: Come on, Felix; I've never *seen* anyone so in love.

FELIX (*hurt*): I thought you were my friend.

OSCAR: That's why I can talk to you like this. Because I love you almost as much as *you* do.

FELIX: Then help me.

OSCAR (*up on one elbow*): How can I help you when I can't help myself? You think *you're* impossible to live with? Blanche used to say, "What time do you want dinner?" And I'd say, "I don't know. I'm not hungry." Then at three o'clock in the morning I'd wake her up and say, "Now!" I've been one of the highest paid sportswriters in the East for the past fourteen years, and we saved eight and a half dollars —in pennies! I'm never home, I gamble, I burn cigar holes in the furniture, drink like a fish and lie to her every chance I get. And for our tenth wedding anniversary, I took her to see the New York Rangers-Detroit Red Wings hockey game where she got hit with a puck. And I *still* can't understand why she left me. That's how impossible *I* am!

FELIX: I'm not like you, Oscar. I couldn't take it living all alone. I don't know how I'm going to work. They've got to fire me. How am I going to make a living?

OSCAR: You'll go on street corners and cry. They'll throw nickels at you! You'll work, Felix; you'll work.

(*He lies back down.*)

FELIX: You think I ought to call Frances?

OSCAR (*about to explode*): What for?

(*He sits up.*)

FELIX: Well, talk it out again.

OSCAR: You've *talked* it all out. There are no words left in your entire marriage. When are you going to face up to it?

FELIX: I can't help it, Oscar; I don't know what to do.

OSCAR: Then listen to me. Tonight you're going to sleep here. And tomorrow you're going to get your clothes and your electric toothbrush and you'll move in with me.

FELIX: No, no. It's your apartment. I'll be in the way.

OSCAR: There's eight rooms. We could go for a year without seeing each other. Don't you understand? I *want* you to move in.

FELIX: Why? I'm a pest.

OSCAR: I *know* you're a pest. You don't have to keep telling me.

FELIX: Then why do you want me to live with you?

OSCAR: Because I can't stand living alone, that's why! For crying out loud, I'm proposing to you. What do you want, a ring?

FELIX (*moves to* OSCAR): Well, Oscar, if you really mean it, there's a lot I can do around here. I'm very handy around the house. I can fix things.

OSCAR: You don't have to fix things.

FELIX: I want to do *something,* Oscar. Let me do something.

OSCAR (*nods*): All right, you can take my wife's initials off the towels. Anything you want.

FELIX (*beginning to tidy up*): I can cook. I'm a terrific cook.

OSCAR: You don't have to cook. I eat cold cuts for breakfast.

FELIX: Two meals a day at home, we'll save a fortune. We've got to pay alimony, you know.

OSCAR (*happy to see* FELIX's *new optimism*): All right, you can cook.

(*He throws a pillow at him.*)

FELIX (*throws the pillow back*): Do you like leg of lamb?

OSCAR: Yes, I like leg of lamb.

FELIX: I'll make it tomorrow night. I'll have to call Frances. She has my big pot.

OSCAR: *Will you forget Frances!* We'll get our own pots. Don't drive me crazy before you move in. (*The phone rings.* OSCAR *picks it up quickly.*) Hello? Oh, hello, Frances!

FELIX (*stops cleaning and starts to wave his arms wildly. He whispers screamingly*): I'm not here! I'm not here! You didn't see me. You don't know where I am. I didn't call. I'm not here. I'm not here.

OSCAR (*into the phone*): Yes, he's here.

FELIX (*pacing back and forth*): How does she sound? Is she worried? Is she crying? What is she saying? Does she want to speak to me? I don't want to speak to her.

OSCAR (*into the phone*): Yes, he is!

FELIX: You can tell her I'm not coming back. I've made up my mind. I've had it there. I've taken just as much as she has. You can tell her for me if she thinks I'm coming back she's got another think coming. Tell her. Tell her.

OSCAR (*into the phone*): Yes! Yes, he's fine.

FELIX: Don't tell her I'm fine! You heard me carrying on before. What are you telling her that for? I'm not fine.

OSCAR (*into the phone*): Yes, I understand, Frances.

FELIX (*sits down next to* OSCAR): Does she want to speak to me? Ask her if she wants to speak to me?

OSCAR (*into the phone*): Do you want to speak to him?

FELIX (*reaches for the phone*): Give me the phone. I'll speak to her.

OSCAR (*into the phone*): Oh. You don't want to speak to him.

FELIX: She doesn't want to speak to me?

OSCAR (*into the phone*): Yeah, I see. Right. Well, good-bye.

(*He hangs up.*)

FELIX: She didn't want to speak to me?

OSCAR: No!

FELIX: Why did she call?

OSCAR: She wants to know when you're coming over for your clothes. She wants to have the room repainted.

FELIX: Oh!

OSCAR (*pats* FELIX *on the shoulder*): Listen, Felix, it's almost one o'clock.

(*He gets up.*)

FELIX: Didn't want to speak to me, huh?

OSCAR: I'm going to bed. Do you want a cup of tea with Fruitanos or Raisinettos?

FELIX: She'll paint it pink. She always wanted it pink.

OSCAR: I'll get you a pair of pajamas. You like stripes, dots, or animals?

(*He goes into the bedroom.*)

FELIX: She's really heartbroken, isn't she? I want to kill myself, and she's picking out colors.

OSCAR (*in the bedroom*): Which bedroom do you want? I'm lousy with bedrooms.

FELIX (*gets up and moves toward the bedroom*): You know, I'm glad. Because she finally made me realize—it's over. It didn't sink in until just this minute.

OSCAR (*comes back with pillow, pillowcase, and pajamas*): Felix, I want you to go to bed.

FELIX: I don't think I believed her until just now. My marriage is *really* over.

OSCAR: Felix, go to bed.

FELIX: Somehow it doesn't seem so bad now. I mean, I think I can live with this thing.

OSCAR: Live with it tomorrow. Go to bed tonight.

FELIX: In a little while. I've got to think. I've got to start rearranging my life. Do you have a pencil and paper?

OSCAR: Not in a little while. Now! It's my house; I make up the bedtime.

(*He throws the pajamas to him.*)

FELIX: Oscar, please. I have to be alone for a few minutes. I've got to get organized. Go on, you go to bed. I'll—I'll clean up.

(*He begins picking up debris from the floor.*)

OSCAR (*putting the pillow into the pillowcase*): You don't have to clean up. I pay a dollar fifty an hour to clean up.

FELIX: It's all right, Oscar. I wouldn't be able to sleep with all this dirt around anyway. Go to bed. I'll see you in the morning.

(*He puts the dishes on the tray.*)

OSCAR: You're not going to do anything big, are you, like rolling up the rugs?

FELIX: Ten minutes, that's all I'll be.

OSCAR: You're sure?

FELIX (*smiles*): I'm sure.

OSCAR: No monkey business?

FELIX: No monkey business. I'll do the dishes and go right to bed.

OSCAR: Yeah.

(*Crosses up to his bedroom, throwing the pillow into the downstage bedroom as he passes. He closes his bedroom door behind him.*)

FELIX (*calls him*): Oscar! (OSCAR *anxiously comes out of his bedroom and crosses to* FELIX.) I'm going to be all right! It's going to take me a couple of days, but I'm going to be all right.

OSCAR (*smiles*): Good! Well, good night, Felix.

(*He turns to go toward the bedroom as* FELIX *begins to plump up a pillow from the couch.*)

FELIX: Good night, Frances.

(OSCAR *stops dead.* FELIX, *unaware of his error, plumps another pillow as* OSCAR *turns and stares at* FELIX *with a troubled expression.*)

CURTAIN

ACT TWO

SCENE I

Two weeks later, about eleven at night. The poker game is in session again. VINNIE, ROY, SPEED, MURRAY *and* OSCAR *are all seated at the table.* FELIX's *chair is empty.*

There is one major difference between this scene and the opening poker-game scene. It is the appearance of the room. It is immaculately clean. No, not clean. Sterile! Spotless! Not a speck of dirt can be seen under the ten coats of Johnson's Glo-Coat that have been applied to the floor in the last three weeks. No laundry bags, no dirty dishes, no half-filled glasses.

Suddenly FELIX *appears from the kitchen. He carries a tray with glasses and food—and napkins. After putting the tray down, he takes the napkins one at a time, flicks them out to full length and hands one to every player. They take them with grumbling and put them on their laps. He picks up a can of beer and very carefully pours it into a tall glass, measuring it perfectly so that not a drop spills or overflows. With a flourish he puts the can down.*

FELIX (*moves to* MURRAY): An ice-cold glass of beer for Murray.

(MURRAY *reaches up for it.*)

MURRAY: Thank you, Felix.

FELIX (*holds the glass back*): Where's your coaster?

MURRAY: My what?

FELIX: Your coaster. The little round thing that goes under the glass.

MURRAY (*looks around on the table*): I think I bet it.

OSCAR (*picks it up and hands it to* MURRAY): I knew I was winning too much. Here!

FELIX: Always try to use your coasters, fellows. (*He picks up another drink from the tray.*) Scotch and a little bit of water?

SPEED (*raises his hand*): Scotch and a little bit of water. (*Proudly.*) And I have my coaster.

(*He holds it up for inspection.*)

FELIX (*hands him the drink*): I hate to be a pest but you know what wet glasses do?

(*He goes back to the tray and picks up and wipes a clean ashtray.*)

OSCAR (*coldly and deliberately*): They leave little rings on the table.

FELIX (*nods*): Ruins the finish. Eats right through the polish.

OSCAR (*to the others*): So let's watch those little rings, huh?

FELIX (*takes an ashtray and a plate with a sandwich from the tray and crosses to the table*): And we have a clean ashtray for Roy (*Handing* ROY *the ashtray.*) Aaaaand—a sandwich for Vinnie.

(*Like a doting headwaiter, he skillfully places the sandwich in front of* VINNIE.)

VINNIE (*looks at* FELIX, *then at the sandwich*): Gee, it smells good. What is it?

FELIX: Bacon, lettuce and tomato with mayonnaise on pumpernickel toast.

VINNIE (*unbelievingly*): Where'd you get it?

FELIX (*puzzled*): I made it. In the kitchen.

VINNIE: You mean you put in toast and cooked bacon? Just for me?

OSCAR: If you don't like it, he'll make you a meat loaf. Takes him five minutes.

FELIX: It's no trouble. Honest. I love to cook. Try to eat over the dish. I just vacuumed the rug. (*He goes back to the tray, then stops.*) Oscar!

OSCAR (*quickly*): Yes, sir?

FELIX: I forgot what you wanted. What did you ask me for?

OSCAR: Two three-and-a-half-minute eggs and some petit fours.

FELIX (*points to him*): A double gin and tonic. I'll be right back. (FELIX *starts out, then stops at a little box on the bar.*) Who turned off the Pure-A-Tron?

MURRAY: The what?

FELIX: The Pure-A-Tron! (*He snaps it back on.*) Don't play with this, fellows. I'm trying to get some of the grime out of the air.

(*He looks at them and shakes his head disapprovingly, then exits. They all sit in silence a few seconds.*)

OSCAR: Murray, I'll give you two hundred dollars for your gun.

SPEED (*throws his cards on the table and gets up angrily*): I can't take it any more. (*With his hand on his neck.*) I've had it up to here. In the last three hours we played four minutes of poker. I'm not giving up my Friday nights to watch cooking and housekeeping.

ROY (*slumped in his chair, head hanging down*): I can't breathe. (*He points to the Pure-A-Tron.*) That lousy machine is sucking everything out of the air.

VINNIE (*chewing*): Gee, this is delicious. Who wants a bite?

MURRAY: Is the toast warm?

VINNIE: Perfect. And not too much mayonnaise. It's really a well-made sandwich.

MURRAY: Cut me off a little piece.

VINNIE: Give me your napkin. I don't want to drop any crumbs.

SPEED (*watches them, horrified, as* VINNIE *carefully breaks the sandwich over* MURRAY's *napkin. Then he turns to* OSCAR): Are you listening to this? Martha and Gertrude at the Automat. (*Almost crying in despair.*) What the hell happened to our poker game?

ROY (*still choking*): I'm telling you that thing could kill us. They'll find us here in the morning with our tongues on the floor.

SPEED (*yells at* OSCAR): Do something! Get him back in the game.

OSCAR (*rising, containing his anger*): Don't bother me with your petty little problems. You get this one stinkin' night a week. I'm cooped up here with Dione Lucas twenty-four hours a day.

(*He moves to the window.*)

ROY: It was better before. With the garbage and the smoke, it was better before.

VINNIE (*to* MURRAY): Did you notice what he does with the bread?

MURRAY: What?

VINNIE: He cuts off the crusts. That's why the sandwich is so light.

MURRAY: And then he only uses the soft, green part of the lettuce. (*Chewing.*) It's really delicious.

SPEED (*reacts in amazement and disgust*): I'm going out of my mind.

OSCAR (*yells toward the kitchen*): Felix! Damn it, Felix!

SPEED (*takes the kitty box from the bookcase, puts it on the table, and puts the money in*): Forget it. I'm going home.

OSCAR: Sit down!

SPEED: I'll buy a book and I'll start to read again.

OSCAR: Siddown! Will you siddown! (*Yells.*) Felix!

SPEED: Oscar, it's all over. The day his marriage busted up was the end of our poker game. (*He takes his jacket from the back of the chair and crosses to the door.*) If you find some real players next week, call me.

OSCAR (*following him*): You can't run out now. I'm a big loser.

SPEED (*with the door open*): You got no one to blame but yourself. It's all your fault. You're the one who stopped him from killing himself.

(*He exits and slams the door.*)

OSCAR (*stares at the door*): He's right! The man is absolutely right.

(*He moves to the table.*)

MURRAY (*to* VINNIE): Are you going to eat that pickle?

VINNIE: I wasn't thinking of it. Why? Do you want it?

MURRAY: Unless you want it. It's your pickle.

VINNIE: No, no. Take it. I don't usually eat pickle.

(VINNIE *holds the plate with the pickle out to* MURRAY. OSCAR *slaps the plate, which sends the pickle flying through the air.*)

OSCAR: Deal the cards!

MURRAY: What did you do that for?

OSCAR: Just deal the cards. You want to play poker, deal the cards. You want to eat, go to Schrafft's. (*To* VINNIE.) Keep your sandwich and your pickles to yourself. I'm losing ninety-two dollars and everybody's getting fat! (*He screams.*) Felix!

(FELIX *appears in the kitchen doorway.*)

FELIX: What?

OSCAR: Close the kitchen and sit down. It's a quarter to twelve. I still got an hour and a half to win this month's alimony.

ROY (*sniffs*): What is the smell? Disinfectant! (*He smells the cards.*) It's the cards. *He washed the cards!*

(*He throws down the cards, takes his jacket from the chair and moves past the table to put his money into the kitty box.*)

FELIX (*comes to the table with* OSCAR'*s drink, which he puts down; then he sits in his own seat*): Okay. What's the bet?

OSCAR (*hurrying to his seat*): I can't believe it. We're gonna play cards again. (*He sits.*) It's up to Roy. Roy, baby, what are you gonna do?

ROY: I'm going to get in a cab and go to Central Park. If I don't get some fresh air, you got yourself a dead accountant.

(*He moves toward the door.*)

OSCAR (*follows him*): What do you mean? It's not even twelve o'clock.

ROY (*turns back to* OSCAR): Look, I've been sitting here breathing Lysol and ammonia for four hours! Nature didn't intend for poker to be played like that. (*He crosses to the door.*) If you wanna have a game next week (*He points to* FELIX.) either Louis Pasteur cleans up *after* we've gone, or we play in the Hotel Dixie! Good night!

(*He goes and slams the door. There is a moment's silence.* OSCAR *goes back to the table and sits.*)

OSCAR: We got just enough for handball!

FELIX: Gee, I'm sorry. Is it my fault?

VINNIE: No, I guess no one feels like playing much lately.

MURRAY: Yeah. I don't know what it is, but something's happening to the old gang.

(*He goes to a side chair, sits and puts on his shoes.*)

OSCAR: Don't you know what's happening to the old gang? It's breaking up. Everyone's getting divorced. I swear, we used to have better games when we couldn't get out at night.

VINNIE (*getting up and putting on his jacket*): Well, I guess I'll be going too. Bebe and I are driving to Asbury Park for the weekend.

FELIX: Just the two of you, heh? Gee, that's nice! You always do things like that together, don't you?

VINNIE (*shrugs*): We have to. I don't know how to drive! (*He takes all the money from the kitty box and moves to the door.*) You coming, Murray?

MURRAY (*gets up, takes his jacket and moves toward the door*): Yeah, why not? If I'm not home by one o'clock with a hero sandwich and a frozen éclair, she'll have an all-points out on me. Ahhh, you guys got the life.

FELIX: Who?

MURRAY (*turns back*): Who? You! The Marx Brothers! Laugh, laugh, laugh. What have you got to worry about? If you suddenly want to go to the Playboy Club to hunt Bunnies, who's gonna stop you?

FELIX: I don't belong to the Playboy Club.

MURRAY: I know you don't, Felix, it's just a figure of speech. Anyway, it's not such a bad idea. Why don't you join?

FELIX: Why?

MURRAY: Why! Because for twenty-five dollars they give you a key— and you walk into Paradise. *My* keys cost thirty cents—and you walk into corned beef and cabbage. (*He winks at him.*) Listen to me.

(*He moves to the door.*)

FELIX: What are you talking about, Murray? You're a happily married man.

MURRAY (*turns back on the landing*): I'm not talking about *my* situation. (*He puts on his jacket.*) I'm talking about *yours!* Fate has just played a cruel and rotten trick on you, so enjoy it! (*He turns to go,*

revealing "PAL" letters sewn on the back of his jacket.) C'mon,
Vinnie.

(VINNIE *waves good-bye and they both exit.*)

FELIX (*staring at the door*): That's funny, isn't it, Oscar? They think
we're happy. They really think we're enjoying this. (*He gets up and
begins to straighten up the chairs.*) They don't know, Oscar. They
don't know what's it's like.

(*He gives a short, ironic laugh, tucks the napkins under his arm
and starts to pick up the dishes from the table.*)

OSCAR: I'd be immensely grateful to you, Felix, if you didn't clean up
just now.

FELIX (*puts dishes on the tray*): It's only a few things. (*He stops and
looks back at the door.*) I can't get over what Murray just said. You
know I think they really envy us. (*He clears more stuff from the
table.*)

OSCAR: Felix, leave everything alone. I'm not through dirtying-up for
the night.

(*He drops some poker chips on the floor.*)

FELIX (*puting stuff on the tray*): But don't you see the irony of it?
Don't you see it, Oscar?

OSCAR (*sighs heavily*): Yes, I see it.

FELIX (*clearing the table*): No, you don't. I really don't think you do.

OSCAR: Felix, I'm telling you I see the irony of it.

FELIX (*pauses*): Then tell me. What is it? What's the irony?

OSCAR (*deep breath*): The irony is—unless we can come to some other
arrangement, I'm gonna kill you! That's the irony.

FELIX: What's wrong?

(*He crosses back to the tray and puts down all the glasses and
other things.*)

OSCAR: There's something wrong with this system, that's what's wrong.
I don't think that two single men living alone in a big eight-room
apartment should have a cleaner house than my mother.

FELIX (*gets the rest of the dishes, glasses and coasters from the table*): What are you talking about? I'm just going to put the dishes in the sink. You want me to leave them here all night?

OSCAR (*takes his glass, which* FELIX *has put on the tray, and crosses to the bar for a refill*): I don't care if you take them to bed with you. You can play Mr. Clean all you want. But don't make *me* feel guilty.

FELIX (*takes the tray into the kitchen, leaving the swinging door open*): I'm not asking you to do it, Oscar. You don't have to clean up.

OSCAR (*moves up to the door*): That's why you make me feel guilty. You're always in my bathroom hanging up my towels. Whenever I smoke you follow me around with an ashtray. Last night I found you washing the kitchen floor, shaking your head and moaning, "Footprints, footprints!"

(*He paces around the room.*)

FELIX (*comes back to the table with a silent butler. He dumps the ashtrays, then wipes them carefully*): I didn't say they were yours.

OSCAR (*angrily sits down in the wing chair*): Well, they *were* mine, damn it. I have feet and they make prints. What do you want me to do, climb across the cabinets?

FELIX: No! I want you to walk on the floor.

OSCAR: I appreciate that! I really do.

FELIX (*crosses to the telephone table and cleans the ashtray there*): I'm just trying to keep the place livable. I didn't realize I irritated you that much.

OSCAR: I just feel I should have the right to decide when my bathtub needs a going over with Dutch Cleanser. It's the democratic way!

FELIX (*puts the silent butler and his rag down on the coffee table and sits down glumly on the couch*): I was wondering how long it would take.

OSCAR: How long *what* would take?

FELIX: Before I got on your nerves.

OSCAR: I didn't say you get on my nerves.

FELIX: Well, it's the same thing. You said I irritated you.

OSCAR: *You* said you irritated me. I didn't say it.

FELIX: Then what *did* you say?

OSCAR: I don't know *what* I said. What's the difference what I said?

FELIX: It doesn't make any difference. I was just repeating what I thought you said.

OSCAR: Well, don't repeat what you *thought* I said. Repeat what I *said!* My God, that's irritating!

FELIX: You see! You see! You *did* say it!

OSCAR: I don't believe this whole conversation.

(*He gets up and paces by the table.*)

FELIX (*pawing with a cup*): Oscar, I'm—I'm sorry. I don't know what's wrong with me.

OSCAR (*still pacing*): And don't pout. If you want to fight, we'll fight. But don't pout! Fighting *I* win. Pouting *you* win!

FELIX: You're right. Everything you say about me is absolutely right.

OSCAR (*really angry, turns to* FELIX): And don't give in so easily. I'm *not* always right. Sometimes *you're* right.

FELIX: You're right. I do that. I always figure I'm in the wrong.

OSCAR: Only this time you *are* wrong. And I'm right.

FELIX: Oh, leave me alone.

OSCAR: And don't sulk. That's the same as pouting.

FELIX: I know. I know. (*He squeezes his cup with anger.*) Damn me, why can't I do one lousy thing right?

(*He suddenly stands up and cocks his arm back, about to hurl the cup angrily against the front door. Then he thinks better of it, puts the cup down and sits.*)

OSCAR (*watching this*): Why didn't you throw it?

FELIX: I almost did. I get so insane with myself sometimes.

OSCAR: Then why don't you throw the cup?

FELIX: Because I'm trying to control myself.

OSCAR: Why?

FELIX: What do you mean, why?

OSCAR: Why do you have to control yourself? You're angry, you felt like throwing the cup, why don't you throw it?

FELIX: Because there's no point to it. I'd still be angry and I'd have a broken cup.

OSCAR: How do you *know* how you'd feel? Maybe you'd feel *wonderful*. Why do you have to control every single thought in your head? Why don't you let loose *once* in your life? Do something that you *feel* like doing—and not what you *think* you're supposed to do. Stop keeping books, Felix. Relax. Get drunk. Get angry. C'mon, *break the goddamned cup!*

(FELIX *suddenly stands up and hurls the cup against the door, smashing it to pieces. Then he grabs his shoulder in pain.*)

FELIX: Oww! I hurt my arm!

(*He sinks down on the couch, massaging his arm.*)

OSCAR (*throws up his hands*): You're hopeless! You're a hopeless mental case!

(*He paces around the table.*)

FELIX (*grimacing with pain*): I'm not supposed to throw with that arm. What a stupid thing to do.

OSCAR: Why don't you live in a closet? I'll leave your meals outside the door and slide in the papers. Is that safe enough?

FELIX (*rubbing his arm*): I used to have bursitis in this arm. I had to give up golf. Do you have a heating pad?

OSCAR: How can you hurt your arm throwing a cup? If it had coffee in it, that's one thing. But an empty cup . . .

(*He sits in the wing chair.*)

FELIX: All right, cut it out, Oscar. That's the way I am. I get hurt easily. I can't help it.

OSCAR: You're not going to cry, are you? I think all those tears dripping on the arm is what gave you bursitis.

FELIX (*holding his arm*): I once got it just from combing my hair.

OSCAR (*shaking his head*): A world full of room-mates and I pick myself the Tin Man. (*He sighs.*) Oh, well, I suppose I could have done worse.

FELIX (*moves the rag and silent butler to the bar. Then he takes the chip box from the bar and crosses to the table*): You're darn right, you could have. A *lot* worse.

OSCAR: How?

FELIX: What do you mean, how? How'd you like to live with ten-thumbs Murray or Speed and his complaining? (*He gets down on his knees, picks up the chips and puts them into the box.*) Don't forget I cook and clean and take care of this house. I save us a lot of money, don't I?

OSCAR: Yeah, but then you keep me up all night counting it.

FELIX (*goes to the table and sweeps the chips and cards into the box*): Now wait a minute. We're not always going at each other. We have some fun too, don't we?

OSCAR (*crosses to the couch*): Fun? Felix, getting a clear picture on Channel Two isn't my idea of whoopee.

FELIX: What are you talking about?

OSCAR: All right, what do you and I do every night?

(*He takes off his sneakers and drops them on the floor.*)

FELIX: What do we do? You mean after dinner?

OSCAR: That's right. After we've had your halibut steak and the dishes are done and the sink has been Brillo'd and the pans have been S.O.S.'d and the leftovers have been Saran-Wrapped—what do we do?

FELIX (*finishes clearing the table and puts everything on top of the bookcase*): Well, we read, we talk . . .

OSCAR (*takes off his pants and throws them on the floor*): No, no. *I* read and *you* talk! I try to work and you talk. I take a bath and you talk. I go to sleep and you talk. We've got your life arranged pretty good but I'm still looking for a little entertainment.

FELIX (*pulling the kitchen chairs away from the table*): What are you saying? That I talk too much?

OSCAR (*sits on the couch*): No, no. I'm not complaining. You have a lot to say. What's worrying me is that I'm beginning to listen.

FELIX (*pulls the table into the alcove*): Oscar, I told you a hundred times, just tell me to shut up. I'm not sensitive.

(*He pulls the love seat down into the room, and centers the table between the windows in the alcove.*)

OSCAR: I don't think you're getting my point. For a husky man, I think I've spent enough evenings discussing tomorrow's menu. The night was made for other things.

FELIX: Like what?

(*He puts two dining chairs neatly on one side of the table.*)

OSCAR: Like unless I get to touch something soft in the next two weeks, I'm in big trouble.

FELIX: You mean women?

(*He puts the two other dining chairs neatly on the other side of the table.*)

OSCAR: If you want to give it a name, all right, women!

FELIX (*picks up the two kitchen chairs and starts toward the landing*): That's funny. You know I haven't even *thought* about women in weeks.

OSCAR: I fail to see the humor.

FELIX (*stops*): No, that's really strange. I mean when Frances and I were happy, I don't think there was a girl on the street I didn't stare at for ten minutes. (*He crosses to the kitchen door and pushes it open with his back.*) I used to take the wrong subway home just following a pair of legs. But since we broke up, I don't even know what a woman looks like.

(*He takes the chairs into the kitchen.*)

OSCAR: Well, either I could go downstairs and buy a couple of magazines—or I could make a phone call.

FELIX (*from the kitchen, as he washes the dishes*): What are you saying?

OSCAR (*crosses to a humidor on a small table and takes out a cigar*): I'm saying let's spend one night talking to someone with higher voices than us.

FELIX: You mean go out on a date?

OSCAR: Yah . . .

FELIX: Oh, well, I—I can't.

OSCAR: Why not?

FELIX: Well, it's all right for you. But I'm still married.

OSCAR (*paces toward the kitchen door*): You can *cheat* until the divorce comes through!

FELIX: It's not that. It's just that I have no—no *feeling* for it. I can't explain it.

OSCAR: Try!

FELIX (*comes to the doorway with a brush and dish in his hand*): Listen, I intend to go out. I get lonely too. But I'm just separated a few weeks. Give me a little time.

(*He goes back to the sink.*)

OSCAR: There isn't any time left. I saw *TV Guide* and there's nothing on this week! (*He paces into and through the kitchen and out the kitchen door onto the landing.*) What am I asking you? All I want to do is have dinner with a couple of girls. You just have to eat and talk. It's not hard. You've eaten and talked before.

FELIX: Why do you need me? Can't you go out yourself?

OSCAR: Because I may want to come back here. And if we walk in and find you washing the windows, it puts a damper on things.

(*He sits down.*)

FELIX (*pokes his head out of the kitchen*): I'll take a pill and go to sleep.

(*He goes back into the kitchen.*)

OSCAR: Why take a pill when you can take a girl?

FELIX (*comes out with an aerosol bomb held high over his head and circles around the room, spraying it*): Because I'd feel guilty, that's why. Maybe it doesn't make any sense to you, but that's the way I feel.

(*He puts the bomb on the bar and takes the silent butler and rag into the kitchen. He places them on the sink and busily begins to wipe the refrigerator.*)

OSCAR: Look, for all I care you can take her in the kitchen and make a blueberry pie. But I think it's a lot healthier than sitting up in your bed every night writing Frances' name all through the crossword puzzles. Just for one night, talk to another girl.

FELIX (*returns, pushes the love seat carefully into position and sits,* *weakenin*g): But who would I call? The only single girl I know is my secretary and I don't think she likes me.

OSCAR (*jumps up and crouches next to* FELIX): Leave that to me. There's two sisters who live in this building. English girls. One's a widow; the other's a divorcée. They're a barrel of laughs.

FELIX: How do you know?

OSCAR: I was trapped in the elevator with them last week. (*Runs to the telephone table, puts the directory on the floor, and gets down on his knees to look for the number.*) I've been meaning to call them but I didn't know which one to take out. This'll be perfect.

FELIX: What do they look like?

OSCAR: Don't worry. Yours is very pretty.

FELIX: I'm not worried. Which one is mine?

OSCAR (*looking in the book*): The divorcée.

FELIX (*goes to* OSCAR): Why do I get the divorcée?

OSCAR: I don't care. You want the widow?

(*He circles a number on the page with a crayon.*)

FELIX (*sitting on the couch*): No, I don't want the widow. I don't even want the divorcée. I'm just doing this for you.

OSCAR: Look, take whoever you want. When they come in the door, point to the sister of your choice. (*Tears the page out of the book, runs to the bookcase and hangs it up.*) I don't care. I just want to have some laughs.

FELIX: All right. All right.

OSCAR (*crosses to the couch and sits next to* FELIX): Don't say all right. I want you to promise me you're going to try to have a good time. Please, Felix. It's important. Say, "I promise."

FELIX (*nods*): I promise.

OSCAR: Again!

FELIX: I promise!

OSCAR: And no writing in the book, a dollar thirty for the cab.

FELIX: No writing in the book.

OSCAR: No one is to be called Frances. It's Gwendolyn and Cecily.

FELIX: No Frances.

OSCAR: No crying, sighing, moaning or groaning.

FELIX: I'll smile from seven to twelve.

OSCAR: And this above all, no talk of the past. Only the present.

FELIX: And the future.

OSCAR: That's the new Felix I've been waiting for. (*Leaps up and prances around.*) Oh, is this going to be a night. Hey, where do you want to go?

FELIX: For what?

OSCAR: For dinner. Where'll we eat?

FELIX: You mean a restaurant? For the four of us? It'll cost a fortune.

OSCAR: We'll cut down on laundry. We won't wear socks on Thursdays.

FELIX: But that's throwing away money. We can't afford it, Oscar.

OSCAR: We have to eat.

FELIX (*moves to* OSCAR): We'll have dinner here.

OSCAR: *Here?*

FELIX: I'll cook. We'll save thirty, forty dollars.

(*He goes to the couch, sits and picks up the phone.*)

OSCAR: What kind of a double date is that? You'll be in the kitchen all night.

FELIX: No, I won't. I'll put it up in the afternoon. Once I get my potatoes in, I'll have all the time in the world.

(*He starts to dial.*)

OSCAR (*pacing back and forth*): What happened to the new Felix? Who are you calling?

FELIX: Frances. I want to get her recipe for London broil. The girls'll be crazy about it.

(*He dials as* OSCAR *storms off toward his bedroom.*)

CURTAIN

SCENE II

It is a few days later, about eight o'clock.

No one is on stage. The dining table looks like a page out of House and Garden. *It is set for dinner for four, complete with linen tablecloth, candles and wine glasses. There is a floral cen-*

terpiece and flowers about the room, and crackers and dip on the coffee table. There are sounds of activity in the kitchen.

The front door opens and OSCAR *enters with a bottle of wine in a brown paper bag, his jacket over his arm. He looks about gleefully as he listens to the sounds from the kitchen. He puts the bag on the table and his jacket over a chair.*

OSCAR (*calls out in a playful mood*): I'm home, dear! (*He goes into his bedroom, taking off his shirt, and comes skipping out shaving with a cordless razor, with a clean shirt and a tie over his arm. He is joyfully singing as he admires the table.*) Beautiful! Just beautiful! (*He sniffs, obviously catching the aroma from the kitchen.*) Oh, yeah. Something wonderful is going on in that kitchen. (*He rubs his hands gleefully.*) No, sir. There's no doubt about it. I'm the luckiest man on earth. (*He puts the razor into his pocket and begins to put on the shirt.* FELIX *enters slowly from the kitchen. He's wearing a small dish towel as an apron. He has a ladle in one hand. He looks silently and glumly at* OSCAR, *crosses to the armchair and sits.*) I got the wine. (*He takes the bottle out of the bag and puts it on the table.*) Batard Montrachet. Six and a quarter. You don't mind, do you, pussycat? We'll walk to work this week. (FELIX *sits glumly and silently.*) Hey, no kidding, Felix, you did a great job. One little suggestion? Let's come down a little with the lights (*He switches off the wall brackets.*) —and up very softly with the music. (*He crosses to the stereo set in the bookcase and picks up some record albums.*) What do you think goes better with London broil, Mancini or Sinatra? (FELIX *just stares ahead.*) Felix? What's the matter? (*He puts the albums down.*) Something's wrong. I can tell by your conversation. (*He goes into the bathroom, gets a bottle of after-shave lotion and comes out putting it on.*) All right, Felix, what is it?

FELIX (*without looking at him*): What is it? Let's start with what time do you think it is?

OSCAR: What time? I don't know. Seven thirty?

FELIX: Seven thirty? Try eight o'clock.

OSCAR (*puts the lotion down on the small table.*) All right, so it's eight o'clock. So?

(*He begins to fix his tie.*)

FELIX: So? You said you'd be home at seven.

OSCAR: Is that what I said?

FELIX (*nods*): That's what you said. "I will be home at seven" is what you said.

OSCAR: Okay, I said I'd be home at seven. And it's eight. So what's the problem?

FELIX: If you knew you were going to be late, why didn't you call me?

OSCAR (*pauses while making the knot in his tie*): I couldn't call you. I was busy.

FELIX: Too busy to pick up a phone? Where were you?

OSCAR: I was in the office, working.

FELIX: Working? Ha!

OSCAR: Yes. Working!

FELIX: I called your office at seven o'clock. You were gone.

OSCAR (*tucking in his shirt*): It took me an hour to get home. I couldn't get a cab.

FELIX: Since when do they have cabs in Hannigan's Bar?

OSCAR: Wait a minute. I want to get this down on a tape recorder, because no one'll believe me. You mean now I have to call you if I'm coming home late for dinner?

FELIX (*crosses to* OSCAR): Not *any* dinner. Just the ones I've been slaving over since two o'clock this afternoon—to help save *you* money to pay your wife's alimony.

OSCAR (*controlling himself*): Felix, this is no time to have a domestic quarrel. We have two girls coming down any minute.

FELIX: You mean you told them to be here at eight o'clock?

OSCAR (*takes his jacket and crosses to the couch, then sits and takes some dip from the coffee table*): I don't remember what I said. Seven thirty, eight o'clock. What difference does it make?

FELIX (*follows* OSCAR): I'll tell you what difference. You told me they were coming at seven thirty. You were going to be here at seven to help me with the hors d'oeuvres. At seven thirty they arrive and we have cocktails. At eight o'clock we have dinner. It is now eight o'clock. *My London broil is finished!* If we don't eat now the whole damned thing'll be *dried out!*

OSCAR: Oh, God, help me.

FELIX: Never mind helping *you*. Tell Him to save the meat. Because we got nine dollars and thirty-four cents worth drying up in there right now.

OSCAR: Can't you keep it warm?

FELIX (*pacing*): What do you think I am, the Magic Chef? I'm lucky I got it to come out at eight o'clock. What am I going to do?

OSCAR: I don't know. Keep pouring gravy on it.

FELIX: What gravy?

OSCAR: Don't you have any gravy?

FELIX (*storms over to* OSCAR): Where the hell am I going to get gravy at eight o'clock?

OSCAR (*getting up*): I thought it comes when you cook the meat.

FELIX (*follows him*): When you *cook the meat?* You don't know the first thing you're talking about. You have to make gravy. It doesn't come!

OSCAR: You asked my advice, I'm giving it to you.

(*He puts on his jacket.*)

FELIX: Advice? (*He waves the ladle in his face.*) You didn't know where the kitchen was till I came here and showed you.

OSCAR: You wanna talk to me, put down the spoon.

FELIX (*exploding in rage, again waving the ladle in his face*): Spoon? You dumb ignoramus. It's a ladle. You don't even know it's a ladle.

OSCAR: All right, Felix, get a hold of yourself.

FELIX (*pulls himself together and sits on the love seat*): You think it's so easy? Go on. The kitchen's all yours. Go make a London broil for four people who come a half hour late.

OSCAR (*to no one in particular*): Listen to me. I'm arguing with him over gravy.

(*The bell rings.*)

FELIX (*jumps up*): Well, they're here. Our dinner guests. I'll get a saw and cut the meat.

(*He starts for the kitchen.*)

OSCAR (*stopping him*): Stay where you are!

FELIX: I'm not taking the blame for this dinner.

OSCAR: Who's blaming you? Who even *cares* about the dinner?

FELIX (*moves to* OSCAR): I care. I take *pride* in what I do. And you're going to explain to them exactly what happened.

OSCAR: All right, you can take a Polaroid picture of me coming in at eight o'clock! Now take off that stupid apron because I'm opening the door.

(*He rips the towel off* FELIX *and goes to the door.*)

FELIX (*takes his jacket from a dining chair and puts it on*): I just want to get one thing clear. This is the last time I ever cook for you. Because people like you don't even appreciate a decent meal. That's why they have TV dinners.

OSCAR: You through?

FELIX: I'm through!

OSCAR: Then smile. (OSCAR *smiles and opens the door. The girls poke their heads through the door. They are in their young thirties and somewhat attractive. They are undoubtedly British.*) Well, hello.

GWENDOLYN (*to* OSCAR): Hallo.

CECILY (*to* OSCAR): Hallo.

GWENDOLYN: I do hope we're not late.

OSCAR: No, no. You timed it perfectly. Come on in. (*He points to them as they enter.*) Er, Felix, I'd like you to meet two very good friends of mine, Gwendolyn and Cecily . . .

CECILY (*pointing out his mistake*): Cecily and Gwendolyn.

OSCAR: Oh, yes. Cecily and Gwendolyn . . . er (*Trying to remember their last name.*) Er . . . Don't tell me. Robin? No, no. Cardinal?

GWENDOLYN: Wrong both times. It's Pigeon!

OSCAR: Pigeon. Right. Cecily and Gwendolyn Pigeon.

GWENDOLYN (*to* FELIX): You don't spell it like Walter Pidgeon. You spell it like "Coo-Coo" Pigeon.

OSCAR: We'll remember that if it comes up. Cecily and Gwendolyn, I'd like you to meet my room-mate, and our chef for the evening, Felix Ungar.

CECILY (*holding her hand out*): Heh d'yew dew?

FELIX (*moving to her and shaking her hand*): How do you do?

GWENDOLYN (*holding her hand out*): Heh d'yew dew?

FELIX (*stepping up on the landing and shaking her hand*): How do you do you?

(*This puts him nose to nose with* OSCAR, *and there is an awkward pause as they look at each other.*)

OSCAR: Well, we did that beautifully. Why don't we sit down and make ourselves comfortable?

(FELIX *steps aside and ushers the girls down into the room. There is ad libbing and a bit of confusion and milling about as they all squeeze between the armchair and the couch, and the* PIGEONS *finally seat themselves on the couch.* OSCAR *sits in the armchair, and* FELIX *snakes past him to the love seat. Finally all have settled down.*)

CECILY: This is ever so nice, isn't it, Gwen?

GWENDOLYN (*looking around*): Lovely. And much nicer than our flat. Do you have help?

OSCAR: Er, yes. I have a man who comes in every night.

CECILY: Aren't you the lucky one?

(CECILY, GWENDOLYN *and* OSCAR *all laugh at her joke.* OSCAR *looks over at* FELIX *but there is no response.*)

OSCAR (*rubs his hands together*): Well, isn't this nice? I was telling Felix yesterday about how we happened to meet.

GWENDOLYN: Oh? Who's Felix?

OSCAR (*a litle embarrassed, he points to* FELIX): He is!

GWENDOLYN: Oh, yes, of course. I'm so sorry.

(FELIX *nods that it's all right.*)

CECILY: You know it happened to us again this morning.

OSCAR: What did?

GWENDOLYN: Stuck in the elevator again.

OSCAR: Really? Just the two of you?

CECILY: And poor old Mr. Kessler from the third floor. We were in there half an hour.

OSCAR: No kidding? What happened?

GWENDOLYN: Nothing much, I'm afraid.

(CECILY *and* GWENDOLYN *both laugh at her latest joke, joined by* OSCAR. *He once again looks over at* FELIX, *but there is no response.*)

OSCAR (*rubs his hands again*): Well, this really is nice.

CECILY: And ever so much cooler than our place.

GWENDOLYN: It's like equatorial Africa on our side of the building.

CECILY: Last night it was so bad Gwen and I sat there in nature's own cooling ourselves in front of the open fridge. Can you imagine such a thing?

OSCAR: Er, I'm working on it.

GWENDOLYN: Actually, it's impossible to get a night's sleep. Cec and I really don't know what to do.

OSCAR: Why don't you sleep with an air conditioner?

GWENDOLYN: We haven't got one.

OSCAR: I know. But we have.

GWENDOLYN: Oh, you! I told you about that one, didn't I, Cec?

FELIX: They say it may rain Friday.

(*They all stare at* FELIX.)

GWENDOLYN: Oh?

CECILY: That should cool things off a bit.

OSCAR: I wouldn't be surprised.

FELIX: Although sometimes it gets hotter after it rains.

GWENDOLYN: Yes, it does, doesn't it?

(*They continue to stare at* FELIX.)

FELIX (*jumps up and, picking up the ladle, starts for the kitchen*): Dinner is served!

OSCAR (*stopping him*): No, it isn't!

FELIX: Yes, it is!

OSCAR: No, it isn't! I'm sure the girls would like a cocktail first. (*To the girls.*) Wouldn't you, girls?

GWENDOLYN: Well, I wouldn't put up a struggle.

OSCAR: There you are. (*To* CECILY.) What would you like?

CECILY: Oh, I really don't know. (*To* OSCAR.) What have you got?

FELIX: London broil.

OSCAR (*to* FELIX): She means to drink. (*To* CECILY.) We have everything. And what we don't have, I mix in the medicine cabinet. What'll it be?

(*He crouches next to her.*)

CECILY: Oh, a double vodka.

GWENDOLYN: Cecily, not before dinner.

CECILY (*to the men*): My sister. She watches over me like a mother hen. (*To* OSCAR.) Make it a *small* double vodka.

OSCAR: A small double vodka! And for the beautiful mother hen?

GWENDOLYN: Oh, I'd like something cool. I think I would like to have a double Drambuie with some crushed ice, unless you don't have the crushed ice.

OSCAR: I was up all night with a sledge hammer. I shall return!

(*He goes to the bar and gets bottles of vodka and Drambuie.*)

FELIX (*going to him*): Where are you going?

OSCAR: To get the refreshments.

FELIX (*starting to panic*): Inside? What'll *I* do?

OSCAR: You can finish the weather report.

(*He exits into the kitchen.*)

FELIX (*calls after him*): Don't forget to look at my meat! (*He turns and faces the girls. He crosses to a chair and sits. He crosses his legs nonchalantly. But he is ill at ease and he crosses them again. He is becoming aware of the silence and he can no longer get away with just smiling.*) Er, Oscar tells me you're sisters.

CECILY: Yes. That's right.

(*She looks at* GWENDOLYN.)

FELIX: From England.

GWENDOLYN: Yes. That's right.

(*She looks at* CECILY.)

FELIX: I see. (*Silence. Then, his little joke.*) We're not brothers.

CECILY: Yes. We know.

FELIX: Although I am a brother. I have a brother who's a doctor. He lives in Buffalo. That's upstate in New York.

GWENDOLYN (*taking a cigarette from her purse*): Yes, we know.

FELIX: You know my brother?

GWENDOLYN: No. We know that Buffalo is upstate in New York.

FELIX: Oh!

(*He gets up, takes a cigarette lighter from the side table and moves to light* GWENDOLYN's *cigarette.*)

CECILY: We've been there! Have you?

FELIX: No! Is it nice?

CECILY: Lovely.

(FELIX *closes the lighter on* GWENDOLYN's *cigarette and turns to go back to his chair, taking the cigarette, now caught in the lighter, with him. He notices the cigarette and hastily gives it back to* GWENDOLYN, *stopping to light it once again. He puts the lighter back on the table and sits down nervously. There is a pause.*)

FELIX: Isn't that interesting? How long have you been in the United States of America?

CECILY: Almost four years now.

FELIX (*nods*): Uh huh. Just visiting?

GWENDOLYN (*looks at* CECILY): No! We live here.

FELIX: And you work here too, do you?

CECILY: Yes. We're secretaries for Slenderama.

GWENDOLYN: You know. The health club.

CECILY: People bring us their bodies and we do wonderful things with them.

GWENDOLYN: Actually, if you're interested, we can get you ten per cent off.

CECILY: Off the price, not off your body.

FELIX: Yes, I see. (*He laughs. They all laugh. Suddenly he shouts toward the kitchen.*) Oscar, where's the drinks?

OSCAR (*offstage*): Coming! Coming!

CECILY: What field of endeavor are you engaged in?

FELIX: I write the news for CBS.

CECILY: Oh! Fascinating!

GWENDOLYN: Where do you get your ideas from?

FELIX (*he looks at her as though she's a Martian*): From the news.

GWENDOLYN: Oh, yes, of course. Silly me . . .

CECILY: Maybe you can mention Gwen and I in one of your news reports.

FELIX: Well, if you do something spectacular, maybe I will.

CECILY: Oh, we've done spectacular things but I don't think we'd want it spread all over the telly, do you, Gwen?

(*They both laugh.*)

FELIX (*he laughs too, then cries out almost for help*): Oscar!

OSCAR (*offstage*): Yeah, yeah!

FELIX (*to the girls*): It's such a large apartment, sometimes you have to shout.

GWENDOLYN: Just you two baches live here?

FELIX: Baches? Oh, bachelors! We're not bachelors. We're divorced. That is, Oscar's divorced. I'm *getting* divorced.

CECILY: Oh. Small world. We've cut the dinghy loose too, as they say.

GWENDOLYN: Well, you couldn't have a *better* matched foursome, could you?

FELIX (*smiles weakly*): No, I suppose not.

GWENDOLYN: Although technically I'm a widow. I was divorcing my husband, but he died before the final papers came through.

FELIX: Oh, I'm awfully sorry. (*Sighs.*) It's a terrible thing, isn't it? Divorce.

GWENDOLYN: It can be—if you haven't got the right solicitor.

CECILY: That's true. Sometimes they can drag it out for months. I was lucky. Snip, cut and I was free.

FELIX: I mean it's terrible what it can do to people. After all, what is divorce? It's taking two happy people and tearing their lives completely apart. It's inhuman, don't you think so?

CECILY: Yes, it can be an awful bother.

GWENDOLYN: But of course, that's all water under the bridge now, eh? Er, I'm terribly sorry, but I think I've forgotten your name.

FELIX: Felix.

GWENDOLYN: Oh, yes. Felix.

CECILY: Like the cat.

(FELIX *takes his wallet from his jacket pocket.*)

GWENDOLYN: Well, the Pigeons will have to beware of the cat, won't they?

(*She laughs.*)

CECILY (*nibbles on a nut from the dish*): Mmm, cashews. Lovely.

FELIX (*takes a snapshot out of his wallet*): This is the worst part of breaking up.

(*He hands the picture to* CECILY.)

CECILY (*looks at it*): Childhood sweethearts, were you?

FELIX: No, no. That's my little boy and girl. (CECILY *gives the picture to* GWENDOLYN, *takes a pair of glasses from her purse and puts them on.*) He's seven, she's five.

CECILY (*looks again*): Oh! Sweet.

FELIX: They live with their mother.

GWENDOLYN: I imagine you must miss them terribly.

FELIX (*takes back the picture and looks at it longingly*): I can't stand being away from them. (*Shrugs.*) But—that's what happens with divorce.

CECILY: When do you get to see them?

FELIX: Every night. I stop there on my way home! Then I take them on the weekends, and I get them on holidays and July and August.

CECILY: Oh! Well, when is it that you miss them?

FELIX: Whenever I'm not there. If they didn't have to go to school so early, I'd go over and make them breakfast. They love my French toast.

GWENDOLYN: You're certainly a devoted father.

FELIX: It's Frances who's the wonderful one.

CECILY: She's the little girl?

FELIX: No. She's the mother. My wife.

GWENDOLYN: The one you're divorcing?

FELIX (*nods*): Mm! She's done a terrific job bringing them up. They always look so nice. They're so polite. Speak beautifully. Never, "Yeah." Always, "Yes." They're such good kids. And she did it all. She's the kind of woman who— Ah, what am I saying? You don't want to hear any of this.

(*He puts the picture back in his wallet.*)

CECILY: Nonsense. You have a right to be proud. You have two beautiful children and a wonderful ex-wife.

FELIX (*containing his emotions*): I know. (*He hands* CECILY *another snapshot.*) That's her. Frances.

GWENDOLYN (*looking at the picture*): Oh, she's pretty. Isn't she pretty, Cecy?

CECILY: Oh, yes. Pretty. A pretty girl. Very pretty.

FELIX (*takes the picture back*): Thank you. (*Shows them another snapshot.*) Isn't this nice?

GWENDOLYN (*looks*): There's no one in the picture.

FELIX: I know. It's a picture of our living room. We had a beautiful apartment.

GWENDOLYN: Oh, yes. Pretty. Very pretty.

CECILY: Those are lovely lamps.

FELIX: Thank you! (*Takes the picture.*) We bought them in Mexico on our honeymoon. (*He looks at the picture again.*) I used to love to come home at night. (*He's beginning to break.*) That was my whole life. My wife, my kids—and my apartment.

(*He breaks down and sobs.*)

CECILY: Does she have the lamps now too?

FELIX (*nods*): I gave her everything. It'll never be like that again. Never! I—I— (*He turns his head away.*) I'm sorry. (*He takes out a handkerchief and dabs his eyes.* GWENDOLYN *and* CECILY *look at each other with compassion.*) Please forgive me. I didn't mean to get emotional. (*Trying to pull himself together, he picks up a bowl from the side table and offers it to the girls.*) Would you like some potato chips?

(CECILY *takes the bowl.*)

GWENDOLYN: You mustn't be ashamed. I think it's a rare quality in a man to be able to cry.

FELIX (*puts a hand over his eyes*): Please. Let's not talk about it.

CECILY: I think it's sweet. Terribly, terribly sweet.

(*She takes a potato chip.*)

FELIX: You're just making it worse.

GWENDOLYN (*teary-eyed*): It's so refreshing to hear a man speak so highly of the woman he's divorcing! Oh, dear. (*She takes out her handkerchief.*) Now you've got me thinking about poor Sydney.

CECILY: Oh, Gwen. Please don't.

(*She puts the bowl down.*)

GWENDOLYN: It was a good marriage at first. Everyone said so. Didn't they, Cecily? Not like you and George.

CECILY (*the past returns as she comforts* GWENDOLYN): That's right. George and I were never happy. Not for one single, solitary day.

(*She remembers her unhappiness, grabs her handkerchief and dabs her eyes. All three are now sitting with handkerchiefs at their eyes.*)

FELIX: Isn't this ridiculous?

GWENDOLYN: I don't know what brought this on. I was feeling so good a few minutes ago.

CECILY: I haven't cried since I was fourteen.

FELIX: Just let it pour out. It'll make you feel much better. I always do.

GWENDOLYN: Oh, dear; oh, dear; oh, dear.

(*All three sit sobbing into their handkerchiefs. Suddenly* OSCAR *bursts happily into the room with a tray full of drinks. He is all smiles.*)

OSCAR (*like a corny M.C.*): Is ev-rybuddy happy? (*Then he sees the maudlin scene.* FELIX *and the girls quickly try to pull themselves to-gether.*) What the hell happened?

FELIX: Nothing! Nothing!

(*He quickly puts his handkerchief away.*)

OSCAR: What do you mean, nothing? I'm gone three minutes and I walk into a funeral parlor. What did you say to them?

FELIX: I didn't say anything. Don't start in again, Oscar.

OSCAR: I can't leave you alone for five seconds. Well, if you really want to cry, go inside and look at your London broil.

FELIX (*he rushes madly into the kitchen*): Oh, my gosh! Why didn't you call me? I told you to call me.

OSCAR (*giving a drink to* CECILY): I'm sorry, girls. I forgot to warn you about Felix. He's a walking soap opera.

GWENDOLYN: I think he's the dearest thing I ever met.

CECILY (*taking the glass*): He's so sensitive. So fragile. I just want to bundle him up in my arms and take care of him.

OSCAR (*holds out* GWENDOLYN'*s drink. At this, he puts it back down on the tray and takes a swallow from his own drink*): Well, I think when he comes out of that kitchen you may have to.

(*Sure enough,* FELIX *comes out of the kitchen onto the landing looking like a wounded puppy. With a protective kitchen glove, he holds a pan with the exposed London broil. Black is the color of his true love.*)

FELIX (*very calmly*): I'm going down to the delicatessen. I'll be right back.

OSCAR (*going to him*): Wait a minute. Maybe it's not so bad. Let's see it.

FELIX (*shows him*): Here! Look! Nine dollars and thirty-four cents worth of ashes! (*Pulls the pan away. To the girls.*) I'll get some corned beef sandwiches.

OSCAR (*trying to get a look at it*): Give it to me! Maybe we can save some of it.

FELIX (*holding it away from* OSCAR): There's nothing to save. It's all black meat. Nobody likes black meat!

OSCAR: Can't I even look at it?

FELIX: No, you can't look at it!

OSCAR: Why can't I look at it?

FELIX: If you looked at your watch before, you wouldn't have to look at the black meat now! Leave it alone!

(*He turns to go back into the kitchen.*)

GWENDOLYN (*going to him*): Felix! Can *we* look at it?

CECILY (*turning to him, kneeling on the couch*): Please? (FELIX *stops in the kitchen doorway. He hesitates for a moment. He likes them. Then he turns and wordlessly holds the pan out to them.* GWENDOLYN *and* CECILY *inspect it wordlessly, and then turn away sobbing quietly. To* OSCAR.) How about Chinese food?

OSCAR: A wonderful idea.

GWENDOLYN: I've got a better idea. Why don't we just make pot luck in the kitchen?

OSCAR: A *much* better idea.

FELIX: I used up all the pots!

(*He crosses to the love seat and sits, still holding the pan.*)

CECILY: Well, then we can eat up in *our* place. We have tons of Horn and Hardart's.

OSCAR (*gleefully*): That's the best idea I ever heard.

GWENDOLYN: Of course it's awfully hot up there. You'll have to take off your jackets.

OSCAR (*smiling*): We can always open up a refrigerator.

CECILY (*gets her purse from the couch*): Give us five minutes to get into our cooking things.

(GWENDOLYN *gets her purse from the couch.*)

OSCAR: Can't you make it four? I'm suddenly starving to death.

(*The girls are crossing to the door.*)

GWENDOLYN: Don't forget the wine.

OSCAR: How could I forget the wine?

CECILY: And a corkscrew.

OSCAR: *And* a corkscrew.

GWENDOLYN: And Felix.

OSCAR: No, I won't forget Felix.

CECILY: Ta, ta!

OSCAR: Ta, ta!

GWENDOLYN: Ta, ta!

(*The girls exit.*)

OSCAR (*throws a kiss at the closed door*): You bet your sweet little crumpets, "Ta, Ta!" (*He wheels around beaming and quickly gathers up the corkscrew from the bar, and picks up the wine and the records.*) Felix, I love you. You've just overcooked us into one hell of a night. Come on, get the ice bucket. Ready or not, here we come.

(*He runs to the door.*)

FELIX (*sitting motionless*): I'm not going!

OSCAR: What?

FELIX: I said I'm not going.

OSCAR (*crossing to* FELIX): Are you out of your mind? Do you know what's waiting for us up there? You've just been invited to spend the evening in a two-bedroom hothouse with the Coo-Coo Pigeon Sisters! What do you mean you're not going?

FELIX: I don't know how to talk to them. I don't know what to say. I already told them about my brother in Buffalo. I've used up my conversation.

OSCAR: Felix, they're crazy about you. They told me! One of them wants to wrap you up and make a bundle out of you. You're doing better than I am! Get the ice bucket.

(*He starts for the door.*)

FELIX: Don't you understand? I cried! I cried in front of two women.

OSCAR (*stops*): And they *loved* it! I'm thinking of getting hysterical. (*Goes to the door.*) Will you get the ice bucket?

FELIX: But why did I cry? Because I felt guilty. Emotionally I'm still tied to Frances and the kids.

OSCAR: Well, untie the knot just for tonight, will you!

FELIX: I don't want to discuss it any more. (*Starts for the kitchen.*) I'm going to scrub the pots and wash my hair. (*He goes into the kitchen and puts the pan in the sink.*)

OSCAR (*yelling*): Your greasy pots and your greasy hair can wait. You're coming upstairs with me!

FELIX (*in the kitchen*): I'm not! *I'm not!*

OSCAR: What am I going to do with two girls? Felix, don't do this to me. I'll never forgive you!

FELIX: I'm not going!

OSCAR (*screams*): All right, damn you, I'll go without you! (*And he storms out the door and slams it. Then it opens and he comes in again.*) Are you coming?

FELIX (*comes out of the kitchen looking at a magazine*): No.

OSCAR: You mean you're not going to make any effort to change? This is the person you're going to be—until the day you die?

FELIX (*sitting on the couch*): We are what we are.

OSCAR (*nods, then crosses to window, pulls back the drapes and opens the window wide. Then he starts back to the door*): It's *twelve* floors, not eleven.

(*He walks out as* FELIX *stares at the open window.*)

CURTAIN

ACT THREE

The next evening about 7:30 P.M. The room is once again set up for the poker game, with the dining table pulled down, the chairs set about it, and the love seat moved back beneath the windows in the alcove. FELIX *appears from the bedroom with a vacuum cleaner. He is doing a thorough job on the rug. As he vacuums around the table, the door opens and* OSCAR *comes in wearing a summer hat and carrying a newspaper. He glares at* FELIX, *who is still vacuuming, and shakes his head contemptuously. He crosses behind* FELIX, *leaving his hat on the side table next to the armchair, and goes into his bedroom.* FELIX *is not aware of his presence. Then suddenly the power stops on the vacuum, as* OSCAR *has obviously pulled the plug in the bedroom.* FELIX *tries switching the button on and off a few times, then turns to go back into the bedroom. He stops and realizes what's happened as* OSCAR *comes back into the room.* OSCAR *takes a cigar out of his pocket and as he crosses in front of* FELIX *to the couch, he unwraps it and drops the wrappings carelessly on the floor. He then steps up on the couch and walks back and forth mashing down the pillows. Stepping down, he plants one foot on the armchair and then sits on the couch, taking a wooden match from the coffee table and striking it on the table to light his cigar. He flips the used match onto the rug and settles back to read his newspaper.* FELIX *has watched this all in silence, and now carefully picks up the cigar wrappings and the match and drops them into* OSCAR's *hat. He then dusts his hands and takes the vacuum cleaner into the kitchen, pulling the cord in after him.* OSCAR *takes the wrap-*

*pings from the hat and puts them in the butt-filled ashtray on
the coffee table. Then he takes the ashtray and dumps it on the
floor. As he once more settles down with his newspaper,* FELIX
*comes out of the kitchen carrying a tray with a steaming dish of
spaghetti. As he crosses behind* OSCAR *to the table, he indicates
that it smells delicious and passes it close to* OSCAR *to make
sure* OSCAR *smells the fantastic dish he's missing. As* FELIX *sits
and begins to eat,* OSCAR *takes a can of aerosol spray from the
bar, and circling the table, sprays all around* FELIX, *then puts
the can down next to him and goes back to his newspaper.*

FELIX (*pushing the spaghetti away*): All right, how much longer is this
  gonna go on?

OSCAR (*reading his paper*): Are you talking to me?

FELIX: That's right, I'm talking to you.

OSCAR: What do you want to know?

FELIX: I want to know if you're going to spend the rest of your life not
  talking to me. Because if you are, I'm going to buy a radio. (*No
  reply.*) Well? (*No reply.*) I see. You're not going to talk to me. (*No
  reply.*) All right. Two can play at this game. (*Pause.*) If you're not
  going to talk to me, I'm not going to talk to you. (*No reply.*) I can
  act childish too, you know. (*No reply.*) I can go on without talking
  just as long as you can.

OSCAR: Then why the hell don't you shut up?

FELIX: Are you talking to me?

OSCAR: You had your chance to talk last night. I begged you to come
  upstairs with me. From now on I never want to hear a word from
  that shampooed head as long as you live. That's a warning, Felix.

FELIX (*stares at him*): I stand warned. Over and out!

OSCAR (*gets up, takes a key out of his pocket and slams it on the
  table*): There's a key to the back door. If you stick to the hallway
  and your room, you won't get hurt.

  (*He sits back down on the couch.*)

FELIX: I don't think I gather the entire meaning of that remark.

OSCAR: Then I'll explain it to you. Stay out of my way.

FELIX (*picks up the key and moves to the couch*): I think you're serious. I think you're really serious. Are you serious?

OSCAR: This is my apartment. Everything in my apartment is mine. The only thing here that's yours is you. Just stay in your room and speak softly.

FELIX: Yeah, you're serious. Well, let me remind you that I pay half the rent and I'll go into any room I want.

(*He gets up angrily and starts toward the hallway.*)

OSCAR: Where are you going?

FELIX: I'm going to walk around your bedroom.

OSCAR (*slams down his newspaper*): You stay out of there.

FELIX (*steaming*): Don't tell where to go. I pay a hundred and twenty dollars a month.

OSCAR: That was off-season. Starting tomorrow the rates are twelve dollars a day.

FELIX: All right. (*He takes some bills out of his pocket and slams them down on the table.*) There you are. I'm paid up for today. Now I'm going to walk in your bedroom.

(*He starts to storm off.*)

OSCAR: Stay out of there! Stay out of my room!

(*He chases after him.* FELIX *dodges around the table as* OSCAR *blocks the hallway.*)

FELIX (*backing away, keeping the table between them*): Watch yourself! Just watch yourself, Oscar!

OSCAR (*with a pointing finger*): I'm warning you. You want to live here, I don't want to see you, I don't want to hear you and I don't want to smell your cooking. Now get this spaghetti off my poker table.

FELIX: Ha! Ha, ha!

OSCAR: What the hell's so funny?

FELIX: It's not spaghetti. It's linguini!

(OSCAR *picks up the plate of linguini, crosses to the doorway and hurls it into the kitchen.*)

OSCAR: Now it's garbage!

(*He paces by the couch.*)

FELIX (*looks at* OSCAR *unbelievingly: what an insane thing to do*): You are crazy! I'm a neurotic nut but *you are crazy!*

OSCAR: *I'm* crazy, heh? That's really funny coming from a fruitcake like you.

FELIX (*goes to the kitchen door and looks in at the mess. Turns back to* OSCAR): I'm not cleaning that up.

OSCAR: Is that a promise?

FELIX: Did you hear what I said? I'm not cleaning it up. It's your mess. (*Looking into the kitchen again.*) Look at it. Hanging all over the walls.

OSCAR (*crosses to the landing and looks in the kitchen door*): I like it.

(*He closes the door and paces around.*)

FELIX (*fumes*): You'd just let it lie there, wouldn't you? Until it turns hard and brown and . . . Yich, it's disgusting. I'm cleaning it up.

(*He goes into the kitchen,* OSCAR *chases after him. There is the sound of a struggle and falling pots.*)

OSCAR: *Leave it alone!* You touch one strand of that linguini—and I'm gonna punch you right in your sinuses.

FELIX (*dashes out of kitchen with* OSCAR *in pursuit. He stops and tries to calm* OSCAR *down*): Oscar, I'd like you to take a couple of phenobarbital.

OSCAR (*points*): Go to your room! Did you hear what I said? *Go to your room!*

FELIX: All right, let's everybody just settle down, heh?

(*He puts his hand on* OSCAR'*s shoulder to calm him but* OSCAR *pulls away violently from his touch.*)

OSCAR: If you want to live through this night, you'd better tie me up and lock your doors and windows.

FELIX (*sits at the table with a great pretense of calm*): All right, Oscar, I'd like to know what's happened?

OSCAR (*moves toward him*): What's *happened?*

FELIX (*hurriedly slides over to the next chair*): That's right. Something must have caused you to go off the deep end like this. What is it? Something I said? Something I did? Heh? What?

OSCAR (*pacing*): It's nothing you said. It's nothing you did. It's *you!*

FELIX: I see. Well, that's plain enough.

OSCAR: I could make it plainer but I don't want to hurt you.

FELIX: What is it, the cooking? The cleaning? The crying?

OSCAR (*moving toward him*): I'll tell you exactly what it is. It's the cooking, cleaning and crying. It's the talking in your sleep, it's the moose calls that open your ears at two o'clock in the morning. I can't take it any more, Felix. I'm crackin' up. Everything you do irritates me. And when you're not here, the things I know you're gonna do when you come in irritate me. You leave me little notes on my pillow. I told you a hundred times, I can't stand little notes on my pillow. "We're all out of Corn Flakes. F.U." It took me three hours to figure out that F.U. was Felix Ungar. It's not your fault, Felix. It's a rotten combination.

FELIX: I get the picture.

OSCAR: That's just the frame. The picture I haven't even painted yet. I got a typewritten list in my office of the "Ten Most Aggravating Things You Do That Drive Me Berserk." But last night was the topper. Oh, that was the topper. Oh, that was the ever-loving lulu of all times.

FELIX: What are you talking about, the London broil?

OSCAR: No, not the London broil. I'm talking about those two lamb chops. (*He points upstairs.*) I had it all set up with that English Betty Boop and her sister, and I wind up drinking tea and telling them *your* life story.

FELIX (*jumps up*): Oho! So *that's* what's bothering you. That I loused up your evening!

OSCAR: After the mood you put them in, I'm surprised they didn't go out to Rockaway and swim back to England.

FELIX: Don't blame me. I warned you not to make the date in the first place.

(*He makes his point by shaking his finger in* OSCAR's *face.*)

OSCAR: Don't point that finger at me unless you intend to use it!

FELIX (*moves in nose to nose with* OSCAR): All right, Oscar, get off my back. Get off! Off!

(*Startled by his own actions,* FELIX *jumps back from* OSCAR, *warily circles him, crosses to the couch and sits.*)

OSCAR: What's this? A display of temper? I haven't seen you really angry since the day I dropped my cigar in your pancake batter.

(*He starts toward the hallway.*)

FELIX (*threateningly*): Oscar, you're asking to hear something I don't want to say. But if I say it, I think you'd better hear it.

OSCAR (*comes back to the table, places both hands on it and leans toward* FELIX): If you've got anything on your chest besides your chin, you'd better get it off.

FELIX (*strides to the table, places hands on it and leans toward* OSCAR. *They are nose to nose*): All right, I warned you. You're a wonderful guy, Oscar. You've done everything for me. If it weren't for you, I don't know what would have happened to me. You took me in here, gave me a place to live and something to live for. I'll never forget you for that. You're tops with me, Oscar.

OSCAR (*motionless*): If I've just been told off, I think I may have missed it.

FELIX: It's coming now! You're also one of the biggest slobs in the world.

OSCAR: I see.

FELIX: And completely unreliable.

OSCAR: Finished?

FELIX: Undependable.

OSCAR: Is that it?

FELIX: And irresponsible.

OSCAR: Keep going. I think you're hot.

FELIX: That's it. I'm finished. *Now* you've been told off. How do you like that?

(*He crosses to the couch.*)

OSCAR (*straightening up*): Good. Because now I'm going to tell *you* off. For six months I lived alone in this apartment. All alone in eight rooms. I was dejected, despondent and disgusted. Then *you* moved in —my dearest and closest friend. And after three weeks of close, personal contact—I am about to have a nervous breakdown! Do me a favor. Move into the kitchen. Live with your pots, your pans, your ladle and your meat thermometer. When you want to come out, ring a bell and I'll run into the bedroom. (*Almost breaking down.*) I'm asking you nicely, Felix—as a friend. Stay out of my way!

(*And he goes into the bedroom.*)

FELIX (*is hurt by this, then remembers something. He calls after him*): Walk on the paper, will you? The floors are wet. (OSCAR *comes out of the door. He is glaring maniacally, as he slowly strides back down the hallway.* FELIX *quickly puts the couch between him and* OSCAR.) Awright, keep away. Keep away from me.

OSCAR (*chasing him around the couch*): Come on. Let me get in one shot. You pick it. Head, stomach or kidneys.

FELIX (*dodging about the room*): You're gonna find yourself in one sweet law suit, Oscar.

OSCAR: It's no use running, Felix. There's only eight rooms and I know the short cuts.

(*They are now poised at opposite ends of the couch.* FELIX *picks up a lamp for protection.*)

FELIX: Is this how you settle your problems, Oscar? Like an animal?

OSCAR: All right. You wanna see how I settle my problems. I'll show you. (*Storms off into* FELIX's *bedroom. There is the sound of falling objects and he returns with a suitcase.*) I'll show you how I settle them. (*Throws the suitcase on the table.*) There! That's how I settle them!

FELIX (*bewildered, looks at the suitcase*): Where are you going?

OSCAR (*exploding*): Not me, you idiot! You. You're the one who's going. I want you out of here. Now! Tonight!

(*He opens the suitcase.*)

FELIX: What are you talking about?

OSCAR: It's all over, Felix. The whole marriage. We're getting an annulment! Don't you understand? I don't want to live with you any more. I want you to pack your things, tie it up with your Saran Wrap and get out of here.

FELIX: You mean actually move out?

OSCAR: Actually, physically and immediately. I don't care where you go. Move into the Museum of Natural History. (*Goes into the kitchen. There is the crash of falling pots and pans.*) I'm sure you'll be very comfortable there. You can dust around the Egyptian mummies to your heart's content. But I'm a human, living person. (*Comes out with a stack of cooking utensils which he throws into the open suitcase.*) All I want is my freedom. Is that too much to ask for? (*Closes it.*) There, you're all packed.

FELIX: You know, I've got a good mind to really leave.

OSCAR (*looking to the heavens*): Why doesn't he ever listen to what I say? Why doesn't he hear me? I know I'm talking—I recognize my voice.

FELIX (*indignantly*): Because if you really want me to go, I'll go.

OSCAR: Then go. I want you to go, so go. When are you going?

FELIX: When am I going, huh? Boy, you're in a bigger hurry than Frances was.

OSCAR: Take as much time as she gave you. I want you to follow your usual routine.

FELIX: In other words, you're throwing me out.

OSCAR: Not in other words. Those are the perfect ones. (*Picks up the suitcase and holds it out to* FELIX.) I am throwing you out.

FELIX: All right, I just wanted to get the record straight. Let it be on *your* conscience.

(*He goes into his bedroom.*)

OSCAR: What? What? (*Follows him to the bedroom doorway.*) Let what be on my conscience?

FELIX (*comes out putting on his jacket and passes by* OSCAR): That you're throwing me out. (*Stops and turns back to him.*) I'm perfectly willing to stay and clear the air of our differences. But you refuse, right?

OSCAR (*still holding the suitcase*): Right! I'm sick and tired of you cleaning the air. That's why I want you to leave!

FELIX: Okay, as long as I heard you say the words, "Get out of the house." Fine. But remember, what happens to me is your responsibility. Let it be on *your* head.

(*He crosses to the door.*)

OSCAR (*follows him to the door and screams*): Wait a minute, damn it! Why can't you be thrown out like a decent human being? Why do you have to say things like, "Let it be on your head"? I don't want it on my head. I just want you out of the house.

FELIX: What's the matter, Oscar? Can't cope with a little guilt feelings?

OSCAR (*pounding the railing in frustration*): Damn you. I've been looking forward to throwing you out all day long, and now you even take the pleasure out of that.

FELIX: Forgive me for spoiling your fun. I'm leaving now—according to your wishes and desires.

(*He starts to open the door.*)

OSCAR (*pushes by* FELIX *and slams the door shut. He stands between* FELIX *and the door*): You're not leaving here until you take it back.

FELIX: Take what back?

OSCAR: "Let it be on your head." What the hell is that, the Curse of the Cat People?

FELIX: Get out of my way, please.

OSCAR: Is this how you left that night with Frances? No wonder she wanted to have the room repainted right away. (*Points to* FELIX's *bedroom.*) I'm gonna have yours dipped in bronze.

FELIX (*sits on the back of the couch with his back to* OSCAR): How can I leave if you're blocking the door?

OSCAR (*very calmly*): Felix, we've been friends a long time. For the sake of that friendship, please say, "Oscar, we can't stand each other; let's break up."

FELIX: I'll let you know what to do about my clothes. Either I'll call— or someone else will. (*Controlling great emotion.*) I'd like to leave now.

(OSCAR, *resigned, moves out of the way.* FELIX *opens the door.*)

OSCAR: Where will you go?

FELIX (*turns in the doorway and looks at him*): Where? (*He smiles.*) Oh, come on, Oscar. You're not really interested, are you?

(*He exits.* OSCAR *looks as though he's about to burst with frustration. He calls after* FELIX.)

OSCAR: All right, Felix, you win. (*Goes out into the hall.*) We'll try to iron it out. Anything you want. Come back, Felix. Felix? *Felix?* Don't leave me like this—you louse! (*But* FELIX *is gone.* OSCAR *comes back into the room closing the door. He is limp. He searches for something to ease his enormous frustration. He throws a pillow at the door, and then paces about like a caged lion.*) All right, Oscar, get a hold of yourself! He's gone! Keep saying that over and over. He's gone. He's really gone! (*He holds his head in pain.*) He did it. He put a curse on me. It's on my head. I don't know what it is, but something's on my head. (*The doorbell rings and he looks up hopefully.*) Please let it be him. Let it be Felix. Please give me one more chance to kill him.

(*Putting the suitcase on the sofa, he rushes to the door and opens it.* MURRAY *comes in with* VINNIE.)

MURRAY (*putting his jacket on a chair at the table*): Hey, what's the matter with Felix? He walked right by me with that "human sacrifice" look on his face again.

(*He takes off his shoes.*)

VINNIE (*laying his jacket on the love seat*): What's with him? I asked him where he's going and he said, "Only Oscar knows. Only Oscar knows." Where's he going, Oscar?

OSCAR (*sitting at the table*): How the hell should I know? All right, let's get the game started, heh? Come on, get your chips.

MURRAY: I have to get something to eat. I'm starving. Mmm, I think I smell spaghetti.

(*He goes into the kitchen.*)

VINNIE: Isn't he playing tonight?

(*He takes two chairs from the dining alcove and puts them at the table.*)

OSCAR: I don't want to discuss it. I don't even want to hear his name.
VINNIE: Who? Felix?
OSCAR: I told you not to mention his name.

VINNIE: I didn't know what name you meant.

(*He clears the table and places what's left of* FELIX's *dinner on the bookcase.*)

MURRAY (*comes out of the kitchen*): Hey, did you know there's spaghetti all over the kitchen?

OSCAR: Yes, I know, and it's not spaghetti; it's linguini.

MURRAY: Oh. I thought it was spaghetti.

(*He goes back into the kitchen.*)

VINNIE (*taking the poker stuff from the bookcase and putting it on the table*): Why shouldn't I mention his name?

OSCAR: Who?

VINNIE: Felix. What's happened? Has something happened?

(SPEED *and* ROY *come in the open door.*)

SPEED: Yeah, what's the matter with Felix?

(SPEED *puts his jacket over a chair at the table.* ROY *sits in the armchair.* MURRAY *comes out of the kitchen with a six-pack of beer and bags of pretzels and chips. They all stare at* OSCAR *waiting for an answer. There is a long pause and then he stands up.*)

OSCAR: We broke up! I kicked him out. It was my decision. I threw him out of the house. All right? I admit it. Let it be on my head.

VINNIE: Let what be on your head?

OSCAR: How should I know? *Felix put it there!* Ask him!

(*He paces around to the right.*)

MURRAY: He'll go to pieces. I know Felix. He's gonna try something crazy.

OSCAR (*turns to the boys*): Why do you think I did it? (MURRAY *makes a gesture of disbelief and moves to the couch, putting down the beer and the bags.* OSCAR *moves to him.*) You think I'm just selfish? That I wanted to be cruel? I did it for you—I did it for all of us.

ROY: What are you talking about?

OSCAR (*crosses to* ROY): All right, we've all been through the napkins and the ashtrays and the bacon, lettuce and tomato sandwiches. But that was just the beginning. Just the beginning. Do you know what he was planning for next Friday night's poker game? As a change of pace. Do you have any idea?

VINNIE: What?

OSCAR: A Luau! An Hawaiian Luau! Spareribs, roast pork and fried rice. They don't play poker like that in Honolulu.

MURRAY: One thing has nothing to do with the other. We all know he's impossible, but he's still our friend, and he's still out on the street, and I'm still worried about him.

OSCAR (*going to* MURRAY): And I'm not, heh? I'm not concerned? I'm not worried? Who do you think sent him out there in the first place?

MURRAY: Frances!

OSCAR: What?

MURRAY: Frances sent him out in the first place. *You* sent him out in the second place. And whoever he lives with next will send him out in the third place. Don't you understand? It's Felix. He does it to himself.

OSCAR: Why?

MURRAY: I don't know why. *He* doesn't know why. There are people like that. There's a whole tribe in Africa who hit themselves on the head all day long.

(*He sums it all up with an eloquent gesture of resignation.*)

OSCAR (*a slow realization of a whole new reason to be angry*): I'm not going to worry about him. Why should I? He's not worrying about me. He's somewhere out on the streets sulking and crying and having a wonderful time. If he had a spark of human decency he would leave us all alone and go back to Blanche.

(*He sits down at the table.*)

VINNIE: Why should he?

OSCAR (*picks up a deck of cards*): Because it's his wife.

VINNIE: No, Blanche is your wife. His wife is Frances.

OSCAR (*stares at him*): What are you, some kind of wise guy?

VINNIE: What did I say?

OSCAR (*throws the cards in the air*): All right, the poker game is over. I don't want to play any more.

(*He paces around on the right.*)

SPEED: Who's playing? We didn't even start.

OSCAR (*turns on him*): Is that all you can do is complain? Have you given one single thought to where Felix might be?

SPEED: I thought you said you're not worried about him.

OSCAR (*screams*): I'm not worried, damn it! I'm not worried. (*The doorbell rings. A gleeful look passes over* OSCAR's *face.*) It's him. I bet it's him! (*The boys start to go for the door.* OSCAR *stops them.*) Don't let him in; he's not welcome in this house.

MURRAY (*moves toward the door*): Oscar, don't be childish. We've got to let him in.

OSCAR (*stopping him and leading him to the table*): I won't give him the satisfaction of knowing we've been worrying about him. Sit down. Play cards. Like nothing happened.

MURRAY: But, Oscar . . .

OSCAR: Sit down. Everybody. Come on, sit down and play poker.

(*They sit and* SPEED *begins to deal out cards.*)

VINNIE (*crossing to the door*): Oscar . . .

OSCAR: All right, Vinnie, open the door.

(VINNIE *opens the door. It is* GWENDOLYN *standing there.*)

VINNIE (*surprised*): Oh, hello. (*To* OSCAR.) It's not him, Oscar.

GWENDOLYN: How do you do.

(*She walks into the room.*)

OSCAR (*crosses to her*): Oh, hello, Cecily. Boys, I'd like you to meet Cecily Pigeon.

GWENDOLYN: Gwendolyn Pigeon. Please don't get up. (*To* OSCAR.) May I see you for a moment, Mr. Madison?

OSCAR: Certainly, Gwen. What's the matter?

GWENDOLYN: I think you know. I've come for Felix's things.

(OSCAR *looks at her in shock and disbelief. He looks at the boys, then back at* GWENDOLYN.)

OSCAR: Felix? My Felix?

GWENDOLYN: Yes. Felix Ungar. That sweet, tortured man who's in my flat at this moment pouring his heart out to my sister.

OSCAR (*turns to the boys*): You hear? I'm worried to death and he's up there getting tea and sympathy.

(CECILY *rushes in dragging a reluctant* FELIX *with her.*)

CECILY: Gwen, Felix doesn't want to stay. Please tell him to stay.

FELIX: Really, girls, this is very embarrassing. I can go to a hotel. (*To the boys.*) Hello, fellas.

GWENDOLYN (*overriding his objections*): Nonsense. I told you, we've plenty of room, and it's a very comfortable sofa. Isn't it, Cecy?

CECILY (*joining in*): Enormous. And we've rented an air conditioner.

GWENDOLYN: And we just don't like the idea of your wandering the streets looking for a place to live.

FELIX: But I'd be in the way. Wouldn't I be in the way?

GWENDOLYN: How could you possibly be in anyone's way?

OSCAR: You want to see a typewritten list?

GWENDOLYN (*turning on him*): Haven't you said enough already, Mr. Madison? (*To* FELIX.) I won't take no for an answer. Just for a few days, Felix.

CECILY: Until you get settled.

GWENDOLYN: Please. Please say, "Yes," Felix.

CECILY: Oh, please—we'd be so happy.

FELIX (*considers*): Well, maybe just for a few days.

GWENDOLYN (*jumping with joy*): Oh, wonderful.

CECILY (*ecstatic*): Marvelous!

GWENDOLYN (*crosses to the door*): You get your things and come right up.

CECILY: And come hungry. We're making dinner.

GWENDOLYN (*to the boys*): Good night, gentlemen; sorry to interrupt your bridge game.

CECILY (*to* FELIX): If you'd like, you can invite your friends to play in our flat.

GWENDOLYN (*to* FELIX): Don't be late. Cocktails in fifteen minutes.

FELIX: I won't.

GWENDOLYN: Ta, ta.

CECILY: Ta, ta.

FELIX: Ta, ta.

(*The girls leave.* FELIX *turns and looks at the fellows and smiles as he crosses the room into the bedroom. The five men stare dumbfounded at the door without moving. Finally* MURRAY *crosses to the door.*)

SPEED (*to the others*): I told you. It's always the quiet guys.

MURRAY: Gee, what nice girls.

(*He closes the door.* FELIX *comes out of the bedroom carrying two suits in a plastic cleaner's bag.*)

ROY: Hey, Felix, are you really gonna move in with them?

FELIX (*turns back to them*): Just for a few days. Until I find my own place. Well, so long, fellows. You can drop your crumbs on the rug again.

(*He starts toward the door.*)

OSCAR: Hey, Felix. Aren't you going to thank me?

FELIX (*stopping on the landing*): For what?

OSCAR: For the two greatest things I ever did for you. Taking you in and throwing you out.

FELIX (*lays his suits over the railing and goes to* OSCAR): You're right, Oscar. Thanks a lot. Getting kicked out twice is enough for any man. In gratitude, I remove the curse.

OSCAR (*smiles*): Oh, bless you and thank you, Wicked Witch of the North.

(*They shake hands. The phone rings.*)

FELIX: Ah, that must be the girls.

MURRAY (*picking up the phone*): Hello?

FELIX: They hate it so when I'm late for cocktails. (*Turning to the boys.*) Well, so long.

MURRAY: It's your wife.

FELIX (*turning to* MURRAY): Oh? Well, do me a favor, Murray. Tell her I can't speak to her now. But tell her I'll be calling her in a few days, because she and I have a lot to talk about. And tell her if I sound different to her, it's because I'm not the same man she kicked out three weeks ago. Tell her, Murray; tell her.

MURRAY: I will when I see her. This is Oscar's wife.

FELIX: Oh!

MURRAY (*into the phone*): Just a minute, Blanche.

(OSCAR *crosses to the phone and sits on the arm of the couch.*)

FELIX: Well, so long, fellows.

(*He shakes hands with the boys, takes his suits and moves to the door.*)

OSCAR (*into the phone*): Hello? Yeah, Blanche. I got a pretty good idea why you're calling. You got my checks, right? Good. (FELIX *stops at the door, caught by* OSCAR's *conversation. He slowly comes back into the room to listen, putting his suits on the railing, and sitting down on the arm of the armchair.*) So now I'm all paid up. No, no, I didn't win at the track. I've just been able to save a little money. I've been eating home a lot. (*Takes a pillow from the couch and throws it at* FELIX.) Listen, Blanche, you don't have to thank me. I'm just doing what's right. Well, that's nice of you too. The apartment? No, I think you'd be shocked. It's in surprisingly good shape. (FELIX *throws the pillow back at* OSCAR.) Say, Blanche, did Brucey get the goldfish I sent him? Yeah, well, I'll speak to you again soon, huh? Whenever you want. I don't go out much any more.

FELIX (*gets up, takes his suits from the railing and goes to the door*): Well, good night, Mr. Madison. If you need me again, I get a dollar-fifty an hour.

OSCAR (*makes a gesture to stop* FELIX *as he talks on the phone*): Well, kiss the kids for me. Good night, Blanche. (*Hangs up and turns to* FELIX.) Felix?

FELIX (*at the opened door*): Yeah?

OSCAR: How about next Friday night? You're not going to break up the game, are you?

FELIX: Me? Never! Marriages may come and go, but the game must go on. So long, Frances.

(*He exits, closing the door.*)

OSCAR (*yelling after him*): So long, Blanche. (*The boys all look at* OSCAR *a moment.*) All right, are we just gonna sit around or are we gonna play poker?

ROY: We're gonna play poker.

(*There is a general hubbub as they pass out the beer, deal the cards and settle around the table.*)

OSCAR (*standing up*): Then let's play poker. (*Sharply, to the boys.*) And watch your cigarettes, will you? This is my house, not a pigsty.

(*He takes the ashtray from the side table next to the armchair, bends down and begins to pick up the butts. The boys settle down to play poker.*)

CURTAIN